CAMBRIDGE GREEK AND LATIN CLASSICS

D1527857

HOMER

ILIAD

BOOK VI

EDITED BY
BARBARA GRAZIOSI

Professor of Classics,
Durham University

JOHANNES HAUBOLD

Leverhulme Senior Lecturer in Greek Literature,
Durham University

CAMBRIDGE
UNIVERSITY PRESS

CAMBRIDGE UNIVERSITY PRESS
Cambridge, New York, Melbourne, Madrid, Cape Town, Singapore,
São Paulo, Delhi, Dubai, Tokyo, Mexico City

Cambridge University Press
The Edinburgh Building, Cambridge CB2 8RU, UK

Published in the United States of America by Cambridge University Press, New York

www.cambridge.org
Information on this title: www.cambridge.org/9780521703727

First published 2010

Printed in the United Kingdom at the University Press, Cambridge

A catalogue record for this publication is available from the British Library

Library of Congress Cataloguing in Publication data
Homer.
[Iliad. Book 6]
Homer Iliad, book VI / [edited by] Barbara Graziosi, Johannes Haubold.
p.   cm. – (Cambridge Greek and Latin classics)
Text in Greek with introduction and commentary in English.
Includes index.
ISBN 978-0-521-87884-5 (hardback)
1. Homer. Iliad. Book 6.   I. Graziosi, Barbara.   II. Haubold, Johannes.   III. Title.
IV. Series.
PA4020.P6   2010
883′.01 – dc22   2010030218

ISBN 978-0-521-87884-5 Hardback
ISBN 978-0-521-70372-7 Paperback

To our parents

CONTENTS

ACKNOWLEDGEMENTS

The first invitation to write this commentary came from Pat Easterling, when we left Cambridge, after our doctoral and postdoctoral studies, and moved to Durham to take up two lectureships. Since then, many colleagues, friends and students have helped us try to make sense of *Iliad* 6. We cannot mention them all by name, but we are very grateful for the help we received with a task that seemed, at times, simply too hard. We have profited greatly from the guidance of the series editors, Pat Easterling and Richard Hunter, and from the detailed comments of Luigi Battezzato, Felix Budelmann, Andrea Capra, Georg Danek and Maria Serena Mirto: we can only hope that we have learnt enough from them. We would also like to thank our copy-editor, Jan Chapman, and Michael Sharp, classics editor at Cambridge University Press, for their work. We are grateful to the Department of Classics and Ancient History, Durham University, to the Arts and Humanities Research Council, and to the Loeb Foundation for granting and funding crucial periods of leave, which we devoted to this commentary. We have relied on excellent recent scholarship on Homeric epic and – especially – the two editions of the *Iliad* by Helmut van Thiel and M. L. West: our debt to them will be obvious to all readers. Magdalene Stoevesandt's commentary on *Iliad* 6, part of the *Gesamtkommentar* edited by J. Latacz and A. Bierl, came out shortly before we submitted ours to Cambridge University Press: it is truly excellent, and we have tried to include its insights in our discussion, but readers are very much advised to consult it too. We wrote most of this commentary in the evenings, after our children had gone to bed. While they slept upstairs, and we worked on the harrowing narrative of *Iliad* 6, we felt – more than ever – grateful for peace.

ABBREVIATIONS

Abbreviations mainly follow those used in the *Oxford Classical Dictionary* with the following variations and additions:

LfgrE   *Lexikon des frühgriechischen Epos*, ed. B. Snell, U. Fleischer and H.-J. Mette *et al.*, Göttingen 1955–

New Pauly   *Brill's New Pauly: encyclopaedia of the ancient world*, ed. H. Cancik and H. Schneider, Leiden 2007

INTRODUCTION

1. THE POET AND THE MUSES

In his *Collection of useful knowledge* Proclus observes that Homer said nothing about his own origins and lineage, and that 'because his poetry gives no express indication on these questions, each writer has indulged his inclinations with great freedom'.[1] This is a perceptive comment: from antiquity to the present there has been much debate about the origin, date and authorship of Homeric epic – a debate fuelled, in part, by a lack of reliable information. And yet the *Iliad* does say something important about its poet, and in order to offer an introduction to Homeric poetry, it seems reasonable to start with the image of the poet presented in the *Iliad* itself, before broaching the many, and difficult, issues on which the poem offers no explicit guidance.

The poem starts with an order: 'Sing, goddess, the wrath of Achilles.' Like all second-person addresses, this opening invocation establishes a specific relationship between speaker and addressee. The poet asks the goddess to sing and she evidently complies with his request: what follows, after the proem, is indeed a song about the wrath of Achilles. Song, ἀοιδή, is a word the poet uses for his own performance: the Muse sings, and the poet sings too, about the same topic. After the proem their voices blend, until the poet faces particularly difficult challenges. Before launching into the massive Catalogue of Ships in book 2, for example, the poet suddenly puts some distance between himself and the Muse, re-establishes his own individual voice with the pronoun μοι, and asks, again, for divine support (2.484–93):

> ἔσπετε νῦν μοι, Μοῦσαι Ὀλύμπια δώματ' ἔχουσαι –
> ὑμεῖς γὰρ θεαί ἐστε πάρεστέ τε ἴστε τε πάντα,
> ἡμεῖς δὲ κλέος οἶον ἀκούομεν οὐδέ τι ἴδμεν –
> οἵ τινες ἡγεμόνες Δαναῶν καὶ κοίρανοι ἦσαν.
> πληθὺν δ' οὐκ ἂν ἐγὼ μυθήσομαι οὐδ' ὀνομήνω,
> οὐδ' εἴ μοι δέκα μὲν γλῶσσαι, δέκα δὲ στόματ' εἶεν,
> φωνὴ δ' ἄρρηκτος, χάλκεον δέ μοι ἦτορ ἐνείη,
> εἰ μὴ Ὀλυμπιάδες Μοῦσαι, Διὸς αἰγιόχοιο
> θυγατέρες, μνησαίαθ' ὅσοι ὑπὸ Ἴλιον ἦλθον.
> ἀρχοὺς αὖ νηῶν ἐρέω νῆάς τε προπάσας.

> Tell me now, you Muses who have your homes on Olympus –
> for you are goddesses, are present and know all things,
> but we hear only the *kleos* and know nothing –
> who were the leaders and commanders of the Danaans.
> I could not tell the masses nor name them,

[1] Proclus, *Chrestomathy* I, trans. M. L. West 2003: 419.

> not even if I had ten tongues and ten mouths,
> a voice that cannot break, and a heart of bronze inside me,
> unless the Muses of Olympus, daughters of aegis-bearing
> Zeus, remembered all of those who came to Ilios;
> but now I will tell the leaders of the ships, and all the ships there were.

The Muses alone 'are present and know all things'. Without their help, the poet is in exactly the same position as his audience: 'we have only heard the κλέος, and know nothing'. κλέος is, literally, 'what is heard': the word sometimes describes the subject matter of epic poetry (e.g. *Od.* 3.204, 8.73; Hes. *Theog.* 99–101; *Hom. Hymn* 32.18–20; cf. *Il.* 9.189). The Muse 'sings', and the audience 'hear': in between, mediating in that complex transaction, stands the poet. At 2.487 the poet asks the Muses to tell him who the leaders of the Danaans were; he then declares he needs their help in order to relate to the audience this information; and finally, at 493, he launches into the grandest and most impressive catalogue in the whole poem. The Muses and the poet sing in unison again for a while; but the invocation establishes the terms of their relationship.[2] The goddesses guarantee the accuracy of the poet's performance (they 'know everything'); while the poet's performance, in turn, guarantees their presence (he states he could not accomplish his poetic feat without their help). Through this interaction, the ability to perform and the accuracy of the performance are tightly woven together.

We may wonder about the meaning of πάρεστε, at 2.485: are the Muses 'present', in the sense that they are in the company of the poet and his audience; or are they 'present' in Troy, at the time of the Trojan expedition? This question admits of no straightforward answer. Clearly, the Muses and the poet enjoy an intimate relationship, and the result of that relationship is the performance itself, in front of an audience. But the 'presence' of the Muses, in our passage, does not just concern their impact on the poet and his audience: it is closely linked to the Muses' own knowledge of the Trojan expedition, and to their divine powers more generally: ὑμεῖς γὰρ θεαί ἐστε πάρεστέ τε ἴστε τε πάντα, 'you are goddesses, are present, and know all things'. Hesiod tells us that the Muses please the mind of Zeus by 'telling what is, what will be, and what was before' (εἰρεῦσαι τά τ' ἐόντα τά τ' ἐσσόμενα πρό τ' ἐόντα; *Theog.* 38). Their knowledge has a temporal dimension in the *Iliad* too: they bridge the gap between the great events at Troy, and the world of Homeric audiences. The poet never describes his audience in any detail, but he does imply that his performance takes place long after the age of the heroes: he repeatedly compares the feats of his heroic characters with the meagre achievements of 'people as they are nowadays' (5.302–4, 12.378–83, 445–9 and 20.285–7).

---

[2] Later the poet asks the Muse to identify the best of the Achaeans (2.761–2). At 11.218–20 and 14.508–10, two important moments in the narrative, he asks the Muses to establish the correct order of events. At 16.112–13 he demands to know how the ships of the Achaeans caught fire. In every case, the poet goes on to provide the information he requested of the goddesses.

The question about the 'presence' of the Muses also applies to the position of the epic singer, as a passage in the *Odyssey* makes clear. When Odysseus arrives at the land of the Phaeacians, he has lost everything: his ship, his comrades, his possessions, even his clothes. The Phaeacians cannot, therefore, establish his identity on the basis of any external evidence; they can only rely on what he says himself – and that, of course, is a risk because travellers often lie. Fortunately, there is one character, in the land of the Phaeacians, who already knows about Odysseus and is thus in a position to corroborate his story. In the course of celebrations in honour of the shipwrecked stranger, the singer Demodocus entertains his audience with three songs: the first is about a quarrel between Odysseus and Achilles (8.73–82); the second is set on Olympus and describes an adulterous love affair between Ares and Aphrodite (8.266–366); the third celebrates the fall of Troy, and Odysseus' stratagem of the Trojan horse (8.499–520). Demodocus is blind: he does not know that Odysseus, a major character in his own songs, is right there, among his audience. It is Odysseus who recognises himself in Demodocus' first song: he pulls up his cloak, covers his head, and cries (8.83–92). Later, before Demodocus' third song, he praises the singer (8.487–91):

"Δημόδοκ', ἔξοχα δή σε βροτῶν αἰνίζομ' ἁπάντων·
ἢ σέ γε Μοῦσ' ἐδίδαξε, Διὸς πᾶις, ἢ σέ γ' Ἀπόλλων.
λίην γὰρ κατὰ κόσμον Ἀχαιῶν οἶτον ἀείδεις,
ὅσσ' ἔρξαν τ' ἔπαθόν τε καὶ ὅσσ' ἐμόγησαν Ἀχαιοί,
ὥς τέ που ἢ αὐτὸς παρεὼν ἢ ἄλλου ἀκούσας."

'Demodocus, greatly I praise you, above all mortals;
either the Muse, daughter of Zeus, taught you, or Apollo.
You sing the fate of the Achaeans precisely, according to order;
what they did and endured and all they suffered,
as if you had been there yourself, or heard from someone who had.'

There is a striking correspondence between the suffering of the Achaeans and Odysseus' own pain, as he listens and remembers his past. It is through tears, and poetry, that Odysseus first begins to reveal himself to his hosts. After paying his compliment to Demodocus, Odysseus asks the bard to sing about the fall of Troy, and the stratagem of the Trojan horse. It is after that performance that he finally reveals his identity: in books 9–12 Odysseus takes over from Demodocus' story and tells what happened after the fall of Troy. The Phaeacians believe Odysseus because he sounds like a singer (11.363–9):

"ὦ Ὀδυσεῦ, τὸ μὲν οὔ τί σ' ἐΐσκομεν εἰσορόωντες
ἠπεροπῆά τ' ἔμεν καὶ ἐπίκλοπον, οἷά τε πολλοὺς
βόσκει γαῖα μέλαινα πολυσπερέας ἀνθρώπους
ψεύδεά τ' ἀρτύνοντας, ὅθεν κέ τις οὐδὲ ἴδοιτο·
σοὶ δ' ἔπι μὲν μορφὴ ἐπέων, ἔνι δὲ φρένες ἐσθλαί,
μῦθον δ' ὡς ὅτ' ἀοιδὸς ἐπισταμένως κατέλεξας,
πάντων Ἀργείων σέο δ' αὐτοῦ κήδεα λυγρά."

'Odysseus, looking at you, we do not liken you
to a fraud or a cheat, the sort that the black earth
breeds in great numbers, widespread people,
who craft their lies – from what sources one does not see.
Your words have beauty, and there is sense in you,
and expertly, as a singer would do, you have set out the story,
of all the Argives' terrible sorrows, and your own.'

Again, a complex exchange links truth to epic performance. Odysseus compliments
Demodocus because he describes the fall of Troy as accurately as if he had been
there; while the Phaeacians believe Odysseus' own account because he performs like
a singer: his words have 'beauty', or 'shape' (μορφή).

There are of course differences between Odysseus and Demodocus: the most
obvious is that the singer will never be an eyewitness: he is blind. It is because of
his relationship with the Muse, rather than any first-hand experience, that he knows
what happened at Troy. By himself, he is not even able to recognise Odysseus, who is
sitting right beside him. Blindness separates Demodocus from his audience; but also
marks a different, divine, kind of vision (8.63–4):

τὸν περὶ Μοῦσ᾽ ἐφίλησε, δίδου δ᾽ ἀγαθόν τε κακόν τε·
ὀφθαλμῶν μὲν ἄμερσε, δίδου δ᾽ ἡδεῖαν ἀοιδήν.

The Muse loved him greatly, and gave him both good and evil:
she took his eyesight but gave him sweet song.

Ancient readers thought that this description of Demodocus was autobiographical:
an image of Homer himself. Modern scholars have often doubted the ancient report
that Homer was blind and have sometimes noted that his poetry is especially vivid
and visual. But this is to miss the point of the ancient legend: Homer's blindness,
just like Demodocus', was thought to compensate for his poetry.[3] And, as a poet, he
could see what went on in Troy: like Demodocus, and the Muses, he could overcome
the barriers of time and space and 'be present'. At the same time, Homer's blindness
symbolised his distance and impartiality vis-à-vis his human audiences.

The poet of the *Iliad* does not address his audience directly, in order to ask
for attention, flatter or make demands. Never does he name specific addressees or
describe the context of his performance. By contrast, he addresses not only the Muses,
but also some characters in his own story.[4] These direct apostrophes are so startling
that some ancient and modern readers have argued that they betray a special concern

---

[3] The idea would have seemed less strange to ancient readers than it might seem to us.
Compare what Socrates has to say about true insight at Plato, *Symp.* 219a: 'The inner eye of
thought (ἡ τῆς διανοίας ὄψις) begins to see clearly when our real eyes start losing their sharpness
of vision.'

[4] The passages are collected and discussed in A. Parry 1972, Block 1982 and
Yamagata 1989.

for the characters addressed.[5] But in one case, at least, there seems to be no reason to suppose an enduring affection or interest on the part of the poet: the direct address seems motivated by the immediate situation at hand, rather than by a long-lasting commitment to certain characters. At 15.582–4 Antilochos has just killed Melanippos and is about to take his spoils, when the poet suddenly addresses the dead Melanippos in the vocative and points out that Hector defended his corpse. The narrative gains in immediacy: what the poet describes is not a routine battlefield occurrence, but something that would have mattered greatly to Melanippos and now matters to the poet, and hence to all those who listen to him. The poet thus engages his audience not by addressing them directly, but by addressing his characters, and thus taking part in the story he tells.

The poet's presence at Troy may help to explain another puzzling feature of Homeric poetry. In an influential study of 1899–1901, Theodor Zielinski argued that Homeric narrative always moves forward: as a result, the poet represents simultaneous actions as sequential. Early responses to 'Zielinski's law' took it as evidence for the primitive state of the Homeric mind, which was supposedly unable to grasp the complexities of time and simultaneity.[6] Such perceptions of Homeric poetry have by now been dispelled: the poems do, in fact, represent simultaneous action by several different means.[7] For example, while Hector leaves the battlefield, Glaukos and Diomedes meet and exchange gifts: in terms of narrative structure, the encounter between the two warriors counterbalances Hector's mission in Troy (see below, Introduction 4.1). What remains true, however, is that the poet often fails to draw attention to simultaneity. As Scodel points out in her judicious appraisal of Zielinski's law, 'there is no single solution for all passages where the Homeric narrator's treatment of time is difficult, because time stands in a complex relationship with his other narrative concerns'.[8] One such concern does, however, help to explain Zielinski's observation. The poet describes events as if he were there. Overt references to simultaneity would dispel that sense of presence: in order to say that an event was taking place while something else was happening elsewhere, the poet would need to stand back from both events, however briefly. That, by and large, he does not do: he often abandons one strand of the story and picks up another without offering explicit guidance to the audience about the transition. He simply, suddenly, looks elsewhere, or changes locale – just like Zeus, who, at the beginning of book 13, momentarily stops looking down at the war raging on the Trojan plain and turns his eyes to the land of the Thracians.

The perspective of the poet is indeed that of the gods. He can offer a god's-eye view of the whole battlefield at 1–4n. and then zoom in to show how the tip of a spear penetrates through a forehead and 'breaks into the bone': 10n. He can observe at close quarters how Adrestos' horses trip over a tamarisk branch, break the chariot's pole and run away – and then zoom out in order to show how the horses

---

[5] S. D. Richardson 1990: 170–4 discusses ancient and modern views.
[6] See, for example, Fränkel 1955.   [7] De Jong 2007: 30–1.   [8] Scodel 2008b: 109.

are just two of many that are stampeding across the plain towards the city (38–41n.). Contemporary readers describe Homeric poetry as cinematic,[9] but in antiquity there were no helicopters from which to take aerial shots, and no cameras zooming in or out. The poet's powers were truly divine: only the gods could view things from above, or descend and observe the fighting at close quarters, without fear of death. The poet makes that point explicitly at 4.539–42, when he describes an especially fierce battle:

> ἔνθά κεν οὐκέτι ἔργον ἀνὴρ ὀνόσαιτο μετελθών,
> ὅς τις ἔτ᾽ ἄβλητος καὶ ἀνούτατος ὀξέϊ χαλκῶι
> δινεύοι κατὰ μέσσον, ἄγοι δέ ἑ Παλλὰς Ἀθήνη
> χειρὸς ἑλοῦσ᾽, αὐτὰρ βελέων ἀπερύκοι ἐρωήν·

> Then no longer could a man have faulted their war work, on arrival –
> someone who, as yet unhurt and unstabbed by the piercing bronze,
> moved about in their midst, as Pallas Athena led him
> taking his hand, and holding off the oncoming spears.[10]

Divine inspiration, then, is not just a matter of conventional invocations to the Muses. It shapes the poet's relationship to space, and his treatment of time. More importantly still, it informs his moral outlook. The poet can always tell whether the gods are present or absent (1n.) and knows what they plan. At the very beginning of the *Iliad* he asks the Muse to sing the wrath of Achilles and tell how 'the will of Zeus was accomplished' (1.5). The characters inside the poem have only a limited understanding of their own circumstances and have no sure knowledge of the future. The poet, by contrast, knows everything: his song follows the plan of Zeus and describes in painful detail what it entails for mortals. There is, then, a wide gap between the poet (and his audience), who know the future and the will of the gods; and the characters inside the narrative, who struggle, in their ignorance, with their hopes and fears (see, for example, 237–41n.). There is just one character, in *Iliad* 6, who does share the perceptions of the poet, at least to an extent. At 357–8n. Helen presents herself, Paris and, indirectly, Hector as future subjects of song – and sees a link between her human suffering, the fate decreed by Zeus and the delight of future epic audiences.

Helen's clear-sightedness is unusual and derives, in part, from her unique position in the poem. As the war rages over her, she – standing in the eye of the storm – sees herself from the perspective of future audiences. Helen thus momentarily comes close to sharing the poet's own vantage point and, like him, draws a connection between Zeus's plans, human suffering, and poetry. And yet her vision does not stem from an objective knowledge of what was, is and shall be – for all that she is the daughter of Zeus (just like the Muses themselves). In the *Iliad* Helen's divinity is played down, and she shapes her vision of the future not like a goddess or a singer,

---

[9] Winkler 2007.

[10] On the complex relationship between the imagined observer, the poet and the audience in this passage, see Mirto 1997: 925.

but like a woman with immediate and pressing concerns. She wants Hector to stay with her: she needs him to focus on her plight and wants him to feel special because of his connection with her. In Helen's handling, future poetry becomes a weapon of seduction (343–58n., 357–8n.). Her words are not an impartial statement of fact, but an attempt to manipulate the situation so as to flatter Hector and persuade him to stay. Helen cannot ultimately escape the pain and uncertainty of her own human condition. At 3.234–42, for example, she looks for her brothers among the Achaean troops and wonders why they are not there: at that point, the poet informs us that they are already dead (3.243–4).

There is a great difference between what we know with utter certainty (because the poet, the Muses and Zeus himself guarantee it), and what the characters themselves think, feel and fear. This gap in knowledge is crucial to the *Iliad* as a whole but is especially important in book 6. We know that Troy must fall; and so, when Hector enters the city, we are confronted with a place and a people that are, from our perspective, already doomed. This is not just a general impression: it is reinforced by many details in the narrative. The women of Troy, for example, pray that Diomedes die in front of the Scaean Gates – but we know that he will survive the war: we thus realise that their prayer is futile (306–7n.), even before the poet describes Athena's response to it (311n.). The poet's narrative is in tune with the plans and actions of the gods, but also with what we already know, as competent epic audiences. It is of course difficult to establish, in every case, what kind of knowledge the poet assumed of his listeners. In some cases, allusions seem clear. When Hector picks up his baby son and tosses him about in his arms, we recognise a familiar gesture, which usually makes babies squeal with fear and elation – but we also remember Astyanax's individual fate: the next time a soldier picks him up, he will throw him off the walls (466–81n.). Other allusions are harder to assess: according to Euripides' *Alexander*, Paris was meant to be killed in infancy, but he survived and returned to Troy as a grown man. Hecuba tried to kill him on his return but then recognized him as her child and welcomed him back into the city. At 280–5n. Hector says to Hecuba, of all people, that he wishes her own son Paris was dead: that is a hard thing for any mother to hear, but to those audiences who knew the legend staged in the *Alexander*, Hector's comment will have seemed particularly harsh – a pointed allusion to Hecuba's own role in saving Paris' life. Early audiences did not have complete mastery of every aspect of the epic tradition: they did not instantly recognise all verbal echoes with the facility of a computer search engine. The point, rather, is that what the poet told his audiences resonated with what they already knew about his characters; and that, conversely, further stories, legends and poems developed around the *Iliad*: as a result of that process, the *Iliad* itself became richer, and more allusive, in the course of time (e.g. 434n.).

The main effect of our knowledge, and of the characters' lack of it, is a sense of tragic irony – a realisation that mortals have no sure understanding of the gods, or even of themselves. The *Iliad* enables us to see the limitations of humankind from the perspective of divine knowledge; but the spectacle is not simply entertaining, because the pain, suffering and uncertainty of Homer's characters are ultimately our own.

Sometimes, characters do have moments of insight: at 447–9n., for example, Hector declares that he knows Troy will fall. And yet he cannot hold on to that realisation: only moments later, with his baby son in his arms, he hopes for a better future (475–81n.). Later still, Hector declares that he does not know what awaits him: he tells himself and his wife that all they can do is behave dutifully, as their destiny unfolds (485–93n.); but even that sense of clarity, and resignation, gives way to wild hope at the very end of the book. As Hector leaves the city and prepares to face the enemy, he depicts an unlikely image of future happiness: one day, after the Achaeans have been defeated, he will raise a toast to freedom together with his brother Paris, and the other Trojan men (520–9n., 526–9n.). This last wish clashes violently with what we know will happen to the Trojans and their city. The prophetic knowledge of the poet, together with the human frailty and uncertainty of his characters, provokes in the audience a mixture of pleasure and pain. As Macleod points out, in Homer we find 'an awareness of the paradox that pain, as recorded in art, can give pleasure – and not only of this aesthetic paradox, but also of the fact it rests on, namely the difference between art and life, tragedy and suffering'.[11] In Homer's *Iliad* we do indeed recognise the seeds of Greek tragedy; but more importantly still, we recognise ourselves.[12] Homeric audiences, and readers, need no special knowledge in order to understand, for example, Hector's sudden surge of hope, as he holds his baby son in his arms; or imagine Hecuba's pain, as she hears one of her sons wish death on another. The Muses guarantee the truthfulness of the poet's song: they are goddesses, are present and can describe with utter precision what happened at Troy. But the poem is true also because it connects with what audiences know, from their own experience, about human life.

2. THE COMPOSITION OF HOMERIC EPIC

The poet never specifies his intended audience, or the context of his performance. This has led to great speculation about the circumstances under which the *Iliad* was composed; but there are, in fact, good reasons for the poet's silence. The poem aspires to be a tale of universal interest, and the poet, as Griffith points out, avoids establishing a privileged relationship with a particular addressee, or audience.[13] Scodel argues that he tells his story in a manner which does not divide audiences over controversial issues: he does not draw attention to mythological innovations, for example.[14] That he shows little interest in local legends and cults has long been recognised.[15] Because of the poet's reticence, and the scarcity of external evidence, it is difficult to establish how and when the *Iliad* was composed, so it seems best to start with two points on which there is general consensus. The poem clearly belongs to a rich and ancient tradition of epic poetry. Its language and compositional techniques were honed over a long

---

[11] Macleod 1982: 7.   [12] See Zajko 2006.   [13] Griffith 1983: 46.   [14] Scodel 2002a.
[15] See, for example, Rohde 1925: 25–6 (German edn 1898).

period of time: they developed for the purpose of singing the deeds of gods and men to a particular rhythm, what we call the hexameter 'line'.

The second point on which there is broad agreement is that, by the second half of the sixth century BCE, the *Iliad* was well known. The material record preserves many late archaic images inspired by the *Iliad*; and the earliest explicit quotation from the poem also dates to this period. Simonides singles out a line from book 6, and calls it 'the finest thing the Chian man said': 146n. Some doubt the authenticity of Simonides' fragment 19 West, but his treatment of Homer fits a late sixth-century or early fifth-century context: we know that at that time artists were selecting and reworking their favourite Iliadic episodes.[16] We also know that Theagenes was writing about Homer in the late sixth century: as Cassio argues, the fact that there were written disquisitions about Homeric epic suggests that there were also written copies of his poems by 530–520 BCE.[17] It thus seems that the *Iliad* was widely known in the late sixth century BCE, and that written copies were available. When precisely the poem came into being is much more difficult to establish: current suggestions range from *c.* 800 BCE to as late as the sixth century itself.[18] Those who champion an early date of composition tend to argue that Homer himself wrote down or dictated a master copy of the *Iliad*.[19] Those who support a sixth-century date often emphasise the importance of an Athenian 'recension'.[20] According to some sources, the tyrant Pisistratus or one of his sons decreed that only Homer had to be recited, in the correct order, at the most important city festival: the Great Panathenaea.[21] Those reports do not speak of a state-owned text; they refer to a situation in which the state monitored the performance of Homeric poetry. The debate over the date of composition of the *Iliad* reflects, in part, a difference in emphasis: some scholars focus on the original contribution by an early poet, others on the earliest known historical context for Homeric recitation. Beyond these differences, all Homerists agree that a sixth-century 'recension' must have captured something older; it is also clear that even if texts of the *Iliad* existed in the seventh century, they did not much affect the reception of the poem: they were scores or scripts, rather than works of literature. Most people appreciated the *Iliad* through listening, not reading.

[16] The visual evidence for Iliadic scenes is collected and discussed in Burgess 2001: 53–94.

[17] Cassio 2002: 118–19.

[18] Powell 1991 suggests that the Greek alphabet was adapted from West Semitic prototypes specifically so as to write down Homeric epic at around 800 BCE. Janko 1982: 231 dates the *Iliad* to *c.* 755/750–725 BCE. Burkert 1976 and M. L. West 1995 detect allusions in the *Iliad* to later events, and on that basis suggest a date of composition in the seventh century BCE. Jensen 1980 argues that the poems were written down in Athens, in the sixth century BCE.

[19] E.g. Janko 1982: 191; Lord 2000: chs. 6–7; Powell 1991: 232–3.

[20] E.g. Wolf 1985 [1795]; Heitsch 1968; Jensen 1980; Seaford 1994: 152–4; for the view that the poems were transmitted orally, but with only minor variations, between the eight and sixth centuries BCE, see Kirk 1962, esp. pp. 98–101. Kirk's idea of the 'life cycle' of an oral tradition (Kirk 1962: 95–8) is developed in G. Nagy 1996a.

[21] See esp. [Plato], *Hipparchus* 228b and Lycurgus, *In Leocratem* 102. Related sources are collected and discussed in Merkelbach 1952; Jensen 1980: chs. 9–10; Kotsidu 1991: 41–4; and G. Nagy 1996a, esp. ch. 3.

Our own love of reading, and appreciation of writing, may lead in fact to wrong assumptions: in the *Iliad* writing (or something close to it) is depicted as an especially nasty and devious business. At 168–70n. Proitos asks Bellerophontes to deliver a folded tablet to the king of Lycia, on which he has inscribed the order to kill the bearer of the message.[22] Bellerophontes thus goes into exile carrying with him his own death warrant. There is no hint, in the Homeric poems, that writing may be used to record great deeds, or help singers compose their songs. This may simply be because Homeric epic is set in a distant, heroic past, where writing did not yet exist or was just being invented by resourceful crooks like Proitos. The actual context of composition of the *Iliad* may have been quite different from the situation depicted inside the poem.[23] What remains true, however, is that the poet of the *Iliad* describes his own work in terms of singing (ἀοιδή) and listening (κλέος): he therefore invites his audience, and indeed his readers, to consider his poem as a live performance. The hexameter rhythm is an integral part of that performance, and shapes the language, grammar, and narrative structures of the *Iliad*.

2.1 The hexameter

1	2	3	4	5	6
—	—	—	—	—	
– ∪∪		– ∪∪		– ∪∪		– ∪∪		– ∪∪		– –

The rhythm of Homeric poetry is the dactylic hexameter.[24] It consists of five dactylic feet or metra (– ∪∪), and a sixth foot that scans – –. The last syllable in the line can be short or long, but is always measured long, because there is a pause in recitation at the end of the verse. Dactyls can be replaced with spondees (– –), though this is rare in the fifth foot (about 5 per cent of lines in the whole of early Greek epic; e.g. 232–3n.). Homeric lines may consist exclusively of dactyls (e.g. 6.13) or, exceptionally, spondees (e.g. 2.544); but most lines are a mixture of the two.

For the purposes of scansion, each verse is divided into syllables, without regard for word division; that is, word divisions can fall within syllables: it is only at the end of the line that there is always a break (for other breaks see below). A syllable is long if it is 'closed' (i.e. ends with a consonant), or if it has a long vowel or diphthong; otherwise it is short. The letters η and ω represent long vowels; ε and ο represent short ones. α, ι, υ may be either long or short.

Syllables begin with the consonant that precedes a vowel, if there is one; otherwise they begin with the vowel itself. When two consonants occur in succession (other than

---

[22] On Proitos' trick and what, if anything, it reveals about the role of writing in the composition of Homeric epic, see Heubeck 1979: 126–46; Powell 1991: 198–200; Ford 1992: 131–8; Brillante 1996; Bassi 1997: 325–9; and J. M. Foley 1999: 1–3.

[23] The extremely regular layout of the inscription on the eighth-century Ischia cup ('Nestor's cup') may reflect the influence of epic texts written on papyrus or leather – though such texts may not have been Homer's poems as we have them; see Cassio 1999: 79.

[24] For Homeric prosody and metre see W. S. Allen 1973, M. L. West 1982 and 1997b, Sicking 1993, Nünlist 2000.

at the beginning of the line), the second consonant starts the following syllable, while the first (normally) belongs to the preceding one, which is therefore closed. This is also true of the consonant clusters which, in the Greek alphabet, are represented by a single letter (ζ, ξ and ψ = *zd*, *ks* and *ps*). The sound *w*, represented by digamma (ϝ), was lost early in the Ionic dialect but continued to affect the rhythm of Homeric epic – even if not consistently.[25] Epic performers knew, for example, that the word (ϝ)ἄστυ behaved as if it began with a consonant; but, in some rare cases, they ignored that and treated it as a normal word starting with α (e.g. 18.274). Similarly, the digamma before the 3rd pers. sing. pronoun (ϝ)ἕ, (ϝ)ἕθεν, (ϝ)οἷ, etc. was generally felt (e.g. 16–17n., ἀλλά οἱ), but not always; some editors try to restore it in all cases, but there is no reason to suppose there was total consistency on the matter: cf. 90n. (ὅς οἱ δοκέει). At the beginning of a word, the sounds represented by μ, ν, ρ, λ and σ are sometimes drawn out to close a preceding syllable, even when no other consonant follows; in some papyri and manuscripts this is marked by a double consonant, see e.g. 91n. (ἐνὶ μεγάρωι).[26] Conversely, plosive consonants (π, β, φ, τ, δ, θ, κ, γ, χ) sometimes start a syllable although they are followed by a second, nasal or liquid consonant (μ, ν, λ, ρ). In those cases, the previous syllable may therefore be open (e.g. 6.163: βασιλῆα προσηύδα, *ba-si-lē-a-pro-sēu-dā*, scanned ∪∪|−∪∪|−−).

When followed by another vowel, a short vowel is elided (e.g. 6.1: δ' οἰώθη); and a long vowel is often shortened (this is called correption, e.g. 6.69: μιμνέτω ὥς, scanned −∪∪|−). Diphthongs too may be shortened when followed by a vowel. In such cases, the second element (ι or υ) was perhaps pronounced like a consonant (like English *y* and *w*), making the syllable open (e.g. 6.1: καὶ Ἀχαιῶν).[27] When two vowels are juxtaposed and there is no elision or correption, they may come together to form a single syllable (so-called 'crasis', 'mixing', cf. 260n.: καὐτός) or each retain their natural length ('hiatus', cf. 6.388: ἐπειγομένη ἀφικάνει).

Greek poetry usually avoids hiatus (lit. the 'gap' or 'opening' in sound, when a word ending in a vowel is followed by a word beginning with one). In Homeric poetry, however, hiatus is much more frequent than in later epic.[28] It arises, for example, when traditional expressions are adapted to new contexts (e.g. δεκάτη ἐφάνη ῥοδοδάκτυλος Ἠώς, 175n.). In many cases the loss of initial digamma at an early stage in the epic tradition resulted in a hiatus that is merely apparent; see, e.g., 16–17n.: ἀλλά (ϝ)οἵ; 6.56: κατὰ (ϝ)οἶκον; 6.75: Ἕκτορι (ϝ)εἶπε; 6.148: φύει (ϝ)ἔαρος; 6.256: περὶ (ϝ)ἄστυ; 6.258: μελιηδέα (ϝ)οἶνον; 6.451: Πριάμοιο (ϝ)ἄνακτος. But there are also several cases of true hiatus: because the tradition allowed hiatus where there had once been a digamma, other cases may have sounded acceptable too. Hiatus is particularly common where the rhythm of the hexameter is interrupted by a word break (caesura); cf. 6.8: υἱὸν Εὐσσώρου || Ἀκάμαντ' ἠΰν τε μέγαν τε.

[25] For a brief overview see Wachter 2000: 72–3.
[26] At the end of a word, the sounds ν, ρ, ς may have the same effect.
[27] W. S. Allen 1973: 224; M. L. West 1982: 12; Nünlist 2000: 110. Wachter 2000: 74 is sceptical.
[28] The same freedom in the treatment of hiatus is evident in the text inscribed on the Ischia cup (n. 23); see Chadwick 1990: 174–5; and Garvie 1994: 32.

The whole hexameter line is hard to pronounce in one breath; word breaks occur at specific places and tend not to occur at others.[29] A word division must occur around the middle of the line, where the break is clearly useful for the performing bard: it takes place either after the first short syllable of the third foot (the so-called 'feminine' caesura, which is the most common), or after the first long syllable of that foot (the 'masculine' caesura) or, less often, after the first long syllable of the fourth foot (the hephthemimeral).[30] Word division is also common between the fourth and the fifth foot (bucolic diairesis): this produces a separate unit $| - \cup\cup | - -$ at the end of the hexameter verse, which often leads on to a runover line. There is usually no word division between the first and the second short syllable of the fourth foot: at that point the rhythm runs smoothly on towards the end of the line. This phenomenon is called 'Hermann's bridge'.[31] Like many other aspects of Homeric rhythm, it too is a strong tendency rather than a hard-and-fast rule.

Oral performance is greatly facilitated by lines that are self-contained units of thought. The performer makes a brief pause at the end of the line, before gathering his thoughts and launching into the next line: when lines express self-sufficient units of thought, the break at the end of each line does not disrupt the performer's train of thought or impair the audience's ability to follow his performance. Most Homeric lines are grammatically complete;[32] though lines often start in enjambment: they elaborate (e.g. 154n.), qualify (e.g. 126n. and 260n.), or modify (e.g. 37–8n.) what has just been said.[33] There are two different kinds of enjambment: most often, a line is grammatically complete and could stand on its own, but an additional phrase extends it, in what we call 'progressive' enjambment.[34] Less frequently, in order to make grammatical sense, a line requires an addition in 'necessary' enjambment (see, e.g., πεφνέμεν, 180n.).[35] In antiquity Homer was considered a master of enjambment: in the *Contest of Homer and Hesiod*, his rival Hesiod challenges him to complete lines that cannot stand on their own without correction or qualification; and Homer always overcomes the challenge, with miraculous resourcefulness.[36] In the *Iliad* there are many cases of striking enjambment, which must have been even more striking in performance: see, e.g., 130–1n. with 139–40n., 341n., 413n. and 496n.

---

[29] Groups of words that were pronounced together may have been marked in early written texts of Homer, as they are on the Ischia cup (n. 23); see Alpers 1969; Heubeck 1979: 115; and Wachter 2000: 66–7.

[30] M. L. West 1997b: 222–3 gives the relative frequencies of the main Homeric caesurae.

[31] Enclitic words are not considered exceptions to Hermann's bridge because they lean heavily on the previous word (i.e. there is no real word break there). There are also words that lean forward and belong to what follows: for example, καί $- \cup\cup | - -$ is frequent at the end of the line and is not thought to disregard Hermann's bridge. See further van Leeuwen 1890: 265–76; and M. L. West 1982: 37–8.

[32] Higbie 1990: 66 gives the percentage of Homeric lines that can stand on their own as just over 75 per cent.

[33] This happens in just over 60 per cent of cases, according to Higbie 1990: 66.

[34] For the term, see Kirk 1985: 30–7.

[35] The term is Parry's; for his discussion of enjambment, see M. Parry 1971: 251–65.

[36] See Graziosi 2001 and D. B. Collins 2004: 185–91.

Enjambment is clearly used to expressive effect: the progressive type, for example, suits the weighty register of epic catalogues.[37] Necessary runovers, by contrast, often convey the urgency and animation of Iliadic speeches (see, e.g., 477n.). This is particularly evident at the beginning of Andromache's speech, when she first addresses Hector: as Bakker points out, Andromache's speech creates 'a rhythmical profile that runs increasingly against the basic rhythm of the hexameter'.[38] In Andromache's speech, units of rhythm, and of thought, often start after the bucolic diairesis, rather than at the beginning of the line: this alternative rhythm seems to reflect her emotional strain and characterises fraught speeches also elsewhere in the poem.[39]

Though rhythm is not generally used to expressive effect in Homer,[40] there are, then, exceptions. At 506–11n., for example, the overlapping runovers match the swift movement of the horse; and the effect is reinforced by the 'galloping' dactyls of 511n., as Kirk points out.[41] At 157n. Glaukos' exceptionally ugly and impressive κάκ' ἐμήσατο θυμῷι, at the end of the line, is made even uglier by the fact that he disregards Hermann's bridge – that is to say, he inserts a word break, where the line usually runs smoothly on. At 164n. Anteia's brutal rhetoric matches the disjointed rhythm of her speech. Elision too can have a powerful impact, especially at the beginning of the line: 165n., 413n. Even hiatus can sometimes be expressive: at 306n. it lends urgency to Theano's prayer. Whether or not the poet of the *Iliad* made use of writing, all this shows that he understood the power of rhythm in performance.

2.2 Formulae and their meaning

Rhythm shapes the language of epic. In composing his song, the poet of the *Iliad* draws on a large and well-established stock of phrases, which fit the rhythm of the hexameter line. Comparative studies show that repeated phrases, or formulae, help bards to compose poetry in real time, as they perform in front of an audience. In the 1930s Milman Parry and Albert Lord recorded the performances of illiterate Bosnian *guslari* and showed that they were able to recite very long poems – not by remembering a script, but by combining formulaic expressions, and by arranging them into well-established narrative patterns, or 'themes'. Formulae and themes were, to a large extent, inherited: they had developed over generations, in order to enable singers to compose, or re-compose, their poems in the course of live performances. The *guslar* had at his disposal a stock of different formulae that described the same character, situation, thing or action, each of which had a specific metrical shape. He could choose the appropriate formula depending on how many beats he needed in order to reach the end of the line.

Parry showed that in Homeric epic there is usually just one formula describing a particular character or action in any given metrical unit: this formulaic economy, or 'thrift', enabled bards to get to the end of the line without having to take too long thinking about different options for describing an action or character. The language

---

[37] See Higbie 1990: 67. [38] Bakker 2005: 55. [39] For discussion, Bakker 2005: 52–5.
[40] M. L. West 1982: 39 and 1997b: 232–3. [41] Kirk 1990: 226.

of Homeric epic is thus characterised by formulaic economy. This characteristic emerges clearly, for example, when we consider some of the more common noun–epithet formulae used to describe Hector, in the nominative, at the end of the line.[42] He is called μέγας κορυθαιόλος Ἕκτωρ after the feminine caesura (e.g. 263n.):

– ∪∪ | – ∪∪ | – ∪ μέγας κορυθαιόλος Ἕκτωρ

A briefer formula is used after the hephthemimeral caesura (116 etc.):

– ∪∪ | – ∪∪ | – ∪∪ | – κορυθαιόλος Ἕκτωρ

After the bucolic diairesis, when only two feet are left, Hector is called φαίδιμος Ἕκτωρ (466n., 472, 494, etc.), or ὄβριμος Ἕκτωρ, in contexts where φαίδιμος Ἕκτωρ is metrically impossible (8.473, 10.200, 11.347, 14.44):

– ∪∪ | – ∪∪ | – ∪∪ | – ∪∪ | φαίδιμος Ἕκτωρ/ὄβριμος Ἕκτωρ

This kind of analysis helps to explain when these formulae are used; what remains to be seen is how they affect the audience. Milman Parry, in an influential study entitled 'The meaning of the epithet in epic poetry', reached rather discouraging conclusions about the significance of noun–epithet formulae: he argued that many epithets had no special meaning in relation to the context in which they were used, that audiences felt indifferent towards them, and that they were perhaps best left untranslated.[43] This sort of approach does not seem entirely satisfactory: traditional epithets, and other formulaic expressions, are not equivalent to an instrumental interlude, or a bit of humming, or some other wordless rhythmical 'filling'. They are words, and affect audiences through their meaning, as well as through their rhythmical qualities.

Modern readers often find the traditional formulations of Homeric poetry repet-itive and burdensome: in his reworking of the *Iliad* the poet Christopher Logue, for example, decided '(mostly) to omit Homer's descriptive epithets'.[44] In antiquity too, the formularity of Homer became increasingly obsolete: in keeping with their liter-ary sensibilities, Hellenistic scholars often championed a less formulaic text of Homer than that found in the mainstream tradition.[45] In order to assess the effect of formulae on early audiences, it is perhaps best to start with the reactions to epic performances described in the Homeric poems themselves.

The Phaeacians trust Odysseus because he sounds like a singer, there is a 'shape of words' to his performance (*Od.* 11.367, quoted above). This is an apt description of traditional epic language: formulae have a specific shape, and they do inspire trust. The poet does not describe actions and characters simply as the fancy takes him; there is a rhythm and an order to his words. Although the formulaic system is used with remarkable flexibility and inventiveness in the *Iliad*, rhetorically, it conveys an impression of stability. Traditional epithets, for example, link specific characters to their aptest attributes. Hector is κορυθαιόλος, 'of the gleaming helmet', throughout the *Iliad*. Most of the time the epithet remains in the background: it reminds the

---

[42] For a full analysis of Hector's epithets see Di Benedetto 1998: 122–39.
[43] M. Parry 1971: 118–72, esp. 171–2.   [44] Logue 2001: vii.   [45] Fantuzzi 2001: 174–7.

audience, unobtrusively, that Hector is an impressive-looking warrior. In book 6, however, the poet reflects on Hector's warlike appearance and brings his epithet into focus. At 467–70n. baby Astyanax suddenly realises that his father is indeed κορυθαιόλος and lets out a mighty scream. The scene makes us smile (471n.), not only because the baby's reaction is described in such vivid and realistic detail, but also because the poet adapts standard battlefield formulations in order to describe a most unwarlike episode (468n., 469–70n.).

There is often a dynamic, expressive tension between the traditional formulations used by the poet and the specific situations he describes. The use of patronymics is a case in point. Sons bear their fathers' names and should live up to their memory: patronymics are precisely a means of remembering the father when describing the son. And yet the narrative shows how the relationship between fathers and sons is seldom straightforward. At 119n. the poet formally introduces 'Glaukos, son of Hippolochos' and Diomedes 'son of Tydeus', as they drive forward ready to fight one another. In the ensuing encounter between the two, Glaukos tries hard to live up to the expectations of his father (206–11n.) and fails; Diomedes, by contrast, claims that he cannot even remember his own father (222–3n.) and proposes an exchange of gifts in honour of a friendship between grandfathers: 215–21n. The use of the patronymic at 401n. is even more devastating: the poet calls Astyanax Ἑκτορίδην, 'son of Hector'. The word is traditional in meaning and formation; but it is, in fact, unique: a *hapax legomenon* – something the poet says only once. There are obvious reasons for this: Astyanax will never grow up to be Hector's heir. The poet makes up a patronymic for him only shortly before the baby dies. And Astyanax will die precisely because he is 'the son of Hector', as Andromache points out: 24.734–8.

Traditional formulations describe the world as it should be: they encapsulate, for example, the orderly succession from father to son. But in fact, the poet often draws attention to the distance between his traditional, inherited 'beauty of words' and the painful tale he sings: Hector 'of the gleaming helmet' frightens his son; and later, when Achilles kills him and drags him from his chariot, the poet describes how 'the dust rose around him, as he was dragged away, and his black hair spread out, and his whole head was in the dust, which had been beautiful before' (22.401–3). That image shows Hector without his shining helmet.

Not all epithets are thrown into relief in quite this way; some remain in the background, but they too add to the texture of the poem: many words, for example, convey a sense of brilliance (cf., e.g., 26–7n.: φαίδιμα γυῖα; and 31n.: δῖος). They also, unobtrusively, express some fundamental values: war is dreadful (1n.); death is terrible (16–17n.). Homer's traditional formulations constitute a powerful language, then; they are not simply a toolkit of metrically convenient expressions, or empty fillers.[46] Like many other aspects of Homeric poetry – ranging from metre, to diction, to grammar – formulae are far from rigidly mechanical. There are some stable

---

[46] Edwards 1986 and 1988 gives an excellent account of scholarship on Homeric formulae. For more recent contributions see the articles assembled in Morris and Powell 1997, Bakker and Kahane 1997, and Létoublon 1997; also Visser 1987, J. M. Foley 1991 and 1999, Bakker 1997a and 2005, Graziosi and Haubold 2005.

patterns; and, even more often, there are recognisable tendencies: some epithets, for example, gravitate towards certain nouns but are not exclusive to them (12n: βοὴν ἀγαθός). Some phrases or lines are repeated just twice: they are not standard formulae or type scenes, therefore, but they are also not unique: 9–11n., 447–9n., 506–11n.[47] It does not seem possible to draw sharp distinctions between inherited, traditional formulations and original contributions on the part of the poet. In fact, any sharp distinction between tradition and innovation seems unhelpful: the poet, inspired by the Muse, sings what happened at Troy 'as if he had been there himself' (Od. 8.491). Traditional formulae help him in this task; but in order to describe unique, and often startling, events – such as the conversation between Glaukos and Diomedes, the encounter between Hector and his son Astyanax, or the defilement of Hector's body – the poet adapts and reworks the language of epic, in order to convey what happened precisely, and in vivid detail.

2.3 Traditional narrative patterns

As well as shorter formulae, the poet also makes use of larger narrative patterns and structures, which help give shape and significance to the story. Catalogues, as has already emerged, are a distinctive feature of Homeric poetry: they enable the poet to express and organise his impressive knowledge of the heroic past.[48] Well-established structures are also employed in the description of common actions or events: Homeric characters arm themselves, bathe, eat, fight, die and lament the dead according to recognisable routines, or 'type scenes'.[49] Speeches also follow standard templates and can be divided into several different categories, depending on their purpose and their formal characteristics: there are, for example, clearly defined martial exhortations, prayers, supplications, laments for the dead and verbal assaults ('flyting': 123–43n.). Formalised lines mark the beginning and end of speeches, and they express something important about their tone, significance and effect (45n., 51n.). Other traditional devices are standardly used to structure the poems: at the end of a speech or episode, for example, the poet often echoes its beginning, in 'ring composition' (e.g. 123–43n., 253–62n. and see below p. 18).[50]

These traditional patterns were doubtless technically helpful, and we can imagine how experienced singers must have taught beginners how to do a supplication speech, or round off a killing. We know that, in the South Slavic tradition, the guslari learnt from

---

[47] On significant lines repeated twice, see Rutherford 1992: 56–7.

[48] Catalogues impressed ancient audiences and readers: Alcinous compliments Odysseus on his ability to 'set out' or 'catalogue' his story like a bard (καταλέξαι: Od. 11.368); see also the comments of ancient readers in the scholia ad Il. 2.484–93. Gaertner 2001, Perceau 2002 and Sammons 2010 discuss Homeric catalogues.

[49] Discussed by Arend 1933 and, from the perspective of oral poetry, Lord 2000 (first published in 1960). For more recent approaches, see Edwards 1992 and Clark 2004: 134–7.

[50] Ring composition was first described by van Otterlo 1948. For an up-to-date anthropological perspective see Douglas 2007. Minchin 1995 and Nimis 1999 focus on Homer; for ring composition in Homeric speeches: Lohmann 1970.

one another how to 'ornament' a horse or a hero (as they put it); they knew, in other words, how to describe the arming of a hero, or the appearance of his beautiful horse, according to standard templates, which facilitated (re-)composition in performance.[51] But the point, for readers of Homer, is not so much to learn traditional techniques of composition, but to appreciate their effect, and the different uses to which they are put in the *Iliad*. Like formulae, traditional narrative patterns contribute to an impression of 'shape and beauty' (μορφή: *Od.* 11.368). They suggest that there is a proper way of doing things: the actions of epic characters often have a formalised quality to them. When Hecuba enters her store room and selects her favourite garment, for example, her actions resemble those of Priam at 24.191–237, when he enters the store room, and those of Helen at *Odyssey* 15.99–108, when she selects a garment for Telemachus. The verbal similarities between these different passages are not uniquely significant (they are not as pointed and deliberate as the rare repeated lines in Virgil, for example); and yet they lend to the passage a distinctive shape (288–95n.).

Sometimes, traditional narrative patterns are put to more specific and pointed use. It is rewarding to pay attention to divergences and adaptations, because the poet often harnesses the expectations of competent listeners to great dramatic effect. At 110–18n., for example, Hector delivers a speech of martial exhortation. He starts in conventional fashion but then makes a radical departure from the norm. Just at the point when exhortations usually feature an appeal for unity and solidarity among men on the battlefield (113n.), Hector declares that he alone will go back into the city and meet up with the wives of his soldiers – while they stay out and fight. This is a shocking statement, not just for Hector's troops, but also for Homeric audiences familiar with the rhetoric of martial exhortation. Even catalogues, which may be thought intrinsically static in form, can actually have dramatic impact, and considerable narrative momentum. The catalogue of killings at the beginning of book 6, for example, is arranged in a steady *crescendo*: in the first entry, Ajax kills one opponent; in the next, Diomedes kills two; Euryalos then kills four men in quick succession; and the catalogue then adds seven deaths in an even shorter compass: 5–36n. By line 36 it is clear that the Achaeans are about to defeat the Trojans, even before the poet says so explicitly.

Traditional patterns, then, should not be regarded as the unwieldy legacy of an oral tradition, but rather as versatile poetic resources. The poet commands a very rich and diverse tradition, from which he draws together and combines many different elements. Glaukos' speech, for example, is cast as a genealogy and invites listeners to reflect on an issue that is more generally relevant to genealogical accounts: in every family history there are rises and falls; there are generations that stand out for their achievements, and others that contribute to a family decline. Glaukos tries hard to present himself as the culmination of his family's hopes and aspirations (206–11n.), but in fact it is his grandfather Bellerophontes who dominates his family history.

[51] For a fascinating description of how the *guslari* learnt and used traditional themes, see Lord 2000: ch. 4, esp. 88.

Often, the poet combines different traditional elements to striking effect: when Andromache addresses Hector as he is about to leave for the battlefield, she opens and closes her speech in a manner that recalls battlefield rebukes – but with a difference. Instead of urging Hector to go forward and fight in the first line of battle, as in ordinary rebukes, she tells him to put the troops forward and to direct operations from inside the walls (431–9). This suggestion shocked ancient readers, but the main part of her speech explains her perspective – in the most direct and harrowing way. Between her opening reproach and her closing suggestion, Andromache performs something close to a funeral lament, in front of her living husband. She thus enacts, for him, the consequences of his actions. The poet later comments explicitly on Andromache's performance: he says that, on returning home, she instilled in all the women a need to mourn, and that 'they lamented Hector in his own home, while he was still living' (500n.). This is one of many lines that mark the end of the book through ring composition: see also 482–3n., 494n., 495n., 497n., 499n., 501–2n., 515–16n. and 520–9n. All these circles close off the last encounter between husband and wife – and foreshadow the end of everything that mattered to them: the death of Hector, the enslavement of Andromache, the murder of Astyanax, the fall of the city.

2.4 *Language*

Almost half the *Iliad* consists of direct speech; book 6 exceeds even that proportion: speeches take up more than 60 per cent of the overall number of lines. Homeric characters use language in an impressive and memorable way: they pun (e.g. 130–1n., 139–40n., 143n., 201n., 284n., 328–9n. with 331n.), quote proverbs and maxims (146n., 261n., 339n., 492–3n.), subvert or parody traditional language (255n., 260n., 336n.) and often use flamboyant turns of phrase (143n., 344n., 413n.). Characters have a recognisable, individual style: Hector tends to be formal and restrained, except for one sudden, frustrated outburst when he talks to his mother (280–5n.). Paris sounds self-indulgent, petulant and insecure (332–41n., 517–19n.); Hecuba uses dramatic gestures and vigorous language (255n.); Helen's words are as inviting as her appearance (343–58n.).

In comparison with the language of his characters, the poet is more even: some words occur only in character speech, because they are too colourful, or imply too strong a value judgement.[52] And yet the language of the poet is far from rigid or monotonous: he too puns on words (500n.) and uses memorable phrases (e.g. 496n.). Objects and situations affect his language: the description of Priam's palace, for example, is solid and painstaking (242–52n.); while the scene where Paris runs towards Hector requires a more free-flowing approach (503–5). The language of

---

[52] Griffin 1986. Restrictions can cut both ways: Homeric characters, who lack the poet's understanding of divine affairs, do not call Helen the 'daughter of Zeus'; the one exception is Penelope at *Od.* 23.218.

the similes is often more varied and idiosyncratic than that of the main narrative: when the poet makes a comparison, he moves away from the battlefield, and this is reflected in the greater variety of his vocabulary and style.[53] The famous simile at 506–14n. is a good example: the poet describes the mood and movement of the horse in a style that recalls the more idiosyncratic language and syntax of character speech.

The language of the poet is often influenced by the concerns and perspectives of his characters: narratologists call the phenomenon 'embedded focalisation'.[54] When Hector looks at Astyanax in silence, for example, the poet uses the language of doting parents, and he piles on words of endearment for the little boy: Ἑκτορίδην ἀγαπητόν, ἀλίγκιον ἀστέρι καλῶι, 'son of Hector, beloved, beautiful like a shining star' (401n., cf. 400–3n.). Later, the poet describes how Astyanax perceives his father, as he looks up to his terrifying helmet: 470n. This is a striking case of focalisation, where the poet describes things from the perspective of a baby who is too young to talk. Sometimes, it is the characters who adopt the tone and register of the poet. At 414–28n., for example, Andromache gives an account of her family history, thus completing the information provided by the poet shortly before (395–8n.). This kind of juxtaposition between main narrative and character speech is typical of Homeric epic and was of interest to ancient readers;[55] sometimes, it involves a drastic change of tone, but not in this case: Andromache sounds almost as distanced and objective as the poet. Her tone reveals, with devastating clarity, that her dependence on Hector is a matter of fact, not just an emotion: if Hector dies, nobody will be able to look after her, because her father, her brothers and her mother are already dead.

Homeric language is, at times, difficult to translate – not because it is particularly erudite or recherché, but because it contains many traditional words and expressions that were not entirely transparent even to the earliest audiences of the *Iliad*. Comparative studies show that traditional texts (whether oral or written) tend to retain archaic words beyond the point when they are easily comprehensible: the liturgical formula 'the quick and the dead', for example, retains a use of 'quick' (= 'living') which is almost extinct in standard, contemporary English. The diction of Homeric epic is likewise characterised by inherited expressions, and the poet sometimes glosses within the text itself: at the very beginning of book 6, for example, φύλοπις is followed by the common noun μάχη. While the exact meaning of φύλοπις was debated in antiquity, the word was powerful and expressive: it sounded warlike, and later Greek poets used it precisely in order to evoke the heroic battles described in early hexameter poetry (1n.). There are, then, some obvious continuities between the glosses contained in the poem itself, the explanations given by ancient scholars and lexicographers, and the definitions offered in standard modern dictionaries. For example, Homer suggests two popular etymologies for the traditional epithet δαΐφρων, indicating that it may mean 'warlike' (cf. δαΐ = 'battle') or 'wise' (cf. δαήμων = 'knowledgeable, understanding'):

---

53 Edwards 1991: 37–8, with further bibliographical guidance.   54 De Jong 2004: ch. 4.
55 Plato famously discusses the phenomenon at *Rep.* 392c.

162n. The same alternative meanings are preserved also in the Homeric scholia; and the LSJ proposes the following translations: 'warlike', 'fiery', 'wise', 'prudent'.

Sometimes, the point of particular words and expressions is not to convey a straightforward meaning in the clearest possible way, but to mirror the most mysterious and difficult aspects of human life and behaviour. It is not entirely clear, for example, what exactly is meant by the description of sacrificial cattle as ἦνις ἠκέστας (93–4n.), but the epithets sound ancient and precise and suggest ritual propriety. Death is shrouded in mysterious expressions (143n., 241n.); and the Chimaira is as impossible as the adjective that characterises her: ἀμαιμακέτην, 179n. Many words try to capture the unfathomable characteristics of the gods (e.g. 269n.: ἀγελείης), and the poet occasionally even offers items of vocabulary in the language of the gods: 4n. (Ξάνθοιο), 1.403, 14.290–1 and 20.74. Items of divine vocabulary suggest, in the most direct way, that the poet's linguistic competence derives from his special relationship with the Muse, but there are also less direct ways in which he tries to explain to ordinary mortals the nature of the gods. He reflects, for example, on the etymologies of divine names and epithets: 419–20n. (κοῦραι Διὸς αἰγιόχοιο). Etymologising passages are frequent also in Hesiod's *Theogony* (e.g. 195–8) and the *Homeric Hymns* (311n.: Παλλάς; 428n.: Ἄρτεμις ἰοχέαιρα); and that is no coincidence, because those texts too have divine authority: according to Herodotus, 'it was Hesiod and Homer … who first established a theogony for the Greeks, gave epithets to the gods, defined their due honours and spheres of influence and described their appearance'.[56]

Particles are also difficult to translate, not because they are obscure, but because there are no straightforward equivalents in the English language. They structure and organise Homeric discourse: their effect is sometimes captured by our use of punctuation, and sometimes by conjunctions and adverbs. Particles fit the hexameter rhythm, and different clusters suit different metrical contexts; but this does not entail their being meaningless padding: they enhance and organise the narrative, and establish a connection with the audience. Bakker has shown in detail, for example, how the particle ἄρ(α) or ῥα directs the attention of the audience to a specific aspect of the story and brings it to life before their eyes.[57] When the poet uses the particle at the beginning of the book, 2n., he invites audiences to visualise how the fighting intensified everywhere across the plain. The poet Christopher Logue captures this aspect of Homeric poetry not by using particles, but by challenging his readers directly: 'See if you can imagine how it looked.'[58] At 9n. Homer uses the particle ῥα to draw attention to a specific event – τόν ῥ̱' ἔβαλε, Ajax 'hit him' – and then invites the audience to follow the tip of Ajax's spear, as it penetrates into the forehead of the enemy: πέρησε δ' ἀ̱ρ̱ ὀστέον εἴσω | αἰχμὴ χαλκείη (10n.). Other particles are more discreet, but they too ensure that the audience stays with the poet. The frequent δέ, for example, unobtrusively reminds the audience that the poet is guiding them

---

[56] Herodotus 2.53.2.   [57] Bakker 1993: 16–23.   [58] Logue 2001: 153.

through the story, in proper order.[59] Together with the rarer μέν, which anticipates important developments, δέ can at times be rather pointed (e.g. 40n. with 42–3n., 167n. and 168n., 212–31n., 279n. and 280n.).

Characters use particles in a more obviously rhetorical way than the poet. Diomedes, for example, employs γε three times in quick succession: the particles express his aggressiveness mixed with uncertainty (125n., 128–9n.). Glaukos uses ἄρα to reveal the details of the plot against Bellerophontes (158n.). Hecuba second-guesses Hector with ἦ μάλα δή (255n.; cf. Paris at 518n.). Helen waves away the issue of her guilt with a casual γε (349n.) and then uses ἄρ(α) twice in one line, in order to establish a special relationship with Hector, at the expense of her husband Paris (352n.). Hector responds by mentioning his own wife, excusing himself and trying hard to sound reasonable: three γάρ-clauses in a row (359–68n.).

2.5 *Grammar*

Like every aspect of Homeric language, grammar is fundamentally shaped by the hexameter rhythm. Different grammatical forms coexist, and make Homeric language more versatile and suited to different metrical combinations. For example, the poet can choose between linguistically older, typically uncontracted forms, and more recent, contracted ones. The early singular genitive ending in -οιο coexists with the contracted -ου; there are genitive plurals in -άων and in -ῶν; earlier and later forms of the same verb are often attested: for example, φοβέοντο (early) and φοβεύμενος (late). Contracted forms may be artificially extended so as to fit the hexameter: the phenomenon is called diectasis; cf. φόως (6n.) and τηλεθόωσα (148n.). Some extended forms were never contracted in the first place, thus we find the dative plural ἐπέεσσι(ν) alongside the expected ἔπε(σ)σι(ν); these alternative forms suit different metrical contexts: 325n. Homeric language fits itself exactly to the hexameter and as a result develops some artificial forms (e.g. εὐχετάασθαι: 268n.).[60] Genuine archaisms are preserved if they are metrically convenient or sound especially grand and impressive. Ancient forms in -φι, for example, are metrically useful alternatives to genitive and dative case endings: 510n.

As well as mixing older and more recent forms, Homeric Greek draws from several different dialects. It was never spoken by any real-life community but rather developed for the specific purpose of singing the deeds of gods and men to the six-foot rhythm.[61] The predominant colouring is Ionic (note, for example, the Ionic ending -η, replacing an older -ᾱ), and this fits with ancient traditions that linked Homer to

---

[59] Bakker 1997a: 74–80.
[60] For a detailed discussion of words designed to fit the hexameter, see Chantraine 1948–53: vol. I, 94–112.
[61] For Homeric language as a *Kunstsprache*, 'artificial language', see Meister 1921. For more recent discussions, Chantraine 1948–53, Hainsworth 1988, Horrocks 1997, Wachter 2000 and Hackstein 2002.

various birthplaces on the coast of Asia Minor, especially Chios.[62] There is also a strong Aeolic component (one of Homer's putative birthplaces was Aeolian Cyme), and there may be remnants of Mycenaean Greek.[63] Scholars have also argued for Euboean and Boeotian influences and pointed to several Attic elements, though some of these have turned out not to be exclusive to the Attic dialect, and many seem to concern matters of spelling.[64] There were other literary languages in the ancient world: in seventh-century Mesopotamia, for example, the deeds of gods and heroes were recorded in Standard Babylonian, an equally composite and artificial language.[65] What distinguishes Homeric Greek from other literary languages is the formative influence of the hexameter: different dialect forms were selected so as to provide metrically useful alternatives for saying the same thing. Infinitives, for example, take many different endings: -ειν, -ναι (Ionic), and -μεν, -μεναι (Aeolic); the Ionic pronouns ἡμεῖς/ὑμεῖς coexist with Aeolic ἄμμες/ὔμμες; both the Ionic particle ἄν and the Aeolic alternative κε(ν) are attested and suit different metrical situations.

Ancient readers claimed that Homer knew *all* the Greek dialects.[66] This is an exaggeration that reflects, in part, his status as a poet of Panhellenic appeal; but it is also true that Homeric epic displays a dazzling number of different words and forms. Homer can say 'to be' in five different ways: εἶναι, ἔμεν, ἔμμεν, ἔμεναι, ἔμμεναι; there are also five forms of 'he was': ἔην, ἦεν, ἤην, ἦν, ἔσκε; and the nearly synonymous verbs γίνομαι, πέλομαι and τέτυγμαι add to this already exuberant number of forms. Most of these alternative words are metrically useful, and many are commonplace, but there is also a sense that the poet commands an unfathomably rich language.

In contrast to morphology, Homeric syntax is relatively simple. Complex sub-clauses are rarer than in other genres, though they do feature, especially in character speech (for example: 476–8n.). Sometimes, characters bend the rules of Homeric grammar, as they struggle to express difficult emotions. A good example is 280–5n.: when Hector wishes death on his own brother, even his morphology and syntax become harsh and twisted. In comparison with his characters, the style of the poet is simpler: he often strings together sequences of main clauses, in what is called 'parataxis'. Oral poets from other traditions typically use parataxis, rather than complex subordinate structures: they track the flow of ideas rather than aim at rhetorical condensation.[67] In an important study Bakker argues that parataxis reflects the

---

[62] See Graziosi 2002: ch. 2 for a discussion of early Greek traditions relating to Homer's birth.

[63] See Janko 1994: 15–19 (Aeolic) and 11–12 (Mycenaean).

[64] On Attic: Wackernagel 1916; Chantraine 1948–53: vol. I, 15–16; Cassio 2002: 117 with n. 55. On possible Euboean and Boeotian influences, see the cautious appraisal by Cassio 2002: 108, 111 and 116.

[65] For the character and use of Standard Babylonian see Huehnergard 2005: 595–8.

[66] Hillgruber 1994–9: vol. I, 102–4.

[67] One of the first scholars to investigate the connections between parataxis and orality is Notopoulos 1949, who compares ancient Greek and Kirghiz narrative traditions. An influential discussion of parataxis as a feature of orality is Ong 1988, esp. 37–8.

structures of spontaneous human thought and speech.[68] Given that the *Iliad* stems from a tradition of composition in performance, it makes sense that it should rely on the structures of improvised speech. But parataxis is not just a natural or convenient arrangement for oral performers: it defines the Homeric style. By using parataxis, the poet describes the story as it unfolds, without drawing attention to himself. At 9–11, for example, he offers a series of main clauses marked by the particle ἄρα, as we have already discussed: Ajax attacks an opponent, thrusts his spear into the man's forehead, and the tip breaks through the bone. The attack, the impact and its result are conveyed by successive sentences which, like camera shots, track the movement of the spear. Straightforward sequences of main clauses, like this one, enhance the impression of objectiveness – and make the narrative exceptionally vivid.

2.6 Vividness

There have been many different responses to Homeric epic in the course of its long history, but listeners and readers of different ages have been impressed by its vividness. In *The Contest of Homer and Hesiod* 13 West, for example, the audience react with amazement (θαυμάσαντες) at a recital of *Iliad* 13.126–33 and 339–44 (a blindingly vivid passage).[69] This is the kind of response that the *Iliad* invites: the poet sometimes uses explicit formulae of amazement in order to underline particularly impressive aspects of his story: θαῦμα ἰδέσθαι, 'a wonder to behold'; cf. ἦ μέγα θαῦμα τόδ᾽ ὀφθαλμοῖσιν ὁρῶμαι, 'that is a great wonder for my eyes to see'.[70] In a famous essay entitled *Laocoön: on the limits of painting and poetry*, the eighteenth-century critic Gotthold Ephraim Lessing singles out Homer for the exceptional vividness of his narrative, pointing out that he does not just paint an image but shows how it evolves and develops over time: 'when Homer wants to show us how Agamemnon was dressed, he has the king put on his garments, one by one, before our eyes'; 'he places a single object in a series of stages, in each of which it has a different appearance'.[71] Lessing praises Homer above any painter because, he argues, he tracks the transformation of an image over time. As we have seen, modern readers find his poetry cinematic.

   Many factors contribute to the exceptional vividness of Homeric poetry, some of which have already been discussed. There are the many bright words that describe the heroic world: the scholia D *ad* 2.522 even gloss δῖος as θαυμαστός, thus making a connection between this standard epic epithet and the overall effect of Homeric poetry. There are the many particles which keep the audience engaged and draw attention to salient details in the narrative. And then there are grand panoramic vistas, and detailed observations at close quarters. The poet's language is precise

---

[68] Bakker 1997a.
[69] Note especially 13.340–1: . . . ὄσσε δ᾽ ἄμερδεν | αὐγὴ χαλκείη κορύθων ἄπο λαμπομενάων: '. . . their eyes were dazzled by the bronze light reflecting off the shining helmets'.
[70] 13.99 etc. Slatkin 2007 explores the connections between seeing, marvelling, and epic fame in the *Iliad*.
[71] Lessing 1962: 80; originally 1766.

and memorable, his syntax transparent; and speeches reveal the character of those
who utter them. But, above all, there is the poet's ability to connect with our own
perceptions, even across a gulf of almost three millennia. It is not difficult to visualise,
for example, Astyanax as he recoils, screaming, into his nurse's arms – because we
have all seen little children behave like that. An ancient commentator praises lines
467–9 as follows (ΣbT *ad* 6.467):

ταῦτα δὲ τὰ ἔπη οὕτως ἐστὶν ἐναργείας μεστά, ὅτι οὐ μόνον ἀκούεται τὰ
πράγματα, ἀλλὰ καὶ ὁρᾶται. λαβὼν δὲ τοῦτο ἐκ τοῦ βίου ὁ ποιητὴς ἄκρως
περιεγένετο τῆι μιμήσει.

These lines are so full of vividness because we do not just hear about the events
but see them too.[72] Taking this scene from real life, the poet achieves the highest
degree of imitation.

The scholiast mentions μίμησις, 'imitation', a key concept in ancient literary
criticism. According to Plato, poetry imitates life, drama is the most mimetic kind
of literature, and Homer is 'the path-finder of tragedy'.[73] There are, indeed, many
theatrical aspects to Homer's poetry. We get a clear sense of how characters look and
behave: in some cases the text comes close to providing implicit 'stage directions'. At
496n., for example, the poet describes Andromache, as she walks home in tears and
'turns back again and again' to look at Hector. The implication must be that Hector
is looking at her and is still standing by the Scaean Gates (the poet later confirms
this: 515–16n.). At 340–1n. we can likewise infer Hector's behaviour from the way
others react to him. Paris asks Hector to wait while he gets ready for battle and then
suddenly changes his mind: Hector should go right ahead. We can easily imagine
Hector's look at the mere suggestion that he should stay around, while his soldiers
die (for the sake of Paris) on the battlefield.

Classical Greek tragedy, modern painting, contemporary film: the *Iliad* has repeatedly been compared to the most vivid and visual means of expression. These com-
parisons are, of course, anachronistic: in the end, it is important to return, in ring
composition, to our opening remarks. To the poet of the *Iliad*, and his early audiences,
vividness was a sign of divine presence, a gift of the Muse. Homeric poetry was, as
Ford has argued, a kind of epiphany.[74]

3. BOOK 6 IN THE STRUCTURE OF THE *ILIAD*

It is difficult to establish when the *Iliad* was divided into twenty-four books, each
represented by one letter of the alphabet.[75] The division was clearly in place in

---

[72] Or perhaps: '. . . so that we do not just hear . . . ', reading ὥστε for ὅτι with Wilamowitz.
[73] Plato, *Rep.* 598d, with Macleod 1982: 1–8. On Homer's 'stagecraft', see esp. Clay 2007.
[74] Ford 1992: 54–5.
[75] [Plutarch] *On Homer* II ch. 4 claims that Aristarchus, or more generally his school, was the
first to divide the *Iliad* and *Odyssey* into books, but this cannot be right: see S. West 1967: 18–25.

Hellenistic times but, as with many other aspects of the Homeric text, we know far less about the situation in the archaic and classical period. At 2.116 Herodotus discusses *Iliad* 6.289–92 and says that the lines are found 'in the exploit of Diomedes' (ἐν Διομήδεος ἀριστείηι), a title that was later reserved for book 5 alone. It follows that even if our book divisions are early, as Jensen and others have argued, there were other ways of dividing up the text in classical Greece.[76] The issue of origins should not, however, distract us from a more important point: the divisions at the beginning and end of book 6 stem from an intelligent ancient articulation of the poem. Book 6 is characterised by the gods' absence: they abandon the battlefield at 6.1 and only enter again at 7.17. The central episode of the book is Hector's visit to Troy: lines 1–71 describe the crisis that leads to his mission; lines 72–118 reveal Helenos' plan to send Hector back and describe him as he runs towards the city; an intervening episode concludes the narrative of Diomedes' exploits (119–236); and finally the poet describes in detail Hector's visit: 237–529. The book ends as Hector and Paris are on the point of leaving the city through the Scaean Gates, and at 7.1 they run out into the battlefield.

The first books of the *Iliad* introduce the main characters and evoke the cause and beginning of the Trojan war: the poem opens with the clash between Achilles and Agamemnon; the Catalogue of Ships in book 2 acts as a reminder of the expedition; book 3 introduces Helen and her two husbands; book 4 dramatises how a private quarrel over a woman can become a war; in book 5 the fighting escalates; and in book 6 – as soon as the gods leave the battlefield – the Achaeans break through the lines and demonstrate their military superiority. The narrative now looks forward to the time when the Achaeans will defeat the Trojans: it anticipates the end of the poem (particularly books 22 and 24) and foreshadows the fall of the city. It is book 6, more than any other, that makes the *Iliad* 'a poem about Troy'.

In comparison with other books, the plot hardly advances in *Iliad* 6: the confrontation between Glaukos and Diomedes results in an exchange of gifts rather than a duel; and Hector's mission fails in its purpose (311n.). The tension in the book does not stem from momentous developments in the narrative, but from a stark contrast between what the audience know will happen to the city and what the characters inside it fear and hope. The issue is introduced as soon as Hector enters the city at 237–41n., and the poet constantly reminds the audience about the future of Troy: the second half of the book focuses on the Trojan women in a manner that recalls early accounts of the fall of Troy.[77] The foreshadowing is, at times,

---

For further discussion see especially Jensen 1999; Taplin 1992: 285–93; Heiden 1998; and Edwards 2002: 39–47.

[76] One ancient commentator actually encourages his readers to ignore the division between *Iliad* 2 and 3 because, he claims, it is not original; cf. Nünlist 2006.

[77] E.g. *Iliou Persis* (Proclus, *Chrestomathy*, pp. 144–6 West); Stesichorus, *Sack of Troy* frr. 197–8, 201 and 204–5 Davies. The women of Troy occupy a prominent place also on Polygnotus' painting of the aftermath of the Trojan War as described by Pausanias (10.25–27, esp. 25.9ff.); and in Euripides' play *Trojan Women*.

uncomfortably vivid: Hector's behaviour, in particular, mirrors the actions of future conquerors. At 318–20n. he enters into Helen's bedroom fully armed, and covered in blood – just like the Achaean soldiers who will soon break into the homes and bedrooms of the Trojans, in order to loot, rape and murder.[78] The poet thus relies not only on the audience's familiarity with the epic tradition, but also on their visual memory: he superimposes iconic images of the fall of Troy onto his narrative of Hector's visit.

Whereas the audience know, in graphic detail, that Troy will fall, the characters inside the story can only imagine what might happen. There is a great sense of foreboding in their words, but there are also occasional glimmers of hope, and self-delusion. The speeches in book 6 convey an extraordinary range of emotions. Fear of the future is obvious in all characters in Troy, with the possible exception of Helen. Andromache cannot keep to her daily tasks, the strain is too great: 381–9n., 485–93n. and 494–502n. Hector himself is far from stable: his speeches vary widely in tone and express many contradictory views about the future in close succession. His vitriolic and frustrated outburst against Paris (280–5n.) is quickly followed by a surprisingly restrained speech to him (325–31n.). Hector is studiously reasonable in his reply to Helen (359–68n.); whereas his first speech to Andromache ends in open despair (440–65n., 464–5n.). He imagines Astyanax in his prime, and victorious over the enemy (475–81n.), and then refuses to contemplate the future at all, insisting instead on the importance of duty and the inscrutability of fate (485–93n.). And then there are his sudden and unlikely hopes at the end of the book, which help him make up with Paris and face the enemy (520–9n.).

Book 6 inspires an overwhelming sense of pity, on the part of the audience, for the characters in the story. Pity also colours the characters' own words and feelings: Andromache asks Hector to take pity on her (407n., 431n.) and, when he sees her smiling tearfully at their baby, he does indeed feel pity for his wife (484n.) but goes on to remind her about fate, and duty and honour. The clash of feelings and values, the irreconcilable difference between social expectations and individual needs, the ignorance of the characters and the psychological complexity of their speeches, the threat of madness (389n.), the aloofness of the gods and the audience's sure knowledge of what will happen – all these aspects of book 6 make it remarkably close to classical Greek tragedy.

3.1 The gods

Book 6 is marked by the temporary absence of the gods – but the characters do not know that the gods have left, and we see them ask themselves whether they are present. When Hector rallies the troops, and the Trojans suddenly make a stand, the Achaeans think that a god in disguise 'descended from starry heaven': 107–9n.

---

[78] Later accounts of the sack of Troy emphasise the violent intrusion of soldiers into bedrooms: see e.g. Eur. *Andr.* 109–12, *Hec.* 914–51; and Virg. *Aen.* 2.479–505, esp. 503–5.

The supposition makes sense, especially as a reaction to the events in the previous book. At 5.334–40 Diomedes wounds Aphrodite, who is rescuing her son Aeneas; he then charges against Apollo, who reminds him of the difference between mortals and gods: 5.436–44. Ares enters the fray at 5.461–2, and his intervention draws Athena to the battlefield: she leaps onto Diomedes' chariot (which creaks under her weight) and drives it against Ares: 5.835–41. Diomedes wounds the god: 5.855–63. It is only at the end of the book that Zeus establishes some order, and the gods settle down on Olympus, while mortals continue fighting. In book 6 we see Diomedes reflect on what has just happened, mindful of the warning issued by Apollo. When Glaukos challenges him, his reaction is a strange mixture of uncertainty and aggression: if Glaukos is a god, then Diomedes will not fight him; but if he is mortal, he should consider himself already dead (123–43n.). His speech includes the cautionary tale of Lycurgus, who dared attack Dionysos and was punished as a result; but it is only in the following speech, delivered by Glaukos, that the inscrutability of the gods and the vulnerability of human beings truly find expression: 144–211. Diomedes still behaves as if he can simply establish where he stands vis-à-vis the gods; whereas in Glaukos' speech, and especially in his tale about Bellerophontes (155–205n.), the gods remain in the background – powerful and incomprehensible. His outlook sets the tone for what follows.

Faced with the imminent fall of their city, the Trojans seek the protection of Athena – but do not see that she rejects their entreaties: that knowledge is reserved for the audience alone. The seer Helenos tells Hector that the women of Troy should pray to Athena, offer her a robe, promise a sacrifice and ask her 'to take pity on the wives of the Trojans, and their little children' (94–5n.). Hector repeats those instructions to Hecuba (269–78n.), and the women put them into practice – in their own way (286–311n.). And then the poet reveals, in a single line, that the ritual fails: no explanation is offered; the goddess simply lifts her head in denial (311n.). The line fits the portrayal of the gods in the rest of the poem. The Iliadic gods show little concern for human communities; they do not take pity on women or little children. In fact, they seem mostly concerned with individual men. Thetis cares only about her son Achilles: she wants the other Achaeans to perish, so that he may receive his due honours. Hera is determined to destroy the entire city of Troy (presumably because Paris offended her by judging Aphrodite more beautiful).[79] Hera is in fact so keen to see Troy fall that she casually tells Zeus he is welcome to destroy her own favourite cities – Argos, Sparta and Mycenae – whenever he likes: 'let us grant these things to each other, I to you, and you to me, and the other gods will follow' (4.62–3). The other gods do indeed share Hera's careless attitude towards human cities: the Trojans worship Athena, they call her 'protector of cities' (ἐρυσίπτολι: 305n.), they have a temple dedicated to her on their acropolis and, at the end of the war, famously

---

[79] Hera and Athena are hostile to Troy throughout the *Iliad*, and indeed until the city falls: 20.313–17. The poet hardly refers to the judgement of Paris, though at 24.27–30 he does say that it offended the goddesses; see further Scully 1990: 38–40.

drag the Trojan horse into the city, as an offering to her.[80] And yet Athena does not care for Troy: Paris offended her too, and so she hates the entire city. She changes her attitude only after the fall of Troy, when Ajax desecrates her statue and rapes Cassandra. After that, she exacts her revenge on the Achaeans, because a single man offended her. Many poems in the Trojan cycle explored Athena's complex attitude towards Trojans and Achaeans.[81] The failed ritual in *Iliad* 6, as so many other aspects of the book, invited early audiences to reflect on the poems, legends and images that depicted the fall of Troy.

The relationship between Athena and Troy remained a prominent issue in the classical period: according to Herodotus, Xerxes presented himself to the Greeks as the avenger of Priam and the champion of Trojan Athena.[82] The failure of the ritual in book 6 must have seemed particularly interesting, and alarming, to audiences at the Panathenaea. We have already seen that recitations of the Homeric poems featured prominently at that festival. The most important event, however, was a ritual procession, which culminated in the offering of a garment to the goddess Athena. The parallels between the Panathenaea and the ritual in *Iliad* 6 are so striking that Lorimer considered the entire episode an Athenian interpolation.[83] It is ultimately impossible to establish the origins of our text; but it remains important to ask how the Athenians experienced the similarities between their own ritual and that depicted in *Iliad* 6. It must have been striking to hear about Athena's rejection of the Trojan robe, at a festival where the Athenians themselves presented the goddess with one. There were, however, some crucial differences between the Trojan and the Athenian offering. In the *Iliad* Helenos asks Hecuba to select 'the most graceful and largest robe, the one dearest to her' (90n., 91n.). Her choice is disastrous: she picks a garment woven by Sidonian women who were abducted by Paris on his way home, after he had already taken Helen (288–95n.). In early epic the history of an object generally determines its significance,[84] and the history of this particular garment was unlikely to please Athena: it evoked the rape of Helen, and hence the judgement of Paris. The history of an object was also important in actual cultic practice: the Athenians closely monitored the design and production of the robe they offered to Athena. Rather than leaving such matters to individual choice, they publicly appointed weavers and helpers.[85] A comparison with Panathenaic practices suggests that Troy, in contrast to Athens, is at the mercy of individual whims, preferences and allegiances. We have already seen that the Iliadic gods care more about individual men than about cities

---

[80] *Iliou Persis* in Proclus, *Chrestomathy*, p. 144 West. No individual god is mentioned at *Od.* 8.509.

[81] See especially the *Little Iliad* (Proclus, *Chrestomathy*, pp. 120–2 West); the *Iliou Persis* (*Chrest.* pp. 144–6 West); the *Nostoi* (*Chrest.* p. 154 West); and cf. *Od.* 1.326–7, 3.130–6 and 143–7, 4.502, 5.105–11, 13.312–51, with Clay 1983. For a later exploration of Athena's attitude to Troy, cf. Eur. *Tro.* 1–97.

[82] See esp. Herodotus 7.43, with Haubold 2007.

[83] Lorimer 1950: 442–9, who builds on earlier work by Bethe 1929: 314–24; for further discussion, see Kirk 1990: 167–8.

[84] See Crielaard 2003 and Grethlein 2008.   [85] See Neils 1992: 112–17.

and communities – but the problem is not limited to the gods. Hecuba's choice of garment reveals that she is too close to Paris: she cherishes his gifts and is therefore implicated in his actions. Even when she tries to act on behalf of the city, she remains first and foremost Paris' mother.

3.2 Men and women

As the Achaeans break through the lines, and the Trojans flee in disarray, the narrative shifts from the battlefield to the city, and to the women who live in it. Agamemnon reminds his brother of what happened in his home when Paris raped Helen and urges him to fight on relentlessly, until he exacts his revenge: all the Trojans must die, even babies still in their mothers' wombs (55–60n.). The speech is an extreme version of a thought that Nestor has already expressed: at 2.354–6 he told the Achaeans that nobody should set sail for home 'until he has lain in bed with the wife of a Trojan, to avenge Helen . . . ' (cf. also 3.301, where rape is again considered an aspect of war). It is quite clear what the fall of the city entails for the women of Troy and, at 73–4n., the Achaeans are poised for victory. It is at this point that Helenos tells Hector and Aeneas to rally the troops 'before they fall into the hands of the women and become a source of joy for the enemy' (81–2n.). The Achaeans are eager to enter, rape and murder – and, precisely for that reason, the Trojans must not withdraw into the arms of their own wives. Helenos insists that, in this moment of extreme danger, the men and women of Troy must keep to their separate tasks: the men must continue fighting, while the women should pray and make an offering to Athena. The problem is that Helenos needs to communicate his plan to the women: for this difficult task he chooses Hector, who alone must enter the city and talk to the women – without falling into their hands.

At the Scaean Gates he is surrounded by the wives and daughters of the Trojans, who anxiously ask him about their relatives. Family concerns threaten to take over, but Hector does not linger on individual circumstances and delivers the same message to each woman: they should all pray (237–241n.). Here, as elsewhere, Hector tries to reinforce cohesiveness and a sense of community, refusing to yield to individual concerns. The poet, however, emphasises the different personal circumstances of the women: he reveals that many are already bereaved, even though they are unaware of it: 241n. There are good reasons why Hector fails to give specific information about those who have fallen in battle: he may not know all the details, and in any case the news would be divisive – some women would feel relieved, while others would abandon themselves to despair and mourning. And yet Hector will eventually have to face the individual concerns of his own womenfolk: his mother, his sister-in-law and his wife will all confront him with their needs.

Under the strain of war it is difficult and dangerous for men and women to meet: despite Hector's encounters, *Iliad* 6 largely depicts 'a divided world'.[86] The poet

---

[86] The description is taken from Arthur Katz 1981.

conveys the impression that the women move and meet inside the city according to their plans and routines, and that Hector's arrival interrupts and startles them. He meets Hecuba in front of the palace, as she returns from some errand together with her daughter Laodike; like Hector, we do not know where she has been.[87] There is a clear sense, in *Iliad* 6, that the women's plans remain largely unknown to the men. Helenos, for example, says that Hecuba should gather the old women of Troy, unlock the temple of Athena, choose a robe for her and utter a prayer on behalf of the community (86–98n.). In the event, however, the women of Troy divide these tasks among themselves: Hecuba tells her maids to gather the old women (286–7), while she selects the garment (288–95n.); it is then Theano, in her official capacity as priestess of Athena, who opens the temple (297–311n.), places the robe on Athena's knees and utters the prayer (304–10). These discrepancies do not mean that Hecuba disobeys her son's instructions; they simply show that Helenos and Hector have no direct access to the world of the women: they tell their mother what needs to be done, and she delegates as appropriate.

This sense of distance and separation between men and women reaches a new intensity when Hector meets Andromache. He first looks for her at home but does not find her. The housekeeper then tells him that she ran out to the rampart 'like a madwoman', together with the nurse and the baby (381–9n.). When Hector finally meets Andromache, she is extremely distressed, but she is not deranged: the housekeeper must have seen Andromache's grief at its rawest and most uncontrolled. When Andromache returns home after talking to Hector, she again shows the extremity of her pain to her maids: rather than supervising their work, as Hector had told her to do, she rouses them to a full funeral lament (494–502n.). All this suggests that Andromache gives full expression to her pain only in front of other women. Eventually, Andromache will follow Hector's advice and return to her normal household duties – weaving, spinning, and supervising her maids (491–2n.). At 22.437–46, when she next appears, she is weaving a robe and giving an order to her maids – that they should prepare a warm bath for Hector. It is at that point that the poet calls her νηπίη, 'poor innocent' (22.445), because then Hector is already dead. Andromache's tempo does not match Hector's: there is a disjunction between her emotional responses and his death. The poet's comment, νηπίη, suggests that Andromache is out of touch with Hector's situation; but it also exposes the limitations of Hector's earlier advice to her.[88] To continue at home, as normal, while men see to the fighting, proves impossible because war destroys everybody; it is ultimately not just 'the concern of men' (492).

It is above all through the perspectives of women that the poet exposes the brutality of war. Never do women in the *Iliad* celebrate war.[89] Andromache makes no moral distinction between killing and being killed – and accuses Hector of being

---

[87] Aristarchus was so puzzled by Hecuba's movements that he offered an unlikely interpretation in order to account for them: 252n.

[88] On 22.445, see further Grethlein 2006a: 245–53.

[89] On women's attitude to war in the *Iliad*, see further Murnaghan 1999: 207–17.

about to make her a widow: 432n. The one exception is Helen, who ultimately commemorates her own powers in a woven robe depicting the wars that Achaeans and Trojans underwent 'for her sake' (3.128).[90] She is also the only woman who taunts her husband, Paris, and tells him to go back to the battlefield, if he dares (3.428–36; cf. 349–53n.). Her behaviour emphasises, by contrast, the attitudes of other women. Andromache desperately tries to keep Hector safe, and close to her, inside the city: she fights against Hector's determination to prove himself in the first line of battle: 'Your own strength will kill you', are her first words to him (407n.), and in her final appeal she tells him not to make her a widow, or her son an orphan: those are the acts of an enemy (432n.). Her attitude is similar to that of other women in the *Iliad*: in general, they focus their attention on the man they love and try to influence his thoughts and ideas; how his behaviour may be determined by other men is not something they consider in any great detail. Hecuba, for example, assumes that Hector retreated into the city on an impulse, in order to pray (256n.); but, in fact, we know that he is carrying out Helenos' instructions, has rallied the troops before leaving and has informed the army of his mission (110–18n.). He is not simply acting on a whim, as Hecuba suggests. The physical separation between men and women affects the knowledge and outlook of Homeric characters: men do not know exactly how women move and organise themselves in the city; while women can only imagine, and try to affect, how their own men behave.

That the feelings, values and priorities of men and women are different is drama-tised most eloquently in the encounter between Hector and Andromache. Hector is torn between the competing demands of the other men, who need him on the battlefield, and Andromache, who wants him to stay inside. This kind of entangle-ment seems typically Trojan: Diomedes too has a wife, as Dione reveals when she comforts Aphrodite (at 5.410–15), but he never mentions her – and this is not just because she is far away, since the Trojan ally Sarpedon does think about his wife and baby son back in Lycia (5.479–81 and 684–8). The point, rather, is that women compromise a man's valour and impair his ability to fight (81–2n.). Hector finds it hard to resist Andromache's appeal for pity. It is only at the end of the *Iliad* that the quest for glory, social responsibility, love and pity are reconciled – but then the drama is played out entirely in the male domain, and Achilles is the protagonist. As Arthur Katz points out, 'Achilles' love for Patroclus brings him back to the battlefield, and ensures victory for the Greeks [. . .] And Achilles' pity for Priam, who reminds him of his own father, induces him to accept Priam's supplication and so to acknowledge the common bond of humanity which unites all men.'[91] Women, however, are left crying at the end of the poem.[92] Hector does imagine a future of perfect harmony between men and women, when he utters a prayer on behalf of his son (475–81n.): he

---

[90] See further Arthur Katz 1981: 26.   [91] Arthur Katz 1981: 38.

[92] The prevailing notion that the *Iliad* ends with the touching encounter between Achilles and Priam is not quite accurate: the poem finishes with the women's laments for Hector, and with his burial.

imagines that, one day, Astyanax will return from the battlefield carrying the spoils of the enemy, and that his mother will 'rejoice in her heart' (481n.). The whole vision is unlikely, doomed even. It implies that Hector and Andromache share the same values, but Andromache never celebrates Hector as a warrior – to her, he is 'father, mother, brother and tender husband' (429–30n.). Even in her final funeral lament, at 24.739–45, she makes a distinction between her own perspective and that of the wider community: the people mourn Hector because he was the strongest warrior, 'but for me above all there will be sharp pain, Hector, because you did not die in your own bed, stretching out your hands to me, and telling me a wise word, that I could cherish always . . . ' That was her preferred vision for the future.

3.3 The city of Troy

The plight of the Trojans is set against the backdrop of their city. Book 6, more than any other, gives a vivid impression of the landmarks, buildings and streets of Troy. Rather than offering a static image of the city, the poet describes it by following Hector's progress through it. The overall impression is of swift movement: images of the city pass quickly before Hector's eyes, and our own. He enters through the Scaean Gates, near the oak tree (237n.); then he presses on to the palace of Priam – an imposing building, all made of polished stone (242–52n.); at the entrance to the palace he meets Hecuba – and the narrative then follows her, as she enters into the innermost chamber of the palace (288n.) and picks her favourite robe (295n.). She then leads the women to the temple of Athena, on the acropolis; Theano unlocks its doors and places Hecuba's robe on the knees of a seated statue of Athena (297n.; 298n. with 88–9n.; and 303 with 92n.). Also on the acropolis, in ominous proximity to the temple, is the palace of Paris: built by the best workmen in Troy, it is beautiful and houses the most beautiful couple (312–17n.). After visiting Paris and Helen in their own bedroom, Hector hurries home, looking for Andromache (369–91n.). The poet says very little about Hector's palace, a case of secondary focalisation: to Hector, it is home, and therefore unremarkable. We see him looking for Andromache inside, then stopping at the threshold, asking after her. He then runs back to the Scaean Gates, retracing his steps through the 'built-up streets' (391n.), of 'the great city' (392n.). Hector's overall trajectory is configured as a linear journey in, and then out of, the city. The innermost point in that journey is Hector's own home.

   Greek audiences of all times thought they knew where Troy was: Homer gives it a precise location on the plain beneath Mount Ida, close to the rivers Scamander and Simoeis, not far from the Hellespont and the islands of Samothrace, Tenedos and Imbros. Heinrich Schliemann excavated an impressive Bronze Age citadel precisely in this area, at Hisarlik in modern Turkey.[93] The relationship between the ongoing

---

[93] For Schliemann's work see Schliemann 1880, Calder and Traill 1986, Calder and Cobet 1990, Cobet and Patzek 1992, Traill 1993 and 1995, Boedeker 1997, Cobet 1997 and Easton 2002.

excavations at Hisarlik and Homer's Troy is complex and much debated.[94] One thing, however, seems clear: imposing Bronze Age fortifications were still visible in the early first millennium BCE. The site at Hisarlik continued to be inhabited, and Athena was worshipped there in historical times.[95] It seems, then, that the Trojan saga found confirmation in the grand ruins of an early citadel; and that the ruins, in turn, inspired stories and explanations. For those communities who lived near the ruins or in any case had seen them, the fall of Troy was a material reality. But for all audiences, the *Iliad* supplied a concrete image of the city. Within the text, a sense of doom is palpable in the mention of specific landmarks. Hector and Andromache meet at the Scaean Gates, and the *Iliad* later reveals that Hector confronted Achilles outside the Gates (22.5–6), and that Andromache stood near them, watching Achilles disfigure her husband's corpse (22.462–4). Specific places contribute to the sense of doom also by reference to a wider net of legends and stories. At 6.433–4, for example, Andromache mentions one part of the wall, 'near the fig tree', which seems particularly vulnerable: according to a myth attested in Pindar, one portion of the wall was built by human hands, rather than the gods, and was therefore vulnerable to attack: 434n. Andromache's fear thus finds confirmation in Pindar's poetry.

The very solidity of the city in *Iliad* 6 emphasises, by contrast, the vulnerability of those who live in it. The palace of Priam boasts fifty bedrooms for his sons and their wives, and twelve bedrooms for his daughters and their husbands (242–52n., 244n., 248–50n.). It is a powerful image of dynastic continuity, but in fact those couples will never live there together again. In *Iliad* 6 the city is configured as a female space. We know that there must be old men inside too, because they featured at 3.146–60, and because Hector mentions them in his initial speech to the troops (see 113n.). After that, however, they remain out of sight. By focusing on the women, the poet not only emphasises the trials of Hector – a man surrounded by women who want to delay him – but also powerfully foreshadows the fall of Troy. The city has fragrant storerooms, bedrooms and lovely women with scented breasts (288n.: κηώεντα; cf. 482–3n.: κηώδεϊ): it is a treasure, a prize for conquerors. Because the city is so starkly female, Hector's final wish, at the end of book 6, seems especially unrealistic. He imagines that one day the Achaeans will sail home, defeated – and that the Trojan men will finally celebrate together, resolve all tensions between them and set up a mixing bowl for freedom 'in the halls' (526–9n.) – thus reclaiming civic space as their own.

The fall of Troy is evoked by the buildings, the landmarks and the people in it. What remains unclear is exactly why Troy must fall. The poet and his characters offer many explanations: the gods came to dislike Laomedon (21.441–60); Paris presumed to judge on divine beauty (24.25–30) and abused his position as Menelaos' guest

[94] See, for example, the debate about the excavations of the late Manfred Korfmann: Latacz *et al.* 2001, Cobet and Gehrke 2002, Haubold 2002, Ulf 2003 and Latacz 2004.
[95] Hertel 2003: 24–86 (the walls of Troy) and 94–122 (the temple of Athena); see also the remarks in Hertel 2008: 86–9.

(3.351–4, 328–9n., 356n.); Helen behaved badly (3.126–8, 164–5 and 173–5; 344–8n.); Pandaros broke the truce (4.155–68, 7.348–53); the Trojans failed to disown Paris and return Helen (7.345–79); Hector failed his people (22.99–110). But there were also larger, more general causes at work in the background: the *Iliad* suggests that the heroes were destined to die.[96] They were much stronger than 'people nowadays', but their social institutions were weaker. The fate of Troy could not be disentangled from the affairs of the ruling family; similarly, the Achaeans perished as a result of Achilles' anger, and Agamemnon's greed (1.1–7). The fall of Troy thus symbolises the death of the heroes, and the end of an entire age (12.22–3 and 14.83–7). And perhaps, it symbolises even more than that: for Achilles, the Trojan War illustrates the general truth that human happiness cannot last (24.543–51).

4. DIFFICULT ENCOUNTERS

With the gods largely withdrawn from the action, the poet explores in detail how human beings interact with one another – on the battlefield, and in the city. Most of book 6 represents their difficult encounters, at a time of extreme tension. When Hector sets off for Troy, the narrative initially remains focused on the battlefield: Glaukos and Diomedes drive forward between the two armies, determined to fight to the death. Their encounter offers a searching exploration of conflicting loyalties on the battlefield. It is memorable and surprising: an exchange of insults between enemies becomes a hospitality scene; while an exchange of gifts between friends turns out to be a source of humiliation for one of them. The placing of the episode, between Hector's departure (117–18n.) and his arrival at Troy (237), offers a starting-point for its interpretation: although some ancient critics placed it elsewhere,[97] it is best understood as a description of what happens on the battlefield while Hector is away.[98] The episode is sufficiently long and elaborate to counterbalance the description of Hector's actions in the second half of the book, and to suggest that nothing momentous takes place while he is away. At the same time, it shows that Glaukos is no substitute for Hector (cf. 119n.), and that Diomedes remains dangerous: the Trojans need Athena to 'break his spear' more than ever (306n.).

In comparison with the long and uneventful encounter between Glaukos and Diomedes, Hector's mission in Troy is swift and to the point. Hector's aims are set out clearly at the beginning of the book: his brother Helenos instructs him to go into the city and tell Hecuba to organise an offering for Athena (86–98n.). In the course of his visit Hector meets not only his mother, but also Helen and Paris, and his wife and child. Each encounter is carefully introduced, so as to show that Hector acts as a responsible soldier, even while away from the battlefield. In the course of

---

[96] Graziosi and Haubold 2005: 103–5, 125–34.   [97] ΣA *ad* 6.119a.

[98] ΣbT *ad* 6.237a; Schadewaldt 1943: 77; Homer inserts an episode of similar length and nature while Trojan heralds are sent from the battlefield to the city in book 3: between their departure (3.116–17) and their arrival (245), the poet offers an extended description of the battlefield (3.121–244).

his conversation with Hecuba, he announces his intention to go and retrieve Paris from his palace and bring him back to the battlefield. His decision is not part of Helenos' original plan but can hardly be faulted: it is – as Hector himself points out – demoralising for the troops to fight on behalf of somebody who absents himself from the battlefield (325–31n.). Later, in response to Helen's seductive speech (343–58n.), Hector suddenly declares that he wants to go and see his own wife (359–68n.). This is the only decision that he cannot justify in military terms. And yet, again, it is hard to fault him for it: Hector needs to wait for Paris, in order to ensure that he does indeed return to the battlefield and, rather than spend time with Helen, he decides to go and see his own wife and son – because, he adds in an alarming moment of insight, this may be the last time they see him alive (367–8n.).

Throughout his mission in Troy, Hector is conscious that the men desperately need him to return to the battlefield as soon as possible. He runs towards Troy, with his shield slung behind him, 'battering his neck and shins' (117–18n.). He quickly dismisses the women of Troy, telling them all to pray (237–41n.); he then reaches the palace of Priam and refuses Hecuba's offer of wine because, he claims, it would sap his strength (265n.). Hecuba tries to delay him (ἀλλὰ μέν': 258n.), but he moves swiftly on. He enters Paris' bedroom and finds his brother sitting idle (318–24n.). When Paris asks him to wait or go ahead without him, he is left speechless (340–1n., 342n.). When Helen invites him to 'sit down' next to her (354–6n.), he says that the Trojan men on the battlefield are 'longing' for him (362n.) – and then, while he waits for Paris, he goes swiftly home to see his own wife (370n.: αἶψα δ᾽ ἔπειτα). When he realises Andromache is not there, he rushes back to the Gates (ἀπέσσυτο: 390n.), where she intercepts him (393n.). There is only one moment, in the whole of book 6, when Hector loses momentum. After his conversation with Andromache, she leaves crying – 'turning back again and again' to look at him (496n.). It is precisely at this moment that Paris appears in full armour, galloping like a stallion towards the battlefield. As soon as he sees Hector, he takes the opportunity to draw attention to his own speed – and this precisely at the one moment when Hector is standing still, with his back to the battlefield 'in the place where he had his sweet talk with his wife' (515–16n.). Despite Paris' provoking words, Hector refuses to get drawn into an argument: any differences, he claims, will be resolved after the war (520–9n.).

Hector's mission in Troy is configured as a set of three trials. First, he must resist Hecuba's offer of wine; then there is the trial of seduction; and finally he is confronted with Andromache's emotional appeal. The tension increases steadily: each trial is harder and more drawn out. Some scholars speak of a 'scale of affection' in the order of Hector's encounters, corresponding to Andromache's description of her relationship with Hector: 'you are to me father, mother, brother and tender husband'.[99] There is, however, no reason to think that Hector loves Paris or Helen more than Hecuba; just as, in Andromache's speech, there is no indication that her brothers are more important to her than her father or mother. The point of

[99] The idea goes back to Kakridis 1949: ch. 1, esp. 49–53.

this arrangement, rather, is that it traces the natural course of a human life: as his
visit unfolds, Hector is cast as a son, brother, husband and father. And it is that
last challenge – of being a good husband and father – that proves most painful.
Hector's different relationships offer precious insights into the dynamics of ancient
families. Ancient commentators observe, for example, that Hecuba behaves like a
typical mother,[100] that Astyanax's reactions are true to life[101] and that Andromache
is torn between her desire to obey Hector and her love for him.[102] When reading
the difficult encounters of *Iliad* 6, it is useful to follow the cues of ancient scholiasts
and ask to what extent we still recognise Homer's characters in our own experience.
Homeric poetry suggests that some aspects of human life, particularly family life, are
remarkably stable. A simile at 15.362–4, for example, reveals that children have been
busy making and destroying sandcastles at the beach for almost three millennia. But
even when the activities, values and situations of Homer's characters are radically
different from our own, the careful way in which they are drawn brings them truly to
life.

4.1 Glaukos and Diomedes

In terms of narrative structure, the episode needs to be substantial in length and incon-
clusive in outcome: it suggests that nothing momentous happens on the battlefield
while Hector is away. The poet takes this as an opportunity to explore, quizzically and
unpredictably, some important themes in *Iliad* 6, such as loyalty in marriage and in
war, divine inscrutability and human self-deception. He uses a wide range of different
narrative forms: exchanges of insults on the battlefield, hymns to the gods, sayings,
children's stories, genealogies, hospitality scenes. These different elements combine
to unexpected effect: the encounter between Glaukos and Diomedes has puzzled
ancient and modern readers alike, and it has attracted comments and explanations
through the ages – starting within the text itself. The poet's own comment at the
end of the episode casts an entirely new light on it (232–6n.), and the exchange of
gifts between Ajax and Hector at 7.277–312 works as an internal elaboration on the
episode.

Diomedes, who has been on a rampage since book 5, is the first to speak. His words
are an example of battlefield 'flyting' (verbal assault): he intimidates his opponent and
boasts about his own prowess: 123–43n. To these standard elements of flyting, he adds
an altogether different observation: if Glaukos is a god, he will not challenge him.
The dangers of fighting with the gods are illustrated by the story of Lycurgus, which
takes the shape of an inverted hymn: 130–40n. Diomedes seems to have learnt from
his own experiences in book 5 and now wants to draw a sharp line between gods
and mortals. He remains convinced, however, that he can simply establish whether

---

[100] ΣbT *ad* 6.260c, discussed below: Introduction 4.2.
[101] ΣbT *ad* 6.467, discussed above: Introduction 2.6.
[102] ΣbT *ad* 6.495–6, discussed at 494–502n.

Glaukos is a man – and then proceed to kill him if he is. Glaukos' answer suggests that human affairs are not as straightforward as Diomedes assumes: the gods are inscrutable.

In answer to Diomedes, Glaukos delivers one of the longest speeches in the whole *Iliad*. Given the context, length is in itself a sign of weakness: the closest parallel to Glaukos' speech is Aeneas' excessively long answer to Achilles' verbal attack at 20.199–258: that speech is followed by his humiliating defeat.[103] Flyting boasts are usually short preambles to actual violence, but Glaukos' speech does not open as a boast at all.[104] He starts with an image of arresting beauty: his identity is unimportant, he suggests, because men constantly die and are born, like leaves on a tree: 146–9n.; after that, he launches into a very long account of his family and identity: 150–211n. Taken as a whole, his speech is best seen as an answer, however strange, to Diomedes' opening challenge.[105] Diomedes claimed he would kill any human opponent (142–3); now Glaukos admits that he is mortal and suggests that this is all that matters, since all mortals must die (146–9n.). Diomedes told the story of Lycurgus, who offended the gods and was punished for it (130–40n.); now Glaukos tells the story of his grandfather Bellerophontes, who was rewarded by the gods after many trials, only to meet with their displeasure in the end. Glaukos does not explain why Bellerophontes became hateful to the gods: either he does not know it or does not care to mention it (200–2n.), but the story of how Bellerophontes tried to ascend to heaven must have been known to many ancient audiences. Glaukos is similarly silent about crimes of his ancestor Sisyphos, who challenged the gods by trying to overcome death (153n.). These omissions contribute to the impression that Glaukos is young and inexperienced: he seems to be repeating the stories he has been told by his elders (see also 185n. and 190n.). His account of his grandfather's life contains many elements familiar from children's stories: Bellerophontes was persecuted by a wicked queen, went into exile, overcame three impossible trials set by the king of a distant land and finally married a princess and inherited half the kingdom. These are the stories Glaukos understands and relates at length; on the causes of his grandfather's downfall he says nothing at all: 155–205n.

Glaukos' genealogical history reaches a high point with Bellerophontes' exploits and the birth of Sarpedon (191n., 198–9n.); after that, the family experiences a sharp decline. Glaukos is acutely aware that his unremarkable father expects great things of him (206–11n.) but he will ultimately fail to make him proud: the poet suggests that this encounter ends in humiliation (232–6n.). Later in the *Iliad* Glaukos again appears eager, but unable, to prove himself to his own satisfaction and that of others. At 12.310–28 Sarpedon addresses him with a famous speech about valour in the face of death. Glaukos dutifully helps to lead the ensuing attack, but already at 12.387–91 he is wounded by an arrow and hides away, afraid that the Achaeans might taunt him

---

[103] See Willcock 1992: 68–72.
[104] For a standard flyting reply, see, for example 5.647–54.
[105] Stoevesandt 2008: 57–8 discusses alternative interpretations.

and gloat. At 16.490–501 Sarpedon, who is about to die, calls on Glaukos to rescue his
armour and threatens him with eternal shame should he fail to do so. Still wounded
by Teucer's arrow, Glaukos is unable to help (16.508–12) and, even after Apollo heals
him, cannot prevent Sarpedon from being stripped of his armour (16.663–5). It seems
clear that Glaukos cannot measure up to Diomedes; but his speech offers a perspective
on human life that early audiences of the *Iliad* are likely to have recognised as close to
their own: the past seems more glamorous than the present; the gods are inscrutable;
and human fortunes unpredictable.[106]

   In his reply Diomedes considers none of these general truths: he is inexplicably
delighted with Glaukos' speech. He soon explains that their families share an ancient
bond of hospitality and proposes that they should avoid one another in battle (224–9n.)
and exchange armour (230–1n.). Though energetic and apparently straightforward,
Diomedes' speech makes a controversial suggestion and offers a genealogical account
that is as selective as Glaukos' own account of his family. Diomedes claims he cannot
remember his father, a comment that the scholia criticise as inappropriate, 'out of
place' (222–3n.). Whether or not Diomedes has any direct memory of his father,[107]
other characters in the *Iliad* keep reminding him about Tydeus and telling him to
be like him (see especially Athena's words at 5.800–13) – and the audience know
what that means: in the *Iliad* Tydeus is remembered as a savage warrior. He marched
against Thebes disregarding the will of the gods and thus played a leading role in
one the greatest disasters described in the poem: 4.370–400, and 4.404–10. Diomedes
wavers between emulating his father when he is on the attack (5.115–17, 10.283–94; cf.
5.252–6), and rejecting him as a model when he chooses to be less extreme, as here.

   At the end of Diomedes' speech the two enemies leap off their chariots, shake
hands and make pledges – and then the poet remarks that 'Zeus must have robbed
Glaukos of his wits', because he exchanged his golden armour for one of bronze: 232–
6n. This is a shocking comment, which exposes as naïve not only Glaukos' actions,
but also our own interpretation of the encounter up to this moment. What seemed
to be a touching example of friendship across battle lines is now presented as an
unequal exchange. In an important essay of 1795–6, Schiller argued that the conclusion of the episode was characteristically Homeric: he praised the 'matter-of-fact
truthfulness' (*trockene Wahrhaftigkeit*) of Homer and contrasted it with the sentimentality of Ariosto.[108] Homer's final comment struck ancient audiences too: 'bronze for
gold' became proverbial in ancient Greece (Pl. *Symp.* 219a), and the passage gave rise
to many different interpretations. Surviving ancient responses can be divided into
three groups. Some focus on the unequal outcome of the exchange: the scholia T
ad 6.234*b*[1], for example, suggest that Homer was trying to please a Greek audience.

---

[106] See further Graziosi and Haubold 2005: 139–47.

[107] Pratt 2009 suggests that he does not.

[108] *Über naive und sentimentalische Dichtung.* The essay is printed in Janz *et al.* 1992: 706–810.
For an English translation see Hinderer and Dahlstrom 1993: 179–260. Schiller discusses the
passage from *Iliad* 6 at Janz *et al.* 1992: 730–2; cf. Hinderer and Dahlstrom 1993: 198–9 (*trockene
Wahrhaftigkeit*: Janz *et al.* 1992: 731).

Others attempt to justify Glaukos' behaviour: ΣbT *ad* 6.234*a* claim that he was trying to emulate Bellerophontes' generosity; cf. Eustathius IV, p. 83: 14–17 and IV, p. 182: 24–6 van der Valk. Aristotle rejects that view and argues that Glaukos should not be blamed because he gave away something too valuable, but because he gave away something he needed: warriors should not relinquish their armour.[109] A third group of comments focuses on Diomedes' actions: ΣbT *ad* 6.230 insist that he was not greedy; ΣbT *ad* 6.235*a*[2] question the wisdom of stripping and contemplate the possibility that Diomedes was as foolish as Glaukos (πῶς οὐ Διομήδης φρένων λείπεται).[110]

Modern readers echo the concerns of ancient ones.[111] Some insist that Glaukos is the loser; Martin 1989: 127–30 argues that Diomedes intimidates Glaukos and manipulates him into a humiliating defeat. Others try to justify his actions: Donlan 1989b draws on the anthropology of gift exchange to suggest that Glaukos tries – but fails – to compensate for a perceived status imbalance. Others still suggest that Diomedes is the real fool of the situation: Scodel 1992b argues that he is misguided about the human condition and the role of the gods, and that he will be taught a lesson at 8.130–71. The conclusion of the episode allows no doubt on one point: Glaukos suffers a symbolic defeat, cf. 230–1n. Beyond this, the poet leaves us with many difficult questions as we return to Troy and follow Hector's purposeful and swift journey into the city. Some of those questions are then taken up in book 7.

At 7.273–82 the Trojan and the Achaean herald interrupt a particularly fierce single combat between Ajax and Hector, because night is falling and it is time to stop fighting. Ajax declares that he is willing to postpone the duel, if Hector is too – and Hector readily settles for a temporary truce: 'You will make all the Achaeans rejoice by the ships, and especially your friends and relatives; and I will please the Trojan men, and the Trojan women of the trailing robes, in the great city of king Priam': 7.294–7. As ever, Hector thinks first of the benefits of the arrangement for his own community. He then proposes an exchange of gifts: 'So that an Achaean or a Trojan may say about us: "They fought in the soul-devouring battle but then joined together in friendship, before they separated" ': 7.300–2. Hector offers a sword and scabbard, and he receives a purple belt: the exchange does not involve stripping.[112] This episode throws into relief the more problematic aspects of the encounter between Glaukos and Diomedes.[113] Those two warriors do not interrupt their confrontation at the request of others: they simply decide to avoid each other in battle, in the name of a private bond of hospitality. Indeed, Diomedes goes as far as observing that

---

[109] Aristotle, fr. 155 Rose = 379 Gigon.

[110] For ancient interpretations of the episode, see further Maftei 1976: 52–4.

[111] For overviews of the modern debate: Calder 1984; Alden 1996; and Stoevesandt 2008: 85–6.

[112] Even that exchange was perceived as problematic in antiquity, see Soph. *Ajax* 661–5 and 1026–39.

[113] The *Little Iliad* described another wartime encounter between guest-friends: see fr. 22 West, where Odysseus spares Helicaon because they share an ancient bond of hospitality. That episode must also have cast an interesting light on the encounter between Glaukos and Diomedes.

there are plenty of other Trojans he can kill and declares that Glaukos is welcome to kill other Achaeans too, if he can: the two thus trade off the lives of their own comrades in a perverse form of gift exchange between guest-friends: 224–9n. As elsewhere in the *Iliad*, personal bonds and interests are pitted against loyalty to one's own wider community – and, as often, personal considerations prove to be stronger.

4.2 Hector and Hecuba

When Hector enters the city, he is confronted with the interests and priorities of the women closest to him. Their needs are pitted against his wider responsibilities: he needs to defend the city and hence return to the battlefield as soon as possible. Hecuba is the first woman who tries to hold him back. She meets him in front of the royal palace, a building that, as we have seen, provides a poignant backdrop for their encounter: it speaks of generational continuity, lasting protection and ordered family life – but it also reminds us that Troy will fall, and sons will die before their mothers: 242–52n. She arrives at the palace together with her prettiest daughter, Laodike, and is startled to see Hector: her first words express her surprise, as she tries to work out what he might be doing there. She guesses, correctly, that he is reacting to an emergency, but she wrongly assumes that he left the battlefield on an impulse (θυμός: 256n.), because he wanted to pray. Without waiting for an explanation from him, she goes on to make plans: he should wait while she goes inside the palace to get some wine for a libation – and then he should drink himself, because wine restores the strength of a tired man. The scholia bT *ad* 6.260c observe that she behaves like a typical mother: 'because mothers always expect children to eat and drink'. There are other aspects of her speech that contribute to her characterisation: she uses emotive and sometimes strong language (254n.: τέκνον; 255n.: δυσώνυμοι . . . Ἀχαιῶν), and concludes her speech with a proverb: 261n. She makes assumptions about Hector, worries about him and wants to keep him close to her. Unlike Andromache, she does not admit to her own needs and fears. Most of her speech is taken up by second-guessing her son: although, as we have seen, she fails to comprehend the discipline and organisation required of men on the battlefield, her views are in other ways very perceptive. Hector is not planning to pray to Zeus, but Hecuba ultimately turns out to be right: when confronted with the uncertain future of his own son, Hector will indeed stop and pray (475–81n.).

Hector is firm, but polite, in refusing his mother's offer: wine, he claims, would only weaken him, and a libation is inappropriate, because his hands are stained with blood (264–8n.). Here, and indeed repeatedly in the course of book 6, we are reminded that Hector looks wrong against the peaceful backdrop of the city. After his polite refusal, Hector goes on to relate Helenos' instructions precisely (269–78n.). And then, all of a sudden, he bursts out in a vitriolic and frustrated complaint about Paris – wishing death on his own brother (280–5n.). This is the only time in the entire *Iliad* when we witness Hector's exasperation and pent-up suffering, as well as his sheer exhaustion. As Edwards remarks, it can be no coincidence that he discloses those feelings to his mother.[114] And yet Hecuba cannot take his side entirely: Paris is her son too. For those audiences who knew the myth staged in Euripides' *Alexander*, Hector's outburst will have seemed especially pointed.[115] But whether or not early audiences knew the myth is perhaps not the point, since it ultimately expresses a more general truth: that mothers love their children regardless of what they do, and that Hecuba cannot therefore forsake Paris.[116] Indeed, Hector is equally unable to distance himself entirely from his brother – as his next encounter amply demonstrates.

4.3 Hector, Paris and Helen

The narrative now picks up a thread abandoned in book 3: Paris has been in his bedroom ever since Aphrodite saved him from sure death on the battlefield, wrapped him up in mist and deposited him there at 3.382. The goddess then forced Helen to join him, and she sat down opposite him, averting her eyes, and venting her frustration in a mocking speech against her Trojan husband (3.428–36). Paris minimised the significance of his defeat: 'This time Menelaos won with Athena, another time I will defeat him – there are gods on our side too' (3.439–40). But the divine powers that support him are no good on the battlefield. The influence of Aphrodite is evident in what he next says to Helen: 'Never has desire so engulfed my senses, not when I first took you from lovely Lakedaimon, and sailed off in seafaring ships and lay with you in love-making on the island of Kranaë, not even then did I love you as I do now, or sweet desire seize me' (3.442–6). After that, they make love – while the war rages outside.

When Hector enters their bedroom, the poet draws attention to his spear and describes how he finds Paris handling his own weapons: the shield, armour and curved bow. Helen is nearby, supervising the weaving of famously beautiful robes (318–24n.).[117] There is an obvious contrast between Hector's menacing spear and Paris' own weapons – which are beautiful, but idle. The weapons comment on the virility of the two brothers, particularly in the charged context of their meeting in a bedroom, in front of Helen. Paris damaged his spear in his encounter with Menelaos (3.346–9), and now he is handling a bow, which becomes his weapon of choice in the rest of the *Iliad* – despite its negative connotations: 321–2n. This is the only time, in book 6, when we see Hector enter a θάλαμος, the most private room in the house: when he looks for Andromache, the poet uses the more neutral expression ἐν μεγάροισιν (371n.). His martial appearance is in sharp contrast with his surroundings and, as we have seen, foreshadows the future violation of Trojan homes. Hector's

---

[114] Edwards 1987: 207.   [115] See above p. 7.

[116] Priam too loves his son Paris: at 3.304–9 he claims he cannot bear to watch him fight with Menelaos.

[117] This is the second of four conversations between Hector and Paris in the *Iliad*; cf. 3.38–76, 6.517–29 and 13.765–88. It is the only direct encounter between Hector and Helen, though she comments on their relationship at the very end of the poem: 24.761–75.

menacing entrance is, however, followed by a surprisingly restrained speech. Some ancient readers speculated that Hector did not want to humiliate Paris in front of Helen: ΣbT *ad* 6.326*b*.[118] More generally, it seems that Hector is afraid he may not manage to get Paris back to the battlefield if he exerts too much pressure.[119] When they were still on the battlefield, Hector was capable of much harsher words (cf. 3.39–57), and it is clear that he feels equally strongly now (cf. 280–5n.); but the situation has become so anomalous that it requires a more delicate approach. Hector starts by suggesting that Paris might have left the battlefield out of anger; it is not at all clear why Paris should feel any anger, but it is the only acceptable reason for a hero not to fight: 326n. Hector goes on to suggest that Paris surely agrees with him and would say the same things to any remiss soldier: this is another conciliatory move, which casts Paris in the role of a fighter (328–9n. and 330n.). Finally, Hector points out the real danger they are all facing: if Troy falls, everything will burn – one implication being that even Paris' bedroom, which now seems so sheltered and inviting, is in fact vulnerable to attack: 331n. (πυρὸς δηΐοιο).

Paris' reply is an embarrassment: 332–41n. He starts by judging Hector's reproach appropriate, rather than excessive (333n.), and continues by correcting Hector: he did not withdraw from the battlefield out of anger, but because he abandoned himself to grief: 335n., 336n. This explanation does not tally with what we already know: Aphrodite removed him from the battlefield, and he was overcome by desire for Helen. And yet, Paris' own account is psychologically convincing: although he slept with Helen (indeed, perhaps because of it), he is now feeling despondent. The situation demands that he fight in the first line of battle, not that he withdraw into the bedroom – and he knows that. Much has been made of 'double motivation' in the *Iliad*: there are human explanations for actions, and divine causes.[120] There is what Paris says about himself, and what the poet reveals about Aphrodite. Rather than dismissing double motivation as an archaic pattern of thought, it is important to bear in mind how difficult it is – at times – to account for human actions. Alternative explanations, then as now, are a sign that situations are complicated, and hard to understand. Paris' behaviour is so bad that it attracts different explanations: Hector tactfully suggests anger, Paris himself speaks of grief, and the poet reveals that Aphrodite was involved. Paris does not linger on the most embarrassing details of his situation, but he does reveal some humiliating information – not just about his state of mind, but more specifically about his marriage. He claims that Helen was encouraging him to return to the battlefield 'with soft words' (337n.). We know that her words at 3.428–36 were far from soft, and she goes on to criticise Paris in the harshest possible way, in front of Hector: 352n., 353n. But even leaving aside her tone, it is bad enough that Helen is trying to persuade Paris to return to the battlefield: her

---

[118] See also Minchin 2007: 33.

[119] Cf. 13.116–22, where Poseidon claims there is no point in upbraiding weaklings.

[120] Lesky 1961 is a classic account of this phenomenon. For an abridged version in English see Lesky 2001. For more recent discussion and bibliography, see Cairns 2001: 14–20.

attitude is in sharp contrast with that of Andromache – who is desperate with anxiety that Hector might be killed and wants to keep him in the city at all costs.[121]

Paris' speech leaves Hector at a loss for words: 342n.[122] And it is at this point that Helen intervenes, filling one of the heaviest silences in the whole poem. Her speech is a lesson in the arts of seduction.[123] She starts by blaming herself and drawing attention to her own terrible plight, then she flatters Hector at the expense of her own husband and finally she imagines a future for herself, Paris and – implicitly – Hector, as subjects of poetry. The context of her speech is particularly charged, because of the dynamics of ancient families: Hesiod's discussion of adultery includes a specific warning against sleeping with the wife of a brother (*Op.* 327–9), and this makes sense, since men would have had more intimate contact with their sisters-in-law than with most other women, excepting slaves and blood relatives. We have already seen that some ancient readers thought that Hector was inhibited by Helen's presence in the room. Helen now weaves her speech around a central request that Hector come and sit next to her (354–6n.): she is the only woman in book 6 who stays at a distance and expects Hector to approach her; all the other women he encounters run or walk towards him.[124] This is, in itself, a seductive ploy. Helen starts by wishing she had died in infancy (344–8n.) then suddenly strikes a realistic note: since the gods decreed that she had to be abducted, she just wishes she had a better husband in Troy – somebody with a sense of shame and proper behaviour (349–53n.).[125] She then criticises Paris in the harshest terms and predicts that he will have his comeuppance. Echoing Hector's own view that Paris was solely responsible for the war (328–9n.), she now casts herself in the role of the victim. This is not how ancient audiences saw her, of course: although Gorgias argued for Helen's innocence (in a deliberately provocative speech), she was generally held to be at least partly responsible for the war.[126] And it has to be said that her behaviour in *Iliad* 6 gives some support to ancient perceptions: her seductive stance towards Hector undermines her protestations of innocence. She is the only woman in early Greek epic who explicitly wishes for a better husband, and she has already had two. By the end of her speech, Helen has effectively set up a new triangle: she, Paris and Hector are inextricably bound together: she and Paris will be the subject of future song, but that is also a promise held out to Hector (cf. 358n.:

---

[121] Eust. II, p. 353: 12–15 van der Valk.

[122] Here as elsewhere, Paris has a powerful hold on his family and people; cf. 7.345–79, 11.122–5.

[123] Helen's ability to seduce depends on her words as well as her beauty: at *Od.* 4.277–9, for example, we are told that she tried to lure the Achaeans out of the wooden horse by imitating the voices of their wives; on Helen, beauty and persuasion, see further Gorgias, *Encomium of Helen*, together with Bergren 1983: 82–6; Worman 1997 and 2001. For a different reading of the speech, see Stoevesandt 2008: 115.

[124] Cf. 238n. (the Trojan women), 251n. (Hecuba) and 394n. (Andromache).

[125] Arthur Katz 1981: 29 rightly points out that Helen's description of a good husband fits Hector.

[126] Gorgias, *Hel.* ch. 7: ὁ μὲν γὰρ ἔδρασε δεινά, ἡ δὲ ἔπαθε ('he did dreadful deeds, she suffered them'). On ancient attitudes towards Helen, see Austin 1994.

πελώμεθ᾽ ἀοίδιμοι). Helen shares, to an extent, the poet's perspective here, and the poet's own portrayal of Helen in the *Iliad* is not unsympathetic. Yet he does show, in only fifteen lines of poetry, how Helen cannot help but be seductive, and he offers us a glimpse of how things might have gone when she first welcomed Paris to come in and sit down near her, in Sparta. Hector is polite but firm in declining her offer: 'Do not make me sit down, Helen, loving as you are' (φιλέουσά περ: 360n.). He 'is careful not to offend her', as the ancient commentators, ΣbT *ad* 6.360*a*, point out. It is in response to Helen's invitation that Hector first mentions his intention to go and see his own wife, Andromache: 367–8n.

4.4 Hector and Andromache

When Hector reaches his house, he does not find his wife there: 369–91n. This detail casts Hector, for the first time, in the role of the pursuer – and delays the encounter between husband and wife. The poet introduces Andromache not by describing her directly, but by dramatising how others perceive her. Hector can think of two explanations for her absence: that she is visiting her sisters-in-law, or that she joined the women who are praying at the temple (374–80n.). As the scholia bT *ad* 6.378*b* point out, 'he gives reasons for which modest women (τὰς σώφρονας) may leave the house' – but we know that he is wrong in his assumptions, because the poet already said that Andromache went to the rampart (372–3n.). Now the housekeeper has the difficult task of telling Hector that his wife ran out to the city wall in a frenzy (381–9n.). The role of the housekeeper is important, in this scene. She looks after Andromache and depends on her: her perspective, both sympathetic and alarmed, adds to the narrative tension and prepares for the later exploration of Andromache's own feelings of dependence, fear and love.[127] There is a stark contrast between Hector's wishful thinking and Andromache's desperate plight, as witnessed by her servant. This contrast reinforces the impression that men and women inhabit separate spheres, and it adds to the sense of foreboding which pervades the book: the war, Hector is now forced to realise, is already disrupting domestic life.

Hector is about to leave the city through the Scaean Gates when Andromache sees him (393n.). As she runs towards him, the poet introduces her formally, through a short 'catalogue' entry outlining her origins, family and marriage (395–8n.); this background information further delays the moment of encounter – the audience can imagine Andromache running down from the rampart, as they hear about her origins and realise that she and Hector had a wedding, share a past and were once unremarkable in their happiness.[128] And then, suddenly, she is in front of him: ἤντησ᾽ (399n.). This is not an easy confrontation: it happens at the last possible moment,[129]

---

[127] For an excellent discussion of the housekeeper, see Di Benedetto 1998: 60–1.

[128] The poet employs a similar technique at 369–91n.: while Hector looks for Andromache inside the house, he tells the audience where she actually is. The time of story and that of the performance match: Hector looks, while the poet tells. Andromache runs, while the poet remembers her past.

and in a transitional place, at the Scaean Gates, halfway between home and the battlefield.[130] Neither partner speaks immediately: Hector is taken by the presence of his baby son and smiles at him in silence: 404n. Andromache takes her cue from Hector's smile (his only one in the poem), and she starts her appeal by telling him that he has no pity for his son, or for her. She then describes his death with prophetic clarity (410n.) and wishes she could die when he does. There will be no warmth or comfort for her when he is gone (θαλπωρή: 412n.), but only pain: ἀλλ' ἄχε' at 413n. is as close as Homeric diction ever gets to an anguished scream. Andromache then explains that Achilles killed her father, destroyed her city, slaughtered her seven brothers and enslaved her mother. And then she adds an interesting detail: Achilles released her mother for ransom, and she died in the palace of her own father: 425–8n. It is the fate of Andromache's mother that highlights, by contrast, Andromache's total dependence on Hector: she has no family that could come to her rescue or pay for her release. When she claims that Hector is a father, mother, brother and tender husband to her, this is not a sentimental line of poetry (as in Catullus 72.3–4), or a piece of aggrandising rhetoric (as in several Near Eastern texts, cf. 429–30n.): it is the truth.

In the final part of her speech Andromache suddenly strikes a pragmatic note: Hector should place the troops in front of the wall, near the fig tree, where it is most vulnerable (433–9). She justifies her suggestion with an empirical observation: the Achaeans have already tried to scale the wall in that place three times (435n.) and may be acting on the advice of a seer (438–9n.). Ancient and modern readers have found Andromache's suggestions extraordinary, and many have objected to them. ΣA ad 6.433–9 report that the lines were athetised in antiquity, on the grounds that Andromache gives alternative military advice to Hector (ἀντιστρατηγεῖ . . . τῶι Ἕκτορι), and that the lines contain a 'lie', since the battle is not that close to the walls (though cf. 73–4n.). Some modern scholars likewise find lines 433–9 suspect: Lohmann 1988: 37–8 argues that they upset the carefully balanced structure of the speech and introduce an unseemly topic, since, in his view, Andromache's address ought to focus on family matters alone. It is true that her final suggestion is, from a military point of view, problematic (433n.), and that it upsets the balanced structure of her speech, but the extremity of her situation has – according to her housekeeper – unbalanced Andromache (389n.), so there is no reason to expect a measured ending to her appeal. As an ancient commentator remarks, the end of her speech defies conventional expectations about the behaviour of women but 'fits Andromache'.[131]

---

[129] Felson and Slatkin 2004: 99, n. 24.   [130] Arthur Katz 1981: 19–20 and 31.

[131] ΣbT ad 6.433: 'Even if it is not fitting for a woman, it is fitting for Andromache, since looking after horses is also not for a woman, but Andromache gives wheat to Hector's horses and mixes wine for them, because loving her husband she also looks after the horses who carry him.' The scholiast is referring to 8.186–90, where Hector remarks good-naturedly to his horses that Andromache feeds them before taking care of her own dear husband. As the scholiast points out, such unconventional details in no way cast doubt on Andromache's love for Hector but make her marriage to him vivid and credible. For modern appreciations of lines 433–9, see Arthur Katz 1981: 32–3; Kirk 1990: 217–18; Schadewaldt 1997: 134; and Van Nortwick 2001: 226–7.

She wants to keep Hector close to her, tries to capture his attention and delay his departure by discussing strategy – a topic that should interest him. As Pope observed in the notes to his translation, 'we shall not think that she talks like a soldier, but like a woman, who naturally enough makes use of any incident that offers, to persuade her lover to what she desires'.[132]

Hector refuses to be drawn into a detailed discussion of military matters, or to view the battlefield from the rampart. He opens his speech with some statements of principle, which summarise what has often been called 'the heroic code':[133] he would feel shame before the men and women of Troy if he stayed away from the battlefield; he has learnt always to fight in the first line of battle; and he wants to win κλέος for his father and for himself: 441–6n. This last thought leads Hector to face the future with unflinching clarity: he knows in his heart that Troy will fall, and Priam and his people perish – it is precisely for this reason that he must fight in the first line of battle, rather than look for alternative courses of action as Andromache suggests (447–9n.). In book 22, moments before dying, he will again reflect on the need to give his best, not for the people of Troy, but for all those who will hear of his deeds in the future: 22.300–5. For now, however, his speech focuses – more painfully – on the future of his immediate family: in the third, longest, and most anguished part of his speech (450–65), he considers the fate of his parents, his brothers, and that of Andromache, the person he loves above all others. Hector imagines her as a slave, carrying water, and weaving. The one task he does not mention explicitly is forced sex with the enemy. Instead, he quotes the words of a passer-by, who will one day recognise Andromache as the former wife of Hector, best warrior among the Trojans: 454–63n. That, he knows, will only be the source of fresh suffering for her: 462n., 463n. And this is when Hector finally breaks down: he would rather be dead, he says, than hear Andromache scream as she is dragged away into slavery (464–5n.). These final lines confirm Andromache's view that Hector is on a death mission (407n.); but they also resonate with her own death wish at 410–11n., and more generally with the tone of her speech, which was close to that of a funeral lament (405–39n.).

Andromache performed a lament in front of her living husband, and now Hector says he had rather be dead than witness her suffering. In many respects, Hector's reply corresponds to Andromache's appeal: both partners have lost, or are about to lose, their closest family; both love and care for each other, above all other people; and both contemplate the imminent fall of Troy, Hector's death and Andromache's terrible future. Husband and wife are 'born to the same fate', as Andromache claims at 22.477–80. And yet their speeches also highlight contrasting perspectives and priorities: Andromache starts with a desperate plea but ends with practical suggestions aimed at protecting Hector and the city walls. Hector, by contrast, starts with a measured statement of principle, but, in the end, sees death as his escape route. His final words

[132] Mack 1967: 354.
[133] For discussions of the heroic code, see, e.g., Dodds 1951: chs. 1–2, Adkins 1960: chs. 2–4; Long 1970; Rowe 1983; Redfield 1994: 99–127; Cairns 1993: ch. 1; and Scodel 2008a, esp. ch. 1.

are, ultimately, an admission of defeat. Hector can hardly face Andromache at this point, and he turns his attention to baby Astyanax, as he had done at the beginning of their encounter (466–81n.). It is the baby's frightened reaction at the sight of his helmet that finally brings Hector and Andromache together: they both laugh out loud (471n.). As Σb *ad* 6.471 point out, in times of hardship even the smallest incident can cause laughter.[134] And it is again the scholia who observe, about the role of Astyanax: 'Making babies binds men and women together' (ΣbT *ad* 6.404*b*: σύνδεσμος γὰρ ἀνδρῶν καὶ γυναικῶν ἡ παιδοποιΐα).

Hector seizes this moment of harmony, lifts up his baby and utters a prayer on his behalf. As we have seen, he hopes for a future of shared values: Astyanax will, one day, bring home the spoils of the enemy, and Andromache will rejoice at the sight. This is an impossible vision, not just because Troy will fall and Astyanax will be killed in infancy – but because we never see Andromache take pleasure in war. When, at the end of his prayer, Hector entrusts Astyanax into her arms, 'she laughs in tears', and Hector feels pity for her (484n.). When he tells her to go home, while he sees to the war, her response is equally ambiguous: she obeys, but she turns back again and again to look at him (496n.). Once home, she mourns him as if he was already dead. Hector's speech clearly failed to reassure her, and his words about shame, duty and glory had no impact on her own views: when he dies, she repeats her initial judgement – that he was killed by his own strength (22.455–9). Hector himself remains committed to his own position: when confronted with Achilles, he reminds himself that he must not chat to him like a girl to a boy (22.127–8).[135] There is no resolution, no common perspective. At the end of this most loving encounter, there is simply a parting.[136]

5. THE ENCOUNTER BETWEEN HECTOR AND ANDROMACHE THROUGH TIME

One of the most rewarding aspects of reading the *Iliad* is that one joins a vast community of other committed readers. For more than 2,500 years, people have studied this poem, tried to explain it and brought to bear on its interpretation all their intelligence, knowledge, experience and creativity. The comments of ancient scholars, which survive in much abbreviated form in the margins of medieval manuscripts

---

[134] The comment reads: ἀπὸ τῆς πολλῆς αὐτῶν λύπης ἡ μικρὰ τοῦ παιδὸς αἰτία φυσικόν τινα κινεῖ καὶ μέτριον γέλωτα; 'out of their great distress, the child's slight cause (sc. for distress) moves them to a natural and fitting laughter'. As often, the b scholia creatively reinterpret a source more faithfully represented by the T scholia: ἀπὸ τῆς πολλῆς λύπης ἐκ μικρᾶς αἰτίας γέλωτα κινεῖ: '[Astyanax] makes them laugh because of *his* great distress from a slight cause.' The intent of b is clearly that of explaining how Andromache and Hector can laugh although they are in such a terrible situation. On the b scholia, see van der Valk 1963–4: vol. I, ch. 5; and cf. 21n. (Αἴσηπον καὶ Πήδασον).

[135] See further Van Nortwick 2001.

[136] Although Hector briefly returns to Troy at 7.307–10, the poet makes little of it and says nothing about Andromache. This is, in effect, their final parting, as Edwards 1987: 212 rightly argues.

(scholia), have already featured prominently; but they are not the only useful resources for commentators and readers of *Iliad* 6.[137] It is not possible, in the short compass of this commentary, to examine the immensely rich and varied responses which the *Iliad* inspired, and yet it is useful to have some awareness of its reception history – for a simple reason. By considering how other readers approached *Iliad* 6, we can begin to explore some important continuities and changes in the history of its interpretation – and, more importantly still, we can position ourselves, as readers, in relation to those who read the poem in radically different historical and cultural circumstances. In what follows we outline some important stages in the reception of the encounter between Hector and Andromache. We focus on this episode because it seems to be the most memorable and important in *Iliad* 6. This judgement does not just reflect modern sensibilities: we know, for example, that Stephanos the Grammarian (who must have been active in the late antique or early Byzantine period) shared that view. He wrote a poem, preserved in the *Palatine Anthology* and in many Homeric manuscripts, which summarised the contents of the *Iliad* book by book. About *Iliad* 6 he stated:

Ζῆτα δ᾽ ἄρ᾽ Ἀνδρομάχης καὶ ῞Εκτορός ἐστ᾽ ὀαριστύς.

Book 6 is the love talk between Andromache and Hector.[138]

For Stephanos, as for modern readers, the encounter between Hector and Andromache is the most important episode in book 6 – even if the word he uses to describe it, ὀαριστύς, is, in some ways, surprising. Hector and Andromache are not just engaged in 'love talk': they speak about their deepest needs, fears and convictions. And yet Stephanos is not wrong or casual in his summary: he is actually paraphrasing the poet's own description of the encounter at the end of the book, when Hector and Paris are about to return to the battlefield (ὀάριζε: 516–17n.). There are at least three lessons to be learnt here. First, the reception of the episode starts within the *Iliad* itself: there is no neutral terrain 'before reception' that we may ever hope to recover. Secondly, reception is contested from the beginning. Finally, a confrontation with Stephanos helps to shed light on a simple truth about the episode, and about the *Iliad* more generally: from the perspective of men engaged in killing one another on the battlefield, any conversation with a loving wife – however difficult – is a sweet alternative.

---

[137] For a useful introduction to the Homeric scholia see Schmidt 2002. The *Iliad* scholia have been edited by Erbse 1969–88; those to the *Odyssey* are currently being re-edited by Pontani, who has so far covered books 1–2 (Pontani 2007). For the other books, it is still necessary to consult Dindorf 1855. The important *Iliad* commentary of Eustathius has been edited in van der Valk 1971–87; the so-called D-Scholia to the *Iliad* are available in a preliminary edition by van Thiel 2000b; see also van Thiel 2000a; Schmidt 1976 studies the bT scholia. On ancient scholarship, see further van der Valk 1963–4, Pfeiffer 1968, Montanari 1979–95, Reynolds and Wilson 1991, and Dickey 2007.

[138] *Anthologia Graeca* 9, epigram 385.6. For critical edition and discussion see Ludwich 1887: 1–9; and Stadtmueller 1906: 364–8. There was a competing version of the poem which emphasised the offering to Athena.

Surviving evidence suggests that the encounter between Hector and Andromache made little impact on archaic and classical art and literature, with one exception: Athenian drama. Vases do not display much interest in the episode,[139] and, although Sappho does celebrate the wedding of Hector and Andromache in fr. 44 Voigt, the relationship between her poem and *Iliad* 6 is hard to characterise – as is, more generally, the relationship between early lyric and Homeric epic.[140] Sappho depicts the joyful first encounter between Hector and Andromache, and that is appropriate to her genre: as Griffith points out, 'lyric in general often seems to relish those very moments and feelings that epic is least capable of including, or at least, of sustaining and approving: romance, courtship, seduction and marriage'.[141] Sappho describes in detail the happy couple, the gifts, the songs and dances: her vision is in some ways antithetical to the sense of loss, the laments and the sheer anguish of *Iliad* 6. But there is no close engagement with our text of the *Iliad*.

The first clear allusions to the Iliadic encounter between Hector and Andromache survive in Athenian drama. Sophocles modelled the meeting between Ajax, Tecmessa and their son Eurysaces (*Ajax* 430–692) on the Homeric episode: ancient and modern commentators have pointed out the close parallels between the two texts.[142] The differences, however, are also important: Tecmessa is a slave rather than a wife and, according to classical Athenian law, her son is therefore illegitimate. As Helene Foley has argued, Sophocles' allusion to Homer fosters a serious and emotionally committed consideration of an issue – the status of illegitimate children – that was controversial in classical Athens.[143] Euripides' *Andromache* investigates similar concerns by recasting the Iliadic Andromache as a slave and mother, after the fall of Troy.[144] *Iliad* 6 also features in comedy: Aristophanes' Lysistrata claims that her husband quotes Hector at her, 'war will be the concern of men', in order to make her shut up – and then declares that from now on 'war will be the concern of women'.[145] At *Acharnians* 580–90, Dicaeopolis behaves just like baby Astyanax: he is terrified by the mighty plume on top of Lamachus' helmet![146] It seems that the helmet scene also

[139] Herter 1973: 160; see also *LIMC* s.v. 'Andromache', vol. 1.1, p. 773. The few vase paintings that undoubtedly represent the parting scene are listed at *LIMC* s.v. 'Andromache' 3.4–6 (vol. 1.1, p. 768). Images 14–21 (vol. 1.1, p. 769) are of doubtful relevance: even if some of the disputed vases were meant to represent Hector and Andromache, the very fact that we can no longer be sure seems significant.

[140] On the relationship between epic and lyric, see further Fowler 1987: 3–52; Hunter 2004: 238–40; and Graziosi and Haubold 2009, with further literature.

[141] Griffith 2009: 82.

[142] See the Sophoclean scholia *ad* 499, 501b, 514, 545a, 550 Christodoulou. See further Easterling 1984; Zanker 1992: 22–3; Farmer 1998; Ormand 1999: 110–19; Zimmermann 2002: 244–5; and Maronitis 2004: 89–97.

[143] H. P. Foley 2001: 90–1.

[144] Note, for example, the parallels between Euripides *Andr.* 164–9 and *Il.* 6.456–8. The image of Andromache carrying water seems to become popular in later literature; cf. ΣA *ad* 6.457a.

[145] Aristoph. *Lys.* 520 and 538. For other citations of, and allusions to, Hector's words, see Aesch. *Sept.* 200–1 with Ieranò 2002: 75–6, and the passages collected in West's *apparatus*.

[146] See Hunter 2004: 242; Zimmermann 2006: 75.

made an impact on tragedy: a fragment from Astydamas' *Hector* suggests that, in one scene, Hector removes his helmet, so as not to frighten his child.[147] These tragic and comic allusions are quite specific but should not come as a surprise: the audience in the theatre of Dionysos were well placed to appreciate them. There was a dynamic relationship between different festivals and performances in classical Athens: at the Great Dionysia, drama offered ever new and challenging perspectives on the epic tradition, whereas at the Great Panathenaea the *Iliad* kept being performed, festival after festival. There was a sense that the *Iliad* was well known and authoritative: at *Trojan Women* 647–58, for example, Euripides portrays Andromache as a rather self-satisfied wife, who knows she is famous for being good. His Andromache claims that she did not deserve her fate, because she always behaved well towards her husband and never yielded to her longing to be outdoors: it is hard not to see in this a rather pointed reference to her behaviour in *Iliad* 6.[148]

The behaviour of Andromache in the *Iliad* remained a source of debate, inspiration and anxiety in later Greek literature too. In popular philosophy and rhetorical education her character became that of the loving wife (φίλανδρος).[149] And yet some concern was expressed, for example, when discussing the etymology of her name: Ἄνδρο – μάχη (man-fighter).[150] In the Second Sophistic, Hector and Andromache were held up as a model couple[151] but also used in order to articulate cultural changes and developments. In his *Advice to bride and groom*, a treatise cast in the form of a wedding address to Pollianus and his bride Eurydice, Plutarch urges the young couple to emulate Hector and Andromache in a way that is appropriate to their different circumstances: the husband will become 'father and honoured mother, and brother' to his wife, but he should also be 'a guide, philosopher and teacher' to her.[152] In the *Brutus* Plutarch again discusses Hector and Andromache as a model for a married couple. He reports that Porcia recognised her own situation in a painting of Andromache, and that the painting made her reveal her pain at the departure of her husband Brutus:

---

[147] Astydamas *TrGF* 1 60 F 2; Carrara 1997 discusses the content and context of this difficult fragment. For a reconstruction of the play on the basis of an Apulian volute-crater in Berlin, see Taplin 2009.

[148] Esp. *Tro.* 650; see also *Tro.* 645–6, where she claims that she always behaved modestly (σῶφρον') in the house of Hector: Iliadic readers know that she was not always there; for further discussion of the *Troades* and Homer, see Davidson 2001.

[149] E.g. ΣT *ad* 6.394b[1]; ΣT *ad* 6.411a[1]; ΣbT *ad* 6.433; ΣbT *ad* 17.207–8b; Maximus of Tyre, *Dissertationes* 40.3; Eust. II, p. 372: 20–1 van der Valk.

[150] See, e.g., Eur. *Tro.* 731–4; *TrGF* v.2 F 1094; Varro, *De Lingua Latina* 7.82 (Ennius takes up the Euripidean etymology); and *Anthologia Graeca* 11, epigram 378.5 (about a dreaded wife who is truly ἀνδρομάχη). The motif of a combative Andromache is attested in vase painting (Capettini 2007: 218–20) and found its way also into ancient Homeric scholarship (see Eust. II, p. 331: 9–11 van der Valk).

[151] See, e.g., Maximus of Tyre, *Dissertationes* 18.8.

[152] Plutarch, *Coniugalia praecepta* 145B6–C2.

παντάπασιν ἀπογνοὺς τῶν πραγμάτων ἔγνω καταλιπεῖν Ἰταλίαν, καὶ πεζῇι
διὰ Λευκανίας εἰς Ἐλέαν ἐπὶ θάλασσαν ἧκεν. ὅθεν ἡ Πορκία μέλλουσα πάλιν
εἰς Ῥώμην ἀποτραπέσθαι, λανθάνειν μὲν ἐπειρᾶτο περιπαθῶς ἔχουσα, γραφὴ
δέ τις αὐτὴν προὔδωκε, τἄλλα γενναίαν οὖσαν. ἦν γὰρ ἐκ τῶν Ἑλληνικῶν
διάθεσις, προπεμπόμενος Ἕκτωρ ὑπ' Ἀνδρομάχης, κομιζομένης παρ' αὐτοῦ
τὸ παιδίον, ἐκείνωι δὲ προσβλεπούσης. ταῦτα θεωμένην τὴν Πορκίαν ἡ τοῦ
πάθους εἰκὼν ἐξέτηξεν εἰς δάκρυα, καὶ πολλάκις φοιτῶσα τῆς ἡμέρας ἔκλαιεν.

Altogether despairing of the situation, Brutus decided to leave Italy and came by
land through Lucania to Elea by the sea. As Porcia was about to return from there
to Rome, she tried to conceal her distress, but a painting betrayed her, although
she had otherwise been very brave. Its subject was Greek: Andromache's farewell
to Hector; she was taking from his arms their little son, while her eyes were fixed
upon her husband. That image of suffering made Porcia burst into tears when
she looked at it – and she would return to it many times a day and weep before
it.[153]

Clearly, Porcia is looking at a painting that depicts the precise moment when Hector
entrusts Astyanax to Andromache: 482–93n. We know from other sources that the
scene was popular in Roman art,[154] but Plutarch uniquely describes an individual
reaction to it. Porcia identifies herself with Andromache to the point of tears. She is not
supposed to display her grief, and indeed she does not want to (unlike Andromache) –
but she cannot help it. Indeed, she submits to the power of the painting 'many times'.
Plutarch uses this story to frame a second response to Hector and Andromache which,
this time, focuses on Brutus, the husband:

Ἀκιλίου δέ τινος τῶν Βρούτου φίλων τὰ πρὸς Ἕκτορα τῆς Ἀνδρομάχης ἔπη
διελθόντος·

Ἕκτορ, ἀτὰρ σύ μοί ἐσσι πατὴρ καὶ πότνια μήτηρ
ἠδὲ κασίγνητος, σὺ δέ μοι θαλερὸς παρακοίτης,

μειδιάσας ὁ Βροῦτος "ἀλλ' οὐκ ἐμοί γ'" εἶπε "πρὸς Πορκίαν ἔπεισι φάναι τὰ
τοῦ Ἕκτορος·

ἱστόν τ' ἠλακάτην τε καὶ ἀμφιπόλοισι κέλευε·

σώματος γὰρ ἀπολείπεται φύσει τῶν ἴσων ἀνδραγαθημάτων, γνώμηι δ' ὑπὲρ
τῆς πατρίδος ὥσπερ ἡμεῖς ἀριστεύσει." ταῦτα μὲν ὁ τῆς Πορκίας υἱὸς ἱστόρηκε
Βύβλος.[155]

[153] Plutarch, *Brutus* 994D–E.
[154] See *LIMC* s.v. Andromache 3.8–9 for two other extant examples of Roman wall painting,
one from a house in Pompeii, the other from Nero's *Domus Aurea*.
[155] Plut. *Brut.* 994E–F.

When Acilius, one of Brutus' friends, recited the verses containing Andromache's words to Hector,

> 'But Hector, you are a father and honoured mother to me,
> and a brother, and a tender husband'

Brutus smiled and said: 'But I, for one, do not intend to speak to Porcia in Hector's words:

> "Ply the loom and the distaff, and give orders to your maids"

for though her body is not strong enough to perform such heroic feats as men do, still, in spirit she valiantly defends her country just as we do.' Bibulus, Porcia's son, tells this story.

By juxtaposing this scene with Porcia's response to the painting, Plutarch sets up a series of contrasts: between men and women, art and poetry, and between Greek and Roman attitudes to marriage and war. Porcia responds to the painted Andromache by submitting to the emotional power of art. Brutus by contrast refuses to play Hector to her Andromache: he quotes the *Iliad* – a text, not an image – and distances himself from it with a knowing smile. His act of resistance is manly, and yet it concerns a woman: Brutus declares that Porcia is just as valiant in spirit, and committed to war, as he is himself. This attempt at rewriting *Iliad* 6 is full of ironies. Although Brutus claims that Porcia is like a man in spirit, she has just shown herself to be very unlike Brutus, and very much like the Homeric Andromache – even though she had initially tried to resist a display of grief.

On the whole, the Roman reception of *Iliad* 6 focuses on Andromache's life after the fall of Troy and is often mediated through tragedy; Hector is less important, partly because he has no future beyond the Trojan War. Naevius may have followed Astydamas in his *Hector proficiscens*;[156] but Ennius' influential *Andromacha* put the emphasis squarely on the post-Iliadic Andromache. Virgil extensively reworked the encounter between Hector and Andromache in *Aeneid* 2: his emphasis is also on Andromache, because Hector recedes into the past.[157] Seneca's *Troades* portrays Andromache as a widow and – alongside Virgil's description of her in exile (*Aeneid* 3.294–505) – defines her persona for much of the Middle Ages and the early modern period.[158] In Racine's *Andromaque* she is – as often in earlier literature – a widow, rather than the anguished wife of *Iliad* 6. It is only towards the end of the seventeenth century that we begin to see a renewed interest in the Iliadic encounter between Hector and Andromache.

---

[156] Marmorale 1950: 149–50 and 190. Too little is left of the play to allow firm conclusions as to its contents.

[157] On Virgil's allusions to *Iliad* 6 in *Aeneid* 2, see esp. Hughes 1997. Elegy, unsurprisingly, does show an interest in Hector and Andromache as a couple, but the focus is more on their sex life than on their final parting: Propertius 2.22 b, 31–4 Heyworth; Ovid, *Amores* 1.9.35–6; cf. *Ars amatoria* 2.709–10, 3.107–10. For Hector as a paradigmatic husband and lover, see *Heroides* 5.107 (*felix Andromache, certo bene nupta marito*), and *Ars am.* 2.645–6. The *Ilias Latina* has Andromache initiate the encounter: 564–74.

[158] For the reception of Seneca's *Troades* see Keulen 2001: 30–5.

Dryden translated it for his *Examen poeticum* of 1693,[159] and Pellegrini painted his *Hector and Andromache* for the first Duke of Manchester *c.* 1708–10.[160] Shortly after, Pope wrote the following note on *Iliad* 6:

> Homer undoubtedly shines most upon the great Subjects, in raising our Admiration or Terror: Pity, and the softer Passions, are not so much of the Nature of his Poem, which is formed upon Anger and the Violence of Ambition. But we have cause to think his Genius was no less capable of touching the Heart with Tenderness, than of firing it with Glory, from the few Sketches he has left us of his Excellency in that way too. In the present Episode of the Parting of *Hector* and *Andromache*, he has assembled all that Love, Grief, and Compassion could inspire.[161]

As Clingham notes, the episode was fast becoming 'a touchstone for pathos and a natural style',[162] and not just in poetry: in his *Tableaux tirés de l'Iliade de l'Odyssée et de l'Enéide* of 1757, the comte de Caylus devoted to the encounter three separate tableaux: 'Andromache and the nurse', 'the farewell of Hector' and 'Andromache laments with her maids'.[163] In Britain the Swiss-born Angelica Kauffmann painted *Hector taking leave of Andromache* (*c.* 1768/9) for the inaugural exhibition at the Royal Academy of Painting and Sculpture; she turns Hector into a 'wistful juvenile who wears his helmet uneasily'.[164] Kauffmann's painting inspired Friedrich Schiller's poem *Hektors Abschied*, which is formally a dialogue between the two partners but concentrates almost entirely on Hector.[165] Schiller returned to and reworked his poem for a period of over twenty years and considered it 'one of his best'.[166] Goethe's newspaper *Propyläen* held a painting competition in 1800: artists could choose whether to depict the Iliadic encounter between Hector and Andromache, or the death of Rhesos in *Iliad* 10. The subjects were designed to showcase different skills: one required 'tender sentiment

---

[159] For discussion see Clingham 2000.
[160] Oil on canvas, Temple Newsam House, Leeds Museums and Galleries. For a reproduction see Lomax 2000: 26.
[161] Mack 1967: 349. Pope himself acknowledged his debt to Dryden in the same context: 'I must not forget, that Mr. Dryden has formerly translated this admirable Episode, and with so much Success, as to leave me at least no hopes of improving or equalling it. The utmost I can pretend is to have avoided a few modern Phrases and Deviations from the Original, which have escaped that great Man.'
[162] Clingham 2000: 54.
[163] Caylus 1757: 50–2, plates 6–8. Note especially his comments on plate 7: he believes that the farewell of Hector 'will always deserve the attention of painters'.
[164] Boime 1987: 112–13; cf. Mellor 1995: 132. The painting is now kept in Saltram House, Plymouth. For a reproduction see Bermingham and Brewer 1995, plate 8.2.
[165] Schiller appears to have known Kauffmann's painting indirectly, through a description of Helfrich Peter Sturz; cf. Ballof 1914: 298 and Thalheim 1980: 834. For discussion of his poem see Borchmeyer 1972.
[166] Letter to Christian Gottfried Körner of 27 May 1793, printed in Nahler and Nahler 1992: 243. The poem had already appeared as an inset song in Schiller's play *Die Räuber* (1781) but was only published as a free-standing work in 1800 (*Gedichte* I/1 pp. 301–2). Schubert set it to music in 1815, published in 1826.

and inner feeling', the other 'artistic effect'.[167] Dönike has argued that the two subjects reflected a tension between German classicism, with its emphasis on inner feelings (Hector and Andromache) and the more dramatic French manner, as represented especially by Jacques-Louis David.[168] In his appraisal of the submissions to the painting competition, Schiller explicitly connected the popularity of Hector and Andromache as a subject with German sentimentality:

> Hector's farewell is a moving subject in and of itself, even without any input on the part of the artist. It could make a telling image without testing the imagination, through simple truth alone. But here one had to reckon with the sentimental tendencies of our nation and our times, which have taken hold to such an extent that they are truly threatening to ruin all art, including that of painting, as it is threatening to ruin poetry.[169]

Schiller praised Homer for his ability to depict sentiments without sentimentality; his judgement proved influential. Schadewaldt's reading of the *Iliad* is deeply influenced by Schiller,[170] and through Schadewaldt's own work, Schiller's views have entered mainstream Homeric scholarship. But Hector and Andromache also had a lasting impact on the visual arts. Giorgio de Chirico painted Hector and Andromache as mannequins and hence deprived them of all inner feeling.[171] His enigmatic *Hector and Andromache* became an icon of the metaphysical movement and was later reconfigured by the post-modern artists Andy Warhol and Mike Bidlo.[172] It seems, then, that from Plutarch to Schiller to de Chirico and beyond, the encounter between Hector and Andromache inspired an extended meditation on poetry, art and human emotion.[173]

---

[167] Meyer 1800; for discussion of the competition and reproductions of some of the submissions see Scheidig 1958: 65–124 and plates 4–10; Lange *et al.* 1988: 422–31 and 1088–96; and Dönike 2005: 236–78.

[168] Dönike 2005: 269–70 and 273–4. David's dramatic *Andromache mourning Hector* (painted after Racine) gained him election to the Académie Royale in 1784; for the much later drawing of *Hector's departure* (1812), see Schnapper 1982: 260.

[169] Schiller in Janz *et al.* 1992: 847. Goethe expressed his agreement with Schiller's remarks in a letter of 30 September 1800: 'You cannot imagine how beautiful, good and appropriate I find [your essay]' (Dörr and Oellers 1999: 79).

[170] Schadewaldt himself praises Schiller's 'deep understanding' of the Homeric scene at Schadewaldt 1959: 232.

[171] De Chirico painted several versions of *Hector and Andromache* between 1917 and 1970. For a reproduction of the 1917 version (Mattioli collection, Milan) see Hirsh 2004: 416; for the 1924 version (Galerie Cazeau-Béraudère, Paris) see Baldacci and Roos 2007: 119. The visual template for the series was de Chirico's own earlier work *Le duo (Les mannequins de la tour rosel)* of 1915. On the mannequin motif see Bohn 1975. For a very different Hector and Andromache by de Chirico, see Quasimodo 1982: 45.

[172] A. Warhol, *Hector and Andromache*, 1982; M. Bidlo, *Not de Chirico (Hector and Andromache, 1918)*, 1989. For reproductions and discussion see Hirsh 2004: 415–31.

[173] Zajko 2006 chooses precisely the Iliadic encounter between Hector and Andromache in order to develop and test her Freudian model for reader identification. The reception history of the episode suggests that readers have indeed found it easy to commit emotionally to Hector and Andromache.

This brief discussion is not intended as a normative guide to the most influential reworkings of the episode, but rather as an open-ended invitation to read *Iliad* 6 together with other readers, as well as scholars, writers and artists. Some modern reworkings can help to capture the overall mood of the episode. Cavafy's *Trojans*, for example, though primarily inspired by *Iliad* 22, recreates the effect of Andromache's ominous lamenting for Hector, while he is still alive:

> Our efforts are those of men prone to disaster;
> our efforts are like those of the Trojans.
> . . .
> and we scurry around the walls
> trying to save ourselves by running away.
> Yet we're sure to fail. Up there,
> high on the wall, the dirge has already begun.[174]

Mandelstam recalls the encounter in *Iliad* 6 from the perspective of Andromache:

> Why did I tear myself away from you before it was time?[175]

Sometimes, poets contribute to our understanding of details. Carol Ann Duffy, for example, expands Homer's compressed line 391, offering a full picture of the built-up city, and Hector's movement through it:

> These words, like shadows, followed Hector's stride
> All through the town, along the avenues, ducking down
> Cool alleyways, his helmet's sudden flash,
> His cape's dark swish, disappearing round the corner
> Of walled lanes, until he reached the Skaian Gates.[176]

Amy Clampitt describes a Greek tutorial in a 'ninth-floor classroom, its windows grimy . . . the noise of traffic, πολυφλοίσβοιο-θαλάσσης-like', and then suddenly identifies with Astyanax:

> We have seen . . .
> . . . Hector's baby, shadowed by the plumes of war
> As we are, pull back from his own father with a shriek.[177]

Michael Longley, in 'The Parting', condenses the whole encounter into two lines of poetry.[178]

> He: 'Leave it to the big boys, Andromache.'
> 'Hector, my darling husband, och, och,' she.

Through his vernacular idiom, Longley sets the encounter in a modern Irish context, against the backdrop of the Troubles. In another poem, 'The Helmet', he reflects on

---

[174] Cavafy 1992: 22.   [175] In Kossman 2001: 226.   [176] Duffy and Graziosi 2005: 7.
[177] Clampitt 1997: 202.   [178] Longley 2006: 226.

the same episode, but focuses on Hector's prayer for Astyanax. Here he implicitly casts Homer as his own literary father – and questions his influence on contemporary literary and moral values.[179]

> When shiny Hector reached out for his son, the wean
> Squirmed and buried his head between his nurse's breasts
> And howled, terrorised by his father, by flashing bronze
> And the nightmarish nodding of the horse-hair crest.
>
> His daddy laughed, his mammy laughed, and his daddy
> Took off the helmet and laid it on the ground to gleam,
> Then kissed the babbie and dandled him in his arms and
> Prayed that his son might grow up bloodier than him.

6. THE TEXT

Editors of Homer are guided in their choices by what they think about two funda-mental, and much disputed, issues: how the *Iliad* came into being, and what happened to it in Alexandria.

Those who believe that Homer dictated or wrote down a master copy of the *Iliad* in the eighth or seventh century BCE privilege readings that look old, find it easier to justify interventions that aim at consistency and tend to emend passages or features that seem recent relative to other aspects of the text.[180] Those who believe that the *Iliad* stems from a more drawn-out process of textual fixation are prepared to allow for a less consistent and early-sounding text.[181] In formulating our own views, we have tried to hold on to one basic point. The origins of the *Iliad* remain obscure: as Cassio points out in a helpful discussion, the poem is 'likely to be the result of extremely complicated processes involving both orality and writing, which we can no longer reconstruct'.[182] Given the limitations of our knowledge, caution seems appropriate.[183] The *Iliad* may be early, but then – as we have seen – there is little evidence that suggests it made much impact before the sixth century. Performances at the Panathenaea were clearly an important factor in the survival and transmission of Homeric epic, but the *Iliad* is not an Athenian poem.[184] The language of epic combines older with more recent elements and shows influences from different dialects; attempts to weed out

---

[179] Longley 2006: 226; for a discussion of the poem, see Hardwick 2007: 58–9.

[180] E.g. the edition by M. L. West 1998–2000, cf. West 2001a; for specific discussions of West's text: 61n., 90n., 237n., 266n., 280n., 285n., 291n., 298n., 344n., 459n., 465n. and 493–4n.

[181] G. Nagy 1996a, 1996b and 2004.   [182] Cassio 2002: 114.

[183] Van Thiel 1996 is exemplary in this respect.

[184] Jensen 1980 argues that 'the *Iliad* and the *Odyssey* were dictated and written at the court of Pisistratus' (p. 159). The Athenians themselves, however, thought that the Homeric poems originated in Ionia, i.e. the coast of Asia Minor, and had been brought to Athens by the Homeridae: for ancient discussions of the origins of the poems, see Graziosi 2002: 201–34. The earliest authors known to have discussed the Homeric poems are Theagenes of Rhegium, Xenophanes of Colophon and Heraclitus of Ephesus, not one of them Athenian.

supposedly un-Homeric forms quickly run into difficulties: even seemingly clear-cut examples of innovative spelling are not always easy to date absolutely and therefore cannot be disregarded as post-Homeric.[185] In view of the gaps in our knowledge, the present edition adopts a pragmatic approach: we have noted instances of *prima facie* archaic forms (e.g. regard for initial digamma) and apparently later usage (e.g. disregard of digamma), but we have not attempted to date these, or to impose consistency on the transmitted text.

The second issue concerns the impact of Alexandrian scholarship on the text of the *Iliad*. It is generally agreed that the vulgate can be traced back to the Hellenistic period. To what extent it is a reliable guide to the pre-Hellenistic text of Homer is a more difficult question. Early papyri show a certain amount of variation, especially in the number of lines.[186] These divergences, however, are small-scale, and do not detract from the general impression of textual unity: the classical text of the *Iliad* must have been close to the medieval vulgate. Early citations by and large confirm this impression.[187] When Herodotus, for example, quotes and discusses *Iliad* 6.289–92, he uses a text that is recognisably the same as our own: we cannot of course exclude the possibility that Herodotus' text was brought in line with the Homeric vulgate at some point in the history of transmission, but it is clear from Herodotus' paraphrase that he must have known essentially the same *Iliad* as we have today: 289–92n. Some variants may have originated in rhapsodic performance, though ancient commentaries do not usually credit rhapsodes with variant readings.[188] A particular problem arises from variants recommended by ancient scholars, but unattested – or only weakly attested – in the textual tradition. There is considerable dispute over the value and origins of such variants.[189] We have tried to approach them with an open mind, assessing each case on its own merits. The result has been that – as far as *Iliad* 6 is concerned – the readings of ancient scholars often seem motivated by a desire to clarify or correct the transmitted text (e.g. 4n., 21n., 31n., 71n., 76n., 148n., 226n., 237n., 241n., 252n., 266n., 285n., 321–2n., 415n., 511n.). Scholarly readings make the Homeric text more context-specific (e.g. 112n.), more idiomatic (e.g. 475n.) or more decorous (e.g. 135n., 160n.) by the standards of Hellenistic readers. Our findings thus confirm Fantuzzi's argument that Hellenistic scholars tended to adjust Homeric poetry to the sensibilities

---

[185] For a striking instance of the Homeric narrator using a late form even when an earlier one can be restored, see 344n. (κακομηχάνου, ὀκρυοέσσης).

[186] S. West 1967.

[187] Although there are differences between early citations and the Homeric vulgate (as emphasised, for example, by Haslam 1997, Dué 2001a and 2001b), they do not seem to us to testify to the existence of radically divergent *Iliads*. The *Iliad* may be called a multiform text in the archaic and classical period, but it is important to emphasise that variations seem to be small scale.

[188] Cassio 2002: 124. The rhapsodes prided themselves on accurate performance (Graziosi 2004), but we do not know against what standards they judged their own faithfulness to Homer's text.

[189] E.g. M. L. West 2001a; Rengakos 2002; Janko 2002: 658–62; G. Nagy 2003; M. L. West 2004. Zenodotus' readings are especially controversial.

of their age.[190] This does not exclude the possibility that some of the readings favoured by the Alexandrians represent genuine early variants,[191] but if that is what they are, they survived because they suited Hellenistic tastes.

The text is our own, though it does not differ significantly from standard editions. Our apparatus adopts the simplified system of reference introduced by Macleod 1982: the letters **a**, **b** and **c** indicate variant readings, including those found in the papyri and scholia. Readings only found in one or more papyri are noted under **p**; in the commentary papyri are sometimes identified by quoting their number in M. L. West 2001a. Suggestions of ancient scholars are cited by their name, when it is known; the following abbreviations are used: Ar. = Aristarchus; Arph. = Aristophanes of Byzantium; Zen. = Zenodotus. The apparatus makes no claim to completeness. Variants are selected either because they are significant in themselves or because they are instructive for readers of *Iliad* 6. Those interested in the details of textual transmission should consult the editions by van Thiel and West.[192]

---

[190] Fantuzzi 2001: 174–7.
[191] As argued by Rengakos 1993.
[192] The papyri are listed in M. L. West 2001a: 88–138. The fullest list of manuscripts can be found in Allen 1931, though his work has been criticised for containing numerous inaccuracies; see van Thiel 1996: VII–VIII. For a more sympathetic view of Allen's contribution, see Haslam 1997.

ΙΛΙΑΔΟΣ Ζ

ΙΛΙΑΔΟΣ Ζ

Τρώων δ' οἰώθη καὶ Ἀχαιῶν φύλοπις αἰνή.
πολλὰ δ' ἄρ ἔνθα καὶ ἔνθ' ἴθυσε μάχη πεδίοιο
ἀλλήλων ἰθυνομένων χαλκήρεα δοῦρα
μεσσηγὺς Σιμόεντος ἰδὲ Ξάνθοιο ῥοάων.
Αἴας δὲ πρῶτος Τελαμώνιος ἕρκος Ἀχαιῶν, 5
Τρώων ῥῆξε φάλαγγα, φόως δ' ἑτάροισιν ἔθηκεν,
ἄνδρα βαλὼν ὃς ἄριστος ἐνὶ Θρήικεσσι τέτυκτο,
υἱὸν Ἐϋσσώρου Ἀκάμαντ' ἠΰν τε μέγαν τε.
τόν ῥ' ἔβαλε πρῶτος κόρυθος φάλον ἱπποδασείης,
ἐν δὲ μετώπωι πῆξε· πέρησε δ' ἄρ ὀστέον εἴσω 10
αἰχμὴ χαλκείη, τὸν δὲ σκότος ὄσσ' ἐκάλυψεν.
Ἄξυλον δ' ἄρ ἔπεφνε βοὴν ἀγαθὸς Διομήδης
Τευθρανίδην, ὃς ἔναιεν ἐϋκτιμένηι ἐν Ἀρίσβηι
ἀφνειὸς βιότοιο, φίλος δ' ἦν ἀνθρώποισι.
πάντας γὰρ φιλέεσκεν ὁδῶι ἔπι οἰκία ναίων. 15
ἀλλά οἱ οὔ τις τῶν γε τότ' ἤρκεσε λυγρὸν ὄλεθρον
πρόσθεν ὑπαντιάσας, ἀλλ' ἄμφω θυμὸν ἀπηύρα,
αὐτὸν καὶ θεράποντα Καλήσιον, ὅς ῥα τόθ' ἵππων
ἔσκεν ὑφηνίοχος· τὼ δ' ἄμφω γαῖαν ἐδύτην.
Δρῆσον δ' Εὐρύαλος καὶ Ὀφέλτιον ἐξενάριξε· 20
βῆ δὲ μετ' Αἴσηπον καὶ Πήδασον, οὕς ποτε νύμφη
νηῒς Ἀβαρβαρέη τέκ' ἀμύμονι Βουκολίωνι.
Βουκολίων δ' ἦν υἱὸς ἀγαυοῦ Λαομέδοντος
πρεσβύτατος γενεῆι, σκότιον δέ ἑ γείνατο μήτηρ·
ποιμαίνων δ' ἐπ' ὄεσσι μίγη φιλότητι καὶ εὐνῆι· 25
ἣ δ' ὑποκυσαμένη διδυμάονε γείνατο παῖδε.
καὶ μὲν τῶν ὑπέλυσε μένος καὶ φαίδιμα γυῖα
Μηκιστηϊάδης καὶ ἀπ' ὤμων τεύχε' ἐσύλα.
Ἀστύαλον δ' ἄρ ἔπεφνε μενεπτόλεμος Πολυποίτης·
Πιδύτην δ' Ὀδυσεὺς Περκώσιον ἐξενάριξεν 30
ἔγχεϊ χαλκείωι, Τεῦκρος δ' Ἀρετάονα δῖον.
Ἀντίλοχος δ' Ἄβληρον ἐνήρατο δουρὶ φαεινῶι
Νεστορίδης, Ἔλατον δὲ ἄναξ ἀνδρῶν Ἀγαμέμνων·

4 μεσσηγὺς ποταμοῖο Σκαμάνδρου καὶ στομαλίμνης p, Ar.: μεσσηγὺς ποταμοῖο Σκαμάνδρου καὶ Σιμόεντος Chaeris 18 οἱ a 21 Πήδασον: Τήρεχον a 31 δ' ἄρ Ἐτάονα a

ναῖε δὲ Σατνιόεντος ἐϋρρείταο παρ' ὄχθας
Πήδασον αἰπεινήν. Φύλακον δ' ἕλε Λήϊτος ἥρως   35
φεύγοντ'· Εὐρύπυλος δὲ Μελάνθιον ἐξενάριξεν.

   Ἄδρηστον δ' ἄρ ἔπειτα βοὴν ἀγαθὸς Μενέλαος
ζωὸν ἕλ'· ἵππω γάρ οἱ ἀτυζομένω πεδίοιο
ὄζωι ἐνὶ βλαφθέντε μυρικίνωι ἀγκύλον ἅρμα
ἄξαντ' ἐν πρώτωι ῥυμῶι αὐτὼ μὲν ἐβήτην   40
πρὸς πόλιν, ἧι περ οἱ ἄλλοι ἀτυζόμενοι φοβέοντο,
αὐτὸς δ' ἐκ δίφροιο παρὰ τροχὸν ἐξεκυλίσθη
πρηνὴς ἐν κονίῃσιν ἐπὶ στόμα· πὰρ δέ οἱ ἔστη
Ἀτρείδης Μενέλαος ἔχων δολιχόσκιον ἔγχος.
Ἄδρηστος δ' ἄρ ἔπειτα λαβὼν ἐλίσσετο γούνων·   45
"ζώγρει, Ἀτρέος υἱέ, σὺ δ' ἄξια δέξαι ἄποινα.
πολλὰ δ' ἐν ἀφνειοῦ πατρὸς κειμήλια κεῖται,
χαλκός τε χρυσός τε πολύκμητός τε σίδηρος·
τῶν κέν τοι χαρίσαιτο πατὴρ ἀπερείσι' ἄποινα,
εἴ κεν ἐμὲ ζωὸν πεπύθοιτ' ἐπὶ νηυσὶν Ἀχαιῶν."   50
   ὣς φάτο, τῶι δ' ἄρα θυμὸν ἐνὶ στήθεσσιν ἔπειθε·
καὶ δή μιν τάχ' ἔμελλε θοὰς ἐπὶ νῆας Ἀχαιῶν
δώσειν ὧι θεράποντι καταξέμεν. ἀλλ' Ἀγαμέμνων
ἀντίος ἦλθε θέων, καὶ ὁμοκλήσας ἔπος ηὔδα·
"ὦ πέπον ὦ Μενέλαε, τίη δὲ σὺ κήδεαι οὕτως   55
ἀνδρῶν; ἦ σοὶ ἄριστα πεποίηται κατὰ οἶκον
πρὸς Τρώων; τῶν μή τις ὑπεκφύγοι αἰπὺν ὄλεθρον
χεῖράς θ' ἡμετέρας· μηδ' ὅν τινα γαστέρι μήτηρ
κοῦρον ἐόντα φέροι, μηδ' ὃς φύγοι, ἀλλ' ἅμα πάντες
Ἰλίου ἐξαπολοίατ' ἀκήδεστοι καὶ ἄφαντοι."   60
   ὣς εἰπὼν ἔτρεψεν ἀδελφειοῦ φρένας ἥρως,
αἴσιμα παρειπών· ὃ δ' ἀπὸ ἕθεν ὤσατο χειρὶ
ἥρω' Ἄδρηστον. τὸν δὲ κρείων Ἀγαμέμνων
οὖτα κατὰ λαπάρην· ὃ δ' ἀνετράπετ', Ἀτρείδης δὲ
λὰξ ἐν στήθεσι βὰς ἐξέσπασε μείλινον ἔγχος.   65
   Νέστωρ δ' Ἀργείοισιν ἐκέκλετο μακρὸν ἀΰσας·
"ὦ φίλοι ἥρωες Δαναοί, θεράποντες Ἄρηος,
μή τις νῦν ἐνάρων ἐπιβαλλόμενος μετόπισθε
μιμνέτω, ὥς κεν πλεῖστα φέρων ἐπὶ νῆας ἵκηται,
ἀλλ' ἄνδρας κτείνωμεν· ἔπειτα δὲ καὶ τὰ ἕκηλοι   70

34 ὃς ναῖε Zen.   45 ἑλίσσετο p   51 ὄρινε a   61 παρέπεισεν a

νεκροὺς ἂμ πεδίον συλήσετε τεθνειῶτας."
ὣς εἰπὼν ὤτρυνε μένος καὶ θυμὸν ἑκάστου.
ἔνθά κεν αὖτε Τρῶες ἀρηΐφίλων ὑπ' Ἀχαιῶν
Ἴλιον εἰσανέβησαν ἀναλκείηισι δαμέντες,
εἰ μὴ ἄρ' Αἰνείαι τε καὶ Ἕκτορι εἶπε παραστὰς   75
Πριαμίδης Ἕλενος, οἰωνοπόλων ὄχ' ἄριστος·
"Αἰνεία τε καὶ Ἕκτορ, ἐπεὶ πόνος ὔμμι μάλιστα
Τρώων καὶ Λυκίων ἐγκέκλιται, οὕνεκ' ἄριστοι
πᾶσαν ἐπ' ἰθύν ἐστε μάχεσθαί τε φρονέειν τε,
στῆτ' αὐτοῦ καὶ λαὸν ἐρυκάκετε πρὸ πυλάων   80
πάντηι ἐποιχόμενοι, πρὶν αὖτ' ἐν χερσὶ γυναικῶν
φεύγοντας πεσέειν, δηΐοισι δὲ χάρμα γενέσθαι.
αὐτὰρ ἐπεί κε φάλαγγας ἐποτρύνητον ἁπάσας,
ἡμεῖς μὲν Δαναοῖσι μαχησόμεθ' αὖθι μένοντες,
καὶ μάλα τειρόμενοί περ· ἀναγκαίη γὰρ ἐπείγει.   85
Ἕκτορ, ἀτὰρ σὺ πόλινδε μετέρχεο, εἰπὲ δ' ἔπειτα
μητέρι σῆι καὶ ἐμῆι· ἣ δὲ ξυνάγουσα γεραιὰς
νηὸν Ἀθηναίης γλαυκώπιδος ἐν πόλει ἄκρηι,
οἴξασα κληῖδι θύρας ἱεροῖο δόμοιο,
πέπλον, ὅς οἱ δοκέει χαριέστατος ἠδὲ μέγιστος   90
εἶναι ἐνὶ μεγάρωι καί οἱ πολὺ φίλτατος αὐτῆι,
θεῖναι Ἀθηναίης ἐπὶ γούνασιν ἠϋκόμοιο,
καί οἱ ὑποσχέσθαι δυοκαίδεκα βοῦς ἐνὶ νηῶι
ἤνις ἠκέστας ἱερευσέμεν, αἴ κ' ἐλεήσηι
ἄστυ τε καὶ Τρώων ἀλόχους καὶ νήπια τέκνα,   95
αἴ κεν Τυδέος υἱὸν ἀπόσχηι Ἰλίου ἱρῆς
ἄγριον αἰχμητήν, κρατερὸν μήστωρα φόβοιο,
ὃν δὴ ἐγὼ κάρτιστον Ἀχαιῶν φημὶ γενέσθαι.
οὐδ' Ἀχιλῆά ποθ' ὧδέ γ' ἐδείδιμεν ὄρχαμον ἀνδρῶν,
ὅν περ φασὶ θεᾶς ἐξέμμεναι· ἀλλ' ὅδε λίην   100
μαίνεται, οὐδέ τίς οἱ δύναται μένος ἰσοφαρίζειν."
ὣς ἔφαθ', Ἕκτωρ δ' οὔ τι κασιγνήτωι ἀπίθησεν.
αὐτίκα δ' ἐξ ὀχέων σὺν τεύχεσιν ἆλτο χαμᾶζε,
πάλλων δ' ὀξέα δοῦρα κατὰ στρατὸν ὤιχετο πάντηι
ὀτρύνων μαχέσασθαι, ἔγειρε δὲ φύλοπιν αἰνήν·   105
οἱ δ' ἐλελίχθησαν καὶ ἐναντίοι ἔσταν Ἀχαιῶν.

71 Τρώων ἂμ πεδίον συλήσομεν ἔντεα νεκρούς Zen.   τεθνηῶτας a, Ar.   76 μάντις τ'
οἰωνοπόλος τε Ar.   86 μετοίχεο a   87 γεραιρὰς a   90 ὅς οἱ: ὃ οἱ p   91 μμεγάρωι
a   95 ἄστύ τε a   96 αἴ: ὣς a, Ar.   101 ἀντιφερίζειν Bentley

Ἀργεῖοι δ᾽ ὑπεχώρησαν, λῆξαν δὲ φόνοιο·
φὰν δέ τιν᾽ ἀθανάτων ἐξ οὐρανοῦ ἀστερόεντος
Τρωσὶν ἀλεξήσοντα κατελθέμεν, ὡς ἐλέλιχθεν.
Ἕκτωρ δὲ Τρώεσσιν ἐκέκλετο μακρὸν ἀΰσας·   110
"Τρῶες ὑπέρθυμοι τηλεκλειτοί τ᾽ ἐπίκουροι,
ἀνέρες ἔστε, φίλοι, μνήσασθε δὲ θούριδος ἀλκῆς,
ὄφρ᾽ ἂν ἐγὼ βείω προτὶ Ἴλιον ἠδὲ γέρουσιν
εἴπω βουλευτῇσι καὶ ἡμετέρῃς ἀλόχοισι
δαίμοσιν ἀρήσασθαι, ὑποσχέσθαι δ᾽ ἑκατόμβας."   115
ὣς ἄρα φωνήσας ἀπέβη κορυθαίολος Ἕκτωρ·
ἀμφὶ δέ μιν σφυρὰ τύπτε καὶ αὐχένα δέρμα κελαινόν,
ἄντυξ ἣ πυμάτη θέεν ἀσπίδος ὀμφαλοέσσης.
Γλαῦκος δ᾽ Ἱππολόχοιο πάϊς καὶ Τυδέος υἱὸς
ἐς μέσον ἀμφοτέρων συνίτην μεμαῶτε μάχεσθαι.   120
οἳ δ᾽ ὅτε δὴ σχεδὸν ἦσαν ἐπ᾽ ἀλλήλοισιν ἰόντες,
τὸν πρότερος προσέειπε βοὴν ἀγαθὸς Διομήδης·
"τίς δὲ σύ ἐσσι, φέριστε, καταθνητῶν ἀνθρώπων;
οὐ μὲν γάρ ποτ᾽ ὄπωπα μάχῃ ἐνὶ κυδιανείρῃ
τὸ πρίν· ἀτὰρ μὲν νῦν γε πολὺ προβέβηκας ἁπάντων   125
σῷ θάρσει, ὅτ᾽ ἐμὸν δολιχόσκιον ἔγχος ἔμεινας.
δυστήνων δέ τε παῖδες ἐμῷ μένει ἀντιόωσιν.
εἰ δέ τις ἀθανάτων γε κατ᾽ οὐρανοῦ εἰλήλουθας,
οὐκ ἂν ἔγωγε θεοῖσιν ἐπουρανίοισι μαχοίμην.
οὐδὲ γὰρ οὐδὲ Δρύαντος υἱὸς κρατερὸς Λυκόοργος   130
δὴν ἦν, ὅς ῥα θεοῖσιν ἐπουρανίοισιν ἔριζεν·
ὅς ποτε μαινομένοιο Διωνύσοιο τιθήνας
σεῦε κατ᾽ ἠγάθεον Νυσήϊον, αἳ δ᾽ ἅμα πᾶσαι
θύσθλα χαμαὶ κατέχευαν, ὑπ᾽ ἀνδροφόνοιο Λυκούργου
θεινόμεναι βουπλῆγι. Διώνυσος δὲ φοβηθεὶς   135
δύσεθ᾽ ἁλὸς κατὰ κῦμα, Θέτις δ᾽ ὑπεδέξατο κόλπωι
δειδιότα· κρατερὸς γὰρ ἔχε τρόμος ἀνδρὸς ὁμοκλῇ.
τῶι μὲν ἔπειτ᾽ ὀδύσαντο θεοὶ ῥεῖα ζώοντες,
καί μιν τυφλὸν ἔθηκε Κρόνου παῖς· οὐδ᾽ ἄρ ἔτι δὴν
ἦν, ἐπεὶ ἀθανάτοισιν ἀπήχθετο πᾶσι θεοῖσιν.   140
οὐδ᾽ ἂν ἐγὼ μακάρεσσι θεοῖς ἐθέλοιμι μάχεσθαι.
εἰ δέ τίς ἐσσι βροτῶν, οἳ ἀρούρης καρπὸν ἔδουσιν,

109 ὣς **a**   111 Τρῶες καὶ Λύκιοι καὶ Δάρδανοι ἀγχιμαχηταί **a**   112 ἀνέρες ἔστε θοοὶ καὶ
ἀμύνετον ἄστεΐ λώβην Zen., ἀμύνετε Leaf   120 ἀμφοτέρω **a**   121 ἰόντε Zen., Arph., Ar.
128 οὐρανὸν Ar.   135 χολωθεὶς Zen.

ἆσσον ἴθ᾿, ὥς κεν θᾶσσον ὀλέθρου πείραθ᾿ ἵκηαι.᾿
τὸν δ᾿ αὖθ᾿ Ἱππολόχοιο προσηύδα φαίδιμος υἱός·
"Τυδείδη μεγάθυμε, τίη γενεὴν ἐρεείνεις;   145
οἵη περ φύλλων γενεή, τοίη δὲ καὶ ἀνδρῶν.
φύλλα τὰ μέν τ᾿ ἄνεμος χαμάδις χέει, ἄλλα δέ θ᾿ ὕλη
τηλεθόωσα φύει, ἔαρος δ᾿ ἐπιγίνεται ὥρη·
ὣς ἀνδρῶν γενεὴ ἣ μὲν φύει ἣ δ᾿ ἀπολήγει.
εἰ δ᾿ ἐθέλεις καὶ ταῦτα δαήμεναι, ὄφρ᾿ εὖ εἰδῇς   150
ἡμετέρην γενεήν, πολλοὶ δέ μιν ἄνδρες ἴσασιν,
ἔστι πόλις Ἐφύρη μυχῶι Ἄργεος ἱπποβότοιο,
ἔνθα δὲ Σίσυφος ἔσκεν, ὃ κέρδιστος γένετ᾿ ἀνδρῶν,
Σίσυφος Αἰολίδης· ὃ δ᾿ ἄρα Γλαῦκον τέκεθ᾿ υἱόν·
αὐτὰρ Γλαῦκος ἔτικτεν ἀμύμονα Βελλεροφόντην.   155
τῶι δὲ θεοὶ κάλλος τε καὶ ἠνορέην ἐρατεινὴν
ὤπασαν· αὐτὰρ οἱ Προῖτος κάκ᾿ ἐμήσατο θυμῶι,
ὅς ῥ᾿ ἐκ δήμου ἔλασσεν, ἐπεὶ πολὺ φέρτερος ἦεν,
Ἀργείων· Ζεὺς γάρ οἱ ὑπὸ σκήπτρωι ἐδάμασσε.
τῶι δὲ γυνὴ Προίτου ἐπεμήνατο δῖ᾿ Ἄντεια   160
κρυπταδίηι φιλότητι μιγήμεναι· ἀλλὰ τὸν οὔ τι
πεῖθ᾿ ἀγαθὰ φρονέοντα δαΐφρονα Βελλεροφόντην.
ἣ δὲ ψευσαμένη Προῖτον βασιλῆα προσηύδα·
'τεθναίης, ὦ Προῖτ᾿, ἢ κάκτανε Βελλεροφόντην,
ὅς μ᾿ ἔθελεν φιλότητι μιγήμεναι οὐκ ἐθελούσηι.᾿   165
ὣς φάτο· τὸν δὲ ἄνακτα χόλος λάβεν οἷον ἄκουσε.
κτεῖναι μέν ῥ᾿ ἀλέεινε, σεβάσσατο γὰρ τό γε θυμῶι,
πέμπε δέ μιν Λυκίηνδε, πόρεν δ᾿ ὅ γε σήματα λυγρὰ
γράψας ἐν πίνακι πτυκτῶι θυμοφθόρα πολλά,
δεῖξαι δ᾿ ἠνώγει ὧι πενθερῶι ὄφρ᾿ ἀπόλοιτο.   170
αὐτὰρ ὃ βῆ Λυκίηνδε θεῶν ὑπ᾿ ἀμύμονι πομπῆι.
ἀλλ᾿ ὅτε δὴ Λυκίην ἷξε Ξάνθον τε ῥέοντα,
προφρονέως μιν τῖεν ἄναξ Λυκίης εὐρείης.
ἐννῆμαρ ξείνισσε καὶ ἐννέα βοῦς ἱέρευσεν.
ἀλλ᾿ ὅτε δὴ δεκάτη ἐφάνη ῥοδοδάκτυλος Ἠώς,   175
καὶ τότε μιν ἐρέεινε καὶ ἤιτεε σῆμα ἰδέσθαι,
ὅττι ῥά οἱ γαμβροῖο παρὰ Προίτοιο φέροιτο.
αὐτὰρ ἐπεὶ δὴ σῆμα κακὸν παρεδέξατο γαμβροῦ,

---

148 τηλεθόωντα Arph.   ὥρηι **a**, Arph.   155 Ἐλλεροφόντην Zen.   157 κακὰ μήσατο
a, Ar.   159 οἳ: μιν **a**   160 Διάντεια **a**   165 ἐθέλουσαν **a**   170 ἠνώγειν **a**, Ar.
171 μετ᾿ Demetrius Ixio   172 Ξάνθόν τε **a**

πρῶτον μέν ῥα Χίμαιραν ἀμαιμακέτην ἐκέλευσε
πεφνέμεν· ἣ δ᾽ ἄρ ἔην θεῖον γένος οὐδ᾽ ἀνθρώπων,   180
πρόσθε λέων, ὄπιθεν δὲ δράκων, μέσση δὲ χίμαιρα,
δεινὸν ἀποπνείουσα πυρὸς μένος αἰθομένοιο.
καὶ τὴν μὲν κατέπεφνε θεῶν τεράεσσι πιθήσας.
δεύτερον αὖ Σολύμοισι μαχέσσατο κυδαλίμοισι·
καρτίστην δὴ τήν γε μάχην φάτο δύμεναι ἀνδρῶν.   185
τὸ τρίτον αὖ κατέπεφνεν Ἀμαζόνας ἀντιανείρας.
τῶι δ᾽ ἄρ ἀνερχομένωι πυκινὸν δόλον ἄλλον ὕφαινε·
κρίνας ἐκ Λυκίης εὐρείης φῶτας ἀρίστους
εἷσε λόχον. τοὶ δ᾽ οὔ τι πάλιν οἶκόνδε νέοντο·
πάντας γὰρ κατέπεφνεν ἀμύμων Βελλεροφόντης.   190
ἀλλ᾽ ὅτε δὴ γίνωσκε θεοῦ γόνον ἠὺν ἐόντα,
αὐτοῦ μιν κατέρυκε, δίδου δ᾽ ὅ γε θυγατέρα ἥν,
δῶκε δέ οἱ τιμῆς βασιληΐδος ἥμισυ πάσης·
καὶ μέν οἱ Λύκιοι τέμενος τάμον ἔξοχον ἄλλων
καλὸν φυταλιῆς καὶ ἀρούρης, ὄφρα νέμοιτο.   195
ἣ δ᾽ ἔτεκε τρία τέκνα δαΐφρονι Βελλεροφόντηι
Ἴσανδρόν τε καὶ Ἱππόλοχον καὶ Λαοδάμειαν.
Λαοδαμείηι μὲν παρελέξατο μητίετα Ζεύς,
ἣ δ᾽ ἔτεκ᾽ ἀντίθεον Σαρπηδόνα χαλκοκορυστήν.
ἀλλ᾽ ὅτε δὴ καὶ κεῖνος ἀπήχθετο πᾶσι θεοῖσιν,   200
ἤτοι ὃ κὰπ πεδίον τὸ Ἀλήϊον οἶος ἀλᾶτο,
ὃν θυμὸν κατέδων, πάτον ἀνθρώπων ἀλεείνων·
Ἴσανδρον δέ οἱ υἱὸν Ἄρης ἆτος πολέμοιο
μαρνάμενον Σολύμοισι κατέκτανε κυδαλίμοισι·
τὴν δὲ χολωσαμένη χρυσήνιος Ἄρτεμις ἔκτα.   205
Ἱππόλοχος δέ μ᾽ ἔτικτε, καὶ ἐκ τοῦ φημὶ γενέσθαι·
πέμπε δέ μ᾽ ἐς Τροίην, καί μοι μάλα πόλλ᾽ ἐπέτελλεν,
αἰὲν ἀριστεύειν καὶ ὑπείροχον ἔμμεναι ἄλλων,
μηδὲ γένος πατέρων αἰσχυνέμεν, οἳ μέγ᾽ ἄριστοι
ἔν τ᾽ Ἐφύρηι ἐγένοντο καὶ ἐν Λυκίηι εὐρείηι.   210
ταύτης τοι γενεῆς τε καὶ αἵματος εὔχομαι εἶναι."
   ὣς φάτο, γήθησεν δὲ βοὴν ἀγαθὸς Διομήδης.
ἔγχος μὲν κατέπηξεν ἐπὶ χθονὶ πουλυβοτείρηι,
αὐτὰρ ὃ μειλιχίοισι προσηύδα ποιμένα λαῶν·
"ἦ ῥά νύ μοι ξεῖνος πατρώϊός ἐσσι παλαιός·   215

Οἰνεὺς γάρ ποτε δῖος ἀμύμονα Βελλεροφόντην
ξείνισ᾽ ἐνὶ μεγάροισιν ἐείκοσιν ἤματ᾽ ἐρύξας.
οἳ δὲ καὶ ἀλλήλοισι πόρον ξεινήϊα καλά·
Οἰνεὺς μὲν ζωστῆρα δίδου φοίνικι φαεινόν,
Βελλεροφόντης δὲ χρύσεον δέπας ἀμφικύπελλον·   220
καί μιν ἐγὼ κατέλειπον ἰὼν ἐν δώμασ᾽ ἐμοῖσι.
Τυδέα δ᾽ οὐ μέμνημαι, ἐπεί μ᾽ ἔτι τυτθὸν ἐόντα
κάλλιφ᾽, ὅτ᾽ ἐν Θήβησιν ἀπώλετο λαὸς Ἀχαιῶν.
τῶ νῦν σοὶ μὲν ἐγὼ ξεῖνος φίλος Ἄργεϊ μέσσωι
εἰμί, σὺ δ᾽ ἐν Λυκίηι, ὅτε κεν τῶν δῆμον ἵκωμαι.   225
ἔγχεα δ᾽ ἀλλήλων ἀλεώμεθα καὶ δι᾽ ὁμίλου·
πολλοὶ μὲν γὰρ ἐμοὶ Τρῶες κλειτοί τ᾽ ἐπίκουροι
κτείνειν, ὅν κε θεός γε πόρηι καὶ ποσσὶ κιχείω,
πολλοὶ δ᾽ αὖ σοὶ Ἀχαιοὶ ἐναιρέμεν, ὅν κε δύνηαι.
τεύχεα δ᾽ ἀλλήλοις ἐπαμείψομεν, ὄφρα καὶ οἵδε   230
γνῶσιν ὅτι ξεῖνοι πατρώϊοι εὐχόμεθ᾽ εἶναι."
ὣς ἄρα φωνήσαντε, καθ᾽ ἵππων ἀΐξαντε
χεῖράς τ᾽ ἀλλήλων λαβέτην καὶ πιστώσαντο.
ἔνθ᾽ αὖτε Γλαύκωι Κρονίδης φρένας ἐξέλετο Ζεύς,
ὃς πρὸς Τυδείδην Διομήδεα τεύχε᾽ ἄμειβε   235
χρύσεα χαλκείων, ἑκατόμβοι᾽ ἐννεαβοίων.
Ἕκτωρ δ᾽ ὡς Σκαιάς τε πύλας καὶ φηγὸν ἵκανεν,
ἀμφ᾽ ἄρα μιν Τρώων ἄλοχοι θέον ἠδὲ θύγατρες
εἰρόμεναι παῖδάς τε κασιγνήτους τε ἔτας τε
καὶ πόσιας. ὃ δ᾽ ἔπειτα θεοῖς εὔχεσθαι ἀνώγει   240
πάσας ἑξείης· πολλῆισι δὲ κήδε᾽ ἐφῆπτο.
ἀλλ᾽ ὅτε δὴ Πριάμοιο δόμον περικαλλέ᾽ ἵκανε,
ξεστῆις αἰθούσηισι τετυγμένον – αὐτὰρ ἐν αὐτῶι
πεντήκοντ᾽ ἔνεσαν θάλαμοι ξεστοῖο λίθοιο,
πλησίοι ἀλλήλων δεδμημένοι, ἔνθα δὲ παῖδες   245
κοιμῶντο Πριάμοιο παρὰ μνηστῆις ἀλόχοισι·
κουράων δ᾽ ἑτέρωθεν ἐναντίοι ἔνδοθεν αὐλῆς
δώδεκ᾽ ἔσαν τέγεοι θάλαμοι ξεστοῖο λίθοιο,
πλησίοι ἀλλήλων δεδμημένοι, ἔνθα δὲ γαμβροὶ
κοιμῶντο Πριάμοιο παρ᾽ αἰδοίηις ἀλόχοισιν –   250
ἔνθά οἱ ἠπιόδωρος ἐναντίη ἤλυθε μήτηρ,

---

217 μμεγάροισιν a   226 ἔγχεσι a   ἀλλήλους Zen.   237 φηγὸν: πύργον a   241
πᾶσι μάλ᾽ a   245 πλησίον a   246 παρ᾽ αἰδοίηις a   249 πλησίον a   250 παρὰ
μνηστῆις a

Λαοδίκην ἐσάγουσα θυγατρῶν εἶδος ἀρίστην·
ἔν τ᾽ ἄρα οἱ φῦ χειρὶ ἔπος τ᾽ ἔφατ᾽ ἔκ τ᾽ ὀνόμαζε·
"τέκνον, τίπτε λιπὼν πόλεμον θρασὺν εἰλήλουθας;
ἦ μάλα δὴ τείρουσι δυσώνυμοι υἷες Ἀχαιῶν   255
μαρνάμενοι περὶ ἄστυ, σὲ δ᾽ ἐνθάδε θυμὸς ἀνῆκεν
ἐλθόντ᾽ ἐξ ἄκρης πόλιος Διὶ χεῖρας ἀνασχεῖν.
ἀλλὰ μέν᾽, ὄφρα κέ τοι μελιηδέα οἶνον ἐνείκω,
ὡς σπείσῃς Διὶ πατρὶ καὶ ἄλλοις ἀθανάτοισι
πρῶτον, ἔπειτα δὲ καὐτὸς ὀνήσεαι αἴ κε πίῃσθα.   260
ἀνδρὶ δὲ κεκμηῶτι μένος μέγα οἶνος ἀέξει,
ὡς τύνη κέκμηκας ἀμύνων σοῖσιν ἔτῃσι."
   τὴν δ᾽ ἠμείβετ᾽ ἔπειτα μέγας κορυθαίολος Ἕκτωρ·
"μή μοι οἶνον ἄειρε μελίφρονα, πότνια μῆτερ,
μή μ᾽ ἀπογυιώσῃς μένεος, ἀλκῆς τε λάθωμαι.   265
χερσὶ δ᾽ ἀνίπτοισιν Διὶ λείβειν αἴθοπα οἶνον
ἅζομαι· οὐδέ πῃ ἐστὶ κελαινεφέϊ Κρονίωνι
αἵματι καὶ λύθρωι πεπαλαγμένον εὐχετάασθαι.
ἀλλὰ σύ γε πρὸς νηὸν Ἀθηναίης ἀγελείης
ἔρχεο σὺν θυέεσσιν ἀολλίσσασα γεραιάς·   270
πέπλον δ᾽, ὅς τίς τοι χαριέστατος ἠδὲ μέγιστος
ἐστὶν ἐνὶ μεγάρωι καί τοι πολὺ φίλτατος αὐτῆι,
τὸν θὲς Ἀθηναίης ἐπὶ γούνασιν ἠϋκόμοιο,
καί οἱ ὑποσχέσθαι δυοκαίδεκα βοῦς ἐνὶ νηῶι
ἤνις ἠκέστας ἱερευσέμεν, αἴ κ᾽ ἐλεήσηι   275
ἄστυ τε καὶ Τρώων ἀλόχους καὶ νήπια τέκνα,
αἴ κεν Τυδέος υἱὸν ἀπόσχηι Ἰλίου ἱρῆς,
ἄγριον αἰχμητήν, κρατερὸν μήστωρα φόβοιο.
ἀλλὰ σὺ μὲν πρὸς νηὸν Ἀθηναίης ἀγελείης
ἔρχευ, ἐγὼ δὲ Πάριν μετελεύσομαι ὄφρα καλέσσω   280
αἴ κ᾽ ἐθέλησ᾽ εἰπόντος ἀκουέμεν. ὥς κέ οἱ αὖθι
γαῖα χάνοι· μέγα γάρ μιν Ὀλύμπιος ἔτρεφε πῆμα
Τρωσί τε καὶ Πριάμωι μεγαλήτορι τοῖό τε παισίν.
εἰ κεῖνόν γε ἴδοιμι κατελθόντ᾽ Ἄϊδος εἴσω,
φαίην κεν φρέν᾽ ἀτέρπου ὀϊζύος ἐκλελαθέσθαι."   285
   ὣς ἔφαθ᾽, ἡ δὲ μολοῦσα ποτὶ μέγαρ᾽ ἀμφιπόλοισι

252 ἐς ἄγουσα a   260 δέ κ᾽ αὐτός a   263 τὴν δ᾽ ἀπαμειβόμενος προσέφη p   266
ἀνίπτησιν Zen.   269 γε: μὲν a   270 γεραιράς a   272 μμεγάρωι a   276 ἄστύ τε
a   280 ἔρχεο a   281 κέ οἱ: καί οἱ a: δέ οἱ p   283 om. p   285 φρέν᾽ ἄτερ που a,
Ar.: φίλον ἦτορ Zen.   286 [ο]ὐδ᾽ ἀπίθησ᾽ Ἑκάβη, ταχὺ δ᾽ ἀ[μ]φιπόλοισι p   μμέγαρ᾽ a

κέκλετο· ταὶ δ' ἄρ ἀόλλισσαν κατὰ ἄστυ γεραιάς.
αὐτὴ δ' ἐς θάλαμον κατεβήσετο κηώεντα,
ἔνθ' ἔσαν οἱ πέπλοι παμποίκιλοι, ἔργα γυναικῶν
Σιδονίων, τὰς αὐτὸς Ἀλέξανδρος θεοειδὴς   290
ἤγαγε Σιδονίηθεν, ἐπιπλὼς εὐρέα πόντον,
τὴν ὁδὸν ἣν Ἑλένην περ ἀνήγαγεν εὐπατέρειαν.
τῶν ἕν' ἀειραμένη Ἑκάβη φέρε δῶρον Ἀθήνηι,
ὃς κάλλιστος ἔην ποικίλμασιν ἠδὲ μέγιστος,
ἀστὴρ δ' ὣς ἀπέλαμπεν· ἔκειτο δὲ νείατος ἄλλων.   295
βῆ δ' ἰέναι, πολλαὶ δὲ μετεσσεύοντο γεραιαί.
    αἳ δ' ὅτε νηὸν ἵκανον Ἀθήνης ἐν πόλει ἄκρηι,
τῆισι θύρας ὤϊξε Θεανὼ καλλιπάρηος
Κισσηΐς, ἄλοχος Ἀντήνορος ἱπποδάμοιο·
τὴν γὰρ Τρῶες ἔθηκαν Ἀθηναίης ἱέρειαν.   300
αἳ δ' ὀλολυγῆι πᾶσαι Ἀθήνηι χεῖρας ἀνέσχον·
ἣ δ' ἄρα πέπλον ἑλοῦσα Θεανὼ καλλιπάρηος
θῆκεν Ἀθηναίης ἐπὶ γούνασιν ἠϋκόμοιο.
εὐχομένη δ' ἠρᾶτο Διὸς κούρηι μεγάλοιο·
"πότνι' Ἀθηναίη, ἐρυσίπτολι, δῖα θεάων,   305
ἄξον δὴ ἔγχος Διομήδεος, ἠδὲ καὶ αὐτὸν
πρηνέα δὸς πεσέειν Σκαιῶν προπάροιθε πυλάων,
ὄφρα τοι αὐτίκα νῦν δυοκαίδεκα βοῦς ἐνὶ νηῶι
ἤνις ἠκέστας ἱερεύσομεν, αἴ κ' ἐλεήσηις
ἄστυ τε καὶ Τρώων ἀλόχους καὶ νήπια τέκνα."   310
ὣς ἔφατ' εὐχομένη, ἀνένευε δὲ Παλλὰς Ἀθήνη.
    ὣς αἳ μέν ῥ' εὔχοντο Διὸς κούρηι μεγάλοιο·
Ἕκτωρ δὲ πρὸς δώματ' Ἀλεξάνδροιο βεβήκει
καλά, τά ῥ' αὐτὸς ἔτευξε σὺν ἀνδράσιν οἳ τότ' ἄριστοι
ἦσαν ἐνὶ Τροίηι ἐριβώλακι τέκτονες ἄνδρες,   315
οἵ οἱ ἐποίησαν θάλαμον καὶ δῶμα καὶ αὐλὴν
ἐγγύθι τε Πριάμοιο καὶ Ἕκτορος ἐν πόλει ἄκρηι.
ἔνθ' Ἕκτωρ εἰσῆλθε Διὶ φίλος, ἐν δ' ἄρα χειρὶ
ἔγχος ἔχ' ἑνδεκάπηχυ· πάροιθε δὲ λάμπετο δουρὸς
αἰχμὴ χαλκείη, περὶ δὲ χρύσεος θέε πόρκης.   320
τὸν δ' εὗρ' ἐν θαλάμωι περικαλλέα τεύχε' ἔποντα,

---

288 ἣ δ' εἰς οἶκον ἰοῦσα παρίστατο φωριαμοῖσιν **a**, Ar.   288*ab* [κέδρινον] ὑψερεφῆ, ὃς
γλήνη πόλλ' ἐκεκεύθει | [ἔνθα δὲ] φωριαμοῖσι παρί[στ]ατο δῖα γυνα[ικῶν] add. **p**   290
Σιδονιῶν Fick   305 ῥυσίπτολι **a**   311 ath. Ar.   319 ἔχεν δεκάπηχυ **a**

ἀσπίδα καὶ θώρηκα, καὶ ἀγκύλα τόξ᾽ ἀφόωντα·
Ἀργείη δ᾽ Ἑλένη μετ᾽ ἄρα δμωῇσι γυναιξὶν
ἧστο καὶ ἀμφιπόλοισι περικλυτὰ ἔργα κέλευε.
    τὸν δ᾽ Ἕκτωρ νείκεσσεν ἰδὼν αἰσχροῖς ἐπέεσσι·   325
"δαιμόνι᾽ οὐ μὲν καλὰ χόλον τόνδ᾽ ἔνθεο θυμῶι.
λαοὶ μὲν φθινύθουσι περὶ πτόλιν αἰπύ τε τεῖχος
μαρνάμενοι, σέο δ᾽ εἵνεκ᾽ ἀϋτή τε πτόλεμός τε
ἄστυ τόδ᾽ ἀμφιδέδηε· σὺ δ᾽ ἂν μαχέσαιο καὶ ἄλλωι,
εἴ τινά που μεθιέντα ἴδοις στυγεροῦ πολέμοιο.   330
ἀλλ᾽ ἄνα μὴ τάχα ἄστυ πυρὸς δηΐοιο θέρηται."
    τὸν δ᾽ αὖτε προσέειπεν Ἀλέξανδρος θεοειδής·
"Ἕκτορ ἐπεί με κατ᾽ αἶσαν ἐνείκεσας οὐδ᾽ ὑπὲρ αἶσαν,
τοὔνεκά τοι ἐρέω· σὺ δὲ σύνθεο καί μευ ἄκουσον·
οὔ τοι ἐγὼ Τρώων τόσσον χόλωι οὐδὲ νεμέσσι   335
ἥμην ἐν θαλάμωι, ἔθελον δ᾽ ἄχεϊ προτραπέσθαι.
νῦν δέ με παρειποῦσ᾽ ἄλοχος μαλακοῖς ἐπέεσσιν
ὥρμησ᾽ ἐς πόλεμον· δοκέει δέ μοι ὧδε καὶ αὐτῶι
λώϊον ἔσσεσθαι· νίκη δ᾽ ἐπαμείβεται ἄνδρας.
ἀλλ᾽ ἄγε νῦν ἐπίμεινον, ἀρήϊα τεύχεα δύω·   340
ἢ ἴθ᾽, ἐγὼ δὲ μέτειμι· κιχήσεσθαι δέ σ᾽ ὀΐω."
    ὣς φάτο, τὸν δ᾽ οὔ τι προσέφη κορυθαίολος Ἕκτωρ.
τὸν δ᾽ Ἑλένη μύθοισι προσηύδα μειλιχίοισι·
"δᾶερ ἐμεῖο κυνὸς κακομηχάνου ὀκρυοέσσης,
ὥς μ᾽ ὄφελ᾽ ἤματι τῶι, ὅτε με πρῶτον τέκε μήτηρ,   345
οἴχεσθαι προφέρουσα κακὴ ἀνέμοιο θύελλα
εἰς ὄρος ἢ εἰς κῦμα πολυφλοίσβοιο θαλάσσης,
ἔνθα με κῦμ᾽ ἀπόερσε πάρος τάδε ἔργα γενέσθαι.
αὐτὰρ ἐπεὶ τάδε γ᾽ ὧδε θεοὶ κακὰ τεκμήραντο,
ἀνδρὸς ἔπειτ᾽ ὤφελλον ἀμείνονος εἶναι ἄκοιτις,   350
ὃς ἤιδη νέμεσίν τε καὶ αἴσχεα πόλλ᾽ ἀνθρώπων.
τούτωι δ᾽ οὔτ᾽ ἂρ νῦν φρένες ἔμπεδοι οὔτ᾽ ἂρ ὀπίσσω
ἔσσονται· τῶ καί μιν ἐπαυρήσεσθαι ὀΐω.
ἀλλ᾽ ἄγε νῦν εἴσελθε καὶ ἕζεο τῶιδ᾽ ἐπὶ δίφρωι,
δᾶερ, ἐπεί σε μάλιστα πόνος φρένας ἀμφιβέβηκεν   355
εἵνεκ᾽ ἐμεῖο κυνὸς καὶ Ἀλεξάνδρου ἕνεκ᾽ ἄτης,
οἷσιν ἐπὶ Ζεὺς θῆκε κακὸν μόρον, ὡς καὶ ὀπίσσω

322 τόξα φόωντα **a**   330 εἴ: ὅν **p**, Ar.   335 νεμέσ(σ)ει **a**   343 προσηύδα δῖα
γυναικῶν **a**: ἀμείβετο δῖα γυναικῶν **b**   349 διετεκμήραντο **a**   350 ἀμύμονος **a**   351
ὅς ῥ᾽ **a**   εἴδη Fick   353 τῶ: τοῦ Herwerden: τῶν Nauck   καί: κέν **a**   356 ἀρχῆς **a**

ἀνθρώποισι πελώμεθ᾽ ἀοίδιμοι ἐσσομένοισι."
τὴν δ᾽ ἠμείβετ᾽ ἔπειτα μέγας κορυθαίολος Ἕκτωρ·
"μή με κάθιζ᾽, Ἑλένη, φιλέουσά περ· οὐδέ με πείσεις· 360
ἤδη γάρ μοι θυμὸς ἐπέσσυται ὄφρ᾽ ἐπαμύνω
Τρώεσσ᾽, οἳ μέγ᾽ ἐμεῖο ποθὴν ἀπεόντος ἔχουσιν.
ἀλλὰ σύ γ᾽ ὄρνυθι τοῦτον, ἐπειγέσθω δὲ καὶ αὐτός,
ὥς κεν ἔμ᾽ ἔντοσθεν πόλιος καταμάρψῃ ἐόντα.
καὶ γὰρ ἐγὼν οἶκόνδ᾽ ἐσελεύσομαι, ὄφρα ἴδωμαι 365
οἰκῆας ἄλοχόν τε φίλην καὶ νήπιον υἱόν.
οὐ γάρ τ᾽ οἶδ᾽ εἰ ἔτι σφιν ὑπότροπος ἵξομαι αὖτις,
ἦ ἤδη μ᾽ ὑπὸ χερσὶ θεοὶ δαμόωσιν Ἀχαιῶν."
ὣς ἄρα φωνήσας ἀπέβη κορυθαίολος Ἕκτωρ·
αἶψα δ᾽ ἔπειθ᾽ ἵκανε δόμους εὖ ναιετάοντας. 370
οὐδ᾽ εὗρ᾽ Ἀνδρομάχην λευκώλενον ἐν μεγάροισιν,
ἀλλ᾽ ἥ γε ξὺν παιδὶ καὶ ἀμφιπόλωι ἐϋπέπλωι
πύργωι ἐφεστήκει γοόωσά τε μυρομένη τε.
Ἕκτωρ δ᾽ ὡς οὐκ ἔνδον ἀμύμονα τέτμεν ἄκοιτιν,
ἔστη ἐπ᾽ οὐδὸν ἰών, μετὰ δὲ δμωῇσιν ἔειπεν· 375
"εἰ δ᾽ ἄγε μοι, δμωιαί, νημερτέα μυθήσασθε·
πῇ ἔβη Ἀνδρομάχη λευκώλενος ἐκ μεγάροιο;
ἠέ πῃ ἐς γαλόων ἢ εἰνατέρων ἐϋπέπλων
ἦ ἐς Ἀθηναίης ἐξοίχεται, ἔνθά περ ἄλλαι
Τρωιαὶ ἐϋπλόκαμοι δεινὴν θεὸν ἱλάσκονται;" 380
τὸν δ᾽ αὖτ᾽ ὀτρηρὴ ταμίη πρὸς μῦθον ἔειπεν·
"Ἕκτορ, ἐπεὶ μάλ᾽ ἄνωγας ἀληθέα μυθήσασθαι,
οὔτέ πῃ ἐς γαλόων οὔτ᾽ εἰνατέρων ἐϋπέπλων
οὔτ᾽ ἐς Ἀθηναίης ἐξοίχεται, ἔνθά περ ἄλλαι
Τρωιαὶ ἐϋπλόκαμοι δεινὴν θεὸν ἱλάσκονται, 385
ἀλλ᾽ ἐπὶ πύργον ἔβη μέγαν Ἰλίου, οὔνεκ᾽ ἄκουσε
τείρεσθαι Τρῶας, μέγα δὲ κράτος εἶναι Ἀχαιῶν.
ἡ μὲν δὴ πρὸς τεῖχος ἐπειγομένη ἀφικάνει
μαινομένηι εἰκυῖα, φέρει δ᾽ ἅμα παῖδα τιθήνη."
ἦ ῥα γυνὴ ταμίη, ὃ δ᾽ ἀπέσσυτο δώματος Ἕκτωρ 390
τὴν αὐτὴν ὁδὸν αὖτις ἐϋκτιμένας κατ᾽ ἀγυιάς.
εὖτε πύλας ἵκανε διερχόμενος μέγα ἄστυ
Σκαιάς, τῇ ἂρ ἔμελλε διεξίμεναι πεδίονδε,
ἔνθ᾽ ἄλοχος πολύδωρος ἐναντίη ἦλθε θέουσα

---

359 [τὴν δ᾽ ἀπαμειβόμενος προ]σέφη **p**   365 οἰκόνδ᾽ ἐλεύσομαι **a**: οἰκόνδε ἐλεύσομαι **b**
367 γάρ τ᾽: γὰρ ἔτ᾽ **a**   373 ἐφειστήκει **a**

Ἀνδρομάχη, θυγάτηρ μεγαλήτορος Ἠετίωνος,   395
Ἠετίων, ὃς ἔναιεν ὑπὸ Πλάκωι ὑληέσσηι,
Θήβηι Ὑποπλακίηι Κιλίκεσσ᾽ ἄνδρεσσιν ἀνάσσων·
τοῦ περ δὴ θυγάτηρ ἔχεθ᾽ Ἕκτορι χαλκοκορυστῆι.
ἥ οἱ ἔπειτ᾽ ἤντησ᾽, ἅμα δ᾽ ἀμφίπολος κίεν αὐτῆι
παῖδ᾽ ἐπὶ κόλπωι ἔχουσ᾽ ἀταλάφρονα, νήπιον αὔτως,   400
Ἑκτορίδην ἀγαπητόν, ἀλίγκιον ἀστέρι καλῶι,
τόν ῥ᾽ Ἕκτωρ καλέεσκε Σκαμάνδριον, αὐτὰρ οἱ ἄλλοι
Ἀστυάνακτ᾽· οἶος γὰρ ἐρύετο Ἴλιον Ἕκτωρ.
ἤτοι ὃ μὲν μείδησεν ἰδὼν ἐς παῖδα σιωπῆι·
Ἀνδρομάχη δέ οἱ ἄγχι παρίστατο δάκρυ χέουσα,   405
ἔν τ᾽ ἄρα οἱ φῦ χειρὶ ἔπος τ᾽ ἔφατ᾽ ἔκ τ᾽ ὀνόμαζε·
"δαιμόνιε, φθίσει σε τὸ σὸν μένος, οὐδ᾽ ἐλεαίρεις
παῖδά τε νηπίαχον καὶ ἔμ᾽ ἄμμορον, ἣ τάχα χήρη
σεῦ ἔσομαι· τάχα γάρ σε κατακτανέουσιν Ἀχαιοὶ
πάντες ἐφορμηθέντες. ἐμοὶ δέ κε κέρδιον εἴη   410
σεῦ ἀφαμαρτούσηι χθόνα δύμεναι· οὐ γὰρ ἔτ᾽ ἄλλη
ἔσται θαλπωρή, ἐπεὶ ἂν σύ γε πότμον ἐπίσπηις,
ἀλλ᾽ ἄχε᾽· οὐδέ μοι ἐστὶ πατὴρ καὶ πότνια μήτηρ.
ἤτοι γὰρ πατέρ᾽ ἀμὸν ἀπέκτανε δῖος Ἀχιλλεύς,
ἐκ δὲ πόλιν πέρσεν Κιλίκων εὖ ναιετάωσαν,   415
Θήβην ὑψίπυλον, κατὰ δ᾽ ἔκτανεν Ἠετίωνα·
οὐδέ μιν ἐξενάριξε, σεβάσσατο γὰρ τό γε θυμῶι,
ἀλλ᾽ ἄρα μιν κατέκηε σὺν ἔντεσι δαιδαλέοισιν
ἠδ᾽ ἐπὶ σῆμ᾽ ἔχεεν· περὶ δὲ πτελέας ἐφύτευσαν
νύμφαι ὀρεστιάδες, κοῦραι Διὸς αἰγιόχοιο.   420
οἳ δέ μοι ἑπτὰ κασίγνητοι ἔσαν ἐν μεγάροισιν,
οἳ μὲν πάντες ἰῶι κίον ἤματι Ἄϊδος εἴσω·
πάντας γὰρ κατέπεφνε ποδάρκης δῖος Ἀχιλλεὺς
βουσὶν ἐπ᾽ εἰλιπόδεσσι καὶ ἀργεννῆις ὀίεσσι.
μητέρα δ᾽, ἣ βασίλευεν ὑπὸ Πλάκωι ὑληέσσηι,   425
τὴν ἐπεὶ ἂρ δεῦρ᾽ ἤγαγ᾽ ἅμ᾽ ἄλλοισι κτεάτεσσιν,
ἂψ ὅ γε τὴν ἀπέλυσε λαβὼν ἀπερείσι᾽ ἄποινα,
πατρὸς δ᾽ ἐν μεγάροισι βάλ᾽ Ἄρτεμις ἰοχέαιρα.
Ἕκτορ, ἀτὰρ σύ μοί ἐσσι πατὴρ καὶ πότνια μήτηρ
ἠδὲ κασίγνητος, σὺ δέ μοι θαλερὸς παρακοίτης.   430

---

398 χαλκοκορύστηι: Ἠεδίωνο[ς] **p**   400 ἐπί: ἐνὶ **a**   κόλπον **a**   407 φθείσει **a**   408
ἐμὸν μόρον **a**   414 ἀμὸν **a**: ἐμὸν **b**: οὐμὸν **c**   415 ναιετόωσαν **p**, Ar.

ἀλλ' ἄγε νῦν ἐλέαιρε καὶ αὐτοῦ μίμν' ἐπὶ πύργωι,
μὴ παῖδ' ὀρφανικὸν θήηις χήρην τε γυναῖκα.
λαὸν δὲ στῆσον παρ' ἐρινεόν, ἔνθα μάλιστα
ἄμβατός ἐστι πόλις καὶ ἐπίδρομον ἔπλετο τεῖχος.
τρὶς γὰρ τῆι γ' ἐλθόντες ἐπειρήσανθ' οἱ ἄριστοι   435
ἀμφ' Αἴαντε δύω καὶ ἀγακλυτὸν Ἰδομενῆα
ἠδ' ἀμφ' Ἀτρείδας καὶ Τυδέος ἄλκιμον υἱόν·
ἤ πού τίς σφιν ἔνισπε θεοπροπίων εὖ εἰδώς,
ἢ νυ καὶ αὐτῶν θυμὸς ἐποτρύνει καὶ ἀνώγει."
τὴν δ' αὖτε προσέειπε μέγας κορυθαίολος Ἕκτωρ·   440
"ἦ καὶ ἐμοὶ τάδε πάντα μέλει, γύναι· ἀλλὰ μάλ' αἰνῶς
αἰδέομαι Τρῶας καὶ Τρωιάδας ἑλκεσιπέπλους,
αἴ κε κακὸς ὣς νόσφιν ἀλυσκάζω πολέμοιο.
οὐδέ με θυμὸς ἄνωγεν, ἐπεὶ μάθον ἔμμεναι ἐσθλὸς
αἰεὶ καὶ πρώτοισι μετὰ Τρώεσσι μάχεσθαι,   445
ἀρνύμενος πατρός τε μέγα κλέος ἠδ' ἐμὸν αὐτοῦ.
εὖ γὰρ ἐγὼ τόδε οἶδα κατὰ φρένα καὶ κατὰ θυμόν·
ἔσσεται ἦμαρ ὅτ' ἄν ποτ' ὀλώληι Ἴλιος ἱρὴ
καὶ Πρίαμος καὶ λαὸς ἐϋμμελίω Πριάμοιο·
ἀλλ' οὔ μοι Τρώων τόσσον μέλει ἄλγος ὀπίσσω,   450
οὔτ' αὐτῆς Ἑκάβης οὔτε Πριάμοιο ἄνακτος
οὔτε κασιγνήτων, οἵ κεν πολέες τε καὶ ἐσθλοὶ
ἐν κονίηισι πέσοιεν ὑπ' ἀνδράσι δυσμενέεσσιν,
ὅσσον σεῖ', ὅτε κέν τις Ἀχαιῶν χαλκοχιτώνων
δακρυόεσσαν ἄγηται ἐλεύθερον ἦμαρ ἀπούρας.   455
καί κεν ἐν Ἄργει ἐοῦσα πρὸς ἄλλης ἱστὸν ὑφαίνοις,
καί κεν ὕδωρ φορέοις Μεσσηΐδος ἢ Ὑπερείης
πόλλ' ἀεκαζομένη, κρατερὴ δ' ἐπικείσετ' ἀνάγκη·
καί ποτέ τις εἴπηισιν ἰδὼν κατὰ δάκρυ χέουσαν·
'Ἕκτορος ἥδε γυνή, ὃς ἀριστεύεσκε μάχεσθαι   460
Τρώων ἱπποδάμων, ὅτε Ἴλιον ἀμφεμάχοντο.'
ὥς ποτέ τις ἐρέει· σοὶ δ' αὖ νέον ἔσσεται ἄλγος
χήτει τοιοῦδ' ἀνδρὸς ἀμύνειν δούλιον ἦμαρ.
ἀλλά με τεθνειῶτα χυτὴ κατὰ γαῖα καλύπτοι,
πρίν γέ τι σῆς τε βοῆς σοῦ θ' ἑλκηθμοῖο πυθέσθαι."   465

432 θείηις a   433–9 ath. Ar.   434 ἀμβατός a, Ar.: ἀμβατή Callistratus   435 τῆιδ'
a   437 Ἀτρείδα Demetrius Ixio   438 θεοπροπέων a: θεοπροπίας b   447 γὰρ: μὲν a
453 πέσωσιν p   456 Ἀργεΐ οὖσα a   ἄλληις a   464 τεθνηῶτα a: τεθνεῶτα p   465
γ' ἔτι a

ὣς εἰπὼν οὗ παιδὸς ὀρέξατο φαίδιμος Ἕκτωρ·
ἂψ δ' ὁ πάϊς πρὸς κόλπον ἐϋζώνοιο τιθήνης
ἐκλίνθη ἰάχων πατρὸς φίλου ὄψιν ἀτυχθείς,
ταρβήσας χαλκόν τε ἰδὲ λόφον ἱππιοχαίτην,
δεινὸν ἀπ' ἀκροτάτης κόρυθος νεύοντα νοήσας·   470
ἐκ δ' ἐγέλασσε πατήρ τε φίλος καὶ πότνια μήτηρ.
αὐτίκ' ἀπὸ κρατὸς κόρυθ' εἵλετο φαίδιμος Ἕκτωρ,
καὶ τὴν μὲν κατέθηκεν ἐπὶ χθονὶ παμφανόωσαν·
αὐτὰρ ὅ γ' ὃν φίλον υἱὸν ἐπεὶ κύσε πῆλέ τε χερσίν,
εἶπεν ἐπευξάμενος Διί τ' ἄλλοισίν τε θεοῖσι·   475
"Ζεῦ ἄλλοι τε θεοί, δότε δὴ καὶ τόνδε γενέσθαι,
παῖδ' ἐμόν, ὡς καὶ ἐγώ περ, ἀριπρεπέα Τρώεσσιν
ὧδε βίην τ' ἀγαθόν, καὶ Ἰλίου ἶφι ἀνάσσειν.
καί ποτέ τις εἴπῃσι 'πατρὸς δ' ὅ γε πολλὸν ἀμείνων'
ἐκ πολέμου ἀνιόντα· φέροι δ' ἔναρα βροτόεντα   480
κτείνας δήϊον ἄνδρα, χαρείη δὲ φρένα μήτηρ."
ὣς εἰπὼν ἀλόχοιο φίλης ἐν χερσὶν ἔθηκε
παῖδ' ἑόν· ἣ δ' ἄρα μιν κηώδεϊ δέξατο κόλπωι
δακρυόεν γελάσασα. πόσις δ' ἐλέησε νοήσας,
χειρί τέ μιν κατέρεξεν ἔπος τ' ἔφατ' ἔκ τ' ὀνόμαζε·   485
"δαιμονίη, μή μοί τι λίην ἀκαχίζεο θυμῶι·
οὐ γάρ τίς μ' ὑπὲρ αἶσαν ἀνὴρ Ἄϊδι προϊάψει,
μοῖραν δ' οὔ τινα φημὶ πεφυγμένον ἔμμεναι ἀνδρῶν,
οὐ κακὸν οὐδὲ μὲν ἐσθλόν, ἐπὴν τὰ πρῶτα γένηται.
ἀλλ' εἰς οἶκον ἰοῦσα τὰ σ' αὐτῆς ἔργα κόμιζε,   490
ἱστόν τ' ἠλακάτην τε, καὶ ἀμφιπόλοισι κέλευε
ἔργον ἐποίχεσθαι· πόλεμος δ' ἄνδρεσσι μελήσει
πᾶσιν, ἐμοὶ δὲ μάλιστα, τοὶ Ἰλίωι ἐγγεγάασιν."
ὣς ἄρα φωνήσας κόρυθ' εἵλετο φαίδιμος Ἕκτωρ
ἵππουριν· ἄλοχος δὲ φίλη οἶκόνδε βεβήκει   495
ἐντροπαλιζομένη, θαλερὸν κατὰ δάκρυ χέουσα.
αἶψα δ' ἔπειθ' ἵκανε δόμους εὖ ναιετάοντας
Ἕκτορος ἀνδροφόνοιο, κιχήσατο δ' ἔνδοθι πολλὰς
ἀμφιπόλους, τῆισιν δὲ γόον πάσηισιν ἐνῶρσεν.
αἳ μὲν ἔτι ζωὸν γόον Ἕκτορα ὧι ἐνὶ οἴκωι·   500
οὐ γάρ μιν ἔτ' ἔφαντο ὑπότροπον ἐκ πολέμοιο

---

470 ἐπ' **a**   κορυφῆς **a**   475 εἶπε δ' Ar.   477 ἐνιπρεπέα **a**   478 βίην ἀγαθόν τε **a**
479 εἴποι **a**   γ' ὅδε **p**, Ar.   484 ἐλέαιρε **a**   493 πᾶσι, μάλιστα δ' ἐμοί **p**, Epictetus
494 χε[ιρὶ παχείηι] (?) **p**

ἵξεσθαι προφυγόντα μένος καὶ χεῖρας Ἀχαιῶν.
οὐδὲ Πάρις δήθυνεν ἐν ὑψηλοῖσι δόμοισιν,
ἀλλ' ὅ γ', ἐπεὶ κατέδυ κλυτὰ τεύχεα ποικίλα χαλκῶι,
σεύατ' ἔπειτ' ἀνὰ ἄστυ ποσὶ κραιπνοῖσι πεποιθώς.
ὡς δ' ὅτε τις στατὸς ἵππος, ἀκοστήσας ἐπὶ φάτνηι,   505
δεσμὸν ἀπορρήξας θείηι πεδίοιο κροαίνων,
εἰωθὼς λούεσθαι ἐϋρρεῖος ποταμοῖο,
κυδιόων· ὑψοῦ δὲ κάρη ἔχει, ἀμφὶ δὲ χαῖται
ὤμοις ἀΐσσονται· ὃ δ' ἀγλαΐηφι πεποιθώς,   510
ῥίμφά ἑ γοῦνα φέρει μετά τ' ἤθεα καὶ νομὸν ἵππων·
ὡς υἱὸς Πριάμοιο Πάρις κατὰ Περγάμου ἄκρης
τεύχεσι παμφαίνων ὥς τ' ἠλέκτωρ ἐβεβήκει
καγχαλόων, ταχέες δὲ πόδες φέρον. αἶψα δ' ἔπειτα
Ἕκτορα δῖον ἔτετμεν ἀδελφεόν, εὖτ' ἄρ' ἔμελλε   515
στρέψεσθ' ἐκ χώρης ὅθι ἦι ὀάριζε γυναικί.
τὸν πρότερος προσέειπεν Ἀλέξανδρος θεοειδής·
"ἠθεῖ', ἦ μάλα δή σε καὶ ἐσσύμενον κατερύκω
δηθύνων, οὐδ' ἦλθον ἐναίσιμον ὡς ἐκέλευες."
τὸν δ' ἀπαμειβόμενος προσέφη κορυθαίολος Ἕκτωρ·   520
"δαιμόνι', οὐκ ἄν τίς τοι ἀνήρ, ὃς ἐναίσιμος εἴη,
ἔργον ἀτιμήσειε μάχης, ἐπεὶ ἄλκιμός ἐσσι.
ἀλλὰ ἑκὼν μεθίεις τε καὶ οὐκ ἐθέλεις· τὸ δ' ἐμὸν κῆρ
ἄχνυται ἐν θυμῶι, ὅθ' ὑπὲρ σέθεν αἴσχε' ἀκούω
πρὸς Τρώων, οἳ ἔχουσι πολὺν πόνον εἵνεκα σεῖο.   525
ἀλλ' ἴομεν· τὰ δ' ὄπισθεν ἀρεσσόμεθ', αἴ κέ ποθι Ζεὺς
δώηι ἐπουρανίοισι θεοῖς αἰειγενέτηισι
κρητῆρα στήσασθαι ἐλεύθερον ἐν μεγάροισιν,
ἐκ Τροίης ἐλάσαντας ἐϋκνήμιδας Ἀχαιούς."

504 ποικίλα χαλκῶι: παμφανόωντα a   511 ῥίμφ' ἑὰ Zen.   528 στήσεσθαι a

COMMENTARY

1–71: CATALOGUE OF KILLINGS

The catalogue of killings gradually tips the balance in favour of the Achaeans and leads to the statement that at this point the Achaeans were about to drive the Trojans all the way back into Troy (73–4): this is the first time in the poem when the defeat of the Trojans is said to be imminent. For an excellent study of this catalogue, see Broccia 1963: 15–51.

1–4 A panoramic view of the Trojan plain (cf. S. D. Richardson 1990: 119–23; and de Jong and Nünlist 2004: 69–70). It summarises the events of book 5: the gods have gradually left the battlefield. The two sides are carefully balanced and command equal attention. The catalogue of killings which begins at 5 is introduced by a subtle shift from passive to active verbs (1–2), from intransitive to transitive ones (2–3) and from abstract nouns (φύλοπις, μάχη) to human agents (the implied subject of ἰθυνομένων). General descriptions of battle like this one often introduce scenes of single combat; see Fenik 1968: 19.

1 δ᾽: the particle typically introduces a new idea, making sure that the audience stays with the narrator and notices the shift, see Bakker 1997a: 79–80; cf. further Introduction 2.4.   οἰώθη: 3rd pers. sing. aor. pass., of a verb *οἰωθῆναι that in epic is exclusively attested in this form (cf. 11.401). From the point of view of the poet, the battlefield is empty because the gods have abandoned it. For the poet's knowledge of the gods, see Jörgensen 1904, with Introduction 1 and 3.1.   Τρώων: 6n., 111n.   καί: unlike δέ, which introduces a new thought, this particle adds to the previous narrative unit, see Bakker 1997a: 71–4.   Ἀχαιῶν: 5n.   φύλοπις αἰνή 'dreadful battle'; for the epithet see Stoevesandt 2008: 13 and, for the unobtrusive value judgement, cf. 16–17n. (λυγρὸν ὄλεθρον). The exact meaning of φύλοπις was debated already in antiquity, see Σb *ad* 6.1c, Ebeling 1880–5: vol. ii, 456. Occasionally it is followed by πολεμοῖο, suggesting that it could be conceived as an aspect of war rather than an unusual word for it. Some ancient commentators speculated that it might refer to the din of battle, but at *Il.* 16.256 Achilles wants to watch (not hear) the φύλοπις of Achaeans and Trojans. The term is heroic (cf. Hes. *Op.* 161) and was used by later authors to evoke the tradition of heroic epic (e.g. Theoc. 16.50). On difficult Homeric words, see further Introduction 2.4.

2 The line captures the energetic movement on the battlefield: for its unusual metrical shape, which disregards Hermann's bridge, see Hoekstra 1969: 64, Stoevesandt 2008: 13, and Introduction 2.1.   πολλά: adverbial, 'much'.   ἄρ: the particle (also ἄρα, ῥα) draws out a detail which may otherwise remain implicit or hidden from sight; cf. Bakker 1993: 16–19, 10n., 215n.; and Introduction 2.4.   ἔνθα καὶ ἔνθ᾽... πεδίοιο 'this way and that... across the plain'; for the construction with the genitive, see Chantraine 1948–53: vol. ii, 59. ἔνθα καὶ ἔνθα is often used in overall descriptions of the action (e.g. 2.476, 15.345, 21.11), panoramic similes (2.462) and other overviews (e.g. 10.264, 18.543, 20.249). The catalogue beginning at 5 zooms in on the fighting and describes specific cases of what is happening across the plain.   ἴθυσε: forms of the verb ἰθύω are often used in battle narrative, where they convey the impression of head-on engagement (cf. the cognate verb ἰθύνω, 'straighten, direct', the noun ἰθύς, 'straight course of action, attack', and the adjective ἰθύς, 'straight, direct').

3 ἀλλήλων ἰθυνομένων 'as they aimed at each other' (ἀλλήλων goes with ἰθυνομένων, which is best taken as a genitive absolute, rather than as a qualifier of μάχη). The phrase echoes ἴθυσε in 2 and prepares the transition to the catalogue of killings; cf. 1–4n.   χαλκήρεα δοῦρα: the phrase is formulaic in heroic epic, especially in this metrical position. Bronze, as a metal, evokes the world of the heroes: although iron is mentioned in the Homeric poems (cf. 48n.), the heroes mostly use weapons and utensils made of bronze, while the gods are closely associated with gold (or, sometimes, silver: e.g. ἀργυρόπεζα Θέτις); cf. 236n. In Hesiod, iron is a marker of the present era, as opposed to the earlier ages of gold, silver and bronze: see *Op.* 106–79 with M. L. West 1978: 172–7. On metals as markers of different ages and beings (gods, heroes, ordinary mortals), see also Most 1997 and Clay 2003: 81–99. This mythical chronology of metals probably reflects a memory that bronze was indeed manufactured earlier than iron: iron working on a significant scale was introduced to the Aegean in the eleventh century BCE and did not spread to all parts of the Greek world until the ninth century BCE; see Snodgrass 1980: 345–55. χαλκήρεα literally means 'fitted with bronze' (ἀραρίσκω).   δοῦρα: the most common plural form of singular δόρυ/δοῦρυ (< *dorw-). For ου as a spelling of long ō, see Chantraine 1948–53: vol. I, 5–6; Wachter 2000: 67; Cassio 2002: 110–11. Wachter 2001: 244–5 and 335–6 points out examples of the practice from the seventh century onwards and suggests that it arose in the context of writing down poetry; see also Wachter 1991: 108–13. δόρυ/δοῦρυ is the shaft of the spear and hence the spear as a whole; see Trümpy 1950: 53.

4 Σιμόεντος ἰδὲ Ξάνθοιο ῥοάων: the battle takes place within a triangle formed by the two rivers and the walls of Troy; for discussion see Elliger 1975: 48–52; Thornton 1984: 154–6; Luce 1984; for the larger geographical context Herzhoff 2008. The Simoeis is prominent at the end of book 5, where we learn that it flows into the river Skamandros, also known as Xanthos: cf. 5.774. The printed text is that of the medieval manuscripts and most papyri. At least two alternative readings were known to ancient scholars: ποταμοῖο Σκαμάνδρου καὶ στομαλίμνης (Aristarchus) and ποτάμοιο Σκαμάνδρου καὶ Σιμόεντος (Chaeris, on whom see M. L. West 2001a: 81). The reading of the medieval vulgate is likely to reflect the majority of the ancient manuscripts. Aristarchus is said to have found his alternative reading in 'the ancient manuscripts' (ἐν τοῖς ἀρχαιοῖς). He initially accepted it but then changed his mind in order better to account for the location of the Achaean camp in relation to the battlefield (ΣA *ad* 6.4, with Nickau 1977: 2–3). Chaeris' reading looks like an attempt to adapt the 'ancient' reading to Aristarchus' changed view of the Trojan plain. On these ancient variants, see further van der Valk 1963–4: vol. II, 88; S. West 1967: 72–3; and Rengakos 1993: 154–5.   Ξάνθοιο: a son of Zeus (*Il.* 21.2) and protagonist of the battle in book 21. At 20.74 we are told that Ξάνθος is the divine name of the river which men call Skamandros. For the poet's familiarity with the language of the gods, see Introduction 2.4; for his divine perspective, see 1n. (οἰώθη).

5–36 Catalogues of killings can be arranged in two ways: chain reactions, where Trojan and Achaean deaths alternate, or series of uninterrupted killings on one side only, as here; cf. Fenik 1968: 10. This catalogue has narrative momentum: it is arranged in a steady *crescendo*, which shows that the Achaeans gradually gain ground. In the first entry Ajax kills just one opponent (5–11), Diomedes follows with one opponent and his charioteer (12–19), Euryalos kills two pairs of men in quick succession (20–8), then the catalogue continues with seven deaths in an even shorter compass (29–36). The verbs add to the effect: βαλών – βάλε for Ajax = 'hit'; ἔπεφνε for Diomedes = 'killed', ἐξενάριξεν – ἐσύλα for Euryalos = '(killed and) despoiled'. As the pace of the narrative quickens, its scope becomes more ambitious: Ajax's opponent is described almost entirely in terms of his behaviour on the battlefield and the details of his death. The vista then widens to take in the former life of Diomedes' victim (13–16). The third entry describes the rise and fall of an entire branch of the Trojan royal family (21–8); then the catalogue continues with a quick, matter-of-fact succession of deaths without detail. Broccia 1963: 17 argues that the catalogue establishes a hierarchy of Achaean fighters: the first ones have the hardest task.

5–11 The catalogue starts with a prominent pair of opponents: Ajax is the best of the Achaeans after Achilles (cf. 2.768–9); his victim, Akamas, is the best of the Thracians (7). In book 5 Ares took the shape of Akamas and joined the battle without fearing for his life; now the human Akamas gets killed.

5 πρῶτος marks the opening entry in the catalogue. The poet introduces a series of specific examples of what is happening everywhere on the battlefield, cf. 2n. (ἔνθα καὶ ἔνθ'), see de Jong and Nünlist 2004: 76–9.   Τελαμώνιος: on patronymics see Introduction 2.2.   ἕρκος Ἀχαιῶν: in this form only of Ajax (3.229, 7.211; but cf. 1.283–4). In early epic he is a defensive warrior (cf. *Od.* 11.555–6), and is expected to defend others also in later texts (e.g. Sophocles' *Ajax*).   Ἀχαιῶν: one of the three collective names used of the warriors who side against the Trojans; the other two are Ἀργεῖοι and Δαναοί (cf. 66n., 67n.). Thuc. 1.3.3 comments on the Homeric words Ἀχαιοί, Ἀργεῖοι, Δαναοί and Ἕλληνες, arguing that Homer does not operate with the mutually exclusive categories of 'Greeks' versus 'barbarians'. This is true but, after the Persian Wars, the Trojan expedition was generally interpreted as a conflict between Greeks and barbarians; see E. Hall 1989 and Haubold 2007. The name Ἀχαιοί may have very ancient origins: Hittite sources mention a western people called *Ahhijawā*; see further Finkelberg 1988; J. Hall 2002: 49–55; Hajnal 2003: 35–42; Latacz 2004: 121–8.

6 Τρώων: placed in striking juxtaposition to Ἀχαιῶν at the end of line 5: Ajax protects the Achaeans and defeats the Trojans. The term refers to the inhabitants of

Troy (Τροίη) and hence its defenders more generally. It may go back to the Bronze Age; cf. 207n.   φάλαγγα 'line of battle', only here in the singular, perhaps emphasising the fragility of the Trojan line.

Ancient audiences seem to have understood the term as a reference to the hoplite phalanx, see Graziosi 2002: 175–8; modern scholars emphasise the differences between Homeric and classical warfare; see Latacz 1977: 45–67 and 178–215; Bowden 1993; Hanson 1999: 38–45; van Wees 2004: 151–97.   φόως δ' ἑτάροισιν ἔθηκεν ~ 8.282, 11.797, 16.39, all in direct speech. Ajax eases the pressure on the Achaeans: the breakthrough starts off as a successful act of defence; cf. 5n. (ἕρκος Ἀχαιῶν).   φόως: an alternative form of φάος, 'light'; closer in sound to Ionic φῶς but lengthened so that it fits the hexameter (the phenomenon is called diectasis, lit. 'stretching'). The Ionic-sounding form φόως, rather than φάος, is generally used when the next word starts with a consonant, i.e. when the metre allows it; see Chantraine 1948–53: vol. i, 81. Here it means 'relief', 'safety', cf. 15.741; Ciani 1974: 7–9; and Lossau 1994: 86.

7 ἐνί: epic form of ἐν.   τέτυκτο: unaugmented pluperfect passive of τεύχω, 'make'. The perfect and pluperfect passive forms of this verb are frequently used simply for 'is' or 'was'.

8 Εὐσσώρου scans ∪ – – –; the final syllable -ου remains long before the main caesura which separates the two words (Εὐσσώρου ‖ Ἀκάμαντ'). For this type of hiatus, see Nünlist 2000: 112; cf. 175n., 293n. Recent editors rightly resist the temptation of restoring the ancient epic genitive -οιο, with elision of final omicron (Chantraine 1948–53: vol. i, 193–4): already the eighth-century Ischia cup spells καλλιστε[φα]νο: Αφροδιτες, i.e. καλλιστεφάνου Ἀφροδίτης, with contraction and hiatus; cf. M. L. West 2001a: 164.   Ἀκάμαντ': the only warrior in this catalogue who also features in the Catalogue of Trojans (2.844); see further 5–11n.   ἠΰν τε μέγαν τε is used mostly of Trojan warriors (Bernsdorff 1992: 21); for epithets which gravitate towards certain nouns, see 12n. (βοὴν ἀγαθός).

9–11 = 4.459–61. For repeated lines, see Introduction 2.2. Here and in book 4 a catalogue of killings opens with a blow to the forehead, a particularly confrontational way to set off the hostilities. At the end of the catalogue, at 36, Phylakos is caught while running away: the sequence suggests that the Trojans are buckling under the pressure (cf. 5–36n.)

9 τόν 'that one, him' (demonstrative pronoun). There are few real articles in early Greek epic: ὅ, ἥ, τό are used as pronouns even when followed by the noun to which they refer; see Chantraine 1948–53: vol. ii, 236–50.   ῥ': unaccentuated (enclitic) form of ἄρα with elision of final alpha, cf. 2n.   ἔβαλε governs two accusatives, first of the person (τόν), then of the part of the body (or, in this case, attire: φάλον), as often in Homer; cf. 355n., and see Chantraine 1948–53: vol. ii, 42.   πρῶτος picks up πρῶτος at 5, a reminder that we are still dealing with the first entry in a larger catalogue.   φάλον: probably a metal plate attached to the helmet; or one of the plates that make up the helmet itself. Cognate expressions suggest various possibilities, with up to four such plates per helmet (cf. τετράφαλος). See Lebessi 1992 and, for older literature, Borchhardt 1972: 7–8 and 1977: 73.

10 We follow the path of Ajax's spear from the 'forehead' into the 'bone'. Descriptions of wounds in Homer tend to be detailed and memorable: the scholia expected listeners to respond with amazement, θαῦμα, at the description of wounds, see ΣbT *ad* 17.314–15. Tatum 2003: ch. 6, discusses the effect of Homeric woundings; Salazar 2000: 127–8 reviews earlier scholarship; for a medical perspective see Robertson 2002, and Saunders 2003. ἄρα is repeated (cf. 9) to draw out the detail; cf. 2n.   ἐν δὲ μετώπωι πῆξε 'he rammed (the spear) into his forehead' (πήγνυμι). The object of πῆξε remains implicit until the beginning of line 11.   εἴσω 'into', after nouns in the accusative or genitive.

11 αἰχμὴ χαλκείη: a frequent expression, usually placed in necessary enjambment, as is the case here. αἰχμή is the tip of the spear; see 319n., 320n., and Trümpy 1950: 54–5. On bronze, see 3n.   τὸν δὲ σκότος ὄσσ᾽ ἐκάλυψεν: a traditional phrase at the end of a killing, cf. Morrison 1999; on darkness and death, see also Bremer 1976: 40–3. Here, σκότος contrasts with φόως (6n.); cf. Broccia 1963: 21.   τόν: cf. 9n.

12–20 From this point onwards, entries are headed by the Trojan victims rather than their Achaean slayers, as the poet's attention shifts to the Trojan side. Axylos is one of many Iliadic characters who are mentioned for the first time at the moment of their death. Although we have not heard of him before, the location of his house and his kindness to strangers make him memorable, and his death is experienced as a loss: Griffin 1980: 103–43, and 12n.

12 ~ 5.69, 6.29, etc.; see Visser 1987: 196–9.   Ἄξυλον: only here. The etymology of the name is unclear; ΣbT suggest 'he who leads (the guests to his place)', cf. the ancient explanation for Καλήσιος (18n.). Axylos' father, Teuthras, has an Achaean namesake (5.705). Unknown characters often sound familiar, giving the impression that we could know more about them, even when in fact we do not. We are not meant to assume that they are created just so that they can be killed (Griffin 1980: 103); rather, we are invited to think of them as full characters about whom we happen to know little. Their names are often plain and plausible: e.g. Δρῆσος (20), Ἀστύαλος (29), Ἀρετάων (31), Ἔλατος (33); or evoke known characters, places or activities: e.g. Ὀφέλτιος (20n.); Αἴσηπος and Πήδασος (21n.); Βουκολίων (22n.); Φύλακος (34–5n.); Μελάνθιος (36n.); Ἄδρηστος (37n.). For Homer's treatment of minor warriors see further Reichel 1994: 279–300.   ἔπεφνε: reduplicated aorist of a root that also forms the noun φόνος, and the present stem θειν-, 'to strike'; see Chantraine 1948–53: vol. 1, 395–8. As often in early Greek epic, linguistically younger forms coexist with older ones; see *LfgrE* s.v. *θείνω, πεφνεῖν B 1 and Introduction 2.5.   βοὴν ἀγαθός 'good at the war-cry', accusative of respect. The phrase can accompany a range of names but tends to be used of either Menelaos or Diomedes at the end of the line. For epithets that gravitate towards specific nouns without being applied exclusively to them, cf. Hainsworth 1993: 22–3; Friedrich 2007: 84–6 argues, rightly, that there is a sliding scale between 'distinctive' epithets (i.e. those joined to only one noun), and 'generic' ones.   Διομήδης: son of Tydeus and one of the most important warriors at Troy; cf. Andersen 1978. He plays a crucial role on the battlefield when Achilles is away: Taplin 1992: 135.

13 Τευθρανίδην: a typical case of progressive enjambment, see Introduction 2.1. The patronymic serves as a link between line 12 and the additional information provided in 13–15. For possible connections between Axylos' father, Teuthras, and the myth of Telephos, king of Teuthrania, see Wathelet 1988: 1529–30; Stoevesandt 2008: 18.   **ἐϋκτιμένηι** 'well built, well settled'; a standard epithet of Homeric buildings (e.g. houses, streets, threshing floors), cities and islands; cf. 391n. (ἐϋκτιμένας κατ' ἀγυιάς).   **Ἀρίσβηι:** a town near Abydos and Perkote, on the southern shore of the Hellespont; see Latacz 2003: 273–4.

14 ἀφνειὸς βιότοιο 'rich in possessions' (gen. part.); for ἀφνειός see 47n. (ἐν ἀφνειοῦ πατρός).   **φίλος δ᾽ ἦν ἀνθρώποισι:** the exact wording is unparalleled but the phrase recalls 24.61, φίλος γένετ᾽ ἀθανάτοισι, and related passages that describe mortals loved by the gods. The difference is significant: now that the gods have left (11n.), fellow human beings are presented as an alternative (and inadequate) source of support. Ancient readers express their disappointment that Axylos is not backed by a god, since his treatment of guests would deserve divine support: ΣbT *ad* 6.16. On φίλος, see Scheid-Tissinier 1994: 122–35 and cf. 67n. For other Trojans who die despite their individual merits, see Stoevesandt 2004: 141–2.

15 γάρ: apart from introducing causal explanations (as here), Homeric γάρ often provides additional detail: Bakker 1997a: 112–15.   **φιλέεσκεν:** 'iterative' forms with -εσκ- express frequent action.   **ὁδῶι ἔπι** 'by the road', with the preposition following the noun (anastrophe), as often in Homer.

16–17 Warriors are often described as helpless at the moment of their death: see Fenik 1968: 15–16.   **οἱ:** 3rd pers. sing. dat. of the personal pronoun. As often in Homer, the original digamma (ϝοι) is still felt: there is no hiatus after ἀλλά; cf. Introduction 2.1.   **τῶν:** see 9n.   **γε:** the particle highlights an authorial comment on an event or character.   **τότ᾽** emphasises the specific circumstances of the encounter; cf. 18n.   **λυγρὸν ὄλεθρον:** a common phrase in this metrical position, and one of the many cases where the narrator unobtrusively 'express[es] his opinion on an . . . element of his story', de Jong 2004: 43.   **πρόσθεν ὑπαντιάσας** 'facing Diomedes by coming up in front of Axylos'. ὑπαντιάσας < ἀντάω/ἀντιάω, 'encounter', and ὑπ-. The meaning of the prefix in this context is debated: perhaps it suggests that the rescuer appears unexpectedly, sneaking in from below, cf. ὑπομένω 'withstand a superior opponent' (17.174) and ὑποδύω 'slip in under' in order to retrieve a corpse or a wounded warrior (8.332, 13.421, 17.717).   **ἀπηύρα:** aorist with final long α. At some point the form must have been interpreted as an imperfect on the model of ἐτίμα (hence the form ἀπηύρων, 'I took away', 'they took away', which retains the meaning of the aorist stem). ἀπηύρα is frequently used of irreplaceable objects such as life, glory or freedom, see *LfgrE* s.v. ἀπηύρων B.

18 Καλήσιον: the only instance of this name. The scholia derive it from καλέω, 'call', and link it to Axylos' hospitality. In this case the name would mean something like 'he who invites', thus Kirk 1990: 157; cf. 12n. (Ἄξυλον).   **ὅς ῥα:** as often in Homer, the relative pronoun is reinforced by the enclitic form of the particle ἄρα (Ruijgh 1971: 438–43): translate 'and he'.   **τόθ᾽:** one papyrus and a manuscript of ΣD read οἱ, but the vulgate text is preferable: it emphasises that Kalesios was in no position to save Axylos 'then'; for the use of τότε with ἔσκεν, cf. 9.561–2 (τότ(ε)... καλέεσκον), and *Od.* 4.518 (τότ᾿ ἔναιε, durative).

19 ἔσκεν 'he used to be'. An alternative form of ἦν, 'was', expressing duration; cf. 15n., Chantraine 1948–53: vol. I, 320–1.   ὑφηνίοχος: the term is unparalleled in epic and its precise meaning has been debated since antiquity; cf. Stoevesandt 2008: 19–20. The prefix ὑφ- may emphasise that Kalesios is in no position to help.   τὼ... ἐδύτην 'they both sank into the earth' (dual). For the root aorist of δύομαι, cf. 185n. For similar formulations see 411n. and *Od.* 24.106. Hades, as the abode of the deceased, was situated beneath the earth; see 284n., 20.61–5.

20–8 The third entry describes two double killings: Euryalos kills Dresos and Opheltios (20), then Aisepos and Pedasos (21–8). The list of pairs culminates with the statement that Aisepos and Pedasos are twin brothers (26); cf. 5.541–61. The poet gives a detailed and rather compressed account of the twins' family, spanning three generations. With their death, one branch of the Trojan royal family comes to an end. Epic poetry is much preoccupied with the survival of family lines and revels in long genealogies. The poet provides recondite information on Boukolion's family and draws attention to this fact: Boukolion and his sons are born in obscure circumstances and marginal settings; see 24n., 25n. Commentators debate whether the genealogy should be considered 'conscious fiction' or whether it reflects a local tradition; see Kirk 1990: 158. The text, however, does not encourage us to view these options as alternatives: the poet tells us about a family that would otherwise remain obscure, and its history has a strong local flavour, rather than enjoying Panhellenic fame.

20 ~ 30, 36, 14.513, and many related verses; cf. Visser 1987: 173–7.   Δρῆσον: only here, cf. 12n. (Ἄξυλον).   Εὐρύαλος: one of the Epigoni, the sons of the 'Seven against Thebes'; see Cingano 2004: 60–2. He plays a minor role in the *Iliad*, appearing twice as a subordinate and close ally of Diomedes (2.565–7, 23.677–84). The Theban War is evoked often in books 4–6, when Diomedes, himself one of the Epigoni, is prominent; cf. 222–3n.   Ὀφέλτιον: nothing is known about the Trojan Opheltios, but there is an Achaean of the same name (11.302); for minor characters, see 12n. (Ἄξυλον).   ἐξενάριξε: the meaning ranges from killing an enemy to taking his spoils. Usually the two actions go together: van Wees 1992: 97–8. Euryalos does both (28n.) but at the end of the catalogue Nestor urges the Achaeans to keep up the momentum and kill men without stopping for spoils (66–71n.).

21 Αἴσηπον καὶ Πήδασον: the names are elsewhere given to a river and a town respectively, see 2.825, 6.34–5n., 20.92, 21.87. On the local colouring of the passage: 20–8n. On personal names, cf. 12n. (Ἄξυλον). ΣΤ report a variant reading Τήρεχον for transmitted Πήδασον, which was allegedly used by 'the other ἱστορικοί'. (For the form Πήρεχον, which Σb mistakenly ascribe to Aristarchus and his school, cf. van der Valk 1963–4: vol. I, 173.)   ποτε: contrast 16–17n., 18n. (τότ᾿, τόθ᾿). The narrative reaches into a more distant past.   νύμφη: cf. 22n., and 419–20n.

22 νηΐς: always used in conjunction with νύμφη, a minor goddess living near or in water (cf. νάω/ναίω = 'flow'); on nymphs and water: Larson 2001:

8.   Ἀβαρβαρέη: only here in early Greek hexameter poetry. The name has been linked with βόρβορος ('mud'), but its etymology remains uncertain (*LfgrE* s.v. Ἀβαρβαρέη).   ἀμύμονι: generic epithet used of a wide range of characters (or, less often, activities, places and objects). The word may derive from μῶμος, 'blame' (cf. Aeol. μῦμαρ), and was understood in antiquity to mean 'blameless', 'excellent'; cf. 155n., 171n. and 190n.   Βουκολίωνι: only here. The name means 'cowherd' and links this character to the circumstances in which his children were conceived; cf. βουκολέω, βούκολος.

23   ἀγαυοῦ 'illustrious', 'impressive'; cf. 4.534 = 5.625 μέγαν . . . καὶ ἴφθιμον καὶ ἀγαυόν. A common epithet, it is often used of famous heroes from an older generation, as here; cf. 5.277 (Tydeus), 17.284 (Telamon), 18.16 (Nestor).   Λαομέδοντος: the father of Priam (20.237), famous for his bad manners: 5.649–51, 21.443–57.

24   σκότιον 'in(to) obscurity' (cf. σκότος = 'darkness'), i.e. 'illegitimate' (ΣbT *ad* 6.24), but the expression also emphasises how difficult it is to know and sing about Boukolion, in contrast with 'illustrious Laomedon' in the line before; for discussion, see Ebbott 2003: 20–36. Bukolion does not feature in the official list of Laomedon's children at 20.237–8 (Λαομέδων δ᾽ ἄρα Τιθωνὸν τέκετο Πρίαμόν τε | Λάμπον τε Κλύτιόν θ᾽ Ἱκετάονά τ᾽, ὄζον Ἄρηος). For the poet's ability to tell us about this character, cf. 20–8n.; for the relationship between what can be seen and what can be known, see Graziosi and Haubold 2005: 80–4.   ἓ 'him'. 3rd pers. sing. acc. of the personal pronoun in its unaccentuated (enclitic) form.

25   ποιμαίνων δ᾽ ἐπ᾽ ὄεσσι ~ 11.106. Boukolion has sex with Abarbaree 'near the sheep'. It is the task of young men to tend flocks in early Greek epic, cf. 424n. While doing so, they sometimes meet and have intercourse with divine partners: cf. 14.444–5, and Hom. *Hymn* 5.53–291; the judgement of Paris is a variation on this theme: 24.29–30. Griffin 1992: 201–4 points out that such liaisons typically involve men fighting on the Trojan side and tend to spell doom.   μίγη . . . εὐνῆι: a resonant phrase in early Greek epic: through this traditional expression, the obscure story of Boukolion evokes other genealogies of gods and heroes where similar phrases are used (e.g. *Od.* 5.126; Hes. fr. 17.5 MW, *Theog.* 125).

26–7   The narrative is arranged in such a way that birth of the twins is directly followed by their death.   ἣ δ᾽ ὑποκυσαμένη ~ 20.225, *Od.* 11.254; Hom. *Hymn* 32.15; and seven times in the Hesiodic corpus; cf. 25n. (μίγη . . . εὐνῆι) and Introduction 2.4.   ἥ: Abarbaree, cf. 9n.   διδυμάονε γείνατο παῖδε = Hes. *Sc.* 49 ~ *Il.* 5.548; Hes. fr. 17.14 MW.   μέν: 'clears the ground for later statements, providing a basis from which further continuation is possible': Bakker 1997a: 82. The fact that μέν rounds off the killing of Aisepos and Pedasos – but not previous killings – suggests that an important transition is about to take place.   τῶν: cf. 9n.   ὑπέλυσε: the compound form is often used with γυῖα (e.g. 15.581), only here with μένος as well; it echoes ὑποκυσαμένη above. For another pair of ὑπό-compounds in close succession, see 17 and 19.   μένος: 'the force of onrushing energy that is manifested in swift physical and mental movement', Clarke 2004: 80. It is lost forever at the moment of death: *LfgrE* s.v. μένος B 1 e. (The epithet ἀμενηνός describes the dead and is explained by ΣD *ad* 5.887 as μένος οὐκ ἔχων.) **φαίδιμα γυῖα:** a frequent phrase in this metrical position. φαίδιμος is almost exclusively used of people or limbs; contrast φαεινός at 32n. For the impression of brilliance conveyed by the epic language, cf. 31n. (δῖος).

28 Μηκιστηϊάδης: in the *Iliad* Mekisteus is one of the 'Seven against Thebes' (also in Hdt. 5.67; but not in Aesch. *Septem*); see Cingano 2002: 47–8 and 60. At 23.679–80 we are told that he competed and won in the funeral games for Oedipus (N. J. Richardson 1993: 243). On the function of patronymics, cf. Introduction 2.4. On the Theban War, cf. 222–3n. **καὶ . . . ἐσύλα** ~ 15.524, 22.368, etc. A traditional phrase at the end of a killing (cf. 11n. τὸν δὲ σκότος ὄσσε κάλυψεν). In the heat of battle it is not always possible to strip the dead (cf. 5.617–26); the fact that Euryalos does so suggests that the Achaeans are gaining ground, cf. 20n. (ἐξενάριξε) – see, however, 68–9n.

29–36 The narrative accelerates further, with seven killings in eight lines. Frequent enjambment (30–1, 32–3, 34–5 and 35–6) and several changes of rhythm, in combination with ellipsis of the verb (31, 33), and different verbs of killing in quick succession (ἔπεφνε . . . ἐξενάριξεν . . . ἐνήρατο . . . ἕλε . . . ἐξενάριξεν), give the impression of rapid and relentless attack. By line 36 the Trojans are in full flight; cf. 9–11n.

29 ~ 5.69, etc.; cf. 12n. **Ἀστύαλον:** only here, perhaps formed as a variation on Εὐρύαλος (20n.); cf. 12n. (Ἄξυλον). **μενεπτόλεμος** < μένω + π(τ)όλεμος (cf. ΣD *ad* 2.740; and Risch 1974: 191). Four times out of nine in the *Iliad* this epithet is used of Polypoites and is thus neither simply generic nor fully distinctive; cf. 12n. (βοὴν ἀγαθός). **Πολυποίτης:** a son of the Lapith Peirithous (2.740–4); he is mentioned again at 12.127–94 for a brief moment of glory. At 23.836–49 he beats Ajax at the discus.

30 Πιδύτην: only here; for a discussion of the name, see Visser 1987: 181–4. **Περκώσιον:** from Perkote on the southern shore of the Hellespont. **ἐξενάριξεν:** cf. 20n.

31 ἔγχεϊ χαλκείωι: frequently found in this metrical position; for the effect of the enjambment see 29–36n. Homer's use of ἔγχος may contain traces of an older Mycenaean meaning 'thrusting spear' (as opposed to δόρυ = 'casting spear'), but this is not certain: see *LfgrE* s.v. δόρυ B 2; and Trümpy 1950: 52–4. For bronze as a marker of the heroic age, see 3n. **Τεῦκρος . . . δῖον:** the first of two clauses in this section with ellipsis of the verb; cf. 29–36n., 33n. **Τεῦκρος:** Ajax's half-brother (8.281–5). He is mentioned here for the first time in the poem; later, in books 8, 12–13 and 15, he becomes prominent as one of the few archers on the Achaean side. He loses the archery contest at the funeral games for Patroclus because he fails to pray to Apollo (23.859–69). For his role in the *Iliad*, see Ebbott 2003: 37–44. **Ἀρετάονα:** only here. The scholia and some manuscripts read ἄρ Ἐτάονα, for which see Wathelet 1988: 309, but the particle ἄρα seems out of place. Since both names are unique in epic, it is possible that the variants reflect ancient controversies about the identity of minor Homeric characters; cf. 21n. (Πήδασον). **δῖον:** generic epithet used of men, women, goddesses and geographical features (e.g. the ground, the sea); it is never applied to male gods. The meaning appears to be 'amazing', 'brilliant', rather than 'divine' in any strong sense, though Hellenistic readers saw it as equivalent to θεῖος in at least some cases (cf. *LfgrE* s.v. δῖος Σχ and B). Generic epithets like δῖος enhance the overall brilliance of the epic world; cf. 26–7n. (φαίδιμα γυῖα), 32n. (δουρὶ φαεινῶι), and Introduction 2.6. The ΣD *ad* 2.522 gloss δῖος as θαυμαστός ('amazing'): Introduction 2.6.

32 A combination of two otherwise distinct formulaic patterns: cf. 5.43 (∼ 5.59, 14.515) Ἰδομενεὺς δ' ἄρα Φαῖστον ἐνήρατο Μηιόνος υἱόν; and 17.304 (∼ 4.496, 5.611, etc.) Ἕκτωρ δ' αὖτ' Αἴαντος ἀκόντισε δουρὶ φαεινῶι. The overall effect is one of condensation and acceleration.   **Ἀντίλοχος:** the son of Nestor and a friend of Achilles (23.556), prominent in the latter half of the *Iliad* and, especially, in the cyclic epic *Aethiopis*, where he is Achilles' favourite comrade (Proclus, *Chrestomathy*, p. 112 West; cf. *Od.* 4.187–8, 24.77–9; Pind. *Pyth.* 6.28–43).   **Ἄβληρον:** only here. Von Kamptz 1982: 279–80 tentatively compares Homeric εὔληρα = 'reins', but the name may have a non-Greek etymology; cf. 12n. (Ἄξυλον).   **ἐνήρατο:** unaugmented aorist middle of ἐναίρω. The original meaning was probably 'to strip of arms' (cf. ἐναρίζω, 20n.), but in Homer ἐναίρω means 'kill' (people, animals) or 'disfigure' (a body).   **δουρὶ φαεινῶι:** very common in this metrical position, often after the verb ἀκόντισε, 'he thrust' (Visser 1987: 80–2). On the many epic words which convey an impression of brilliance, see 31n. (δῖον).

33 Νεστορίδης: cf. 13n. The enjambment breaks up the rhythm of the hexameter line and contributes to the overall effect of breathless forward movement; cf. 29–36n.   Ἔλατον . . . Ἀγαμέμνων: another elided verb, cf. 31n. (Τεῦκρος . . . δῖον). Elatos is mentioned only here, cf. 12n. (Ἄξυλον).   ἄναξ ἀνδρῶν Ἀγαμέμνων: ἄναξ ἀνδρῶν is not used exclusively of Agamemnon but is closely associated with him: see M. Parry 1971: 93. The form *wanax* appears as the title of kings and gods on Mycenaean tablets. In early Greek epic it is an honorific title for divine and human characters ('lord'), unlike the term βασιλεύς, 'king', which describes a political office; see Carlier 1984: 140–50 and 215–30; Yamagata 1997; Carlier 2006; Schmidt 2006.

34–5 The only digression of any length in this section.   ναῖε δέ: here and at 13.172, Zenodotus read ὃς ναῖε (scanned – ∪∪, *ʰos-na-ye*). Both readings are possible; cf. Janko 1994: 68 and 81. For the readings of Zenodotus, see Introduction n. 189. The verb ναίω can be transitive, as here ('dwell in' + acc. of the place), intransitive ('be situated') or causative ('found').   Σατνιόεντος: the river is mentioned again as the birthplace of the eponymous Satnios at 14.445. It has its source on Mount Ida and reaches the Aegean in the southern Troad.   Πήδασον: cf. 21n. Pedasos was founded by the Leleges (21.86–7) and destroyed by Achilles (20.92). Agamemnon offers to Achilles a different city called Pedasos in the Peloponnese (9.152, 9.294).   αἰπεινήν: a common epithet of mountains and cities (especially Troy). The alternative form αἰπήεις/-εσσα is used of Pedasos at 21.87.   Φύλακον . . . ἥρως ∼ 15.340; cf. 23.779, 839. This Phylakos appears only here; the Argonaut Iphiklos is the son of a different Phylakos (Φυλακίδης: 2.705 and 13.698; cf. Apoll. Rhod. 1.45–8); on

names of minor warriors, cf. 12n. (Ἄξυλον).   Λήϊτος: one of the Boeotian leaders (2.494), mentioned again at 13.91 and in more detail at 17.597–606.   ἥρως:
the term is primarily used to place characters in a distant age, when human beings
were closer to the gods and greater than now (cf. Hes. *Op.* 160: προτέρη γενέη).
It is applied, apparently without discrimination, to more or less impressive fighters
(Kirk 1990: 162), and even to men (never women) who do not fight at all: *Od.* 8.483.
Early audiences of Homeric poetry worshipped the heroes, typically at their tombs
(Antonaccio 1995, Deoudi 1999, and Ekroth 2002); but there is little reference to this
practice in the *Iliad*: the poem forces us to contemplate the heroes' death from their
own perspective, not that of later generations, see further Clarke 2004: 78–80; Currie
2005: 48–57; and Graziosi and Haubold 2005: 122–5.

36 φεύγοντ᾽: Phylakos is the first Trojan who is said to be running away, but
by 41 there is a general stampede towards Troy. On enjambment, see 29–36n. and
Introduction 2.1; on the increasing pressure experienced by the Trojans in the opening
lines of book 6, see 1–71n.   Εὐρύπυλος . . . ἐξενάριξεν: cf. 20n.   Εὐρύπυλος:
one of the Thessalian leaders (2.734–7) and a prominent warrior on the Achaean
side (esp. 7.167 and 11.575–95, where he is wounded by Paris). It is unclear exactly
where he rules in Thessaly; cf. Kirk 1985: 234–5; Visser 1997: 698–708; Latacz 2003:
237.   Μελάνθιον: only here in the *Iliad*. In the *Odyssey* Μελανθεύς/Μελάνθιος is
the name of an Ithacan who sides with the suitors against Odysseus; Μελανθώ is the
only named maid among those killed by Odysseus.

37–65 Formally, this is the last and longest entry in the catalogue of killings.
Supplication is presented as the last means by which the Achaean onslaught may
be delayed – but it fails: Agamemnon urges Menelaos to kill the suppliant as a step
towards the extermination of all Trojans, even babies still in their mothers' wombs
(58n., 59n.).

37–8 Line 37 may look like yet another killing, but instead of the expected δ᾽
ἄρ ἔπεφνε (cf. 12 and 29), we get δ᾽ ἄρ ἔπειτα, which cues us for something new:
the enjambment reveals that Menelaos has captured his victim alive. For the use of
enjambment as an effective way of changing or redirecting what has been said before,
see Introduction 2.1.   Ἄδρηστον: two other characters called Adrestos fight on the
Trojan side: one is mentioned in the Catalogue of Trojans (2.830–4) and dies with his
brother at 11.328–34, the other is killed at 16.694. This specific Adrestos is mentioned
only here, but his name sounds familiar: the audience may well not realise that he is
mentioned only at the moment of his death, cf. 12n. (Ἄξυλον). For possible parallels
with the more famous Adrestos of the Theban Saga, see Murray 1934: 223; and Aloni
1986: 96–8.   ἄρ ἔπειτα: cf. 37–8n.; and Stoevesandt 2008: 25.   βοὴν ἀγαθός
Μενέλαος: cf. 12n.

38–41 The poet focuses on Adrestos' horses, offering a detailed view of how they
trip over a tamarisk branch and where exactly they break the chariot. The syntax at
this point is strikingly unencumbered by line breaks (cf. Bakker 1997b: 303). At 41 the
poet widens his perspective and shows us that Adrestos' horses are just two of many
that are stampeding towards Troy.

38 γάρ: 15n.   **ἀτυζομένω πεδίοιο** ~ 18.7. 'Stampeding across the plain'; for the genitive with a verb of motion, see Chantraine 1948–53: vol. 1, 58–9.

39–41 In the *Iliad* horses often obey their masters 'not unwillingly'; cf. the formulaic phrase τὼ δ᾽ οὐκ ἀέκοντε πετέσθην (5.366 etc.). The fact that now they are out of control adds to the panic; cf. 16.370–1. For a similar incident, cf. 23.392–7.

39 βλαφθέντε: dual.   **μυρικίνωι:** in the *Iliad* tamarisks typically grow on river banks, cf. Kirk 1990: 159. The battle takes place between two rivers (4n.), so Adrestos seems to find himself near one of them, at the edge of the battlefield.   **ἀγκύλον ἅρμα** 'curved', usually of bows; cf. 322n. The epithet may point to the curved front of the chariot; see Kirk 1990: 159; Plath 1994: 139–43.

40 ἐν πρώτωι ῥυμῶι 'at the front of the pole', i.e. where the chariot is attached to the yoke.   **αὐτὼ μέν:** we are asked to keep our focus on the horses, as they flee towards the city, but μέν implies that our attention will soon shift elsewhere; cf. Bakker 1997a: 84–5 and 26–7n.

41 ~ 21.4 (cf. 21.554).   **πρὸς πόλιν:** the city comes into view as the object of the Trojans' panicked retreat. Later, we are shown how the spectre of their defeat affects those left inside.   **περ:** this particle places a given word or phrase at a specific point on an imaginary spectrum of meaning: ἧι περ = 'just where', 'exactly where'; cf. Bakker 1988.   **ἀτυζόμενοι:** cf. 38n.   **φοβέοντο:** the third verb of flight in six lines. In Homer φοβέομαι usually means 'flee' rather than 'fear'; for discussion see Cheyns 1985: 37–8; Stoevesandt 2008: 25. For ἀτύζομαι together with φοβέομαι, see 21.4 and *LfgrE* s.v. ἀτύζομαι B.

42–3 The sequence of prepositions traces Adrestos' fall in vivid detail: 'from' the chariot, 'near' the wheel, 'into' the dust, 'on' his mouth; see Introduction 2.6.   **αὐτὸς δ᾽:** cf. 40n. (μέν).   **ἐκ δίφροιο παρὰ τροχόν:** Adrestos' fall symbolises defeat: in Homer, and more generally in Near Eastern and Mediterranean art and literature, victors typically stand on the chariot, whereas defeated warriors fall and lie next to the wheels; cf. 16.378–9. For an Egyptian example, see the decoration on the chariot of Thutmose IV, in Müller 1979: 116.   **ἐξεκυλίσθη:** epic κυλίνδω and its derivatives are often used of corpses. For living warriors being treated like inanimate objects, see Weil 2003: 20–2 and 46–8.   **πρηνὴς... στόμα:** Adrestos lies face down, in a position which is typical of corpses, cf. 2.418 and 4.544.   **πὰρ... ἔστη:** in Homeric Greek the two components of the verb have not yet fully coalesced; the technical term tmesis ('splitting') is therefore misleading. The sudden, looming presence of Menelaos has the uncanny quality of a divine apparition.

44 Ἀτρείδης: used of both Agamemnon and Menelaos (contrast Ἀτρείων, only of Agamemnon). Menelaos is first mentioned without reference to his brother or father (37), now he is 'Menelaos son of Atreus', and at 46 Adrestos calls him simply 'son of Atreus', a phrase equally applicable to Agamemnon; cf. 46n. This gradual shift leads on to 53–65, where Agamemnon actually takes over from Menelaos.   **δολιχόσκιον ἔγχος:** from δόλιχος (long) and possibly σκιά (shadow), cf. *LfgrE* s.v. δολιχόσκι(ος) Σχ and B. For ἔγχος see 31n. The epithet is used only of ἔγχος, most commonly at the end of the line (for exceptions see 126n. and *Od.* 22.97).

45 ~ 21.71, *Od.* 10.264. As often in Homer, the line which introduces a speech also gives some guidance as to what we might expect to hear; see de Jong 2004: 195–208. For different types of speech introduction: Edwards 1970; and Beck 2005: 32–43; Riggsby 1992 discusses the composition of speech-introductory lines. λαβών... γούνων: the scene has been carefully set up: Adrestos lies in the dust face down and Menelaos looms over him (cf. 42–3n.). Now Adrestos grabs his knees in supplication; for this gesture in Homer and other literature, see Naiden 2006: 45–6. ἄρ ἔπειτα: cf. 37n. ἐλίσσετο: λ is drawn out and closes the preceding syllable, which is then measured long. The phenomenon is familiar at word boundary; see Introduction 2.1. Within words, one might have expected syllable length to be marked by a double consonant; cf. ἐλλίσσετο in papyrus 270 West. However, West's apparatus here and *ad* 9.585, 21.71, 22.414 – as well as the parallels at *Od.* 7.145, 10.264, etc. – suggest that the preferred spelling for ἐλ(λ)ίσσετο and ἐλ(λ)ιτάνευε, with long first syllable, had one λ rather than two. Both forms are justifiable: ἐλλίσσετο attempts to capture pronunciation, ἐλίσσετο represents the grammatical form.

46–50 ~ 11.131–5; cf. 10.378–81. The first of many battlefield supplications in the *Iliad*: they are always made by Trojans and are never successful (cf. 10.378–81, 11.130–5, 20.463–5, 21.71–98). We know that earlier in the war suppliants were sometimes captured alive and sold, or returned for a ransom (21.34–44, 74–80, 99–105; cf. 2.229–31, 22.46–51; Wilson 2002: 31–2; see also 427n.). In this episode, and in the course of the war, pity gives way to the brutal killing of suppliants.

46 Ἀτρέος υἱέ: here of Menelaos; elsewhere in the *Iliad* this phrase in the vocative applies to Agamemnon (cf. 2.23 and 60, 11.131; contrast *Od.* 4.462 and 543); cf. 44n. ἄξια: here Adrestos suggests that the ransom will be 'worthy' or 'suitable', though later he describes it as 'infinite', ἀπερείσια, an adjective which is much more commonly used of ἄποινα (49n.). The narrator never uses the phrase ἄξια ἄποινα and indeed Adrestos cannot name a suitable price for his own life: his father will give all he can. For differences between the words used by the poet and those of his characters, see Introduction 2.4. ἄποινα 'ransom'; it is typically offered by a father who hopes to save his son or daughter. The term should be distinguished from ποινή, 'compensation', which is offered or demanded to atone for some wrongdoing. Those who offer ransom are not in a position to make or even meet demands; they can only hope that their offer will be accepted: Wilson 2002: 25–39.

47 ἐν ἀφνειοῦ πατρός 'in the house of my wealthy father'; a dative noun after ἐν must be supplied; cf. 378n. Adrestos does not name his father (contrast 11.132) but emphasises his wealth and prestige, see Coin-Longeray 1999 on ἀφνειός. κειμήλια: valuable goods which lie in a house; often, as here, in the phrase κειμήλια κεῖται, which draws attention to the word's etymology; cf. 194n. (τέμενος). Beyond their material value, κειμήλια symbolise the stability and wellbeing of a family or even an entire city (cf. 18.288–92); they are often material tokens of long-standing relationships with other families and friends (e.g. 23.618–50). See further Scheid-Tissinier 1994: 41–3; and Bichler 2007.

48 = 11.133, 10.379, *Od.* 21.10. The three metals listed are valuable and long-lasting, as befits family possessions (for the durability of bronze: 5.292 etc.; iron: 24.205 etc.; gold: 13.22). πολύκμητος 'much worked', 'laboriously wrought'. Iron is much harder than bronze or gold. **49** τῶν: 9n. κέν = ἄν; cf. Latacz 2000b: 92. τοι = Attic σοι. χαρίσαιτο 'will give you for your pleasure'; a desperate attempt to establish a bond with the enemy. χαρίζεσθαι characterises the relationship between allies (15.449 = 17.291), comrades (*Od.* 8.584), guest-friends (*Od.* 24.273, 283), spouses (5.71) and more generally anyone who qualifies as φίλος (cf. *Od.* 10.43). On giving pleasure to the enemy: 82n. (χάρμα). It may be attempted only as a last resort in supplication; cf. 10.380, 11.134. πατήρ: cf. 47n. ἀπερείσι᾽ ἄποινα: Adrestos first promised a 'worthy ransom' (cf. 46n.) but now uses the traditional phrase 'infinite ransom' (ἀπερείσια < ἀ + πέρας), thus accepting that all the bargaining power is with the victor; cf. Scodel 2008a: 77–80.

50 Adrestos begins to envisage the possibility that he might be saved.   εἴ κεν with optative rather than simple εἰ is commonly used in Homer to introduce hypothetical subclauses: Chantraine 1948–53: vol. ii, 277–8.   ζωόν echoes ζώγρει at the beginning of the speech (46).   πεπύθοιτ᾽: 3rd pers. sing. opt. of the reduplicated aorist (πυνθάνομαι).   ἐπὶ νηυσὶν Ἀχαιῶν: a common phrase at the end of the line, often used to describe the place where the booty is stored (spoils: 7.78 etc.; horses: 5.25–6 etc.; captives: 10.381, 11.111–12 and 135; cf. 1.12–13).

51–65 Agamemnon and Menelaos clash over the future of Adrestos, but their encounter also brings into view the entire history of the Trojan War, from its origins (56–7) to the future sack of Troy (57–60). Mentioning the two brothers together is an effective way of evoking the expedition as a whole, both here and more generally in Greek literature: Pind. *Ol.* 9.70, *Isthm.* 5.38 and 8.51; Bacchyl. 11.123; Aesch. *Ag.* 40–7, with Fraenkel 1950: 27–8. Menelaos is the reason why the expedition takes place; Agamemnon is in charge of it: these different roles tally with the characterisation of the two brothers. Menelaos emerges here as relatively kind and ineffectual, Agamemnon as bent on success to the point of savagery (58–60n.). On the characterisation of Menelaos as a 'soft' warrior, cf. 17.588, and ΣbT *ad* 6.51*a*; on his reluctance to cause pain, cf. also *Od.* 4.97–103, where he regrets the death of his own men in Troy. In tragedy his character degenerates: he becomes even more ineffectual and can also be unpleasant (e.g. Eur. *Andr.*); for Menelaos in the *Iliad* see Willcock 2002; and Schmit-Neuerburg 1999: 155–6; on the characterisation of Agamemnon, see 55–60n., 62n., and Taplin 1990.

51 ~ 2.142, 3.395, etc. Lines that conclude a speech usually offer authorial guidance on how to interpret it and/or describe the reaction it elicits; Beck 2005: 43–4 and 290–4 collects and discusses speech-concluding formulae; cf. 45n.   ὣς φάτο: cf. ὣς ἔφατ᾽ before a vowel (102n.).   θυμόν: the basic meaning seems to be 'breath'; cf. Clarke 1999: 79–83, but θυμός is more generally associated with strong feelings and compelling thoughts: for example, it typically drives a subject towards a certain course of action but does not usually recommend idleness or easy options (one clear exception is *Od.* 9.302, where Odysseus presents prudence as an act of valour; see also 444n.). Persuasion typically appeals to the θυμός: *LfgrE* s.v. θυμός B 6 c.   ἔπειθε: the imperfect of πείθω expresses both the process of persuasion and its (however provisional) realisation; cf. 4.104 τῶι δὲ φρένας ἄφρονι πεῖθεν, with Chantraine 1948–53: vol. II, 190. The reading adopted here is found in an unedited Oxyrhynchus papyrus (1044 West), and in some of the more important MSS. Most manuscripts, however, have ὄρινε, 'he stirred him'. θυμὸν ὀρίνω can be used when a highly emotional act of supplication is successful (cf. 9.595 and 24.465–7), but Adrestos does not make an especially strong appeal for pity. The variants, both here and at 61n. (ἔτρεψεν), suggest that Menelaos' exact state of mind was a matter of interest and debate in antiquity.

52–3 καί: cf. 1n.   δή . . . τάχ' ἔμελλε: δή confirms the previous statement and draws out its consequences; see Bakker 1997a: 75–6. τάχ' ἔμελλε means 'was about to', i.e. 'very nearly did'; cf. 10.365 and *LfgrE* s.v. τάχα B 1 d. Menelaos is persuaded – 'indeed' (δή) he is about to (τάχ' ἔμελλε) send Adrestos to the ships.   μιν: 3rd pers. sing. acc. of the personal pronoun (enclitic).   ἔμελλε . . . δώσειν . . . καταξέμεν 'he was about . . . to hand him over to his servant so that he might lead him away'.   θοάς: frequently of ships (see M. Parry 1971: 109–13; and *LfgrE* s.v. θοός B I). The epithet describes an essential quality of ships, even in a context where they are beached; cf. Introduction 2.2.

53–4 καταξέμεν is postponed long after ἐπὶ νῆας Ἀχαιῶν and makes the transition to ἀλλ' Ἀγαμέμνων particularly abrupt. Agamemnon arrives running and speaks in a stream of runover lines: changing Menelaos' mind and killing Adrestos is a matter of urgency: 55–60n., 61–5n.

53 ὧι: 3rd pers. sing. dat. of the possessive pronoun.   καταξέμεν: Aeolic infinitive of the mixed aorist (136n.; cf. 24.663; *Hom. Hymn* 3.103).   ἀλλ' Ἀγαμέμνων: cf. Hes. fr. 197.14 MW, where the phrase recurs in the same metrical position and to similar effect.

54 The line prepares us for a reproachful speech, cf. 45n.   ἀντίος ἦλθε θέων: cf. 15.584 and 17.257, where a warrior attacks the enemy in battle; cf. 53–4n.   ὁμοκλήσας: the verb is used when a person of higher status reprimands an inferior (god to mortal, commander to soldier, man to woman, father to son, driver to horse, master to dog). It can imply strong reproach; cf. 2.199.

55–60 After a series of killings, Menelaos is prepared to spare Adrestos' life, but Agamemnon insists that no exceptions will be made: all Trojans must pay for the rape of Helen. In effect, Agamemnon answers Adrestos' offer of ransom by demanding compensation for an act of wrongdoing; cf. 46n. and Wilson 2002: 165–7. Agamemnon's rhetoric fits the narrative development of lines 1–71n.: from individual scenes of conflict we are led to contemplate the overall defeat of the Trojans. Agamemnon's speech is relentless and was admired as a rhetorical tour de force in antiquity (cf. ΣbT *ad* 6.56–7 and 6.62*a*). At the same time, both ancient and modern readers have expressed shock at his harshness (58–60n.), and at the poet's apparent endorsement of it (62n.). For Agamemnon's determination to rape and kill the Trojan women, see Introduction 3.2.

55 ὦ πέπον ὦ Μενέλαε ~ 17.238. The elaborate address suggests Agamemnon's outrage at his brother's actions.   πέπον establishes intimacy but also expresses more or less open disapproval: cf. 2.235 (strong reproach), 15.437 (mild reproach), *Od.* 13.154 (implied criticism). Only in direct speech, from superior to inferior (e.g. Ajax to Teucer, Sarpedon to Glaukos, Zeus to Poseidon; contrast the deferential ἠθεῖ': 518n.).   τίη δέ: τίη tends to express surprise, disbelief or outrage. The effect is further strengthened by δέ: 123n., Stoevesandt 2008: 29. For τίη, cf. 145n., 1.365, 11.407–8. Translate: 'How can you...?'   κήδεαι: in the active, κήδω means 'cause pain'; in the middle it means 'take pains' = 'care about'. κήδομαι often arises from a sense of pity (2.27 = 2.64 = 24.174, 11.664), or even a feeling of friendship (cf. 1.196 = 209, 7.204, etc.). Here, the implication is that Menelaos cares about the wrong people: 56n.

56 ἀνδρῶν: the plural fits Agamemnon's rhetoric. Menelaos is not depicted as caring about a particular man, but as failing to fight the Trojans. As Nestor says at 70, the Achaeans should 'kill men', not look after them.   ἦ expresses surprise, disbelief or indignation, see Latacz 2000b: 73.   σοί: Agamemnon is careful to point out that he is acting in Menelaos' own best interest.   ἄριστα: sarcastic; cf. 3.351 κάκ', 3.354 κακά.   κατὰ οἶκον: Agamemnon implies that the rape of Helen should take precedence over any other consideration.

57 πρὸς Τρώων '(were you treated so very well...) by the Trojans?' For πρός with the genitive see Chantraine 1948–53: vol. II, 134; George 2005: 68–9; and cf. 456n., 524–5n. Agamemnon implicates all the Trojans in Paris' act.   μή τις: cf. μήδ' 58 and 59, relentlessly driving home the message that no exceptions are possible.   ὑπεκφύγοι... ὄλεθρον = *Od.* 12.287 ~ *Od.* 9.286, 12.446 etc. ὑπέκφυγον/ὑπεξέφυγον is an expressive compound used only in the aorist, 'escape'; cf. ὑπεξαλέομαι, 'flee out from under' (15.180); ὑπεξφέρω, 'carry off' (5.318 etc.); see also 16–17n. (πρόσθεν ὑπαντιάσας).   αἰπὺν ὄλεθρον: common at the end of the hexameter line. In contrast with αἰπεινός (34–5n.), αἰπύς can be used of a wide range of nouns. It is unclear to what extent its basic meaning 'steep' is felt in this formula (ΣbT *ad* 14.99 gloss ἀνυπέρβλητος, 'that cannot be surpassed').

58–60 Agamemnon outlines a miniature 'Sack of Troy' of shocking brutality. The scholiasts were much exercised by the 'beastliness' (θηριότης) of his words (ΣbT *ad* 6.58–9b). They try to justify him by rehearsing his own arguments and by drawing attention to the Trojans' violation of the truce in book 4; cf. Agamemnon's own speech at 4.158–68. The sack of Troy has been mentioned before, but only as a frustrated ambition (2.29–30, 66–7, 113, 132–3, 286–8, 4.32–6, 5.715–16), a memory of the distant past (Heracles' previous sack: 5.638–42), or an equally distant future (4.160–8, 415–16). Now it seems imminent and is countenanced in all its horror.

58 χεῖράς θ' ἡμετέρας: so far, Agamemnon used the 2nd pers. sing. (κήδεαι, σοί), now he shifts to the 1st pers. plur.: Menelaos is addressed as one of 'us', i.e. the Achaeans. On the strategic use of the 1st pers. plur. towards the end of an exhortation, cf. 70n., 99–100n., 114n., 226n.   γαστέρι 'in the womb' (locative).

59 κοῦρον: the scholia rightly point out that Agamemnon focuses on male off-spring. The tender portrayal of Andromache and her baby son at 394–502 jars with this image. For the premature death of children as a source of pathos in Homer: Griffin 1980: 108; Golden 1988: 152.   **μηδ' ὅς** 'not even he'; for ὅς used as a demonstrative pronoun after καί and οὐδέ/μηδέ, see Chantraine 1948–53: vol. I, 276.   **φύγοι:** babies still in their mothers' wombs cannot 'escape', but the language assimilates them to the soldiers who are running away; cf. 57n.

60 Ἰλίου: the ultimate goal of the Achaean onslaught is finally named. Ἴλιος is almost always feminine in early epic (*Il.* 15.71 is the only clear exception). The identification between (ϝ)Ἴλιος and Hittite *Wilusa* is debated; cf. Heinhold-Krahmer 2003; and Latacz 2004: 75–92.   **ἐξαπολοίατ' =** ἐξαπόλοιντο, with vocalisation of Indo-European *n* (Schwyzer 1939: 671).   **ἀκήδεστοι** echoes κήδεαι at 55 (ring composition), but with a sinister twist: ἀκήδεστος means not only 'without care' but also 'unmourned' and hence 'without funerary rites' (*LfgrE* s.vv. ἀκήδεστος, ἀκηδέστως; cf. Alexiou 2002: 10–11).   **ἄφαντοι** is used to describe the disappearance of an entire family line, or even a people (cf. 20.303); contrast ἄϊστος (14.258, *Od.* 1.235, 242), and ἄπυστος (*Od.* 1.242).

61–5 The series of runover lines continues, as Adrestos is dispatched in a swift and brutal fashion; cf. 55–60n.

61 ∼ 7.120, 13.788.   **ἔτρεψεν:** some manuscripts read παρέπεισεν, but in the *Iliad* that verb is otherwise used when the speaker has a restraining effect; ἔτρεψεν is more appropriate here. These variants and those at 51n. suggest that Menelaos' precise reaction after the speeches was a matter of interest to ancient and medieval readers.   **ἀδελφειοῦ:** genitive of ἀδελφεός, 'brother' (cf. Attic ἀδελφός). Here, as also at 5.21 etc., the Homeric form ἀδελφειοῦ stems from pre-Homeric *ἀδελφεόο, which should not be restored (*pace* West); cf. 344n. (ὀκρυοέσσης).   **φρένας:** an inner organ, situated in the chest and associated with a wide range of thoughts and emotions (Sullivan 1988; Clarke 1999: 83–92). φρένες are often closely associated with the θυμός (e.g. 12.173–4); cf. 51n. and see further Jahn 1987, Caswell 1990.   **ἥρως:** cf. 34–5n.

62 αἴσιμα παρειπών ∼ 7.121, 'advising what was apportioned'; cf. 333n. (κατ' αἶσαν . . . οὐδ' ὑπὲρ αἶσαν). A problematic addition which has challenged ancient and modern readers (e.g. Goldhill 1990: 376); as elsewhere, the poet invites scrutiny of Agamemnon's behaviour (see esp. 2.1–420). Ancient commentators wondered whether αἴσιμα simply means 'in accordance with fate' (ΣT *ad* 6.62*a*), or whether the poet endorses Agamemnon's speech as 'appropriate', even though it seems especially savage (ΣbT *ad* 6.62*a*, cf. 58–60n.). As Kirk 1990: 191 points out, 'αἴσιμα . . . refers to Agamemnon's invocation of the laws of hospitality in 56 more than anything else'; see esp. *Od.* 15.68–71. ΣbT *ad* 6.58–9*b* argue that the speech is appropriate, because the truce has been broken: at 3.300–1, Trojans and Achaeans agreed that, should they break the truce, they ought to have 'their brains poured out like wine, and those of their sons too, and their wives raped'. For further discussion, see esp. Fenik 1986: 26; Yamagata 1994: 118; Wilson 2002: 166–7; Stoevesandt 2004: 152–5. For another surprising authorial comment: 232–6n. with Introduction 4.1.   **ὃ δ' ἀπὸ**

ἔθεν ὤσατο χειρί: the suppliant is rejected with a gesture that ends direct physical contact; cf. Naiden 2006: 130. ἔθεν is gen. sing. of the reflexive pronoun (< ϝέθεν, closing the final syllable of ἀπό). The old separative ending -θεν ('away from') is treated as a metrically convenient alternative to ἕο, εἷο, εὗ.
63 ἥρω᾿ Ἄδρηστον: cf., e.g., 13.428, *Od.* 11.520, with different names. On ἥρως, see 34–5n. κρείων: mostly used of gods and men, esp. Agamemnon (the fem. κρείουσα is used once in the *Iliad*, at 22.48, of Laothoe). Ancient audiences heard in it the root κρατ- (cf. κράτος, κρατέω, κρατερός); modern scholars debate its etymology and exact meaning: *LfgrE* s.v. κρείων. Translate 'powerful', 'ruler'.
64 After the expansiveness of the supplication scene, we return to the brisk brutality of the previous killings, with swift changes of subject.   οὖτα . . . λαπάρην ~ 14.447 and 517. οὖτα, 'wounded', is an aorist with final short alpha (Chantraine 1948–53: vol. 1, 380); it alternates with the aorists οὔτασε and οὔτησε, which are also common in Homer.   λαπάρην: the soft part of the body between ribs and hip; wounds in Homer often target soft and painful spots (e.g. 13.567–75: lower abdomen between ὀμφαλός and αἰδοῖα; 16.345–50: through the mouth). The lambda in λαπάρην closes the final syllable of κατά (*ka-tal-la-pa-rēn*); see Introduction 2.1.   ἀνετράπετ᾿ 'fell on his back', cf. 14.447.   Ἀτρείδης: cf. 44n.
65 The line closes the episode which started at 38.   λὰξ ἐν στήθεσι βάς 'stepping with one foot on his chest' (cf. λακτίζω; for λάξ, see Radif 1998: 39–40). Usually the gesture is followed by taking spoils (cf. 5.620–2, 13.618–19, and 16.503).   ἐξέσπασε: Agamemnon recovers his own weapon but does not strip Adrestos, cf. Nestor's speech at 66–71n.   μείλινον ἔγχος: frequent at the end of the hexameter line. Unlike the metrically equivalent χάλκεον ἔγχος, the phrase is not used with verbs of striking or wounding: Stoevesandt 2008: 32. Hes. *Op.* 144–5 suggests a close connection between ash wood, bronze, and warriors of an earlier age: Ζεὺς δὲ πατὴρ τρίτον ἄλλο γένος μερόπων ἀνθρώπων | χάλκειον ποίησ᾿, οὐκ ἀργυρέωι οὐδὲν ὁμοῖον, | ἐκ μελιᾶν . . .
66–71 Nestor's role in the *Iliad* is primarily that of military advisor, as befits his old age: Roisman 2005. He is especially close to Agamemnon and typically reminds him (and others) to put the common cause before individual interests. At the beginning of the poem he tries to mend the quarrel between Achilles and Agamemnon (1.247–84); and he later advises Agamemnon to send an embassy to Achilles (9.93–113). In this speech too he obliquely alludes to the quarrel (68–9n.). More generally, he translates Agamemnon's personal rebuke to his brother into a rallying speech for all the Achaeans. The Achaeans have gathered momentum and should now continue to 'kill men'. Hector similarly urges the Trojans to press on without stopping for spoils when they get close to the ships: 15.346–51.
66 ~ 110n., 8.172, etc., introducing the speech as a rallying cry.   Ἀργείοισιν: often used interchangeably with Ἀχαιοί and Δαναοί, as here (5n.); cf. ΣD *ad* 1.79 (Ἀργεῖοι = Ἕλληνες), and 152n. For Ἀργεῖοι = 'the inhabitants of Argos', cf. 159n.   ἐκέκλετο: reduplicated aorist of κέλομαι. The verb characterises Nestor's speech as martial exhortation; cf. 45n. on speech-introductory lines.

67 = 2.110, 15.733, 19.78. The line falls into three sections, each defining the relationship between the speaker and his listeners from a slightly different perspective. ὦ φίλοι establishes an affective bond (opp. ἐχθροί, δυσμενέες). Konstan 1997: 28–31 discusses the meaning of φίλος in Homer ('dear' rather than simply 'one's own'), cf. also 14n., 360n. For the army as a group of φίλοι see Cairns 1993: 86. ἥρωες Δαναοί identifies the addressees collectively as Danaans and implies an opposition with Τρῶες. Note that Δαναοί = Ἀργεῖοι in the line above: 5n. The name Δαναοί may be attested in Egyptian sources of the Bronze Age (*Danaja/Tanaja*); cf. Burkert 1998: 49; and Latacz 2004: 128–33. For ἥρωες cf. 34–5n. θεράποντες Ἄρηος defines the addressees as warriors (lit. 'attendants of Ares') and prepares them for the military advice to come. The phrase is used only of the Achaeans; though Ares actually supports the Trojans (see esp. books 5 and 21). There is a tension between Ares as the personification of war (203n.) and Ares as an Olympian god with his own plans and favourite side; cf. Burkert 1985: 169; Erbse 1986: 162–3; and Prieto 1996.

68–9 μή τις . . . μιμνέτω 'Let nobody stay behind hankering after spoils.' Nestor gives advice on how the troops should behave elsewhere too (e.g. 4.303–9); for his concern with the common cause, see also 66–71n. μή τις echoes Agamemnon's generalisations; cf. 57n. νῦν: Nestor emphasises that the Achaeans should press on 'now' that the Trojans are in flight. ἐνάρων ἐπιβαλλόμενος 'throwing himself upon the spoils'. The phrasing is unique in Homer, but compares closely to Sappho 107 Voigt, where the poet wonders how she can still hanker after youth: ἦρ' ἔτι παρθενίας ἐπιβάλλομαι. The noun ἔναρα refers to the armour of enemy soldiers after they have been killed (hence formulaic ἔναρα βροτόεντα; cf. 480n.). μετόπισθε: the best Homeric warriors are expected to fight in the forefront of battle (ἐνὶ προμάχοισιν); cf. 445n. In victory, the emphasis shifts towards the idea that no one should lag behind. πλεῖστα φέρων: Nestor obliquely recalls the quarrel between Achilles and Agamemnon over their share of the booty. Any concerns about personal gain should be set aside for the common cause. ἐπὶ νῆας ἵκηται: cf. 50n., 52–3n.

70 ἀλλ' ἄνδρας κτείνωμεν: Nestor switches to the 1st pers. plur.; cf. the rhetoric at 58n., 99–100n., 114n., 226n. καὶ τά 'those things too', referring to ἐνάρων; cf. 68–9n. The pronoun suggests that Nestor is being somewhat dismissive; cf. his use of ἕκηλοι ('at your leisure') and the 2nd pers. plur. at 71n.

71 Cf. 68–9 (ring composition). Nestor switches back from the 1st to the 2nd pers. plur. This is unusual at the end of an exhortation (58n., 70n., 99–100n., 114n.) but effectively makes the point that Nestor does *not* care about spoils. Zenodotus preferred to read Τρώων ἄμ πεδίον συλήσομεν ἔντεα νεκρούς, apparently because he wanted Nestor to join the others in the taking of spoils (ΣAbT *ad* 6.71*ab*). His text is less convincing rhetorically than that of the vulgate. νεκρούς . . . τεθνειῶτας ~ 18.540. The redundant addition of τεθνειώς is common with νέκυς, though rare with νεκρός. Here and elsewhere in epic the transmission wavers between forms with ει = *ē* and with η. Aristarchus recommended τεθνηῶτας (cf. ΣA *ad* 6.71*a*², 7.89*e* and 409, 9.633, etc.), whereas the mainstream Hellenistic transmission appears to have favoured the linguistically younger form τεθνειῶτας, with Ionic 'metathesis' of vowels (i.e. transfer of quantity: -ηότας > -εῶτας) and compensatory lengthening (-εῶτας > -ειῶτας); cf. 113n. (βείω). For discussion of metathesis, see Meister 1921: 146–76; cf. also Chantraine 1948–53: vol. I, 68–73 and 429–31; Wachter 2000: 77–8 and 101. **ἄμ:** shortened form of the preposition ἀνά, with assimilation before π-. **συλήσετε** 'you will be able to take spoils', i.e. 'you may take spoils'; for the concessive use of the future tense see Chantraine 1948–53: vol. II, 202.

72–118: THE TROJAN REACTION

The Trojans are about to retreat inside the walls, when the seer Helenos gives advice: Aeneas and Hector should rally the troops, then Hector alone should enter the city and instruct Hecuba on how to make an offering to Athena. There is an implication that he is chosen for the task because he alone will not 'fall into the hands of the women' (cf. 81–2n.).

72 The line still focuses on individual reactions (ἑκάστου) but describes unanimity; it seamlessly leads on to a general assessment of the conflict in the next two lines, mirroring the transition from a panoramic view of the battlefield to individual scenes of single combat at the beginning of the book, cf. 1–4n. **μένος:** cf. 26–7n. **θυμόν:** cf. 51n.

73–4 = 17.319–20 (cf. 336–7), where Apollo intervenes in support of the Trojans. Several passages in the *Iliad* describe events that almost happened: they serve to change the direction of the narrative, mark climactic points, highlight the intervention of particular characters and explore the limits of the epic tradition. Here, the phrase draws attention to the possibility that Troy might have fallen before it did and helps to present Hector's visit inside the city not as a retreat, but as part of a plan for the defence of the city. On counterfactual statements in Homer, see further Lang 1989, Morrison 1992, Nesselrath 1992, Louden 1993, and de Jong 2004: 68–81.

73 ἔνθα marks the specific point at which the Trojans would have retreated into Troy; for the frequent use of ἔνθα in counterfactual statements see Lang 1989: 25; and Louden 1993: 183–4 with n. 6. For the accentuation of ἔνθά κεν, see 251n. αὖτε introduces a shift of focus: we have just heard about the Achaeans, the Trojans 'for their part' were about to retreat. The particle often introduces a reply in a dialogue 'then, in turn' (cf. 144n., 381n.). ἀρηϊφίλων: lit. 'dear to Ares', i.e. 'warlike'. In the plural, the epithet is used only of the Achaeans, and only in contexts where they are about to defeat the Trojans: 17.319 and 336; cf. 16.303. The spelling as one word suggests that the Achaeans' relationship with Ares is not the main point of the expression (and indeed Ares himself is on the side of the Trojans); cf. common ἀρήϊος, 'warlike', and contrast 318n. (Διὶ φίλος). See also 67n. (θεράποντες Ἄρηος).

74 Ἴλιον εἰσανέβησαν: in the *Iliad* the phrase is always used of the Trojans as they are driven back into the city. In the *Odyssey* the same phrase always refers to the Achaean expedition: after the fall of Troy only the Achaean perspective survives; cf. *Od.* 2.172, 18.252, 19.125. Here, as often, εἰς can be interpreted as a postposition: Ἴλιον εἰς ἀνέβησαν; though at *Od.* 16.449 εἰσαναβαίνω must be treated as a compound verb.   ἀναλκείηισι δαμέντες 'overcome by their own weakness', 'discouraged'; cf. 17.336–7, where Aeneas berates the Trojans because they are defeated on account of their own weakness. Lack of ἀλκή is typical of women (cf. 5.349); Hector is about to tell the Trojan fighters to 'be men' and remember their own ἀλκή: 112n., cf. 265n.

75   Cf. 13.725, 23.155, and, for the second half of the line, 12.60 and 210, etc.   εἰ μή: for its frequent use in counterfactual statements, see Lang 1989: 25.   ἄρ introduces what actually happened after the thought experiment at 73–4.   Αἰνείαι: in the *Iliad* Aeneas is second in command of the Trojans. Here he is mentioned before Hector, but he then drops out of the narrative altogether, cf. 102–9n. This abrupt disappearance tallies with his rather marginal role in the poem: at 13.460–1 Aeneas himself is upset that Priam neglects him. At 20.179–83 Achilles taunts him precisely by saying that Priam will never care about him, because he is not his son. The gods twice remove him from the battlefield when he is about to be killed (Aphrodite at 5.311–17; Poseidon at 20.288–340): in a poem fundamentally concerned with death, Aeneas the survivor is marginal; see Horsfall 1979: 372.   Ἕκτορι: Hector is introduced with little emphasis, after Aeneas. In his speech Helenos implies that reorganising the troops on the battlefield is a joint effort, and includes himself in the act of resistance; cf. 84n. He then singles out Hector as the only man who is going to enter the city: 86n. For Hector's role in the book, and in the poem as a whole, see 441–6n., and Introduction 4.   παραστάς: formulaic at the end of the line, often in combination with εἶπε. Here it marks the moment at which resistance begins: while the Trojans are running away, Helenos makes a stand.

76   Cf. 1.69. In the *Iliad* it is often a god who prevents 'something that was about to happen': Lang 1989: 23–4; Morrison 1992: 66–8; Louden 1993: 184 with n. 8. Here, however, the gods have left the battlefield (cf. 1n.), and it is the seer Helenos who changes the course of events.   Πριαμίδης: most frequently of Hector but occasionally also of other sons of Priam. Helenos is unobtrusively presented as Hector's brother, and this becomes important later: 87n. and 102n.   Ἕλενος: the most prominent seer on the Trojan side, he is also a warrior. He is mentioned here for the first time: the instructions he is about to give to Hector do not achieve their ultimate aim, which is that of pleasing Athena (cf. 311n.), but his prophetic powers are vindicated in the next book (see 7.44–53; cf. 77–101n.) and here his intervention is successful in arresting the Trojan retreat. In the *Little Iliad* he predicts the fall of Troy to Odysseus (Proclus, *Chrestomathy*, p. 120 West; cf. Soph. *Phil.* 604–13). In Eur. *Andr.* 1243–5 he becomes Andromache's husband after the fall of Troy and the death of Neoptolemos. Many characters in book 6 are prominent in texts dealing with the sack of Troy; see Introduction 3. The last syllable of Ἕλενος is measured long before caesura; it is possible that final sigma is drawn out and closes the syllable; see Introduction 2.1.   οἰωνοπόλων ὄχ' ἄριστος: we are cued to expect a speech which concerns the gods; cf. 45n. The Alexandrian scholar Ammonius (M. L. West 2001a: 79–80) cites as known to Aristarchus the alternative ending μάντις τ' οἰωνοπόλος τε (cf. also Zenodotus' alternative reading at 1.69, of Calchas). This may be an attempt to describe Helenos' expertise more precisely (he is not about to interpret the flight of birds), or to avoid contradiction with 1.69 (Calchas and Helenos cannot both be 'the best reader of birds'). Aristarchus discussed the meaning of μάντις and other terms for seer, cf. ΣΑ *ad* 1.62 with van der Valk 1963–4: vol. II, 100. For variants in Hellenistic scholarship, see Introduction 6.

77–101 Helenos' speech begins like a standard rallying cry but at 86 takes a surprising turn.

Helenos is careful to present Hector's mission as viable and beneficial to the whole community: in the first section of his speech he organises the Trojan resistance so that Hector can leave without opening a gap in the battle line (77–85); then he gives precise instructions as to how the women of Troy should seek Athena's support (cf. 86–98n.); finally, he emphasises the immediate crisis on the battlefield (cf. 98–101 with nn.). Hector himself is aware that the Trojans must not think he is about to do what no warrior is supposed to, namely retreat to the safety of the city and the loving care of his wife: cf. his speech to the troops, 110–18n. Later in the book Hector criticises Paris precisely because he is enjoying Helen's company while the other men fight on his behalf, cf. 325–31n. Three passages echo Helenos' instructions, with some significant differences, cf. 110–18n., 269–78n., 286–311n. On Athena's reaction to the offering and prayers recommended by Helenos, cf. 311n.

77 Αἰνεία τε καὶ Ἕκτορ: cf. 77–101n. Ancient commentators suggest that by addressing himself first to Aeneas, Helenos avoids direct confrontation with Hector (ΣbT *ad* 6.77*a*). On Aeneas, cf. 75n.   πόνος: the toil of battle. Aristarchus argued that in Homer the word has no connotations of suffering (i.e. 'the work of battle'), but his interpretation seems too narrow: cf. 355, 524–5n.; *LfgrE* s.v. πόνος B I 2. On Aristarchus' theory, cf. 107n.; ΣAT *ad* 21.249*c*; and Lehrs 1882: 73–5.

78 Λυκίων: the Lycian leader Sarpedon has just been wounded (5.663–98) and is therefore no longer available to lead his people: the task falls on Aeneas and Hector. For the role of the Lycians in the *Iliad* and possible connections to the Lukka people of the Bronze Age, see Bryce 1986: 1–41 and 1992; Hiller 1993; and Mellink 1995. They are the most important Trojan allies and, as ΣbT *ad* 6.78 point out, 'Lycians' can be used as a shorthand reference to all allies, cf. 4.197, 11.285 = 15.424 = 485, 16.685.   ἐγκέκλιται 'leans upon you'; the verb evokes many expressions which describe the pressure of war: the Achaeans push back the Trojans (5.37; cf. 14.510 and *Od.* 9.59); warriors 'lean' their shields against their shoulders as they brace themselves for an attack (11.593, 13.488; cf. 22.4, with N. J. Richardson 1993: 106).   ἄριστοι: Helenos introduces a typically Homeric ideal of excellence, which is described in greater detail in the next line. The implication of his address is that the best warriors have an obligation to solve the present crisis; cf. Adkins 1960: 46–9.

79 πᾶσαν ἐπ' ἰθύν 'in every emergency'; = *Od.* 4.434, cf. *Il.* 14.403 (with variant readings) and 21.303. πᾶσαν suggests that the best warriors should always succeed (cf. 208n., 445n.); on ἰθύς see further 2n. The present situation is presented as a test for Aeneas and Hector.   μάχεσθαί τε φρονέειν τε: a typical definition of male excellence in Homer; cf. 9.440–3 with Griffin 1995: 128.

80 στῆτ' αὐτοῦ: the first and most urgent task is to 'make a stand here', cf. 75n. Then Aeneas and Hector must go everywhere (πάντηι ἐποιχόμενοι, 81n.)

until all the Trojans finally 'stand' and face the Achaeans (ἐναντίοι ἔσταν Ἀχαιῶν, 106n.). **λαὸν ἐρυκάκετε:** the term λαός is closely associated with the responsibilities of leaders in relation to their people: Haubold 2000: ch. 1. On Helenos' appeal to Aeneas' and Hector's obligations to the Trojans, cf. 78n. The verb ἐρύκω ('hold back') is frequently used of containing the enemy, not of rallying one's own troops. Helenos' choice of language suggests a shift of focus from fighting the enemy to rallying one's own side; cf. 81–2n.   **πρὸ πυλάων** suggests that the Trojans were about to flee into their city, as they in fact do later in the poem; cf. 21.526–42.

81–2 Agamemnon has just expressed the wish that the Trojans fall into the hands of the Achaeans: 58n. Helenos now contemplates another danger: that they might 'fall into the hands' of their own women. The martial language makes it clear that such a meeting would weaken the men and benefit the enemy. Helenos' words here have clear implications for Hector's future conduct: when he enters the city, he must not be delayed by the women or surrender to their anxiety; see Introduction 3.2 and 4.

81 **πάντηι ἐποιχόμενοι:** a common expression in this metrical position, suggesting a concerted effort to turn the tide of battle; cf. 16.496 = 533 and 5.508 παντόσ' ἐποιχόμενος (of Ares). The verb ἐποίχομαι is used of people attending to their own tasks (cf. *Od.* 17.226–8 ∼ 18.362–4). These can be the tasks of men, as here, or of women: e.g. 491–2n. (ἔργον ἐποίχεσθαι).   **πρίν:** measured long, as often; for discussion, see Chantraine 1999 s.v.   αὖτ': cf. 73n.   **ἐν χερσὶ γυναικῶν:** in the *Iliad* men are in the hands of their female relatives when they are dead. This is most prominently the case with Hector, whose funeral concludes the poem; see 24.710–12, 724, and cf. 22.426. Kirk 1990: 164 notes the ominous implications of this phrase and points out that seeking comfort in the arms of women is demeaning; cf. Σb *ad* 6.81, and Hector's words to Paris: 325–31n.

82 **φεύγοντας πεσέειν:** in combination, the two verbs suggest a tumultuous and disorderly flight. Contrast the purposeful πάντηι ἐποιχόμενοι at 81, in the same metrical position.   **πεσέειν:** aorists in -έειν are relatively common in early Greek epic; cf. Chantraine 1948–53: vol. 1, 492–3.   **δηΐοισι δὲ χάρμα γενέσθαι:** mortals should only be a source of joy to those who wish them well, never the enemy: cf. 3.51, 10.193, 23.342–3; Arnould 1990: ch. 2, esp. 31–6 (on not pleasing opponents); 17.636, 24.706, *Od.* 6.184–5 (on pleasing those whose joy can be reciprocated). The gods, by contrast, can be a universal 'source of joy' for all mortals: cf. 14.325; *Hom. Hymn* 3.25, *Hom. Hymn* 16.4. For the scansion of δηΐοισι, see Chantraine 1948–53: vol. 1, 107.

83 **αὐτάρ:** more emphatic than δέ, the particle introduces a new thought and articulates narrative development: Bakker 1997a: 96, with nn. 18–19. Here it marks the transition to the central section of Helenos' speech.   **φάλαγγας:** cf. 6n.   **ἐποτρύνητον:** subj. dual. ἐποτρύνω is typically used to urge others, or occasionally oneself, to fight bravely in battle (cf. ὀτρύνω, with the same basic meaning). Participles of the verb often introduce or conclude speeches of martial exhortation (e.g. 8.92, 13.94 = 480 = 17.219, 17.553; 12.442 ∼ 20.364 ∼ 373). Hector exhorts the troops already at 105 (ὀτρύνων), but his speech is delayed until 110;

cf. 110–18n.   ἀπάσας: Helenos makes it clear that 'all' the lines need to be restored before Hector can enter the city; cf. 81n.

84 ἡμεῖς μέν: the scholia remark that Helenos 'persuasively' switches to the 1st pers. plur., thus claiming his share in the danger (πιθανῶς: ΣbT *ad* 6.84). Speakers often include themselves in exhortations to fight (cf. 58n., 70n.), but here ἡμεῖς followed by μέν promises a contrasting 'you', which is introduced at 86: Hector alone should leave the battlefield and return to Troy.   Δαναοῖσι: 67n.   αὖθι μένοντες: the phrase anticipates a change of scene; cf. πόλινδε μετέρχεο (86n.).

85 Helenos' bleak assessment of the Trojan plight on the battlefield informs Hector's actions in Troy.   τειρόμενοί περ 'worn down as we are'; cf. τείρουσι (255n.), τείρεσθαι (387n.). The verb is used to describe the collective plight of the Trojans only in book 6; otherwise, when used collectively, it describes the hardships of the Achaeans (9.248, 302, 11.801, etc.). περ is concessive here, but the particle has a broader range of meanings than English 'although'; cf. 41n.   ἀναγκαίη γὰρ ἐπείγει 'for necessity weighs on us'. The phrase evokes the oppressive πόνος ... ἐγκέκλιται at 77–8 (ring composition), but the sense of pressure is even greater now; cf. 8.57, where ἀναγκαίη is used to express a similar sentiment.

86–98 In the central section of his speech Helenos tells Hector that he should enter the city and instruct Hecuba on how to seek the support of Athena. Contact between the male and the female sphere happens through family connections (cf. 87n. and 88–9n.). The religious role envisaged for the Trojan women is similar to that of real women in archaic and classical times, cf. Lefkowitz 1996, and aspects of Helenos' instructions resemble closely the ritual performed in honour of Athena at the Panathenaic festival in Athens; see Introduction 3.1. The syntax of this section is unusually complex, giving the impression that Helenos speaks with the precise attention to detail necessary for the successful performance of ritual. Athena is envisaged as the protector of the city (cf. 305n.), although in the *Iliad* she favours the Achaeans and especially Diomedes, whom she is now asked to restrain; cf. 96n. This tension in her relationship to the city is typical not only of the *Iliad*, but also of the wider epic tradition: Introduction 3.1.

86 Ἕκτορ, ἀτὰρ σύ: ἡμεῖς μέν (84n.) suggested that there would be an exception to the general injunction to stay and fight; now Hector is emphatically singled out: the formulation is stronger than a sentence containing a simple δέ.   πόλινδε μετέρχεο: μετ(ά) in μετέρχεσθαι is redundant after πόλινδε, as ancient readers noted: ΣT *ad* 6.86. The compound can suggest the idea of attending to one's business, a shade of meaning which may be relevant here; cf. 5.429, *Od.* 16.314. See also 81n. (πάντηι ἐποιχόμενοι).   δ᾽: 1n.   ἔπειτα marks the central message in Helenos' speech; cf. 37–8n.

87 μητέρι σῆι καὶ ἐμῆι: Hecuba is introduced here as the mother of Helenos and Hector and continues to be described as a mother (251, 264; cf. 254) until she chooses the robe for Athena: at that point she is called by name for the first time in the poem; cf. 293n.   ἥ: 9n.   ξυνάγουσα γεραιάς: this is the only gathering of old women in early Greek epic, though cf. Sappho 44.31 Voigt. The gathering seems to be modelled on the meetings of γέροντες: at 9.574–5 and 18.448–9, for example, delegations of 'elders' entreat a powerful warrior on behalf of the community and offer him gifts but are ultimately rejected. The masculine term emphasises authority rather than age (113n.), as does the variant γεραιράς (ΣbT *ad* 6.87*b*, who explain it as 'priestesses'; cf. Schulze 1892: 500–3; van der Valk 1963–4: vol. I, 456–7; Wickert-Micknat 1982: 31). The transmitted γεραιάς is preferable and does seem to emphasise age: Hector assumes that Andromache will be at home. When she is not there, he imagines that she may have gone to visit women of her generation, at their own homes; finally, in order to account for her absence, he suggests that all the Trojan women may have gone to the temple, cf. 379n. (ἔνθά περ ἄλλαι) and 380n. (Τρωιαὶ ἐϋπλόκαμοι). For a different reading, see Stoevesandt 2008: 38.

88–9   ΣbT *ad* 6.88–9 describe these lines as 'superfluous' (περισσοί). Line 89 may seem suspect for two reasons: (a) this is the only Iliadic passage where κληΐς means 'key' or 'hook' as opposed to 'bolt'; (b) the line seems to contradict the poet's later narrative: Helenos says that Hecuba should open the temple, but in fact it is the priestess Theano who does so at 298. (a) is not a problem: the meaning 'key' is attested in the *Odyssey* and must be old; cf. Mycenaean *ka-ra-wi-po-ro* = *κλᾱϝι-φόρος (key-bearer), with Aura Jorro 1985: 324. (b) emphasises Helenos' perspective: discrepancies between character speeches and the main narrative are not uncommon and tend to reflect different priorities and levels of knowledge: de Jong 2004. Men have access to the world of the women primarily through their female relations, so Helenos appeals to Hector by focusing on what their own mother can do to help; the women then share the tasks: Introduction 3.2.

88   νηόν: the abode of a god (cf. ναίω, 'dwell') in a landscape frequented by mortals. In some contexts the word refers specifically to a temple, in others it may refer more generally to the whole sanctuary, cf. 93–4n. The accusative of goal without preposition is often employed after ἰκνέομαι, ἵκω and ἰκάνω, but it is also found with other verbs, including ξυνάγω, 'gather'. For discussion and further examples see Chantraine 1948–53: vol. II, 45–6.   γλαυκώπιδος: a standard epithet of Athena, trans. 'having bright, gleaming eyes'; cf. γλαυκός = 'gleaming', γλαυκιάω = 'glare' (of lions). In epic, Athena is never associated with the owl, γλαῦξ.   ἐν πόλει ἄκρηι: the central elevated area of Troy reserved for palaces and temples; it is also called Πέργαμος (512n.) and, in the *Odyssey*, ἀκρόπολις (8.494, 504). On the location of Paris' house in relation to the temple of Athena: Introduction 3.3.

89   ἱεροῖο δόμοιο: on Olympus the gods live in 'houses' (δώματα); here the house of Athena is qualified as 'sacred'; cf. 88n. (νηόν). The epithet 'sacred' is standardly used of the whole of Troy: the city is defined by its temples and more generally by its religious significance; cf. Ἰλίου ἱρῆς, 96n.

90–7   ~ 271–8. Hector repeats these instructions to Hecuba word for word. In Homeric epic, messengers report fully and faithfully; cf. de Jong 2004: 180–5 and 241–3; M. L. West 1997a: 190–3 discusses comparative material. Messenger speeches remind us that precision and attention to detail can be expected of oral performance just as much as of written documents; see Introduction 1.

90–1 Helenos recommends that Hecuba offer Athena a πέπλος, a 'pinned blanket-dress' worn by women (van Wees 2005: 4–10). His instructions follow two episodes which prominently featured such cloaks: at 5.315–17 Aphrodite uses her *peplos* to shield Aeneas from the enemy, but Diomedes eventually pierces it with his spear and wounds the goddess (5.337–8). When Athena enters into battle on Diomedes' side, she discards her *peplos* – a beautiful garment she wove herself – and wears Zeus's tunic instead (5.733–7; cf. 8.384–8). Now Hecuba is supposed to offer Athena another *peplos* and ask her to restrain Diomedes: the goddess will refuse, cf. 311n. We later learn that the *peplos* chosen by Hecuba is woven by mortal women who were abducted by Paris on his way back to Troy, and is therefore unlikely to please the goddess: see 288–95n. A beautiful *peplos* is a status symbol in Homer (van Wees 2005: 12–25); it is a suitable gift for women and goddesses, and also a gift typically offered by women: Lyons 2003: 107–8; and Kauffmann-Samaras and Szabados 2004. Athena, for example, was offered a *peplos* at the Panathenaea: when the Athenians heard performances of the *Iliad* at that festival, they must have thought about the parallels between Hecuba's offering and their own ritual; see Introduction 3.1.

90 ὅς οἱ δοκέει: Helenos emphasises that it is Hecuba's responsibility to choose the right garment; cf. 91n., 288–95n. ὅς (relative pronoun) is the reading of the manuscripts; ὃ οἱ (demonstrative pronoun) is attested in one papyrus (270 West). The reading ὅς disregards digamma (ϝοι; cf. 16–17n.) but is difficult to dismiss either as a mere corruption or as an intervention on the part of a late editor. Although manuscripts usually acknowledge digamma before οἱ (cf. 281n.: κε οἱ; and Chantraine 1948–53: vol. I, 147; for exceptions, see 100–1n.: τίς οἱ; 91n.: καί οἱ; and 289n.: οἱ), they generally read ὅς οἱ rather than ὃ οἱ, even where a short syllable is required; cf. 13.561, *Od.* 1.300 = 3.198, 21.416 (exceptions: 13.211 and *Od.* 14.3). The scribe of papyrus 270 West (who wrote ἐλλίσσετο at 45n.) may have followed Aristarchus' theory that Homer preferred ὃ to classical ὅς. Aristarchus went as far as athetising two lines, 8.524–5, because they contradicted that theory (Matthaios 1999: 434); and we know that he recommended ὃ οἱ against transmitted ὅς οἱ at *Od.* 1.300 (ΣMᵃ *ad loc.*). ὅς οἱ should stand, though both spellings seem old (cf. West's apparatus *ad* 13.561). χαριέστατος: the adjective emphasises the beauty of the garment and its pleasing effect on the viewer. χάρις is crucial in all human attempts to please the gods; cf. Parker 1998. It is also an appropriate quality for a cloak: at 5.338 we are told that the Χάριτες wove Aphrodite's *peplos*; see further Wagner-Hasel 2002.   ἠδέ emphasises the completeness of a statement, typically by combining near synonyms (e.g. πολεμίζειν ἠδὲ μάχεσθαι), or items that together make up a whole (e.g. βίον ἠδὲ φαρέτρην), or a concrete description of an action, followed by its ultimate goal (as at 113–15; cf. 4.322–3, 341–2 ~ 12.315–16).   μέγιστος: the best *peploi* are generously proportioned; cf. van Wees 2005: 4 and 15–16.

91 ἐνὶ μεγάρωι: a public room, or more generally a dwelling; cf. 371n. (ἐν μεγάροισιν). We later see Hecuba instruct her servants in the μέγαρα, pl. (286–7n.), though she then proceeds into the θάλαμος, an inner room, in order to retrieve her favourite robe (288n.) For this and other differences between Helenos' instructions and Hecuba's actions, see 286–311n.; for the men's limited awareness of female spaces and activities, see Introduction 3.2. The iota of ἐνί is measured long, because μ in μεγάρωι is drawn out and closes the syllable; see Introduction 2.1. Some manuscripts and a papyrus mark the phenomenon with a double consonant: ἐνὶ μμεγάρωι; cf. M. L. West 1998–2000: vol. 1, xxvi. **καί οἱ πολὺ φίλτατος αὐτῆι:** Helenos emphasised the more objective qualities of gracefulness and size; now he adds that Hecuba should offer the garment that she likes best. The idea is that there should be a close correspondence between Hecuba's feelings and Athena's own – though that turns out to be a problem, because Hecuba chooses a garment that is unlikely to please the goddess: 288–95n. καί is measured short (perhaps read *ka-yoi*, Introduction 2.1), without regard for digamma before οἱ, cf. 90n.

92 At the Panathenaea the Athenians also seem to have placed their *peplos* on the knees of a seated image of Athena Polias; see Introduction 3.1. For early examples of seated statues, see Kirk 1990: 167; and Stoevesandt 2008: 40–1. **ἠϋκόμοιο:** a standard epithet of women and goddesses. In the *Iliad* it is never used of Athena, except in book 6 where it describes her cult statue; cf. 273 and 303. This is the only book where Athena's relationship to women is explored; see Introduction 3.1.

93–4 The women are asked to promise a sacrifice rather than make one; animal sacrifices are performed by men in the Homeric poems, cf. 270n. (σὺν θυέεσσιν). **δυοκαίδεκα:** the number 12 typically expresses a sense of completeness (contrast 9, discussed at 174n.). It is therefore appropriate for sacrifices, which should be perfect, cf. 115n. On sacrificing twelve animals, cf. *LfgrE* s.v. δυώδεκα B 2. For significant numbers, see 421n. **ἐνὶ νηῶι:** sacrifices do not usually take place inside the temple. The word νηός may denote the whole sanctuary as the abode of the goddess; cf. 88n. See further Latacz 2000b: 42. **ἤνις ἠκέστας** 'one year old, untamed', according to ancient explanations (cf. 10.292–3 = *Od.* 3.382–3, where ἄδμητος, 'untamed', is used in place of ἤκεστος). The expression, formulaic in this position, is only used of female cattle offered to Athena. It was probably already obscure when the *Iliad* was composed; Hoekstra 1965: 120 and Reece 1999–2000: 196–7 argue that the formula arose out of incorrect word division early in the tradition. More important than the precise meaning of the words is the sense of arcane propriety they convey: ritual language is often obscure. For difficult Homeric words, see Introduction 2.4.

94–5 Hecuba should ask Athena to take pity and restrain Diomedes, cf. 96–8n. Pity is a central concern in book 6, as it is also in books 22 and 24; see Introduction 3. In this book the women and children of Troy are its focus: Agamemnon has just urged Menelaos to spare no one, not even babies in their mothers' wombs; cf. 55–60n. Now Athena should take pity on the city, the women and the little children: she will not, cf. 311n. Later Andromache begs Hector to take pity on herself and baby Astyanax: 407n., 431n., with 405–39n. Hector does feel pity for her but must return to the battlefield nonetheless: 484n., 485–93n.

94 Cf. *Od.* 13.182. **αἴ κ' ἐλεήσηι:** in Homeric Greek, conditional clauses with verb in the subjunctive (Aeolic αἴ = Ionic/Attic εἰ) can express a purpose: 'in the hope that she might take pity'. For ἐλεήσηι see 94–5n.

95 ἄστυ in Homer often refers to one's own city and therefore can have an emotional appeal; cf. Schmidt 2006: 440–1. Such a connotation fits the present context since ἄστυ is followed by mention of its women and children. There might be an opposition with the citadel, πόλις ἄκρη (88n.), where the temples are located; see also Lévy 1983; *LfgrE* s.vv. ἄστυ, πόλις/πτόλις. Some of the best manuscripts accentuate ἄστύ τε, which may be closer to ancient practice than the more widely attested ἄστυ τε; see M. L. West 1966: 438–42; and Probert 2003: 148–50.   καὶ νήπια τέκνα: formulaic at the end of the line. νήπιος is someone who lacks experience and, therefore, understanding. When applied to adults, the term implies reproach; when used of children it underlines their vulnerability and need for protection, cf. 400n. For discussion of its meaning and possible etymology, see Edmunds 1990; and Ingalls 1998: 17–19 and 32–4.

96–8 The hope that Athena might take pity on the Trojans is translated into a very concrete wish: that she restrain Diomedes. Helenos adds that he believes him to be the strongest of the Achaeans: the description evokes Achilles, cf. 98n. and 99–100n. Though the poet never calls Diomedes 'best of the Achaeans', two characters do so during his *aristeia*: 5.103 and 414. The poet calls Diomedes ἀνὴρ ἄριστος at 5.839.

96 αἴ κεν... ἀπόσχηι: cf. 94n. ΣAT *ad* 6.96a report that Aristarchus read ὥς κεν, and the reading is also found in a few MSS. Aristarchus had strong views about the proper use of αἰ (ΣAbT *ad* 1.100a, with Matthaios 1999: 375) and may have wanted to differentiate the second clause by giving it a more obviously final force; on ὡς see Chantraine 1948–53: vol. ii, 267.   Τυδέος υἱόν: formulaic in this position; on Tydeus: 222–3n.   ἱρῆς: a standard epithet of cities and, especially, of Troy: the city was built by the gods (21.441–9) and yet is doomed to fall; the gods will eventually punish the Achaeans for their transgressions when they take it. The epithet draws attention to the complex relationship between the city and the gods; see further Scully 1990: 16–40.

97 ἄγριον αἰχμητήν: a striking juxtaposition. Describing someone as a 'spearman' usually implies a positive judgement; cf. 1.290, 5.602. ἄγριος is less straightforward: it is used of animals or, in character speech, of enemy warriors on a rampage (cf. 8.96, 21.314). The women of Troy pick up on this description of Diomedes: Theano specifically asks Athena to 'break his spear', 306n. Diomedes' spear is also prominent in the intervening encounter with Glaukos, cf. 126n., 213n., 226n.   μήστωρα φόβοιο: a standard phrase in this metrical position. μήστωρ (< μήδομαι, 'contrive, plan'; cf. ΣD *ad* 4.328) is closely associated with proficiency in battle. Hector is described as a κρατερὸς μήστωρ φόβοιο at a point when he is most frightening to the Achaeans: 12.39.

98 δὴ ἐγώ... φημί: the particle draws out the implications of the previous statement (cf. 52–3n.), and, as often, emphasises what follows. Helenos polemically articulates his own assessment of the situation against what people generally say; cf. φασί, 99–100n. Translate: 'I, indeed, say that...'   κάρτιστον... Ἀχαιῶν: Diomedes is κρατερός in the previous line and more generally in the poem (cf. the formula κρατερὸς Διομήδης); Helenos develops this description of Diomedes and makes it much more extreme: he now claims that he is 'strongest of the Achaeans'. The phrase evokes Diomedes' exploits in book 5, cf. 96–8n., and recalls standard descriptions of Achilles as 'best of the Achaeans', ἄριστος Ἀχαιῶν, cf. G. Nagy 1999. Helenos continues by comparing Diomedes with Achilles; cf. 99–100n. Parallels between these two heroes emerge also later in the book; cf. 120n., 127n., 145n., 150–1n., 228n., 307n.

99–100 Helenos compares the present situation to previous experiences on the battlefield, when Achilles was still fighting. There is some vagueness about the past (ποθ᾽, φασί), which throws the immediate crisis into even sharper focus.   ὧδέ γ᾽ 'so much', γε emphasises the previous word and draws attention to Helenos' perception, cf. 16–17n.   ἐδείδιμεν 'we feared'; pluperf. of perf. δείδω/δείδια (< *δέδϝογα/*δέδϝια; cf. Chantraine 1948–53: vol. I, 425). An alternative form of the perfect, δείδοικα, is also attested in Homer: as often, competing forms of the same verb coexist. After singling out Hector, Helenos returns to the inclusive 1st pers. plur., cf. 84n. As appropriate for a speech of martial exhortation, he draws attention to the Trojans' shared experience in battle; cf. 70n.   ὄρχαμον ἀνδρῶν: formulaic in this position, and used of a wide range of characters. The etymology of ὄρχαμος is unclear (perhaps of the same root as ἀρχ-: for discussion see Chantraine 1999 s.v.); in the *Iliad* it is often treated as equivalent to ἀρχός, 'leader', and it sounds similar; cf. *LfgrE* s.v. ὄρχαμος B. For difficult Homeric words, see Introduction 2.2.   ὅν περ 'the very man' (41n.).   ὅν ... φασὶ θεᾶς ἐξέμμεναι: that Achilles is the son of a goddess is central to the whole *Iliad* and accounts for his exceptional strength and status; cf. 1.280, etc., and Slatkin 1992. Here, Achilles' genealogy is viewed from the perspective of the Trojans, as distant hearsay.

100–1 The closing lines drive home the central point of Helenos' speech: Hector must go on his mission because Diomedes is rampant.   ὅδε: the deictic pronoun presents Diomedes as dangerously near; cf. Chantraine 1948–53: vol. II, 168–9.   μαίνεται: a striking verb, especially at the beginning of the line. It refers to extreme energy (cf. μένος), which usually manifests itself in the form of battlefield frenzy; see Henrichs 1994: 43. It is often used in character speech, in order to spur the addressee into action: cf. 389n. Diomedes is said to 'rave' in one other passage: 5.185–6.   τίς οἱ: one of the relatively rare cases in Homer where digamma before οἱ (personal pronoun) is disregarded; cf. 90n. (ὅς οἱ).   μένος ἰσοφαρίζειν 'match in strength'. This is the manuscript reading, which also finds support in papyrus 270 West. Bentley suspected the transmitted text because it neglects initial digamma (ἶσος < ϝῖσος) and emended to ἀντιφερίζειν. Kirk 1990: 101 accepts the emendation, but ἀντιφερίζω in Homer means 'pit oneself against', with defeat as the likely outcome, and is only used of gods challenging other gods. Initial digamma cannot always be restored before ἶσος and its derivatives (Chantraine 1948–53: vol. I, 144; *LfgrE* s.v. ἶσος E). For μένος, see 26–7n.

102–9 Hector puts Helenos' advice swiftly into practice, Aeneas is no longer mentioned: 75n. A sequence of short δέ-clauses suggests brisk efficiency: the first four describe Hector's actions; the next four report the result. We then see the reaction of the Achaeans, who think that a god has intervened; cf. 107–9n. The fighting that started in book 4 now draws to a close as the Trojans make a stand and the Achaeans hold back. This temporary break is marked by the encounter between Glaukos and Diomedes, who meet 'in the middle, between the battle lines' (120); see Introduction 4.1. It also enables Hector to go back to Troy: cf. 110–18n.

102 Hector is depicted as complying with his brother's advice, not as eagerly welcoming the opportunity to return to Troy; cf. 72–118n.   **ὡς ἔφαθ':** cf. 51n. (ὡς φάτο).   **κασιγνήτωι:** already at this stage in the book the poet emphasises family relationships; cf. 76n. (Πριαμίδης).

103–5 = 5.494–6 ~ 11.211–13. In all three instances Hector leads a Trojan recovery.

103 This line occurs frequently in the *Iliad*: it typically describes a warrior who, in response to exhortation, gets down to the task at hand, either by facing the enemy or by rallying his own troops (as here).   **αὐτίκα:** often used when a character responds promptly to a speech (Erren 1970: 27–8).   **σὺν τεύχεσιν:** Hector is ready for combat; cf. 104n., 117–18n. His weapons remain prominent during his visit in Troy: 318–20n., 467–70n., 494n., 495n. and Introduction 4.   **ἆλτο:** aorist of ἅλλομαι, 'leap'; cf. Chantraine 1948–53: vol. 1, 383. As often in Homer, forms with and without aspiration coexist within the same family of words; cf. ἐπᾶλτο (rather than *ἐφᾶλτο) at 13.643, 21.140, but καθαλλομένη at 11.298.

104 **πάλλων δ' ὀξέα δοῦρα:** Hector remains determined to fight, cf. 103n. **δοῦρα:** 3n.   **πάντηι:** Hector needs to rally the whole army before he enters into the city; cf. Helenos' advice: 81n. (πάντηι ἐποιχόμενοι) and 83n. (ἀπάσας).

105 **ὀτρύνων:** Helenos told Hector and Aeneas to exhort the troops; now Hector does so; cf. 83n. His speech of exhortation is delayed until 110–15, when he tells the troops that he needs to return to Troy, cf. 110–18n.   **ἔγειρε:** literally 'he awakened'. Early readers are likely to have felt the literal meaning: cf. Solon, fr. 4.19 West, with discussion in Irwin 2005: 98. In epic, ἐγείρω is frequently said of war or battle (Ἄρης, μάχη, πόλεμος, φύλοπις), but its use is otherwise limited to people, animals, or their fighting spirit (μένος, θυμός).   **φύλοπιν αἰνήν:** cf. 1n. Hector's intervention is about to rekindle the fighting; but the Argives withdraw, so the battle comes to a temporary halt; cf. 107n.

106–7 Ἀχαιοί/-ῶν etc. is, for metrical reasons, favoured at verse end; Ἀργεῖοι etc. at verse beginning, cf. Burkert 1998: 48, and 66n.

106 οἱ δ': 9n.   **ἐλελίχθησαν** 'they turned round'. The verb is best analysed as an aorist of ἐλίσσω, 'turn around' (perhaps < ἐϝελίχθησαν), though it is identical with the corresponding aorist of ἐλελίζω, 'shake' (e.g. 22.448). For the relationship between the two verbs, see Chantraine 1948–53: vol. 1, 132. In early epic the aorist ending -θην is often intransitive rather than passive.   **καί** suggests that the actions of turning round and making a stand are part of the same process; cf. 1n.   **ἐναντίοι ἔσταν:** all the Trojans make a stand. The process of resistance began with Helenos (75n.), Aeneas and Hector (80n.).

107–9 The Achaeans suddenly retreat: they fear that a god has intervened. In book 5 the gods repeatedly fought mortals on the battlefield, so their fear is understandable:

Introduction 3.1. This is Hector's most decisive intervention since the fighting began in book 2 (Erbse 1979: 4).

107 λῆξαν δὲ φόνοιο: the idea is unusual. Homeric warriors are more often said *not* to relent in battle because of their fury etc.; cf. *Od.* 22.63.   φόνοιο 'slaughter'. The ancient variant πόνοιο, 'toil', is less good. It might have been inspired by Aristarchus' theory that πόνος in Homer always describes military action, with no implications of suffering; cf. 77n. and 524–5n.

108 φάν: unaugmented 3rd pers. plur. impf. of φημί. The verb often features in Homer where we would use 'think', as here.   τιν' ἀθανάτων: in the Homeric poems ordinary mortals are rarely in a position to identify specific gods; by and large, they suspect the involvement of 'the gods' or 'a god' in general; cf. Jörgensen 1904, and Introduction 3.1. Here, of course, no god is involved at all.   ἐξ οὐρανοῦ ἀστερόεντος: as ΣbT *ad* 15.371 point out, the poet refers 'not to the sky as it appeared then, but to its nature' (οὐ τὸν τότε ἀλλὰ τὸν φύσει), cf. Hes. *Theog.* 126–7 (Sky is born 'starry'). The gods who dwell in heaven are implicitly contrasted with 'human beings who walk on the ground' (e.g. 5.442: χαμαὶ ἐρχομένων ἀνθρώπων).

109 ὡς '(seeing) how they turned round'; for the flexible use of ὡς, see 16.17, *Od.* 17.218, and cf. 262n.   ἐλέλιχθεν: 3rd pers. plur. aor., ending in -θεν rather than Attic -θησαν, as often; for the intransitive use of the form and its derivation from ἐλίσσω, cf. 106n.

110–18 Hector has already urged the troops to fight (105n.), but his speech of exhortation is delayed until now, because he must make one more demand on them: he tells them to resist on the battlefield, so that he may go back to Troy. Before Hector's intervention, all the Trojans were about to return to the safety of the city and fall into the arms of their women (81–2n.); so the announcement that Hector alone is going back is potentially difficult to deliver. Hector's speech begins like a standard piece of martial exhortation, which traditionally encourages solidarity among men on the battlefield, cf. 112n. and Introduction 2.3. Then, the speech takes a surprising turn (113n.): he announces that he must return to Troy to talk to the elders and the Trojan wives and ask them to pray to the gods and promise sacrifices. Hector makes three strategic changes to Helenos' instructions (77–101n.). Rather than mentioning the old women, he refers to the council of old men, thus avoiding the impression that he is moving from the sphere of men (the battlefield) to that of women (the city), cf. 114n. Secondly, Helenos' emphasis on Hector's mother and personal family ties (87n.) is replaced by a reference to all the Trojan wives. Rather than making vague allusions to the women, or arousing suspicion by keeping silent about them, Hector engages specifically with the men's desire to see their wives. When he decides to look for Andromache, he is not acting behind the men's backs (365–8 with nn.). Thirdly, rather than repeating Helenos' detailed ritual instructions (90–7 with nn.), he makes a general reference to prayer and sacrifice: that is all the men need to know (115n.). Although he does not stay with the other men on the battlefield, Hector feels bound by his word to them also when he is inside the city: Introduction 4.

110 = 8.172 = 15.346, and many similar lines that introduce martial exhortations, cf. 66n.

111 = 9.233 = 11.564, with Friedrich 2007: 110, who points out that Hector's line replaces the more common, but blander, address Τρῶες καὶ Λύκιοι καὶ Δάρδανοι ἀγχιμαχηταί (attested here in some manuscripts). The Trojans and their allies are listed separately. Sometimes the term 'Trojans' is used of both the inhabitants of Troy and their allies (cf. 6n.), but there is no other collective name to describe all those fighting against the Achaeans.   ὑπέρθυμοι: of individual warriors on both sides, and of the Trojans as a group. In the *Iliad* the adjective is broadly positive; in the *Odyssey* and in Hesiod it acquires negative connotations (of the Giants and Titans). Hector uses it again at 20.366, to spur the Trojans into fighting against Achilles.   τηλεκλειτοί: a common epithet of the Trojan allies, emphasising their fame and geographic diversity (cf. 14.321: Φοίνικος τηλεκλειτοῖο). An emphasis on the far-flung allies of the Trojans was clearly embedded in the tradition: in the *Iliad* Sarpedon and the Lycians fight on the Trojan side (e.g. 2.877: τηλόθεν), as do Rhesos and his Thracian contingent. The even more exotic Amazons and Ethiopians join the Trojans in the cyclic *Aethiopis*.   ἐπίκουροι is the normal term for 'allied warriors' in Homer and is most commonly used of the Lycians; for discussion see Lavelle 1997: 230–5.

112 A common verse in the *Iliad*: injunctions to be men are always addressed to groups of warriors (no individual is told to 'be a man' in the *Iliad*) and are frequently followed by an appeal to male solidarity on the battlefield; e.g. 5.529–32, with Graziosi and Haubold 2003: 68. In this case Hector goes on to tell the men that he alone is about to leave for Troy: his plan may seem to undermine any notion of male solidarity, but his behaviour inside the city makes it clear that he feels bound by his word to the men; see Introduction 4. Zenodotus read ἀνέρες ἔστε θοοὶ καὶ ἀμύνετον ἄστεϊ λώβην. His reading is less idiomatic than that of the manuscript tradition: the dual ἀμύνετον is problematic (ἀμύνετε Leaf, West), and the phrase λώβην ἀμύνειν cannot be paralleled in Homer. Moreover, the noun ἄνδρες is not normally qualified by adjectives in injunctions to 'be men'. *Pace* Rengakos 1993: 60, Zenodotus' line seems to be a typically Hellenistic attempt to make Homeric diction more sensitive to the immediate narrative context: Introduction 6, see also Duentzer 1848: 147; Kelly 2007: 392.   φίλοι: the word suggests a sense of comradeship; cf. Nestor's address, 67n.   μνήσασθε δὲ θούριδος ἀλκῆς 'remember your courage', i.e. 'concentrate on it'; cf. *LfgrE* s.v. μιμνήσκω B. When Hector enters the city, he refuses to drink the wine his mother offers him because he is afraid that he might 'forget his courage'; cf. 265n. On ἀλκή, see D. B. Collins 1998: 78–125; and cf. 74n. (ἀναλκείῃσι δαμέντες). θοῦρις (cf. masc. θοῦρος) means 'impetuous', 'rushing' (esp. of Ares). The word acquired negative connotations in post-Homeric poetry ('furious'); e.g. Aesch. *PV* 354 (of Typhon).

113 ὄφρ᾽ ἂν ... βείω: an unusual development in a speech of martial exhortation: usually the point is to achieve victory together, not for one warrior to leave the battle line. (17.186–7 provides a partial parallel.)   ἐγώ marks a strong contrast between the role of Hector and everybody else's; cf. 86n.   βείω: 1st pers. sing. subj. aor. of βαίνω, 'go', with Ionic metathesis (βήω > βέω) and compensatory lengthening (βέω > βείω, with ει = ē̄); cf. 71n. (νεκρούς . . . τεθνειῶτας).   ἠδέ: 90n.   γέρουσιν 'elders', usually honorific, rather than simply indicating age (cf. γέρας, 'gift of honour'); though in this case only old men are left inside the city (cf. 3.146–53).

114 βουλευτῆισι 'councillors'. The word is used only here. Unlike the common term βουληφόρος/-οι, it suggests a group of expert advisers different from the men who fight on the battlefield. On councils and good counsel in Homer, see Schofield 1999. Helenos gave instructions on how to mobilise the old women of Troy (87n.); now Hector mentions the old men instead: 110–18n.   ἡμετέρηις ἀλόχοισι: rather than focusing on his own family (87n.), or on the women of Troy in general (81–2n.), Hector mentions 'our wives'. The 1st pers. plur. suggests that he considers himself part of the group he addresses: this is a typical pose in speeches of martial exhortation; cf. 58n., 70n., etc. Hector attempts to retain cohesion among men by addressing openly the very issue that might divide them: rather than letting each man think of his own wife, he mentions them together and makes them part of a common plan. For the danger that women may weaken the solidarity of men on the battlefield, see Introduction 3.2.

115 The men need not concern themselves with the details of the ritual; cf. Broccia 1963: 56.   δαίμοσιν: the word emphasises the gods' power to determine people's lives, often in a negative sense (cf. δαίομαι, 'apportion'); it is not normally used in descriptions of sacrifice or prayer in early Greek epic (though cf. *Od.* 15.261). Hector's words convey briefly how the wives are expected to help.   ἀρήσασθαι: cf. 240n. and 304n.   ἑκατόμβας: literally an offering of 100 oxen (ἑκατόν + βοῦς), though the word is used more generally of any large-scale sacrifice, e.g. of lambs. Hector translates Helenos' precise instructions (93–4n.) into a general reference to a large and proper sacrifice.

116 Speech-concluding lines typically offer guidance on how to interpret the speech; cf. 51n. Here, Hector's words are immediately translated into action: he leaves. The narrative may continue either with the character who leaves or with those who stay behind, as is the case here.   ἄρα is used for the first time since line 75 and marks the moment when, after much deliberation and preparation, Hector goes to Troy; cf. 232n.   κορυθαίολος 'of the gleaming helmet', only of Hector and, once, of Ares: Stoevesandt 2008: 47; Introduction 2.2. The Homeric κόρυς is made of bronze, contrast κυνέη, a leather cap: Borchhardt 1977: 58. For the accent, see M. L. West 1998–2000: vol. 1, xxi.

117–18 'And around him the dark skin – which circled the shield in a rim – battered his shins and neck.' Hector has slung his shield behind him: we see his back, as he runs away towards Troy. On the poet's vantage point, see Introduction 1. The animal skin that surrounds his shield forms a dark aura: cf. the description of Agamemnon's weapons at 11.32–42; and contrast Diomedes' aura of fire at 5.4–7. For further discussion of such auras, see Rollinger 1996: 159–66, who compares Near Eastern texts. Inside the city of Troy, Hector remains swift and martial, just as he is now.   ἀμφὶ δέ μιν 'around him'.   τύπτε 'battered', cf. 11.306 (the West Wind batters the clouds); and 11.560–1 (children beat a donkey). The word gives a measure of Hector's strength and endurance: we are most certainly not witnessing a cowardly retreat.   ἄντυξ: the rim of a chariot or shield; probably predicative (for the attraction of ἥ to the nearest noun ἄντυξ see Chantraine 1948–53: vol. II, 19). Some understand it as an apposition to δέρμα ('. . . a dark skin, a rim which ran around the shield').   ὀμφαλοέσσης 'with a navel' (ὀμφαλός), i.e. a central boss. The narrator has endowed Hector's body shield with features that properly belong to the round shield; cf. Kirk 1990: 169–70; and Stoevesandt 2008: 48.

119–236: THE ENCOUNTER BETWEEN GLAUKOS AND DIOMEDES

119–22 The lines are carefully balanced, suggesting that both men are eager to fight: note the arrangement of names and patronymics at 119 and the use of duals at 120. Line 122 tips the balance, casting Diomedes as the aggressor.   **119** A solemn line taken up by the names of the two opponents; cf. 20.160. Patronymics are standard (Introduction 2.3); but in the course of this encounter we are shown in greater detail how fathers shape the aspirations, character and fate of their sons: Introduction 4.1.   Γλαῦκος is introduced first and takes up most of the line, perhaps because this is the first time he plays a prominent role in the *Iliad*; cf. Diomedes' insulting remark: 124–5n. In the Catalogue of Trojans he was introduced as second-in-command of the Lycians after Sarpedon (2.876). Now that both Hector and Sarpedon are unavailable (cf. 5.655–98; and ΣbT *ad* 6.124), he suddenly advances, eager to prove himself. Given his lack of prominence earlier in the poem, the audience may wonder whether he is equal to the situation in which he has put himself – as does Diomedes, and indeed Glaukos himself; see Introduction 4.1.   Ἱππολόχοιο: a minor character, who, however, has great influence on Glaukos: 206–11n.   πάϊς: scanned as two syllables, as often in Homer.   Τυδέος υἱός: cf. 96n., 222–3n.   **120** = 20.159 (of Aeneas and Achilles).   συνίτην: i.e. they drew close to each other on their chariots (cf. 232n.; and for εἶμι = 'drive', cf. 23.7–9); on the dual, cf. 119–22n.   μεμαῶτε μάχεσθαι: μεμαῶτε is the dual participle of μέμονα, 'be eager'. The phrase is formulaic in this position and presents single combat as a matter of mutual agreement.   ἐς μέσον ἀμφοτέρων: the two armies keep apart while Glaukos and Diomedes drive forward. The phrasing makes it clear that battle is not about to resume, and that the two warriors are about to engage in a duel; cf. Kirk 1990: 171 and 3.341, 23.814. In epic the phrase ἐς μέσ(σ)ον places an event, person or object in the public sphere: e.g. 3.77–8, 3.264–6, 4.79–80, 23.704 and cf. ἐν μέσ(σ)ωι at 3.69–70, 18.263–4; see Detienne 1996: 90–103. Two of the best manuscripts (A and V in West's edition) read ἀμφοτέρω, dual nominative ('both men'), as opposed to the genitive plural ('between the two armies'), but a reference to the Trojans and the Achaeans seems effective and likely here. The same alternative readings are attested at 20.159 (where two papyri confirm ἀμφοτέρων, and their reading is followed by most editors) and at 23.814 (where recent editors prefer ἀμφοτέρω). Fluctuation between duals and plurals is attested in many other passages: see, for example, 5.156, 9.503, 22.396 and 121n. Aristarchus believed that Homer was an Athenian and that, for this reason, he was fond of using duals: ΣA *ad* 13.197, cf. Matthaios 1999: 381–2. Aristarchus' theory may have inspired attempts to correct plurals to duals where possible: this would help to account for the frequent wavering between duals and plurals in the manuscripts.

121 δή: the particle highlights the confrontation; cf. 52–3n.   ἐπ᾽... ἰόντες: the manuscripts read ἰόντες, plural; this is not a problem after the duals of 120, because, in Homeric Greek, plurals and duals are often used of the same subjects within the same passage. It seems, however, that Zenodotus, Aristophanes and Aristarchus read ἰόντε (dual); cf. 120n. (ἐς μέσον ἀμφοτέρων).

122 Diomedes has been on the attack since the beginning of book 5. Here, again, he takes charge.   προσέειπε 'he addressed (him)'; ἔειπε is a reduplicated and augmented aorist (*e-we-wk^w; root *wek^w, cf. Latin *vox*).   βοὴν ἀγαθὸς Διομήδης: 12n.

123–43 For Diomedes' speech as an example of 'flyting' (verbal assault), see Martin 1989: 126–8; and, more generally on flyting, Parks 1990. The speech is arranged in concentric circles: the cautionary tale of Lycurgus is surrounded by questions about the identity of Glaukos and assertions that Diomedes is ready to take him on; cf. Lohmann 1970: 12–13; and Kirk 1990: 172–3. The structure of the speech is not static: by the end, Diomedes' threats carry more conviction. On the dynamic use of ring composition, Introduction 2.3. The most interesting aspect of the speech is Diomedes' insistence that he will not challenge the gods. This is a crucial issue for him, both as the son of Tydeus and in light of his recent experiences on the battlefield: see further Introduction 3.1 and 4.1. Yet it also shows that Diomedes' state of mind is similar to that of the other Achaeans: 108n. We later discover that Glaukos wears golden armour: audiences who already knew the conclusion of the episode may have wondered whether his armour, as well as his sudden daring, prompted Diomedes' question; cf. 236n.

123 Construe: τίς... ἀνθρώπων (partitive genitive), literally, 'who among mortals'; cf. 15.247: τίς... θεῶν, 'who among the gods', with Janko 1994: 253. Diomedes is not simply asking for a name: he needs to establish whether Glaukos is mortal, especially after Apollo warned him not to attack the gods: 5.439–42; cf. Harries 1993: 136.   δέ after τίς expresses his surprise at seeing Glaukos ('but who are you?'); cf. 55n., 1.540, 10.82, 15.247 etc.   φέριστε is a polite form of address (Bassett 1934: 144) but in this context also suggests uncertainty as to whether the addressee is divine or mortal, see Lowry 1995: 199; cf. 15.247, of a manifest god; and 24.387, of a god in disguise. In the *Odyssey* φέριστε is ironic (cf. 1.405, 9.269), and some degree of irony may be involved here too.   καταθνητῶν ἀνθρώπων: the epithet καταθνητός occurs only here in the *Iliad*, though it is more common in the *Homeric Hymns*, the *Odyssey* and the Hesiodic corpus. It evokes a range of similar attributes that define human beings as mortal; cf. Kirk 1990: 172.

124–5 Diomedes' remark is meant as an insult: warriors are supposed to be prominent: cf., for example, 4.340–8 and 5.2–3 (the latter of Diomedes himself). Diomedes dramatises our own surprise at Glaukos' sudden appearance: we have not seen him on the battlefield either, in the course of the *Iliad*; cf. 119n. Although the poem covers only a short period of time, here as elsewhere there is a sense that the *Iliad* comes to represent, for the audience, the whole war.   μὲν γάρ: μέν points ahead to lines 125–7, γάρ looks back to 123; cf. 26–7n. and 15n.   κυδιανείρηι: from κῦδος, 'glory' and ἀνήρ, 'man'. Diomedes perhaps insinuates that Glaukos has not been acting as fighting men should: Martin 1989: 127. The gods have κῦδος and they typically bestow it on men (never on women), cf. Redfield 1994: 33–4. κυδιάνειρα is one of the few positive epithets of μάχη (cf. 1n.); it is also used of the assembly.

125–7 A stunning example of verbal aggression. Diomedes first describes his opponent as moving forward on the attack (προβέβηκας, 125), then as making a stand (ἔμεινας, 126), and finally, inevitably, meeting with defeat (127).

125 τὸ πρίν: the 'corrective' enjambment emphasises the novelty of the situation; see Introduction 2.1.   ἀτὰρ μέν: the particles impel the speech forward; cf. 125–7n.   γε occurs several times in Diomedes' speech (cf. 128–9n.) and contributes to its animated tone: Diomedes is astonished at Glaukos' daring and is not quite sure what to make of it. On γε, cf. 16–17n.   προβέβηκας ἁπάντων: suddenly, Glaukos presents himself as the bravest of the Trojans and as a match for Diomedes, 'strongest of the Achaeans' (98n.). His daring comes as a surprise to us as well as to Diomedes (119n.). His motivations become clearer in the course of his own speech: cf. 206–11n.

126 σῶι θάρσει: an undermining addition in progressive enjambment. The only reason why Glaukos could possibly face Diomedes is 'because of his own daring', and Diomedes goes on to suggest that Glaukos' daring is misplaced.   ὅτ' 'because'. ὅτε is most commonly used in a temporal sense ('when') but can also express a reason ('since'), especially after νῦν (cf. 125). For its use and spelling in Homer, see Ruijgh 1971: 810–23, esp. 815.   δολιχόσκιον ἔγχος: the phrase is normally found at the end of the line: cf. 44n. Diomedes' spear is the source of great concern in book 6: cf. 97n. and 306n. (and contrast the sense of relief at 213n.)   ἔμεινας: the usual verb for standing one's ground. Diomedes goes on to suggest that nobody can withstand him (127n.) and Helenos has already said as much in his speech to Aeneas and Hector (100–1n.).

127 = 21.151 (Achilles to Asteropaios; for the similarities between Achilles and Diomedes, cf. 98n.).   δυστήνων ... παῖδες ... ἀντιόωσιν 'wretched are the parents whose sons pit themselves against my might'; a memorable phrase, evoking the common Homeric image of the grieving parent and patronisingly treating Glaukos as young and inexperienced – fundamentally a son. Elsewhere Diomedes boasts about causing grief to the wife and children of his enemy (11.391–5). For grieving parents, cf. 59n. and Priam's speech to Hector at 22.38–76, esp. line 59 (δύστηνον); for Glaukos' characterisation as young: Introduction 4.1.   δέ signals the main point after the two μέν clauses.   τε: Diomedes' boast takes the form of a general statement and is marked as such by the epic τε; cf. Ruijgh 1971: 1–60, 648–50 (δέ τε) and especially

696. ἐμῶι μένει ἀντιόωσιν ~ 21.431, in direct speech, and expressing an extreme imbalance of power. On the meaning of μένος see 26–7n. On ἀντιόωσιν cf. 16–17n. For the form with diectasis, see 6n. and 148n.

128–9 Diomedes' speech takes a new turn. The scholia rightly point out that he echoes the thoughts of the Achaeans, as described at 108 (ΣbT *ad* 6.128). οὐρα-νοῦ: Aristarchus recommends οὐρανόν (perhaps on grammatical grounds, cf. ΣA *ad* 6.128c), but the accusative is not commonly used to describe a point of departure, see Chantraine 1948–53: vol. II, 112–14. εἰλήλουθας: perfect of ἐλθεῖν with long initial vowel; for this way of spelling long *ē*, cf. 113n. (βείω). For εἰλήλουθας describing an unexpected visit, see Létoublon 1985: 90–1. ἔγωγε: the third time in five lines that Diomedes uses the particle γε, cf. 125n.; his tone is a mixture of boasting ('I know how to handle this'), uncertainty ('who is this man?') and sarcasm ('you know what I mean'); cf. Kirk 1990: 172. ἐπουρανίοισι: the difference between gods and humans continues to be expressed with reference to the space they inhabit: cf. 108n.

130–40 Diomedes' cautionary tale falls into three sections: a brief introduction (130–1), a conclusion that summarises the main point (139–40) and a middle section that sets out the story of Lycurgus and Dionysos (132–9). The framing sections use evidential particles to draw out the moral of the story (131 ῥα, 139 ἄρ), which is simple enough: those who challenge the gods come to grief. In fact, the events which frame Diomedes' speech suggest a more complex picture: Diomedes himself attacked the gods with impunity in book 5 (see Introduction 4.1), while to Glaukos human fortunes seem random and unpredictable (155–205n., 200–2n.); cf. Gaisser 1969: 175; and Scodel 1992b: 77–8. This is the only episode featuring Lycurgus in extant epic, though Eumelos described the same incident in a now lost epic and set it in Thrace, fr. 27 West; later sources suggest that Lycurgus was a significant figure in Greek myth: Stes. fr. 234 Davies; Aesch. *Lykourgeia* (Radt 1985: 234); and Soph. *Ant.* 955–65; ΣT *ad* 6.130, like the tragedians, identify him as king of the Edonians. This is one of the few passages which mention Dionysos in early epic, see Privitera 1970: 53–74. Dionysos' concerns (primarily: wine, revelry, madness, orgiastic sex, life after death) are marginal to the Trojan saga and, as a god who blurs the boundaries between gods and mortals, he may not suit a poem that insists on the differences between the two (M. Davies 2000). In this episode he is mentioned precisely as a limit-case: even the least martial of gods should not be attacked. As a side effect, Diomedes' choice of god ensures that he pays no compliment to Glaukos: Dionysos is infantile, the only reason why he should not be attacked is his divinity. Diomedes' tale recalls specific Dionysiac rituals (Granata 1991: 627; Henrichs 1994: 43–4; M. Davies 2000: 23–5), as well as evoking the themes and structure of the *Homeric Hymns*, thereby further emphasising Lycurgus' perverse behaviour. The *Hymns* often start with the birth of a god, tell of his or her ascent to Olympus and show how the newcomer is accepted by Zeus and the other gods; see Clay 1989. This episode begins with a newborn Dionysos (132n.), then follows him downwards, into the depths of the sea (136n.) and ends with Zeus acting on his behalf (139–40). Hom. *Hymn* 26 (of uncertain date; cf. Càssola 1975: 407–9 and 581) offers some close points of comparison, as do *Hymns* 1, 3, 4, 7 and 19.

We should not expect specific intertextual allusions: the tale of Lycurgus recalls the *Homeric Hymns* because they represent the appropriate genre in which to recount the adventures of a god. For traditional story patterns, see Introduction 2.3.

130–1 οὐδὲ . . . οὐδέ: the expression is emphatic; cf. Chantraine 1948–53: vol. ii, 337–8. γάρ introduces an embedded narrative, as often in Homer; cf. de Jong 1997. υἱός: the first syllable is open and hence measured short (ʰu-yos). κρατερὸς Λυκόοργος: cf. the recurrent κρατερὸς Διομήδης, in the same metrical position. Diomedes is exceptionally strong (cf. 98n.); yet in book 5 Dione claims that his κράτος is no adequate protection against the gods (cf. 5.410–11). δὴν ἦν: placed in necessary enjambment, this is the first of three rhymes in Diomedes' speech: cf. 139–40n. (using the same words in a different metrical context) and 143n. For δήν, cf. Dione's complaint at 5.407.

131–2 ὅς ῥα . . . ὅς ποτε: the two relative clauses have complementary tasks: the first states the main point of the story (ῥα + imperfect tense); the second introduces a detailed account of what happened (ποτε + aorist). The first clause matches closely line 129: Lycurgus did precisely what Diomedes says he would never do; cf. also 140–1n. θεοῖσιν ἐπουρανίοισιν ἔριζεν: cf. 129 (θεοῖσιν ἐπουρανίοισι μαχοίμην) and 130–1n. for Lycurgus as Diomedes' *alter ego*. ἔριζεν: translate 'he challenged'; cf. Hes. fr. 30.23 MW. ἔρις is thematic in the *Iliad* (e.g. 1.6) and central to the heroes' existence (e.g. *Cypria*, fr. 1 West, with Hogan 1981), but it is not an appropriate response to a god.

132 μαινομένοιο: Dionysos and his followers were closely associated with madness in ancient Greece; cf. Burkert 1985: 161–7. The god's madness corresponds to the experience of his followers (Henrichs 1994: 41–7; cf. ΣA *ad* 6.132a); for frenzied Dionysiac females in early hexameter epic, cf. Hes. fr. 131 MW; *Il.* 22.460; and *Hom. Hymn* 2.386. For other uses of the verb, see 100–1n., 160n. and 389n. Διωνύσοιο: in this passage and in *Hom. Hymns* 7 and 26, Dionysos already displays the main characteristics we know from later portrayals, esp. Eur. *Bacchae*. He is not virile (in this story not so much effeminate as babyish), he shares the company of nursing females in a bucolic setting (cf. the suckling maenads at *Bacch.* 699–702), he is slighted by an aggressive man who fails to recognise his power and eventually exacts his revenge not by using violence himself, but by relying on female support. On the continuities in the portrayal of Dionysos, see Wathelet 1991. τιθήνας: *Hom. Hymn* 26 tells us that Zeus entrusted baby Dionysos to the nymphs of Nysa, but in the *Iliad* the identity of his nurses is left entirely vague; Dionysos appears in the company of his nurses also in later texts (e.g. Soph. *OC* 680).

133 σεῦε: a strong word, elsewhere used of chasing dogs and other animals; cf. 11.293–4, 15.680–2, *Od.* 6.88–9, 14.35–6; *Hom. Hymn* 2.375–9. ἠγάθεον < ἀγα- + θεός, primarily of places inhabited or frequented by the gods (Vermeule 1974: 125–6). Νυσήϊον: the birthplace of Dionysos, also called Νύση and usually described as a mountain (*Hom. Hymns* 1 A 9 West and 26.5). Its location varies from source to source and its main characteristic is remoteness (cf. *Hom. Hymn* 1 A 7–14 West; *Hom. Hymn* 2.17 with N. J. Richardson 1974: 148–9). Ancient readers already linked it to the name (Dio)nysos: ΣT *ad* 6.132*b*.   αἳ δ᾽ ἅμα πᾶσαι: Dionysos and his retinue are persecuted as a group, as is typical of later stories of this type, cf. Eur. *Bacchae*.

134 θύσθλα: objects associated with the cult of Dionysos, possibly thyrsos staffs (Krauskopf 2001, esp. p. 47); though the exact meaning of this word was debated in antiquity (ΣbT *ad* 6.134) and remains unclear today (*LfgrE* s.v. θύσθλα; Kirk 1990: 174). As often, the language of cult is at once precise and impenetrable; cf. 93–4n. The addition of θύσθλα in enjambment makes it clear that Lycurgus is not simply chasing women but engaging in an act of profanation.   χαμαί 'on the ground' or 'to the ground', as here. The word evokes Lycurgus' violence: it is used of weapons or limbs falling to the ground when somebody is killed or wounded; see 5.582–3, 13.529–30 and 578; cf. 16.802–3, 22.448.   ὑπ᾽: best construed with Λυκούργου rather than βουπλῆγι; cf. George 2005: 62.   ἀνδροφόνοιο: the epithet describes warriors (mostly Hector), especially when they are seen through the eyes of the enemy; cf. 498n. It underlines how inappropriate Lycurgus' behaviour is in this context; he is not about to kill a man; rather, he is attacking an immortal god and his female retinue; cf. 137n.

135 θεινόμεναι βουπλῆγι: an extreme example of necessary enjambment, which adds a shocking detail: the nurses are chased with an implement that seems designed to coerce cattle. The precise meaning of βουπλήξ was debated already in antiquity, but it was always taken to be formed on the basis of βοῦς, 'ox', and πλήσσω, 'strike'. Dionysos is often depicted as having the attributes of a bull, cf. Eur. *Bacch.* 100, with Seaford 1996: 160.   φοβηθείς: for the meaning of φοβέομαι ('panic, flee' rather than simply 'fear'), see 41n. Zenodotus read χολωθείς, 'angered', perhaps in order to restore some dignity to the god, but this does not fit the story. For Zenodotus' preoccupation with 'propriety' (τὸ πρέπον) especially concerning the gods, see van der Valk 1963–4: vol. II, 11–22. For an alternative explanation concerning Zenodotus' reading, see Nickau 1977: 193.

136 δύσεθ᾽ ἁλὸς κατὰ κῦμα: for the association between Dionysos and the sea, cf. *Hom. Hymn* 7; Otto 1965: 162–4; Burkert 1985: 166; M. Davies 2000: 21, n. 22; *LIMC* s.v. *Dionysos* 788–90 and 827–9. Dionysos' downward journey underlines Lycurgus' crime: cf. the parallels with Hephaistos' fall from Olympus, discussed below.   δύσεθ᾽: a so-called 'mixed' aorist, with σ and thematic vowel ε (Risch 1974: 250; Roth 1990); some manuscripts have the form in -σάτο. Manuscripts often report alternatives of this kind, and the matter was much debated also in antiquity; cf. van der Valk 1963–4: vol. II, 172–4. Modern editors prefer the mixed aorist here because it is better attested; cf. van Thiel 1991: xxv.   κατά: cf. κατέχευαν at 134. The downward movement is emphasised by the repeated use of κατά.   Θέτις also rescued baby Hephaistos when Hera cast him out of Olympus and into the sea: 18.394–405, and cf. *Hom. Hymn* I as discussed by M. L. West 2001b: 3. More generally, in the *Iliad*, Thetis is conceived of as a primordial mother and a counterweight to Olympian power: Slatkin 1992.   κόλπωι: the bosom, and more specifically the part of the *peplos* which covers it in a deep fold (van Wees 2005: 7), see further 400n.

The nymphs take baby Dionysos to their bosom in *Hom. Hymn* 26.4; Eurynome and Thetis welcome the newborn Hephaistos to their bosom at *Il.* 18.398.

137 Dionysos is depicted as utterly helpless. He deserves respect not on account of his courage (he has none), but because he is a god. Diomedes emphasises the categorical difference between gods and mortals and never suggests that he is impressed by Glaukos' daring. δειδιότα is used in progressive enjambment, as often in epic. Thetis' embrace is brief (contrast 18.394–405): the emphasis remains on the trauma sustained by Dionysos. For δειδιότα (participle of the perfect δείδω/δείδια), cf. 99–100n. κρατερός: cf. κρατερὸς Λυκόοργος (130–1n.). All that seems 'mighty' about Dionysos is his fear, though he is in fact much more powerful than his opponent. In *Hom. Hymn* 7, Dionysos seems equally helpless until he reveals himself as a καρτερὸς θεός (17–18). ἀνδρὸς ὁμοκλῆι: ὁμοκλῆι implies that Lycurgus feels superior to Dionysos (cf. 54n. with 12.413 and *Od.* 17.189); ἀνδρός exposes the fact that is not.

138 This is the first line which does not start in enjambment since the beginning of the story at 132. Lycurgus' irruption had momentarily upset the proper order of hexameter verse: Introduction 2.1. τῶι μέν prepares for a shift in focus from Lycurgus to Diomedes; cf. 140–1n. (οὐδ᾽ ἂν ἐγώ). ἔπειτ᾽ signals a crucial turning point in the story of Lycurgus; cf. 37–8n. ὀδύσαντο 'they became angry'. The verb is used almost exclusively of the gods: cf. *LfgrE* s.v. ὀδύσ(σ)ασθαι. Whereas the *Homeric Hymns* typically end with the gods rejoicing, this story ends with their anger. On the similarities between Diomedes' tale and the *Homeric Hymns*, cf. 130–40n. θεοὶ ῥεῖα ζώοντες = *Od.* 4.805, 5.122, both in direct speech. The rare phrase pointedly contrasts the carefree existence of the gods with the miseries of mortals (cf. 24.525–6). It also underlines the futility of Lycurgus' violence: ultimately, he cannot affect the gods' blissful existence.

139–40 Zeus sides with the newborn Dionysos; for parallel patterns in the *Homeric Hymns*, cf. 130–40n. καί: 106n. τυφλόν: only here and at *Hom. Hymn* 3.172 in early Greek epic; the standard word for 'blind' in epic is ἀλαός. Blindness may be perceived as analogous to death (cf. 11n. and formulae such as ὁρᾶν φάος ἠελίοιο = 'to be alive'); it is a standard punishment for transgressions against the immortals, cf. Hes. fr. 275 MW; Stesichorus, fr. 192 Davies, and Graziosi 2002: 138–50. Κρόνου παῖς: cf. 234n. and Introduction 2.4. ἄρ: 130–40n. δήν < δϝήν: the last syllable of ἔτι is measured long. ἦν: one of the bluntest cases of necessary enjambment in Homeric poetry. The rhythm of line 139 comes to an abrupt halt, as does Lycurgus' life. Cf. 130–1n. for the same phrase in ring composition; on rhyming words in Diomedes' speech (δήν | ἦν): 143n.

140–1 The point of the story is straightforward: the gods hated Lycurgus for his behaviour, therefore Diomedes plans to act differently. Glaukos will shortly use similar words in order to paint a different picture: for him, the gods are inscrutable and their anger sudden and unpredictable: 200–2n. Diomedes' conclusion echoes his opening statement (128–9n.) but puts greater emphasis on his intentions (ἐθέλοιμι): he has learnt from Lycurgus' bad example. ἀπήχθετο: from ἐχθάνομαι, 'become hateful'. Diomedes has recently demanded Athena's friendship (5.117, φῖλαι), now he considers what it means to be hated by the gods.   οὐδ' ἂν ἐγώ takes up 138n. (τῷ μέν), and echoes line 139 (οὐδ' ἄρ), with potential ἂν in place of evidential ἄρ. For Diomedes and Lycurgus as contrasting foils, cf. 130–1n.

142 Diomedes returns to his original hypothesis: 123n.; for ring composition, cf. 123–43n.   οἳ ἀρούρης καρπὸν ἔδουσιν ∼ 21.465. Mortals are grain-eaters, the gods are not: 5.341–2, 13.322; cf. Kitts 1994: 136–42.

143 ἄσσον... θᾶσσον = 20.429 (Achilles to Hector). Another striking rhyme in Diomedes' speech, cf. 130–1n. and 139–40n. Word play and rhymes are common in epic, especially in speeches; cf. Macleod 1982: 50–3; Louden 1995; and Introduction 2.4. They are especially frequent in Diomedes' speech and add to his aggressive and patronising tone. At 5.440 Apollo used a similar jingle to put Diomedes in his place (φράζεο... καὶ χάζεο). There is a sense that Diomedes is responding to his experiences in book 5; cf. Introduction 4.1.   ὀλέθρου πείραθ' ἵκηαι: the phrase concludes Diomedes' challenge in a grim and memorable way. It recalls phrases of the type πείρατα γαίης (πείρατα = 'limit'), though expressions such as ὀλέθρου πείρατ' ἐφῆπται (πείρατα = 'bonds') are also relevant, see further Bergren 1975: 35–40.

144–211 On this speech, and on Glaukos' characterisation in the *Iliad* more generally, see further Introduction 4.1.

144 There is no authorial comment rounding off Diomedes' speech; this line moves straight to Glaukos' reply.   αὖθ': 73n.   Ἱππολόχοιο: 119n. and 206–11n.   φαίδιμος: 26–7n.

145 ∼ 21.153 (Asteropaios to Achilles). Glaukos rephrases Diomedes' question (cf. 123n.), thus shifting the emphasis from his behaviour, as compared with that of other men on the battlefield, to his identity as revealed by his ancestry. Ultimately, it is because of his family connections, rather than his prowess, that he survives the encounter with Diomedes: 212–31n. On Glaukos' speech as a 'lineage boast', see Lang 1994. On genealogy and personal identity in epic: cf. 206–11n.; Grethlein 2006a: 65–84; and Introduction 2.2.   Τυδείδη: 96n., 222–3n., 235n. Unlike Diomedes, Glaukos knows the identity of his opponent.   τίη: 55n. Translate 'why ever?'.   γενεήν: an individual family line, a generation (e.g. 1.250), or an entire race (Hes. *Op.* 160). Glaukos exploits the semantic range: 146n. and 149n.

146–9 The simile of the leaves, much admired also in antiquity: 146n. The basic comparison between leaves and human life seems to have been a widespread motif: cf. 21.464–6; Musaeus, fr. 5 DK; Mimnermus, fr. 2 West; Aristoph. *Birds* 685; for further discussion see Sider 1996; Susanetti 1999; Burgess 2001: 117–26; and Grethlein 2006a: 85–94. Glaukos employs the motif as a form of εἰκάζειν, a comparison calculated to gain the rhetorical upper hand; cf. Pelliccia 2002. Glaukos' formulation emphasises the shared fate of all humankind (147–8n.), thus implicitly revealing that he is not a god (cf. 128–9n.) and exposing Diomedes' boasts as futile (cf. 123–43n.). The passage sets the tone for the rest of Glaukos' speech: although he eventually gives a long genealogical account of himself, he emphasises the vagaries of human fate (cf. 147n., 150–211n.).

146 Simonides praises this line as 'the finest thing the Chian man said' (fr. 19.1–2 West): this is the earliest explicit quotation from the *Iliad*; see Introduction 2. Simonides goes on to complain that although the phrase rings in people's ears, few take it to heart: most people insist on nourishing empty hopes for themselves (19.3–5 West). Although Simonides treats the line as a nugget of Homeric wisdom, his interpretation also fits the context in which the line is uttered: Glaukos suggests that Diomedes' interest in individual identity and achievement is futile; cf. 150–1n. **οἵη . . . τοίη:** the placing of these two words makes the line balanced and memorable; on rhyming words, cf. 143n. This line can stand on its own, with οἵη picked up by τοίη, but Glaukos expands it into a longer comparison governed by ὥς (149). **περ** invites us to contemplate the precise nature of the comparison; cf. 41n. **φύλλων:** a pun on φῦλα, 'tribes', which is close in meaning to γενεή = 'race'; cf. the formulaic phrases φῦλ' ἀνθρώπων and φῦλα θεῶν (e.g. 14.361, 15.51; cf. 5.441–2), and 148n. The version of the leaf simile attributed to Musaeus makes the pun explicit: ὣς δὲ καὶ ἀνθρώπων γενεὴ καὶ φῦλον ἑλίσσει (5.3 DK). Punning language is a feature of wisdom literature and is also found in competitive εἰκάζειν. Here, it encourages a shift in meaning from γενεή = 'family' to γενεή = 'race'; cf. 145n. For δέ after subordinate clauses, see Bakker 1997a: 70 and 475n.

147–8 The lines follow the seasonal pattern: first autumn, then spring. Apollo at 21.464–6 and Mimnermus, fr. 2 West contemplate human lives from youth to old age; Glaukos focuses on generational change, rather than the life of an individual person (Piccaluga 1980: 248); for Simonides' interpretation of Glaukos' simile, cf. 146n.

147 **μέν τ'. . . δέ θ':** generalising τε; cf. 127n. The combination of μέν τε and δέ τε is found only eight times in Homer (Ruijgh 1971: 662), in similes or maxims. Glaukos chooses a particularly rare and striking way of expressing a time-less truth. **ἄνεμος . . . ὕλη:** Diomedes emphasised human choice, Glaukos likens human beings to leaves entirely at the mercy of the winds and seasons; cf. 146–9n., Introduction 4.1. **ἄνεμος χαμάδις χέει:** trees lose their leaves in autumn (cf. Hes. *Op.* 417–21; *Od.* 5.483–5); winds announce the arrival of the cold season (Hes. *Op.* 504–11 and fr. 204.124–6 MW): seasonal change is implied here and explicitly mentioned in the next line.

148 Aristophanes of Byzantium read: τηλεθόωντα φύει, ἔαρος δ'ἐπιγίνεται ὥρῃ 'the wood generates others as they bloom, and they appear again in spring time' (ΣΑΤ *ad* 6.148a), thus keeping the focus on the leaves throughout. Homeric similes, however, often veer off the immediate point of comparison, so a parenthetic clause is not in itself unlikely: 'the blooming wood generates others, and springtime appears again'. Aristophanes' τηλεθόωντα cannot be right: τηλεθάω is never used of leaves in early epic (whereas it is, conversely, used of blossoming woods, cf. ὕλη τηλεθόωσα, *Od.* 5.63.), and the epic form of the participle is in any case τηλεθάοντα (cf. 22.423 etc.), not τηλεθόωντα. ὥρῃ is attractive, especially in view of 2.468 and *Od.* 9.51; it is, however, problematic to accept only half of Aristophanes' text. For a close parallel see Mimnermus, fr. 2.1–2 West: φύλλα φύει πολυάνθεμος ὥρη | ἔαρος. **τηλεθόωσα:** a frequent epithet of plants and especially trees (from a lengthened form of θάλλω, 'blossom'). For the ending -όωσα with diectasis, cf. 6n. (φόως), and see Chantraine 1948–53: vol. ι, 75–83.   φύει echoes φύλλα above; for word play, cf. 143n. and 146n.   ἔαρος δ᾽ ἐπιγίνεται ὥρη: the seasons are closely connected to the rhythms of ordinary human life in early hexameter epic: in Hesiod's *Theog.* 901–3 the ῟Ωραι are born towards the end of the creation of the universe, for the specific purpose of attending to (ὠρεύω) the works of humankind; in the *Works and Days* those human activities are carefully planned according to the seasons. In the heroic world, seasonal change hardly features (Graziosi and Haubold 2005: 88–9); in the *Iliad* the noun ὥρη (as opposed to the divine name) occurs predominantly in similes: 2.468 and 471, 16.643; cf. 21.450 (in direct speech).

149 After describing the seasonal cycle of nature from autumn to spring Glaukos now inverts the order: human beings grow and then die; cf. Susanetti 1999: 99– 100.   **ὡς ἀνδρῶν γενεή** looks back to οἵη περ φύλλων γενεή at 146 (γενεή = 'race'), suggests the idea of generational renewal (γενεή = 'generation') and looks ahead to γενεή = 'family' at 151. For the hiatus after γενεή see 8n.   **ὥς:** 146n.   **ἣ μὲν . . . ἣ δ᾽:** translate 'one (generation) . . . the other'. Grethlein 2006b: 8–9 insists on the translation 'partly (the race of humans) . . . partly', but Glaukos uses the different meanings of γενεή to forge a transition back from the general to the particular: cf. 150– 1n. (ἡμετέρην γενεήν).   **φύει:** in the active, this verb usually takes an accusative. The rule is broken here in the interest of creating a close verbal echo; cf. Pelliccia 2002: 218–20 with reference to Hes. *Op.* 5. Translate: 'thrives'.

150–211 After his simile, Glaukos offers a long account of his family history, which he presents as a concession to Diomedes' interest in his identity (150–1n.). For all that Glaukos boasts about his ancestors and feels he must not shame them (206–11n.), the overall effect of his genealogical account tallies with his opening simile: human fortunes are changeable and beyond individual control (Grethlein 2006a: 94– 5). Genealogies can be constructed in such a way as to converge on one individual, lending him special strength and authority. In Glaukos' account, Bellerophontes takes centre stage (155–205n.) and is surrounded by minimal outlines of the two generations that preceded him (153–5) and the two that followed (196–210). The portrayal of Bellerophontes remains enigmatic, however: 155–205n., 191n. Glaukos draws little attention to himself and is partly eclipsed, in his own account, by the brief description of his cousin Sarpedon (198–9n., 199n.).

150–1 = 20.213–14 (Aeneas to Achilles); for other echoes between this episode and Achilles' actions in books 20 and 21, cf. 120n. and 145n. The line is disparaging: after the simile of the leaves, Diomedes' interest in his opponent's identity is presented as futile. Cf. Simonides, fr. 19 West, discussed at 146n.   **ἐθέλεις:** Glaukos echoes Diomedes' ἐθέλοιμι at 141; cf. 140–1n.   **καὶ ταῦτα:** the only lesson of any importance has already been taught; for the dismissive tone, cf. 70n. (καὶ τά).   **δαήμεναι** 'learn'; inf. aor. of a root *da*- (cf. διδάσκω), the present is not attested.   **ἡμετέρην γενεήν:** the phrase, placed in necessary enjambment, functions as a heading for the genealogy that follows; cf. 206–11n.   **πολλοὶ δέ μιν ἄνδρες ἴσασιν:** a putdown, answering Diomedes' insults (124–5n.).

152 ἔστι πόλις Ἐφύρη: the formulation with ἔστι introduces an obscure place that acquires sudden prominence; cf. 2.811–15 (Batieia), 11.711–12 (Thryoessa), 722–4 (Minyeios), 13.32–4 (an unnamed cave where Poseidon leaves his horses), with Fornaro 1992: 40–3. Unlike the above parallels, this passage lacks a connective particle, because it is the main clause in the period that started at 150: 'But if you want to learn those things too, so that you may know well my genealogy, and many men know it, there is a city . . .' Ἐφύρη: ancient readers (ΣAbT *ad* 6.152*a-c*) took this to be a reference to Corinth. The idea is first attested in Eumelos, *Corinthiaca*, frr. 15–19 West, and became widely accepted: in the later mythographical tradition Sisyphos did indeed come from Corinth (e.g. Pind. *Ol.* 13.49ff.) and Bellerophon was thought to have tamed Pegasos in that city. (Pegasos also featured on Corinthian coinage.) There is, however, no evidence that Ἐφύρη was an alternative name for Corinth in Homer (for Κόρινθος, see 2.570, 13.664; cf. Hes. fr. 204.48 MW). Aristarchus got round the problem by claiming that Homer called the city 'Corinth' in his own voice, but 'Ephyre' in character speech; cf. Lehrs 1882: 228. A city called Ἐφύρη, on the river Selleeis in western Greece (Thesprotia or Elis?), is mentioned at 2.659, 15.531 and perhaps again at *Od.* 1.259. The Ἔφυροι mentioned at 13.301 appear to come from Thessaly. In early epic, places of this name seem shrouded in mystery: they refer to the distant origins of an exotic piece of weaponry (15.529–34, *Od.* 1.259–62), a bride (2.659) or an entire family (as here); for ancient and modern speculations about them, see Janko 1994: 85, 287.   μυχῶι: the phrase suggests that Ephyre is located in a secluded and hidden area; cf. *Od.* 3.263; Hes. *Theog.* 119 and 1015–16.   Ἄργεος: in epic the name is used of the city of Argos, of the Peloponnese and even of the whole of the Achaean world, when contrasted to the city of Troy: Wathelet 1992; Burkert 1998; and Cingano 2004. The latter meaning is relevant here: though Glaukos now fights on the Trojan side, his family originally came from a remote place in 'Argos'.   ἱπποβότοιο: cf. ἵππος, βόσκω, 'nourishing horses'; a frequent epithet of Argos.

153 Σίσυφος: the well-known trickster (cf. Hes. fr. 10a.26 MW Σίσυφος αἰολομήτης), punished for his crimes with perennial suffering. The story of how he tried to cheat death is not told in extant epic but is certainly old: cf. Alcaeus, fr. 38a Voigt, and Theognis 702–12. Some crime against the gods is implied at *Od.* 11.593–600 (cf. *Od.* 11.580–1, on Tityos). At Hes. fr. 43a.75–80 MW we hear that Zeus thwarted Sisyphos' plans for his son. Glaukos thus starts his genealogy with a character who challenged the gods, much like Lycurgus in Diomedes' speech (130–40n.), but fails to mention his ancestor's crime: we are left to wonder how much Glaukos deliberately leaves out, and how much he does not know; see Introduction 4.1. Later Glaukos offers a similarly opaque account of Bellerophontes' relationship to the gods: 200–2n.   ἔσκεν, like ἔστι at line 152, emphasises Diomedes' ignorance; for the form, cf. 19n.   κέρδιστος: a reference to Sisyphos' notorious cunning. The superlative is directly derived from the noun κέρδος ('gain, advantage'): cf. 410n. (ἐμοὶ δέ κε κέρδιον εἴη), with Risch 1974: 89.

154 Σίσυφος Αἰολίδης: a ponderous repetition of Sisyphos' name in progressive enjambment: it introduces the genealogy proper, see Fornaro 1992: 40, n. 68. Aiolos heads his family line in the Hesiodic *Catalogue of Women*: frr. 9 and 10a.25–34 MW; cf. *Od.* 11.237.   **Γλαῦκον:** a marginal character; Glaukos junior seems to be named after the most insignificant character in the genealogy he offers. For traditional stories linked to Glaukos, son of Sisyphos, and other characters of that name, see Paladino 1978.

155–205 The rise and fall of Bellerophontes, the central character in Glaukos' genealogy. Most of Bellerophontes' story follows a pattern familiar from children's stories and folk tales; see Thompson 1955–8: τ68 and cf. 160–5n., 170n., 178–86n., 178n., 187–90n., 191–5n. Pindar retells part of Bellerophontes' story at *Ol.* 13.83–92. Glaukos does not explain why the gods suddenly forsook Bellerophontes: either he does not know the reason or he does not want to reveal it; contrast Pind. *Isthm.* 7.43–8, though Pindar too is reluctant to discuss Bellerophontes' disgrace at *Ol.* 13.91. Early audiences may well have thought they knew what had happened: cf. 200–2n., Gaisser 1969: 170–4; and Alden 2000: 138–9. Glaukos invests the story of Bellerophontes with great significance, but it is hard to see what conclusions should be drawn from it. At least two readings are suggested within Glaukos' speech itself: that of his father Hippolochos, who uncompromisingly demands that Glaukos live up to the family's glorious past (cf. 206–11n.); and that implied by Glaukos' simile of the leaves, which presents fate as variable and ultimately beyond human control (cf. 146–9n., Susanetti 1999). Diomedes draws yet another conclusion from Glaukos' account of Bellerophontes: 212–31n.

155 In Hes. fr. 43a.81–3 MW and in other sources, Bellerophontes is the son of Poseidon; though in fr. 43a.82 MW, we are also told that he was born 'to Glaukos'. It is not unusual for epic characters to have a divine and a human father; cf. the traditional epithets for Heracles: Ἀμφιτρυωνιάδης and Διὸς υἱός. Later in this speech Bellerophontes is described as 'the offspring of a god' (θεοῦ γόνος), but his relationship to the gods remains opaque: 191n., 200–2n. Bellerophontes shares some other similarities with Heracles: he completes a series of challenges set by a king (cf. 1.78–86n.), he is a monster slayer (cf. 179–83n.) and is famous both for his excellence and his crimes (cf. 200–2n. and Introduction 4.1.)   **αὐτάρ** marks an important moment in Glaukos' genealogical account; cf. 83n.   **ἔτικτεν:** used of both men and women. For the imperfect, see Kirk 1990: 178. Translate: 'he fathered'.   **ἀμύμονα:** at the moment of his birth Bellerophontes is introduced by his standard epithet: cf. 190n., and 216n. At 171n. ἀμύμων is associated with the divine favour he enjoys. On the meaning of the epithet, cf. 22n.   **Βελλεροφόντην:** never Βελλεροφῶν in epic. Zenodotus discussed the alternative form Ἐλλεροφόντης, probably in an attempt to etymologise his name (ἔλλερα = κακά; Ἐλλεροφόντης = 'killer of evil things'); cf. M. L. West 2001a: 43. The etymology of transmitted Βελλεροφόντης is unclear and was discussed also in antiquity; see Gaisser 1969: 169 with n. 15; von Kamptz 1982: 29 and 186; Watkins 1995: 385, n. 4; Katz 1998: 325–8; and Stoevesandt 2008: 63–4.

156 We are not told why the gods favour Bellerophontes, though other epic sources say that he was the son of Poseidon and some such connection may be implied here: 155n., 191n. In the Hesiodic *Catalogue of Women* we are told that Poseidon gave the magic horse Pegasos to his son Bellerophontes, and that he killed the Chimaira with the help of the horse (Hes. fr. 43a.84–8 MW; cf. Hes. *Theog.* 325); others add that he used it to ascend to heaven, but was thrown off (Pind. *Isthm.* 7.43–8; cf. Hes. *Theog.* 284–6, where *only* Pegasos ascends to heaven). Here Bellerophontes receives more ordinary gifts – beauty and lovely manliness – though they too turn out to be very dangerous for him, 160–5n.   κάλλος: a straightforward and positive quality in some contexts (e.g. 21.108, of Achilles), though potentially destructive in others (as Paris and Helen demonstrate).   ἠνορέην ἐρατεινήν: usually, ἠνορέη involves solidarity with other men and respect for their households (Graziosi and Haubold 2003); but Bellerophontes' manliness is qualified as 'lovely' (ἐρατεινή – the adjective is not otherwise used of men) and attracts Anteia, thus bringing him into conflict with her husband Proitos: 160–5n.

157 ὤπασαν: a striking case of necessary enjambment, emphasising the role of the gods in shaping Bellerophontes' life.   αὐτάρ οἱ Προῖτος κάκ' ἐμήσατο θυμῶι: a drastic change of tone from Glaukos' genealogical catalogue. The particle αὐτάρ (83n., 155n.) marks a new phase in his speech; the lack of an epithet for Proitos and the brisk κάκ' ἐμήσατο add to the sense that Bellerophontes' life is being brutally disrupted. As it stands, the line is also metrically uncomfortable: it disregards Hermann's bridge, see Introduction 2.1. Aristarchus read κακὰ μήσατο, which ensures metrical regularity (cf. 10.52, 14.253, and *Od.* 24.199); but the transmitted text should not be emended for the sake of smoothness; cf. van Thiel 1991: xxiv–xxvii.   Προῖτος: only here in the *Iliad* and *Odyssey* but prominent in the Hesiodic *Catalogue of Women*: fr. 37.10 MW implies that he rules in Argos; fr. 129.10–17 MW seems to claim that his brother Akrisios rules in Argos, whereas he founds Tiryns. Bacchyl. 11.59–81 tells the story of how Akrisios ousted Proitos from Argos. The *Iliad* remains vague about the exact nature of Proitos' power; cf. 158n., 159n. According to the *Catalogue* and later authors, he is the husband of Stheneboia (fr. 129.18 MW) and father of the Proitids (frr. 129–33 MW). His daughters angered Hera and perhaps Dionysos (Henrichs 1974; M. L. West 1985: 78–9) and were punished with madness; cf. Hes. fr. 131 MW; Bacchyl. 11.43–112. One Hesiodic fragment (fr. 132 MW) mentions the Proitids' μαχλοσύνη, a sexual derangement affecting women (and Paris); cf. Hes. *Op.* 586. Here the emphasis is on the sexual incontinence of Proitos' wife: 160–5n.   κάκ' ἐμήσατο θυμῶι: the phrase functions as a headline; the poet then works backward to the causes of Proitos' evil plan (160–5n.), and describes it in greater detail (167–70n.).   θυμῶι: 51n.

158 ῥ': 2n. Throughout this section, the particle ἄρα draws attention to the details of Proitos' schemes, and those of his father-in-law: cf. 167n., 177n., 179n., 180n., 187n.   δήμου: here, and more generally in early epic, 'land' and the people who inhabit it. Only occasionally does the term describe the common people as opposed to the élite in Homer; cf. 2.198–9, 12.212–14 with *LfgrE* s.v. δῆμος B.   ἐπεὶ πολὺ φέρτερος ἦεν: a standard formula. We are not told exactly why Proitos is more powerful than Bellerophontes, though the implication here, and in the next line, is that he has royal privileges; cf. 157n. and 163n.

159 Ἀργείων: best taken with δήμου ('the land of the Argives'), rather than φέρτερος ('more powerful than the [other] Argives'). The difficult syntax results in a 'floating' runover whose main effect is to suggest Proitos' power over Bellerophontes, without going into any details about his exact position in Argos (for the story of how Proitos was ousted from Argos by his brother Akrisios, cf. 157n.). There is no need to suspect a later interpolation, as Kirk does (1990: 179). Ζεὺς ... ἐδάμασσε expresses Proitos' power over Bellerophontes; the compound verb ὑποδάμνημι emphasises Proitos' position of absolute control and perhaps suggests the use of violence (cf. *Od.* 3.304; *Hom. Hymn* 3.543); according to later sources (e.g. Eur. *Stheneboia, TrGF* v.2 (61) F 661.16–18), Bellerophontes sought Proitos' protection after he had committed a murder. γάρ: 15n. οἱ '(subjected) to him'. The alternative reading μιν ('him', i.e. Bellerophontes) looks like an attempt at clarification.

160–5 No women have been mentioned up to this point, although they often feature in genealogical accounts; cf. 196n., 198–9n.; Hes. *Catalogue of Women*. Now Anteia enters the narrative and defies female roles as encoded in genealogical poetry (for which see, e.g., Osborne 2005): she has sexual designs of her own and, when Bellerophontes rejects her, manipulates her husband so as to ensure Bellerophontes' death. She is the only character whose words Glaukos reports verbatim (for speeches within speeches in Homer, see Beck 2008, esp. 177–81). This is striking: according to Telemachus, speaking is 'the business of men' (*Od.* 1.356–9). The blunt and brutal way in which Anteia addresses her husband fits with her disrespectful behaviour towards him. Bellerophontes eventually asserts himself against transgressive women (178–90n., 186n.) and lawfully marries Anteia's sister (192n.). The story of Anteia and Bellerophontes is based on a widespread folk-tale motif: a married woman tries to seduce a man of lower standing, fails and accuses him of having tried to seduce her; for parallels see Thompson 1955–8: κ2111; Strömberg 1961; Astour 1967: 256–61; M. L. West 1997a: 365; and Hansen 2002: 332–52. Stories of this kind often involve reflections about divine justice. Cf. Eur. *Hippolytus* and the story of Joseph and Potiphar's wife in the Bible, where we hear that 'the Lord was with Joseph and gave him success in whatever he did' (Genesis 39:23; cf. 39:20–1). At first, Glaukos' story seems to imply a similar moral, but the gods' attitude towards Bellerophontes is more complicated: 191n., 200–2n.

160 ἐπεμήνατο 'went crazy over him' (τῶι); the expressive compound ἐπιμαίνομαι occurs only here in epic. For the sexual derangement which, in other stories, affects the daughters of Proitos, cf. 157n. Madness is mentioned repeatedly in book 6: 100–1n., 132n., 389n.; cf. Fineberg 1999: 18–21. δῖ᾽ Ἄντεια: a standard noun–epithet combination; cf. 31n. Proitos has not yet been honoured with one and is subordinated to his wife. For traditional epithets as a means of drawing attention to significant characters, see Bakker 1997a: ch. 7. Aristarchus took exception to the attribute δῖα, which he thought inappropriate for a woman with adulterous designs: ΣA *ad* 6.160a; for Aristarchus' views on epithets see Matthaios 1999: 237–9; and Fantuzzi 2001: 174–5. Some ancient readers tried to get round the problem by declaring her name to be Dianteia (ΣbT *ad* 6.160c). Anteia was not a well-known name for Proitos' wife; cf. 157n. The name may suggest ἀντίος, 'opposite, against'; cf. 186n.

161 κρυπταδίηι φιλότητι μιγήμεναι: the exact wording is unparalleled in epic, though cf. Mimnermus fr. 1.3 West. Similar formulations are used of a male adulterer (cf. Hes. *Op.* 328–9) and, frequently, of gods mating with mortal women (cf. *Od.* 11.244; *Hom. Hymn* 1 A 8 West); see also 25n. Anteia is exceptional, as a woman, in taking the initiative, and her designs remain unfulfilled. Later she claims that it was Bellerophontes who wanted to have sex with her: on that occasion she uses a similar phrase in a more conventional (and hence persuasive) way; cf. 165n. Bellerophontes is the victim of other secret schemes: 167–70n., 187–90n.

162 Cf. *Od.* 1.43.   πεῖθ': trans. 'could not persuade': Stoevesandt 2008: 66.   ἀγαθὰ φρονέοντα δαΐφρονα: in direct contrast to κάκ' ἐμήσατο θυμῶι at 157n. ἀγαθὰ φρονέοντα seems to be modelled on more common phrases combining φίλα, πύκα, ἀταλά, ἐΰ with φρονέω; and in opposition to the frequent κακὰ φρονέων (7.70, in the same metrical position; 10.486, 12.67, 16.373, etc.). Here it comments on δαΐφρονα, whose meaning was debated already in antiquity: the scholia explain it either as 'warlike' or as 'wise, prudent' (e.g. ΣbT *ad* 2.23*a*). Within the *Iliad*, several passages already suggest those explanations: e.g. 5.277 καρτερόθυμε δαΐφρον, and 11.482 δαΐφρονα ποικιλομήτην. Glaukos suggests that Bellerophontes' traditional epithet δαΐφρων (also used at 196n.) means he had 'good thoughts', unlike those of the people who were plotting against him.

163 Glaukos bluntly presents Anteia's speech as a lie; the poet does not usually introduce lies so explicitly (though Hera is often said to speak deceptively: 14.197, 300, 329, 19.106) – thus keeping his own view in the background; see *Od.* 14.191, 19.164, 24.243 and, for a partial exception, *Od.* 13.254–5, with Higbie 1995: 72. Glaukos firmly controls our perception of Anteia. The language of characters is often more partisan than that of the poet: Introduction 2.4.   βασιλῆα: after several expressions which hinted at Proitos' great power (158n., 159n.) he is finally called 'king' precisely at the moment when he receives orders from his wife. This is the only time he is granted an epithet, and the word actually underlines his subordination to Anteia; cf. 160n. (δῖ' Ἄντεια).

164 Anteia moves swiftly and ruthlessly from cursing her husband (τεθναίης) to ordering the death of Bellerophontes (κάκτανε). Her syntax changes halfway through the line: τεθναίης suggests a conditional (εἰ μὴ . . .), but Anteia switches to an alternative clause (ἤ); thus her curse ('may you be dead') turns into a threat ('kill him, or else die'). A change of rhythm (first spondees, then dactyls) underlines the two options presented by Anteia.   τεθναίης: perf. act. opt. of (ἀπο-)θνήισκω. Only Achilles is this blunt in the *Iliad*: 21.106 (θάνε), 22.365 (τέθναθι); cf. 18.98 (τεθναίην).   κάκτανε: from κατάκτανε (κατακτείνω), with apocope of the second α, assimilation of τ, and simplification of the consonant cluster (*κάτ-κτανε > κάκ(κ)τανε); for parallels: Chantraine 1948–53: vol. I, 87. This cacophonous word recalls κάκ' ἐμήσατο at 157n.

165 μ': elided μοι, agreeing with ἐθελούσηι. The elision of the dative pronoun is so harsh that MS Z West reads μ' (i.e. με) . . . ἐθέλουσαν, which is less good syntactically.

For parallel cases of elision, see e.g. 1.170 and *Od.* 4.367, both in direct speech; cf. Wachter 2000: 75. **ἔθελεν . . . οὐκ ἐθελούσηι:** Anteia's choice of words is again harsh and effective. There are similar uses of ἐθέλω elsewhere (e.g. *Od.* 3.272 and 5.155) but her emphasis on who wants what strikes to the core of the issue. **φιλότητι μιγήμεναι:** the same phrase as in 161, and in the same metrical position: Anteia directly contradicts Glaukos' words; cf. 161n.

166 Proitos' reaction is typical of the husband in this kind of story: e.g. Genesis 39:19. **ἄνακτα:** cf. 33n. The word prepares us for the ease with which Proitos dispatches Bellerophontes. **χόλος:** the flow of bile and hence anger as an emotion; cf. Clarke 1999: 92–7. **οἷον ἄκουσε** 'at what he heard'. The phrase is modelled on exclamations of the type ὦ μοι Τυδέος υἱὲ δαΐφρονος, οἷον ἔειπες (8.152), 'Oh son of valiant Tydeus, what did you say!' It suggests the lively tone of direct speech and helps focalise the scene through the eyes of Proitos. For similar cases of embedded focalisation see de Jong 2004: 118–22.

167–70 Proitos believes Anteia but is reluctant to kill Bellerophontes: 167n. Instead, he dispatches him to Lycia to Anteia's father, together with a folded tablet containing the request that he be killed: 168–70n. Proitos' reaction suggests weakness or indecision (contrast, e.g., the way in which Odysseus deals with his wife's suitors: he certainly does not send them off to Ikarios' palace). In classical Athens, when the husband of an adulterous wife stopped living with her, she usually returned to her family of origin (Cohen 1991: 121–4; Cantarella 2009: 302). Here Bellerophontes receives the treatment which – according to ancient audiences – Anteia deserved.

167 **μέν:** the particle cues us for Proitos' alternative plan. **ῥ'** takes the story back to Proitos' plot; cf. 158n. **ἀλέεινε:** the verb tends to be used when a character avoids something dangerous to himself (e.g. κῆρα, βέλεα, etc.). Anteia has just suggested that Proitos should either kill Bellerophontes or die himself, 164n. We later find out how difficult it is to kill Bellerophontes and how dangerous he is to those who try to do so: 178–86n. **σεβάσσατο γὰρ τό γε θυμῶι** = 417n., where Andromache recalls how Achilles refrained from taking her father's spoils. σέβας is a form of shame or awe which prevents people from doing, or allowing to happen, something which they feel is wrong or impious: Cairns 1993: 137–8. Proitos may be concerned with the stigma that attaches to a murderer. In the *Iliad* σέβας and its derivatives σέβομαι and σεβάζομαι only occur in direct speech and always concern the behaviour of other people: the speaker thus expresses his limited understanding of somebody else's actions; contrast the use of σέβας in the *Odyssey*, where it always describes the speaker's own feelings; e.g. 3.123. **τό γε** 'that particular act'. Glaukos emphasises the limitations of Proitos' piety: he shies away from attempting to kill Bellerophontes; but he does arrange for him to be killed by someone else. **θυμῶι:** cf. 51n.

168–70 The narrative gathers momentum: Proitos' plan unfolds and Bellerophontes reaches Lycia in three brisk δέ-clauses. The sequence culminates with αὐτάρ at line 171. Proitos' tablets have been much discussed. It is not clear whether he writes his message, uses a private code or makes some kind of drawing:

ancient readers already wondered about different possibilities. More generally, the issue whether heroes could write was much debated in antiquity: this passage fuelled that kind of speculation without providing any straightforward answers (Maftei 1976: 29–33). Modern scholars also debate what, if anything, the passage tells us about early scripts, orality and the role of writing in the composition of Homeric poetry: see 169n., and Introduction 2. The passage emphasises the cunning and secrecy involved in Proitos' plan but remains vague about how exactly it is meant to work: Bassi 1997: 325–9. Clearly, Bellerophontes does not understand that he is carrying his own death warrant: either he cannot decode the σήματα inscribed by Proitos, or he does not open the folded (and sealed?) tablets; cf. 168n. and 169n. The overall impression is that Proitos uses, or even invents, a nasty trick very close to writing. For the related story of Uriah in the Bible, cf. 2 Samuel 11:14–17. On Greek and Near Eastern accounts of the invention of letters and writing, see more generally Ceccarelli 2002.

168 πέμπε: cf. 171n.   δέ: cf. 167n. (μέν).   Λυκίηνδε: the connection between Argos and Lycia features prominently in Diomedes' reply: 224n., 225n.   ὅ γε marks Proitos' alternative plan, contrast τό γε in the line above.   σήματα 'signs'; in Homer, the word σῆμα can apply to a range of phenomena which, in particular contexts and circumstances, acquire a specific meaning; cf., for example, 7.175–89 (the mark on Ajax's lot); 8.170–1 (thunder), 10.465–8 (a landmark made by Odysseus in order to find his way back); *Od.* 11.126–32 = 23.273–9 (the oar mistaken for a winnowing fan: a wrong decoding which in turn becomes a sign); 23.73–4 (Odysseus' scar). The plural here suggests the complexity of the signs inscribed in the tablets; compare 169n. (θυμοφθόρα πολλά) and contrast σῆμα in the singular at 176 and 178, with 176n. For discussion of Homeric σήματα see G. Nagy 1983; Steiner 1994: 10–29; Scodel 2002b; and cf. 418–19n. (ἠδ' ἐπὶ σῆμ' ἔχεεν).   λυγρά: the epithet λυγρός typically accompanies ὄλεθρος, destruction (16–17n.). Its traditional connotation is relevant here: Proitos' signs are meant to destroy Bellerophontes; cf. 170n. (ὄφρ' ἀπόλοιτο).

169 γράψας: in epic γράφω means 'scratch', and not necessarily 'write'; ancient readers already remarked on this: ΣΑ *ad* 6.169*a*; cf. *LfgrE* s.v. γράφω. The verb does not settle the question of whether Proitos wrote, used some other kind of code or made a drawing: 168–70n.   ἐν πίνακι πτυκτῶι: a wooden diptych, perhaps coated in wax; cf. Kirk 1990: 181. A similar set of tablets, from the Mycenaean period, has been found in the shipwreck of Ulu Burun, off the coast of Lycia: Payton 1991, cf. Shear 1998, and Perna 2007; similar tablets must have been in use also later, when the *Iliad* was composed; see Heubeck 1979: 143–5. Brillante 1996: 41–2 argues that Proitos' tablets resemble ancient letters of reference.   θυμοφθόρα πολλά: the signs scratched by Proitos are numerous and lethal. At *Od.* 2.329, θυμοφθόρος (from θυμός and φθείρω) is an attribute of poison.

170 ἠνώγει: pluperfect of perfect ἄνωγα, 'tell, command', often used when somebody gives an order from a position of strength and expects it to be carried out. A range of forms is attested for this verb, not all of them easy to categorise; see *LfgrE* s.v. ἄνωγα. Aristarchus recommended the alternative form ἠνώγειν, which appears in some of the best MSS. Most witnesses read ἠνώγει, however, and that must be the mainstream Hellenistic reading. **ὧι πενθερῶι** 'his father-in-law'. Since antiquity, commentators have speculated about the man's name: ΣAT *ad* 6.170*bc* suggest Iobates or Amisodaros. The fact that Glaukos only describes him as an in-law of Proitos and, later, Bellerophontes (cf. 192n.) is significant: whereas in epic characters are usually named and placed within a recognisable genealogical tree, folk tales and children's stories often operate with anonymous types; cf. Thompson 1946: 456. For folk-tale motifs in Glaukos' account, cf. 155–205n. For the relationship between son- and father-in-law, cf. 167–70n. and 248–50n. **ὄφρ' ἀπόλοιτο:** the elaborate and mysterious description of Proitos' plan at lines 167–70 ends with a brisk and chilling statement of its aim.

171 The line echoes 168 (cf. Λυκίηνδε in the same metrical position, πέμπε ~ πομπῆι) but implicitly corrects what has been said before: Bellerophontes may seem like a victim, but in fact enjoys divine support. This shift is accompanied by a grammatical change: for the first time in Glaukos' speech Bellerophontes is the subject of a sentence. Up to now things have happened to him; now we expect him to overcome any impending difficulties. His success is embedded in the folk-tale pattern of the story; cf. 160–5n. **αὐτάρ:** cf. 83n. **ὅ:** 9n. **ὑπ':** cf. Eng. 'under escort'; cf. *Od.* 7.193 and Chantraine 1948–53: vol. II, 140. The ancient alternative μετ' does not yield the required sense (μετά + dative = 'among, in'). **ἀμύμονι:** a standard epithet of Bellerophontes; cf. 155n. Here it characterises the divine support he enjoys. **πομπῆι:** the help and support that is needed for a successful voyage, in Homer usually of return journeys (a good host provides his guest with πομπή at the end of his stay); see further Reece 1993: 39.

172–7 This section is made up of two, carefully balanced, three-line components, each introduced by ἀλλ' ὅτε δή. First Bellerophontes receives a warm welcome and lavish hospitality (172–4); then we are reminded that Proitos' insidious message will precipitate the crisis (175–7).

172 ἀλλ' ὅτε δή is often used to mark the end of a journey and resume the narrative in a new setting. In Glaukos' speech it marks four crucial stages in the life of Bellerophontes; cf. 175n., 191n., 200n., with Broccia 1963: 92. **δή:** cf. 52–3n. **Ξάνθον:** the defining landmark of Lycia in the *Iliad*. Mention of the river Xanthos helps to set the scene for the second half of the story; cf. 2.876–7, 5.479, 12.313. Several manuscripts transmit Ξάνθόν τε, which may be closer to ancient pronounciation; cf. 95n. (ἄστυ).

173 προφρονέως: Proitos' father-in-law is not intrinsically evil. He gives Bellerophontes a warm welcome and only changes attitude when he sees Proitos' message. **τῖεν:** proper behaviour demands that guests be honoured; cf. *Od.* 20.129–43, and contrast *Od.* 22.414–15 = 23.65–6. For τιμή and related terms, cf. 193n. **ἄναξ:** as with Proitos, the emphasis is on power and social status; for the meaning of ἄναξ, cf. 33n. For the failure to name Proitos' father-in-law, cf. 170n. **Λυκίης εὐρείης:** the epithet is used to characterise many geographical entities, but especially Troy, Crete and Lycia.

174 ἐννῆμαρ . . . ἐννέα: the number nine typically indicates incompleteness and ten invariably brings about an important change; cf. 2.326–9; *LfgrE* s.vv. ἐννέα Β 1; δέκατος Β 1 a. For other significant numbers in Homer, cf. 421n. ἐννῆμαρ < ἐννέα + ἦμαρ, adverbial; cf. Chantraine 1948–53: vol. 1, 212–13. ξείνισσε: unaugmented aorist of ξεινίζω. For the institution of guest-friendship in Homer, see Reece 1993; for a broader discussion, see Herman 1987. For the original digamma (*ξένϝος > epic ξεῖνος, Attic ξένος), see further Chantraine 1948–53: vol. 1, 162. The form with double sigma (contrast 217, ξείνισ᾽) closes the previous syllable; see Introduction 2.1.
        175 ἀλλ᾽ ὅτε δή signals another turning point in Bellerophontes' fortunes; cf. 172n. and, later, 191n., 200n.   δεκάτη: cf. 174n. (ἔννημαρ . . . ἐννέα).   ἐφάνη ῥοδοδάκ-τυλος Ἠώς: a common formulation; the full-line version, ἦμος δ᾽ ἠριγένεια φάνη ῥοδοδάκτυλος Ἠώς, occurs twice in the *Iliad* (1.477 and 24.788) and some twenty times in the *Odyssey*. The formula is adapted to suit the context (cf. 9.707, 23.109), and the line presents a hiatus before ἐφάνη as a result of that adaptation. There are parallels for this kind of prosodic licence elsewhere in Homer, cf. 8n. For discussion of metrical irregularities stemming from the adaptation of formulae, see M. Parry 1971: 197–221; Hoekstra 1965. Formulaic descriptions of daybreak are a feature of Near Eastern narratives. In the *Poem of Gilgamesh* they serve to structure the story and mark important transitions, see M. L. West 1997a: 174–5 with n. 15.
        176 According to the etiquette of guest-friendship, a host must first welcome his guest and make him comfortable then ask for his identity and/or circumstances; cf. Reece 1993: 26. The king of Lycia entertains Bellerophontes for nine days; then, however, instead of asking him who he is or what he wants, he demands to see the tablets. This is when things go wrong: the departure from traditional patterns of behaviour results in a mistaken assessment of Bellerophontes; cf. 191n. The decisive break with convention occurs after the main caesura, halfway through the line: ἐρέεινε still fits with standard descriptions of guest-friendship; cf. *Od.* 4.61 εἰρησόμεθ᾽. As often, a departure from standard formulations indicates that the story is taking a worrying turn.   καὶ τότε μιν echoes the opening of line 175 and further emphasises that we have reached a crucial point in the story. For καί after subordinate clause, cf., e.g., 1.494, with Denniston 1954: 308; and Bakker 1997a: 79.   μιν ἐρέεινε: μιν is measured long because ν is drawn out and closes the syllable (cf. 501, Introduction 2.1).   σῆμα: note the singular; and contrast the plural at 168n. Glaukos has just emphasised the complexity of Proitos' signs (cf. 168n. and 169n.); now he presents Proitos' whole message as a single and simple σῆμα. For a similar fluctuation between singular and plural, cf. *Od.* 23.202 (Odysseus emphasises the uniqueness of his marriage bed as a σῆμα) and 23.206 (Penelope sees it as an image of the σήματα she shares with her husband; cf. *Od.* 23.109–10).
        177 ὅττι = ὅ τι, 'which'; the form tends to introduce a significant subclause; see Chantraine 1948–53: vol. 11, 239.   ῥά: after the interlude of the hospital-ity scene, the particle takes us back to Proitos' plan and highlights the moment when his father-in-law takes over from him; cf. 158n.   γαμβροῖο: here and at 249 'son-in-law'; the word can be used of other relatives by marriage, see

Gates 1971: 24. Glaukos emphasises again Proitos' reliance on his father-in-law; cf. 167–70n.

178–86 The king sets Bellerophontes three formal challenges: πρῶτον . . . (179n.), δεύτερον . . . (184n.), τὸ τρίτον . . . (186n.); for the phrasing, cf. Hes. *Theog.* 308–15. Bellerophontes meets them all and, after surviving one last, treacherous attack, is rewarded with the hand of the king's daughter and half the kingdom. The pattern is familiar from many folk tales (Thompson 1955–8: H1211) and resembles Heracles' labours: for parallels between the two characters cf. 155n. The challenges are arranged in decreasing order of difficulty (Assunção 1997: 47): first Bellerophontes must vanquish a divine monster, then a tribe of men, then one of women. The narrative gathers momentum as Bellerophontes speeds through the challenges: four lines are devoted to the Chimaira, two to the Solymoi and one to the Amazons.

178 αὐτὰρ ἐπεὶ δή: the cluster of particles marks the point at which the king becomes hostile, cf. 175n. and 176n.   σῆμα κακόν: for the singular, cf. 176n. (σῆμα). Bellerophontes' story is built on stark oppositions, which are typical of folk tales; cf. 157n. (κάκ᾽ ἐμήσατο), contrast 162n. (ἀγαθὰ φρονέοντα). The apparent simplicity of the story ultimately emphasises its ambiguous ending: cf. 155–205n.   παρεδέξατο: the king instantly decodes the message; contrast the elaborate and mysterious description of the tablets: 168–70n. It will take him much longer to recognise that Bellerophontes actually deserves good treatment: 191n. (γίνωσκε)   γαμβροῦ: 177n.

179–83 The feat is mentioned also at Hes. *Theog.* 325, fr. 43a.87 MW, where it is a sign of Bellerophontes' excellence (ἀρετή), and divine ancestry; here it has a similar function. On theogonic monsters and their slayers, see Clay 2003: 151–61; and Haubold 2005.

179 πρῶτον marks the beginning of a catalogue; cf. 5n., 178–86n.   μέν: cf. 183n.   ῥα: cf. 158n.   Χίμαιραν: literally 'The Goat'; Hesiod also describes it as part goat, part lion and part snake: *Theog.* 321–3. For visual representations in Greece and beyond see *LIMC* III.1: 249–69 with III.2: 197–217. The monster was notoriously difficult to defeat, cf. *Hom. Hymn* 3.367–8 (οὐδέ τί τοι θάνατον . . . ἀρκέσει . . . Χίμαιρα δυσώνυμος); it is associated with Lycia also at 16.326–9.   ἀμαιμακέτην: the meaning and etymology of the adjective are unclear. Ancient readers derive it from μαιμάομαι ('be eager, rage') or equate it with ἀ(κατα)μάχητος, 'invincible'; see ΣT *ad* 6.179. Pindar appears to have cherished the word for being suitably grand and obscure: see Pind. *Pyth.* 1.14, 3.32–3, 4.208, *Isthm.* 8.35; and cf. Bacchyl. 11.64. For discussion see Maehler 1982: 228; Braswell 1988: 291. In the *Iliad* it is used only of the Chimaira and characterises her as *sui generis*; cf. 16.329; and Hes. *Theog.* 319.

180 The line suggests that the task is impossible. The Chimaira is divine, not human, yet Bellerophontes must kill her. He succeeds because he relies on the help of the gods, cf. 183n. Through his achievement, he reveals his own divine parentage, cf. 191n.   πεφνέμεν: see 12n. The word, in necessary enjambment, comes as a shock.   ἄρ draws attention to the enormity of Bellerophontes' task; cf. 158n.   θεῖον γένος οὐδ᾽ ἀνθρώπων: as is typical in the *Iliad*, a sharp distinction is drawn between the divine and the human. Theogonic monsters, however, generally elude such straightforward classification, and it soon turns out that the Chimaira is divine but mortal. For the redundant phrasing, see Tzamali 1997.   θεῖον γένος: the formulation is unusual, cf. *Op.* 159 (of the race of the heroes). The closest parallel in the *Iliad* is perhaps δῖον γένος at 9.538–40, if it refers to the boar sent by Artemis, rather than to the goddess herself. See also δῖον γένος at *Hom. Hymn* 1 A 3 West; and Hes. *Op.* 299.

181 = Hes. *Theog.* 323. The line is made up of three rhythmic units of growing length; on 'rising threefolders', see Kirk 1985: 20–1. The rhythm emphasises the composite nature of the beast, which is not assembled in any 'natural' order (back to front or front to back).   λέων: the fierce animal *par excellence* in early Greek epic and more generally in Greek and Near Eastern iconography; cf. Lonsdale 1990; Clarke 1995; *New Pauly* s.v. 'lion'. For composite monsters involving lions see also *Reallexikon der Assyriologie* s.vv. 'Löwenadler', 'Löwendrache', 'Löwenmensch' (vol. VII, pp. 94–102).   δράκων: in the visual arts the Chimaira was depicted as having the tail of a snake; cf. *LIMC* III.2, pp. 198–208. Snakes are associated with fire at Hes. *Theog.* 825–8 and so is the Chimaira, both here and at *Theog.* 319; details, however, remain unclear: Kirk 1990: 183.   χίμαιρα: an incongruous animal, which becomes terrifying in context. The middle section determines the name and gender of the beast: like many other epic monsters, the Chimaira is female; cf. Clay 2003: 150–61, esp. 153.

182 = Hes. *Theog.* 324.   δεινόν: best taken adverbially; cf. 3.342, 14.401, *Od.* 12.236, etc.   μένος: 27n. For fire and μένος see *LfgrE* s.v. μένος B 2 b α.

183 καὶ τὴν μὲν κατέπεφνε 'and yet he killed her', emphasising Bellerophontes' achievement against the odds; cf. 9.499–501 with Kühner 1904: 141. κατέπεφνε echoes πεφνέμεν at 180, in ring composition. The challenge has now been accomplished. Pegasos plays a prominent role in other accounts of the slaying of the Chimaira, cf. 156n.; ΣA *ad* 6.183a remark on the fact that the horse is not mentioned here. Pegasos was Poseidon's gift; the relationship between Bellerophontes and Poseidon remains unexplored in Glaukos' account; cf. 155n.   θεῶν τεράεσσι πιθήσας = 4.398, of Diomedes' father Tydeus. Both characters must prove themselves in official contests abroad and must then withstand a final, treacherous attack on the part of their host, which they do, heeding the warnings of the gods: cf. 187–90n. τέρας is a portent, not simply a sign: *LfgrE* s.v. Both warriors initially enjoy divine favour, both lose it eventually. The similarities between Tydeus and Bellerophontes are significant, especially since Diomedes is about to recognise in Glaukos a family friend: 212–31n.; and Alden 2000: 137–42.

184–5 After defeating a monster, Bellerophontes proves his valour in war. This progression matches the development from theogonic to heroic narratives: for example, Hesiod's *Theogony* features the slaying of several monsters while its sequel, the *Catalogue of Women*, seems to culminate in an account of the Trojan War: fr. 204 MW.

184 δεύτερον αὖ: 178–86n. αὖ signals 'continuation within a series consisting of two (occasionally, more) members' (Klein 1988: 251).   Σολύμοισι: all that we learn about the Solymoi in epic is that they live far away, and that their land is mountainous: *Od.* 5.283. Hdt 1.173 identifies them as an indigenous population of Lycia; the scholia also locate them in southern Asia Minor: ΣT *ad* 6.184. Bellerophontes defeats them but does not exterminate them. As Kirk 1990: 185 observes, they will come back to haunt his offspring: 204n. This detail may explain why Herodotus and other ancient readers thought of them as a local population.   κυδαλίμοισι: from κῦδος, 'glory', for which see 124–5n. The epithet is used of Menelaos and several other Iliadic characters, though only here of an entire people.

185 'That, he claimed, was the hardest battle with men in which he had engaged.'   καρτίστην: superlative of κρατερός, a frequent epithet of ὑσμίνη, 'battle'.   δή: 52–3n.   τήν γε '*that* particular battle'.   φάτο: cf. 98n. ΣbT *ad* 6.185 remark on the sudden intrusion of Bellerophontes' point of view. The passage reminds us that Glaukos himself is not an impartial narrator: he heard the story from members of his own family; cf. 206–11n. The Solymoi continue to pose a threat to the family in the next generation (184n., 204n.); family views and traditions understandably focus on them.   δύμεναι 'sink into, immerse oneself in'; root aorist of δύομαι; cf. δύνω/δύω. The verb suggests eagerness to fight; cf. 11.537, 19.312–13, 20.76. It is used in a wide variety of contexts, cf. 19n.   ἀνδρῶν: see 178–86n.

186 τὸ τρίτον αὖ: 178–86n.   κατέπεφνεν: cf. 183n.   Ἀμαζόνας ἀντιανείρας ∼ 3.189. The epithet means 'equal to men', 'manlike' (on ἀντί, cf. 199n.); but was also interpreted as 'hostile to men' (*LfgrE* s.v. ἀντιάνειρ(α) Σχ). In epic the Amazons are described as a tribe of women who engage in war – an activity which otherwise defines men: 492–3n. In the *Iliad* Priam claims to have fought the Amazons as an ally of the Phrygians: 3.184–9; the obscure Myrine, whose tomb is mentioned at 2.814, was thought to be an Amazon: ΣD *ad* 2.814. In the cyclic *Aethiopis* the Amazons joined the Trojans against the Achaeans, and Achilles eventually killed their queen, Penthesileia: Proclus, *Chrestomathy*, p. 110 West. ΣT *ad* 24.804*a* and papyrus 104 West both mention 'the Amazon' in lines which join the end of the *Iliad* to the beginning of the *Aethiopis*; for discussion see M. L. West 2001a: 283–5. For the Amazons in ancient Greek mythology, see further duBois 1982, Tyrell 1984, Blok 1995.

187–90 After the three official challenges, Bellerophontes must survive one last, treacherous attack. The pattern is familiar from folk tales: the brave little tailor, for example, meets three challenges set by the king, marries the princess and is then ambushed by the king's servants in his own bed; see Uther 1996: 110–19; for the folktale character of Glaukos' story, cf. 155–205n. The last, treacherous attack implies that subalterns cannot expect fair treatment, but also marks the point at which the king loses confidence. Tydeus, Diomedes' father, survives a similar ambush after winning a formal contest at 4.387–90. For similarities between Tydeus and Bellerophontes, cf. 183n.; for specific verbal echoes, see also 187n., 189n., 190n.

187 cf. 4.392 (of Tydeus).   τῶι δ' ἄρ ἀνερχομένωι 'on his way back'; cf. *Od.* 4.529–37: Aegisthus ambushes and kills Agamemnon as he arrives home. Both men are caught off guard, when they think they no longer face danger. Ancient readers saw the parallels between the two passages, cf. 188n. Two textual variants circulated already in antiquity: ἀπερχομένωι, 'as he was leaving' and ἐπερχομένωι, 'as he approached'. Hellenistic readers may have objected to ἀνερχομένωι because Bellerophontes never leaves Lycia and cannot therefore be said to 'return', if this implies 'from another country'; cf. ΣbT *ad* 6.186*a*, where the Amazons are thought to be an invading force; and contrast 4.385–92, where, despite various textual problems, the verb ἀνέρχομαι is hardly in doubt. Aristarchus certainly discussed the line, but the scholia do not allow us to reconstruct with certainty his preferred reading; see further Introduction 6. **ἄρ:** cf. 158n. **πυκινὸν δόλον:** a variation on the formulaic πυκινὸν λόχον, for which see 4.392, 24.779, etc. The emphasis here is on cunning and deviousness, cf. 3.202 δόλους καὶ μήδεα πυκνά; but the expression also evokes other descriptions of ambushes, particularly the attack on Tydeus at 4.392. The reading πυκινὸν λόχον is attested in several medieval manuscripts. **δόλον... ὕφαινε:** literally 'he (sc. the Lycian king) wove a plot', cf. *Od.* 5.356 and 9.422. The verb is also standardly applied to μῆτις, μήδεα, and emphasises the intricacy and deviousness of the thinking involved.

188 ~ *Od.* 4.530. **Λυκίης εὐρείης:** cf. 173n. The variant reading ἐείκοσι, 'twenty', is unmetrical but demonstrates that readers had *Od.* 4.530–1 in mind. **φῶτας:** in epic, the noun φώς, φωτός is generally treated as a synonym for ἀνήρ, cf. 17.377–8; the two terms are used in complementary formulaic systems: e.g. ἀνδρὶ ἐοικώς after consonant, φωτὶ ἐοικώς after vowel. Unlike ἀνήρ, however, φώς is used only in poetry and late prose; by the Hellenistic period, it had a heroic ring; cf. *Hom. Hymn* 32.18–19; Ap. Rhod. *Argon.* 1.1; Theoc. *Id.* 12.10–13. For the reception of Homeric words in Hellenistic poetry, cf. 111. (φύλοπις). **ἀρίστους:** the ambush is presented as a context in which the best men display their valour; cf. 13.275–87.

189 **εἶσε λόχον:** factitive aorist of the root **sed-* (cf. ἵζω, 'sit down'). Lit. 'he sat an ambush', trans. 'he set an ambush'; cf. 4.392, *Od.* 4.531 (in the same metrical position); and Hes. *Theog.* 174. The difficulties of sitting still and waiting during an ambush are emphasised at 13.280–5. **τοὶ δ'... νέοντο:** an economic description; the next line explains what happened to them.

190 **πάντας... κατέπεφνεν** 'because noble Bellerophontes killed them all', a triumphant ending. Glaukos seems to revel in this straightforward conclusion; on the tone of his speech and its affinity to children's stories, see further Introduction 4.1. At 4.397 Tydeus kills all the ambushers but one. Here Bellerophontes kills all his opponents and becomes himself the survivor who returns to tell the tale. We are cued to expect that from now on Lycia will be his homeland. **ἀμύμων Βελλεροφόντης:** standard epithet of Bellerophontes; it is first used at the moment of his birth, cf. 155n.; it now features at the moment when his true nature is revealed, cf. 191n. Diomedes will use it later, when describing his guest-friendship with Oineus; cf. 216n.

191–5 The king finally recognises that Bellerophontes enjoys divine support, and the story of their confrontation ends like a folk tale: the king grants Bellerophontes the hand of his daughter and half the kingdom; the Lycians likewise offer him a prominent place among them. On folk-tale elements, cf. 155–205n. This is not the end of the story, however: Glaukos' genealogical account resumes at line 196 and eventually reveals a far less comforting image of the gods and their relationship to Bellerophontes' family: cf. 200–2n. and Introduction 3.1 and 4.1.

191 ἀλλ' ὅτε δή announces another drastic change in Bellerophontes' life; cf. 172n., 175n. and 200n.   γίνωσκε... ἐόντα: an apparently straightforward recognition, which becomes problematic in the context of Glaukos' speech. According to the logic of the story, the king should finally recognise qualities that are obvious to us. However, Glaukos never mentioned Bellerophontes' divine ancestry: he introduced him as the son of a mortal man (155n.) and made no reference to the horse Pegasos, which was traditionally the gift of Bellerophontes' divine father, Poseidon (156n. and 183n.). In Glaukos' speech, Bellerophontes' relationship with the gods remains obscure: the gods grant him beauty and manliness – gifts that almost cost him his life: 156n., 160–5n.; and their portents guide him when he confronts the Chimaira: 183n. Later, Glaukos says that the gods ruin Bellerophontes, without explaining the cause of their anger: 200–2n. The simple folk-tale ending in which the deserving champion wins the king's favour is undermined here by Glaukos' elliptical portrayal of Bellerophontes and of his relationship to the gods. See further 155–205n. and Introduction 4.1.   θεοῦ γόνον 'offspring of a god', cf. γίνομαι, γενεή (145n.).   ἠΰν 'good', 'valiant', also in the form ἐΰς; cf. the adverb εὖ. The gods are traditionally 'givers of good things', δωτῆρες ἐάων: *Od.* 8.325, 335; cf. *Il.* 24.528; and N. J. Richardson 1993: 330–1. For their gifts to Bellerophontes, cf. 156n.

192 = 11.226, of a foster son who marries the daughter of the house.   κατέρυκε: normally against somebody's will (cf. 518n., *LfgrE* s.v. ἐρύκω II 2), but all power now rests with Bellerophontes.   δίδου... θυγατέρα ἥν: the girl remains unnamed: this is a characteristic of the folk tale; cf. 170n. Bellerophontes marries Anteia's sister and thus becomes, like Proitos, the son-in-law of the king of Lycia; on Anteia and Proitos, cf. 160–5n., 167–70n. For δίδου, 'gave in marriage', see Scheid-Tissinier 1994: 106–10; and Lyons 2003: 102.   ἥν: originally with two initial consonants (*swe* > ϝϝήν; cf. Latin *suam*). Here they close, and thus lengthen, the preceding syllable, as often elsewhere: cf. 5.371, 11.226, 13.376. See Chantraine 1948–53: vol. i, 146.

193 Inheriting half the kingdom is a common folk-tale motif; cf. Thompson 1955–8: Q112. In epic, couples usually settle in the husband's ancestral home, but staying with the bride's family is also a possibility; cf. 248–50n.   τιμῆς βασιληΐδος: the term τιμή refers to social status and its material expression, in terms of power and possessions; for a helpful discussion see Scodel 2008a: ch. 1. For the idea of sharing royal honours as a sign of affection and respect, cf. 9.616.

194–5 ~ 20.184–5 (Achilles taunts Aeneas because he will never receive a plot of land in Troy).

194 καὶ μέν: the story continues; cf. 26–7n.   Λύκιοι: a τέμενος is generally the gift of an entire community, not of an individual.   τέμενος: a plot of land, lit. what is 'cut out' (τάμνω/τέμνω). The land is set aside by the people for a particularly prominent member of the community, from whom they can in turn expect leadership and protection; cf. 9.574–80, 12.310–21, 20.184–5. A τέμενος can be inherited, but the moment when it is first cut and assigned remains important and is evoked in the expression τέμενος τάμνειν; cf. 47n. (κειμήλια κεῖται). How exactly a τέμενος was allotted, and from what land, seems to have been unclear to the poet of the *Iliad*: see

Link 1994, who takes issue with Donlan 1989a.   **τάμον:** unaugmented aorist of
τάμνω, cf. Attic τέμνω. The stem in α prevails in epic, though τέμνω is also attested
(*Od.* 3.175).   **ἔξοχον ἄλλων** qualifies τέμενος here, though elsewhere the phrase is
used adverbially; cf. ἔξοχα (ἁ)πάντων at 14.257 etc., *Od.* 24.78; *Hom. Hymn* 3.88. The
transition from adverbial to adjectival usage is facilitated here by the position of the
verb τάμον.

195 ∼ 12.314, 20.185.   **καλόν:** the alpha is long in early epic (< καλϝόν).
Beauty is often a quality that is added on after the main description, in progressive
enjambment; cf. 314n.   **φυταλιῆς καὶ ἀρούρης:** the genitives depend on τέμενος,
cf. 9.578–80; translate: 'comprising orchards and fields'. φυταλιή, lit. 'planted land',
usually of vineyards or orchards, as opposed to ἄρουρα, 'corn-land'. The Homeric
τέμενος consists of first-rate farm land: cattle and sheep are never said to pasture in a
τέμενος; they are usually herded in the mountains or near river banks, on less valuable
land.   **ὄφρα νέμοιτο:** the variant πυροφόροιο is attested in some manuscripts,
cf. 12.314. The printed text retains the focus on Bellerophontes.   **νέμοιτο:** the
meaning of Homeric 'νέμομαι' (middle) ranges from 'have as one's portion', to 'enjoy'
or 'consume' (also of fire: 23.177), to 'inhabit' (frequently in the Catalogue of Ships).

196–9 The speech changes tone: the tale of Bellerophontes seems to have reached
its happy ending, and Glaukos resumes his genealogical catalogue. Each new character is now introduced briskly and with a name, contrast 170n., 192n. Bellerophontes'
downfall will dramatically interrupt Glaukos' genealogical exposition: 200–2n.

196 **ἣ δ' ἔτεκε:** women in their traditional role as wives and mothers dominate the
catalogue at this stage, contrast 154–5, and 160–5n.   **δαΐφρονι Βελλεροφόντηι:**
162n.

197 **Ἴσανδρον:** only here. Strabo read Πείσανδρον both here and at 203; for
ancient speculation about minor characters, cf. 21n., 31n.   **Ἱππόλοχον:** cf. 119n.
and 206–11n.   **Λαοδάμειαν:** only here, though the name will not have struck
audiences as unusual, cf. Λαοδίκη (252n.), Λαοθόη (21.85, 22.48), Λαονόμη (Hes. fr.
253 MW); and the masculine Λαοδάμας (15.516, *Od.* 7.170, etc.). Female names in epic
are often based on male ones; cf. Neumann 1991: 316. The wife of Protesilaos was
also called Laodameia, though her name does not feature in extant early epic.

198–9 The divine ancestry of Bellerophontes was never entirely clear, and no specific god was mentioned in connection with his birth: cf. 155n., 191n. Now Glaukos
offers a straightforward account: Laodameia slept with Zeus and gave birth to Sarpedon; cf. 198n. This is a high point in the family saga: in early epic the gods choose
the best women as their partners, cf. Hes. fr. 1.3 MW, αἳ τότ' ἄρισται ἔσαν. For
Bellerophontes' privilege in becoming Zeus's father-in-law, cf. 201n. Sarpedon, as the
son of Zeus, eclipses Glaukos (though he is now wounded and unable to fight: 78n.).
Two of Bellerophontes' descendants die in the next lines: 203–5n.; while Glaukos, a
survivor, feels responsible for the reputation of the entire family: 206–11n.

198 In the *Catalogue of Women* and Bacchylides, the mother of Sarpedon is Europa:
this makes him roughly three generations older than the Trojan War and a member
of the Inachid family; cf. Hes. fr. 140 MW = Bacchyl. *Dith.* *10 Maehler; Hes.

fr. 141 MW; ΣA *ad* 6.199; and Hdt. 1.173. Glaukos' version avoids the chronological difficulties posed by the dominant genealogy and is consistent with the portrayal of Europa in the *Iliad*: 14.321–2. See further Maftei 1976: 41–4.   παρελέξατο: aorist of παραλέχομαι, 'go to bed (λέχος) alongside of'. In early Greek epic the verb is used of gods sleeping with goddesses or women, exceptions: 24.676 (Briseis and Achilles); *Od.* 4.305 (Helen and Menelaos); Hes. fr. 176.6 MW (Clytaemnestra and Aegisthus). Not normally of lawfully wedded human couples.   μητίετα Ζεύς: a frequent formula; for the μῆτις of Zeus, see Hes. *Theog.* 886–900; Hes. fr. 343 MW; and Detienne and Vernant 1978: chs. 3–4. The form μητίετα may derive from an older *mētiwetās*, 'rich in intelligence'; cf. Meier-Brügger 1989.

199   ἣ δ' ἔτεκ': cf. 196n.   ἀντίθεον: the epithet is used of many heroes and expresses equivalence of power, rather than family resemblance; cf. ἀντί, 'of equal value', 'exchangeable for'. Here, however, the genealogy reinforces the epithet.   Σαρπηδόνα: an important character in the poem who, in may ways, acts as a counterpart to Hector. He too has a wife and child (5.480), but they are safe in Lycia, so for him the war becomes a test of more abstract notions of heroism. Sarpedon and Glaukos are cousins, but Sarpedon is introduced much earlier in the genealogical account, giving the impression that he is the older of the two. As the son of Zeus, he is an emblematic figure of the mortal hero; see further Redfield 1994: 100–2.   χαλκοκορυστήν 'bronze-clad'; cf. κορύσσω/κορυστής; in the *Iliad* otherwise only of Hector. On bronze as the metal of heroes, cf. 3n.

200–2   The downfall of Bellerophontes. According to Pind. *Isthm.* 7.43–8 Bellerophontes tried to ascend to heaven on his horse Pegasos and was punished for his arrogance. In that account he is presented as a man who challenged the gods and came to grief, like Lycurgus in Diomedes' speech; cf. 130–40n. Glaukos, however, previously suggested that Bellerophontes was an innocent man who suffered unjustly and, after many trials, managed to win a princess and a kingdom: 191–5n. The story of his downfall is delayed until the genealogical account which follows the folk-tale happy ending: the reappearance of Bellerophontes at 200 is so abrupt that some modern readers have been tempted to move lines 200–2 to somewhere else (e.g. after 205), or remove them altogether; for a compelling defence of the transmitted text, see Grethlein 2006a: 340–2. Glaukos delays his account of Bellerophontes' downfall and remains silent about its causes. He never mentions Pegasos (cf. 156n., 183n.), though it seems that audiences linked Glaukos' account to ancient traditions about the horse: 152n. Because there are gaps in Glaukos' story, audiences of all times must have tried to supplement it with what they knew or imagined about Bellerophontes. See further Gaisser 1969; Alden 2000: 138–9; and on allusion in Homer, Introduction 1. On Glaukos' vagueness about Bellerophontes' crimes (as well as those of Sisyphos, 153n.; and perhaps those of Laodameia, 205n.), see Introduction 4.1.

200   ~ 140. For the parallels between Lycurgus and Bellerophontes: 200–2n.   ἀλλ' ὅτε δή marks another reversal in Bellerophontes' fortune; cf. 172n., 175n., 191n.   καὶ κεῖνος 'he too'; looking back to the story of Lycurgus, but also beyond, to the inevitable fate of all humankind; for a similar formulation see 24.538,

ἀλλ' ἐπὶ καὶ τῶι θῆκε θεὸς κακόν. For an overview of ancient and modern interpretations, see Avery 1994: 499, n. 8. The fact that Bellerophontes is not named
enhances the generalising rhetoric. For Glaukos on the human condition, see Introduction 4.1.   ἀπήχθετο: 140–1n.   πᾶσι θεοῖσιν: Glaukos remains vague about
Bellerophontes' downfall.

201 A lonely and nomadic existence is presented as the worst human fate also
at 24.531–3; see Graziosi and Haubold 2005: 141–2; and contrast 217n.   ἤτοι is
similar in meaning and grammatical function to μέν, but more emphatic, cf. 404n.
and 414n., Ruijgh 1996. The final syllable becomes short: for diphthong followed by
vowel, see Introduction 2.1.   ὅ: 9n.   κάπ < κατά with apocope of final vowel
and assimilation of τ before πεδίον; cf. 164n. (κάκτανε), and see further Wachter 2000:
88.   πεδίον . . . Ἀλήϊον: the pun on ἀλᾶτο (Rank 1951: 37–8) suggests that this
is a place of wretched wanderings, cf. 202n. (ἀλεείνων); White 1982: 126–7 discusses
a striking parallel in the Hebrew Bible (Genesis 4:12–16). Symbolically, the Aleian
plain is the opposite of the Ἠλύσιον πεδίον mentioned at *Od.* 4.563–9: Menelaos will
avoid all misery and toil in the Elysian plain, because he is the son-in-law of Zeus;
Bellerophontes, by contrast, is relegated to this place of utter misery, even though he
has just become the equivalent of Zeus's father-in-law. Herodotus identifies a place
called Aleion in Cilicia, to the east of Lycia: *Hist.* 6.95. For ancient speculation on
Homeric place names, cf. 152n. (Ἐφύρη).   οἶος: loneliness is presented as a cause
of extreme suffering.

202 ὃν θυμὸν κατέδων expresses the physicality of grief, 'eating his heart out',
cf. *Od.* 9.75. Bellerophontes is depicted first as a monster-slayer, then a warrior,
and then a vagrant whose suffering is intense but ordinary; on this life-trajectory, see
Graziosi and Haubold 2005: ch. 5.   πάτον ἀνθρώπων ἀλεείνων: the verb puns on
Ἀλήϊον and ἀλᾶτο in the line before; on word play in Homer, cf. 143n. On ἀλεείνω =
'avoid' something harmful, cf. 167n. Bellerophontes, who once defeated monsters and
warriors, has become fearful of ordinary human beings. A similar expression
describes an uninhabited island at *Od.* 9.119.

203–5 Two of Bellerophontes' descendants also meet a bad end. Glaukos finally
mentions specific gods, but his account again obscures any personal connection
between gods and humans. Ares generally represents war, so Isandros is said to die in
battle: 203n. Artemis often inflicts death on women; if she has specific reasons to hate
Laodameia, they are not mentioned: 205n. On the portrayal of the gods in Glaukos'
speech, see further Introduction 4.1. Glaukos adopts the briskly paratactic style of the
epic catalogue, cf. δέ at 203, 205, 206.

203 Ἴσανδρον: 197n.   οἱ: the 'dative of affect' describes the death of Isandros in
terms of Bellerophontes' loss.   Ἄρης: the god represents war at its most senseless
and destructive, cf. Burkert 1985: 169–70; Erbse 1986: 156.   ἆτος: from ἄατος
(Hes. *Theog.* 714) < *ἄ-σατος; cf. Latin *satis*, 'enough'. Translate 'insatiable'.

204 Bellerophontes defeated the Solymoi and now they kill his son:
184n.   μαρνάμενον > μάρναμαι, 'fight' (usually in battle). Unlike the common
μάχομαι, this verb occurs only in poetry.

205 Like her father, Bellerophontes, Laodameia first enjoys divine favour (197n.) and then meets with divine hostility. Artemis is generally responsible for the death of women: e.g. 428n., 19.59, *Od.* 11.171–3. In those cases, however, she is not said to act in anger. Other women who anger Artemis in epic are Niobe (24.605–9) and Callisto (Hes. fr. 163): their story is told in detail. There may be a suggestion here that Glaukos is, once again, failing to give a full account of his relatives' faults, cf. 153n., 200–2n.   χολωσαμένη: cf. 166n. (χόλος).   χρυσήνιος 'of the golden reins'; a rare epithet which Artemis shares only with Ares in extant epic; cf. *Od.* 8.285. Gold features in Artemis' standard epithet χρυσηλάκατος, 'of the golden distaff' (16.183 etc.); this may have facilitated the choice of χρυσήνιος here.   Ἄρτεμις: an important goddess in cult, particularly for women, but presented as infantile and generally marginalised as a character in the *Iliad*, cf. 21.479–513.   ἔκτα: athematic aorist of κτείνω, 'kill'; see Chantraine 1948–53: vol. 1, 380–1.

206–11 Hippolochos, the only survivor in his generation, does not distinguish himself through his own actions and rests all his hopes on Glaukos. The expectations of fathers are important also for other Iliadic warriors (207n., 475–81n., 479n.), but the fluctuating fortunes in Glaukos' genealogy make it especially important that he prove himself. The concluding lines of his speech thus help to explain why he dares to face Diomedes in battle and provide an answer to Diomedes' aggressive questioning (123–43n.). This passage and the speech as a whole show how Iliadic warriors are motivated by their role in their family line as well as by the desire to excel among peers; see Introduction 4.1. Note the many words formed with the root *gen*- : γενέσθαι (206), γένος (209), ἐγένοντο (210), γενεῆς (211). Glaukos concludes his speech in ring composition, by offering a reflection on the nature and significance of genealogy; cf. 145n., 150–1n.

206 First the father generates the son, then the son pays homage to the father.   Ἱππόλοχος: 119n.   ἔτικτε: as elsewhere, Glaukos emphasises fatherhood (cf. 154–5, 209n. and contrast 196n.)   καί: 1n.   τοῦ: genitive of the demonstrative pronoun ὅ; cf. 9n.   φημί 'I claim', 'I assert'; cf. 98n.

207 The father who instructs the son before he leaves for Troy is a common motif. It often occurs in contexts where the son forgets, or fails to heed, an important piece of advice; cf. 5.197–201, 9.252–9 and 11.785–90.   Τροίην: the region (e.g. 24.542) as well as the city itself (e.g. 1.129); cf. Eustathius I, p. 723: 8–12 van der Valk. The name may derive from Hittite *Taruwisa / Tru(w)isa*, a country mentioned in Hittite sources of the Bronze Age; cf. Latacz 2004: 92–100. For a sceptical assessment of the evidence see Heinhold-Kramer 2003: 150–6.   καί: sending Glaukos and imparting fatherly advice are part of the same process; cf. 1n.   ἐπέτελλεν 'instructed'.

208 = 11.784 (Peleus' words to Achilles as reported by Nestor; contrast the allegedly more moderate advice given by Menoitios to his son Patroclus: 11.785–9). A succinct and memorable statement of the Iliadic code of war; cf. Kirk 1990: 187. Glaukos illustrates quite how difficult it is to put such advice into practice.   ἀριστεύειν: to be the 'best', ἄριστος. The verb is relatively rare in the *Iliad*: it tends to be used when a warrior dies, or after his death; cf., e.g., 460n., 7.90, 11.745–6. Hippolochos' advice leads us to expect a fatal confrontation; cf. 232–6n. **ὑπείροχον:** cf. ὑπερέχω, 'surpass'. For ει = ē̆, see 71n. (νεκροὺς . . . τεθνειῶτας), and 113n. (βείω).

209 The idea that men should not shame their ancestors is traditional in epic and is particularly important for the relationship between father and son; cf. *Od.* 24.508 (Odysseus tells Telemachus that they should not shame their ancestors) and *Od.* 24.512 (Telemachus replies that he is up to the task); cf. Crotty 1994, ch. 2, and Bouvier 2002a: 111–17. αἰσχυνέμεν 'disfigure, spoil' and hence 'disgrace' (cf. αἶσχος, 'ugliness, object of shame'); see also 351n. **ἄριστοι:** cf. 208n. (ἀριστεύειν). In fact, Glaukos' ancestry does not provide straightforward models of excellence; cf. esp. 200–2n.

210 An elegant cap to the whole saga; cf. 152n. (Ἐφύρη) and 168n. (Λυκίη). Since it was Bellerophontes who moved from Ephyre to Lycia, Glaukos implies again that he is the central character in the genealogy.

211 = 20.241 (Aeneas to Achilles). In this flyting exchange, Glaukos is supposed to answer Diomedes' boasts in kind. Now he finally manages one boastful line, but it comes very late, and his family history ultimately suggests that Glaukos still has everything to prove; see Introduction 4.1. **τοι:** 49n. The dative of affect draws attention to the perceived needs of the addressee: 'here, for your benefit, is my genealogy'; 'there you have it'. The whole account was introduced as an answer to a futile request on the part of Diomedes: 145n., 150–1n. αἵματος: see *LfgrE* s.v. αἷμα B 2; the notion that members of the same family share the same blood is attested in many cultures, cf. Eng. 'blood relations'. **εὔχομαι** 'I claim' or 'boast'. The verb is often used to express pride in one's family or place of origin (*LfgrE* s.v. (ἐπ)εύχομαι* B 2 d) but may also occur in a broad range of other contexts: from prayer (304n.) to gloating over a defeated foe (e.g. 11.449); see further Muellner 1976.

212–31 Diomedes' reaction to Glaukos' speech is astonishing: he is overjoyed (212n.) and no longer wants to fight (213n.). Then he delivers some 'gentle words' (214n.): he explains that there is an ancient bond of hospitality between his family and that of Glaukos (215–21n.), and concludes that they should avoid one another in battle (224–9n.). Finally, he proposes that they exchange armour as a token of friendship (230–1n.). His speech explains his reaction but in turn raises several questions. First, Diomedes' views about hospitality on the battlefield are unprecedented and problematic: 224–9n. Secondly, his account of his family, while shorter and sharper than that of Glaukos, seems to be equally selective: 222–3n. Thirdly, the exchange of armour becomes a symbolic defeat for Glaukos, rather than a token of friendship: 232–6n. The closest parallel to the exchange proposed by Diomedes can be found at 7.277–312, for discussion see Introduction 4.1. The theme of reciprocity is central to Diomedes' speech and determines its form: cf. ἀλλήλοισι(ι)/ἀλλήλων at 218, 226 and 230, and the parallel structures at 219–20 (μέν – δέ), 224–5 (μέν – δέ) and 227–9 (μέν – δ' αὖ); for the importance of reciprocity in guest-friendship see Herman 1987. Diomedes persuades Glaukos, and he may initially persuade us too; but eventually we realise that there can be no equality in friendship between the two warriors.

212 ὣς φάτο, γήθησεν δέ: the phrase is traditional, and is sometimes used when the listener realises that the speaker is on his side, cf. 17.567–8 and *Od.* 18.281–3. The reasons for Diomedes' spectacular change of attitude emerge only later.   βοὴν ἀγαθὸς Διομήδης: 12n.

213 Diomedes' spear is his most threatening attribute, both in his own view and in that of his enemy: 97n., 126n., 278; the women of Troy specifically ask Athena to break it: 306n. Tydeus too was famous for his spear: 14.124–5. Now Diomedes plants his in the ground, thus suggesting a formal end to his hostility: cf. 3.135. Later in his speech Diomedes qualifies his gesture: his spear will avoid Glaukos but will continue killing other Trojans and allies: 224–9n.   ἔγχος: 31n.   ἐπὶ χθονί: lit. 'on the ground'; χθών is the ground as a surface: objects can be placed 'on' it (ἐπί) or below 'it' (ὑπό), but not normally 'in' it; contrast the frequent ἐν(ὶ) γαίῃ, 'in the earth'. Bekker's emendation ἐνὶ χθονί is unidiomatic, *pace* Kirk 1990: 187. The focus now is not on the tip of Diomedes' spear (contrast e.g. 11.378, ἐν γαίηι), but on his conciliatory gesture (thus ΣAbT *ad* 6.213); cf. Hector who later takes off his helmet and places it ἐπὶ χθονί, in order to reassure his son: 472–3n., with Di Benedetto 1998: 16. In hospitality scenes the host takes the guest's spear before entering the house: that gesture may be relevant here; cf. *Od.* 1.121, 127–9, 15.282, 16.40; cf. *Hom. Hymn* 3.6–9.   πουλυβοτείρηι 'feeding many', used only of χθών. On mortals as grain-eaters, cf. 142n.

214 The line introduces Diomedes' speech as an attempt to persuade Glaukos; cf. 45n.   αὐτάρ: 83n.   ὅ: 9n.   μειλιχίοισι 'soothing, gentle', often taken to mean 'honey-sweet' in antiquity, as if derived from μέλι, 'honey'; for problems with this etymology see Chantraine 1937. The adjective is used to introduce a persuasive speech, as opposed to a 'blunt' one (στερεός 12.267). A gentle speech can be experienced as devious or improper (cf. 343n. with 343–58n. and 359–68n.) and can provoke a 'harsh' answer (cf. ἀμείλικτος ὄψ, at 11.137). Glaukos, however, is charmed: 232–6n.   ποιμένα λαῶν: a common description of leaders in epic, which expresses their duty of care towards their people; cf. Haubold 2000: 17–24. Its use here draws attention to a fundamental problem: Diomedes is about to strike a private agreement with the enemy and envisages that it might harm other Achaeans: 224–9n.

215–21 There are other examples of hospitality between Achaeans and Trojans in the *Iliad* (cf. 3.207), but only here are the bonds of guest-friendship invoked on the battlefield: 224–9n. and Introduction 4.1. Before Diomedes explores how the rules of hospitality might apply to armed combat, he establishes a tradition of guest-friendship between the two families. Bellerophontes is, again, a key figure. Several details in Glaukos' speech had suggested an analogy between Bellerophontes and Diomedes' father Tydeus, cf. 183n., and 187–90n; now Diomedes reveals a connection between Bellerophontes and his grandfather Oineus and then claims he does not remember his father: 222–3n.

215 Diomedes is prone to omitting vocatives (as, indeed, is Achilles); cf. Bassett 1934: 148. Here, his abrupt opening betrays his surprise.   ἦ ῥά νύ μοι: a lively opening, which suggests genuine excitement; cf. 3.183.   ἦ: cf. 441n.   ῥα marks the process of realisation, cf. 2n., 10n.   μοι: cf. 211n. (τοι).   ξεῖνος: 174n.   παλαιός 'of old'; the adjective normally applies to old people (e.g. 14.108) or people of earlier times (e.g. 11.166).   **216** Οἰνεύς: father of Tydeus (cf. Οἰνείδης 5.813, 10.497) and Meleager (2.641–2, 9.535 and 581–3), grandfather of Diomedes. In the Hesiodic *Catalogue of Women* he is ousted by his brothers and reinstated by Tydeus, who kills his uncles: Hes. fr. 10a.55–7 MW. At 14.118, Diomedes suppresses some such story and describes Oineus as the best of three brothers; cf. Janko 1994: 163–4.   γάρ: 15n.   δῖος: 31n.   ἀμύμονα Βελλεροφόντην: the central character in Glaukos' speech plays a crucial role in Diomedes' reply; on the epithet, cf. 22n. and 155n.   **217** ξείνισ': 174n.   ἐνὶ μεγάροισιν: that Oineus is the host is an important detail: cf. 202n. (on Bellerophontes as the homeless wanderer); 218n. On the scansion of ἐνί, cf. 91n.   ἐείκοσιν ἤματ' ἔρυξας: an exceptionally long visit inaugurates this important friendship. The number twenty is often used in descriptions of lengthy periods of time, cf. *LfgrE* s.vv. (ἐ)είκοσι(ν) and (ἐ)εικοστός.

218 καί: it seems that Aristarchus found the word superfluous (ΣA *ad* 6.218) although it is rhetorically effective: it presents an unusual gift exchange as a natural consequence of Bellerophontes' stay.   ἀλλήλοισι: a recurrent word in Diomedes' speech; cf. 212–31n.   ξεινήϊα καλά: gifts are an important aspect of guest-friendship (for which, see 174n.). They are not usually exchanged within the course of a single visit: normally, the host offers a gift to the guest; cf. 18.408; *Od.* 8.389 and 24.271–3, with Reece 1993: 35–6. Perhaps Diomedes has conflated two visits; but it may be significant that Bellerophontes reciprocates when he need not have done.

219 Οἰνεύς: 216n.   μέν: cf. 220n. (δέ).   ζωστῆρα: a warrior's belt; it was probably made of leather and studded with metal: Lorimer 1950: 245–50 and Brandenburg 1977. Epithets such as παναίολος and δαιδάλεος elsewhere characterise it as an artful and elaborate object.   φοίνικι φαεινόν: cf. 7.305, 15.538, *Od.* 23.201. φοῖνιξ is a purple dye obtained from sea snails (Arist. *Hist. an.* 546b-547b; Plin. *HN* 9.124–38), though the scholia claim that in Homer it comes from the flowers of the holm oak (e.g. ΣbT *ad* 4.141d). Objects dyed with φοῖνιξ were thought to be precious: cf. the cheek-piece for a horse described at 4.141–5, and see Blum 1998: 68–75. It is difficult to assess the value of Oineus' gift relative to that of Bellerophontes' offering: Donlan 1989b: 11–15 argues that Bellerophontes loses out, and that his grandson Glaukos is about to make an even greater loss. This conclusion stems from a rereading of Diomedes' speech, in the light of the authorial comment at the end of the episode: cf. 232–6n. Even the earliest audiences of the *Iliad* may have been unsure about the relative value of the two objects, at least on first hearing.

220 δέ after μέν in the line above emphasises the parallel between the two men's gifts.   χρύσεον δέπας ἀμφικύπελλον: a cup is an appropriate gift (e.g. 24.234–7) or prize (e.g. 23.656). ἀμφικύπελλον, a distinctive epithet of δέπας, probably means 'with handles on both sides'; ἀμφι- compounds often suggest perfection. The combination with χρύσεον is unique: this is a particularly valuable cup; cf. *Od.* 3.63 (καλὸν δέπας ἀμφικύπελλον). Bloedow 2007 discusses the archaeological record. For the relative

value of this gift compared with that of Oineus, cf. 219n. Mention of gold prompts
Glaukos to part with his golden armour: 232–6n. and 236n.   χρύσεον: read as
two long syllables, with εο as a diphthong.

221 For precious gifts that are kept at home, cf. 47n. and Reece 1993: 36. It is
not clear at this stage how the presence of the cup in Argos might affect the situation
on the battlefield. On the disruptive effect of war on peacetime relationships, cf. 12–
20n.   μιν: probably 'it' (i.e. the cup), rather than 'him' (i.e. Oineus); cf. 9.364,
for possessions left behind; and Chantraine 1948–53: vol. 1, 264 for μιν.   ἐγώ:
more emphatic than English 'I'; translate 'and I then left it'.   κατέλειπον: 222–
3n.   ἐν δώμασ' ἐμοῖσι takes up line 217 and emphasises that the home is the place
where hospitality is displayed. The issue becomes important later: 224–9n.

222–3 Guest gifts are tokens of social memory (Reece 1993: 35), and it is surprising
that Diomedes makes a point of not remembering his father in a speech where he is
trying to establish a connection between himself and his 'paternal guest-friend' (ξεῖνος
πατρώϊος, 215). Ancient commentators complain that these verses are inappropriate,
'out of place' (ἄτοποι); cf. ΣT ad 6.222–3. However, they are highly effective in the
context of Diomedes' speech: Tydeus is a problematic role model, and Diomedes now
distances himself from him and tries to forge a relationship with Glaukos; cf. Introduction 2.2 and 4.1. Contrast his boasts about Tydeus at 14.110–27.   τυτθὸν
ἐόντα: the phrase evokes a well-established formulaic pattern (ἔτρεφε τυτθὸν ἐόντα,
ἔθρεψε δόμοις ἐνὶ τυτθὸν ἐόντα) and reminds us that Diomedes needed to be looked
after.   κάλλιφ': from *κάτ-λιπε > κατέλιπε, 'he left', with elision of final vowel
and π > φ before rough breathing. The verb, in necessary enjambment, reveals that
Tydeus left his son behind and played no role in bringing him up; for discussion
see Pratt 2009, and contrast Hippolochos' active role in Glaukos' upbringing: 206–
11n.   Θήβησιν: the city in Boeotia, known in epic either as Θήβη, singular, or
Θῆβαι, in the plural, as here. The 'Seven against Thebes' famously marched against
it, cf. 4.370–410 and the cyclic epic known as the *Thebaid*. The descendants of the
Seven conquered it, cf. 4.405–9, 20n. and the cyclic epic *Epigoni*. In the *Iliad* the citadel
of Thebes no longer exists; only a lower city is mentioned: Ὑποθῆβαι, at 2.505. Two
other cities called Thebes feature in the *Iliad*: the fabulously rich Egyptian Thebes
(9.381–4), and the home town of Andromache: 397n.   ἀπώλετο λαὸς Ἀχαιῶν:
a formulaic phrase that evokes the responsibility of leaders towards their people;
cf. 214n. (ποιμένα λαῶν), and 327n. Diomedes depicts the Theban War as a disaster;
one implication may be that he needs to adopt a different set of values.   Ἀχαιῶν:
5n. The same term refers to the army of the Seven against Thebes and those who
took part in the Trojan expedition.

224–9 Diomedes states, uncontroversially, that Glaukos should be his guest in
Argos, and his host in Lycia. He then explores how they should behave towards one
another on the battlefield. First, he suggests that they avoid each other's spears, even
when they meet in the thick of battle (καὶ δι' ὁμίλου). Then, he consoles himself by
contemplating the many Trojans he can kill and, in an act of reciprocity, encourages

Glaukos to kill as many Achaeans as he can manage, cf. 229n. (δύνηαι). This proposal echoes the exchange of gifts between Oineus and Bellerophontes: cf. ἀλλήλοις at 218 and ἀλλήλων at 226; but the idea of trading off the lives of comrades as a sort of gift exchange is problematic; on the importance of not pleasing the enemy, cf. 82n. Diomedes implies that Glaukos may not be able to kill anybody anyway, but his speech remains puzzling, and Glaukos' endorsement of it even more so.

224 τῶ 'therefore': after dealing with Tydeus, Diomedes focuses again on the friendship between his grandfather and Bellerophontes.   νῦν: Diomedes now explores the consequences of the past for the present situation.   μέν: cf. 225n.   φίλος: cf. 67n. For a similar friendship across battle lines (though not at the expense of the larger community), cf. 7.301–3: there as here, nothing more is heard of the friendship. At 21.106 φίλος is used of an enemy, but sarcastically; cf. Goldhill 1991: 88–9. Diomedes' attitude is in sharp contrast to that of Agamemnon: 55–60n.   Ἄργεϊ μέσσωι: an important qualification; Diomedes goes on to work out how he should relate to Glaukos on the battlefield. For Argos as the home of Diomedes, cf. 2.559–63 with Cingano 2004: 60–8; for Argos as Glaukos' remote place of origin, cf. μυχῶι Ἄργεος, 152n. μέσος is a frequent epithet of Argos especially in the *Odyssey*; cf. the formulaic κατ' Ἑλλάδα καὶ μέσον Ἄργος.

225 Diomedes again qualifies his statement: Glaukos is his dear guest-friend – especially if he were to visit him in Lycia; for a similar qualification, cf. 229n. (ὅν κε δύνηαι).   δ' takes up μέν in line 224; for reciprocal constructions in the speech, cf. 212–31n.   τῶν: the Lycians.   δῆμον: cf. 158n.

226 ἔγχεα δ' ἀλλήλων ἀλεώμεθα 'let us avoid each other's spears'. The assonance between ἀλλήλων and ἀλεώμεθα makes for a memorable turn of phrase. The verb in the 1st pers. plur. suggests intimacy: cf. 58n., 70n., 99–100n., 114n.; it is rarely used of warriors fighting on opposite sides, but see 3.94 (the truce is proposed) and 7.299 (Ajax and Hector exchange gifts in an episode that echoes the present one). The printed text reflects the Homeric notion of combat as deliberate confrontation: 17.373–5, 20.257–8; cf. 126n. Many manuscripts and one papyrus read ἔγχεσι δ' ἀλλήλων ἀλεώμεθα. Zenodotus appears to have read ἔγχεσι δ' ἀλλήλους ἀλεώμεθα: 'let us spare each other with our spears'. The variants suggest that ancient readers were worried about the cowardice implied in 'let us avoid' and suggested a more active and therefore heroic alternative: 'let us spare'; cf. ΣAbT ad 6.226a–c. However, ἀλέομαι is not construed with the genitive in Homer, nor does it mean 'spare': it is best to account for that usage as an attempt at improvement.   ἔγχεα: on the prominence of Diomedes' spear in book 6, cf. 213n.   ἀλλήλων suggests reciprocity, cf. 212–31n. and 224–9n.   ἀλεώμεθα: cf. 167n. (ἀλέεινε).   καὶ δι' ὁμίλου 'also in the thick of battle'. The prepositional phrase δι' ὁμίλου is used elsewhere when one warrior singles out and kills another in the thick of battle (cf. 12.191–2, 17.293–4); here it emphasises Diomedes' departure from conventional expectations. ὅμιλος can refer to any crowd, but in the *Iliad* it usually describes the host of Achaeans and Trojans fighting on the battlefield.

227–9 Diomedes devotes two lines to himself and one to Glaukos. The exchange is supposed to be equal, but here and in other details we see the balance tipping in favour of Diomedes, cf. 229n. (ὄν κε δύνηαι) and 232–6n.

227 πολλοὶ μὲν γὰρ ἐμοί 'for there are many . . . for me to kill', with ellipsis of εἰσίν; cf. 229n.   Τρῶες . . . ἐπίκουροι = 18.229, ~ 3.451, 17.14 and many related expressions: cf. 111n. Diomedes' proposal ought to worry Glaukos: he is talking to a Trojan ally about his eagerness to kill other Trojans and allies, cf. 224–9n.   κλειτοί 'famous' (κλείω); as an epithet of the Trojan allies, κλειτός alternates with τηλεκλειτός, for which see 111n.

228 ὄν κε . . . πόρῃι . . . κιχείω: Diomedes continues to emphasise the role of the gods in his life, yet without detracting from his own ability. On double motivation, see Introduction 4.3.   γε qualifies the boast, adding an element of piety; cf. 128–9n., 21.103–4.   πόρῃι echoes πόρον at 218: Diomedes continues to adapt aspects of the ancestral gift exchange to the present circumstances on the battlefield.   καὶ ποσσὶ κιχείω: cf. 11.367 (Diomedes) and 20.454 (Achilles). Swiftness is an important quality in a warrior, cf. 15.569–70. Achilles is the swift-footed hero *par excellence*, Diomedes is the best of the Achaeans now that Achilles is away: cf. 98n., 99–100n.   κιχείω: aor. subj. κιχάνω may simply mean 'encounter, catch' (498n.), but forms of the verb are also used of deadly and inescapable powers: cf., e.g., 17.478 (death), 19.165–6 (hunger and thirst), *Od.* 9.477 (one's own evil deeds).

229 πολλοὶ δ' αὖ σοί echoes 227, thus suggesting a balanced exchange between friends; for the difficulties involved, cf. 224–9n., 227–9n.   αὖ: cf. 184n. (δεύτερον αὖ).   Ἀχαιοί: cf. 5n., 222–3n.   ἐναιρέμεν: cf. 32n.   ὄν κε δύνηαι: Diomedes doubts Glaukos' abilities as a warrior, cf. Kirk 1990: 189. The scholia, by contrast, read the line as an attempt, on the part of Diomedes, to give Glaukos some credit, cf. ΣT *ad* 6.227–9*b*. In his list of casualties, Hyginus, *Fab.* 114–15, claims that Glaukos killed four people in total during the war, whereas Diomedes killed eighteen: there is clearly a disparity between these two warriors.

230–1 Diomedes suggests an exchange of armour, as a public token of friendship. The offer is persuasive, but later the poet reveals that Diomedes profited from the exchange, and that Glaukos was a fool to agree to it: 234–6. Ancient readers worried about Diomedes' apparent greed and also about the wisdom of stripping on the battlefield: Introduction 4.1. Usually, weapons are won as spoils: Nestor insisted that the Achaeans should not stop and take spoils but concentrate on killing instead, see 66–71n.; now Diomedes strikes a private agreement and gains an armour of gold without fighting.   ἀλλήλοις: cf. 212–31n., 224–9n.   ἐπαμείψομεν 'let us exchange'; aorist subjunctive with short stem vowel, as often in early Greek epic. The short vowel is older and survives in contexts where a long vowel is metrically impossible (as here); cf. Introduction 2.5. The 1st pers. plur. suggests intimacy, cf. 226n.   ὄφρα καὶ οἵδε | γνῶσιν: a striking case of necessary enjambment. It reminds us that the confrontation between Glaukos and Diomedes is on public display and forces us to consider how it may look from the perspective of the Achaeans and the Trojans: cf. 120n. (ἐς μέσον ἀμφοτέρων). It is rare that the Achaeans and the Trojans are referred to as one group (οἵδε). γνῶσιν is a contracted form of expected γνώωσιν (1.302 etc.). ξεῖνοι πατρώϊοι: echoes 215 in ring composition, though now the emphasis is on agreement. εὐχόμεθ᾽ εἶναι: a common phrase in this metrical position. It echoes Glaukos' boast at the end of his speech (211n.): rather than a proud warrior, he is now Diomedes' guest-friend – and a dupe, as we soon discover: 232–6n. On the 1st pers. plur., cf. 226n.

232–6 The first two lines after Diomedes' speech invite us to read the episode as a rare example of human friendship across battle-lines; but in the next three lines the poet exposes this reading – together with the exchange of armour – as naïve. The last sentence forces us to reconsider the whole encounter: it draws attention to an underlying imbalance between the two warriors – an imbalance which Diomedes' rhetoric of equality had temporarily obscured – and poses some difficult questions about Glaukos' motives and those of Diomedes: Introduction 4.1.

232–3 The seven spondees lend the lines an air of solemnity. The effect is further enhanced by the rhyming verbs φωνήσαντε . . . ἀΐξαντε, and πιστώσαντο, which round off the scene. Duals are rare in speech-concluding lines and suggest harmony between interlocutors; cf. 10.349–50, *Od.* 24.361. Here they recall the opening of the episode: 119–22n., 120n. Normally, descriptions of single combat start with two opponents equally eager to fight and end with a winner and a loser. Here it seems that the two warriors are still on a par, but we soon realise that the exchange itself produces a glaring inequality.

232 ἄρα: the evidential particle marks, as often, the transition from direct speech to main narrative, cf. 116n., 312–13n., 369, 390n. and 494n.   καθ᾽ ἵππων ἀΐξαντε: the movement indicates trust: warriors are sometimes killed as they leap off their chariots, cf. 11.423–5 and 20.401–2.   ἵππων: chariot horses and hence the chariot.

233 For the shaking of hands as a way of ratifying an agreement see 2.341 = 4.159. Kitts 2005: 79–82 discusses the gesture in Greece, in the Near East and in this specific passage.   ἀλλήλων: a recurrent word in Diomedes' speech, cf. 212–31n.   πιστώσαντο: from πιστόομαι, in epic only in the aorist. This is a rare verb and its meaning seems to fluctuate considerably according to context, cf. *LfgrE* s.v. πιστώσασθαι; here: 'gave each other assurances'.

234 Homeric characters often invoke Zeus when they try to account for events they do not understand: Jörgensen 1904; Graziosi and Haubold 2005: 82–3; cf. 159n. and 198–9n. on the inscrutability of Zeus in Glaukos' account. Here it seems that the poet himself is puzzled by the implications of the exchange.   ἔνθ᾽ marks an important moment in the story; cf. 73n.   αὖτε introduces a shift of focus; cf. 73n.   Κρονίδης: in early Greek epic the epithet is used exclusively of Zeus, because he is Kronos' successor as well as one of his sons.   φρένας ἐξέλετο Ζεύς = 19.137; Hes. *Sc.* 89; Hes. fr. 69 MW; cf., e.g., 9.377. Expressions of this kind refer to obvious and serious misjudgements, which have disastrous consequences for those who make them and are therefore barely comprehensible; cf. 18.310–13, 19.134–8. It is ironic, for a descendant of Sisyphos, to be duped so easily; cf. Mazon 1948: 164–5.

235 Τυδεΐδην: the patronymic defines Diomedes' identity, whether or not he remembers his father (222–3n.) or wishes to follow his example, see Graziosi and Haubold 2005: 58. On traditional epithets, see further Introduction 2.2. τεύχε' ἄμειβε ~ 14.381 (the Achaeans exchange armour among themselves); cf. 17.192 (Hector swaps his armour with that of Patroclus – after he has killed and stripped him). The phrase evokes the common line-ending τεύχε' ἐσύλα, 'he stripped him of his armour', and helps to recast the exchange of arms as a notional defeat. Ancient readers found the exchange unlikely and problematic: ΣbT ad 6.235a suggest that the two warriors did not strip but only exchanged a belt and a sword, like Hector and Ajax at 7.303–5. The term τεύχεα, however, more naturally refers to the whole armour (specifically defensive armour), rather than to individual items: Trümpy 1950: 75–9.

236 The line brings the encounter to a memorable end. Glaukos aspired 'to be the best always' (208n.); but he will be remembered, above all, for the humiliating conclusion to this episode. χρύσεα χαλκείων: Glaukos' golden armour is introduced abruptly and thus seems all the more incongruous; cf. Glaukos' own sudden and incongruous prominence at the beginning of the episode: 119n., 124–5n. Weapons are usually made of bronze, although gold does feature, especially in armour made by Hephaistos; for Achilles' armour, cf. 18.475, 517 etc., 20.265–72 and Edwards 1991: 202–3; for Heracles' armour in Hesiod's *Aspis*, cf., e.g., Hes. *Sc.* 124–5, 142. The scholia AT ad 8.195 infer that Hephaistos made Glaukos' armour too; cf. ΣT ad 6.234b[1]. On gold as the metal of gods see Avery 1994: 500–1; and Piccaluga 1980: 243–4, who quotes 10.440–1; on Diomedes' concern that Glaukos may in fact be a god, cf. 123–43n. Displaying gold on the battlefield can be a sign of prestige (8.192–3, on the shield of Nestor), but also of foolishness: see 2.871–5 on Nastes (or, according to the scholia, his brother Antimachus), who enters battle decked in gold 'like a maiden' and comes to a bad end. The scholia also remark, perceptively, that Glaukos offers a gift of gold, just like his grandfather Bellerophontes: ΣbT ad 6.234a. ἑκατόμβοι' ἐννεαβοίων 'worth one hundred oxen' and 'worth nine oxen' respectively. Oxen are a standard currency in Homeric epic; cf. Macrakis 1984 and Mondio 1996. The number one hundred expresses completion and magnitude, cf. 115n.; the number nine tends to express incompleteness and a need for resolution, cf. 174n.

237–41: HECTOR ENTERS THE CITY

As soon as Hector reaches the Scaean Gates, he is surrounded by women asking after their loved ones – a highly dramatic scene which classical audiences may have perceived as especially close to tragedy; cf., for example, Eteocles' exchange with the chorus of women in the besieged city of Thebes at Aesch. *Sept.* 78–286, with Ieranò 2002: 79. Helenos had already warned Hector about the dangers of 'falling into the hands of the women' (81–2n.); now he must not be weakened or delayed. He tells each of the women to pray to the gods – this is exactly the message he said he would deliver to them when describing his mission to the other men on the battlefield: 114n. And it is also the only message relevant to all women – regardless of their personal circumstances which, the poet reveals, are very different: Introduction 3.2. This opening scene sets up Hector's future meetings with his own loved ones. The order in which the different relationships are introduced here (παῖδας… κασιγνήτους… ἔτας… πόσιας) loosely suggests the order of Hector's own encounters: Hecuba with Laodike, then Helen and finally Andromache.

237 ~ 9.354, 11.170.   Σκαιὰς… πύλας: an important landmark in the *Iliad*, indicating the line between city and battlefield, cf. 307n., 373n.; Introduction 4.4; Elliger 1975: 60; and Scully 1990: 42–4. Hector meets the women as he enters the Scaean Gates and later meets Andromache on his way back to the battlefield: 392–3n.   φηγόν: one of two significant trees outside Troy. The oak suggests safety and respite for the Trojans (Thornton 1984: 150–2), the fig tree marks the most vulnerable part of the walls (433n., 434n.), cf. 11.166–71: the Trojans flee past the fig tree and make a stand by the Scaean Gates and the oak. Scully 1990: 10–14 discusses the oak and other landmarks on the Trojan plain. The alternative line-ending πύργον ἵκανεν, though well attested since antiquity, has no parallel in Homer. The gates and the oak tree together mark the boundary between the city and the plain, and they symbolise safety; πύργον is best explained as an attempt, on the part of ancient readers, to answer the kind of objection raised also by M. L. West 2001a: 196 (who points out that the tree is outside the walls while the women stay inside).

238 The women swirl around Hector; cf. Hecuba and Andromache at 251n. and 394n., and contrast Helen at 354n.   ἄρα: the evidentiary particle suddenly brings the women into focus, as they swarm around Hector; cf. 2n.   Τρώων… θύγατρες: the phrase describes the Trojan women in general (note the inclusive particle ἠδέ: 90n.), though the emphasis is on women in their prime, see Introduction 3.3. For ἄλοχοι: 337n. The women are described in relation to their male relatives. In the next line the focus shifts and we look at the men through the eyes of their women.

239 εἰρόμεναι: from εἴρομαι, 'ask about', often – as here – with an accusative.   ἔτας τε: the exact meaning of ἔτης is uncertain and may be unclear to the poet: Gates 1971: 31. All passages where it occurs suggest a close relationship; almost all instances are accompanied by more familiar terms for 'friends' or 'relations': cf., e.g., 7.295 (together with ἑταῖροι, of the people closest to Ajax), 9.464–5 (together with ἀνεψιοί, of the people closest to Phoenix), *Od.* 15.273 (with κασίγνητοι, of the people who are closest to a murdered man and might avenge him). Here it must describe men who are particularly close and dear to the women, e.g. other relatives. For the meaning of the word in Hecuba's speech, cf. 262n.

240 καὶ πόσιας: particular emphasis is placed on this word, in enjambment.   ἔπειτα: an unusual deployment of the word, hinting perhaps that Hector lets some of the excitement die down before replying.   θεοῖς εὔχεσθαι: Hector entered the city in order to tell the women to pray; now he repeats the message to each of them, without lingering on the fate of individuals, cf. 115n. and 304n.   ἀνώγει: cf. 170n. (ἠνώγει).

241 A moving line: all women are told to pray, though some are already bereaved while others are not. As often, the poet knows more than the characters within the story: Introduction 1 and 3.1. Later Andromache finds herself in the same situation as that of the bereaved women mentioned here: at 22.437–46 we see her think and behave like a wife, while we know that she has already become a widow. For the balance struck, within a line, between communal tragedy and individual grief, cf. 21.524. **πάσας ἑξείης:** construe with ἀνώγει, not εὔχεσθαι. Hector tells the women to pray, addressing them one by one as each asks about her relatives. The scholia report an ancient variant πᾶσι μάλ' ἑξείης, 'to all of them (i.e. all the gods), one by one'; cf. *Od.* 11.134 ~ *Od.* 23.281. The variant misses the point: Hector has one answer for each individual concern. **πολλῆισι δὲ κήδε' ἐφῆπτο** ~ 2.15 = 32 = 69. Translate 'but many had grief (already) tied to them' (pluperfect). The phrase evokes a formulaic expression which ties men to death: ὀλέθρου πείρατ' ἐφῆπται/-ο at 7.402, 12.79, *Od.* 22.33 and 41. The equivalent to death, for women, is grief; cf. 22.477–84, where Andromache claims that she and Hector were born to the same fate, since his death corresponds to her grief. For a similar example of evocative if slightly obscure language, cf. 143n.

242–85: THE ENCOUNTER BETWEEN HECTOR AND HECUBA

242–52 This section is elaborately structured: lines 251–2 contain the main clause, which follows after the temporal subclause in line 242–3; in between, the narrator places an arresting description of Priam's palace, which is itself carefully designed: lines 244–6 correspond to 248–50. The description is as bulky as the palace itself: we are confronted with a massive construction in polished stone, quite unlike any other building in early hexameter epic; modern commentators often comment on its 'air of unreality', Kirk 1990: 193; see also Alden 1990. Dalby 1995 argues that palaces in Homer are grandiose versions of ordinary homes, rather than realistic descriptions of eighth-century palaces; for other Homeric palaces see Rougier-Blanc 2002 and 2005; for possible real-life models for the palace of Priam, see Hertel 2003: 157–8. Drerup 1969, Fagerström 1988 and Weiler 2001 discuss the archaeology of Iron Age palaces. Priam's palace does not stand out for its riches (as do those of Menelaos and Alcinous: *Od.* 4.71–5, 7.86–132), nor does it exhibit supernatural features (such as Alcinous' immortal dogs, made of silver and gold: *Od.* 7.91–4). Rather, the poet emphasises its solidity and its capacity to accommodate an exceptionally large family within an ordered structure: see Taplin 1992: 117 ('the breeding ground of a great dynasty'). The fact that sons-in-law live with Priam adds to his power but also suggests that Priam needs help: at least one of them has moved to Troy specifically in order to lend support during the war; cf. 248–50n. It is understandable that the women who live in this enormous place find it hard to distinguish between the city and the family; in fact, Hector himself is accused of doing the same: 5.473–4. In many ways, the palace symbolises the fortified citadel itself; cf. Taplin 1992: 117 with n. 14; Introduction 3.3.

242 ~ *Od.* 6.85.   ἀλλ᾽ ὅτε δή: 172n.

243 ξεστῇς αἰθούσῃσι τετυγμένον: cf. 20.11. An αἴθουσα is a roofed space outside the main hall of the house, which typically protrudes into the courtyard (αὐλή) and may be situated in an extension (πρόδομος). The αἴθουσα is often used for putting up guests (24.644, *Od.* 3.397–9, 4.296–7, 7.335–6, 344–5, with Rougier-Blanc 1996 and 2005: 97–111). Apart from Priam's palace, only the palaces of Alcinous and Zeus are said to have more than one αἴθουσα: in those cases, as here, the emphasis is on the large number of people, or gods, hosted in the palace: 20.10–12, *Od.* 8.56–8. Hector approaches the outer buildings first, though by the end of the line we are introduced to the palace proper: ἐν αὐτῶι.   ξεστῆς: cf. 244n.   τετυγμένον: perfect passive participle of τεύχω, 'make'.   αὐτάρ introduces the digression on Priam's palace; cf. 83n.   ἐν αὐτῶι: Priam's sons live inside the palace proper, unlike his daughters: 247n.

244 πεντήκοντ᾽: for Priam's fifty sons see 24.493–7; and Wöhrle 1999: 73–5, who points out that the poet mentions only twenty-two. Fifty is a significant number in early epic, cf. *LfgrE* s.v. πεντήκοντα. It suggests a large and useful group: fifty men make up a ship crew (2.719, 16.170) or a platoon (4.393, 8.563). Important households have fifty maidservants: *Od.* 7.103 and 22.421–2. Aigyptos has fifty sons (Hes. fr. 127 MW), and Nereus has fifty daughters (*Theog.* 263–4): having many children is generally presented as a good thing in early Greek epic, but they can also spell disaster – as Achilles tells Priam at 24.602–9; cf. 421n.   θάλαμοι: the θάλαμος is any private room (opp. μέγαρον) but especially the bedroom; cf. Rougier-Blanc 2005: 189–213, esp. 212–13; for θάλαμος as 'store room' cf. 288n. It is often explicitly associated with marriage: cf. 3.174, 11.227, 17.36, *Od.* 4.263.   These θάλαμοι will soon be invaded: 22.63.   ξεστοῖο λίθοιο: seats of honour are typically made of polished stone (cf. 18.504, *Od.* 3.406–12, 8.6), and the material is also used for the house of the immortal Circe: *Od.* 10.210–11. The stone suggests beauty, stability and continuity through time. Drerup 1969: 132 suggests that the present description reflects actual building techniques in the geometric period.

245–6 This image of peaceful and proper family life is in stark contrast to the immediate situation described in book 6.   πλησίοι ἀλλήλων: the plan of the palace reflects the structure of Priam's family; his daughters' rooms are located elsewhere: 247n., 248–50n. The variant πλησίον ἀλλήλων (adverb) is grammatically possible (cf. 3.115, *Od.* 14.14) but is less well attested, and early epic prefers forms of the adjective πλησίος to the adverb πλησίον where both are metrically possible; cf., e.g., 4.21, 6.249, 8.458   δεδμημένοι: perfect participle of δέμω, 'build'; cf. δόμος, 'building'.   παρὰ μνηστῇς ἀλόχοισι 'by their wedded wives' (cf. μνάομαι). The standard expression is (παρ᾽) αἰδοίῃς ἀλόχοισιν, see 250. Variant readings are attested both here and at 250, for a good discussion: Di Benedetto 1998: 88 with n. 4. For ἀλόχοισι see 337n.

247 κουράων δ᾽ 'the daughters' (sc. of Priam). On its own, κούρη usually describes a girl, though it can also refer to a married woman when she is seen primarily as her father's daughter; cf. the frequent references to Penelope as κούρη Ἰκαρίοιο. Here the daughters of Priam live in the outer buildings of their father's palace, even though they are married. On the possible reasons for this arrangement, cf. 248–50n.   ἑτέρωθεν ἐναντίοι ἔνδοθεν αὐλῆς 'elsewhere, opposite, inside the courtyard'. The exact location and arrangement of the daughters' rooms has puzzled modern readers (cf. Kirk 1990: 193), but the poet stresses that Priam's daughters and their husbands live in some outer buildings, rather than inside the palace proper: the spatial arrangement reflects the family structure, which matters in the context of book 6. Elsewhere Priam's daughters and his daughters-in-law are simply said to be in the palace: 24.166.   αὐλῆς: the courtyard around a palace, enclosed by a wall or fence and marking the outer limit of the property, cf. 316n. It is sometimes used for animal husbandry (e.g. 4.433, 24.161–5, 640) but does not normally feature θάλαμοι. Telemachus' bedroom is located in the courtyard at *Od.* 1.425–6: this is a sign of his uncertain status in the household while Odysseus is away. The courtyard may contain extensions of other kinds, especially the αἴθουσα; cf. 243n. Since αἴθουσαι are primarily intended for guests, Priam's married daughters and their husbands are perhaps thought to be similar in status to guests; cf. 13.170–6: Medesikaste, a daughter of Priam, married Imbrios and moved to his place in Pedaios; however, Imbrios has now returned to Troy to fight in the war, and he lives in the palace. Relatives by marriage are expected to help their in-laws (cf. 167–70n., 5.473–4, 13.463–6), though they remain subordinated, in the family hierarchy, to blood relations.

248–50 ~ 244–6. Homeric husbands may, in some circumstances, reside with the family of their wives, as is the case here; cf. Snodgrass 1974: 120; I. Morris 1986: 107; and most recently Finkelberg 2005: 65–89, who argues that the arrangement reflects actual Bronze Age practice. The normal pattern in epic is for the woman to move to her husband's ancestral home upon marriage (*LfgrE* s.v. γαμέω B); this was also standard practice among early Greek audiences of the *Iliad*, and it is described as the norm in Hesiod's post-heroic world: *Op.* 695. In heroic epic, exceptions to the rule are possible if the husband cannot offer a suitable home of his own, or if he is recruited into his wife's family on the basis of her father's superior power and wealth: cf. 193n., 14.115–25, and *Od.* 6.244–5 (Nausicaa hopes Odysseus may marry her and stay in Scherie); and for the more complicated case of Iphidamas at *Il.* 11.221–45 see Mirto 1997: 1096–7. As a group, sons-in-law who reside in their wives' home enhance the power of their father-in-law. Thus, for example, Nestor hosts his sons and his sons-in-law: this is a sign of his status, cf. *Od.* 3.386–7. Priam's power is also enhanced by the presence of his sons-in-law, though in this case their presence also indicates an emergency: 247n.   δώδεκ': cf. 93–4n., and 244n. (on the twelve children of Niobe). This is an impressive number of daughters, though clearly inferior to that of the sons.   τέγεοι 'roofed over', only here. The adjective strengthens the impression that the chambers of the daughters and their husbands are located outside the main building; cf. 247n.   γαμβροί: cf. 177n.   παρ᾽ αἰδοίηις ἀλόχοισιν: cf. 245–6n.

251 Like the Trojan women at the Scaean Gates (238n.), and Andromache later in the book (394n.), Hecuba approaches Hector as soon as she sees him. She walks (ἤλυθε) whereas the younger women run, but her eagerness is obvious. Helen, by contrast, invites Hector to walk towards her, and sit down – one of her many seductive ploys: 354n. On Hecuba's movements, see further 252n.   ἔνθα: Hector meets his mother at the palace, Helen in her bedroom, and Andromache at the Scaean Gates: those locations are crucial for the encounters that follow, cf. 318n. with 321–2 and 392–3n., 394n. On the accentuation of ἔνθά οἱ, see Probert 2003: 148–50; for this passage, it is attested in all the major manuscripts.   ἠπιόδωρος: only here in epic (but cf. Stes. 223.2 Davies), perhaps 'she who gives soothing presents'. The word ἤπιος often characterises fathers who cherish their children, cf. 8.40 = 22.184, 24.770, etc. The scholia compare 22.83, where Hecuba reminds Hector of the breast she offered him as a child, memorably describing it as λαθικηδής 'making (babies) forget their sorrow'. The suggestion is perceptive, for Hecuba will soon offer Hector another drink that instils forgetfulness: 265n. (ἀλκῆς τε λάθωμαι). In his reply, Hector reverts to more conventional language, calling his mother πότνια (the standard epithet of μήτηρ) and refusing her offer of wine.   μήτηρ: Hecuba is introduced in relation to Hector: cf. 87n. and contrast 293n.

252 ~ 3.124. Ancient and modern readers have wondered about Hecuba's movements: it seems that she is arriving at the palace from elsewhere, together with Laodike, and that she encounters Hector in front of the door: M. L. West 2001a: 196–7. Others have supposed that she comes from within the palace, but this reading makes Λαοδίκην ἐσάγουσα difficult to understand. Aristarchus took it to mean: 'going towards/entering the house of Laodike'; cf. ΣAbT *ad* 6.252ab. However, ἄγειν is not used in this way in Homer, and Aristarchus' reading is not adopted in the medieval manuscripts; cf. *LfgrE* s.v. ἄγω B VII d. The arrival of Hecuba and Laodike from elsewhere reinforces the impression that Hector has entered a sphere where women meet and move according to their own routines and patterns; cf. Introduction 3.2. The presence of Laodike is important: lone women are rare in epic, both within the home and outside it. Later in the book Andromache is accompanied by a wet nurse (389n. and 399n.), and even in book 22, when she dashes out fearing that Hector might be dead, she asks two maids to follow her: 22.450.   Λαοδίκην: daughter of Priam and wife of Helikaon, son of Antenor. She was first mentioned at 3.121–4, when Iris took on her semblance and told Helen to go out and watch the battle from the city walls. As the most beautiful daughter of Priam, and as someone who was last seen together with Helen, she reminds the audience that Helen is not far off – and indeed Hector goes on to meet Helen herself in the next scene: 312–69. Later authors report that Laodike was not taken captive after the fall of Troy: see, e.g., Lycophron, *Alexandra* 316–22 with Hurst and Kolde 2008: 146; Pausanias 10.26.7–9; Apollodorus, *Epitome* 5.25; cf. *LIMC* s.v. Laodike II. It is possible that her presence in this passage already alludes to ancient traditions about the sack of Troy. On Laodike's mother-in-law, Theano, cf. 298n.

253–62 Hecuba's speech is loosely structured in ring composition around her central request: ἀλλὰ μέν', 258n.; cf. 262n. On its contents, and the characterisation of Hecuba in this scene, see further Introduction 4.2.

253 A common speech-introductory line both in the *Iliad* and the *Odyssey*; cf. 406n. It suggests a degree of intimacy between speaker and addressee but also signals that the speaker wants to establish even greater closeness: cf. 18.384 and 423. Physical contact is not just a spontaneous gesture: it typically introduces an attempt at winning over the addressee, sometimes against considerable odds; cf., e.g., 14.232–62, *Od.* 2.302–22. ἔν τ'... οἱ φῦ χειρί 'she took his hand', not 'she clung to him with her hand'. χειρί is best taken with ἐν, rather than explained as an instrumental dative. At *Od.* 2.302 (cf. 321) the phrase clearly describes the holding of hands, see also *Il.* 7.108 and *Od.* 3.374. Further parallels for the use of ἐν tell against taking χειρί as an instrumental dative: *Od.* 1.381 = 18.410 = 20.268 (ὀδὰξ ἐν χείλεσι φύντες) and *Od.* 10.397 (ἔφυν δ' ἐν χερσίν). See also 1.513 ἐμπεφυῖα: Thetis clasps Zeus's knees; she certainly does not clasp him with her knees. φῦ: root aorist without thematic vowel. For the long υ, see Chantraine 1948–53: vol. i, 378. ἔπος: no hiatus: ϝέπος, cf. Latin *vox*. ἐκ τ' ὀνόμαζε 'she addressed him', a personal appeal, whether or not it includes the proper name (ὄνομα) of the addressee.

254 τέκνον 'son' – the word is used of grown-up sons or daughters in the *Iliad*; cf., e.g., Thetis to Achilles at 1.362 and 414, with Minchin 2007: 180–2. The next time Hecuba addresses Hector as τέκνον, he is about to die: 22.82 and 84; at 22.431 he is already dead. Priam calls Hector φίλον τέκος at 22.38; cf. 22.56. τίπτε < τί ποτε, 'why ever?', expresses strong surprise. πόλεμον θρασύν: cf. 10.28. The epithet θρασύς, 'fierce', is often used of warriors, and especially of Hector (seven times in the *Iliad*). The battlefield is where he belongs, and Hecuba cannot work out why he has left. εἰλήλουθας: cf. 128–9n.

255 ἦ μάλα δή 'no doubt', cf. 518n. The phrase betrays great animation in the speaker; cf. Griffin 1986: 45–6. It tends to introduce suppositions which are in some way problematic, either (a) because they are unfounded (*Od.* 4.770–2, 23.149–52); or (b) because they are likely to upset the addressee (*Il.* 15.90–1); or (c) because they are upsetting for the speaker (18.12–13). (a) and (b) are combined at 5.422, (a) and (c) at 21.55–6, (b) and (c) at 15.14–15. Hecuba starts off with a combination of (b) and (c) but then drifts off into (a): 256n. ἦ: 55n. δή: 52–3n. τείρουσι: cf. 85n. Hecuba is not wide of the mark. δυσώνυμοι... Ἀχαιῶν 'the accursed sons of the Achaeans', in contrast with her own dear son: even to mention the Achaeans is ill-omened (δυσ- + ὄνομα; cf. ΣAbT *ad* 6.255). δυσώνυμος is a strong word, good for cursing: the poet uses it at 12.116 (of Moira), but its impact emerges especially in character speech: see *Od.* 19.571–2; *Hom. Hymn* 3.368; cf. Δύσπαρι (*Il.* 3.39 = 13.769) and Κακοΐλιον οὐκ ὀνομαστήν (*Od.* 19.260). Hecuba often expresses herself vigorously: cf. 22.80 and 83, 24.201–2, 207, 212–13; here she twists a standard expression according to her point of view: Macleod 1982: 40. υἷες Ἀχαιῶν is common at verse end, cf. κοῦροι Ἀχαιῶν (used after vowel); it recalls well-known Near Eastern phrases: 'the sons of Israel', 'the sons of Assyria' etc.; cf. Roussel 1960: 162; M. L. West 1997a: 226. Early audiences may have heard in it a reference to the generation of the ἐπίγονοι (cf. *Epigoni*, fr. 1 West and Eur. *Supp.* 1213–15: παῖδες Ἀργείων); the older Achaeans who fought in the Theban War are never called υἷες Ἀχαιῶν/κοῦροι

Ἀχαιῶν in extant epic. Classical audiences may have experienced it as patriotic: Pindar is among the first poets to replace υἷες Ἀχαιῶν with παῖδες Ἑλλήνων in the context of the Trojan War: *Isthm.* 3/4.54b; for the patriotic ring of that phrase, see Aesch. *Pers.* 402; cf. also Eur. *Hec.* 928–32.

256 ἄστυ: cf. 95n.   **θυμὸς ἀνῆκεν:** Hecuba is wrong about that: Hector's presence in Troy is part of a carefully thought-out strategy, not an impulsive decision prompted by his θυμός; cf. 72–118n. and Introduction 4.2. Later Hector claims that his θυμός actually impels him to fight in the first line of battle, not to stay in the city: 361n. and 444n. On θυμός, cf. 51n.

257 Hecuba continues to mix wild guesses with acute intuition. Hector has indeed come to appease the gods, though his mission is not to pray to Zeus – but rather to tell the women to appease Athena. Eventually, though, he will pray to Zeus: 475–81n.; Introduction 4.2.   **ἐξ ἄκρης πόλιος:** cf. 88n. For offerings to Zeus made at the highest point in the city, cf. 22.170–2.   **χεῖρας ἀνασχεῖν:** formulaic in epic, and a typical gesture of ancient prayer; cf. 301n., Lateiner 1997: 244 and 250; Pulleyn 1997: 188–9.

258–60 Hecuba moves seamlessly from the idea of a libation to the suggestion that Hector himself drink some wine: note the striking enjambment at 260n. and see Casabona 1966: 233. Above all, she wants to look after Hector (cf. 258: ἀλλὰ μέν'). Hector seems to sense this: he replies first to her suggestion that he drink some wine and then explains why a libation would also be inappropriate: 264–8n. For the libation, cf. 24.283–9 and 300–1.

258 ἀλλὰ μέν': in a prominent position at the beginning of the line. This is Hecuba's central request. Like all the other women Hector meets in Troy, Hecuba tries to delay him; cf. 354–6n. (Helen) and 431n. (Andromache).   **ὄφρα κε . . . ἐνείκω** 'so that in the meantime I bring you'; the basic sense is temporal, but ὄφρα κε also conveys a purpose; cf. 113 (ὄφρ' ἄν), and Chantraine 1948–53: vol. II, 262–3.   **μελιηδέα οἶνον:** a frequent noun–epithet phrase: wine, in Greek epic, is the 'honey-sweet' drink *par excellence* and is therefore tempting. The epithet usually characterises wine intended for consumption rather than libation, cf. 4.346, *Od.* 18.151, 426. Hecuba is already thinking of offering Hector the wine to drink: 260n. No hiatus before (ϝ)οῖνον; cf. Latin *vinum*.   **ἐνείκω:** cf. ἤνεικα, Attic ἤνεγκον, 'I carried'.

259 After the temporal/final ὄφρα κε, Hecuba becomes more explicit about her intent: ὡς introduces a straightforward purpose clause.   **Διὶ πατρὶ καὶ ἄλλοις ἀθανάτοισι:** this is a vague guess on the part of Hecuba, cf. 475n.

260 πρῶτον, ἔπειτα δέ: a striking case of 'corrective' enjambment, cf. Introduction 2.1. Hecuba betrays her motherly instincts: she wants to nourish Hector, as ΣbT *ad* 6.260c point out.   **καὐτός:** the letters ΚΑΥΤΟΣ are best interpreted as καὶ αὐτός, with crasis. Some ancient readers and many medieval manuscripts prefer κ' αὐτός = κε(ν) αὐτός: cf. ΣΑΤ *ad* 6.260ab. This is grammatically possible (for κε(ν) with the future tense see 353n. καί μιν) but is unlikely: Hecuba's point is precisely that Hector too (καὶ αὐτός) should have his share of the wine. Aristarchus seems to have treated the passage as a test case for his view that 'redundant κε is typical of

Homer' (ΣA *ad* 6.260*b*), which would explain the popularity of the variant reading; cf. 13.734 with Janko 1994: 139; Matthaios 1999: 367 and 578–9.   ὀνήσεαι 'you will feel better'; 2nd pers. sing. fut. middle of ὀνίνημι. The suddenness of Hecuba's afterthought suggests a fresh main clause; for a different interpretation (ὀνήσεαι = subjunctive dependent on ὡς), see Stoevesandt 2008: 93.   αἴ κε πίηισθα 'if you drink'. The phrase is modelled on the common verse ending αἴ κε πίθησθα: 'if you listen to me'. In this case, to listen is to drink; cf. Kirk 1990: 195.

261 For wine as a source of strength in war cf. 9.705–6, and especially 19.160–1 and 167–70, with Lardinois 1997: 219. This is a persuasive final flourish on the part of Hecuba: the proverbial tone suits the elderly mother who tries to persuade her son; for Homer's use of proverbial expressions and their role in characterisation, see Lardinois 2000. Wine is a common and accepted way of restoring a man's strength but it is also a notorious test of his restraint and social competence; cf., e.g., *Od.* 9.345–61, 14.463–6, 21.295–8, with Arnould 2002. Ancient commentators discuss at length whether Hector was right to refuse Hecuba's offer of wine. Among other things, they consider the fact that wine needs to be consumed along with food, and at the right time, i.e. in the evening, not in the middle of a fighting day; ΣbT *ad* 6.260*cd*.   κεκμηῶτι: part. perf. act. of κάμνω; for this form as a 'compromise' between Ionic -ότι and Aeolic -οντι, see Chantraine 1948–53: vol. i, 431; Wachter 2000: 101.   μένος: cf. 26–7n.   μέγα: best taken with ἀέξει ('greatly increases') rather than construed as a proleptic adjective ('so as to be great').   οἶνος: for the apparent hiatus see 258n.

262 The line recapitulates 255–6 in ring composition. However, this time Hecuba places greater emphasis on Hector's exhaustion.   ὡς 'just as'; one might perhaps have expected ὧς, 'thus, that way', but comparative clauses are flexible in early Greek epic; cf. 109n.   τύνη ~ σύ (emphatic).   κέκμηκας picks up κεκμηῶτι in the line above.   ἀμύνων σοῖσιν ἔτηισι 'defending your dear ones'. For ἔτηισι cf. 239n. Hecuba presents the Trojan War as a family matter. From Hector's perspective, however, his duties to the family and his role as a warrior are not easy to reconcile, see Introduction 4.

263–85 Hector makes three points in reply: he declines Hecuba's offer (264–8n.), repeats Helenos' instructions (269–78n.) and declares he will go to see Paris (280–5n.). Hector is respectful and precise – until he entirely loses his temper at the mention of Paris: wine is not the point – he implies – only the death of Paris would enable him to forget his sorrows; cf. λάθωμαι, 265n. and ἐκλελαθέσθαι, 285n.; with Mackie 1996: 103–5. On Hector's sudden outburst, see further Introduction 4.2.

263 = 359n. A common line introducing replies, cf. Edwards 1970: 4–5. Other lines of broadly equivalent meaning were available to the poet: see 440n. and 520n., with Friedrich 2007: 68–77. Three papyri (among which West's 270, cf. 45n., 90n.) read: τὴν δ' ἀπαμειβόμενος προσέφη κορυθαίολος Ἕκτωρ; cf. 520n. The printed text creates a sharper contrast between Hecuba's address to her 'son' (τέκνον: 254n.) and the 'great' (μέγας) Hector who answers her.

264–8 Hector first explains why he should not drink any wine, thus addressing Hecuba's need to look after him (264–5). He then explains why it would be inappropriate for him to make a libation and pray to Zeus (266–8). His considerations naturally lead on to the request that she organise the prayers and offering for Athena: 269–78n. Implicit in Hector's words is a rationale for his mission: while the women rely on the men to keep them safe, the men rely on women to uphold proper ritual activity, especially in this time of crisis. Their sphere is one of relative purity, away from the blood, violence and death of the battlefield. For Hector's martial appearance and its inappropriateness in the domestic setting of *Iliad* 6, cf. 318–20n. and 467–70n.

264 ἄειρε 'lift up' and hence 'offer'. The expression is slightly elliptic: it takes up ἐνείκω in line 258; cf. 293 (ἀειραμένη . . . φέρε), and *Od*. 1.141 = 4.57 (παρέθηκεν ἀείρας). μελίφρονα: a common epithet of wine, food and sleep, and one of Hector's favourite words: it highlights, by contrast, his sense of duty, see Mackie 1996: 104. Unlike μελιηδέα (above), μελίφρονα evokes the effect of wine on the mind, cf. ΣbT *ad* 6.264*b* τὸν ἀναγκάζοντα ἡδέα διανοεῖσθαι. Hector goes on to describe the negative effects wine would have on his mental state; on the effects of wine, see Sullivan 1997. πότνια μῆτερ: a respectful address (Vermeule 1974: 78–9). πότνια is used either of mothers (cf. 413n., 429, 471n.) or of goddesses (cf. 305n.).

265 According to Hector, Hecuba's wine would make him forget his strength (μένος, ἀλκή) and hence compromise his virility. On wine and forgetfulness: Arnould 2002: 10. μή μ᾽ ἀπογυιώσηις μένεος 'lest you strip me of my strength'; an expression of intense physicality, cf. γυῖα 'limbs' and γυιόω = 'paralyse' at 8.402, 416 and Hes. *Theog*. 858. It evidently impressed ancient readers; cf. Pl. *Crat*. 415a. Forms of the verb (ἀπο)γυμνόω are likewise used, before the main caesura, to suggest the idea of emasculation: cf. *Od*. 10.301 (∼ 341) μή σ᾽ ἀπογυμνωθέντα κακὸν καὶ ἀνήνορα θήηι, where the verb refers to actual, as well as metaphorical, nakedness. μένεος: contrast μένος at 261. Hector contradicts Hecuba's proverb. ἀλκῆς τε λάθωμαι: contrast 112n. (μνήσασθε δὲ θούριδος ἀλκῆς). Hector describes a typical effect of magic potions (φάρμακα): cf. *Od*. 4.219–27 and 10.233–6.

266 Cf. Hes. *Op*. 724–5. χερσὶ δ᾽ ἀνίπτοισιν 'with unwashed hands'; cf. νίζω/νίπτω, 'wash'. Priam washes his hands before taking, from Hecuba, some wine and making a libation: 24.299–306. More generally, it is important to have clean hands when performing rituals: cf., e.g., 1.447–9, 9.171–8, 16.230–2, with Lateiner 1997: 252. ἀνίπτοισιν < ἄνιπτος, -ον, two-ending adjective. This is the reading of the MSS and one papyrus. West adopts Zenodotus' reading ἀνίπτηισιν, but the parallel in Hes. *Op*. 725 confirms the much better attested form ἀνίπτοισιν. In Attic, compound adjectives such as ἄνιπτος do not form a feminine in -η. They sometimes do in Homer, and Zenodotus appears to have regarded ἀνίπτηισιν as more properly Homeric; for a defense of his reading see van der Valk 1963–4: vol. II, 131–2. For Zenodotus on adjectives, see also 285n. (ἀτέρπου). αἴθοπα οἶνον 'sparkling wine' (cf. αἴθομαι, 'blaze'); the third epithet for wine in only eight lines. αἴθοψ typically describes wine in the context of libations; by contrast, μελιηδέα (258n.) and μελίφρονα

(264n.) relate to its consumption. The three epithets help to articulate the exchange between Hecuba and Hector.

267–8 Hector counters Hecuba's proverb (261n.) with an equally general statement about ritual propriety. Both speakers treat Hector's visit as a test case for proper social and religious behaviour. ἅζομαι expresses religious restraint, or a sense of awe, before the gods, their servants, or a ritual act; cf. Cairns 1993: 136. When characters are described as feeling this way, they are almost always right, though other characters may not think so, cf. 1.20–5. This is one of only two passages in early Greek epic where someone uses the verb ἅζεσθαι to describe his own feelings; cf. *Hom. Hymn* 2.76. οὐδέ πηι ἐστί = 24.71 = *Hom. Hymn* 1 d 9 West = *Hom. Hymn* 7.58. The enclitic adverb πηι ('anywhere', 'in any way') makes Hector's assertion stronger still; cf. *LfgrE* s.v. πῆι, πηι, πη B 3 c α. κελαινεφέϊ 'of the dark clouds'. A distinctive epithet of Zeus as lord of the sky. Κρονίωνι: an alternative form of Κρονίδης, used only of Zeus; cf. 234n.

268 ∼ *Od.* 22.402, 23.48. As the Odyssean parallels bring out, Hector describes himself as intruding, violently, into the domestic sphere. For blood-spattered warriors, cf. 11.169 ∼ 20.503 (note the emphasis on soiled hands in those passages, and compare Hector's concern with his own hands: 266n.). λύθρωι πεπαλαγμένον: λύθρωι (only in this form) is the defilement caused by blood. The noun is always used together with the verb παλάσσω, 'spatter', which is itself associated with bodily fluids and defilement: cf. *Od.* 13.395, Hes. *Op.* 733. εὐχετάασθαι: from εὐχετάομαι, cf. εὔχεσθαι (211n., 304n.). This extended form in -τα- allows the poet to use the verb more flexibly; see Risch 1974: 321. For the diectasis (-άα-), cf. 6n. (φόως), 148n. (τηλεθόωσα).

269–78 Cf. the instructions originally imparted by Helenos (86–98n.), and the ritual performed by the women (297–311n.). Hector has just explained why he is in no fit state to offer a libation to Zeus: this naturally leads on to his central request that Hecuba organise the offering for Athena, cf. 264–8n. Hector reports Helenos' instructions with few variations. Apart from some necessary syntactical adjustments, he mentions θύεα (270n.), and, more significantly perhaps, does not report the injunction to 'unlock the temple' (88–9n.); eventually it will be Theano, the priestess of Athena, who opens the sanctuary (298n.). The slight differences between Helenos' speech, that of Hector, and the ritual which the women actually perform are best explained by taking into consideration the different perspectives and circumstances of the characters involved: Introduction 3.2; Hector, when talking to Hecuba, insists specifically on what she herself must do.

269 σύ γε: emphasising the contrast between Hector, who cannot offer sacrifice, and Hecuba who must; for γε see also 16–17n. The alternative reading μέν seems less apt here than at 279. νηόν: cf. 88n. ἀγελείης: a distinctive epithet of Athena in Homeric and Hesiodic epic (*Sc.* 197). The precise meaning was already debated in antiquity: some readers derived it from ἄγειν and λεία/ληΐη/ληΐς, 'she who brings in the booty' (cf. ληΐτις at 10.460), while others thought of ἄγειν + λαός, 'leader of the people' (cf. λαοσσόος at e.g. 13.128); see *LfgrE* s.v. ἀγελείη Σχ. As often with divine

names and epithets, ambiguous or obscure language reflects the mysterious nature
of the gods. On obscure words associated with ritual, cf. 93–4n. (ἦνις ἠκέστας) and
134n. (θύσθλα), with Introduction 2.4.

270 ἔρχεο: uncontracted imperative (contrast -ou in Attic); cf. Chantraine
1948–53: vol. 1, 62 and below, 280n.   σὺν θυέεσσιν: probably 'with burnt offerings', as opposed to animal sacrifice or libations (cf. 9.499–500, Hes. *Op.* 336–9); see
Stoevesandt 2008: 97. This is an addition on the part of Hector (neither Helenos nor
the poet mention θύεα when describing the ritual for Athena: 86–98n. and 297–311n.)
and may emphasise the women's own contribution: burnt offerings are smaller and
easier to handle than the animal sacrifice they promise for later, cf. 93–4n.   ἀολλίσσασα: the rare verb ἀολλίζω (4 times in early epic) suggests a large, but rather *ad
hoc*, gathering (cf. 15.588, 19.54; cf. 19.42–5).   γεραιάς: cf. 87n.

271–8 See nn. *ad* vv. 90–7.

279 ~ 269 (ring composition), with μέν instead of γε. The particle leads on to
Hector's own plans in the next line: ἐγὼ δέ (280n.)   ἀλλά marks the transition to
a new section, as often in direct speech.

280–5 Hector now departs from Helenos' instructions, though it would be hard
to fault him for that: Paris should certainly fight, since everybody else is doing so on
his behalf. For a similar change of direction, cf. 365n., 366n., where Hector suddenly
announces he will go and see Andromache and Astyanax. As soon as Hector mentions Paris, he launches into a tirade against him. This is not the first time that Hector
complains about Paris (cf. 3.39–57), but his words here are extreme: even his syntax
becomes twisted and harsh. Ancient and modern readers find fault with Hector's
language; cf. 281–2n. (ὥς κέ οἱ . . . χάνοι), 285n. (ἀτέρπου), and M. L. West 2001a:
197. Yet his strained language is best explained as a sign of his mounting agitation
(Kirk 1990: 198). Hector feels as helpless against Paris as against fate or the gods
(281–2n., 282–3n.), and he is clearly ashamed of his brother (note the wish that the
earth may swallow him up). And yet Hector's attitude is problematic: in early Greek
epic, loyalty to 'brothers of one womb' is an absolute duty, cf. 24.46–8. Later, Hector
spares Paris' feelings (325–31n.), and by the end of the book he is even prepared to
make it up to him, delivering a speech which blatantly contradicts this one: 520–9n.
It is important to bear in mind that he is now talking to Hecuba, the one person
who cannot entirely forsake Paris, since he too is her son. According to one tradition, Paris was going to be killed in infancy (by exposure on a mountain), because
Hecuba had dreamed that he would cause the fall of Troy. However, he survived
and returned to Troy as a grown man. Hecuba tried to kill him, but then recognised
him as her child. The story featured prominently in Euripides' *Alexandros*: see further
Scodel 1980: ch. 1; Euripides *Alexandros*, *TrGF* v.1 (3) testimonia iii–iv. We do not know
how old it was, though Pindar mentions Hecuba's dream and may have gone on to
relate the ensuing events, cf. fr. 52i (A) Maehler, and the *Iliad* seems to imply that
Paris only returned to live in Troy as an adult: cf. 24.29 with Reinhardt 1997, *pace*
Wehr 2006: 41–5; and 312–17n. See also Proclus' summary of the *Cypria*, *Chrestomathy*,
pp. 68–70 West; and Sophocles *Alexandros TrGF* iv F 91a–100a. For those audiences

who knew the myth, Hector's speech will have sounded particularly pointed:
Introduction 1.

280   The line announces two simultaneous actions: Hecuba should organise the
ritual, while Hector looks for Paris. As often in Homer, the two actions are then
described in succession (312–13n.); on the treatment of simultaneous events, see further
Introduction 1.   ἔρχευ: the main manuscripts read ἔρχευ, with 'Ionic' contraction
(cf. Attic ἔρχου) and shortening of the final syllable before vowel. One of the main
manuscripts and a second-century papyrus have an uncontracted, unelided ἔρχεο. In
this reading, -εο either forms a single syllable which is shortened in hiatus or must
be interpreted as *scriptio plena* for ἔρχε', see Bolling 1923: 171, 174–5. Scholars have
tended to assume that Ionic contraction was reflected in writing only from *c.* 400 BCE
onwards (Chantraine 1948–53: vol. I, 62 and M. L. West 1998–2000: vol. I, XXII)
but recent work suggests that it was employed much earlier than that; cf. Wachter
2000: 80, n. 25; and Passa 2001.   ἐγὼ δέ: cf. 279n., and 86n. The division of
labour conveyed by μέν – δέ helps Hector introduce his new plan without giving
the impression that he is acting on a whim.   Πάριν: the name Paris is relatively
rare: it is used eleven times in the *Iliad*, cf. Δύσπαρις at 3.39 and 13.769. Ἀλέξανδρος
is much more common: forty-five times. Both names are firmly rooted in the epic
tradition, though why they coexist remains unclear. Some other epic characters have
two names: e.g. Skamandros/Xanthos (where one is the name used by humans, the
other that of the gods: 4n.) Skamandrios/Astyanax (the significance of those two
names is explained by the poet: 402–3n.) and Pyrrhos/Neoptolemos (*Cypria*, fr. 19
West). The name Πάρις does not seem to be Greek in origin; Ἀλέξανδρος may be
linked to Alakšandu, prince of Wilusa, mentioned in a Hittite treaty of the early
thirteenth century BCE (Latacz 2004: 103–10). For other Homeric names which have
been more or less securely identified in non-Greek sources of the Bronze Age, cf. 5n.
(Ἀχαιῶν), 67n. (Δαναοί), 60n. (Ἰλίου), 78n. (Λυκίων) and 207n. (Τροίην). On the
names Paris and Alexandros, see further Wathelet 1988: 817; Gartziou-Tatti 1992: 74,
n. 4.   μετελεύσομαι: cf. 86n.

281–2   αἴ κ' ἐθέλησ' εἰπόντος ἀκουέμεν: cf. 94n. (αἴ κ' ἐλέησηι), 96n. (αἴ
κεν . . . ἀπόσχηι), repeated at 275 and 277. Hector's attempt to persuade Paris echoes
the Trojans' attempt to persuade Athena. Paris seems to be as inscrutable, distant and
destructive as a god, cf. 282–3n.   ὥς κέ οἱ . . . χάνοι: for the necessary enjambment, see Higbie 1990: 116–17. Shame sometimes prompts characters to wish they
could disappear, cf. 4.182, 8.150, 17.415–17 (of a group that includes the speaker). This
is the only passage where a character wishes that somebody else may disappear from
the face of the earth. Hector already wished death on Paris at 3.40–2; cf. the curse
of Trojans and Achaeans at 3.320–3. Here, his choice of words reveals how much he
identifies with his brother; cf. 523n., 524–5n. (where he describes how bad he feels
when people criticise Paris). Hector's anguish manifests itself also in his strained syntax: while Homeric wishes or curses do take the optative and may be introduced by
ὥς, they do not usually take the modal particle κε(ν). The effect of Hector's κε seems
to be that of toning down the harshness of his curse; see Stoevesandt 2008: 98, with

further literature. Two variant readings attempt to smooth the broken syntax (καί in some MSS, δέ in one papyrus), but the harsh asyndeton is appropriate to Hector's mounting agitation; cf. Kirk 1990: 197.   κέ οἱ: cf. 16–17n. (no hiatus). Note that the main manuscripts do not write κεν in order to avoid hiatus, see Chantraine 1948–53: vol. I, 147; cf. 90n.   αὖθι 'on the spot'.

282–3 μέγα...παισίν: a sharp comment, especially because addressed to Hecuba. Hector claims that it was Zeus who raised Paris, as a bane to Priam, his children and Troy at large. He thus distances his brother from the house of Priam, and suggests that Zeus – not Hecuba – was responsible for bringing him up; cf. 280–5n., and Introduction 4.2.   γάρ: 15n.   Ὀλύμπιος: Zeus as the master of Olympus. The word may be used in the plural of all the Olympian gods (e.g. 1.399, 20.47), but in the singular it is almost exclusively applied to Zeus (once in direct speech of a messenger from Zeus), both as an epithet and on its own; cf. 234n. (Κρονίδης).   ἔτρεφε πῆμα: the expression describes the breeding of monsters at *Hom. Hymn* 3.305–6 and Hes. *Theog.* 328–9. More generally, πῆμα often describes a bane or curse sent by a god; see Mawet 1979: 111–13. From the perspective of characters in the narrative, such a bane may take the shape of a particular person: cf. 3.50 (Hector of Paris), 3.160 (the Trojan elders of Helen), 11.347 (Diomedes of Hector), 22.288 (Hector of Achilles), 22.421–2 (Priam of Achilles). Hector's choice of words here suggests that he considers his brother more dangerous and intractable than an ordinary mortal, cf. 281–2n. (αἴ κ' ἐθέλησ' εἰπόντος ἀκουέμεν).   Τρωσὶ...παισίν: as often, Priam's family and the Trojans at large seem to merge, cf. 242–52n.   Πριάμωι μεγαλήτορι: cf. 24.117, 145. μεγαλήτωρ is a generic epithet (31n.) used of a wide range of characters, and their θυμός. The meaning was always taken to be 'noble, great-hearted' etc.: cf. ΣD *ad* 2.547. Hesiod uses it to evoke the grandeur of heroic epic: *Op.* 656, see also Pindar *Isthm.* 5.34–8 (of Aeacus and his descendants, who twice sacked Troy).   τοῖο: cf. 9n.

284 κεῖνόν γε 'that man', cf. Helen's equally spiteful τούτωι 352n.   κατελθόντ' Ἄϊδος εἴσω: sc. δόμον, i.e. 'into the house of Hades' (cf. 3.322 etc.); similar expressions describe those who died in the Trojan War: cf. 1.3, 422. For εἴσω see 10n. Hector now says explicitly that he wants Paris dead – and he is talking to Paris' mother, as well as his own: 280–5n.   Ἄϊδος, Ἄϊδι (< *Ἄϊς), perhaps originally 'underworld' (cf. 23.244), but already in Homer treated as an alternative name for the god Hades, Gk. Ἀΐδης, Ἀϊδωνεύς (cf. 13.415). As befits this mysterious god and his hidden realm, the two meanings are not always clearly distinguished. The house of Hades is one of the four realms of the Homeric universe, together with the sky, the sea and the earth: cf. 15.190–2 and, for parallels in other Mediterranean and Near Eastern traditions, M. L. West 1997a: 110, 137–9. It is the abode of the dead, envisaged as a place beneath the earth (20.61–6; cf. 19n.) and/or at its limits (*Od.* 10.487-end, and book 11); cf. Sourvinou-Inwood 1995: 59–61. Ancient audiences associated it with the verb ἰδεῖν, 'to see' (ἀ-ίδης = 'the invisible one'): cf. 5.845 (δῦν' Ἄϊδος κυνέην, μή μιν ἴδοι...), 24.244–6 (...πρὶν...ὀφθαλμοῖσιν ἰδεῖν βαίην δόμον Ἄϊδος εἴσω). Hector plays on this etymology when he says he wants to *see* Paris go down to (the house of) 'the invisible one' (ἴδοιμι . . . Ἀΐδος): his wish is studiously paradoxical. Initial alpha in Ἀΐδος is lengthened to fit the metre.

285 'Then I dare say my heart would forget its joyless misery.' The Greek is difficult: on Hector's strained use of language, cf. 280–5n.   φρέν' recalls οἶνον . . . μελίφρονα at 264n.; Hector does long for joy, but not through wine. For φρήν cf. 61n.   ἀτέρπου: the form ἄτερπος, whence ἀτέρπου, is unexpected for ἀτερπής. Homeric adjectives may, however, follow more than one declension (e.g. common ἐρίηρες ἑταῖροι vs. ἐρίηρος ἑταῖρος at 4.266) and ἀτέρπου, although rejected by Zenodotus and Aristarchus (see apparatus), is overwhelmingly supported by the ancient and medieval texts.   ὀϊζύος 'misery', 'woe', a characteristic aspect of the human condition (it does not usually afflict the gods). War is closely associated with ὀϊζύς; cf. 13.1–3, 14.480–1, Od. 3.103–4; Hes. Sc. 351.   ἐκλελαθέσθαι: inf. aor. middle, with reduplication; Chantraine 1948–53: vol. I, 396. The expressive compound ('forget utterly') fills the space after bucolic diairesis and brings Hector's speech to a rhetorically effective conclusion.

286–311: THE RITUAL OFFERING FOR ATHENA

Hecuba immediately sets about organising the offering; as is normal in Homer, she does not reply to Hector's request: Edwards 1987: 207. The poet now offers a glimpse into the world of women (Introduction 3.2), and even into the most remote corner of the innermost room of the palace (288n., 295n.; contrast 91n.: Helenos imagined she would find the garment in the μέγαρον). Then, in a chilling line, we are told that Athena rejects the women's offering (311n.). Athena's reaction prompts readers to re-evaluate the ritual just described; for another conclusion that invites a reassessment of a whole episode, see 232–6n. Two details seem significant: Hecuba's choice of garment (cf. 288–95n.), and Theano's request that Diomedes be killed, rather than simply restrained (304–10n. and 306–7n.)

286–7 The narrative moves swiftly, the tone is matter-of-fact (δέ 286, 287). An evidential particle marks the moment when Hector's orders become reality (ἄρ 287). Hecuba starts by enlisting the help of her maids.   ἣ δὲ . . . ἀμφιπόλοισι: one papyrus preserves the alternative reading [ο]ὐδ' ἀπίθησ' Ἑκάβη, ταχὺ δ' ἀ[μ]φιπόλοισι; but ταχύ is not used as an adverb in early Greek epic, and while ὣς ἔφατ' οὐδ' ἀπίθησ(ε) etc. is traditional, it is not normally followed by a δέ-clause in the same line.   ποτὶ μέγαρ': a public room, or the palace as a whole imagined as a public space; opposed to θάλαμος, cf. 288n. For scansion, and for the differences between Helenos' instructions and Hecuba's execution, cf. 91n. (ἐνὶ μεγάρωι).   κέκλετο: cf. 66n.   ταί: metrically useful alternative to αἵ, 'those', 'they' (fem.); cf. 9n. (τόν), and see further Chantraine 1948–53: vol. I, 275–6.   ἀόλλισσαν: cf. 270n.   ἄστυ: 95n.   γεραιάς: cf. 87n., 296n.

288–95 The scene follows a standard sequence of motifs: entering the room (288), description of the storeroom and its contents (288–92), selection of a specific object (293) and description of its history and special value (289–95); cf. 24.191–237 and *Od.* 15.99–108; with 288n. and de Jong 2001: 505–6 and 598. Whereas Hector asked Hecuba to choose the robe that was 'most graceful, largest, and dearest to her' (χαριέστατος . . . μέγιστος . . . φίλτατος; 90–1 ~ 271–2), when she sets about the task, her personal connection with the robe features before its objective qualities: first we hear about its history (289–92); then we are told that it is beautiful and large (κάλλιστος . . . μέγιστος: 294n). The history of the garment is unlikely to please Athena: it shows that Hecuba is close to Paris and that she, her family and the whole city are implicated in his actions: contrast Hector's attempt to cast Paris as an outsider (282–3n.). On Hecuba's choice, see further Introduction 3.1.

288 ~ 24.191 = *Od.* 15.99. After addressing her maids in the μέγαρα (cf. 286–7n.) Hecuba goes to an inner chamber (θάλαμος), where valuable possessions are typically stored; see Rougier-Blanc 2005: 210–12. θάλαμοι can be described as remote and inaccessible (cf. *Od.* 21.8–9: θαλαμόνδε . . . ἔσχατον), or as located on an upper storey (e.g. *Od.* 22.142–3). The present passage, as well as 24.191, *Od.* 2.337, and 15.99, may suggest a basement, but καταβαίνω in early epic need not involve a strong sense of downward movement, cf. *Od.* 11.523 αὐτὰρ ὅτ' εἰς ἵππον κατεβαίνομεν, ὃν κάμ' Ἐπειός; Ebeling 1880–5: vol. 1, 665, col. 2; and *LfgrE* s.v. βαίνω B II 9 c β. The line could suggest that Hecuba is entering the innermost part of the palace. The variants (see *app. crit.*) attest to a long-standing interest in the details of Hecuba's θάλαμος and suggest that this passage was compared to 24.191–2 and *Od.* 15.99–108. **κατεβήσετο:** for the mixed aorist in -σετο, see 136n. (δύσεθ'). **κηώεντα** 'fragrant'; ancient readers derived it either from καίω, 'burn' (i.e. 'fragrant like incense'), or from κεῖμαι, 'lie' (of the riches, κειμήλια, that 'lie' in the storeroom, cf. 47n.). The latter suggestion is based on the fact that *κηώεις is mostly used in connection with the θάλαμος, as a storeroom (but cf. 3.382, of Paris' bed chamber). The first explanation tallies with an internal gloss at 3.382, εὐώδεϊ κηώεντι ('fragrant and κ.'). Another gloss, at 24.191–2, κηώεντα, κέδρινον ('κ. and made of cedar') also suggests a scented storeroom: Lilja 1972: 47–9; van Wees 2005: 14. Later poets take the word to refer to fragrance: cf. *Anth. Pal.* 7.218.9 (μύρον) and Nonnus, *Dion.* 12.257 (ἄνθεα).

289–92 Herodotus 2.116–17 quotes these lines as evidence that the *Cypria* was not by Homer: he observes that, according to the *Cypria* (fr. 14 West), Paris and Helen sailed back to Troy in three days, whereas according to this passage they strayed off course. Herodotus' comment suggests that in the course of the fifth century Homer's *oeuvre* started to be more strictly defined, that the *Iliad* held special authority, and that consistency was used as a criterion for authenticity; see further Graziosi 2007 and Introduction 3 and 6.

289 cf. *Od.* 15.105. **ἔσαν:** some of the best manuscripts follow the ancient grammarian Herodian (M. L. West 2001a: 46) in accentuating ἔσάν οἱ; cf. M. L. West 1966: 442. **οἱ:** the dative of advantage suggests that these are Hecuba's very own, treasured garments; cf. οἱ at 90n., 91n. and 271–2 (τοι . . . τοι). The poet disregards digamma: cf. 90n. (ὅς οἱ). **πέπλοι:** cf. 90–1n. **παμποίκιλοι:** the adjective ποικίλος is associated with beautifully crafted objects, such as garments, military equipment, and pieces of furniture. The derivatives ποίκιλμα (294n.), ποικίλλω

(18.590) and παμποίκιλος (cf. *Od.* 15.105, *Hom. Hymn* 5.89) are rare: they describe objects in a league of their own, such as the most beautiful robe made by Helen, the necklaces worn by Aphrodite when seducing Anchises and the dancing-floor depicted on Achilles' shield.   ἔργα γυναικῶν: cf. *Od.* 7.97, where the expression is also used of πέπλοι. The phrase reminds us that we are here very much in the world of women, contrast 'the work of men', primarily understood as war: 490–3n., 7.234–7.

290 Sidon was a city on the Levantine coast, famous for its wealth; in the Bible it is known as *Ṣîdôn*, and to the Assyrians as *Ṣīdūnu*; cf. Eiselen 1907, Jidejian 1971, Krings 1995. Some ancient readers thought that the name referred to the wider region which was later called Phoenicia; cf. ΣV *ad Od.* 13.285; but *Od.* 4.83–4 distinguishes between the two, as does Herodotus at 2.116 (for a compromise solution see ΣA *ad* 6.291*b*). Sidon is reputed for its craftsmanship; cf. N. J. Richardson 1993: 250–1. Sidonian textiles are not mentioned elsewhere in epic but, for the skills of Phoenician women, see *Od.* 15.418 (ἀγλαὰ ἔργ᾽ εἰδυῖα) with Holeschofsky 1969: 171–2; and, for Phoenician textiles more generally, cf. Bartoloni 1995: 360. The skill of the abducted women seems to match that of the Sidonian metalworkers, for which cf. 23.740–3 with ΣbT *ad* 23.743; *Od.* 4.615–19 = 15.115–19, 15.425.   Σιδονίων: 'Sidonian (women)', not '(women) of the Sidonians': in early epic, the noun γυναῖκες is never followed by a reference to husbands in the genitive, whereas it can be qualified by an adjective of origin, cf., e.g., γυναῖκας | Λεσβίδας (9.128–9 ~ 270–1). The transmitted accent is difficult (we would expect Σιδονιῶν < Σιδονίη, fem.) but does not look like an error. The most likely explanation is that the accent marks a distinction between Σιδόνιος = 'Sidonian' and Σιδονίη = 'Sidon' in the following line (cf. 291n.). Aristarchus believed that Homer could use the masculine form of an adjective with feminine nouns (see Matthaios 1999: 274–7) and on that basis could justify Σιδονίων.   τάς: i.e. the women, not τούς (the garments). In early epic, women can be taken as booty (e.g. 9.128–30, 139–40); they can function as prizes in competitions (23.257–61); and they can even be given away as gifts (*Od.* 24.271–9; Hes. fr. 197.1 MW). These particular women seem to have been abducted; cf. 291n. For the value of captive women who could weave, cf. 456n.   αὐτός: Alexandros himself, emphasising his central role in the story.   Ἀλέξανδρος θεοειδής: a frequent formula. In the *Iliad* θεοειδής is used primarily of Alexandros and his father Priam (Bernsdorff 1992: 30–1); for epithets that gravitate towards certain nouns, cf. 12n. (βοὴν ἀγαθός). For the name Ἀλέξανδρος, see 280n. (Πάριν).

291 ἤγαγε: the verb suggests that Paris abducted these women, just as he abducted Helen, cf. ἀνήγαγεν 292, ἄγηται 455. On the verb, and the practice of abduction, cf., e.g., 3.46–9, 4.238–9, 8.165–6; Gartziou-Tatti 1992: 84, n. 47.   Σιδονίηθεν 'from Sidon' (Σιδονίη), with separative ending -θεν; cf. 9.664 τὴν Λεσβόθεν ἦγε, Radif 1997.   ἐπιπλώς < ἐπιπλέω, participle of the root aorist; cf. ἐπέπλων, 'I sailed'. The expected form ἐπιπλούς (cf. γνούς < γιγνώσκω) is not attested. The irregular participle seems to be modelled on ἐπέπλων, ἐπέπλως etc. before bucolic diaeresis, as here; see Chantraine 1948–53: vol. 1, 378. Ancient readers heard it as a shortened form of ἐπιπλώσας; cf. 3.47 with ΣA *ad loc.*, of the same voyage; 17.197 (γηράς), with ΣAbT *ad loc.* M. L. West 2001a: 23 suggests that the transmitted reading is a transcription error from ΕΠΙΠΛΟΣ in the Attic alphabet, but there is little evidence that the Attic script influenced Homeric spellings; cf. Heubeck 1979: 164–9; and 353n. (τῷ). **εὐρέα πόντον:** a frequent formula in this position. Hesiod parodies the phrase at *Op.* 650–1. εὐρέα is an alternative form of the expected accusative εὐρύν, formed on the basis of dat. εὐρέϊ (cf. formulaic εὐρέϊ πόντωι) and other forms in epsilon: Chantraine 1948–53: vol. ɪ, 97.

292 τὴν ὁδὸν ἦν ∼ *Od.* 6.165, of another journey that brings misfortune. ὁδός is both the road (15n.) and a route or voyage; for the latter meaning see *LfgrE* s.v. ὁδός B 2.   **τήν:** *that* journey, a demonstrative pronoun rather than article, cf. 9n. and Chantraine 1948–53: vol. ɪɪ, 162. Why Paris travelled back to Troy via Sidon was debated already in antiquity; cf. 289–92n.; and ΣAbT *ad* 6.291a; with Kirk 1990: 183; and Stoevesandt 2008: 101–2.   **Ἑλένην:** this mention of Helen evokes the distant origins of the Trojan War: she arrived a long time ago, the women of Sidon have since woven the robes, and the robes have been safely stored away.   **ἀνήγαγεν:** cf. 3.48–9 and 291n.   **εὐπατέρειαν** 'well-born', with emphasis on the father. The epithet looks like an artificial formation, perhaps on the basis of εὐπάτωρ; see Kirk 1990: 199; *LfgrE* s.v. with further literature. It recurs twice in the *Odyssey*, of Helen herself (22.227) and of Tyro (11.235). Helen's father was Zeus (cf. the formula Διὸς ἐκγεγαυῖα); Tyro's father, Salmoneus, tried to emulate Zeus (cf. Hes. fr. 30 MW).

293 ∼ *Od.* 15.106, with hiatus at the main caesura, as here; for this prosodic licence see 8n.   **τῶν:** Hecuba chooses the most beautiful garment out of a pile of ill-omened robes.   **Ἑκάβη:** this is the first time Hecuba is mentioned by name; contrast 87n. (μητέρι σῆι καὶ ἐμῆι), 251 and 264. The proper name emphasises her individual agency as she chooses the fateful robe. For its form and meaning: Stoevesandt 2008: 102.

294 = *Od.* 15.107.   **κάλλιστος... ποικίλμασιν** 'most beautiful in its decorations'. For ποικίλμασιν cf. 289n. (παμποίκιλοι). Note the variation: Helenos and Hector instructed Hecuba to choose the robe that is χαριέστατος ἠδὲ μέγιστος (90 = 271). While κάλλιστος describes the objective quality of beauty, χάρις also evokes the pleasure of the gods as viewers: see 90n. As we soon realise, Athena takes no pleasure in this gift: 311n.   **ἠδέ:** 90n.   **μέγιστος:** cf. 90n., 271.

295 = *Od.* 15.108.   **ἀστὴρ δ' ὡς ἀπέλαμπεν:** cf. 19.381, of Achilles' helmet. Star similes are frequent in the *Iliad* and are often ominous (e.g. 11.61–5 and 22.25–32; for a possible exception: 401n., though Astyanax too is doomed). The simile adds to the sense of foreboding: the *peplos* shines like a star, but may not bring good fortune.   **ὥς:** with ἀστήρ, i.e. after the noun, as often. The original consonant before ὥς is not felt, contrast 443n.   **ἀπέλαμπεν** 'shone'. In early epic this verb is more often construed with a beautiful object or body part in the genitive and its beauty (κάλλος, χάρις) in the nominative: cf. *Hom. Hymn* 5.174 κάλλος παρειάων ἀπέλαμπεν. For shining garments in Homer, and the Mycenaean practice of anointing cloth, see Shelmerdine 1995 and cf. 482–3n. (κηώδεϊ).   **ἔκειτο δὲ νείατος ἄλλων:** the fact that Hecuba stores this *peplos* underneath all the others suggests that she cherishes it especially; cf. *Od.* 21.5–14, where Penelope retrieves Odysseus' bow from the most remote room in the palace. We now are in the most remote corner of the most secluded room in the palace – but we are also at the heart of a problem: Hecuba's dearest possession is the gift of Paris, and a reminder of his abduction of Helen.   νείατος: an isolated superlative derived from the IE root *ni*, 'low' (cf. 5.539 νειαίρηι δ' ἐν γαστρί, 'in the lower part of the belly'; 10.10 νειόθεν ἐκ κραδίης, 'from deep down in his heart'). As often in epic, the superlative is construed with a genitive; cf. Chantraine 1948–53: vol. II, 60.

296 βῆ δ' ἰέναι: a frequent formula in this position. The infinitive is consecutive or final in origin ('she set off so as to go'), but in extant epic it is used primarily to add weight and ceremony to a character's departure, as here. On the syntax, see Schwyzer 1950: 359–60; Chantraine 1948–53: vol. II, 301; Létoublon 1985: 136.   πολλαὶ . . . γεραιαί: picking up γεραιάς at 287, in ring composition. Preparations for the ritual are now complete.   μετεσσεύοντο 'rushed after her'; cf. 21.423 and 23.389, where the verb is more clearly transitive. μετεσσεύοντο casts Hecuba in the role as leader and adds to the sense of urgency; cf. 361n. (ἐπέσσυται), 390n. (ἀπέσσυτο).

297–311 The ritual departs in two significant ways from the instructions originally imparted by Helenos (86–98n.) and faithfully related by Hector (269–78n.). First, Theano – rather than Hecuba – leads the sacrifice. Secondly, Theano does not just ask that Diomedes be kept away from Troy, but that he die in front of the Scaean Gates: the structure and emphasis of her speech are different (304–10n.), as is her central request (306–7n.). The narrative context partly accounts for these differences: Helenos' instructions were clear and calm, while Theano's words express the pressure felt by the women and, indeed, the entire community. But there is more: Helenos' instructions sounded reasonable, whereas Theano's prayer that Diomedes die in Troy will have struck ancient audiences as doomed: 306–7n. Seers are usually right in Homer, and the discrepancy between the instructions imparted by the seer Helenos and the actual ritual carried out by the women helps to account for Athena's negative reaction: 311n.

297 cf. 88n.   αἵ: cf. 9n. This is the first in a series of demonstrative pronouns which help us to visualise the interaction between the priestess and the group of women: 298 (τῆισι), 300 (τήν), 301 (αἵ), 302 (ἥ), 312 (αἵ).

298 τῆισι: cf. 297n.   ὦϊξε: aorist of οἴγνυμι, 'open'. West prints ὦειξε against the manuscripts, but the transmitted form is defensible: Forssmann 2005.   Θεανώ is mentioned also at 5.70–1 and 11.221–4, where we learn more about her immediate and extended family. She seems to have been a prominent character in myth: Beazley 1958: 241–2; Kullmann 1960: 276; M. I. Davies 1977; Espermann 1980: 22–3; and especially Danek 2005 and 2006a. Theano is the wife of Antenor, a prominent Trojan elder who once hosted Odysseus and Menelaos, when they went to Troy in an attempt to retrieve Helen: 3.205–8; cf. 7.348–53, where Antenor would like to see Helen returned. We know of several historical women, some of them priestesses, who were named Theano: this detail adds to the impression that the Trojan priestess was a prominent and positive figure in the Greek imagination; see B. Nagy 1979; and Lefkowitz 1996: 80–1.   καλλιπάρῃος 'of the beautiful cheeks' (παρειαί); Theano's most characteristic epithet (302, 11.224) and one she shares with other attractive women and goddesses.

299 Κισσηῒς: the patronymic, in progressive enjambment, enables the poet to expand on Theano's family background, cf. 13n. Her father Kisses is said to live in Thrace at 11.222–4. Later authors make him the father of Hecuba too (e.g. Eur. *Hec.* 3). Ἀντήνορος: cf. 298n. (Θεανώ). ἱπποδάμοιο 'horse-taming' (δαμάζω). In the singular, the epithet is used of both Trojan and Achaean characters; in the plural, of the Trojans only. See 461n. and M. Parry 1971: 66, 184–7.

300 Theano represents the entire community who elected her, cf. ΣbT *ad* 6.300. The line highlights an implicit tension in the performance of the ritual: on the one hand there is Hecuba's robe – a symbol of the Trojans' support for Priam, his family and even his wayward son Paris; on the other, there is Theano's public office and the attempt, on the part of the Trojans, to interact with the gods in a way that benefits the whole community. On the difficulties of distinguishing between family concerns and public duty, see Introduction 4.4: the issue is at the heart of book 6 and affects Hector above all others.   τήν: 297n.   Ἀθηναίης ἱέρειαν: Theano is portrayed as a priestess of Athena also on the Astarita Crater of *c.* 560 BCE; see M. I. Davies 1977: 78–81; Danek 2005: 12–16. She is the only female priest in early hexameter poetry.

301 αἵ: 297n.   δ᾽: the first of three δέ-clauses which briskly describe the ritual as it unfolds; cf. 302, 304.   ὀλολυγῆι: a ritual female cry, only here in the *Iliad*, though cf. Sappho fr. 44.31 Voigt, where the old women of Troy utter an ὀλολυγή at the wedding of Hector and Andromache. At *Od.* 4.767 it is uttered after a prayer; at *Od.* 3.450 (ὀλόλυξαν) it accompanies the axe blow which paralyses the sacrificial animal, before its throat is cut; see Wickert-Micknat 1982: 31–2.   Ἀθήνηι χεῖρας ἀνέσχον ~ 3.318 = 7.177; cf. 257n. For raised hands accompanying the ὀλολυγή, see Pulleyn 1997: 179.

302 ἤ: 297n.   δ᾽: 301n.   ἄρα marks the moment at which Theano carries out Helenos' instructions; cf. 303n.   Θεανὼ καλλιπάρῃος: cf. 298n.

303 ~ 92n. ~ 273. The identical phrasing suggests that Helenos' instructions are followed to the letter. In her prayer, however, Theano will make some significant changes: 304–10n.

304–10 Theano's prayer is reported verbatim: her precise words matter in this ritual context, and we immediately realise that she reverses the order of Helenos' instructions and makes a more extreme request. According to Helenos, the women were supposed to promise a sacrifice first and then ask for Diomedes to be kept away from Troy (93–7, cf. 274–8). Now Theano starts by asking Athena to break Diomedes' spear and let him die in front of the Scaean Gates (306–7n.); and then she promises a sacrifice (note the addition of αὐτίκα νῦν: 308n.). It is only at the end of her prayer that she echoes precisely the words uttered by Helenos and repeated by Hector (309–10n.). Theano's choice of words expresses the agony and fear of the Trojan women; yet her central plea will have struck ancient audiences as ultimately doomed to fail: 306–7n. At the beginning of his *aristeia*, Diomedes successfully prayed to Athena for strength (5.114–21); as we soon realise, the goddess is still on his side: 311n. For further discussion of Diomedes' prayer in relation to Theano's, see Graziosi and Haubold 2005: 113–14. Lang 1975: 310–11 collects parallels for Theano's promise of future sacrifice and argues that the terms of her prayer are potentially insulting to the goddess; Morrison 1991 discusses Theano's prayer as an instance of a type scene.

304 εὐχομένη δ᾽ ἠρᾶτο: the participle εὐχόμενος/-μένη is often combined with a verb of speech, though only here with a form of ἀράομαι, 'pray, vow'; cf. the metrically and phonetically similar εὐχόμενος δ᾽ ἄρα εἶπεν (16.513 = *Od.* 7.330), and cf. 311n. (ὣς ἔφατ᾽ εὐχομένη). ἀρᾶσθαι is used primarily of solemn vows or wishes, also as uttered by priests (cf. 1.11 ἀρητῆρα and 35 ἠρᾶθ᾽, of the priest Chryses); epic εὔχεσθαι has a broader range of meaning, cf. 211n. In some cases the verbs are used as synonyms (*LfgrE* s.v. ἀράομαι, ἀρήμεναι B) and both have previously described prayers uttered by the women of Troy: 115 (ἀρήσασθαι), 240 (εὔχεσθαι). Now, in combination, they add solemnity to Theano's speech and mark the moment at which the prayer to Athena is finally uttered; for alternative explanations: Stoevesandt 2008: 104.   Διὸς κούρηι μεγάλοιο: of Athena, in the context of prayer, also at 312, 10.296, *Od.* 6.323, and 24.521; she is the maiden daughter of Zeus *par excellence*.

305 An unusual and solemn opening, which draws attention to Theano's role in shaping the prayer. Contrast Theano's formulations at the end of her speech: 309–10n.   πότνι᾽ Ἀθηναίη 'lady Athena'; cf. Mycenaean *a-ta-na-po-ti-ni-ja*, Aura Jorro 1985: 112. The phrase occurs only here in early epic, though Odysseus addresses Athena as πότνα θεά at *Od.* 13.391 (see also *Od.* 5.215 and 20.61, of other deities). πότνια is used exclusively of mothers and goddesses: 264n.; it is a standard epithet of Hera.   ἐρυσίπτολι < (ϝ)ἔρυμαι, 'protect, save' (cf. Latin *seruare*; no hiatus) + πτόλις (cf. Att. πόλις). Theano addresses Athena as the protector of cities, though in the *Iliad* she does not act in that capacity (18.516–19 is an exception). The epithet occurs only here in the poem; by contrast, it features in the two *Homeric Hymns* to Athena: 11.1 and 28.3. Ancient audiences will have recognised in Theano's words an appeal to a well-known trait of the goddess, which, however, does not manifest itself in the *Iliad*. On Athena's relationship to the city, see further 311n. and Introduction 3.1. Linguistic considerations lend support to the transmitted form ἐρυσίπτολις (Chantraine 1999 s.v. ἔρυμαι), which is also attested in the *Homeric Hymns*, and Callimachus, fr. 626 Pfeiffer. For the reading ῥυσίπτολις, which the scholia recommend (ΣA and T *ad loc.*), cf. Aesch. *Sept.* 129; and *TrGF* III F 451q 7.   δῖα θεάων 'brilliant one among the goddesses' (partitive genitive); a frequent formula in early Greek epic, though only here in a direct address. On δῖος, see 31n.

306–7 Up to now, ancient audiences might have thought they were witnessing a successful ritual, despite Hecuba's problematic choice of garment (288–95n.). When, however, Theano asks for Diomedes to be killed in front of the Scaean Gates, the futility of the women's plea becomes more obvious: ancient readers knew that Diomedes was not destined to die at Troy. Theano's words resemble those used of two characters who famously did die there: Patroclus (16.801) and Achilles (22.360).

306 ἄξον δὴ ἔγχος: this is not what Helenos suggested (96–7 = 277–8), though he too was especially worried about Diomedes' spear, cf. 97n. (ἄγριον αἰχμητήν). The phrase is metrically awkward (hiatus after δή; ἔγχος uniquely spread across two feet); for expressive uses of metre, see Introduction 2.1.   δή: the request is urgent.   ἔγχος: cf. 31n.   ἠδέ: cf. 90n.

307 πρηνέα δὸς πεσέειν: as often in the *Iliad*, falling face down is equivalent to dying; cf. 42–3n. For the form πεσέειν (aorist), see 82n.   δός: the verb δίδωμι is standardly used of divine gifts; cf. 22.379, also of the death of an enemy.   Σκαιῶν προπάροιθε πυλάων: in full view of the Trojan people (cf. 373n.). This is also where Achilles will die (22.359–60); for Diomedes as a substitute Achilles, cf. 98n.

308 αὐτίκα νῦν: this is Theano's addition, contrast Helenos' words (93–4 = 274– 5). The adverbs correct the order of her speech by emphasising that the sacrifice will happen 'immediately'. Her phrasing betrays her sense of urgency. In fact, women never sacrifice cattle in the *Iliad*, so all they can do is promise, at this stage; cf. 93–4n. and 270n.

309–10 The final lines in Theano's prayer match exactly Helenos' phrasing (94–5 = 275–6); contrast the overall structure and content of her prayer (304–10n.), and its distinctive opening (305n.).

311 A brief and shocking conclusion to the ritual, without exact parallels in Homeric poetry (though see esp. 2.419–20; and Lateiner 1997: 260–1); contrast the formulaic ὣς ἔφατ᾽ εὐχόμενος, τοῦ δ᾽ ἔκλυε Παλλὰς Ἀθήνη: 5.121 = 23.771 = *Od.* 3.385 = *Od.* 6.328; cf. *Od.* 2.267 and similar phrases involving other gods. The poet does not tell us why Athena turns down the women's offer, though some aspects of their ritual seem unlikely to please her: cf. 288–95n. (on Hecuba's choice of garment) and 306–7n. (on Theano's request that Diomedes be killed). Athena remains firmly on the Achaean side and does not forsake Diomedes – whom she has just supported during his *aristeia*. In book 5 the goddess took off her own self-made *peplos*, brandished her spear (5.733–47) and helped Diomedes use his (5.855–7); now she refuses the gift of another *peplos* made by human hands, preserves Diomedes' spear and does not grant his death. After the fall of Troy, Athena will change sides: here, as elsewhere, the narrative invites the audience to reflect on what they know about the fall of Troy, see further Introduction 3. Ancient readers found this line difficult: Aristarchus marked it for deletion (ΣΑ *ad* 6.311a ἀθετεῖται), but for no good reason. It is certainly not 'superfluous' (περισσός), as he alleged: 311 picks up 304, in ring composition. 312 rounds off the communal ritual as a whole and does not therefore make 311 redundant; cf. 17.423–4, 22.515–23.1 with Bolling 1944: 99; Broccia 1967: 48, n. 5; and, for the alternating focus on the women and the priestess, 297n. Nor is Athena's gesture 'ridiculous' (γελοῖον), if we bear in mind that ἀνένευε is the standard way of describing a god's rejection of a prayer, and that the verb covers the entire semantic spectrum from actual physical movement to mere refusal (*LfgrE* s.v. νεύω B II 1); ancient readers focused on the statue and therefore understood the verb to describe physical movement. For Virgil's reading, see *Aen.* 1.482 with Barchiesi 1998; and Schmit-Neuerburg 1999: 344, n. 919.   ὣς ἔφατ᾽ εὐχομένη: a common speech-concluding formula, cf. 51n. The adaptation of the standard pattern ὡς ἔφατ᾽ εὐχόμενος, τοῦ δ᾽ ἔκλυε Παλλὰς Ἀθήνη results in hiatus after εὐχομένη, which is, however, mitigated by the main caesura; cf. 175n.   Παλλὰς Ἀθήνη: a frequent noun–epithet combination (Venturi Bernardini 1999: 61). The meaning of the epithet was debated already in antiquity: cf. Rank 1951: 65; Burkert 1985: 403 n. 4; *LfgrE* s.v. Παλλάς Σχ. One popular ancient derivation linked the epithet to Athena's brandishing of the spear (e.g. Eur. *HF* 1003: Παλλὰς κραδαίνουσ᾽ ἔγχος; cf. ΣD *ad* 1.200 ἀπὸ τοῦ πάλλειν καὶ κραδαίνειν τὸ δόρυ). The folk etymology seems relevant to *Hom. Hymn* 28.9; cf. also Eur. *Ion* 209–11 (of Pallas Athena brandishing her shield).

312–69: THE ENCOUNTER BETWEEN HECTOR, PARIS AND HELEN

312–17 As Hector approaches the palace of Paris, we are treated to a description of the building and its history. The palace is beautiful, like its owner – and new. We are not told why Paris had his own palace built by the best workmen in Troy: the other sons and daughters of Priam live in their father's palace (242–52n.), with the exception of Hector (317n.). The passage may imply that Paris did not grow up in Troy but only settled there as an adult. Paris' past is relevant also to the interpretation of Hector's words to Hecuba: 280–5n.; see further Introduction 1 and 4.2.

312–13 Hector went to look for Paris, while Hecuba set off to organise the ritual; now the two actions are presented in succession; cf. 280n. Line 312 concludes the ritual, while shifting the emphasis from Theano's actions to those of all the women; cf. 311n.   αἱ μέν: the demonstrative pronoun articulates the description of the ritual, cf. 297n.; for μέν, cf. 279n.   ῥ᾽ highlights the scene of prayer before the narrative moves on to Hector's actions; cf. 232n.   Διὸς κούρηι μεγάλοιο: 304n.   βεβήκει 'was on his way' (unaugmented pluperfect).

314–17 The best workmanship was also employed in order to build Paris' ships: 5.59–64. They marked the 'beginning of evil' (νῆας ἐΐσας | ἀρχεκάκους 5.62–3); the palace seems equally ill-fated.

314 καλά: 195n. Paris' palace is described as very beautiful (δόμον περικαλλέα) at 3.421.   αὐτός: this is the second reference, in a short compass, to the deeds of 'Alexandros himself': 290n. Both passages remind us that Paris was very able to act of his own accord, in the past – and highlight, by contrast, his present inactivity.   σὺν ἀνδράσιν: Paris typically enlists the help of others: cf. 5.59–64 and 11.123–5; contrast *Od.* 23.183–204.   οἳ τότ᾽ ἄριστοι: an ambitious project; cf. Hes. fr. 1.3 MW (αἳ τότ᾽ ἄρισται ἔσαν). Some ancient readers saw in this passage a parallel between Paris' palace in Troy and that of Menelaos in Sparta: ΣbT *ad* 6.315.

315 ἐνὶ Τροίηι ἐριβώλακι: ἐριβῶλαξ and its variant ἐρίβωλος mean 'with big clods' and hence 'fertile', 'good for ploughing' (βῶλος = 'clod of arable earth', with intensifying ἐρι-). The epithet is sometimes used of other places, and of fields in general, but it most typically characterises Troy (Létoublon 2003: 29–30). The formula is common in this metrical position, also in the accusative.   τέκτονες ἄνδρες: skilled 'builders' of a wide range of objects, cf., e.g., 4.110–11, 13.390–1, 23.712–13. For the formulation, cf., e.g., αἰπόλοι ἄνδρες (2.474), ἄνδρες θηρητῆρες (12.170), χαλκῆες ἄνδρες (4.187 ∼ 216).

316 οἵ οἱ ἐποίησαν rephrases αὐτὸς ἔτευξε σὺν ἀνδράσιν, drawing attention to the work others do on behalf of Paris, cf. 314n. ποιέω emphasises the activity of building whereas τεύχω places more emphasis on the result, but it is not always possible to distinguish clearly between the two verbs (cf. 18.483 ἐν μὲν γαῖαν ἔτευξ' and 18.490 ἐν δὲ δύω ποίησε πόλεις). θάλαμον καὶ δῶμα καὶ αὐλήν: the workmen start from the innermost chamber and build outwards; cf. *Od.* 23.190–204 (Odysseus builds his θάλαμος around a tree, which will become part of his marriage bed). Hector will soon enter the palace and go all the way into the θάλαμος: 318–24n.

317 The location of the palace is a powerful reminder that Paris is at the heart of the city, and very close to Priam and Hector. On his position in Troy, see Introduction 3.3. Ἕκτορος: apart from Paris, Hector is the only son of Priam who lives in his own palace, cf. 312–17n. This arrangement emphasises his status as the best of the Trojans and may also reflect family structures: he is the only son of Priam who is also himself portrayed as a father. ἐν πόλει ἄκρηι: the same formula describes the location of Athena's temple, where the women pray for relief (88n. and 297); and of the assembly, where the Trojans anxiously debate their fate: 7.345.

318–24 Hector enters the palace, wielding an enormous spear, and finds Paris in the θάλαμος, looking after his weapons. Helen, meanwhile, supervises her handmaids' weaving in exemplary female fashion (324n., cf. 491–2n.): there is an air of unreality about her, but her presence reminds us that Paris, as well as Hector, is out of place in this female sphere: cf. ΣT *ad* 6.321. It is a memorable tableau, which leads on to two of the most difficult conversations in the whole poem. See further Introduction 4.3.

318–20 ∼ 8.493–5. Aristarchus thought that the lines fitted the martial context of book 8; Zenodotus thought that they properly belonged here: ΣA *ad* 8.493a. It is of course unnecessary to suppose that they originally appeared in one passage only; here they create a contrast with Hector's domestic surroundings; later they show that his appearance suits the battlefield.

318 ἔνθ' brings the narrative back to Hector. The setting for each of Hector's encounters in book 6 is marked by this adverb at line beginning: cf. 251n. (ἔνθα); 394 (ἔνθ'). εἰσῆλθε: Hector enters the palace but later refuses Helen's invitation to 'come in', εἴσελθε: 354n. As always, he knows that he must not be delayed; see Introduction 4. Διὶ φίλος: only in the *Iliad* (in early hexameter), and often of Hector. The spelling of the manuscripts (two words rather than one) accurately reflects the fact that φίλος, 'dear', has retained much of its original force in this expression; contrast 73n. (ἀρηϊφίλων). Zeus's special concern for Hector is dramatised at 22.168–76. For final long iota in Διί, see Chantraine 1948–53: vol. i, 227, n. 1. ἐν δ' ἄρα χειρί: the evidential particle draws attention to the spear in Hector's hand. There is an obvious contrast between Hector's martial appearance and his domestic surroundings: cf. 264–8n. It is standard etiquette to leave spears outside the house: e.g. *Od.* 1.121–9.

319 ἔγχος: cf. 3In.   ἑνδεκάπηχυ: only here and in the identical line 8.494. Since the Giants are ἐννεαπήχεες . . . | εὖρος, 'nine cubits wide', at *Od.* 11.311–12, this weapon is obviously meant to be huge. Achilles too is famous for his huge spear (cf. 16.141–4) and Ajax wields a naval weapon of 22 cubits, i.e. twice the length of Hector's spear, at 15.677–8. The ancient variant ἔχεν δεκάπηχυ, based on different word division, is less well attested and seems less likely; cf. ΣA *ad* 6.319*ab*. It does, however, show that ancient readers were fascinated by Hector's spear and speculated about its exact length.   λάμπετο: the shining tip of Hector's spear is awe-inspiring rather than pretty; on the gleaming menace of metals, cf. 469n., 473 (παμφανόωσαν), 11.61–6, 12.462–6, 20.44–6 and 20.156, where the whole Trojan plain gleams with bronze.   δουρός: cf. 3n.

320 The description of Hector's spear is detailed and frightening, cf. 319n. No metals are mentioned in connection with Paris' weapons, cf. 321–2n. (περικαλλέα τεύχε᾽ ἕποντα).   αἰχμὴ χαλκείη: a typical battlefield formula; cf. 11n.   περί 'around it', here used as an adverb rather than a preposition.   χρύσεος . . . πόρκης: evidently a ring that tightens the socket of the spearhead onto the shaft; cf. ΣAbT *ad* 6.320*a*. Only here, at 8.495, and in the *Little Iliad*, fr. 5 West (of Achilles' spear, which likewise has a golden ring). For uncontracted χρύσεος, cf. 220n.

321–2 Translate: '. . . looking after his exceedingly beautiful weapons, both shield and body armour, and handling his curved bow'. The combination of weapons is jarring: shield and bow are not normally used together. What is obviously missing here is a spear: Paris damaged his when fighting against Menelaos; cf. 3.346–9. Now he is handling a bow, which becomes his main weapon from this point onwards: cf. 11.385 (his bow was first mentioned at 3.17, but in book 6 he has not used it yet). The bow is repeatedly disparaged in the *Iliad* as ineffectual (5.197–216) or treacherous (11.369–95), though it has different associations in the hands of Apollo (1.43–52), and there are prizes for good archery (23.850–83). Ancient readers will have been keenly aware of its ambivalent connotations; see, e.g., Eur. *HF* 159–64 and 188–203; for modern discussion see Hijmans 1976, Sutherland 2001, and Farron 2003. The other weapons mentioned here are defensive. The description of the weapons evokes Paris' humiliating defeat at the hands of Menelaos, his miraculous survival and his failure to return Helen.   τὸν δ᾽ εὖρ᾽ ἐν θαλάμωι: Hector finds Paris in the most private room in the palace, cf. 316n. The θάλαμος need not always be a bedroom (cf. 244n. and 288n.), but here it must be: Paris was last mentioned in bed, in the θάλαμος, having sex with Helen: Introduction 4.3.   περικαλλέα τεύχε᾽ ἕποντα ~ *Od.* 24.165; cf. *Il.* 17.436.   περικαλλέα: not usually of weapons, the scholia pour scorn on Paris' ostentation: ΣbT *ad* 6.321.   ἕποντα: what exactly Paris is doing with his weapons remains unclear, but it seems to be rather leisurely. The verb ἕπω (< *sep-) = 'occupy oneself with' was originally distinct from ἕπομαι (< *sekʷ-) = 'follow', but forms of the two roots are conflated already in Homer; see Chantraine 1948–53: vol. 1, 308–9 and 388. The construction without preposition/preverb (e.g. περί) is unique; perhaps περικαλλέα was deemed sufficient, cf. *LfgrE* s.v. ἕπω B 5.   ἀγκύλα τόξ᾽: cf. 5.209 and *Od.* 21.264, also ἀγκυλότοξος at 2.848, 10.428. A less frequent alternative of the common καμπύλα τόξα; see also 39n.   ἀφόωντα: only here. The compound ἀμφαφάω, 'touch', 'handle', 'inspect', is used of bows at *Od.* 8.215 and 19.586. At 338 Paris claims that he is preparing for battle, so he may be getting his bow ready, but there seems to be a certain vagueness to this description. Uncertainty over the precise nature of Paris' activities may have resulted in the variant reading τόξα φόωντα, 'shining the bow', according to some ancient readers, but it is perhaps better understood as 'the shining bow' (φάε is intransitive at *Od.* 14.502; cf. Hesychius s.v. φῶντα = λάμποντα). The vulgate reading is preferable.

323 Ἀργείη: a common epithet of Helen (otherwise only of Hera); it describes her origin and is a powerful reminder of the conflict she caused, first when suitors gathered from the whole of Greece and competed for her hand (Hes. frr. 200.1–2, 204.42–3 and 54–5 MW), and then when she caused the war between Argives (= Greeks, 66n.) and Trojans (2.160–2, 4.173–5, 7.350–1, *Od.* 17.118–19). In this context, the epithet immediately characterises Helen as an outsider; the modern description 'Helen of Troy' is not attested in Homeric epic.   μετ' ἄρα δμωιῆισι γυναιξίν: cf. *Od.* 17.505 and 22.427; see also *Il.* 9.477 and 375n. δμῶες/δμωιαί are servants who may have been acquired as booty (*Od.* 1.398), passed on within the family (*Od.* 4.736) and perhaps even bought (*Od.* 14.449–52; though Mesaulios is not expressly called a δμώς). *Od.* 24.210 suggests that destitute people could become δμῶες out of necessity.   μετ' 'among'.   ἄρα emphasises Helen's presence. She is, as ever, the centre of attention.

324 ἧστο: in necessary enjambment, as often with forms of this verb; cf., e.g., 13.523–4; and *Od.* 4.438–9.   καί: 1n.   ἀμφιπόλοισι: always of female servants in Homer; the term implies a closer, more personal relationship than δμώς/δμωιή; cf. 372n (καὶ ἀμφιπόλωι ἐϋπέπλωι).   περικλυτὰ ἔργα κέλευε: the women must be weaving, cf. 289n. and 491–2n., with Wickert-Micknat 1982: 38–9. The adjective περικλυτά is used of female work only here, but fits that activity: it usually describes gifts (e.g. 9.121; 18.449) and is a standard epithet of Hephaistos, the divine craftsman (18.383, 587, 590 etc.). The works supervised by Helen are famous and beautiful, like all things connected with her: περικλυτά echoes περικαλλέα at 321 (of Paris' weapons) but also evokes the robe Helen was weaving in book 3, which depicted the many trials suffered by Trojans and Achaeans on her behalf (πολέας... ἀέθλους 3.126; cf. θέσκελα ἔργα at 3.130). That robe was indeed famous – and has been discussed at length by modern scholars: Bergren 1979–80 and 1983; Kennedy 1986; Lynn-George 1988: 28–30; Taplin 1992: 97–8; Austin 1994: 37–41; Pantelia 1993; and Roisman 2006: 8–11, with further bibliography.

325–31 Hector's speech is short and to the point: the people are perishing on Paris' behalf, and he should return to the fighting immediately – before the city goes up in flames. The speech is introduced as a harshly worded reproach (325n.), though in fact it is relatively restrained. The frequent runovers (327–30) may betray Hector's exasperation, but he does not explicitly accuse Paris of being a coward (as ΣbT *ad* 6.327–8 point out) and stops short of saying that Paris should fight harder than everyone else (as Kirk 1990: 202–3 observes). The situation is so difficult that it requires a more delicate approach: Introduction 4.3.

325 = 3.38 (again of Hector to Paris); cf. 13.768. The line introduces Hector's speech as an instance of νεῖκος ('harsh reproach', 'strife'); cf. Martin 1989: 68–77. The Trojans often refer to Paris as the cause of νεῖκος (3.87, 7.374, 388, 22.116); and at 24.29 he is said to have 'found fault' (νείκεσσε) with Athena and Hera, when he judged their beauty. The actual speech, however, is less openly insulting than this line suggests: cf. 325–31n.   νείκεσσεν ἰδών ~ 4.368, cf. 4.336 = *Od.* 17.215. At an early stage of the epic tradition the phrase is likely to have been νείκεσσε (ϝ)ἰδών.   αἰσχροῖς ἐπέεσσι 'with ugly words'. There is a stark contrast between Hector's martial words and appearance, and the beauty of Paris' palace, bedroom, weapons and wife. The expression ὀνειδείοις ἐπέεσσι would be less strong; cf. Cairns 1993: 58 and 60. For the suggestion that αἰσχροῖς ἐπέεσσι derives from αἰσχροῖσι ϝέπεσσι, see Chantraine 1948–53: vol. I, 119 and 206 with n. I. In the *Iliad* the preferred form is ἐπέεσσι, cf. Blanc 2007: 17; Cassio 2006 argues that the form featured in Aeolic dialects and is not artificial.

326 Hector opens his speech by suggesting that Paris may be angry – which raises the question of why he should be angry and at whom; cf. ΣAbT *ad* 6.326ab. Rather than assuming that Hector knows the cause of Paris' behaviour, it seems better to understand, with the bT scholia, that he is giving Paris 'a pretext for his inactivity'; cf. Plut. *De adulatore et amico* 73E. Even great warriors such as Meleager and Achilles withdraw from battle out of anger (cf. 9.553–99), so this is the one explanation that allows Paris to save face; cf. 325–31n. For other interpretations: Hijmans 1975; L. Collins 1987 and 1988: 27–35; Heitsch 2001; Stoevesandt 2008: 110–11.   δαιμόνι': no one in the *Iliad* ever addresses Paris by name; Hector comes closest when he calls him Δύσπαρι at 3.39 = 13.769. δαιμόνιε is used always in the vocative and only in character speech: its precise meaning is difficult to define (Brunius-Nilsson 1955), but the word refers to somebody who is familiar to the speaker and yet behaves in an extraordinary and objectionable way; e.g. 2.189–90 and 199–200, with J. M. Foley 1999: 193. It features repeatedly in the second half of book 6 and indicates that tensions are running high; cf. 407n., 486n. and 521n., with Van Nortwick 2001.   οὐ μὲν καλά = *Od.* 17.381 = 483; ~ *Il.* 8.400, 13.116, etc. Paris and his palace may be beautiful (314n., 321–2n.), but his behaviour is not.   μέν: emphatic, another μέν follows (327n.), and then the central δέ-clause (328–9n.).   χόλον: cf. 166n. Homeric characters can be 'gripped' (αἱρέω, λαμβάνω, ἔχω) or 'overcome' (ἱκάνω, ἐμπίπτω, δύομαι) by χόλος; but they are also responsible for 'putting' it into their heart (*Od.* 24.248).   τόνδ' emphasises Hector's perspective: Hijmans 1975: 180. Translate 'this anger of yours'.   ἔνθεο: 2nd pers. sing. aor.; for the uncontracted form, cf. 270n.   θυμῶι: cf. 51n.

327 λαοὶ μὲν φθινύθουσι: a highly charged phrase in early Greek epic, and a damning indictment of Paris' behaviour. Leaders must not let the people perish: it is their duty to fight at the forefront of battle and protect them; cf. 5.643 (σοὶ δὲ κακὸς μὲν θυμὸς ἀποφθινύθουσι δὲ λαοί); 8on. (λαὸν ἐρυκάκετε), 214n. (ποιμένα λαῶν), 222–3n.

(ἀπώλετο λαὸς Ἀχαιῶν) and *Od.* 8.523–4. Paris' behaviour is entirely unacceptable: he remains safe inside the city while others fight on his behalf; note that, in her anxiety, Andromache later suggests that Hector should do the same: 433n. μέν adds to the previous line, cf. 326n. (μέν), and builds up to the central accusation in the next, cf. 328–9n. (δ'). περὶ πτόλιν αἰπύ τε τεῖχος ~ 11.181, *Od.* 14.472; cf. 34–5n. (αἰπεινήν).

328–9 μαρνάμενοι: progressive runover, as often with participles of μάρνασθαι. σέο δ' εἵνεκ'... ἀμφιδέδηε: a striking variation on the traditional view that the war was fought because of Helen (e.g. 3.28 and 156–7, *Od.* 11.438; Hes. *Op.* 165, fr. 196.4 MW [ε]ἵνεκα κούρης). Hector tries to hold Paris solely responsible for the war (cf. 3.57 and 100, and 524–5n.); but Helen soon intervenes and emphasises her own role in the matter; cf. 356n. (εἵνεκ' ἐμεῖο κυνός). δ' marks the core of Hector's speech, cf. 326 (μέν) and 327 (μέν). ἀϋτή τε πτόλεμός τε = 16.63 ~ 1.492; *Hom. Hymn* 11.3; cf. *Il.* 14.37. As often in Homer, this is a vivid combination of an abstract noun (πτόλεμος) with one that appeals to the senses (ἀϋτή is the clamour of battle, and hence the battle itself); cf. 373n. (γοόωσά τε μυρομένη τε). τόδ': the pronoun brings the war right into Paris' secluded chamber. ἀμφιδέδηε 'rages around the city' (perfect); cf. 12.35–6, ἀμφὶ μάχη ἐνοπή τε δεδήει | τεῖχος ἐϋδμητον, also 13.736, 17.253, 20.18; Hes. *Sc.* 155. Epic δαίω is an expressive, menacing word (cf. 20.316–17) and often occurs in metaphors; in the perfect and pluperfect it never describes actual fire, but rather fighting, rumour that stirs soldiers to battle, groaning, flashing eyes, and dust on the battlefield. Here, the 'burning' battle anticipates the image of the burning city at the end of the speech: 331n. σὺ δ' ἂν μαχέσαιο καὶ ἄλλωι: Hector now tries to cast Paris in a more positive role. For the rare use, inspired by context, of μάχομαι = 'attack verbally', cf. 5.875, 9.32 and 13.118–19.

330 Hector invites Paris to share his point of view. His words suggest that Paris' present behaviour is as bad as that of any soldier who neglects to fight. In fact, it is worse, because he caused the war in the first place; cf. 325–31n. μεθιέντα 'letting go of, relenting in his pursuit of' (with a term for battle in the genitive). μεθίημι and the derivative μεθημοσύνη are often used of warriors who do not pull their weight in battle; cf. 523n. Hector's rhetoric gains strength from the close association between war, anger and this verb for relenting; cf. 1.283, 2.241, 15.138, with 326n. ἴδοις: by implication, this is how Hector sees Paris; cf. ἰδών at 325. στυγεροῦ 'hateful', one of many negative epithets of war.

331 A brisk end to a brisk speech. ἀλλ' ἄνα 'but come!' (lit. 'but up!'). Also used to encourage Achilles to fight after a prolonged period of inactivity, at 9.247 and 18.178. μὴ... θέρηται ~ 11.667; lit. 'lest the city be warmed by fire'. The precise tone of the expression is difficult to gauge but seems sarcastic. Both here and at 11.167 the fire is seen as the responsibility of an inactive leader. ἄστυ: cf. 95n. πυρὸς δηΐοιο 'enemy fire'. δήϊος is an attribute of fire as a war weapon, cf. 9.347 etc.; it is also used of the enemy, and of war; cf. 82n., 481n. and 7.119. Hector makes clear that the war is about to enter the city; not even Paris' bedroom is safe. Some ancient readers heard in the expression an echo of δαίω = 'burn'; cf. ΣD *ad* 2.415.

332–41 Paris' reply reveals many humiliating details about his state of mind, his marriage and his relationship to Hector. He considers Hector's reproach appropriate (333n.), though many ancient and modern readers have actually found it restrained: 325–31n. He then corrects Hector: his motivation was grief, not anger: 335n., 336n. He then states that he was about to return to the battlefield anyway (though he seems unhurried; cf. 321–2n.); and that Helen was sweetly encouraging him to do so (we know, however, that her words were far from 'soft': 337–9n.). Finally, he invites Hector to stay while he gets ready – only to change his mind and suggest that he go ahead: 340–1n. On this speech, double motivation and the difficulties of explaining Paris' behaviour, see Introduction 4.3.

332 = 3.58, 13.774; the line follows a standard pattern; see Edwards 1970: 4–5. In contrast with Hector's speech-introduction (325n.), that given to Paris is entirely unremarkable. αὖτε: cf. 73n. προσέειπεν: cf. 122n. Ἀλέξανδρος θεοειδής: cf. 290n.

333 = 3.59. Here as in book 3, Paris claims he is going to answer because he judges his brother's words to be acceptable (ἐπεὶ... | τοὔνεκα). For Paris' tendency to pass judgement on those who address him, cf. 7.356–8. Ἕκτορ: Paris addresses Hector by name, contrast 326n. κατ' αἶσαν... οὐδ' ὑπὲρ αἶσαν: for a similarly ambivalent reaction, cf. Od. 22.46–7; Il. 17.716 is a more straightforward endorsement. αἶσα is the appointed share (cf. 18.327, Od. 5.40; Hes. Theog. 422, Op. 578), and hence a measure of propriety in a wide range of contexts: Yamagata 1994: 116–19, with LfgrE s.v. αἶσα; see also 487n. ἐνείκεσας: cf. 325n.

334 The expression, with variations in the first half of the line, is used when a character with better knowledge than his addressee explains things 'as they really are'; at Od. 18.129 this takes the form of a gentle reproach. There tends to be a difference in authority between speaker and addressee: Odysseus to Eumaeus (Od. 15.318), to Telemachus (Od. 16.259), to a suitor (Od. 18.129) and to Laertes (Od. 24.265). Paris' choice of words here suggests that he is presumptuous or petulant. τοὔνεκά τοι ἐρέω: cf. 333n. καί: 1n. μευ: for the Ionic contraction see 28on.

335 'It is not so much out of anger at the Trojans or blame' (that I have stayed in the bedroom). A vague statement that suggests a certain carelessness on Paris' part. χόλος picks up Hector's suggestion that Paris is angry (326n.), and the parallels at 8.407 and Od. 23.213 suggest that Paris has his own indignation in mind (Τρώων is an objective genitive). However, νέμεσις more naturally describes the Trojans' attitude to Paris; cf. LfgrE s.v. νέμεσις B. Helen later complains that Paris does not understand νέμεσις (351n., with 343–58n.). τοι echoes τοι in the line above, emphasising Paris' one-upmanship ('actually... '). τόσσον: Paris does not altogether deny he was angry. νεμέσσι: the unexpected form with double sigma seems to be modelled on Aeolic plurals such as πολίεσσι (< πόλις).

336 ἥμην ἐν θαλάμωι: Hector tactfully failed to describe Paris in quite those terms, though ἄνα (331n.) implied idleness: 'sitting down' is appropriate for women (324), but among men it attracts blame when there is a war to fight: cf. 7.94–102, esp. 100; 18.101–6; and Callinus 1.1–4 West. At 3.390–4 Aphrodite described Paris as sitting in the bedroom, looking more like a dancer than a warrior. Later in this episode Hector declines Helen's invitation to 'sit down', claiming that the Trojans need him to return to the battlefield: 354n. and 360n. ἔθελον δ' ἀχεΐ προτραπέσθαι 'I wished to abandon myself to grief'; cf. 10.79, where Nestor refuses to give in to old age: οὐ μὲν ἐπέτρεπε γήραϊ λυγρῶι. A self-defeating statement on Paris' part: προτραπέσθαι elsewhere describes defeated soldiers on the battlefield: 5.700; cf. 16.304 προτροπάδην φοβέοντο 'they were in headlong flight'. ἀχεΐ: at 3.412 Helen feels ἄχος when Aphrodite orders her to go and join Paris in bed; here Paris uses the same word to describe his own relocation to the bedroom. Uniquely, he presents ἄχος as a matter of personal choice: the word usually describes a character's immediate response to pain inflicted by others or by circumstance, cf. Andromache's grief (413n.) and Hector's (524–5n.); see further Mawet 1979: 392; Rijksbaron 1997; and, for ἄχος as an important Iliadic theme, G. Nagy 1999: ch. 5. For Paris *wanting* to turn to grief, cf. 523n. (οὐκ ἐθέλεις); for his motivations and the role of Aphrodite, see further Introduction 4.3.

337–9 Paris reveals an embarrassing detail: Helen already told him that he ought to return to the battlefield. He claims her words were soft but at 3.427–36 they were not. Although Helen's attitude is problematic (esp. when compared to Andromache's), Hector later enlists her support, in order to ensure that Paris does in fact return to the battlefield: 363n.

337 νῦν δέ marks the beginning of a new section. παρειποῦσ': cf. 62n. ἄλοχος: when used of human beings, the term normally refers to legitimate wives (cf., e.g., *Od.* 1.36: Clytaemnestra remains Agamemnon's ἄλοχος, even though she now sleeps and lives with Aegisthus); cf. Chantraine 1946–7: 223. The poet never calls Helen the ἄλοχος of Paris; the Trojan messenger speaking at 7.392–3 diplomatically calls her the κουριδίη ἄλοχος of Menelaos. Paris' description is thus at odds with how others see his relationship to Helen. μαλακοῖς ἐπέεσσιν: Homeric characters are advised to use 'soft words' when they are the weaker party: cf., e.g., 1.582 (Hephaistos to Hera on how to approach Zeus); *Od.* 16.286 and 19.5 (Odysseus advises Telemachus on how to address the suitors); cf. *Od.* 10.70 (Odysseus to Aiolos); *Hom. Hymn* 2.336 (Hermes to Hades). This is how Helen should speak to Paris; cf. 337–9n. For the dative ἐπέεσσιν see 325n.

338 ὥρμησ' ἐς πόλεμον: the causative use of ὁρμάω ('stir') is rare and tends to describe the influence of gods on mortals, cf. *LfgrE* s.v. ὁρμάω B. Paris hints that Helen has extraordinary power over him; cf. also 363n. (ὄρνυθι) and Introduction 4.3. δοκέει δέ μοι ὧδε καὶ αὐτῶι: contrast *Od.* 5.360, and many similar passages. Paris' own opinion is presented as an afterthought: cf. 363n. where Hector tells Helen what to say, and hopes that Paris may take her advice.

339 λώϊον 'better', often, as here, in the speaker's personal opinion (with forms of δοκεῖν). νίκη δ' ἐπαμείβεται ἄνδρας 'victory alternates between men'. At 3.438–40 Paris used similar words in order to excuse himself from fighting. There, as here, he seems supremely casual about the consequences of his defeat (or victory) for those around him. Hector offers a similarly glib maxim at 18.309 (ξυνὸς Ἐνυάλιος), with devastating consequences for himself and the Trojans: 18.310–13. Aristotle argued that maxims revealed the character of the speaker: *Rhet.* 2.21 (1394a19–1395b20, esp. 1395b11–17).

340–1 Paris echoes Hector's ἀλλ' ἄνα (331n.) with an ἀλλ' ἄγε, though in fact he is making a very different point: Hector wanted Paris to return immediately to the battlefield; Paris, by contrast, asks his brother to wait a little. Then he suddenly changes his mind: he suggests that Hector may want to go ahead and claims he will easily catch up with him. He may be reacting to some sign of impatience on the part of Hector, who is anxious to return to the battlefield as soon as possible: here as elsewhere Homer's poetry is so vivid that we can visualise not just the speaker but also the reaction of his interlocutor; see Introduction 2.6. Perhaps, rather than sounding 'efficient' (Kirk 1990: 204), or merely polite (Stoevesandt 2008: 114), the last lines in Paris' speech present him as indecisive and boastful.

340 ∼ *Od.* 1.309, 4.587, both of host to guest (in both cases the guest is in a hurry and refuses to stay). Cf. also 19.142 and 146–50: Achilles is determined to return to the battlefield and refuses to sit around while his gifts are delivered.   ἀλλ' ἄγε 'but come', a common structuring device in direct speech; J. M. Foley 1999: 224–5. The normal expectation is that the addressee will do as told, but in *Iliad* 6 the phrase is used three times to advise Hector, and each time he refuses to comply: cf. 354n., 431n.   ἐπίμεινον: Paris, like the women of Troy, tries to delay Hector; cf. 258n. (Hecuba); 354n. (Helen) and 431n. (Andromache); cf. also 237–41n.   ἀρήϊα τεύχεα δύω ∼ Hes. *Sc.* 108. The phrase ἀρήϊα τεύχεα describes weapons that are about to be used in battle, cf., e.g., 14.381, *Od.* 16.284. For the subjunctive ('let me put on . . .') see Basset 1989: 114; and Stoevesandt 2008: 114.

341 The line is an afterthought and betrays signs of improvisation, as Paris strings together three clauses in a single verse; cf. 340–1n.   ἢ ἴθ' 'or go' (ἰέναι). The apparent hiatus is not likely to have been felt (< ἠ(ϝ)έ with elision of epsilon). The conjunction can be monosyllabic ἤ or bisyllabic ἤ(ϝ)ε; the manuscripts do not mark elision.   κιχήσεσθαι δέ σ' ὀΐω: this and related phrases with ὀΐω express a confident prediction, rather than a simple belief; they sometimes imply an element of threat, as at 353. Paris' boast here sounds grand but hollow: in the end he does catch up with Hector (515–16n., 517–19n.), but only because Andromache has intercepted and delayed him (393n.).

342 One of the heaviest silences in the whole poem. Like all speech-concluding lines, it tells us something crucial about the preceding speech and its reception, cf. 51n. Other speeches meet with a silent response, though reasons for the silence vary from case to case, cf., e.g., 1.511–12, 3.418–20, 4.401–2, 5.689–91, 7.92–3, 8.484, 9.29–30 and 430–1, 21.478–9 and *Od.* 20.183–4. Readers have speculated about Hector's state of mind here, and the scholia suggest that he has become fully aware of Helen's influence over Paris, which is why he later tells her to send him back to the battlefield: ΣbT *ad* 6.342, cf. 363n.   ὣς φάτο: cf. 51 n.

343–58 Helen's speech is structured as a grand account of her life – from distant, elemental origins, to the present war, to future songs. Temporal markers articulate its main sections: 345n. (ἤματι τῶι, ὅτε), 349n. (αὐτὰρ ἐπεί), 350n. (ἔπειτ'), 352n. (οὔτ' ἄρ νῦν . . . οὔτ' ἄρ ὀπίσσω), 354 (νῦν) and 357 (ὀπίσσω). Helen starts with her own birth, an event of cosmic significance: 344–8n. She then complains about Paris and wishes she had a better husband: 349–53n. An invitation for Hector to come in and sit down immediately follows: 354n. Finally, she looks to the future, drawing together the cause and purpose of the war and implicating Hector in her own narrative. In effect, she sets up a new triangle: 358n. (πελώμεθ' ἀοίδιμοι). For Helen's ability to see the war, and her own situation, from the perspective of the poet, cf. 324n., 357–8n., and Introduction 1. For an analysis of this speech, Introduction 4.3.

343 A common type of speech introduction (cf. 3.437, 23.794, *Od.* 19.252), but there is nothing routine about it here; contrast the more neutral alternatives at 3.171, 228 and *Od.* 15.171. The line introduces Helen's speech as an attempt to persuade Hector to stay: cf. 214n. and, for Hector's reply, 360n.   μύθοισι: the word is invested with authority; contrast ἔπος, which can describe any utterance; see Martin 1989: 22–6. Telemachus claims that 'μῦθος is a matter for men' at *Od.* 1.358; and indeed women rarely utter μῦθοι in Homer; Helen does so more often than any other woman in the *Iliad*: 3.171, and 3.427; cf. 381n.   μειλιχίοισι: gentle words (214n.) can range in tone from mild persuasion (e.g. 10.542) to deviousness; see further Worman 2001: 27–8. The ancient variant δῖα γυναικῶν (attested also in the scholia; cf. 3.171) may have come about as a result of speculation about the precise tone of Helen's speech.

344–8 This is an effective opening, as it inhibits others from making Helen feel even worse than she already does; for a similar move, cf. her speech at 3.172–6. The need to elicit sympathy at the beginning of a speech was widely recognised as important in ancient rhetorical theory (cf. Arist. *Rhet.* 3.14 (1415); [Cic.] *Ad Herennium* 1.4–7; Quint. *Inst.* 4.1); Helen's speech is a good example of what was later called *insinuatio*, or 'the subtle approach', which was recommended when the speaker had already disgraced himself or when his case was prejudiced in some way (cf. [Cic.] *Ad Her.* 1.6–7; Quint. *Inst.* 4.42–50). Hector has just expressed the view that Paris alone was responsible for the war (328–9n.); now Helen asserts her own role in the matter and suggests that she, unlike Paris, is ready to contemplate the magnitude of her sins (on Helen's guilt: Introduction 4.3). She then claims that she wants to be dead and offers a grand and elaborate vision of how she ought to have died in infancy. A gust of wind should have blown her away: in Greek myth, girls at the point of marriage are sometimes abducted by winds (346n.); now Helen suggests it would have been best for her to have been taken away right on the day she was born. The wind should have taken her to a mountain – or to the sea, where a wave should have swept her away (cf. 347n., 348n.). The imagery recalls Penelope's prayer at *Od.* 20.61–5, though Helen's emphasis on the wind, the sea and the waves may also suggest that she should have died in the way Aphrodite was born, cf. Hes. *Theog.* 188–99; and *Hom. Hymn* 6. Helen's vision is inflected with wider mythical narratives concerning marriage, abduction and love; cf. the account of her birth from Zeus and Nemesis in *Cypria*, fr. 10 West. In the next section of her speech, she strikes a more pragmatic note.

344 The first two words emphasise Helen's close relationship with Hector; she then goes on to pile insults on herself – but this only highlights Hector's fundamental predicament: Helen and Paris have caused the war and thus put the lives of all the Trojans, himself included, at risk; yet at the same time they are members of his own family, and so it pains him to see them treated harshly or criticised, cf. 524–5n. and 24.761–75. δᾶερ 'husband's brother', cf. 3.180 where Helen describes Agamemnon as her former δαήρ; the term is more specific than Eng. 'brother-in-law', which can mean both 'husband's brother' and 'sister's husband'. Homeric Greek also seems to have separate terms for 'sister of a husband' and 'wife of a husband's brother': 378n. κυνός: a common term of abuse in epic; Helen is the only character who uses it of herself: 3.180, 356n. and *Od.* 4.145 (κυνώπιδος); see further Graver 1995; and Worman 2001: 21. κακομηχάνου 'devising evil'; cf. ΣD *ad* 9.257; *Od.* 3.213 (κακὰ μηχανάασθαι). This punchy adjective occurs only in direct speech, cf. 9.257 and *Od.* 16.418. κακός and related words punctuate Helen's speech: 346n., 349n. and 357n.; on the tradition of blame attached to Helen, see also Gorgias, *Hel.* ch. 7: κακολογηθείη. ὀκρυοέσσης 'dreadful'. The adjective ὀκρυόεις appears to have developed out of κρυόεις = 'bloody, cruel' through wrong word division, see Leumann 1950: 49–50. Some editors restore κακομηχάνοο κρυοέσσης and cite 9.64 (πολέμου) ἐπιδημίου ὀκρυόεντος > ἐπιδημίοο κρυόεντος. However, when the Homeric poems were composed, the genitive in -οο had already been replaced with -ου, see Chantraine 1948–53: vol. I, 46–7; Reece 1999–2000: 198; Wachter 2000: 79–80, n. 24; cf. 61n. (ἀδελφειοῦ). The transmitted text should therefore stand. For comparative evidence on wrong word division, see Lord 1974: 255; Danek 2003: 67. The form may be modelled on the adjective ὀκριόεις meaning 'rugged, jagged' (Kretschmer 1912: 308).

345 ὥς μ' ὄφελ' expresses deep regret or scorn; similar phrases are frequent in death wishes; cf., e.g., 3.40, 173, 428, 7.390, 19.59; see further Chantraine 1948–53: vol. II, 228–9. Helen repeatedly uses this expression in order to negotiate her fraught position in Troy, cf. 350n. and see further Worman 2001: 24–9. ἤματι τῷ, ὅτε: the expression singles out a crucial moment in one's life or that of the community, e.g. 2.351–2, 8.475–6, 22.359–60. The idea that one's fate was determined at birth was widespread in the ancient world, cf., e.g., *Reallexikon der Assyriologie* s.v. 'Schicksal' A § 5 (vol. XII, p. 149, on Mesopotamia), and esp. B § 2 (vol. XII, p. 156, on Hittite Anatolia); for Greek epic see, e.g., 489n., 20.127–8, 23.78–9, with Chadwick 1996: 246–7. πρῶτον: cf. 489n. τέκε μήτηρ: formulaic at the end of the hexameter line, together with the alternative γείνατο μήτηρ. Helen never describes Zeus as her father, though the poet does so repeatedly.

346 ~ *Od.* 20.64. οἴχεσθαι προφέρουσα: the expression οἴχομαι + participle often refers to sudden disappearance through theft or abduction (Létoublon 1985: 106–7; *LfgrE* s.v. οἰχνέω/οἴχομαι B 2 b). Helen introduces the notion of *force majeure*, which dominates much of her speech. κακή picks up κακομήχανος at 344n.: an evil wind for an evil woman. For the hiatus after caesura (here the hephthemimeral), see 8n. θύελλα: a gust of wind, often envisaged as a minor deity, cf. 15.26, *Od.* 20.66

and 77 (where Θύελλαι = Ἅρπυιαι). θύελλαι typically snatch away women just before marriage, cf. 20.61–78 (though see also *Od.* 4.727–8: Penelope imagines that they have abducted Telemachus). On divine seizure, see further Vernant 1991: 102–3.

347 εἰς ὄρος: where unwanted babies were traditionally exposed. There is no reference to the practice in extant epic, though later texts claim that Paris was exposed on the mountains as a baby; cf. 280–5n. εἰς κῦμα πολυφλοίσβοιο θαλάσσης 'to the waves of the loud-roaring sea', a common formula. Zephyr blew Aphrodite 'on the waves of the loud-roaring sea' all the way to Cyprus, where she was born: *Hom. Hymn* 6.3–4; cf. also Hes. *Theog.* 188–93.

348 ἀπόερσε 'would have washed me away'; the verb is part of Helen's wish, for this use of the aorist without κε; cf. 351n., *Od.* 1.217–18; and Chantraine 1948–53: vol. II, 249. The verb is rare in early Greek epic (only here, at 21.283 and 21.329), and ancient readers debated its meaning (e.g. ΣD *ad* 6.348 'drown'; Nic. *Ther.* 110, 'remove'). The etymology is unclear, though the verb seems to refer specifically to obliteration through water, cf. *LfgrE* s.v. ἀποέρσαι E and B. πάρος τάδε ἔργα γενέσθαι: τάδε ἔργα is deliberately vague: the scholia bT *ad* 6.348c suggest that Hector may not want to be reminded of the details; for similar expressions, see *Od.* 22.49, 24.455. Epic poetry typically glorified the 'deeds' (ἔργα) of gods and men (cf., e.g., *Od.* 1.338); Helen goes on to describe the deeds she mentions here as the subject of future song: 357–8n.

349–53 Helen now resigns herself to the situation and blames the gods; cf. 3.164–5; Gorgias *Hel.* 6; and Eur. *Tr.* 948–50. An appraisal of her present situation leads Helen to wish for a better husband. The focus is now firmly on her own feelings, as opposed to any pain inflicted on others. For Helen's seductive stance towards Hector, see Introduction 4.3.

349 αὐτὰρ ἐπεί: the cluster of particles marks a change of tone, cf. 178n. ἐπεί articulates the chronology of Helen's account (343–58n.) but also turns chronology into argument; cf. 350n. (ἔπειτ'). τάδε... κακά takes up τάδε ἔργα (348n.). κακός and related terms recur in Helen's speech and express her concern with apportioning blame; cf. 344n. γ' casually ascribes Helen's predicament to divine causes; she then goes on to claim that there is no excuse for Paris' behaviour. τεκμήραντο 'they decreed' (cf. τέκμωρ = 'goal', 'boundary'). Often used of decisions made by the gods or their agents that have a negative effect on mortals: cf., e.g., 7.69–70, *Od.* 10.563.

350 ἀνδρὸς... ἀμείνονος: a striking case of hyperbaton. At 3.428–36 Helen told Paris that Menelaos was the better husband. Now, however, she is envisaging a better husband in Troy: she seems to have in mind someone like Hector, cf. Arthur Katz 1981: 29. ἔπειτ': for Helen's use of temporal markers, see 343–58n.; ἔπειτα has a causal or consecutive inflection here: 'Given that the gods decreed these bad things for me, then at least I wish I had a better husband.' ὤφελλον takes up 345n. (ὥς μ' ὄφελ'), but in the first person: Helen is now thinking about what she wants and needs, rather than what might have been best for others. ἄκοιτις 'partner', 'wife', as opposed to concubine, παλλακίς, cf. 9.449–50. The term is sometimes treated as synonymous with ἄλοχος but generally places greater emphasis on the personal relationship between two partners; see Gates 1971: 18. ἄλοχος (especially when coupled with the epithets κουριδίη and μνηστή, which are never used of ἄκοιτις) points to marriage as an institution; cf. 337n.

351 ὃς ἤιδη . . . ἀνθρώπων: for similar expressions with οἶδα = 'know, be aware of', cf. *LfgrE* s.v. οἶδα B 2 a δ. The description fits Hector very well; cf. 343–58n., 354–6n., 524–5n.   ἤιδη: the unfulfilled wish continues in the past tense indicative. The second example of this rare construction in only four lines reflects the tortured and regretful tone of Helen's speech; cf. 348n. (ἀπόερσε). For the possibility that early texts read (ϝ)εἴδη, without augment, see M. L. West 1998–2000: vol. I, XXXIII.   νέμεσιν 'blame', 'retribution', a crucial mechanism of social justice in Homeric society, cf. Cairns 1993: 51–4; Redfield 1994: 113–17; Yamagata 1994: 149–58. In some accounts Helen is the daughter of Nemesis: cf. *Cypria*, fr. 10 West; and see further Clader 1976: 18–23 with nn. 30–1; Austin 1994: 43, 46; and Worman 2001: 21–30. Paris' own statement at 335n. suggests that he does not understand νέμεσις.   αἴσχεα 'can refer both to the state considered disgraceful and the reaction of others to that state': Cairns 1993: 55; cf. 209n. (αἰσχυνέμεν), 325 (αἰσχροῖς) and 524 (αἴσχε'). Helen herself is said to have 'shamed' (ᾔσχυνε) Menelaos' bed at Hes. fr. 176.7 MW and claims she is in disgrace at *Il.* 3.242. Austin 1994: ch. 1 discusses Helen's paradoxical connection with disgrace and ugliness.   ἀνθρώπων: in the pl., often used to reflect on human life in general.

352 τούτωι: a put-down. Helen speaks about Paris in the third person; Hector will do so too, in his reply to her: 363n.; see also Lohmann 1970: 101–2.   οὔτ' ἄρ νῦν . . . οὔτ' ἄρ ὀπίσσω: 'neither now . . . nor in the future'. Paris is beyond redemption. On temporal markers and the structure of Helen's speech, cf. 343–58n.   ἄρ . . . ἄρ: the repeated particle presents the verdict as a realisation, rather than a simple statement on Helen's part.   φρένες ἔμπεδοι: cf. *Od.* 10.493 and 18.215; the adjective is also used of νόος (11.813), though it is more frequent with βίη, 'might' and ἴς, 'strength'. Lack of mental strength is an issue with Paris, cf. 3.45; Sullivan 1988: 54–5.

353 Helen invites Hector to give up on his brother ('he will get what he deserves'); her prediction is phrased as a threat to Paris.   τῶ 'therefore' (he will reap the consequences). Helen's words are harshly judgemental, emphasising the necessary consequences of Paris' attitude; cf. *Od.* 22.317 and 416 (τῶ καί), and contrast Andromache's positive assessment of Hector at *Il.* 24.740 (τῶ καί μιν), Briseis of Patroclus at 19.300 (τῶ), Helen of Hector at 24.773 (τῶ) and Agamemnon's words about the φρένες of Penelope at *Od.* 24.194–8 (τῶ, 196). West adopts the conjecture τοῦ (< ΤΟ̄, with wrong transcription from the Attic alphabet, but cf. 291n. ἐπιπλώς), because ἐπαυρίσκω takes the genitive. The genitive object can, however, remain implicit (*Od.* 17.81), and τοῦ as a way of referring to verses 352–3 is rhetorically and syntactically difficult, for three reasons. (1) It breaks the line of personal pronouns which set up a contrast between Hector and Paris (ὃς . . . τούτωι . . . μιν). (2) It refers to a complex verbal clause, which is unparalleled with ἐπαυρίσκω. (At 13.732–3, τοῦ ∼ νόον ἐσθλόν.)

(3) Its significance remains unclear until later in the sentence, resulting in a rhetorical weakness at the heart of Helen's speech. The transmitted text should stand: its syntactical harshness is appropriate to the harshness of Helen's views; cf. some of Hector's more tortured remarks about Paris: 280–5n., 281–2n., 285n.   καί: the well-attested alternative reading κεν seems grammatically difficult (even if taken with the fut. inf.; cf. Chantraine 1948–53: vol. II, 311) and would introduce a note of uncertainty. *Pace* van der Valk 1963–4: vol. II, 109, Helen is not known to spare Paris (cf. 3.427–36), and the blunter καί seems in keeping with the rest of her speech.   ἐπαυρήσεσθαι: the verb is used of reaping both positive and negative consequences; cf. 1.410, 13.733.

354–6   Now Helen turns her attention to Hector and delivers her central plea. She invites him to approach her; see Introduction 4.3. She acknowledges that Hector is weighed down by worry and responsibility (just the kind of trait she would welcome in a husband: 351n.) and states that he is fighting on her behalf and because of Paris' folly: this creates a sense of intimacy. For all that Helen distances herself from Paris, she actually reinforces his previous attempt to make Hector stay: 340n. (ἐπίμεινον).

354   Cf. Hecuba's central plea that Hector 'wait' while she gets some wine for him: ἀλλὰ μέν᾽, 258n.   ἀλλ᾽ ἄγε νῦν εἴσελθε = *Od.* 16.25. Hector evidently stopped near the door when addressing Paris; cf. Lateiner 2005: 419.   ἕζεο: potentially seductive, cf. 3.406 (Helen tells Aphrodite she should sit with Paris herself), and *Od.* 10.314–15 (Circe offers Odysseus a seat before attempting to bewitch him); cf. also Hector's reply: μή με κάθιζ᾽, Ἑλένη, φιλέουσά περ... 360. For further discussion, see Arthur Katz 1981: 29.   τῶιδ᾽ ἐπὶ δίφρωι: Helen shows Hector precisely where he should sit; the deictic τῶιδε suggests that the chair or stool (Laser 1968: 36–9) is close to her. The scene parallels 3.424–6, where Aphrodite makes Helen sit on a δίφρος opposite Paris – that situation quickly leads to their love-making.

355   δᾶερ: an intimate word, cf. 344n.   σε... φρένας ἀμφιβέβηκεν ~ *Od.* 8.541. Helen echoes Hector's own words (cf. ἀμφιδέδηε, 328–9n.) but turns the plight of the city into Hector's personal affliction. ἀμφιβέβηκεν governs accusatives of the person (σε), and the part of the body (φρένας); cf. 9n. (ἔβαλε). For πόνος see 77n., 525n.

356   The line marks a sudden change in register: Helen's personal plea gives way to the resonant patterns of the epic tradition: Helen the bitch, Paris and his blind folly. This change leads on to Helen's closing remarks on future song.   εἵνεκ᾽ ἐμεῖο κυνός ~ 344n. (ring composition). Helen is not simply trying to pre-empt Hector's criticism (thus ΣbT *ad* 6.356), but also to assert her own central role in the war, and hence in Hector's life (he, by contrast, focused exclusively on Paris: 328–9n.).   καὶ Ἀλεξάνδρου ἕνεκ᾽ ἄτης ~ 3.100, 24.28: both ἄτης ('blind folly', and the 'ruin' that results from it) and ἀρχῆς ('beginning') are attested in all three passages, though there is always a clear preference (for ἀρχῆς at 3.100; for ἄτης here and at 24.28). ἄτης suits the present context because it emphasises retribution: unlike ἀρχή, ἄτη can be sent by the gods and is sometimes represented as a deity in her own right (e.g. 9.504–12, 19.91–4); it tends to be invoked by characters in direct speech, see Hershkowitz 1998: 128–32; Mülke 2002: 261–5, with further passages and bibliography.

357–8 A famous passage, where Helen adopts the perspective of the poet; cf. *Od.* 8.579–80: τὸν [sc. Ἰλίου οἶτον] δὲ θεοὶ μὲν τεῦξαν, ἐπεκλώσαντο δ᾽ ὄλεθρον | ἀνθρώποις, ἵνα ᾖσι καὶ ἐσσομένοισιν ἀοιδή; see also *Od.* 24.196–202; and *Hom. Hymn* 3.299. The scholia bT *ad* 6.358 comment: 'she subtly aggrandizes the poem', thus remarking on the effectiveness of Helen as a metapoetic figure. Many readers have commented on Helen's position at the centre of the war, and on her detachment as its observer, see, e.g., Clader 1976: ch. 1; Pantelia 2002; and esp. Taplin 1992: 96–103, who compares her to the poet, and also discusses 3.125–8, where Helen weaves a robe depicting the war fought on her behalf; see 324n. with further bibliography. Although Helen is able to view the war, and her own plight, from the perspective of future epic audiences, she has an immediate purpose: Introduction 1 and 4.3. Hector too is very much concerned with his future fame (cf., e.g., 446n. and 7.81–91); but at this point in time he sees his imminent death as a reason to focus on Andromache's plight, rather than Helen's: 367–8n., cf. 450–3n. and 454–63n.

357 Ζεύς: after mentioning the gods in general (349n.), Helen now singles out Zeus as the cause of the war, cf. 14.85–7 and 'the plan of Zeus' at 1.5, with *Cypria*, fr. 1 West; and Hes. fr. 204.96ff. MW. Her perspective is close to that of the poet, see also *Od.* 1.346–9 (Zeus causes events; the bard memorialises them), and Introduction 1.   κακὸν μόρον: a rare and powerful expression, describing an especially cruel fate (cf. 21.133, *Od.* 1.166, 11.618). For μόρος = 'fate of death', see *LfgrE* s.v. B. This is the only passage in Homer where the word is used of a woman's fate: Helen considers her destiny as grand and significant as that of the heroes. In the context of her speech, the expression κακὸν μόρον resonates with Helen's emphasis on 'evil' in her own life, cf. 344n. (κακομηχάνου), 346n. (κακή), 349n. (τάδε... κακά).   ὡς 'so that' (purpose clause).

358 ἀνθρώποισι... ἐσσομένοισι: Helen is one of the few characters who is able to see her own existence through the eyes of future epic audiences; Hector is another: 22.304–5.   πελώμεθ᾽ ἀοίδιμοι 'so that we become worthy of song' rather than simply 'the subject of song'. At 357 οἶσιν refers to Helen and Paris alone; but the speech is addressed to Hector, and concluding remarks often include both speaker and addressee in a final first person address: cf. 58n. Hector too will certainly be the subject of song, so it is difficult to exclude him from Helen's last remarks. By using the term ἀοίδιμος, Helen sidesteps the issue of blame; contrast *Od.* 24.200 (στυγερὴ ἀοιδή), 201 (χαλεπὴ φῆμις); Hes. fr. 176.2 MW (κακὴ φήμη). Helen's mention of future song is likely to flatter Hector: Martin 1989: 136–7; and Murnaghan 1999: 213–14.

359–68 The structure of Hector's speech mirrors the main points made by Helen: she expressed her wish for a better husband (350n., 351n.); he now talks about his men's longing for him (362n.). She claimed that Paris was beyond hope (353n.); he urges her to tell him to return to the battlefield (363n.). She invited her to join her in her own bedroom (354–6n.); he claims he must go and see his own wife (366n.). She imagined herself, Paris and, by implication, Hector as future subjects of song (357–8n.); he envisages his own death and makes it a priority to see his wife and child (367–8n.). This is the only time Hector addresses Helen in the course of the *Iliad*.

When lamenting Hector at the end of the poem, Helen claims that he was always gentle to her and defended her when she was blamed (24.767–72); what we see here is polite disengagement. For Hector's reasonable tone (γάρ at 361, 365 and 367), see Introduction 2.4. On the speech, see further Lohmann 1970: 101; and Introduction 4.3. For a comparison with other speeches that decline an invitation, Minchin 2001 and 2007: ch. 2, esp. pp. 62–3.

359 = 263n. The traditional line presents Hector's speech as more neutral in tone than his speech to Paris (325n.), and Helen's speech to him (343n.).

360 ~ 18.126 (Achilles to Thetis).   μή με κάθιζ': Hector refuses to 'be sat down' (καθίζω). Warriors engaged in a war should not spend their time sitting down: cf. 336n. and 354n.   Ἑλένη: Hector's address is polite rather than intimate; contrast Priam's φίλον τέκος at 3.162; and Helen's own δᾶερ ἐμεῖο κυνός (344n.) and δᾶερ (355n.).   φιλέουσά περ: φιλέω can describe affection between sexual partners (cf. 9.340–3) but need not have sexual connotations: at 18.126 φιλέουσά περ is used of Thetis' concern for her son; cf. also 1.196 = 209 (of Hera's feelings for Achilles and Agamemnon). Helen's feelings for Hector feature prominently at the very end of the poem: in her funeral lament for Hector she claims that he was 'by far the dearest (πολὺ φίλτατε) of all her brothers-in-law' (24.762), and in the last line of her speech she claims that he was her only φίλος, and that everybody else hates her (24.775). For concessive περ see 85n.   οὐδέ με πείσεις = 11.648, 18.126, etc. The expression is often used in contexts when somebody refuses to be held back.

361 Throughout his mission inside the city, Hector is very aware that the Trojan troops need him on the battlefield: Introduction 4.   ἤδη γάρ: ἤδη conveys Hector's urgency and γάρ offers the first of several explanations: cf. 359–68n.; Introduction 2.4.   θυμός: contrast 256n.; see also 444n.   ἐπέσσυται 'is eager' (perfect tense), continuing the theme of urgent action that runs through the book; cf. 296n., 390n., 505n., 518n., 7.1.

362 Τρώεσσ': emphatically at the beginning of the line, in necessary enjambment. The Trojan soldiers on the battlefield are Hector's priority: their longing for him is more important than Helen's invitation; see Van Nortwick 2001: 233.   οἳ . . . ἔχουσιν: Hector's assessment is borne out in the Trojans' relief when they see him: 7.4–7.   ποθήν: soldiers often 'long' for their absent leaders (ποθέω, ποθή); cf., e.g., 1.240, 11.471. Contrast Paris' 'desire' for Helen (ἔρως, ἵμερος), which keeps him away from the battlefield: 3.442–6.

363 Now that Hector has established his priorities, he tells Helen what she can do to help him. His request is humiliating for Paris (a man should not need his wife to tell him to fight); but it is also problematic for Hector, for he should not need to enlist Helen's help. The scholia try to excuse him: 'He did not think it appropriate to talk to Paris directly, since Paris had entrusted everything to his wife' (ΣbT ad 6.363). The situation between Helen and Paris is now exposed in all its difficulty: at 3.421–47 the poet described how they met in their bedroom, complained about one another and made love; Paris himself revealed that Helen had already told him to return to the battlefield (337–9n.).   ἀλλά: Hector takes control, cf. his previous attempt to impose his will at 331n. (ἀλλ᾽ ἄνα); then Paris' request for time at 340n.; and Helen's invitation to sit down at 354n.   σύ γ᾽ emphasises that Helen can do something and prepares for line 365, καὶ γὰρ ἐγών.   ὄρνυθι 'encourage, incite'; the verb is often used of gods but is not as striking as ὥρμησ᾽ at 338n.   τοῦτον echoes Helen's τούτωι at 352n.   ἐπειγέσθω δὲ καὶ αὐτός: cf. 338n., where Paris admitted to taking his cue from Helen. Note Hector's emphasis on speed: the verb is used specifically in contexts where there is outside pressure; cf. 85n. (ἀναγκαίη γὰρ ἐπείγει) and 388n. (ἐπειγομένη). Paris draws attention to his own speed when he joins Hector at the end of the book: 517–19n.

364 Paris should catch up with Hector while he is still in the city, so that they join the army together (cf. 7.1–7 and especially the duals at 7.7). Hector wants to ensure that Paris really does leave his bedroom and knows that their joint appearance will boost troop morale; but his insistence that he should join him before he leaves the city also enables Hector to introduce and justify a new plan: that of visiting his own family while Paris gets ready.   ὥς κεν introduces a final clause with verb in the subjunctive; on this construction see Chantraine 1948–53: vol. II, 270.

365 The second γάρ-clause explains how Hector plans to ensure that Paris catches up with him but also introduces a new idea; see below (καὶ γὰρ ἐγών). Helenos had warned Hector about the dangers of 'falling into the hands of the women' (81–2n.), so his plan carries some risk of delay and criticism; but the context suggests that it is reasonable for Hector to look for his wife.   καὶ γὰρ ἐγών 'and I, for my part, will go home'. καί in combination with γάρ suggests something more than a straightforward explanation: in fact, Hector introduces a new idea; for γάρ cf. 15n.; for further discussion of καὶ γάρ, see Stoevesandt 2008: 120.   οἶκόνδ᾽ ἐσελεύσομαι combines two ideas: that of going home and that of entering the house (for a similarly complex construction, cf. 86n.). οἶκόνδε expresses the idea of home (cf. formulaic οἶκόνδε νέεσθαι), while εἰς οἶκον refers primarily to a building (490n.) and can be used of somebody else's house (*Od.* 2.52 etc.).

366 Hector first mentions his home (οἶκόνδε), then the people who work there (οἰκῆας), then his dear wife and young child. When talking to the men on the battlefield he told them upfront that he was going to see 'our wives', cf. 114n. (ἡμετέρηις ἀλόχοισι); now he is more reticent. When talking to Helen, Hector is keen to present himself as somebody in charge of a household, rather than as a husband who cannot keep away from his wife. His future encounters follow the order outlined here: first he meets the servants, then his wife and child.   οἰκῆας: the word seems to be a rather vague term for people who belong to the household; cf. 5.413 (of a widow wailing through the night and keeping the οἰκῆες awake: the word must refer to all those who sleep in the house, though she may be living only with servants); see further *LfgrE* s.v. οἰκεύς B. ΣA *ad* 6.366 gloss οἰκῆας as 'servants'; ΣbT *ad* 6.365–6 suggest the more inclusive 'everyone in the house'. The debate has left traces elsewhere in the Homeric scholia; cf. Erbse 1969–88: vol. II, 194. For sigma closing the final syllable of οἰκῆας, see 76n. (Ἔλενος).   ἄλοχόν τε φίλην καὶ νήπιον υἱόν ~ 5.480, 688. Helen, though affectionate (φιλέουσά περ: 360n.), is not Hector's 'dear wife'. For φίλος in Homer, see 67n.; on ἄλοχος, see 337n. Andromache is first mentioned by name at 371n., cf. Hecuba, who is first introduced as 'our mother' (87n.) and is only later mentioned by name (293n.). A baby son completes the family; cf. 5.480 (Sarpedon on his wife and baby son). Helen and Paris, by contrast, have no children; and Helen, most beautiful of women, only managed to give birth to one baby daughter, Hermione, with Menelaos; cf. 3.175, *Od.* 4.12–14; and Hes. fr. 204.94–5 MW.

367–8 A third and last γάρ-clause explains why Hector wants to see his own family; for a similar statement about the future, cf. *Od.* 18.265–6. A series of adverbs ἔτι . . . αὖτις . . . ἤδη conveys Hector's perception that time is running out; cf. Broccia 1956/7: 174. The passage responds to 357–8n., where Helen contemplated the future from the perspective of epic audiences: Hector, by contrast, envisages his own death from the perspective of those closest to him. These lines look forward to the encounter between Hector and Andromache and form a ring with 501–2n.

367 οὐ γάρ τ' οἶδ' ~ *Od.* 10.190, 17.78. At 447–9n. Hector admits he knows that Troy will fall; and later he contemplates his own death in the light of that knowledge.   τ': epic τε usually marks a generalisation or a timeless truth (cf. 127n., 147n.); this does not seem to be the case here, but Hector uses the particle rhetorically, in order to express his (and indeed any warrior's) constant state of uncertainty about the future; see Ruijgh 1971: 737, who discusses this and other examples of rhetorical γάρ τε in direct speech. For ancient attempts to dispense with τε see *app. crit.*   ἔτι: cf. 367–8n., 500n.   σφιν 'for them'; the dative emphasises Hector's concern; cf. 203n.   ὑπότροπος 'returning home'; in the *Iliad* only here and at 501n., but cf. *Od.* 20.332, 21.211 and 22.35 (where it contrasts with Odysseus' defining epithet πολύτροπος, 'of many turns'); and *Hom. Hymn* 3.476. The adjective underlines the distance between the battlefield and home.   ἵξομαι: future of ἱκάνω/ἱκνέομαι/ἱκέσθαι/ἵκω (classical ἀφικνέομαι).   αὖτις: cf. 367–8n.

368 ἤ: for the apparent hiatus see 341n. (ἤ ἴθ').   ἤδη: cf. 361n. and 367–8n. Hector's urgency throughout his visit to Troy is transmuted into a sense of impending doom.   ὑπὸ χερσὶ . . . Ἀχαιῶν: Hector takes up what Helen says about divine power (349n. and 357n.) but gives it a different emphasis: she sounded a note of acceptance, and even relief at the limitations of her own power; Hector feels the tragedy of his own death, because he thinks of the people who love him.   δαμόωσιν: contracted future of δάμνημι, 'subdue, kill': δαμάσουσιν > δαμάουσιν > δαμῶσιν > δαμόωσιν, with diectasis; cf. 148n. (τηλεθόωσα). For this and similar uses of the verb, see *LfgrE* s.v. δάμνημι, δαμνά(ω), δαμνάζω B II 2 d.

369–502: THE ENCOUNTER BETWEEN HECTOR AND ANDROMACHE

369–91 Hector's disappointment at not finding Andromache is palpable in the simple οὐδ' εὗρ' placed at the beginning of the line (371n.); the poet then tells us where she is (372–3n.), while Hector looks for her inside. Then, as he is about to leave, he stops at the threshold and asks the maids where she has gone (375n.). His words, here as elsewhere, show that he has only limited knowledge of how the women live and move inside the city; cf. 374–80n.; and Introduction 3.2. It is the housekeeper's answer that reveals to him a fundamental connection between his own actions and Andromache's: while he is looking for her at home, she is on the city rampart, hoping to see him on the battlefield (381–9n.); see further Schadewaldt 1997: 131–2. Both Hector and Andromache act out of a sense of foreboding, and both feel the urgent need to see one another: he leaves the house at speed (390n.), and she later runs towards him (394n.). This transitional section before their encounter is unusually long and complex; it builds up the narrative tension and plays with the possibility that Hector and Andromache may fail to meet. For the parallels between this scene and Andromache's realisation that Hector is dead (22.437–72), see Segal 1971b; and Grethlein 2006a: 245–53. See also Broccia 1956/7.

369 = 116n. Hector loses no time in implementing his decision to leave. In contrast with 116, the poet now stays with Hector and follows him on his progress home.

370 = 497n.; cf. 514n. (αἶψα δ' ἔπειτα). Hector is as ever conscious that he needs to be quick, Introduction 4.   αἶψα δ' ἔπειθ' emphasises speed; contrast the more common αὐτὰρ ἔπειτα; cf. *LfgrE* s.v. αἶψα B *A* I.   ἵκανε: cf. 367n. In contrast with 391n., the journey is quickly over. The shock of not finding Andromache at home is the greater for it: 371n.   δόμους εὖ ναιετάοντας: a standard phrase (cf., e.g., 11.769, *Od.* 17.28); contrast the elaborate descriptions of Priam's solid stone place (242–52n.) and Paris' luxurious abode (312–17n.). For the form ναιετάοντας (ναιετάω < ναίω), cf. 268n. (εὐχετάασθαι).

371 οὐδ' εὗρ': an alarming revelation. Hector later tells Andromache to return home and attend to her normal duties (485–93n.); ancient readers found her absence from home remarkable, cf. Eur. *Tro.* 647–50, with Introduction 5.   Ἀνδρομάχην: this is the first time Andromache is mentioned by name; on the etymology of her name, see Neumann 1991: 316. The poet does not pun on it overtly (though see 492–3n., with Wathelet 1988: 282). Some ancient readers found her name significant: Introduction 5. We hear more about her life at 414–28n.   λευκώλενον: paleness was an important aspect of female beauty (e.g. *Od.* 18.196); cf. Thomas 2002. White arms are singled out because other parts of the female body were not generally exposed to public view. The epithet is used of Andromache (cf. 377n. and 24.723) and of several other characters, including domestic servants, but it is especially associated with Hera, the Olympian wife: 1.55 etc.   ἐν μεγάροισιν: formulaic at the end of the line. 'Hall(s)' or simply 'dwelling', 'house', esp. when used in the plural, cf. *LfgrE* s.v. μέγαρον B 3; Rougier-Blanc 2005: ch. 3; see also 91n., together with 286–7n. and 288n. Paris and Helen were in their θάλαμος when Hector met them (321–2n.).

372–3 While Hector looks, the poet explains Andromache's absence; as often, the audience know more about the situation than the characters inside the poem; cf. 374–80n.

372 ἀλλ' ἥ γε 'but she, for her part, had gone'. γε draws attention to the poet's knowledge of the situation, cf. 16–17n.   ξὺν παιδί: at 366n. Hector said that he wanted to see his son; now we discover that Andromache has taken him away with her. The baby will feature prominently in the ensuing encounter: 400–3n., 466–81n., esp. 471n.   καὶ ἀμφιπόλωι ἐϋπέπλωι: women do not leave the house on their own, cf. 3.142–4 and esp. 22.460–1 (Andromache leaves in a frenzy, while her maids follow her). Hector and Andromache meet as a family, complete with offspring and a servant; even though their meeting is later recast as a romantic encounter: 515–16n.; see further Introduction 4.4 and 5. ἀμφιπόλωι ἐϋπέπλωι (only here) is a variation on ἀμφιπόλοισιν ἐϋπλοκάμοις at 22.442 and *Od.* 6.198; cf. *Od.* 6.222. It suits the context of the scene: the maid's *peplos* and its folds will feature later (400n., 467n.).

373 ~ 23.106 (of the shade of the dead Patroclus, which is likewise said to be 'lamenting and wailing'). Andromache fears that Hector may be dead; cf. his own words: 367–8n. Later, at 22.460–7, she again leaves home in a frenzy of fear and anxiety – and discovers that Hector *is* dead.   πύργωι: the rampart or bastion near or above the Scaean Gates. The word can be used quite generally of any bastion, or the city wall in its entirety (cf. *Od.* 6.262–3; *LfgrE* s.v. πύργος B); but in the *Iliad* the Trojans often view the battlefield from a bastion at the Scaean Gates: Priam and Helen watch the troops from that vantage point (3.145, 149 and 153–4), as does Priam when he sees Achilles approaching (21.526–37) and Hector waiting for him (22.5–6 and 25–36). Hector's later prediction that Achilles will die in front of the Scaean Gates (22.360) envisages him dying in full view of the Trojans – who are at this point in the narrative witnessing Hector's own death. At 22.447 Andromache hears a great commotion 'from the bastion' (ἀπὸ πύργου) and fears that the Trojans might have seen Hector die. Theano prays that Diomedes die in front of the Scaean Gates: 306–7n.   ἐφεστήκει: pluperfect intransitive, 'she stood upon'.   γοόωσά τε μυρομένη τε: the two verbs have similar meaning and often occur together. γοάω is the act of mourning someone by delivering a funerary lament (cf. 499n.: γόον); μύρομαι refers to wailing in a more physical sense, see *LfgrE* s.v. μύρομαι. For the combination of a more abstract word with one that appeals directly to the senses, cf. 328–9n.

374–80 Hector is about to leave but stops at the threshold and calls back to the servants. He is conscious he must return immediately to the battlefield but still wants to know where Andromache is: his question betrays his anxiety at not finding her, though his tone is exceptionally calm, even stilted (Kirk 1990: 208). Hector suggests two possible explanations for Andromache's absence: 378n. and 379–80n. Both involve the company of other women in an enclosed space; cf. ΣbT *ad* 6.378*a*; and Introduction 4.4.

374 The line recalls *Od.* 13.42–3 (Odysseus expects to find blameless Penelope at home with her maids); cf. also *Od.* 15.14–15 (Athena urges Telemachus to return to Ithaca while his blameless mother is still at home).   ἀμύμονα . . . ἄκοιτιν: the epithet is commonly found in the phrase γυναῖκα(ς) ἀμύμονα ἔργ᾽ εἰδυίας/-υῖαν, but it does not usually qualify female personal names (*Od.* 24.194, in direct speech, and Hes. fr. 26.7 MW are exceptions) and is rare with ἄλοχος or ἄκοιτις (otherwise only at *Od.* 13.42, in direct speech). Here it may reflect Hector's point of view ('embedded focalisation'): he sees Andromache as 'blameless'. On the meaning of ἀμύμων, see

22n.   τέτμεν: Hector did not 'find' or 'meet' Andromache; the verb is always used of people, cf. 515. The form τέτμεν is a reduplicated, athematic aorist of a stem *tem- of uncertain etymology; cf. Chantraine 1999 s.v. τετμεῖν.

375 The line introduces Hector's speech as an afterthought.   ἔστη ἐπ᾽ οὐδὸν ἰών ~ Od. 20.128, 21.124, 149, 24.178, 493. 'He stepped onto the threshold and stood.' The phrase is almost always used of somebody coming from *inside* the house, as must be the case here: Hector has been looking for Andromache ἐν μεγάροισιν (371n.). For the participle construction, cf., e.g., 7.303–4 (δῶκε... φέρων), and see further Chantraine 1948–53: vol. II, 319–20.   οὐδόν: probably the threshold of Hector's house, though some readers (e.g. Stoevesandt 2008: 124) argue that it is the threshold to the women's quarters. Hector's question is presented as a last-minute request for information; he then immediately speeds away: 390n. Thresholds are significant places, especially for masters and potential masters of the house: Od. 21.124; cf. 149, and Od. 22.2; see also Od. 24.178.   δμωῇσιν: cf. 323n.; Hector addresses female servants specifically; no male servants (δμῶες) are mentioned in the *Iliad* – in this time of war, the city is the domain of women.

376 A request for accurate information. This kind of request is rare in the *Iliad*, though it features repeatedly in the *Odyssey*; it often betrays some anxiety on the part of the speaker, as s/he braces herself/himself for an uncomfortable truth (cf. 24.407–9, Od. 23.35–8, etc.; Hom. Hymn 2.71–3).   εἰ δ᾽ ἄγε: cf. ἀλλ᾽ ἄγε (340n., 354), but without the contrast which that expression implies; see further Chantraine 1948–53: vol. II, 274. Though ἄγετε is attested (22.381), ἄγε can be used when addressing more than one person (cf., e.g., 1.62). The particle δέ is formulaic in this phrase, also at the beginning of direct speech; cf. 16.667, Od. 12.112, 23.45. For δέ introducing direct speech see also 123n. and 479n.   δμωιαί: cf. 323n.   νημερτέα μυθήσασθε ~ Hom. Hymn 2.294; a request for a straightforward answer, which 'does not miss the mark' (νημερτής < νη- + ἁμαρτάνω); cf. similar expressions at Il. 6.382, Od. 14.125, etc.; and 343n. (μύθοισι).

377 Hector's language is very similar to that of the poet at 371n., though in his mouth it sounds more ponderous; on Hector's tone: 374–80n. For similar formulations, cf. Od. 18.198 and 19.60, with M. Parry 1971: 98.   Ἀνδρομάχη: 371n.   πῆι: cf. 378n. (πηι).   λευκώλενος: 371n. ΣbT ad 6.377 observe that the epithet fits the language of the poet rather than that of his characters.   μεγάροιο: cf. 371n. (ἐν μεγάροισιν).

378 ~ 24.769. Hector's first suggestion is that Andromache's absence fits the normal peacetime routine of visits among female relatives.   πηι (shortened before vowel) picks up πῆι at 377. Hector wants to qualify his initial question by suggesting two specific destinations for Andromache.   ἐς γαλόων ἢ εἰνατέρων ἐϋπέπλων: i.e. to their homes. γαλόως is the sister of one's husband, cf. 3.122 (e.g. Laodike is Helen's and, indeed, Andromache's γαλόως); εἰνατέρες are the wives of a husband's brothers, i.e., as ΣD ad 6.378 point out, 'what Helen and Andromache are to each other'. Homeric terms of kinship are often more precise than their English equivalents; see also 344n. (δᾶερ). For ἐϋπέπλος, cf. 372n.

379–80 Hector's second suggestion acknowledges that Andromache's absence may be linked to the extreme danger the Trojans are facing but assumes that she is responding to the instructions he gave to Hecuba, and thus contributing to the coordinated effort recommended by Helenos at 77–101n. Hector is out of touch: the audience know that Andromache has actually run to the rampart in a frenzy of anxiety (372–3n.) – and they also know that the women's attempt to appease Athena fails (311n.). This is the last time the ritual is mentioned in the *Iliad*. Against the backdrop of the women's communal action, Andromache seems isolated and vulnerable; cf. 425–8n., 429–30n., with Van Nortwick 2001: 226.

379 ἤ: for the apparent hiatus see 341n. (ἢ ἴθ᾽).   ἐς Ἀθηναίης: cf. 378n. (ἐς γαλόων ἢ εἰνατέρων ἐϋπέπλων).   ἐξοίχεται 'has gone out'. The present tense is used like a perfect, as often with forms of οἴχομαι; cf. *LfgrE* s.v. οἰχνέω, οἴχομαι B II 4.   ἔνθά περ ἄλλαι: Hector's phrasing is defensive; note the use of περ (cf. 41n.). The expression follows a standard pattern at the end of a line, cf. ἔνθά περ ἄλλοι, πὰρ δέ οἱ ἄλλοι, αὐτὰρ οἱ ἄλλοι, etc. in the same position. On the accentuation, see 251n.

380 Τρωιαὶ ἐϋπλόκαμοι: only here and at 385. The epithet is relatively rare in the *Iliad*, though cf. 22.442 and 449 (of Andromache's maidservants). It seems to characterise younger women and so helps Hector express the thought that maybe Andromache has joined the γεραιαί who went to pray to Athena (87n.).   δεινὴν θεόν: a common description of Athena. Here it seems particularly appropriate, cf. 5.839 and 738–42; 311n.); but Hector's language also fits traditional prayers to Athena, cf. *Hom. Hymn* 11.2 (to Athena).   ἱλάσκονται: the technical term for securing divine favour either through sacrifice (e.g. 1.147, 444) or by some other means (e.g. song: 1.472, cf., e.g., *Hom. Hymns* 1 D 8 West, 3.165, 19.48). In epic, attempts to secure divine favour (ἱλάσκεσθαι) are usually successful (*Od.* 21.364–5 is an exception): Hector's use of this verb thus highlights his misplaced hope that his mission might succeed.

381–9 This is the only mention of Hector's and Andromache's housekeeper in the *Iliad*. Other housekeepers (esp. Eurycleia: *Od.* 2.344–7, etc.; cf. *Hom. Hymn* 2.103–4) have a close relationship with their masters, and this seems to be the case here too: the trusted housekeeper not only knows where Andromache is but can also describe how she broke down at the news that the Achaeans were crushing the Trojans. Her speech is introduced as a truthful answer to Hector's questions (381n., 382n.) and falls into two parts: first it deals with his guesses (383–5n.) and then reveals what has actually happened (386–9). As the speech unfolds, Hector's expectations are shattered, until he is confronted with the truth that Andromache left home 'looking like a madwoman' (μαινομένηι εἰκυῖα). This description of Andromache, seen from the perspective of her housekeeper, is alarming for both Hector and the audience, who are drawn into his world: it opens a question about Andromache's feelings, which later become the focus of attention. On the relationship between Andromache and her housekeeper, see Introduction 3.2 and 4.4.

381 ~ *Od.* 17.495 = 18.169.   αὖτ᾽: cf. 73n. (αὖτε).   ὀτρηρὴ ταμίη: a variation on the more common αἰδοίη ταμίη (at *Od.* 1.139 = 4.55, 7.175, etc.).

For the epithet's emphasis on trustworthiness and efficiency, see 1.321, *Od.* 4.735 (ὀτρηρῶς); and more generally *LfgrE* s.v. ὀτρηρός.   πρὸς ... ἔειπεν: on tmesis, cf. 42–3n.   μῦθον: cf. 343n.

382 The emphasis is on truth, as Hector had demanded: cf. 376n.   Ἕκτορ: the first-name address is not particularly intimate in early Greek epic (Weise 1965: 184), though it is rarely used by servants.   ἄνωγας: cf. 170n. (ἠνώγει).   ἀληθέα μυθήσασθαι: cf. 376n. (νημερτέα μυθήσασθαι).

383–5 ~ 378–80. Precision matters, so the housekeeper repeats Hector's guesses verbatim, addressing them one by one; cf. 90–7n.

386 ἀλλ' begins the second half of the speech, which contains alarming news about Andromache's behaviour.   πύργον ... μέγαν Ἰλίου: the housekeeper must refer to the bastion near the Scaean Gates (373n.), though Troy has other bastions too, cf. 18.274, 278 and 22.195.

387 τείρεσθαι Τρῶας: this striking enjambment marks Andromache's terrifying realisation; for τείρεσθαι cf. 85n. and 255n.   μέγα ... Ἀχαιῶν: a powerful epic phrase, cf. formulaic μέγα κράτος ἐγγυάλιξε, τοῦ γὰρ κράτος ἐστὶ μέγιστον and many similar expressions. κράτος is often used of superior 'power', and hence victory, as here; see further *LfgrE* s.v. κράτος/κάρτος B 1.

388 μὲν δή summarises the information about Andromache and points forward to Astyanax, who is mentioned in the next line: cf. δ' at 389.   τεῖχος: very close in meaning to πύργος, cf. 373n., and ΣD *ad* 3.153.   ἐπειγομένη 'rushing'; the verb expresses the theme of urgent action which pervades book 6; cf. 363n.   ἀφικάνει 'has gone'; cf. Chantraine 1948–53: vol. II, 190.

389 μαινομένηι εἰκυῖα 'looking like a madwoman'; cf. 100–1n. (μαίνεται). Later, at 22.460, the poet describes Andromache leaving the house and running to the rampart 'like a maenad' (μαινάδι ἴση). One difference between the two descriptions is that the poet offers a precise likeness, whereas the housekeeper gives her subjective impression of Andromache's behaviour: her words resemble verse-initial formulae of the type noun + εἰκυῖα (3.386, 19.350, *Od.* 2.383, etc.) which describe goddesses in disguise; and the verb she uses, μαίνεσθαι, features often in character speech, especially when the speaker wants to tell the addressee that a third party is out of control, and urgent action is needed; see further Hershkowitz 1998: 132–42. Many scholars detect in the housekeeper's words an allusion to Dionysiac religion (e.g. Privitera 1970: 60–1; Arthur Katz 1981: 30; Seaford 1994: 330–3, esp. n. 6; Gagliardi 2006: 16–17; Tsagalis 2008: ch. 1), but that implication is only spelled out at 22.460. For another madwoman in *Iliad* 6 (certainly not a maenad), see Anteia at 160n. On this passage and 22.460, see also Segal 1971b: 47–8.   φέρει ... τιθήνη: at 22.460–1, in the extremity of her distress, Andromache leaves without her child; but at this stage in the poem she still wants him near her. He becomes the focus of attention for both parents later: 400–3n. and 466–81n.

390 The speech-concluding line (51n.) effectively conveys Hector's immediate departure, cf. ΣbT *ad* 6.390. After ἦ ῥα, the narrative usually stays with the speaker; here, by contrast, we follow Hector: the effect is especially abrupt; cf. *LfgrE* s.v. ἦ B

III 3 a.   ἥ 'she said'; frequent speech-concluding verb, attested in early epic only in the 3rd pers. sing.   ῥα: 232n.   γυνὴ ταμίη: cf. *Od.* 2.345, 3.479 (in the same metrical position); see also 323n. (μετ᾽ ἄρα δμωῇσι γυναιξίν).   ὃ δ᾽: the change of subject with demonstrative pronoun (cf. 9n.) and δέ (1n.) replaces the more usual construction with καί and no change of subject.   ἀπέσσυτο: cf. 361n., though here the emphasis is on leaving home, rather than going towards the battlefield.   δώματος: in the same position as the standard epithet φαίδιμος, cf. ἐξέσσυτο φαίδιμος Ἕκτωρ at 7.1. δώματος draws attention to the fact that Hector is leaving his home.

391 Hector was not coming directly from the Scaean Gates, but the poet constructs a neat reversal of direction: Introduction 3.3.   ὁδόν: 292n.   ἐϋκτιμένας κατ᾽ ἀγυιάς: up to now, the focus was on individual buildings, which were Hector's destinations: the palace of Priam (242–52n.), that of Paris (312–17n.) and Hector's own home (370n.). Now that Hector is ready to leave the city, the poet offers a more general impression of its built-up streets, which is in stark contrast with the openness of the battlefield. The phrase is unique, though compare ἐϋκτίμενον πτολίεθρον, etc.

392–3 πύλας . . . Σκαιάς: the hyperbaton places the significant toponym at the beginning of a new line, in enjambment. Hector rushed home to see Andromache (αἶψα δ᾽ ἔπειτα: 370n.), and she rushed towards the battlefield to see him (ἐπειγομένη: 388n.). Now they meet between home and the battlefield. At the end of their encounter, Hector insists they should return to their respective spheres: 485–93n. On the significance of their meeting point, see Introduction 4.4.

392 εὖτε: for the lack of connecting particles, see Chantraine 1948–53: vol. II, 254.   διερχόμενος μέγα ἄστυ: Hector crosses the great city at speed: Introduction 3.3 and 4. On the great city of Troy, cf. 2.332, 9.136 = 278, 16.448 and esp. 22.251. For ἄστυ as one's own city, 95n.

393 ἄρ brings out the significance of the Scaean Gates, as they come into view.   ἔμελλε emphasises that it is Andromache who intercepts Hector; cf. ΣbT *ad* 6.394*a*; Schadewaldt 1997: 131; and Felson and Slatkin 2004: 99, n. 24. According to Kirk 1990: 21, 'it is inconceivable that, having been told precisely where Andromakhe was, he should rush past without even looking for her'. But Hector is under pressure to return to the battlefield as soon as possible (Introduction 4), and Andromache certainly thinks he is about to enter into battle.   πεδίονδε: the open plain, where the battle is raging (2n., 38n.); contrast the previous lines, which describe the built-up streets (391n.), the great city (μέγα ἄστυ: 392n.) and the gates (392–3n.).

394 Andromache runs towards Hector: the delay at 395–8n. only heightens the anticipation before husband and wife face one another at 399n.   ἔνθ᾽: cf. 251n. and 318n.   ἄλοχος πολύδωρος = 22.88 (of Andromache) and *Od.* 24.294 (of Penelope). The expression emphasises Andromache's role as Hector's precious, wedded wife. In Homer brides have a dowry and also receive wedding gifts: Snodgrass 1974; and Scheid-Tissinier 1994: 87–106. The expression πολύδωρος may refer to both kinds of offerings; cf. ΣD *ad* 6.394; *LfgrE* s.v. πολύδωρος. For Andromache's wedding gifts, cf. 22.470–2; for her lavish dowry, cf. Sappho fr. 44.8–10 Voigt, with Introduction 5. The emphasis on gifts suggests a contrast between Andromache and Helen, whose union with Paris is based on theft, cf. 3.70–2 and 91–3, 7.362–4.   ἦλθε θέουσα 'came running'. Andromache's behaviour recalls that of the other women Hector met during his mission in Troy: 237–41n. The phrasing closely resembles 251n., though Hecuba moves more slowly, as befits her age; another difference is that Hecuba was entirely startled by Hector's appearance, whereas Andromache was hoping to see him, even if only from afar.

395–8 Andromache's name, in progressive enjambment, triggers a short biography: the poet mentions her father Eetion, her place of origin and her marriage to Hector. The information provided resembles a standard entry in an epic catalogue; the poet says nothing about the most tragic events in Andromache's life: Eetion's defeat and the fall of Thebes already featured at 1.366–7, and Andromache will soon describe her father's death, the fall of her city, the death of her brothers and that of her mother: 414–28n. As well as providing a foil to Andromache's narrative, these lines further delay the encounter between Hector and Andromache: she started running towards him at 394n. but faces him only at 399n. (in ring composition); the intervening lines slow the pace of the narrative and introduce Andromache in a 'grand and formal' manner (Easterling 1995: 163).

395 = 8.187 ∼ *Od.* 6.17 = 213, etc.: a standard line. For enjambment leading to further information on a character, cf. 13n.   Ἀνδρομάχη: 371n.   μεγαλήτορος: 282–3n. (Πριάμωι μεγαλήτορι).   Ἠετίωνος: for Eetion, king of Cilician Thebes, cf. 1.366–7, 22.479–81, and see further 414–28n. There is also a Trojan warrior called Eetion (17.575 and 590), and another Eetion from Imbros, a guest-friend of the Trojans (21.43); for a fourth Eetion, brother of Dardanos ancestor of the Trojans, see Hes. fr. 178.5–12 MW. All these characters are associated with Troy; the etymology of the name is unknown (Wathelet 1988: 563–4) and may be non-Greek (von Kamptz 1982: 135 and 372).

396 Ἠετίων: an unusual form of progressive enjambment: Hoekstra 1965: 34. It may be relevant that Ἠετίων ὅς sounds like Ἠετίωνος (Wackernagel 1926: 56), but the change of grammatical case hardly needs justifying (*pace* Jacquinod 1994).   ἔναιεν: for background information, the imperfect tense is standard, cf. ἔχεθ᾽ at 398n.   ὑπὸ Πλάκωι ὑληέσσηι = 425, and 22.479; cf. Sappho fr. 44.6 Voigt (Θήβας ἐξ ἱέρας Πλακίας τ᾽ ἀπ᾽ [ἀϊ]ν<ν>άω). ὑλήεις, 'wooded', is a standard epithet of mountains (cf. 21.449; *Od.* 1.186; and Hes. fr. 40.2 MW); it can also characterise glens (e.g. *Hom. Hymn* 14.5), promontories (e.g. 17.747–8) and islands (e.g. 13.12, of Samos).

397 Θήβηι Ὑποπλακίηι 'in Thebes beneath Mount Plakos', with dative of place (locative); cf. Chantraine 1948–53: vol. ii, 78. The epithet is used only here (though cf. *Od.* 3.81 ἐξ Ἰθάκης Ὑπονηΐου) and differentiates this Thebes from more famous cities of the same name, for which see 222–3n. (Θήβηισιν). Ancient readers located Thebes beneath Mount Plakos in the plain near Adramyttion, opposite the island of Lesbos; cf. Hdt. 7.42; ΣbT *ad* 1.366*c*.   Κιλίκεσσ᾽ ἄνδρεσσιν ἀνάσσων: cf., e.g., 17.308. The older formulation must have been ἀνδρέσσι ϝανάσσων. The possible connections between Eetion's 'Cilicians' and Cilicia in south-eastern Asia Minor are debated; see Ulf and Rollinger 2010.

398 τοῦ περ δή 'and the daughter of this man, then . . .' The demonstrative pronoun (9n.) with περ (41n.) and δή (52–3n.) resumes the main narrative after a short digression; cf. 11.126, 12.256 and 15.707. ἔχεθ᾽ Ἕκτορι: men standardly 'have' a wife in early Greek epic; for women, the passive construction is used, as here. Formally, the construction seems to be modelled on phrases that describe the taming of an animal or a woman (δάμνημι), cf. George 2005: 51–5. For the word play Ἕκτωρ – ἔχειν, cf. 5.472–4, 6.403n., 24.730, with Taplin 1992: 116. χαλκοκορυστῆι: cf. 199n. One papyrus reads Ἡεδίωνο[ς] (i.e. Ἡετίωνος): this seems to be an attempt to make Homeric diction more sensitive to the immediate narrative context, cf. 112n.

399 The line resumes the narrative of 394, cf. ἔνθ᾽. . . ἐναντίη ἦλθε θέουσα.   ἦ: cf. 9n.   ἔπειτ᾽: for the resumptive use of this particle, see West in Heubeck, West and Hainsworth 1988: 163, ad Od. 3.62.   ἤντησ᾽: Andromache faces Hector, though he will first focus his attention on the child: 404n.   ἀμφίπολος: the servant is Astyanax's wet nurse (τιθήνη: 389, 467n.), but from Andromache's point of view (ἅμα. . . αὐτῆι), she is her maid; cf. 372n.

400–3 The baby was briefly mentioned twice (cf. 372n., 389n.); this full description is matched by 466–83, in ring composition. The poet adopts the language and perspective of a parent, as he accumulates epithets and words of endearment: ἀταλάφρονα, νήπιον, Ἑκτορίδην ἀγαπητόν, ἀλίγκιον ἀστέρι καλῶι (400–1); see de Jong 1987a: 108, and, for the poet's language and embedded focalisation, see further de Jong 2004: 136–46. For the sympathetic portrayal of children and parenting in the *Iliad* see van Wees 1996, Ingalls 1998 and Pratt 2007. The next two lines, 402–3, widen the perspective to include the views and hopes of the people of Troy: Hector calls his son Skamandrios, but the Trojans call him Astyanax, because Hector protects the city. Hector's role as father is thus inextricably linked to his wider responsibilities towards the community, cf. Introduction 4.4 and Redfield 1994, esp. 123–7. The alternative names for the baby interested ancient readers: at Pl. *Crat.* 392c–393a, Socrates uses the two names Astyanax/Skamandrios in order to draw a distinction between the language of men and that of women, though in Homer the distinction is actually between family and wider community.

400 παῖδ᾽ ἐπὶ κόλπωι ἔχουσ᾽ ~ *Hom. Hymn* 2.187; for the 'bosom' (κόλπος) as the natural place for a baby, cf. 136n., 467–70n. and 482–3n.   κόλπωι: the ancient variant κόλπον (accusative) is well attested but difficult to construe; it may stem from an ancient debate about the meaning of Homeric κόλπος. Commenting on the vulgate text, the scholia argue that the word usually refers to the upper part of the *peplos* rather than a part of the female body; but they add that here it means 'arms' (ΣA *ad* 6.400a; cf. ΣA *ad* 14.219a; ΣbT *ad* 22.80c), see also 136n. (κόλπωι), 372n. (καὶ ἀμφιπόλωι εὐπέπλωι) and 467n.   ἀταλάφρονα, νήπιον αὔτως: Lattimore translates 'a little child, only a baby', which captures the tone of the phrase.   ἀταλάφρονα: cf. 18.567, ἀταλὰ φρονέοντες. The epithet emphasises Astyanax's babyish mind; cf. ἀταλός, 'young, playful', ἀτάλλω, 'be playful'; ἀτιτάλλω, 'raise (young children)'. The exact meaning of the word was debated also in antiquity: ΣD *ad* 6.400 associate it with ἀπαλός, 'tender' (cf. the variant ἀπαλὰ φρονέοντα at Hes. *Theog.* 989); ΣAbT *ad* 6.400*ab* derive it from τλῆναι, 'to endure' (ἀ-ταλάφρονα = 'not enduring', 'soft'); the latter derivation may already inform the punning πολύτλητοί τε γέροντες | παρθενικαί τ' ἀταλαί at *Od.* 11.38–9. For difficult words in Homer, see Introduction 2.4. νήπιον αὔτως ~ 22.484, 24.726. For νήπιον, see 95n. For αὔτως in combination with νηπ-, cf. *LfgrE* s.v. αὔτως B, and ΣΑ *ad* 6.400*c* οὔτως ὡς οἱ παῖδες, 'just like children'.

401 Ἑκτορίδην: only here. The patronymic expresses the bond between Hector and his child, especially in combination with ἀγαπητόν ('dear', 'beloved'); but it also reminds the audience that Astyanax has, in fact, no future: he will not continue his father's line, and there will be no further occasion to call him a Hectorid; cf. Introduction 2.2. ἀλίγκιον ἀστέρι καλῶι: another endearing description, cf. Carol Ann Duffy's rendition: 'in Hector's eyes... a swaddled star' (Duffy and Graziosi 2005: 7). The phrase, however, also has more ominous connotations, see Moulton 1977: 24–6, who compares 295 and comments on the sense of foreboding evoked by star similes. ἀλίγκιον 'like in appearance (or effect)'; the word occurs only here and at *Od.* 8.174, but cf. the common ἐναλίγκιος, with the same meaning (e.g. 5.5, of a star). The emphasis is on how the baby looks (to Hector), cf. 400–3n.

402 τόν: cf. 9n. ῥ': the evidential particle marks the process of recognition (9n.): the audience now hears the name of the baby – first the one Hector uses, then the name given to the child by the whole community. καλέεσκε: the iterative form evokes family usage; cf. 9.561–4; Hes. *Theog.* 207–10; and *Naupactia*, fr. 1 West. Σκαμάνδριον: a minor Trojan character is also called Skamandrios (5.49), and several other Trojans are named after rivers: Αἴσηπος (21n.), Σιμοείσιος (4.474) and Σάτνιος (14.443). Hector's chosen name for his son expresses a connection with the Trojan landscape and may also express the wish that the river might protect the boy (as it in fact protects the Trojans against Achilles: 21.130–8, 211–382); at 23.144–9 we are told that Peleus prayed to the Spercheios, the main river in his own homeland, for the safe return of his son Achilles. The consonants σ and κ in Σκαμάνδριον do not lengthen the preceding syllable; cf. Chantraine 1948–53: vol. i, 110. αὐτάρ: cf. 83n.

403 The views and hopes of the community find expression in another name for Hector's child. Andromache remembers those hopes, and the people's name for her child, in her lament for Hector at 22.506–7; and Hector alludes to them at 478n. Ἀστυάνακτ' 'lord of the city' (cf. 95n. (ἄστυ), 33n. (ἄναξ), 478n. (Ἰλίου ἶφι ἀνάσσειν)); this name features also elsewhere in the *Iliad* (22.500 and 506) and in other early hexameter poetry (*Iliou Persis* in Proclus, *Chrestomathy*, p. 146 West). There is no easy hierarchy between the two names given to the child: they suggest a tension between family concerns and public expectations; for discussion see Kirk 1990: 212–13. οἶος... Ἕκτωρ: cf. 24.499. Hector's name was understood to mean protector or 'holder' (ἔχειν) of Troy (398n.) The son's name reflects the role of the father; see Higbie 1995: 11. The fate of Hector, and hence of his son, comes to represent that of the city: when Hector dies, it is as though Troy had already fallen: 22.410–11. ἐρύετο: imperf. middle of ἐρύομαι/ῥύομαι/ῥῦμαι/ἔρυμαι, 'save'. Chantraine

1948–53: vol. 1, 294 derives it from ἐρύομαι without augment, but the precise nature of the form may well have been unclear to the poet himself; cf. Hainsworth 1993: 96–7. Ἴλιον: cf. 6on.

404 A rare moment of tenderness: this is Hector's only smile in the entire poem. His loving silence is equally rare, in a poem full of noise and speeches. Astyanax is too young to talk, so Hector's silent response seems especially appropriate. The line marks an important moment of transition in Hector's encounter with Andromache. In her appeal to Hector, Andromache takes her cue from his reaction, asking him to take pity on the baby, and on herself: 405–39n., 407n. Astyanax thus eases the difficult encounter between his parents: Introduction 4.4. ἤτοι: cf. 201n. ὃ μέν sets up Ἀνδρομάχη δέ in the next line; on ὅ see 9n. (τόν). μείδησεν: Homeric smiles express a range of emotions, from sarcasm to affection: Levine 1982–3. Hector's is among the most affectionate in the poem. ἰδὼν ἐς παῖδα: Hector turns his attention on his child: the description of Astyanax at 400–3n. was already largely focalised through him. For verbs of seeing as markers of 'embedded focalisation', cf. de Jong 2004: 102–7. σιωπῆι: a rare, loving silence. When characters fall silent in the *Iliad*, it is often out of embarrassment, fear or sadness, cf. 342n. and see also 7.427–8.

405–39 The speech is initially organised in concentric circles but takes a surprising turn towards the end. Andromache starts on a note of reproach (407n.), claiming that Hector takes no pity on his child (he has been smiling at the baby: 404n.). She then turns to her own plight (407–13n.). In the next section (414–28n.) she explains how her father, brothers and mother have died. She then returns to her fear and dependence: Hector is everything to her – father, mother, brother and tender husband (429–30n.): this statement is the emotional core of her speech. In the final section she asks Hector to take pity on the child and herself, in ring composition, and to stay ἐπὶ πύργωι (431n.); she then adds a concrete suggestion, which follows from her initial word of criticism: 433–9. In some respects, her speech resembles a formal rebuke, particularly in the opening words and the final suggestion (Minchin 2007: 160–3); but, as a rebuke, it is unparalleled: elsewhere warriors are upbraided for not fighting, whereas Andromache is alarmed by Hector's courage. The central part of her speech closely resembles a funeral lament, though again it is unique, because she performs it in front of her living husband (cf. 500n.). Just like Briseis and Helen in their own laments for the dead, Andromache offers a tragic account of her past (cf. 19.291–4; 24.763–6), emphasises her utter dependence on the addressee (cf. 19.295–9, 24.768–72) and dreads the future without him (cf. 19.300, 24.773–5); her speech also prefigures her own future laments for the dead Hector at 22.475–515 and 24.723–46; see further Kirk 1990: 214; J. M. Foley 1999: 188–98; Tsagalis 2004: 118–29; Gagliardi 2006; and, especially for the parallels with Briseis' lament, Lohmann 1988: 19–20 and 39–40, and Dué 2002: 68–72. The rhythm of Andromache's words is strained: Introduction 2.1 and Bakker 2005: 52–5. For a discussion of the speech as an example of *schetliasmos* (an emotional plea not to go on a dangerous mission), see Stoevesandt 2008: 133.

405 ∼ 5.570; cf. 16.2 etc.   Ἀνδρομάχη δέ picks up ὃ μέν at 404n. and shifts the focus back to Andromache.   ἄγχι παρίστατο: cf., e.g., formulaic ἄγχι παρέστη/παραστάς, often in lines that introduce a speech (e.g. 23.304–5, *Od.* 9.345, etc.).   δάκρυ χέουσα: formulaic at the end of the line (cf. 22.79 etc.). Andromache's tears foreshadow her imminent bereavement: δάκρυ χέουσα are the last two words in the lament she performs at Hector's funeral: 24.745. For Andromache's tears, see also 373n., 455n., 459n., 484n., 496n., 499n., 500n.

406 = 253n. Andromache's emotional appeal and affectionate gesture mirror Hecuba's earlier address to Hector; cf. 394n.

407–13 Andromache, who has just seen Hector run towards the battlefield, now warns him that his impulse to fight (μένος: 26–7n.) will kill him. She accuses him of feeling no pity for his child – or for his wife, who will soon be a widow. Andromache's language is anguished (τάχα . . . τάχα: 408–9), and the repeated enjambments, especially when paired with bucolic diaeresis (cf. 407/8, 408/9, 411/12), create a forward rhythm that breaks up the natural cadences of the hexameter: Introduction 2.1. She envisages Hector's death, as all the Achaeans rush forward and attack him together (410n.): her vision is grimly prophetic since, although Achilles alone kills Hector, all the Achaeans surround his corpse and stab it at 22.369–75. Andromache then contemplates her future. If Hector is killed, she wants to die too; her wish fits a funerary lament: 410–11n. Three γάρ-clauses of increasing length and complexity gradually bring order to her turmoil; cf. 409n. (γάρ), 411 and 414–28n. Andromache's intensive use of personal pronouns, which characterises this opening section, presents her fate as interwoven with Hector's: σε, σόν (407); ἔμ' (408); σεῦ, σε (409); ἐμοί (410); σεῦ (411); σύ (412); μοι (413); cf. Andromache's funerary lament at 22.477: 'We were born to the same fate . . .'

407 δαιμόνιε: Hector uses the same word to address his brother (326n., 521n.) and calls Andromache δαιμονίη at 486n.   φθίσει . . . μένος: Andromache fears that Hector is brave to the point of recklessness, cf. 22.455–9. For the dangers of excessive bravery, and the criticism it attracts in the Homeric poems, see Graziosi and Haubold 2003 and Clarke 2004.   σε . . . σόν: cf. 407–13n.   οὐδ' ἐλεαίρεις ∼ 21.147 (of Achilles), *Od.* 23.313 (of the Cyclops). Hector does take pity on Andromache (ἐλέησε: 484n.) but does not remain with her ἐπὶ πύργωι as she asks at 431n. For Andromache's appeals for pity, see further Burkert 1955: 86–8; Crotty 1994: 46–51; and Konstan 2001: 61–2.

408 Andromache mentions first the child and then herself, in necessary enjambment; see further 407–13n.   νηπίαχον: meaning and etymology are unclear, though certainly connected to νήπιος (Risch 1974: 176, 208 and 216); some ancient readers heard in the adjective νήπιος + ἰάχω/ἰαχέω, 'cry' (Eustathius II, p. 347: 8–12 van der Valk); cf. ἰάχων at 468n. It is only used of young children, and in contexts that emphasise their lack of valour (cf. 2.337–8 and 16.262). Eustathius *ad loc.* (II, p. 347: 12–14 van der Valk) claims that the word is more emotive than simple νήπιος (400n.). At 22.502 Andromache uses the verb νηπιαχεύω to describe Astyanax's former life, in contrast with the harsh realities he will have to face after Hector's death.

καὶ ἔμ' ἄμμορον = 24.773 (Helen laments her fate after Hector has died). ἄμμορος derives from ἀ- + μόρος, lit. 'without a share' and hence 'abandoned' (cf. 18.489 = *Od.* 5.275 and *Hom. Hymn* 2.481; see also ἀμμορίη at *Od.* 20.76). Several compounds in -μορος express wretchedness (e.g. αἰνόμορος, δύσμορος, κάμμορος); the emphasis of ἄμμορος is on loss. At 22.485 and 24.727 Andromache calls Hector and herself δυσάμμοροι, an even more extreme word for grief and loss; cf. Ferrari 1986: 65–6. The variant ἐμὸν μόρον (also at 24.773) yields less good sense and was criticised also in antiquity (cf. ΣA *ad* 6.408: οὐκ εὖ). **ἔμ':** cf. 407–13n. **τάχα:** 407–13n. Hector also feels that his death is imminent: 367–8n. **χήρη:** usually 'widow' in Homer, but here followed by a genitive in enjambment, hence 'bereft'. The word features five times in Andromache's speeches: 432, 22.484, 22.499 and 24.725; but it occurs only once in the rest of early hexameter epic: χῆραι at 2.289, though cf. χηρεύω ('lack': *Od.* 9.124), χηρόω ('bereave': *Il.* 5.642, 17.36), χηρωσταί (bereaved relatives: 5.158; Hes. *Theog.* 606–7). For Andromache as the archetypal Homeric widow, see Taplin 1992: 125–6, and Introduction 5.

409 The necessary enjambment underscores Andromache's loss, cf. 407–13n. **σεῦ:** this form, with Ionic contraction (cf. 280n.), is transmitted here and elsewhere at the beginning of the hexameter line. West prints σεῖ' ἔσομαι, which avoids hiatus; cf. the transmitted σεῖ' at 454n. (not at the beginning of the line). **τάχα:** 407–13n. **γάρ:** the first of three γάρ-clauses which explain Andromache's plight; cf. 407–13n. **κατακτανέουσιν Ἀχαιοί:** only here, though cf. 14.481 (κατακτανέεσθε καὶ ὔμμες), also in direct speech. For the unusual future which seems to have been formed on the basis of the aorist stem (cf. ἔκτανον), see Chantraine 1948–53: vol. I, 449–50.

410–11 Andromache's death wish is a characteristic of funeral laments (cf. Tsagalis 2004: 119) but also fits other speeches in book 6. Hector wished death on his brother Paris at 281–2n.; then Helen wished death on herself at 344–8n.; in his reply to Andromache, Hector will claim that he had rather die than witness her enslavement: 464–5n.

410 The line, in progressive enjambment, develops a specific scenario, where Hector is isolated, surrounded by all the Achaeans and killed. This prediction points to Andromache's even more accurate vision of his death at 22.454–9. In both cases, Andromache believes (with some justification: 492–3n.) that Hector's excessive bravery will impel him forward on his own, and therefore make him vulnerable to attack. Andromache's fears fit into a wider Homeric discourse about the dangers of excessive bravery, especially as perceived by women; see Graziosi and Haubold 2003. **πάντες ἐφορμηθέντες** 'attacking together', cf. 24.800; in early epic the aorist ending -θην is usually intransitive rather than passive (106n.). For a similar situation, cf. 11.401–84 where Odysseus is surrounded by the Trojans. **ἐμοὶ δέ κε κέρδιον εἴη** = *Od.* 2.74; cf. *Il.* 3.41, 5.201 = 22.103, 7.28, etc. The phrase 'identifies an action or event that will not or did not happen and forecasts something dire as a result' (J. M. Foley 1999: 195). For the comparative κέρδιον 'advantageous, preferable', cf. 153n. (κέρδιστος). **ἐμοί:** cf. 407–13n.

411 σεῦ ἀφαμαρτούσηι: an arresting expression; Andromache provides the only parallel at 22.505. Forms of (ἀφ-)αμαρτάνω (mostly in the aorist) mean 'miss a goal or target' rather than 'lose something' (*Od.* 9.512, in direct speech, is another exception). Andromache extends the use of this verb to personal bereavement: if Hector dies, her life no longer has a goal. For σεῦ see 409n. and 407–13n.   χθόνα δύμεναι 'sink beneath the earth'; no direct parallels but cf. 19n., 281–2n., 3.322, 7.131 (δῦναι δόμον Ἄϊδος εἴσω), 23.100–1 (ψυχὴ δὲ κατὰ χθονός . . . ὤιχετο). For the form δύμεναι cf. 185n.   γάρ: cf. 407–13n.

412 For the necessary enjambment see 407–13n.   θαλπωρή: etymologically related to θάλπω ('heat') but always used metaphorically of human warmth and comfort, cf. 10.223, *Od.* 1.166–7, with Zink 1962: 11–12; Arthur Katz 1981: 32. Translate: 'and there will be no other comfort left'. For the accent see Probert 2006: 36–8.   ἐπεὶ ἄν 'once'. The only uncontracted example in Homer, otherwise ἐπήν; cf. 489n., Chantraine 1948–53: vol. II, 258–9.   σύ γε: cf. 407–13; for γε, see 16–17n.   πότμον ἐπίσπηις: a common formula in this position; for πότμος, 'fate of death', cf. Clarke 1999: 241, 251–3. ἐπίσπηις is aor. subj. of ἐφέπω, cf. 321–2n. (ἔποντα). The meaning of the phrase πότμον ἐπισπεῖν (in the aorist or future) is not fully transparent but must be something like 'to meet with one's fate' (euphemistic); for another semantically difficult expression for 'dying' cf. 143n.

413 Andromache thinks about her own family as the only other possible source of comfort; cf. 429n. in ring composition. The blood relatives of a married woman continued to take an active interest in her life, particularly in times of crisis; cf. 167–70n. and 425–8n.   ἀλλ' ἄχε': another harsh runover (cf. 407–13n.), this time of the progressive type. The expression comes close to an anguished scream. ἄχε' is a rare occurrence of ἄχος in the plural; for which see 336n. The dual elision and the slightly elliptical syntax make the phrase memorable, see Introduction 4.4.   οὐδέ μοι ἐστὶ πατὴρ καὶ πότνια μήτηρ: a statement of devastating simplicity, expressed in traditional language: πατὴρ καὶ πότνια μήτηρ is formulaic at the end of the line, cf., e.g., 9.561. Andromache now relies on Hector alone: 429–30n.

414–28 A third γάρ-clause explains Andromache's despair; cf. 407–13n. This account of her family's tragic end is in stark contrast with the standard biographical details (birth, marriage) provided by the poet at 395–8n., though Andromache's tone is more restrained in this section than in her opening address; see Introduction 4.4. This section of her speech falls into three parts: she recalls how Achilles sacked her city and killed her father Eetion (414–20); how her seven brothers died at the hands of Achilles (421–4); and how Achilles captured her mother and released her for a ransom, only for her to die at home (425–8). This is an elaboration of 413: between the father's death and the mother's, Andromache recalls the death of all their sons; the motif of the orphan girl, bereaved of her seven brothers, recalls folk-tale patterns: 421n. On Achilles in Andromache's account, see Minchin 2007: 262–3: his behaviour is destructive but will become even harsher later in the poem. Hector's fate is worse than Eetion's; likewise Andromache's fate is even more horrific than that of her mother: 425–8n. Achilles' destruction of Thebes is mentioned repeatedly in the *Iliad*

(1.366–7, 9.188, 16.153, 23.826–9) and also featured in the *Cypria* (Kullmann 1960: 287–91; Jones 1995): it serves as a model for what will happen to Troy (Easterling 1995). Andromache's account gives the impression that she is drawing on a well-developed saga about Thebes, partly because she adopts the tone of a bard, cf. 414n. (δῖος Ἀχιλλεύς), 418–19n. (ἄρα) and 423n. (ποδάρκης δῖος Ἀχιλλεύς). However, we need not suppose that the poet was alluding to an actual tradition or poem (*pace* Zarker 1965: 110; and Kirk 1990: 214–15).

414 ἤτοι is taken up by δέ at 421 (Andromache's brothers), and 425 (her mother); cf. 201n.   γάρ introduces, as often, a substantial digression; cf. 130–1n.   ἀμόν 'my', a reminder that Andromache speaks about her own bereavement, cf. 421n. The adjective is probably an archaic form of the 1st pers. plur. (cf. ἡμέτερος), which was then understood also as a 1st pers. sing.; cf. Chantraine 1948–53: vol. 1, 272. It is used as a plural at 13.96 (~ ἡμέτερος) and looks like a singular (~ ἐμός) at *Od.* 11.166–7 = 481–2; in other passages it remains ambiguous. The adjective was extensively discussed in antiquity, see ΣAbT *ad* 6.414*bc*. Both ἁμός and ἀμός are attested; the majority of manuscripts has ἀμόν, suggesting the ancient derivation from ἐμόν (which is also attested as a variant reading).   δῖος Ἀχιλλεύς: frequent line-ending formula; for δῖος cf. 31n. The phrase is uncommon in character speech, though both Hector and Andromache use it elsewhere (18.305, 22.102 and 455). Here it suggests a change in register after the raw despair of lines 407–13; cf. 414–28n. Achilles remains the grammatical subject until line 419.

415 cf. 1.366–7, where Achilles describes the campaign from his perspective.   ἐκ... πέρσεν: cf. 42–3n. (πὰρ... ἔστη).   Κιλίκων: cf. 397n. εὖ ναιετάωσαν 'well-settled'; cf. 370n. The form embarrassed ancient commentators; by the normal rules of Homeric grammar, one would expect either ναιετόωσαν with diectasis (cf. 148n.), or uncontracted ναιετάουσαν. Aristarchus favoured ναιετόωσαν, ΣΑ *ad* 6.415*b*, but ναιετάωσ- is the transmitted form in many passages in extant epic and should stand.

416 Θήβην ὑψίπυλον: elsewhere the epithet is used only of Troy (16.698, 21.544; and cf. Bacchyl. 9.46); for the analogies between these two cities, see Easterling 1995: 165 and 414–28n. For Thebes underneath Mount Plakos, 397n.; for Boeotian and Egyptian Thebes, cf. 222–3n. (Θήβησιν).   κατὰ δ᾽ ἔκτανεν: cf. ἀπέκτανε at 414n., before bucolic diairesis, as here. For κατά as a free-standing word, see 42–3n.   Ἠετίωνα: the personal name recalls 395n. Andromache's mother remains unnamed: 425n.

417–20 Although Eetion's city has fallen, a landmark still commemorates his life. Andromache now tells Hector about Achilles' respectful handling of Eetion's body (417n.); later, at the point of death, Hector will beg Achilles for the privilege of a burial, but with no success: 22.337–54.

417 οὐδέ μιν ἐξενάριξε 'and he did not take his spoils', cf. 20n. Being robbed of one's arms is a relatively mild form of dishonour (cf. 7.77–80), though it may lead to more shameful acts: Segal 1971a: 18–21. At the end of the poem Achilles will not only take Hector's spoils but deny him burial and defile his corpse: 22.367–404 and 24.12–18. For other signs that the war has become more brutal, cf. 46–50n. and 55–6on. Achilles reflects on his own increased brutality at 21.100–5.   σεβάσ-σατο . . . θυμῶι: a sudden and unexpected display of mercy, cf. 167n.

418–19 It is Achilles who buries Eetion; contrast his later, reluctant release of Hector's body, so that his people can organise a funeral: 24.559–70. Burial is crucially important to Homeric warriors (for the fear of being eaten by birds and dogs, cf., e.g., 1.4–5, 22.335–54, *Od.* 3.258–60; and see Segal 1971a, esp. ch. 3). To be buried with one's weapons is rare (cf. *Od.* 11.74) and only happens when there is nobody left to inherit them: Bouvier 2002b. Easterling 1995: 164 compares Andromache's burning of Hector's clothes after his death.   ἄρα marks what actually happened; cf. 75n. (ἄρ). Andromache's tone now resembles that of the poet; cf. 414–28n., 426n.   κατέκηε < κατακαίω, 'burn completely', often of sacrifice or funeral pyres.   σὺν ἔντεσι δαιδαλέοισιν = 13.331 and 719. ἔντεα refers to the armour and weapons (Trümpy 1950: 79–81); for δαιδάλεος ('well-wrought') and related terms, see S. P. Morris 1992: 3–35. Eetion's beautifully crafted possessions also feature at 9.186–8 (καλῆι δαιδαλέηι).   ἠδ' ἐπὶ σῆμ' ἔχεεν ~ 24.799. After cremation, the pyre is covered with earth and turned into a burial mound; cf. 23.250–7, with Sourvinou-Inwood 1995: 122–5. For the commemorative function of a σῆμα ('sign' at 168n., but more specifically 'burial mound'), cf. 7.84–91; see also 2.811–14 (the hill of Batieia known to the gods as the funeral mound of Myrine); and 10.415, 11.166, 371–2 (the funeral mound of Ilos). The tomb as σῆμα is discussed in Vermeule 1979: 45; Ford 1992: 138–46; Sourvinou-Inwood 1995: 131–6; and Grethlein 2008: 31–2.

419–20 περὶ δὲ πτελέας ἐφύτευσαν | νύμφαι ὀρεστιάδες 'and around it the mountain nymphs planted elm trees'; the trees make Eetion's burial site more distinctive and recognisable; cf. 13.437 where the poet compares a wounded warrior to a 'stele or a towering tree', thus suggesting a parallel between man-made and natural landmarks and memorials. The gods orchestrate other prominent burials too, see esp. 16.666–83 (Sarpedon), but Eetion's burial remains anomalous; cf. Andronikos 1968: 33. It signals the end of a family and a city, not just a person.   πτελέας: Virgil, *Aen.* 6.282–4 associates elm trees with dreams and the underworld; Plin. *HN* 16.72 claims they are infertile (for the infertility of underworld trees, cf. *Od.* 10.510).   νύμφαι ὀρεστιάδες ~ *Hom. Hymn* 19.19. For hills and mountains as the habitat of nymphs see Larson 2001: 8–9; cf. 22n.   κοῦραι Διὸς αἰγιόχοιο: formulaic at the end of the line; the expression is used either of nymphs or of the Muses. The aegis is Zeus's most significant, but also most mysterious weapon, probably best understood as a goatskin used as protection, or a goatskin shield embellished with gold; cf., e.g., 4.166–7, 15.308–10, 24.20–1. The precise meaning of αἰγιόχοιο is unclear and was already obscure to the epic poets, who subjected the word to etymologising speculation; see *LfgrE* s.vv. αἰγίς B, αἰγίοχος Σχ and B, with discussion of Hes. *Sc.* 443–4 (αἰγιόχοιο ~ αἰγίδ' ἔχουσα); *Il.* 7.59–60 (where αἰγιόχοιο is associated with αἰγύπιοι, 'vultures', derived from αἴξ, 'goat', by popular etymology); and *Od.* 9.154–7, with αἰγιόχοιο ~ αἶγας ('goats') and αἰγανέας ('spears', again derived from αἴξ in antiquity).

421–4 Between the death of her father, and that of her mother, Andromache places the demise of her seven brothers. Achilles killed them all on a single day, while they were tending cattle and sheep. This activity is typical of young men (25n.): Andromache's brothers were killed before they reached their prime.   οἳ δὲ . . . | οἵ . . . : the register and grammatical structure is typical of catalogues, cf. 2.511–12 etc., 2.828–30 etc. Andromache lists her misfortunes.

421 Translate: 'but as for the seven brothers I had in the house'.   οἳ δέ: relative pronoun ('those who'); δέ follows after ἤτοι at 414 and introduces the whole sentence at 421–2, not merely the relative clause at 421.   μοι: a reminder that the story is told from the perspective of Andromache.   ἑπτά: numbers are often significant in Homer, cf. three (435n.), nine (174n.), twelve (93–4n., 248–50n.), twenty (217n.), fifty (244n.), one hundred (115n.). Children are frequently six or multiples of six (248n., 24.603–4, *Od.* 10.6, 24.497; cf. *Il.* 5.270, 20.225), but in those cases the emphasis is on the parents' achievement; here the perspective is that of the only surviving sister. For the folk-tale motif of the little girl and her seven brothers, see Thompson 1955–8: z71.5.1. For Briseis and her three brothers, cf. 19.293–4.   ἐν μεγάροισιν: cf. 371n.

422 The cause of death is only revealed in the next line.   οἳ μέν takes up 421n. (οἳ δέ) and keeps the audience focused on Andromache's brothers until attention shifts to her mother at 425n. (μητέρα δ'); for this use of μέν see Bakker 1997a: 84–5.   ἰῶι . . . ἤματι refers emphatically to 'one and the same', esp. when that is unexpected; cf. *LfgrE* s.v. ἴα, ἰῶι (only these forms); for the dative of time, see Chantraine 1948–53: vol. II, 81.   κίον 'went', 3rd pers. pl. of (ἔ)κιε, only attested in the aorist stem.   Ἄϊδος εἴσω: 284n.

423 ~ 190n., 23.828.   γάρ explains how the seven brothers died: it turns out that Achilles is, again, responsible for the massacre.   κατέπεφνε: cf. 12n. (ἔπεφνε).   ποδάρκης δῖος Ἀχιλλεύς: only here in direct speech. For the similarities between Andromache's tone and the voice of the poet, cf. 418–19n. (ἄρα): her family's demise is best expressed in the language of heroic epic, cf. 414–28n. For the formulaic system 'swift-footed Achilles' and its significance in the *Iliad*, see further Graziosi and Haubold 2005: 49–53. For δῖος, cf. 31n., 414n.

424 βουσὶν ἐπ' εἰλιπόδεσσι: cf. Hes. fr. 193.17 MW (restored), in a similar context. The phrasing is traditional: cf., e.g., *Od.* 20.221; *Hom. Hymn* 4.272; Hes. *Theog.* 290. The preposition ἐπί ('at', 'among'; cf. 25n.) suggests that Andromache's brothers were taken by surprise. Wars and battles over cattle are common in epic: cf. 1.154, 11.671–6, 18.527ff., *Od.* 17.471–2; Hes. *Theog.* 289–91, *Op.* 163. Achilles also attacked Aeneas while he was tending cattle, though he managed to escape with the help of Zeus: 20.89–93. Griffin 1992: 197–9 discusses this and other examples of bucolic seclusion disrupted by war.   εἰλιπόδεσσι: only of oxen. Ancient readers connected it with ἑλίσσω (cf. ΣD *ad* 6.424) and took it to refer to the rolling gait of cattle (contrast μῆλα ταναύποδα, ἵπποι ἀερσίποδες).   καὶ ἀργεννῇς ὀΐεσσι ~ *Od.* 17.472; cf. *Il.* 3.198, 18.529, 588. *ἀργεννός = 'white, bright' (of sheep and woven wool).

425–8 Achilles captures Andromache's mother and later releases her for a ransom; she then returns to her own family of origin and dies in the ancestral home of her father; cf. Chryseis, who is captured in Thebes, presumably where she lived with her husband (1.366–9), and is then returned to her father, who lives in Chryse (1.98–100 etc.). The fate of Andromache's mother is terrible, but this passage suggests that Andromache's own future will be worse. If Troy falls, there will be nobody in a position to pay ransom for Andromache, nor will she be able to return to her own parents, because Achilles has already sacked her city, and all her family are dead. These lines lead on to Andromache's famous statement that Hector is everything to her: 429–30n. Married women could normally rely on the help of their family of origin, particularly in times of crisis: cf. 167–70n. and 413n.

425 μητέρα δ' takes up ἤτοι πατέρ' ἀμόν (414n.) and οἳ δὲ...κασίγνητοι (421n.).   βασίλευεν 'was queen' (imperfect). The verb is rarely used of women: Andromache remembers her own mother as the queen of Thebes under Mount Plakos, before moving on to her enslavement and death. Euripides' Hecuba, another fallen queen, remarks on the effectiveness of juxtaposing accounts of earlier happiness with later misfortunes at *Tr.* 472–3: πρῶτον μὲν οὖν μοι τἀγάθ' ἐξᾷσαι φίλον· | τοῖς γὰρ κακοῖσι πλείον' οἶκτον ἐμβαλῶ.   ὑπὸ Πλάκωι ὑληέσσηι: cf. 396n.

426 τήν: cf. 9n.   ἄρ: cf. 418–19n.   δεῦρ' 'here', i.e. to Troy.   ἄμ' ἄλλοισι κτεάτεσσιν ~ 23.829 (also of the spoils Achilles took from Eetion; on which see also 9.186–8). For captive women as material goods, cf. 290n.: Andromache adopts the language of her mother's captors when she talks about her in this way. Her shift in tone (contrast βασίλευεν: 425n.) accompanies her mother's drastic change of fortune.

427 ὅ γε: sc. Achilles; he dominated Andromache's account of her family's demise: 414–28n. Just as he buried Eetion with his armour (418–19n.), he was also prepared to free his widow for a ransom. Warriors never release prisoners for ransom in the main narrative of the *Iliad*, though this happened earlier in the war: 46–50n. For the increasing brutality displayed by warriors in general, and Achilles in particular, cf. 414–28n. and 417n. γε after the demonstrative pronoun sets up a contrast with line 428; cf. Chantraine 1948–53: vol. II, 159.   τήν: cf. 9n. For the ransom of women, see *LfgrE* s.v. ἄποινα B I b.   ἀπέλυσε: a technical term for releasing a person in exchange for ransom (simple λύομαι can also mean 'ransom'); cf. *LfgrE* s.v. λύω B I 1 d and II 2 b.   λαβὼν ἀπερείσι' ἄποινα ~ 1.13 = 372, cf. 24.502. For ἀπερείσι' ἄποινα, cf. 49n. (also at verse end). The line suggests a happy ending, but Andromache's mother dies in the next line.

428 Cf. *Od.* 15.478. Artemis is generally held responsible for the death of women (205n.). This passage suggests a specific parallel between the goddess and Achilles, who has just killed Andromache's male relatives. Achilles is repeatedly presented as a human counterpart to Apollo, Artemis' twin brother, in the *Iliad*; see G. Nagy 1999, Rabel 1990.   πατρὸς δ' ἐν μεγάροισι ~ Hes. fr. 43a.33 MW (restored); cf., e.g., 21.475.   Ἄρτεμις ἰοχέαιρα 'Artemis the arrow-shooter', a frequent formula at verse end. The epithet is unique to Artemis; its exact meaning was debated also in antiquity, cf. Hesychius s.v. ἰοχέαιρα: 'spreading/shooting arrows' (< χέω), or 'rejoicing in arrows' (< χαίρω). Both ancient etymologies take their cue from early poetry: cf. *Hom. Hymn* 27.2–6, where ἰοχέαιρα ~ πέμπουσα στονόεντα βέλη, and

Hom. Hymn 27.11–12, with τερφθῆι and εὐφρήνηι as internal glosses on ἰοχέαιρα ~ χαίρουσα τοῖς ἰοῖς. For χέω see also 21.492 ('the one whose arrows are spilled'). For the alternative modern derivation from χείρ, 'hand', see Hagen 2000.

429–30 take up 413, though the emphasis is now on trust, comfort and love. In Near Eastern sources, rulers or gods are often said to be 'like father and mother' to their people, cf. a Phoenician inscription from Sam'al in northern Syria (Donner and Röllig 2002: 5 (n. 24), ll. 10–11): 'but for some I was a father, for some a mother, for some a brother'. The bilingual Luwian/Phoenician Karatepe and Çineköy Inscriptions from south-eastern Turkey (eighth/early seventh century BCE) describe rulers as 'mother and father' to their subjects; cf. Lanfranchi 2007: 187, 195–6. For an Egyptian example see Parkinson 1997: 61 (of a high Egyptian official); for Mesopotamia see Foster 2005: 681, 683 (of the Babylonian god Marduk). Andromache adapts this motif in order to describe an intimate relationship of love, trust and affection; cf. Catullus 72.3–4: 'I loved you not as any man loves his girlfriend, but as a father loves his sons and his sons-in-law.' Andromache's appeal to Hector is powerful and direct: because she has lost all her family, she is now entirely dependent on him, cf. esp. 425–8n. See Introduction 4.4.

429 Ἕκτορ, ἀτὰρ σύ: cf. 86n. Andromache finally calls Hector by name; contrast 407n. (δαιμόνιε). On the simple and poignant form of her address here see Wendel 1929: 63.   σύ μοί ἐσσι: the first time the pronouns 'you' and 'I' are close together in the speech, cf. 407–13n.   πατὴρ καὶ πότνια μήτηρ: cf. 413n., 429–30n.

430 ἠδὲ κασίγνητος: the progressive enjambment with ἠδέ (cf. 90n.) picks up 421–4n., where Andromache describes the death of her brothers.   σὺ δέ μοι: cf. 429n. (σύ μοί ἐσσι).   θαλερὸς παρακοίτης: a warm description of Hector as Andromache's husband. The adjective θαλερός literally means 'blooming' (cf. θάλλω) and hence 'young', 'full of vitality'; Andromache's tears are later described as θαλερὸν . . . δάκρυ (496n.), but the word can have happier connotations too: it is used, for example, of wives and husbands in their prime (3.53, 8.156), and of the marriage between young partners (θαλερὸς γάμος at *Od.* 6.66 and 20.74); see Schein 1976: 3 and 2002: 197. παρακοίτης is a rare word for 'husband' which emphasises the emotional bond between the partners; cf. Gates 1971: 19. It is used in contexts where the perspective of the wife is important; cf. 8.156; and Hes. *Theog.* 928; contrast 8.190, where Hector describes himself as Andromache's θαλερὸς πόσις.

431 The line echoes 407 in ring composition but opens the possibility that Hector might do the right thing, as Andromache sees it.   ἀλλ' ἄγε νῦν ἐλέαιρε: appeals for pity do not usually start with the peremptory ἀλλ' ἄγε νῦν, but the phrasing fits Andromache's unique role as Hector's wife: it conveys her feelings of dependence and need for pity but also expresses her confident ease in addressing her husband. Paris and Helen have already tried to hold back Hector, using similar language: ἀλλ' ἄγε νῦν ἐπίμεινον (Paris to Hector: 340n.); ἀλλ' ἄγε νῦν εἴσελθε καὶ ἕζεο (Helen to Hector: 354n.). Unlike the others, Andromache manages to delay Hector, but only temporarily (515–16n.): he will soon leave, although he feels pity for her (484n.).   μίμν' ἐπὶ πύργωι: Andromache wants Hector to stay right where she has been: in the next lines she tries to convey the impression that it is an excellent vantage point from which to survey the battlefield and direct military operations. At 22.84–5 Hecuba, standing on the walls, tells Hector he should return inside the city and join her.

432 The line corresponds to 408–9 and suggests that Hector behaves exactly like the enemy; cf. 11.393–4, where Diomedes boasts that his spear turns women into widows, and children into orphans. Andromache's control over the war is limited to what she can persuade Hector to do or not to do; so it is not surprising that, from her perspective, Hector is responsible for the war and all its consequences, including her own bereavement: Introduction 3.2. Hector later suggests that Andromache might rejoice in the spoils of the enemy (481n.); but in her speech she does not distinguish between killing and being killed and thus presents the war as a disastrous male activity. Andromache not only makes an appeal for pity but also suggests the possibility of blame: the moral obligation to look after widows and orphans, particularly on the part of leaders, was keenly felt in ancient Greece and the Near East (Hes. *Op.* 330; Solon T 10 Ruschenbusch; for non-Greek sources, see e.g. Exodus 22:21–3; Deuteronomy 14:28–9. For further sources and discussion see Fensham 1962 and Patterson 1973). Andromache has explained that nobody will be in a position to look after her when Hector dies, so she now holds him responsible for her future (425–8n. and 429–30n.). Hector replies to this appeal when he paradoxically states that he had rather be dead than see her widowed and enslaved (464–5n.).   ὀρφανικόν: a rare word (cf. 11.394, 22.490), always of the traumatic moment of bereavement. It is derived from ὀρφανός, 'orphan', also rare (*Od.* 20.68; Hes. *Op.* 330).   θήῃς: 2nd pers. aor. subj. of τίθημι.   χήρην: cf. 408n.

433–9 For ancient and modern reactions to Andromache's unconventional suggestion, including the view that these lines are spurious, see Introduction 4.4. For Andromache's fear that the Achaeans may be acting on the advice of a seer, see 438–9n.

433 λαὸν δὲ στῆσον: the details of Andromache's scheme remain unclear, but there may be a suggestion that she wants Hector to use his people as a shield for himself and his family. Such behaviour would be entirely reprehensible: Homeric leaders are supposed to protect their λαός: 8on., 214n., 222–3n. and 327n. Later, at 22.99–110, Hector decides to stay outside the walls while the Trojan troops withdraw inside: he claims he has lost too many men (ὤλεσα λαόν) and would rather face death on the battlefield than blame inside the city. On Andromache's suggestion see further Haubold 2000: 88–9.   παρ' ἐρινεόν: unlike the oak that also grows near the walls of Troy (237n.), the fig tree is a symbol of impending defeat; cf. Thornton 1984: 152–3; Tsagalis 2004: 125–6.

434 Andromache uses the technical language of siege warfare (ἄμβατος, ἐπίδρο-μος) in an attempt to draw Hector into a military discussion, rather than see him leave; cf. ΣbT *ad* 6.434b. According to Pindar, *Ol.* 8.31–46, there was one vulnerable section of the Trojan walls, built by the mortal Aeacus, rather than by Apollo and Poseidon. It is possible that this line alludes to the same legend, or that the legend originated from this passage; Kirk 1990: 218; ΣbT *ad* 6.438; and Introduction 3.3. On the text of the *Iliad* becoming richer and more allusive in the course of time: Introduction 1. **ἄμβατος:** a rare adjective that appropriately describes a tall structure (< ἀναβαίνω; cf. *Od.* 11.316, of the Giants' attempted conquest of heaven) but is used also for other places that may offer specific openings (cf. Hes. *Op.* 681, of the sea). It seems that Aristarchus accentuated ἀμβατός, though the majority of the manuscripts read ἄμβατος. For the ancient variant ἀμβατή, cf. 266n. (ἀνίπτοισιν). **ἐπί-δρομον:** only here in epic and rare in general; cf. ἐπιδραμεῖν, 'to storm forward, follow up' after killing or wounding (4.524, 14.421), or when there is an opening (10.354, 18.527).

435 τρίς: when used in the context of battle narrative, the number three is followed by success or failure at the fourth attempt; cf. 5.436–9, 16.702–6, 18.155–67, 20.445–8. For significant numbers, cf. 421n.   **γάρ:** not a causal explanation of what goes before but an additional reason; cf. 15n.   **τῆι γ'** 'at that particular point'; for γε cf. 16–17n.   **οἱ ἄριστοι:** the article is used with comparatives and superlatives, to single out a specific group, cf. Chantraine 1948–53: vol. II, 162.

436–7 Andromache's catalogue conjures the enemy before Hector's eyes and lends weight to the suggestion that he should stay on the rampart and direct operations from there. Each line mentions a pair of warriors and a third name with epithet; the overall trajectory is from defence (Ajax) to attack (Diomedes); cf. 5–36n., 5n. Achilles does not feature because he is not fighting at all. Andromache's language resembles closely that of the epic narrator, though the events she describes remain unconfirmed in the main narrative. Some ancient readers thought that these lines contained 'a lie' and disputed their authenticity, for further discussion: Introduction 4.4.

436 Cf. 15.301.   **ἀμφ':** the preposition describes the group of soldiers led by the two Ajaxes and emphasises cohesion; cf. *LfgrE* s.v. ἀμφί B I 2.   **Αἴαντε δύω:** Telamonian Ajax (5n.) and Ajax son of Oïleus, from Locri. In the *Iliad* they are often mentioned together, although they are unrelated and come from different parts of Greece. Telamonian Ajax is the more prominent of the two (cf. 2.527–9, 768). Ajax son of Oïleus acquires a more individual profile towards the end of the *Iliad* (23.473–98 and 754–97) and, especially, during the sack of Troy and the journey home of the Achaeans, where he offends Athena and perishes as a result (*Iliou Persis* and *Nostoi* in Proclus, *Chrestomathy*, pp. 146 and 154 West; *Od.* 4.499–511). Together, the two Ajaxes are particularly effective in defence and counter-attack: 12.265–77, 13.46–84, 701–18, etc. The dual Αἴαντε appears originally to have referred to Telamonian Ajax and his half-brother Teucer (31n.); see Wackernagel 1953; Page 1959: 235–8; and Nappi 2002.   **ἀγακλυτὸν Ἰδομενῆα** = *Od.* 14.237; cf. *Od.* 21.295, 24.103 and the common formula Ἰδομενεὺς δουρικλυτός. The epithet ἀγακλυτός is used only here in the *Iliad* but is common in the *Odyssey*; cf. ἀγακλειτός at *Il.* 2.564 etc. Compared with the metrically equivalent ἀρήϊον Ἰδομενῆα (11.501), Andromache's phrase emphasises glory rather than danger; and it may therefore suggest to Hector that he could pursue glory *and* stay on the walls.

437 **ἠδ':** cf. 90n.   **Ἀτρείδας:** cf. 44n.   **Τυδέος ἄλκιμον υἱόν:** cf. 11.605 Μενοιτίου ἄλκιμος υἱός, etc.: a standard formulation; only here of Diomedes, but cf. the common Τυδέος υἱόν *et sim.* (96n.). When father and son are mentioned in formulae of this kind, only one of the two tends to have an epithet: in the case of Tydeus and Diomedes, it is normally Tydeus who receives further emphasis (4.370 etc.); but Andromache wants to emphasise the threat posed by Diomedes; cf. 96–8n., 98n., 100–1n.

438–9 Andromache adds a further thought about the situation, openly wondering whether the Achaeans have been instructed by a seer, or whether they are acting on their own instincts. Hector himself was instructed by the seer Helenos to go to Troy and organise a ritual offering for Athena (86–98n.), though we know that that offering failed (311n.). Andromache's final question seems designed to engage Hector in a discussion of what the Achaeans are planning outside the wall and thus persuade him to look out from the rampart; it also adds to the sense of foreboding that pervades book 6. In early epic several prophecies predict the fall of Troy: 2.299–330 (esp. 322, θεοπροπέων), *Od.* 8.73–82; *Cypria* and *Little Iliad* in Proclus, *Chrestomathy*, pp. 72 and 120 West. This passage makes the audience view such prophecies from Andromache's perspective.

438 ἤ που: Andromache speculates; cf. *LfgrE* s.v. πού, που B 2 b θ. ἔνισπε: aorist of ἐν(ν)έπω, 'tell, announce'; used of important matters, often concerning the gods. θεοπροπίων εὖ εἰδώς: θεοπρόπιον (more commonly in the form θεο-προπίη) usually describes a divine message known to and conveyed by a seer (μάντις); cf. 1.85. For the construction (εἰδέναι with genitive = 'to understand, have knowledge of'), see, e.g., 12.228–9, *Od.* 1.202; and *LfgrE* s.v. οἶδα B 2 b β. The alternative reading θεοπροπέων (< *θεοπροπέω) does not command support: it is weakly attested, and the verb θεοπροπέω is always construed with a form of ἀγορεύω in Homer; cf. 1.109, 2.322, *Od.* 2.184.

439 ~ 15.43. ἤ νυ καί: the use of καί suggests that this is a weak alternative to Andromache's first explanation. Contrast 2.367–8, where divine will is the secondary explanation (εἰ καί). αὐτῶν 'their own'. ΣΑΤ *ad loc.* report an ancient variant αὐτούς, which weakens the contrast between lines 438 and 439. θυμὸς ἐποτρύνει καὶ ἀνώγει: formulaic at the end of the line; the verbs often describe the actions of a god or a leader. For θυμός, cf. 51n. and 444n.; for ἐποτρύνει see 83n.; for ἀνώγει = 'commands' (present tense); see Stoevesandt 2008: 141.

440–65 A traditional, formal line introduces Hector's reply (440n.), which is itself – in the opening section – formal and conventional (441–6n.). Rather than lingering on the thought of future fame, as Helen had invited him to do (357–8n.), Hector then considers the fall of Troy, and its consequences for those he loves, and especially for Andromache – the person for whom he cares the most. The shift in focus from himself to Andromache is marked by Hector's use of pronouns: 441 (ἐμοί), 444 (με), 446 (ἐμὸν αὐτοῦ), 447 (ἐγώ), 450 (μοι), 454 (σεῖ'), 462 (σοί), 464 (με), 465 (σῆς, σοῦ). He envisages Andromache's future as a slave and as a living memorial to his glory (454–63n.), and then he breaks down, claiming that he had rather be dead than see Andromache dragged into slavery: 464–5n. On this speech, see Introduction 4.4 and, for its structure, Lohmann 1970: 96–101 and 1988: 34–45.

440 There is no formal conclusion to Andromache's speech (cf. 144n.). This conventional line introduces Hector's reply; cf. 263n., and 359n.   κορυθαίολος Ἕκτωρ: the expression already featured five times in book 6: 116n., 263, 342, 359 and 369. Hector's helmet is about to become the focus of attention: 472–3n.; see further Introduction 2.2.

441–6 Hector shares Andromache's concerns (441n.) but now lists his own reasons for returning to the battlefield: his sense of shame (441–3); the possibility of blame (note the opposition between κακός (443n.) and ἐσθλός (444n.)); his instinct and training (444–5); and his desire to win glory for his father and himself (446n.). These are all conventional motivations for fighting, but Hector presents them in a way that is characteristic of him: his sense of duty and responsibility towards his people and his father, as king of Troy, emerge clearly. He also suggests that he has learnt to be brave: his determination to fight is not just a matter of temperament but of social conditioning. On Hector's character, see Schadewaldt 1970, Erbse 1979, Redfield 1994, de Romilly 1997; and cf. esp. 442n. (αἰδέομαι).

441 ~ 5.490 (Sarpedon chides Hector).   ἦ: the particle, prominently placed at the beginning of the line, expresses Hector's lively reaction to Andromache's speech; cf. 215n. (ἦ ῥά νύ μοι).   καὶ ἐμοί: 440–65n.   τάδε πάντα is a vague acknowledgement of what Andromache has been saying: Hector does not discuss her suggestions in detail.   μέλει covers a wide range of meaning, from 'caring about' to 'taking care of'. In combination with forms of πᾶς, μέλω is used of people or gods who take charge of all aspects of an operation; cf., e.g., 5.430 (Ares and Athena); 5.490 (Hector); 23.724 (Zeus); *Od.* 6.65 (Nausicaa). Hector's dilemma in *Iliad* 6 is reflected in his shifting use of the verb: he 'cares about' Andromache above all others (450n. μέλει); yet he must also 'take care of' the war (492–3n.: μελήσει).   γύναι: Hector addresses Andromache as a woman and a wife (γυνή means both: Gates 1971: 17); and he does not discuss her idiosyncratic views about the deployment of troops (cf. 433–9n. and esp. ΣbT *ad* 6.433: 'not fitting for a woman, but fitting for Andromache'). Cf. 264n. (where Hector addresses Hecuba as his mother) and 293n. (on the use of her proper name).   ἀλλὰ μάλ' αἰνῶς = 10.38, 19.23, 22.454, where it is followed by δείδω, 'I fear', in the next line. Here Hector continues by saying 'I am ashamed', but the sentiment is close to fear of judgement; for fear and shame, cf., e.g., 24.435–6 and *Od.* 17.188–9.

442 = 22.105. The line is characteristic of Hector, who often views himself through the eyes of the community. Here he assumes that the men and women of Troy will judge him exactly in the same way (cf. 481n.), though many passages in book 6 suggest that male and female perspectives on war differ significantly: see Introduction 3.2 and 4.4.   αἰδέομαι: the feeling of shame, αἰδώς, is 'a responsiveness to social situations and to the judgment of others' (Redfield 1994: 115), and hence an awareness of social standards on the part of the individual: Cairns 1993: 139–46. It primarily inhibits behaviour that may attract blame ('αἰδώς prevents me from doing x'). For Hector as the 'hero of αἰδώς, see Redfield 1994: 119; cf. Cairns 1993: 79–83. αἰδώς is often mentioned in conjunction with ἔλεος (e.g. 24.44–5), though in this context Hector feels a sharp contrast between Andromache's need for pity (407n., 431n.), and his sense of shame before the people of Troy; on ἔλεος and αἰδώς see further Karp 1994; and Crotty 1994: ch. 3.   Τρῶας καὶ Τρωιάδας: Hector repeatedly refers to 'the men and women of Troy': 7.297, 22.105. They in turn look to him for help and support; cf. 22.433–4, 514, 24.215–16 and 704–6.   ἑλκεσιπέπλους: probably 'of the trailing robe' (thus ΣADT ad 6.442; van Wees 2005: 7–8) rather than 'drawing up the[ir] robe' as tentatively suggested in LfgrE s.v. ἑλκεσίπεπλ(ος), and Stoevesandt 2008: 143; for a similar epithet, cf. εἰνατέρων ἐϋπέπλων at 378n.

443 Hector does not oppose his own views to those of Andromache but rather appeals to the opinions of others.   κακὸς ὥς: the opposite of ἀγαθός or ἐσθλός (444n.); cf. 2.190, 8.94, with Adkins 1960: 31–40; LfgrE s.v. κακός B 1. For Hector's concern that he may be considered κακός see 17.180, 24.214–16 (Hecuba recalls the valour of her dead son); cf. also 22.106, where Hector imagines a lesser person (κακώτερος) criticising him. Later in his encounter with Andromache, Hector will let go of this distinction and point out that both the good man (ἐσθλός) and the bad one (κακός) are subject to fate: 489n. The second syllable of κακός is measured long: the original consonant before ὥς (*yōs, only when postponed) is still felt; see M. L. West 1997b: 229; contrast 295n.   νόσφιν . . . πολέμοιο: to Andromache, the fighting seemed very near, as she stood on the rampart (436–7n.); now Hector describes the same location as 'far from the war'.   ἀλυσκάζω: a rare intensive form of ἀλύσκω, 'avoid'. In the *Iliad* this verb suggests cowardice; contrast simple ἀλύσκω/ἀλεείνω (167n., 202n.).

444 οὐδέ με θυμὸς ἄνωγεν: the θυμός usually impels warriors forward, and into action (51n., 439n.); Hecuba speculated that Hector's θυμός made him return to Troy (256n.); Hector, by contrast, told Helen that his θυμός urged him to join his men on the battlefield (361–2). Now he makes the negative claim that his θυμός fails to recommend caution; this contorted statement is unparalleled in the *Iliad*: it suggests that Hector is at pains to seem reasonable rather than impulsive and may be influenced by αἰδώς, which also inhibits action (442n.). For με, see 440–65n.   ἐπεὶ μάθον ἔμμεναι ἐσθλός: Hector shifts the emphasis from his instincts to what he has learned. ΣAbT ad 6.444b comment that 'the virtues can be learned' but prefer to gloss μάθον ('I have learned') with εἴωθα ('I am accustomed to'): ancient readers saw the line as making a controversial point about nature and nurture. The verb μαθεῖν (only in the aorist) is rare in epic and is close in meaning to English 'internalise' (i.e. learn and make one's own). For ἐσθλός see 443n.

445 αἰεί: the Homeric scholar Nicanor (second century CE) rightly took this word with line 444 (ΣbT ad 6.445b; cf. ΣA ad 6.445a) rather than μάχεσθαι, thus preserving one of the most significant cases of enjambment in Homer. 'Always' being best is a core precept in Homeric battlefield pedagogy (208n.), but it is unlikely to reassure Andromache; cf. 407n., 460n.   καὶ πρώτοισι . . . μάχεσθαι: another cliché, typically invoked in direct speech, as characters remind one another of their obligations in battle: e.g. 4.340–55, 12.310–21. Hector is eminently susceptible to that kind of pressure.

446 Winning glory, κλέος, is another standard motivation for fighting, cf. Redfield 1994: 30–5. What is typical of Hector is that he thinks about his father's κλέος as well as his own; for examples of κλέος as a family concern, see Scodel 2008a: 23–4. Throughout this opening section Hector emphasises his duty to do what others expect of him: 441–6n. For κλέος (cf. κλύω, 'listen') and epic poetry, see Introduction 1. ἀρνύμενος 'trying to secure', typically on behalf of somebody else. The genitives πατρός... ἠδ' ἐμὸν αὐτοῦ suggest the added nuance of 'preserving' something that already belongs to Priam and Hector (cf. *Od.* 1.5); contrast the datives of advantage at 1.159 and 5.552–3. μέγα κλέος: in the *Iliad* this phrase (as opposed to the more common κλέος ἐσθλόν) describes major, glorious events: 11.21–2, 17.129–31; in the *Odyssey* μέγα κλέος is much more frequent; cf. also Hes. fr. 199.9 MW.

447–9 A simple, truthful and devastating statement; Agamemnon predicts the fall of Troy in the same words at 4.163–5; for the different effect of the two statements, see Kirk 1990: 220; and Di Benedetto 1998: 184–7. Hector answers Andromache's suggestions and fears about a possible prophecy (438–9n.), by confronting her with his certainty that Troy will fall; see Tsagalis 2004: 126–7. For his line of thought, cf. 447n. (γάρ). In the next section he sets out the implications of the fall of Troy for his family (450–3n.), for Andromache (454–63n.) and finally for himself (464–5n.). He opened his speech by stating that he would behave like a warrior (441–6n.); and he ends it by claiming that he wants to die before Andromache is enslaved (464–5n.)

447 = 4.163, *Od.* 15.211; cf., e.g., *Il.* 20.264.   εὖ... οἶδα picks up ἐΰ εἰδώς at 438n.; Hector does not need to speculate about what the Achaeans have been told about Troy; the basic truth is that the city is doomed.   γάρ 'for'. Hector's train of thought seems to be: 'I must fight because Troy is bound to fall' (Taplin 1992: 123–4; see also Görgemanns 2001: 116); cf. Sarpedon, who claims he must fight in the first line of battle because he knows he is going to die: 12.322–8, esp. 326 γάρ. The variant reading μέν is not well attested, though some editors prefer it because they find γάρ difficult to explain (cf. M. L. West 2001a: 199).   ἐγώ: Hector's statement, as well as being the plain truth, concerns him first and foremost.   κατὰ φρένα καὶ κατὰ θυμόν: cf., e.g., 5.671, 8.169, and many passages in the *Odyssey*. For φρένα, see 61n. For Hector's θυμός, cf. 444n.

448–9 For this description of Troy in terms of the 'sacred city, the king and his people', cf. 4.46–7, 164–5; and [Plato] *Alc.* II 149d.   ὀλώληι: intransitive perf. subjunctive (Chantraine 1948–53: vol. 1, 424–6) of transitive ὄλλυμι, 'destroy'.   Ἴλιος ἱρή: 96n.   λαὸς... Πριάμοιο: the people of Troy, not just the 'army'; cf. *LfgrE* s.v. λαός B 1 a α.   ἐϋμμελίω 'of the good spear' (εὖ + μελίη), the nominative is unattested, for the genitive in -ω (< -αο) see Chantraine 1948–53: vol. 1, 64–5. ἐϋ- is disyllabic in this word, and is scanned ∪ –. The Homeric manuscripts and papyri seem to prefer the spelling with double μμ, without, however, achieving full consistency, see West's apparatus ad 4.47, 165; cf. 45n. (ἐλίσσετο).

450–3 Hector considers the consequences of the fall of Troy for those he loves. He starts with the people of Troy (450n.); then he mentions his parents (451n.) and his brothers (452–3n.), and finally the person dearest to him: Andromache (454–63n.). His affection for her finds expression through a priamel, 'a series of detached statements which through contrast or comparison lead up to the idea with which the speaker is primarily concerned' (Fraenkel 1950: 407–8, n. 3). Hector slowly comes to declare his feelings for Andromache: 'the priamel provides a measure of intensity that the mere statement of fact would otherwise lack' (Race 1982: 42). It also suggests that Hector can focus on Andromache only after he has imagined himself fulfilling the expectations of the community (441–6n.), and after that community has ceased to exist. His statement here corresponds to Andromache's description of the fall of Thebes and the death of her family (414–28n. and esp. 429–30n.) though Andromache speaks about her own grief (413n.: ἀλλ' ἄχε'), while Hector talks about his care for the pain (450n.: ἄλγος) of those he loves. On the correspondence between the two speeches, see further Schadewaldt 1997: 135–6; Lohmann 1988: 40–1; and Introduction 4.4.

450 Hector eventually reveals that he cares for Andromache more than for the Trojans; contrast 361n. and 362n., where he declines Helen's invitation to stay because the Trojans long for him to return to the battlefield.   ἀλλ' introduces the first statement in the priamel, cf. 464n. (ἀλλά): after outlining what is expected of him (441–6n.), Hector turns to his own feelings.   οὐ . . . τόσσον: the rhetorical build-up (οὐ . . . οὔτ' . . . οὔτε . . . οὔτε) reaches its climax with the runover ὅσσον σεῖ' at 454n.   μοι: cf. 440–65n.   Τρώων: subjective genitive, 'of the Trojans'; it is unusual for someone to care about somebody else's ἄλγος in early epic; but it is characteristic of Hector.   μέλει: here primarily in the sense of 'caring about'; cf. 441n. (μέλει).   ἄλγος: acute hardship, pain or grief, largely seen as an objective given, in contrast with Andromache's preferred term ἄχος (413n.; cf. 486n.), which refers to a person's subjective response to difficulties; see Mawet 1979: 387–8; Rijksbaron 1992; Cingano 2002–3: 60–2. The noun ἄλγος is thematic in the *Iliad* (1.2 etc., with Holmes 2007) and in heroic epic more generally (cf. formulaic ἄλγεα πάσχειν/-ων). In the context of social relationships, it is often used of the suffering caused to dependants by the loss of someone who cares for them: e.g. leader and people (22.54–5), son and parents (22.52–3), husband and wife (462–3, 24.742, *Od.* 21.87–8). Hector is thinking about his own death, and the pain it will cause to the Trojans; cf. 462n., 463n.

451 Hector now thinks about his very own mother, and Priam the king. The cause of their pain (ἄλγος: 450n.) is not openly stated, but the end of the poem dramatises their terrible suffering when Hector faces Achilles (22.25–91) and dies (esp. 22.405–36).   αὐτῆς: Hector cares deeply for his mother, but Andromache is even more important to him: 454n. His train of thought here corresponds to his actual progress through the city: first he meets his mother (242–85), and finally his wife (369–502).   Πριάμοιο ἄνακτος: formulaic in this position, elsewhere always in combination with ἄστυ or πόλις: here too the city has just been mentioned (448–9n.).

452–3 Priam laments the death of his sons at 24.255–60 and 493–8. Mestor and Troilos died before the narrative of the *Iliad* begins; ten more of Hector's brothers are killed in the course of the poem (Wöhrle 1999: 75, n. 5); then Hector himself dies – and his death comes to symbolise the fall of Troy: 22.410–11.

For Priam's fifty sons, see 244n. οὔτε: cf. 450n. πολέες τε καὶ ἐσθλοί: cf. 24.166–8 (Priam's daughters and daughters-in-law grieve for their slain men, who are πολέες τε καὶ ἐσθλοί); and 24.204–5 ~ 520–1 (the sons of Priam slain by Achilles are πολέες τε καὶ ἐσθλοί). Only once in the *Iliad* is the phrase πολέες τε καὶ ἐσθλοί used of living men, and there it describes a group of Achaean warriors: 4.298. ἐν κονίῃσι πέσοιεν = 23.437, cf., e.g., 15.423. ὑπ᾽: Hector's brothers will be killed 'by', 'at the hands of' the enemy. For this use of ὑπό with the dative, cf., e.g., 5.646, 13.98; with Chantraine 1948–53: vol. II, 141; and George 2005: 63–4. ἀνδράσι δυσμενέεσσιν: the phrase is formulaic at the beginning of the line; there are two Odyssean parallels at the end of the line: *Od.* 3.90 and 22.234. The word δυσμενής (hostile, enemy) is highly partisan and occurs only in direct speech (*Il.* 22.403 is the one exception but is an example of embedded focalisation).

454–63 Now Hector contemplates the worst: images of Andromache's future overlap and the syntax becomes loose. Her captivity is introduced by ὅτε at 454, followed by a subjunctive (ἄγηται: 455n.). Two parenthetic main clauses in the optative follow: they are introduced by καί κεν in anaphora (456, 457). A third καί, with ποτε, refers back to ὅτε (454) and returns to the subjunctive: the sequence is framed by Andromache's tears, in ring composition. Hector spares Andromache (and himself) any detail about her relationship to a future master, cf. ΣbT *ad* 6.457*b*; the two parenthetic sentences (456n. and 457n.) outline what she will have to do for a mistress. Overt references to forced sex are avoided, but that particular threat is implied by πόλλ᾽ ἀεκαζομένη (458n., cf. ἐλκηθμοῖο at 465n.). Hector then imagines that somebody will see Andromache's tears and recognise her as the former wife of Hector, best of the Trojan warriors, at the time when they fought over Troy. Hector is especially prone to stating what people might say of him and, more generally, to taking seriously the expectations of others; for his other τις-speeches cf. 479n., 7.87–91, 22.106–10; with de Jong 1987b: 76–9; Mackie 1996: 98–9; Beck 2008: 168–70. Usually, the opinion of an imagined speaker influences Hector's behaviour, though the situation here is more complicated, because the anonymous speaker comments on Andromache's plight (459n.) and elicits a response from her (462n.). For Andromache as a memorial to Hector, see Scodel 1992a: 59. For a comparative example, see 'The Kosovo Girl', in Karadžić 1953, no. 51: the Serbian heroes give an item of their clothing or jewellery to a girl, who thus becomes a living memorial for them after they die. In her own speech Andromache saw her fate as intertwined with Hector's (see esp. 407–13n.); now Hector cannot disentangle his future glory from her suffering. At the end of his speech Hector no longer appeals to duty or glory as reasons for fighting but rather claims it is Andromache's future suffering that drives him to death: 464–5n. Easterling 1991 discusses some connections between female suffering and male glory.

454 ὅσσον σεῖ᾽: the culmination of Hector's priamel (450–3n.), underlined by the opening spondee. In early Greek epic the form σεῖ᾽ with elision is attested only here and at *Hom. Hymn* 1 D 10 West; for contracted, unelided σεῦ, see 409n. τις Ἀχαιῶν χαλκοχιτώνων: some Achaean man will take possession of Andromache and replace Hector; cf. 1.112–15, where Agamemnon assesses the physical and mental accomplishments of his slave Chryseis and declares her better than his own wife. For Neoptolemos as Andromache's new master, see *Little Iliad*, frr. 29–30 West; and *Iliou Persis* in Proclus, *Chrestomathy*, p. 146 West. The adjective χαλκοχίτων suggests that the heroes are warriors whose very garments are made of bronze (a χιτών is usually made of cloth: Marinatos 1967: 7–9), or whose armour is like a garment; on bronze as the metal of heroes, see 3n. In the *Iliad* the epithet χαλκοχίτων is used most often of the Achaeans; in other early hexameter poems it is used exclusively of them and is associated specifically with the Trojan War (*Od.* 1.286, 4.496; cf. Hes. fr. 165.14 MW). ΣT *ad* 11.805a¹ disparage the phrase Ἀχαιῶν χαλκοχιτώνων as 'cyclic', i.e. commonplace. For the possible connections between the epithet and Mycenaean armour, cf. Kirk 1990: 66–7.

455 δακρυόεσσαν: at the beginning of the line the adjective is used predicatively and means 'in tears' (cf., e.g., 16.10, 18.66); at the end of the line it is used as an attribute, 'grievous', esp. of 'war' or 'battle'. Andromache is already crying (405n.).   ἄγηται: cf. 291n. (ἤγαγε); for the subjunctive cf. 454–63n.   ἐλεύθερον ἦμαρ ἀπούρας = 16.831, 20.193, of captive women; cf. ἀμύνειν δούλιον ἦμαρ: 463n., with Raaflaub 1981: 188–9. The adjective ἐλεύθερος is rare in early epic and occurs mostly in this phrase (*LfgrE* s.v. ἐλεύθερος*), though see 528n. for a different usage. Homeric words related to freedom emphasise one's ties with one's family and people. The opposite is slavery, which severs those ties; cf. Jacquinod 1992. ἀπούρας < ἀπόϝρας, participle of ἀπηύρα: 16–17n.

456 καί κεν takes up ὅτε κεν at 454, but without referring to a specific point in the future.   ἐν Ἄργει ἐοῦσα: the land of the Achaeans, rather than any specific location in Thessaly or the Peloponnese; cf. 152n.; Kirk 1990: 221. For 'Argive Helen', cf. 323n.; in Euripides' *Andromache*, Helen's daughter Hermione becomes Andromache's mistress.   πρὸς ἄλλης: for πρός with a noun in the genitive = 'on behalf of', 'at the command of', cf. 1.238–9, and Chantraine 1948–53: vol. II, 134.   ἱστὸν ὑφαίνοις ~ 3.125 (of Helen), *Od.* 15.517, etc. Captive women who could weave were prized possessions; cf. 1.31, 290n. (τάς). For the optative, see 454–63n.

457 καί κεν: 454–63n., 456n. The repetition expresses Hector's tortured frame of mind as he contemplates the details of Andromache's future.   ὕδωρ φορέοις: this is the task of female servants (*Od.* 3.427–9, 10.358; cf. *Il.* 24.302–4) or young girls (e.g. *Od.* 10.105–8; *Hom. Hymn* 2.105–10); mistresses of the house do not do it. ΣA *ad* 6.457a point out that later authors took their cue from this line and portrayed Andromache carrying water; cf. Eur. *Andr.* 166–7. For the optative see 454–63n.   Μεσσηΐδος ἢ Ὑπερείης: names of springs are feminine. Ancient and modern readers have speculated about the precise location of these springs (Strabo 9.5.6 and 18; Pausanias 3.20.1), but geographical accuracy is hardly what matters to Hector, and Kirk 1990: 221–2 rightly points out that the names are generic ('Middle Spring' and 'Upper Spring'): Andromache's forced labour could take place anywhere in the land of the Argives. For Ὑπέρεια, cf. 2.734–5 and Pind. *Pyth.* 4.125.   ἤ: 341n. (ἤ ἴθ').

458 πόλλ' ἀεκαζομένη ~ *Od.* 13.277; *Hom. Hymn* 2.344 and 432. The verb
*ἀεκάζομαι (only attested in the present participle) expresses a strong resistance or
extreme reluctance, often in the context of violent abduction; cf. esp. Persephone in
Hom. Hymn 2.30, 344 and 432. For the intensifying combination with πολλά (adverbial)
compare ἤϊε πόλλ' ἀέκων at 11.557 ~ 17.666.　　κρατερὴ δ' ἐπικείσετ' ἀνάγκη ~
Od. 10.273; *Hom. Hymn* 5.130, of characters confronted with a terrible fate. The Trojans
have already confronted 'necessity' at the beginning of the book: 85n.
459 ~ 479n., 7.87, etc. The line introduces an anonymous 'τις-speech'; for Hector's repeated references to what others might say, cf. 454–63n.　　καί ποτε takes
up καί κεν at 456n., 457n., but with a clearer reference to a specific time in the
future.　　εἴπῃσιν: subjunctive, cf. 454–63n., 479n. The later future ἐρέει makes
the speech seem even more real: cf. 462n. West believes that the Homeric spelling
was εἴπησιν (cf. πίησι on the Ischia cup), but the transmitted form εἴπῃσιν may
be old, see Peters 1998: 594–6.　　ἰδών is traditional in this position; elsewhere the
speaker turns to his addressee and looks at him (cf., e.g., *Il.* 2.271, 4.81). For τις-
speeches responding to a specific sight, cf., e.g., 4.79–81, 22.370–2.　　κατὰ δάκρυ
χέουσαν: Andromache is already crying (405n.); so Hector imagines an Achaean man
witnessing what he already sees in front of his eyes; see also 455n.
460–1 [Plutarch], *On Homer* II, ch. 215, perceptively calls the lines an epigram; see
also ΣbT *ad* 6.460b; Vox 1975: 70; Hillgruber 1994–9: vol. II, 434–5; and Elmer 2005.
Epigrams typically adorned funerary monuments. The speaker praises Hector for his
actions (460n. ἀριστεύεσκε μάχεσθαι), thus offering confirmation that Hector should
now return to the battlefield (441–6n.). For a close parallel, cf. 7.89–90. Andromache
functions as a σῆμα, a living memorial of Hector's past achievements in war (418–
19n. ἠδ' ἐπὶ σῆμ' ἔχεεν) – but the problem is that Hector's prowess only adds to her
pain (462n.). Hector finds it impossible to contemplate Andromache's suffering and
effectively chooses death as his escape route (464–5n.).
460 Ἕκτορος ἥδε γυνή: Andromache is described as the wife of Hector and hence
in terms of her Trojan past. Hector has just addressed her with γύναι (441n.), so his
words and views tally with those of the anonymous speaker. Here, as throughout his
speech, Hector points out to Andromache that his decision to fight is not his own
personal choice, but a socially sanctioned response to the war – one shared not just
by the Trojans but also by the Achaean man who comments on Andromache's tears.
For this type of phrase in funerary epigrams, cf. 7.89 (ἀνδρὸς μὲν τόδε σῆμα), and see
Elmer 2005: 5, with n. 13; and 7–8.　　ὃς ἀριστεύεσκε μάχεσθαι = 11.746, 16.292,
551, 17.351, always of a warrior who has died in battle; cf. 208n. Here the expression
harks back to 444–5.
461 Τρώων ἱπποδάμων: a typical addition in progressive enjambment. The formula is common in the *Iliad* but unattested elsewhere; ἱππόδαμοι in the plural only
of the Trojans (with one exception: Hes. fr. 35.8 MW); in the singular it can characterise warriors on either side, cf. 299n. Horses need plains (*Od.* 4.601–8, cf. Ἄργεος
ἱπποβότοιο: 152n.), so it is appropriate that the epithet characterises the Trojans who
live on a plain. The Trojan horses are famous (e.g. 5.221–5 ~ 8.105–8, 16.383–93);

esp. those of Erichthonius (20.221–9), Tros (5.263–73) and Laomedon (5.640; Hes. frr. 43a.64 and 165.10–11 MW). Hector himself is remembered as ἱππόδαμος in the last line of the *Iliad*; for Andromache's special care for his horses, see 8.186–90. ὅτε Ἴλιον ἀμφεμάχοντο: cf. 329n. (ἀμφιδέδηε).

462 Speech-concluding line which, unusually, focuses on the reaction of the person mentioned in the speech (Andromache), rather than on the person who imagined that the speech would be uttered (Hector).   ὥς ποτέ τις ἐρέει = 4.182, 7.91; cf. 22.108. The future tense picks up the previous subjunctive and makes the speech seem more real with hindsight, as Hector contemplates its terrifying implications; cf. *Od.* 6.275 (subj.) with 285 (fut.). Willmott 2007: 64 argues against a distinction between the subjunctive and the future in this passage, but whereas Homer uses the future both to introduce and round off hypothetical speeches (e.g. 4.176 and 182), he uses the subjunctive only to introduce such speeches, never to round them off. For Homeric speakers warming to their own scenarios, cf. 22.106 (lest they say, subj.) and 108 (thus they will speak, fut.), and *Od.* 21.324 with 329. For subtle shifts in emphasis through ring composition, cf. Introduction 2.3.   σοὶ δ' αὖ νέον ἔσσεται ἄλγος: another prediction in the future indicative, echoing ἄλγος at 450n., in ring composition. For δ' αὖ expressing a weak contrast see Klein 1988: 256–8. νέον is usually an adverb, though is more naturally taken as an adjective here.

463 χήτεϊ 'for lack of'. The word is used rarely, only in the dative. It features only in direct speech and is highly emotional: it speaks of desolation and bereavement; cf. 19.324 with Di Benedetto 1998: 311; *Od.* 16.34–5; *Hom. Hymn* 3.78; Hes. *Theog.* 605.   τοιοῦδ' ἀνδρός: Hector describes himself as a great man, but in the context of failing to save Andromache from slavery. Typically, Hector has high aspirations but is also keenly aware of his own shortcomings.   ἀμύνειν δούλιον ἦμαρ 'who can ward off slavery'; cf., e.g., 11.484, 588, 13.514. For the infinitive after demonstrative pronoun, see Chantraine 1948–53: vol. II, 302. Hector casts himself in the role of the defender, cf. his words at 12.243, as well as Priam's remembrance speech at 24.499–501. For δούλιον ἦμαρ, cf. *Od.* 14.340, 17.323; there are many similar expressions with adjective + ἦμαρ: they mark a dramatic change in somebody's life; cf. 455n. (ἐλεύθερον ἦμαρ).

464–5 Hector's concluding lines are as unconventional as the conclusion to Andromache's speech. Both partners fail to return to their opening statements: Andromache started her speech with her need for pity (407n.) and ends it by giving strategic advice, and speculating about the military intelligence of the Achaeans (433–9n., 438–9n.). Hector began with his sense of honour, courage and quest for fame (441–6n.); but now he claims that he had rather die than witness Andromache's suffering. She ends her speech by offering practical suggestions for action; he finishes on a note of resignation and defeat. Both speeches defy conventional gender roles, and Hector later tries to restore them: 490–3n. Hector's final answer to Andromache is devastating in its simplicity: he had rather die – not despite her suffering, but because of it. For an excellent reading of these lines, see Mirto 1997: 983–4.

464 ἀλλά marks a final turning point in Hector's speech; cf. 450n.   με: Hector has not referred to himself in the first person since 450n. (μοι). For the use of personal pronouns in the speech see 440–65n.   τεθνειῶτα: for the form in ει cf. 71n. (νεκρούς . . . τεθνειῶτας).   χυτὴ κατὰ γαῖα καλύπτοι: cf. Andromache's own death wish at 410–11n. Hector's words are more concrete (χυτὴ . . . γαῖα = 'burial mound'), and indeed he alone faces an imminent death. The verb καλύπτω is elsewhere used of burial (see the close verbal parallel at 14.114), and of death and darkness more generally (cf. 11n.); it also frequently describes a protective covering, either before or after death, cf., e.g., 5.23, 11.752, 24.20; see further Bremer 1976: 66–73. Hector combines these different associations: for him, the earth is not only a resting place after death but also a shield against the suffering of Andromache. For the earth as a refuge in funeral laments, see Tsagalis 2004: 119.

465 πρίν γέ τι: γε emphasises the preceding πρίν, cf. 16–17n. (γε). τι further emphasises Hector's revulsion: he insists that he must die before Andromache becomes a slave. The variant reading πρίν γ' ἔτι, adopted by West, seems less effective rhetorically; see also Stoevesandt 2008: 148.   σῆς . . . σοῦ: cf. 440–65n.   ἑλκηθμοῖο: the noun (< ἕλκω) occurs only here in early epic, but the idea of 'dragging' women into captivity is attested elsewhere in the *Iliad* (22.62, 65) and in the epic cycle (esp. *Iliou Persis* in Proclus, *Chrestomathy*, p. 146 West, where Ajax drags away Cassandra, and the statue of Athena to which she clings). It has clear connotations of sexual violence, cf. εἷλκες at Lysias 1.12.

466–81 At the end of his speech to Andromache, Hector had wished for death as the only escape from future suffering (464–5n.); now, as he reaches for his child, his mood changes. Children embody the hopes of their parents, and Hector now hopes that Astyanax will grow up good and strong and continue to be a source of happiness for his mother (for the difficulties involved in his wish, cf. esp. 481n.). The audience, however, know that his prayer is destined to remain unanswered: another soldier (Neoptolemos in *Little Iliad*, frr. 18 and 29 West; Odysseus in *Iliou Persis*, p. 146 West) will snatch Astyanax from his nurse's bosom, lift him up and throw him off the walls (cf. 467n. and 474n.). Some scholars have argued that the poet of the *Iliad* did not know what would happen to Astyanax (Kullmann 1960: 186–7), but this seems overly sceptical, especially in view of 24.734–8, where Andromache fears that some Achaean will hurl Astyanax off the bastion (ἀπὸ πύργου), with Burgess 2001: 65–7. Some later accounts of Astyanax's death also mention the bastion (Paus. 10.25.9; Quintus of Smyrna 13.252), though others mention the walls more generally (Eur. *Andr.* 10 and *Tro.* 725; Apollod. *Epit.* 5.23), cf. 474n. The possibility of domestic happiness, which glimmers briefly in his passage, is set against the fall of Troy and the brutal death of Astyanax – but the language of war is also used here to comic effect: Astyanax beats a retreat into the arms of his nurse. The episode is designed to elicit a smile, even before the audience hear that Hector and Andromache are laughing too. Andromache's own feelings, as Hector returns Astyanax to her, reflect the complex emotions dramatised in the encounter: δακρυόεν γελάσασα (484n.). On the episode see also Schadewaldt 1997: 136–9; Lohmann 1988: 47; and Van Nortwick 2001: 227–9. ΣbT *ad* 6.466 rightly point out that the episode starts a long tradition of scenes involving children in tragedy; cf. Sifakis 1979.

466 The line suggests that Andromache's speech interrupted Hector's encounter with Astyanax, cf. 404n.   οὗ παιδός: references to Astyanax as 'Hector's child' frame the episode, cf. 482–3n.; contrast the more neutral παῖδα (without possessive adjective) at 404n.   ὀρέξατο 'reached for' (in order to embrace).   φαίδιμος Ἕκτωρ: a common noun–epithet formula. φαίδιμος is occasionally used also of other men (e.g. Ajax at 5.617 etc., Odysseus at *Od.* 10.251 etc.) but most typically describes Hector; for his appearance, cf. 11.61–6 and 12.462–6 (a striking elaboration of the traditional epithet). This episode explores the relationship between martial Hector and his baby son, and the epithet punctuates their encounter: first 'brilliant' Hector frightens Astyanax, then he takes off his helmet, which is itself 'shining' (473n.) and finally he picks it up again (494n.). When Neoptolemos takes away Andromache and kills Astyanax at *Little Iliad*, fr. 29 West, he is called φαίδιμος too.

467–70 The scholia bT *ad* 6.467 praise Homer for the extraordinary vividness (ἐνάργεια) of these lines, and they comment that we can see, as well as hear, the action; cf. Introduction 2.6. The passage invites the audience not only to visualise Astyanax, but also to view Hector from the perspective of his frightened baby: 469–70n. Up to now Hector made no concession to his domestic surroundings: he refused Hecuba's offer of wine because, he pointed out, he was covered in blood (264–8n.); and later he entered Paris' bedroom wielding an enormous spear (318–24n., 319n.). Now, finally, he relinquishes his helmet in an attempt to soothe Astyanax: 472–3n.

467 Cf. *Little Iliad*, fr. 29 West: παῖδα δ᾽ ἑλὼν ἐκ κόλπου ἐϋπλοκάμοιο τιθήνης.   ἄψ: the tone of the adverb is mock-military (cf. 3.32 = 11.585 = 13.566 etc.).   πάϊς takes up οὗ παιδός at 466n. but now with emphasis not on the relationship between father and son but on Astyanax's tender age. The word is scanned as two syllables; cf. 119n.   κόλπον: 400n.   ἐϋζώνοιο τιθήνης: the housekeeper introduced the servant as Astyanax's nurse (389); the poet initially described her as Andromache's maid (ἀμφίπολος: 372n. and 399n.) but now uses τιθήνη, thus emphasising her relationship to Astyanax. ἐΰζωνος is a common epithet of women in epic (cf. 1.429 etc.): the ζώνη is a belt or girdle worn by goddesses and women (Marinatos 1967: 12); when applied to men, ζώνη simply means waist.

468 ἐκλίνθη 'shrank back' (< κλίνω), the aorist ending -θην is intransitive rather than passive, cf. 106n. (ἐλελίχθησαν). The same verb is used of warriors avoiding a blow (3.360 = 7.254).   ἰάχων < ἰάχω, 'scream'; cf. νηπίαχον at 408n. In the *Iliad* the participle ἰάχων is otherwise used of warriors whose war cry is terrifying to the enemy: cf. the formulaic σμερδαλέα ἰάχων; contrast the feminine ἰάχουσα of the wounded Aphrodite at 5.343. The hiatus before ἰάχων is merely apparent (< ϝιάχων), though Homer often treats this verb as though it did not have an initial consonant; for discussion see Chantraine 1948–53: vol. I, 139–40.   φίλου: a standard epithet of πατήρ, cf. 4.354 etc., 471n., and *Od.* 1.94 ~ 2.360 (in the same metrical position).

The expression φίλος υἱός is even more common (474n.).   ἀτυχθείς: another item of battlefield vocabulary; cf. 38n. (ἀτυζομένω πεδίοιο) and Schein 1984: 175; though the verb also describes Andromache's reaction when she sees Hector's corpse: 22.474. Only here in the aorist.

469–70 The lines are a variation on a common verse in arming scenes: 3.337 = 11.42 = 15.481 = 16.138. Now, the baby focuses on one of Hector's most prominent attributes: his helmet was a gift of Apollo (11.352–3 with Edwards 1987: 211) and features in Hector's most common epithet: κορυθαίόλος (Introduction 2.2; for statistics on Hector's epithets, see M. Parry 1971: 142).

469 ταρβήσας: the same verb is used of the fear Hector instils in the enemy: 17.586.   χαλκόν: cf. 116n., and χαλκήρης at 13.714 and 15.535. Bronze weapons are often said to gleam (319n.); but Hector is particularly associated with gleaming bronze, not just through his epithet κορυθαίόλος (116n.), but also in similes and the main narrative (11.61–6, 12.462–4).   ἰδέ: a rarer alternative to ἠδέ (90n.); cf. Latacz 2003: 164. The final syllable is closed: 91n. (ἐνὶ μεγάρωι) and Introduction 2.1.   λόφον ἱππιοχαίτην: the adjective is unique but recalls the frequently used ἵππουριν (of Hector's helmet: 495n.); and related terms such as ἵππειος, ἱπποδάσεια (9), ἱππόκομος and ἱπποκορυστής. The unusual word emphasises the animal-like features of the helmet and reflects Astyanax's distorted perception of his father: Hector appears to him as a strange composite monster.

470 δεινόν: adverbial in Homer; cf. 182n.   ἀπ' ἀκροτάτης 'from the very top'. The phrasing is unusual: Astyanax is looking up to Hector and his terrifying, gleaming, nodding helmet; see Di Benedetto 1998: 116.   κόρυθος echoes κορυθαίόλος Ἕκτωρ.   νεύοντα 'nodding', often of helmets: cf. 13.132–3 = 16.216–17, 20.162, 22.314, and the passages cited at 469–70n. Carol Ann Duffy captures Astyanax's perception: 'a bristling horsehair plume / alive on top' (see Duffy and Graziosi 2005).   νοήσας: the verb now explicitly focalises the description of the helmet through Astyanax.

471 ἐκ δ' ἐγέλασσε: the line opens with ἐκ, expressing the spontaneous, open reaction of both Hector and Andromache. The compound ἐκγελάω (for the tmesis see 42–3n.) occurs only here in the *Iliad*; cf. *Hom. Hymn* 4.389, also a reaction to the amusing behaviour of a child; for more sarcastic uses of the verb, cf. *Od.* 16.354, 18.35; and Hes. *Op.* 59. For Homeric laughter more generally, see Levine 1982–3, Jäkel 1994, Pisanello 1999, Halliwell 2008: ch. 2; cf. 484n.   πατήρ τε φίλος echoes 468n. Hector was already smiling at 404n.   καὶ πότνια μήτηρ: this is the first time Andromache is called a mother; cf. 264n. where the same expression is used of Hecuba. Andromache will not remain a mother for long: there are only two other passages where she is called μήτηρ in the *Iliad*, and both describe a future shared with Astyanax, which she will never have: 481, 22.499. For Andromache as a mother in later literature, see esp. Eur. *Andromache*, with Introduction 5.

472–3 This is the only time Hector adapts to the domestic situation in which he finds himself and lets go of his martial appearance, cf. 467–70n. On the battlefield losing one's helmet signifies defeat, cf. 21.50 and especially 3.369–78. The next time we see Hector without his helmet is when Achilles drags his corpse in the dust: 22.401–4. In Virg. *Aen.* 12.434, Aeneas kisses his child without removing his helmet.

472 αὐτίκ᾽: a spontaneous gesture in response to his son: Erren 1970: 27. κρατός: genitive singular of κάρη; for the declension of this noun see Chantraine 1948–53: vol. I, 230–1. κόρυθ᾽: cf. 470n., 472–3n. φαίδιμος Ἕκτωρ: cf. 466n.

473 ἐπὶ χθονὶ παμφανόωσαν: the expected epithet after χθονί would be πουλυβοτείρηι, 'nourishing' (213n.); the unusual final participle focuses on Hector's gleaming helmet, cf. Edwards 1987: 211: 'The unexpected effect, startling to anyone familiar with the usual formulae, directs attention both to the sight of the helmet lying on the ground and to its glitter, the reason for the child's fright.'

474 Hector kisses his baby son and tosses him in his arms – a natural gesture for a father; but, in this context, tinged with foreboding: 466–8in. ὅ γ᾽: the particle singles out Hector's gesture; cf. 16–17n. Expected digamma before ὅν can be restored by deleting γε (Chantraine 1948–53: vol. I, 147), but Homer does not always acknowledge digamma, and the transmitted text should stand: 90n. (ὅς οἱ). φίλον υἱόν corresponds to 'dear father' at 468n. and 471n.; cf. 401n. (Ἑκτορίδην). κύσε: the only loving kiss in the *Iliad*; the other two are (real or imagined) gestures of submission: 8.371, 24.478. In the *Odyssey* people kiss more frequently, and for a variety of reasons; cf. *LfgrE* s.v. κύνει, κύσ(σ)αι. πῆλέ τε χερσίν: often translated as 'dandled', but πάλλω implies an energetic gesture; the verb normally describes the throwing of objects, especially spears and stones, on the battlefield; see also Eur. *Hec.* 1157–62 (of children about to be killed).

475–81 At 447–9n. Hector told Andromache he knew that Troy was going to fall. Now, with baby Astyanax in his arms, he suddenly becomes hopeful: as the scholia put it, 'he melts, and forgets his previous words' (ΣbT *ad* 6.476 διαχυθεὶς δὲ ἐπιλέλησται τῶν πρώην); see also Taplin 1992: 123 on the discrepancy between this passage and 447–9. The language and syntax of Hector's prayer show signs of improvisation, cf. 477n. (ὡς καὶ ἐγώ περ), 478n. (ὧδε; βίην τ᾽ ἀγαθόν), 479n. (καί ποτέ τις εἴπηισι), 480n. (ἐκ πολέμου ἀνιόντα). Hector hardly adheres to the formal conventions of prayer (476n.: Ζεῦ ἄλλοι τε θεοί), see Pulleyn 1997: 26–38, with 304–10n. What he says remains a mere wish – and substitutes for the conversation he cannot yet have, and will never be able to have, with his son. Structurally, his speech replaces the traditional prayer warriors utter before entering into battle, cf. Arthur Katz 1981: 34; this reinforces the strong sense of identification of the father with the son. The speech ends with an unlikely image: one day Astyanax will return home with the spoils of the enemy – and Andromache will rejoice at the sight. There is a clear echo of this passage at 17.206–8, where Zeus points out that Hector will never manage to present Andromache with Achilles' spoils; see further Taplin 1992: 125; Bouvier 2002a: 100; and Introduction 3.2 and 4.4. For Michael Longley's 'The Helmet', based on this passage, see Introduction 5.

475 Prayers to 'Zeus and the other gods' remain vague plans, complaints, intentions and speculations; the expression is never used by the poet to describe a precise and successful ritual; cf., e.g., 259n., 3.298–302, 8.526–8, see further Jörgensen 1904, who argues that characters invoke 'Zeus' and 'the gods' when they are unsure about which god is responsible for a particular situation.   εἶπεν: Aristarchus read εἶπε δ'; cf. ΣAT *ad* 6.475. He believed that Homer used 'apodotic' δέ (i.e. δέ after a subordinate clause) as a matter of habit: Matthaios 1999: 571–3; and he noted instances also when the main tradition does not seem to have δέ, as here.   ἐπευξάμενος: cf. 304n. (εὐχομένη).

476–8 The syntax of these three lines gives the impression that Hector puts together his prayer as he speaks; cf. 475–81n. Construe: δότε... τόνδε γενέσθαι... ἀριπρεπέα... βίην τ' ἀγαθόν... καὶ... ἀνάσσειν.

476 Ζεῦ ἄλλοι τε θεοί: without the expected (Ζεῦ) πάτερ, or any other epithets, Hector's address sounds improvised (475–81n.). Elsewhere, only Athena addresses her father without an epithet, and only at the end of a speech that is introduced by an elaborate address (*Od.* 1.62; cf. 45); for the gods addressing each other, see also *Od.* 5.7 = 8.306 = 12.377, and cf. 12.371 (the closest parallel in prayer). Hiatus after Ζεῦ further suggests improvisation. (No close parallels; contrast Ζεῦ ἄνα at *Il.* 3.351 etc., with digamma still felt.)   δότε: cf. 307n. (δός).   δή adds urgency to the prayer, cf. 52–3n.   καὶ τόνδε 'this one too'; the deictic pronoun suggests that Hector is presenting Astyanax to the gods. καί, here and at 477n., expresses Hector's identification with his son, cf. 475–81n.

477 The line, in necessary enjambment, is supposed to complete and thus clarify Hector's wish; though in fact two parentheses separate γενέσθαι from ἀριπρεπέα and make the speech seem disjointed: Hector is trying to express his affection for his child, and his hopes for the future, all at the same time.   παῖδ' ἐμόν: the phrase, in apposition, draws attention to Hector's close relationship with his son.   ὡς καὶ ἐγώ περ: a second parenthesis suggests that Hector is ahead of himself: ἀριπρεπέα is already on his mind and strikes him as an aspiration both for himself and for his son. περ invites us to reflect on the point of the comparison: 146n.; ἐγώ suggests a separate clause with ellipsis of εἰμί, 'am'; cf. Stoevesandt 2008: 151–2.   ἀριπρεπέα: not simply 'excellent' but 'recognised for his excellence'. The word sometimes describes a young man's transition into adulthood and the public arena (it is never used of women): 9.438–41; *Hom. Hymn* 5.103–6; cf. *Od.* 11.540 (ἀριδείκετος).   Τρώεσσιν: Hector first considers Trojan society, and then Andromache's perspective, as in his previous speech: 440–65n., 450–3n. The locative dative ('among the Trojans') seems inspired by ἀριπρεπέα and its similarity in sound and meaning to μεταπρεπέα, μεταπρέπω + dative (cf. 18.370, μεταπρεπέ' ἀθανάτοισι; 13.175 etc., μετέπρεπε δὲ Τρώεσσι; *Hom. Hymn* 5.104, μετὰ Τρώεσσιν ἀριπρεπέ' ἔμμεναι).

478 A further elaboration on what Hector has already said; again the syntax is strained; cf. 475–81n. His words emphasise both power and physical force: Astyanax, like his father, is expected to be the strongest warrior and, eventually, the ruler of Troy.   ὧδε: another comparison with Hector, and another unexpected turn of phrase; ὧδε follows ὡς καὶ ἐγώ περ in line 477 and is best taken as enjambment with ἀριπρεπέα in 477: 'distinguished to such an extent' (i.e. like me); cf. Stoevesandt 2008:

151. Some ancient texts and many medieval manuscripts read ὧδε βίην ἀγαθόν τε ('so valiant and'), in an attempt to do away with the harsh enjambment. The result is unconvincing.   βίην τ' ἀγαθόν: there are no close parallels, but cf. 15.139 (βίην καὶ χείρας ἀμείνων); see also 1.404, 15.165, 181, etc. At the level of sound and rhythm, the frequent βοὴν ἀγαθός (12n.) provides a model – and is attested in one manuscript. βίη, '(violent) force', is not always positive, cf. esp. Hector's view about how others might assess him at 22.107.   Ἰλίου Ἶφι ἀνάσσειν: cf., e.g., 1.38 = 452, Od. 17.443. The traditional expression further strains the syntax (ἀριπρεπέα... ἀγαθὸν... ἀνάσσειν). Hector reflects on Astyanax's public name (ἀνάσσειν ~ Ἀστυ-άναξ; 403n.).   Ἶφι 'with might' (ἴς); for the ending in -φι see Chantraine 1948–53: vol. I, 235, and cf. 510n.

479 The Trojans already have high hopes for Astyanax (403n.); now Hector imagines that one day somebody will recognise his son as the strongest man in a distinguished family line; for the aspirations of fathers, cf. 206–11n., 209n.; and Arthur Katz 1981: 35. Hector is, as ever, mindful of what others will say, cf. 454–63n.   καί ποτέ τις εἴπῃσι: the free-standing subjunctive fits Hector's animated, improvised prayer; his use of the subjunctive at 459n. is almost as abrupt; see also his words at 7.85–8. The phrase ποτέ τις εἴπῃσι sometimes follows after μή (see 22.106, 23.575, Od. 21.324) but can also feature in positive formulations: the closest parallel is Od. 6.275, which harks back to μή τις... | μωμεύηι at Od. 6.273–4. This reading is preferable to the optative εἴποι attested in the papyri and some medieval manuscripts; εἴποι agrees with φέροι in the next line; but here Hector is not simply expressing a wish, he is imagining a situation; for discussion see also Ludwich 1885: 351–4. For the expressive grammar of character speech, see e.g. 280–5n., and Introduction 2.5.   πατρὸς δ' ὅ γε πολλὸν ἀμείνων: cf. 1.404 and, for the metrical shape of the expression, 7.114, 16.709, etc. The particle δέ does not normally introduce direct speech in Homer, though see 123n. In the present context the effect is elliptical, also because the speech starts midway through the line: '(the father was great) but (δέ) he is even better than his father'. There is only one other speech in the *Iliad* which does not start at the beginning of the line: 23.855, with Edwards 1970: 27. According to ΣAT ad 6.479a, Aristarchus read πατρὸς γ' ὅδε, which makes the text grammatically smoother and avoids δέ; cf. van der Valk 1963–4: vol. II, 124–5.

480 Hector describes Astyanax 'returning from the war', just like himself, except that he imagines a victorious return with spoils – and then, in the next line, he describes what he would most like to see: a happy Andromache; cf. Zeus's comment at 17.206–8.   ἐκ πολέμου ἀνιόντα '(seeing him) as he returns from the war'. The accusative exercised ancient readers (ΣAT ad 6.479–80) but fits Hector's elliptical and improvised prayer (475–81n.).   φέροι δ' ἔναρα βροτόεντα: cf., e.g., 8.534, 17.540; for ἔναρα, see 68–9n. The last man to be killed and despoiled in the *Iliad* is Hector himself: 22.367–9.

481 Hector now imagines Andromache's happiness – in response not to his own actions, but those of Astyanax, who has just managed to make her laugh (471n.). Cassandra is the first who sees Priam return with Hector's corpse at the end of the poem and remembers how the whole community used to rejoice whenever they saw Hector returning alive from the battlefield: 24.704–6. This passage foreshadows Hector's death, but also that of Astyanax. 17.38–40 provides only a partial parallel: Euphorbos wants to kill Menelaos in order to avenge his brother Hyperenor, and he imagines that his parents would rejoice at the sight of Menelaos' head and weapons; Hector's vision is less specific and is at odds with what Andromache says about the war: cf. 405–39n., esp. 432n., and Introduction 3.2.   κτείνας . . . ἄνδρα echoes one of Hector's traditional epithets: ἀνδροφόνος (498n.). Astyanax continues to be seen as an *alter ego* of his father.   δήϊον ἄνδρα: in the singular, the adjective is otherwise used only of fire and war – except at 22.84–5, where Hecuba describes Achilles as the ultimate enemy, in the singular; for the plural, see 82n.   μήτηρ: 471n.

482–93 After a character utters a prayer, the poet usually describes how the god responded or did not respond to it (cf. 311n.), but this is not the case here: Hector's wish is so far removed from what will actually happen that the poet does not linger on it; for a similarly unrealistic prayer followed by silence about the god's intentions, cf. 3.351–5 with Lateiner 1997: 260, n. 39. Rather than comment explicitly on the future, the poet focuses on the immediate situation: 'a statement of Zeus's intentions would fall too heavily into the delicate and responsive exchange between husband and wife' (Macleod 1982: 42). Hector now places Astyanax in Andromache's arms: it was the nurse who carried him when Hector first picked him up (cf. 389n. φέρει . . . τιθήνη, 400n.), but now he entrusts the baby to his mother (482–3n.). His gesture, like the speech that follows, reminds Andromache of her role and responsibilities, while also trying to comfort her. She responds with laughter and tears. Her complex, entangled reaction makes Hector take pity on her (484n.), which is exactly what she hoped to elicit (407n.; 431n.). His final words, however, suggest a very different course of action from the one she recommended at 433–9n.; see 485–93n., with Schadewaldt 1997: 137–8. For a Roman painting of this scene, see Introduction 5.

482–3 ἀλόχοιο φίλης: one of several expressions that emphasise the affection shared by family members (cf. 468n.: πατρὸς φίλου; 474n.: φίλον υἱόν); the focus now shifts from the relationship between parents and child, to that between Hector and Andromache.   παῖδ' ἑόν, in necessary enjambment, picks up παῖδ' ἐμόν at 477n. Andromache wants to keep Hector close to her, but he entrusts 'his son' to her, while he prepares to leave. Cf. 400 and 467–8, in ring composition.   κηώδεϊ: probably 'fragrant'. The description is focalised through Astyanax, who can smell his mother's bosom, as she carries him; cf. Lilja 1972: 146. Van Wees 2005: 13–14 discusses the practice of treating garments with scented oils. The related κηώεντα at 288n. (of Hecuba's storeroom) may point to the same practice. Ancient readers related both adjectives to κεῖσθαι and here paraphrased 'in which babies are put to sleep' (ἐν ὧι τὰ βρέφη κοιμίζεται): see ΣAT *ad* 6.483 with Erbse's apparatus. Their interpretation is not accurate in linguistic terms but suggests that ancient readers too understood the word in relation to Astyanax.   δέξατο κόλπωι: cf. 136n.

484 δακρυόεν γελάσασα: ancient readers state that 'this powerful description is impossible to interpret', δυνατῶς ῥηθὲν ἀνερμήνευτόν ἐστιν; ΣAbT *ad* 6.484. For Andromache's laughter, cf. 471n.; for her tears, cf. 373n., 455n., 459n., 496n., 499n. and

500n. She is breaking down under the strain of conflicting emotions; see further 482–93n. This is the only instance in Homer where somebody laughs and cries at the same time (for later examples see Arnould 1990: 93–4), but paradoxical forms of laughter feature prominently in both *Iliad* and *Odyssey*: cf. 471n. and 2.270, 15.101–3, *Od.* 18.100 and 163. πόσις corresponds to ἄλοχος at 482 and emphasises the reciprocity between husband and wife; for Hector as Andromache's 'husband', cf. 8.190 and 22.439. ἐλέησε νοήσας: cf. 407n., 431n. The alternative reading ἐλέαιρε is well attested but less suitable, because it describes a general attitude rather than a sudden pang of feeling; for ἐλέησε, cf., e.g., 8.350, 15.12, 17.346; for ἐλεαίρω, cf., e.g., 9.302, 13.15. νοήσας, in the aorist, focalises the scene through Hector's eyes and emphasises the onset of pity; for the use of an aor. part. with a main verb in the aor. to express concomitant actions, see Chantraine 1948–53: vol. ii, 188.

485–93 Hector tenderly touches Andromache and talks to her one last time: his words are more vigorous than line 485n. suggests. She should try not to upset herself (or, implicitly, him) too much: 486n. There is a shape to human life: nobody can escape fate (οὐ κακὸν οὐδὲ μὲν ἐσθλόν: 489n.). This assertion may seem to contradict Hector's earlier insistence on the difference between being bad (κακὸς ὥς: 443n.) and learning to be good (ἐπεὶ μάθον ἔμμεναι ἐσθλός: 444n.); but the underlying thought, in the opening sections of both his speeches, is the same: it is precisely because all mortals must die, and cannot escape fate, that they must behave well and do their duty; cf. 447n. (γάρ) and 487–9n. After this general proposition, in the second part of his speech, Hector describes Andromache's duties and his own: 490–3n. Andromache complies but is not reassured: 494–502n. When we next see Andromache, in book 22, she is attending to her domestic duties – weaving and telling her maids to prepare a bath for Hector – when she hears a commotion outside and immediately fears that Hector's excessive manliness in war will have cost him his life: her behaviour and thoughts at 22.437–59 seem directly inspired by Hector's last words to her: Graziosi and Haubold 2003: 69–71.

485 Similar lines introduce the words of mothers when they try to console their children: 1.361, 5.372 and 24.127. Andromache has just said that Hector is 'a father and a mother' to her (429–30n.); in the *Iliad* Hector is the only male character who caresses (κατέρεξεν) another person.

486 Hector tells Andromache that she should not indulge in excessive grief; his opening words betray his alarm: Andromache's despair affects him too (note the dative of affect: μοι; cf. 203n.); the conclusion to his previous speech already revealed that he finds her suffering difficult to bear: 464–5n. Excessive grief impairs proper behaviour: cf. Paris' revelation at 336n. (ἔθελον δ' ἄχεϊ προτραπέσθαι). δαιμονίη: not an affectionate word, *pace* Kirk 1990: 224; see 326n. and 521n. (in both cases Hector is talking to Paris). Andromache used the same word when she addressed Hector and complained that he felt no pity (407n.). Ancient readers thought of his words as a reproach: 494–502n. μὴ . . . λίην: for the importance of proper measure, even in suffering, cf. 24.46–9, 522–6 and 602–20. ἀκαχίζεο: the form is used as the imperative of ἄχνυμαι etc., 'have ἄχος (524–5n.), both here and at *Od.* 11.486;

contrast *Od.* 16.432 where ἀκαχίζω is causative. In all three cases the speaker says, or strongly implies, that the addressee is behaving inappropriately.   θυμῶι: cf. 51n. and 524–5n. For the locative dative, 397n. and 510n.

487–9 An elaborate anaphora (οὐ . . . οὐ . . . οὐ . . . οὐδέ) takes up the negative command in line 486n. Hector's thinking is traditional: mortals must do their duty not because they can hope to transcend their condition, but precisely because they are mortal; he reasons along similar lines at 447n. (γάρ); for a famous statement of the same principle in the *Iliad*, cf. 12.322–8.

487 Hector's words evoke the fated death of the heroes as described, prominently, in the proem: 1.3; cf. 11.54–5; and, with slightly different inflection, Hes. fr. 204.118 MW. For the idea that nobody can send another man to Hades (Ἀΐδωνῆϊ προϊάψειν) against the will of the gods, see 5.190–1.   οὐ . . . τις . . . ἀνήρ: cf. 487–9n.   ὑπὲρ αἶσαν: an impersonal reference to what is destined (cf. 333n.); μοῖραν in the next line refers more specifically to Hector's fate.   Ἄϊδι προϊάψει: cf. the related expressions ψυχὴν Ἄϊδι δοῦναι (5.654 = 11.445 ~ 16.625) and εἰς Ἀΐδαο (προ)πέμψαι (8.367, 21.48). Early epic uses προϊάψαι (or ἀπιάψαι: Hes. fr. 204.118 MW) only in the aorist and future, and always in the context of hurling somebody to Hades. Later readers thought that the expression described a particularly cruel and untimely death: ΣbT *ad* 1.3*c*; cf. Aesch. *Sept.* 321–2 (of the city of Thebes).

488 μοῖραν: a person's fate, often envisaged as a powerful deity who shapes human affairs: 24.49; Hes. *Theog.* 904–6; cf. Redfield 1994: 131–6; Yamagata 1994: 105–16; Graziosi and Haubold 2005: 89–92. Etymologically, μοῖρα is one's 'share' (cf. μείρομαι); it is closely associated with a person's death as the limit of his or her share in life; cf., e.g., 3.101–2, *Od.* 2.99–100; *Hom. Hymn* 5.269; and Hes. fr. 35.4 MW. When Hector dies, that is his μοῖρα: cf. 22.5, 303.   οὔ τινα . . . ἀνδρῶν: cf. 487–9n.   φημί: as often in Homer, φημί expresses a confident assertion rather than a mere opinion; cf. 206n. For its use with sayings, see Lardinois 1997: 220.   πεφυγμένον ἔμμεναι 'has escaped from', i.e. 'is safe from', an elaborate periphrasis that illustrates the present meaning of the perfect tense (cf. ἀφῖγμαι, εἰλήλουθα, 'I am here'; Chantraine 1948–53: vol. II, 198); but also emphasises that there is no escape: cf. 22.219, *Od.* 1.18, 9.455; *Hom. Hymn* 5.34, all of them negative.

489 = *Od.* 8.553 (about the fact that everybody has a name).   οὐ κακὸν οὐδὲ μὲν ἐσθλόν: this collapse of social and moral categories comes as a shock after the careful distinctions drawn at 443n. (κακὸς ὥς) and 444n. (ἐπεὶ μάθον ἔμμεναι ἐσθλός). However, it is precisely *because* moral choices make no difference to Hector's apportioned fate that they are of crucial importance to him as a human being, cf. 485–93n.   οὐδὲ μέν 'nor again' (emphatic); cf. Denniston 1954: 362–3.   ἐπὴν . . . γένηται: πρῶτα emphasises that the event is irreversible; see Latacz 2000b: 21. For the idea that one's fate is determined at birth see also 345n. ἐπήν (< ἐπεί + ἄν) here links a specific statement to a general truth, cf. 19.223–4 etc.   τά: for the use of the article with ordinal numbers (first, second, etc.), cf. Chantraine 1948–53: vol. II, 162.

490–3 ~ *Od.* 1.356–9 and 21.350–3 (Telemachus addresses his mother and claims that μῦθος, or τόξον, is the business of men – and his especially, since he rules in the household). This and the two Odyssean passages conclude extensive scenes at the end of which the male speaker feels he needs to assert his authority and role. On these lines as an articulation of gender roles, see further Felson and Slatkin 2004: 99; for their reception in Athenian drama, see Introduction 5.

490 εἰς οἶκον ἰοῦσα: Hector's matter-of-fact tone is in stark contrast with the picture the poet paints at 496n.   τὰ σ᾽ αὐτῆς = τὰ σὰ αὐτῆς; cf. 446 (ἐμὸν αὐτοῦ)   ἔργα: for the works of women, cf. 289n. and 324n.   κόμιζε 'attend to', 'look after', used both of people (e.g. 24.541) and things (e.g. *Od.* 23.355); κομίζω and the related noun κομιδή are often used of domestic work: 8.185–90, *Od.* 16.73–7, 20.337; seamen and vagrants (ἄνδρες ἀλῆται) do not enjoy proper κομιδή: *Od.* 8.232–3 and 451–2.

491–2 Weaving and spinning are important female tasks in Homer (Pantelia 1993), and indeed in the ancient world more generally: a bilingual Luwian/Phoenician inscription from Karatepe (eighth or early seventh century BCE) describes territories that were once dangerous for men, but where women now walk freely, carrying their spindles; cf. Lanfranchi 2007: 197. The tasks Hector recommends are appropriate in peacetime but, in time of war, become difficult: Introduction 3.2.   ἱστόν τ᾽ ἠλακάτην τε 'the loom and the distaff': these concrete objects stand for the activities of weaving and spinning respectively. The distaff holds the unspun wool, cf. *Od.* 4.121–35 with S. West in Heubeck, West and Hainsworth 1988: 203 (Helen has a gold distaff and keeps her spun wool in a silver basket on wheels).   ἔργον: the collective singular ἔργον picks up ἔργα at 490: Andromache and her servants are essentially engaged in the same activities. Hector earlier imagined Andromache's future life as a slave, weaving for somebody else: 456n.   ἐποίχεσθαι: cf. 81n.

492–3 πόλεμος δ᾽ ἄνδρεσσι μελήσει: the same proverbial expression distinguishes men from gods at 20.137; here Hector uses it both to justify his instructions to Andromache (she must act like all women) and to clarify his own exceptional role in the war; see Lardinois 1997: 219; and, for a discussion of ἄνδρεσσι μελήσει, Prauscello 2007. Hector previously used the verb μέλει when he claimed that he cared for Andromache more than for anyone else: 450n.; now, by contrast, he insists that he cares for the same thing as all other men: war. His words imply that Andromache should not concern herself with war, and they perhaps draw attention to her name: Ἀνδρο-μάχη: 371n.   πᾶσιν, ἐμοὶ δὲ μάλιστα: the progressive runover, as often, makes the previous statement more specific, see Introduction 2.1. Here the contrast between 'all men' and Hector emerges emphatically from the sequence πᾶσιν, ἐμοί at the beginning of the runover line. Hector's insistence that he cares for war more than all the other men does not reassure Andromache: 494–502n., and Graziosi and Haubold 2003: 70. The alternative reading πᾶσι, μάλιστα δ᾽ ἐμοί, preserved in one papyrus and cited by Epictetus, dilutes the stark contrast between πᾶσιν and ἐμοί and will have intruded from *Od.* 1.359, 11.353 and 21.353, where it alone is metrically possible. Some modern editors prefer πᾶσι, μάλιστα δ᾽ ἐμοί because it respects digamma before Ἰλίωι, but it is unlikely that their concern would have been shared by Epictetus or the scribe of papyrus 21 West; cf. van der Valk 1963–4: vol. II,

570–1. Digamma cannot always be restored before Ἴλιος (e.g. 386) and is not felt at 17.145, where the transmitted text is λαοῖσι τοὶ Ἰλίωι ἐγγεγάασιν. ἐγγεγάασιν makes a striking rhyme with πᾶσιν at the beginning of the line; cf. 143n. (ἄσσον . . . θᾶσσον).

494–502 Hector and Andromache now part: he picks up his helmet, and she walks home in tears, turning back again and again to look at him. 'The rebuke made her leave; but the affection made her turn back' comments an ancient reader: ΣbT *ad* 6.495–6. The narrative then follows Andromache as she enters the house: she already came close to performing a funeral lament in front of her living husband (405–39n.), now the poet makes the funerary overtones of the episode explicit. It is, of course, ill-omened to mourn a living man (Alexiou 2002: 4–5), and ancient readers called Andromache's lament παράνομος (ΣbT *ad* 6.499); see also Cavafy's 'Trojans' quoted in Introduction 5. The alternative – to carry on as normal and assume that Hector will come back – is, as the poet later reveals, also impossible: see Introduction 3.2.

494 ~ 472n. (ring composition); the gesture puts an end to Hector's encounter with his wife and child – though he does not yet leave (503–29n.). **ὣς . . . φωνήσας:** cf. 116n. **ἄρα:** 232n. **κόρυθ᾽ εἵλετο φαίδιμος Ἕκτωρ:** Hector resumes his traditional persona by putting on his helmet. One papyrus seems to preserve the variant χε[ιρὶ παχείηι] (cf. 10.31), which attempts to make Homeric diction more responsive to the immediate narrative context.

495 ἵππουριν 'with a horse-tail' (< ἵππος + οὐρή), standardly employed at the beginning of the line, as here; the adjective is otherwise used in arming scenes, just before a warrior enters into battle (cf., e.g., 3.337), and is normally followed by a description of the terrifying plume: δεινὸν δὲ λόφος καθύπερθεν ἔνευεν. 'The normal continuation is suppressed here because the horse-tail crest has already figured when its movement frightens Astyanax' (Macleod 1982: 42): the adjective looks back, in ring composition, to 469–70n. – but also anticipates Hector's return to the battlefield. The creative adaptation of traditional formulae captures Hector's situation: he is now fully armed and ready to fight but is still looking back at Andromache, rather than moving forward: 496n., and 515–16n. ἄλοχος . . . βεβήκει echoes 394n., in ring composition; it also echoes the last speech: Hector's 'dear wife' (482–3n.) does what he asked her to do (490n.). The phrasing is traditional, cf. *Od.* 1.360 = 21.354, 23.292, etc.

496 After a plain and traditional line, the poet continues with an arresting word in enjambment. ἐντροπαλιζομένη 'turning back again and again' (τροπέω/τρέπω); see Risch 1974: 300 for the formation in -αλίζω; the verb otherwise belongs to battlefield narratives, where it describes retreats that are particularly reluctant or costly: 11.544–57, 17.106–13 and 21.490–6. The participle takes up the first half of the line, up to the main caesura, and becomes all the more striking as a result, cf., e.g., προπροκυλινδόμενος at 22.221 and *Od.* 17.525. One implication must be that Hector is still there, looking at Andromache (Edwards 1987: 212); the poet later confirms this: 515–16n. (στρέψεσθ᾽ ἐκ χώρης), cf. Introduction 2.6. On Mandelstam's reflection on this line, see Introduction 5. θαλερὸν κατὰ δάκρυ χέουσα ~ 24.9,

Od. 4.556, 10.201, etc. For Andromache's tears, cf. 405n.; for the meaning of θαλερόν, cf. 430n. (θαλερὸς παρακοίτης).

497 = 370n., in ring composition: Hector went home while Andromache was outside; now she returns home while he is about to leave for the battlefield.

498 Ἕκτορος ἀνδροφόνοιο: the epithet *ἀνδροφόνος is used pointedly in the *Iliad* (Schein 1984: 125, n. 30; Friedrich 2007: 104–6): it most frequently characterises Hector, especially at the end of the line, where it competes with the metrically equivalent but more neutral ἱππόδαμος: the emphasis is either on the threat he poses to the Achaeans (1.242, 9.351, 16.840, 17.616, 638 and 18.149) or on the Trojans' loss when he dies (24.509 and 724). Both aspects are relevant here.　κιχήσατο δ᾽ ἔνδοθι πολλάς ∼ *Od.* 6.51; cf. *Il.* 4.385 and 22.226. Andromache immediately gets hold of her many servants (on the verb, cf. 228n. κιχείω); contrast Hector's uncertain movements and questions at 369–91n.　ἔνδοθι 'inside', with adverbial suffix -θι; cf. οἴκοθι, ῾in the house' (e.g. 8.513), ἄλλοθι, 'elsewhere' (e.g. *Od.* 16.44).

499 τῇσιν … ἐνῶρσεν 'and roused up lamentation in them all'. We expect Andromache to set her servants to work (491–2n.): this line comes as a surprise, and shows – again – that Andromache shares the full extent of her despair with the other women in the house: cf. 381–9n. and Introduction 3.2.　γόον takes up 373n. in ring composition, but now the set-up resembles closely the arrangement at Hector's funeral: a γόος is a lament uttered by a female relative of the deceased, which inspires a collective wailing; cf. 24.723 and 746; 747 and 760; 761 and 776; see Ferrari 1986: 59–69; Murnaghan 1999; and Alexiou 2002, esp. 11–14.　ἐνῶρσεν: cf. the common ὑφ᾽ ἵμερον ὦρσε γόοιο and similar phrases. ἐνόρνυμι tends to describe the effect of gods on mortals, though it is also used of Idomeneus and Hector on a rampage (13.362 and 15.62 respectively), and of a singer instilling a desire for song and dance (*Od* 23.144). The effect of Andromache's grief on her maids is overwhelming.

500 A devastating line, memorable and detailed. At its heart is a paradox, expressed by the assonant ζωὸν γόον. Hector urged Andromache not to abandon herself to grief (486n.) and earlier told all the women of Troy to pray, i.e. behave constructively (237–41n.). Excessive grief is crippling and, as Paris pointed out, impairs the ability to do one's duty (336n.); that those closest to Hector should now lament him as if he was dead is terrible, but also understandable: 494–502n.　αἳ μέν adds new detail and prepares us for a change of scene; cf. 312–13n. (αἳ μέν).　ἔτι: an ominous qualification, repeated again in the next line.　γόον: 3rd pers. plur. imp. or aor. of γοάω, 'lament'; the form is unique and difficult to explain in purely grammatical terms; for discussion, see Leumann 1950: 186–7; and Frisk 1960: 317. Chantraine 1948–53: vol. i, 392 may be right in suggesting that γόον was derived from the noun γόος (cf. ἔκτυπε > κτύπος); what is clear is that the form echoes γόον at 499n., and ζωόν at 500; cf. the unusual γηρὰς … ἐγήρα at 17.197. For difficult forms characterised by assonance, see Hackstein 2002: 115–16 and 2007.　ὧι ἐνὶ οἴκωι: frequent at the end of the line, and always emphatic; e.g. 8.284 (raising an illegitimate child in one's own home), *Od.* 23.153–4 (Odysseus being finally washed and anointed 'in his own house'), 9.478 (the Cyclops eating his visitors 'in his own home'), etc. The phrase draws attention to Hector's plight: he is still fighting but is already considered dead in his own home.

501–2 pick up 367–8n., in ring composition: Hector feared he would never see his own family again; see Di Benedetto 1998: 272–3. Andromache and her maids seem certain that he will not – but eventually will start to hope again: 22.442–4. Hector does in fact return to Troy one more time, though the poet does not emphasise this: see Introduction 4.4 n. 136.   οὐ... ἔτ'... ἵξεσθαι 'they were convinced he was no longer going to come back'.

501 μιν: cf. 176n.   ἔτ': cf. 500n. (ἔτι).   ἔφαντο is otherwise used of false hopes or promises: 12.125–7, 17.377–80, *Od.* 1.194–5, 4.638–40, 13.211–12; and (dramatically) *Hom. Hymn* 7.11–14; cf., e.g., ἐφάμην at *Il.* 3.366, and contrast 488n. (φημί). In the present context, all hope has already been shattered.   ὑπότροπον: only here and at 367n. For the hiatus after main caesura (ἔφαντο ‖ ὑπότροπον), cf. 8n.

502 ~ 7.309.   ἵξεσθαι: cf. 367n.   προφυγόντα... Ἀχαιῶν: the compound προφυγεῖν (only aor.) is used of narrow or unlikely escapes: cf., e.g., 11.339–42, 14.81. For another expressive compound, cf. 57n. (ὑπεκφύγοι).   μένος καὶ χεῖρας Ἀχαιῶν = 13.105. The phrase is a rare variant of the frequent μένος καὶ χεῖρας ἀάπτους (7.309, 12.166, etc.); experienced listeners are likely to have thought of ἀάπτους in this context and considered the hands of the Achaeans 'inescapable', or 'invincible', also here.

503–29: HECTOR AND PARIS MEET BEFORE
ENTERING BATTLE

Hector has been watching, rooted to the spot, as Andromache leaves (496n., 515–16n.); Paris catches up with him and immediately takes the opportunity to draw attention to his own speed (517–19n.). The poet compares Paris to a horse that has broken free from its manger (506–11n.): the image effectively contrasts the duty-bound Hector with his blindingly beautiful, unfettered brother. Just as the horse's instinct leads him out of the stable and into the open, so Paris finally leaves his bedroom and rushes towards the battlefield, where he should have been all along. His attitude has an immediate effect on Hector too, who now acknowledges Paris' prowess and then briefly mentions his own pain when others deny it; he then quickly shakes off that thought and ends on a wildly optimistic note: 520–9n. After the long and anguished encounter between Hector and Andromache, the narrative gathers momentum in this section. The brief conversation between the two brothers does not slow the action, even if Paris is – as ever – warped and self-important, and Hector can only snap out of his painful sense of responsibility by entertaining wild hopes for the future. The fast pace carries on into the next book: 7.1–7.

503 After Hector and Andromache parted, the narrative followed Andromache (494–502n.), and now we might expect a sentence about Hector; but Paris suddenly appears. Hector remains in the background and we are left to wonder how he copes with the swift transition from talking to his tearful wife to dealing with his jubilant brother (καγχαλόων: 514n.); his feelings can partly be inferred from the way in which others relate to him, cf. 340–1n. and 496n.   οὐδὲ... δήθυνεν suggests that Paris started to get ready as soon as Hector left (363n., 364n.): for Homer's treatment of simultaneous action, see Introduction 1.   οὐδέ, as often, marks an abrupt change of scene.   Πάρις: cf. 280n.   ἐν ὑψηλοῖσι δόμοισιν: cf. 24.281, *Od.* 7.131, etc. Here the phrase recalls the earlier description of Paris' beautiful palace on the acropolis (312–17n.); and points forward to 512, where the poet describes Paris running κατὰ Περγάμου ἄκρης towards the gates and the plain.

504 The line briefly confirms that Paris armed himself, while Hector talked to Andromache. After an arming scene, the warrior usually enjoys an *aristeia*: here Paris' arming is reported only *en passant*, and no *aristeia* follows.   ὅ γ': cf. 474n.   ἐπεί: a brisk subclause brings up a second strand in the story (cf. 505, ἔπειτα); the two are then joined up with αἶψα δ' ἔπειτα (514n.).   κατέδυ κλυτὰ τεύχεα ποικίλα χαλκῶι: the phrase combines two distinct traditional expressions, one associated with arming scenes (κλυτὰ τεύχεα δύω etc.); the other with the moment in battle when a warrior falls wounded to the ground (ἀμφὶ δέ μιν βράχε τεύχεα ποικίλα χαλκῶι; cf. 12.396, 13.181 and 14.420). Paris' weapons are again prominent (cf. 321–2n.) and impressed ancient readers: one manuscript reads κλυτὰ τεύχεα παμφανόωντα as at 18.144 (of Achilles' weapons).

505 The line suggests a sense of confidence, and self-satisfaction; cf. ΣbT *ad* 6.505: ἑαυτῶι πρόεισι ἀρέσκων ('he goes forth pleased with himself').   σεύατ' 'he sped' (aor. middle).   ἔπειτ': cf. 504n. (ἐπεί).   ποσὶ κραιπνοῖσι πεποιθώς: the only exact parallel is 22.138 (Achilles chases Hector); for similar expressions, cf. *Cypria* fr. 16 West and the passages listed at *LfgrE* s.v. πείθω, πιθήσ- Β 1 c α. Paris resembles 'swift-footed' Achilles (423n.) in this passage, cf. 512–14n., though the similarities are limited to his appearance. There is a sense that this sudden show of bravado is precisely that: a show.

506–11 = 15.263–8, ancient readers, and some modern scholars too, tried to establish whether this simile belongs here or in book 15 (of Hector) but, as Janko 1994: 256 points out, it suits both contexts – as do other repeated similes in the *Iliad*; cf. Scott 1974: 127–40; Beye 1984, esp. 10–11; and Di Benedetto 1998: 148–51. Just as the horse, after taking his fill at the manger, breaks free from his shackle and returns to his natural habitat, so Paris finally leaves Helen's bedroom, after having had sex with her, and re-enters the battlefield; cf. ΣbT *ad* 6.507*a*: δεσμὸς Ἀλεξάνδρου ἡ Ἑλένη ('Helen was Alexandros' fetter'). Homeric similes often describe the natural world (Fränkel 1921; Edwards 1991: 34–7; Buxton 2004: 145–6); horse similes typically mark a warrior's return to battle, as at 22.22–4 (Krischer 1971: 41–3). For further discussion of Homeric similes and their functions, see, e.g., Moulton 1977, Lonsdale 1990, Erbse 2000, Nannini 2003 and Danek 2006b; for detailed interpretations of this simile, see Fränkel 1921: 77–8; and Fagan 2001: 102–13. Stylistically, the many runover lines imitate, at the level of syntax and metre, the galloping rhythm of the horse. For the unusual vocabulary and grammar, see 506n. (στατός, ἀκοστήσας ἐπὶ φάτνηι), 507n. (κροαίνων), 509–11n.; 509n. (ὑψοῦ δὲ κάρη ἔχει), 510n. (ὃ δ' ἀγλαΐηφι πεποιθώς), 511n. (ῥίμφά ἑ γοῦνα φέρει), with Introduction 2.4 and Chantraine 1948–53: vol. 11,

356. The simile was much admired in antiquity: Apollonius 3.1259–61; Ennius fr. sed. inc. lxxxii = 535–9 Skutsch; and Virg. *Aen.* 11.492–7; with Williams 1968: 695–6 and 732–3; von Albrecht 1969; Wülfing-von Martitz 1972: 267–70; and Skutsch 1985: 683–5.

506 στατός 'kept in a stable'; only here and at 15.263. The exact meaning of this rare word was debated in antiquity; it derives from ἵστημι and helps to depict a static tableau, before the sudden escape of the horse.   ἀκοστήσας ἐπὶ φάτνηι 'having had its fill at the manger' (< ἀκοστή, 'barley'). ἀκοστήσας is used only here (= 15.263): Ennius fr. sed. inc. lxxxii.1 = 535 Skutsch translated it as *fartus* ('sated'). Other ancient readers speculated that it punned on ἄκος ('remedy') and στάσις; or even on ἄχος (the horse is, quite literally, 'fed up'). See *LfgrE* s.v. ἀκοστῆσαι Σχ; and Schlunk 1974: 26–7.

507 A sharp change of tone and pace replicates, within the simile, the transition from the protracted encounter between Helen and Paris (and between Hector and Andromache) to the sudden release of the two brothers into the battlefield; cf. 503–29n. Animals in the Homeric similes are not usually under the control of human beings, and when they are, they may display a will of their own, as here; cf. 11.558–62 (a stubborn donkey), and 20.403–5 (a bull that needs to be dragged to the altar), with Graziosi and Haubold 2005: 87–8.   δεσμὸν ἀπορρήξας: the runover drastically changes the direction of the narrative. δεσμός (literally 'shackles, chains') suggests imprisonment; ἀπόρρηξας points to a rare and exhilarating escape.   θείηι: 3rd pers. sing. pres. subj. of θέω, 'run'.   πεδίοιο 'across the plain'; for the genitive see 2n.   κροαίνων 'stamping'; another rare and obscure word: only here and at 15.264. Ancient readers gave the following explanations: (1) 'beating with his feet' (ἐπικροτῶν/ἐπικρούων τοῖς ποσίν), cf. 5.503–4; Hes. *Sc.* 61–3, etc. This is the modern explanation too; cf. Chantraine 1999 s.v. κρούω. (2) 'neighing' (χρεμετίζων). (3) 'longing for' (ἐπιθυμῶν), which allegedly goes back to Archilochus; cf. ΣAbTD *ad* 6.507; Schlunk 1974: 27. In his reworking of the simile at *Arg.* 3.1260 Apollonius combines 'stamping' (1) and 'neighing' (2); Ennius and Virgil focus on the horse's 'spirit' (3); and Virgil's horse neighs too (2): *Aen.* 11.496.

508 The horse's natural habitat is the open countryside, not the stable (Fagan 2001: 110); similarly, Paris and Hector were out of place inside the city.   εἰωθώς 'used to', from ἔωθα, the initial epsilon is lengthened to fit the metre; for εɩ = *ē*, cf. 113n. (βείω).   λούεσθαι . . . ποταμοῖο 'to bathe in the river'. Epic λούομαι usually takes the dative, except for rivers, which are in the genitive (e.g. 5.6; cf. *Od.* 6.216: λοῦσθαι ποταμοῖο ῥοῆισι). Horses do not usually 'have baths': the verb λούω is used of people washing horses; cf. 23.282. At *Aen.* 11.495 Virgil has *perfundi* (rather than *lauari*), which is appropriate for animals (Varro, *Rust.* 1.13.3 *boues . . . perfunduntur*).   ἐϋρρεῖος ποταμοῖο (< ἐϋρρεής, cf. ἐϋρρείτης, -ρροος) is formulaic in this position; Virgil has *flumine noto* (cf. 511n. ἤθεα καὶ νομόν), which is more sensitive to context.

509–11 The description starts with the horse's head (509), then moves down to his shoulders (510) and finally his knees (511); swiftness is the main point of comparison with Paris, who is running fast (512–14n.), but beauty is important too. Some ancient readers saw the mane as a source of pride for the horse and drew a parallel with Paris' hair: ΣbT *ad* 6.509; with Schlunk 1974: 27–8. The grammatical subject changes frequently in these lines (the horse: 509; the mane: 509–10; the horse again: 510; its knees: 511). The sequence culminates in an expressive break in the syntax at 510–11, which parallels the unencumbered movement of the horse: Kirk 1990: 226.

509 κυδιόων 'rejoicing', 'glorying' (< κῦδος; cf. 124n. (κυδιανείρῃ), 204n. (κυδαλί-μοισι)). A rare verb, mostly used in the participle at the beginning of a runover line, as here: 2.579, 15.266; Hes. *Sc.* 27. It describes a sense of pleasure, esp. about one's own superiority over others; cf. 2.579–80 and 21.519. The word is characteristic of gods and human beings rather than animals (*LfgrE* s.v. κυδιάω); here it suggests that Paris is well pleased with himself (cf. ΣbT quoted at 505n. and καγχαλόων at 514n.).   ὑψοῦ δὲ κάρη ἔχει: a sign of high spirits; contrast the grieving horses at 17.437 and 23.283–4. As often in Homeric similes, an initial subjunctive marks the comparison as hypothetical, while vivid parenthetic descriptions follow in the indicative; see Chantraine 1948–53: vol. II, 355–6.   ἀμφὶ δὲ χαῖται: ἀμφί is typically used as an adverb with parts of the body (Chantraine 1948–53: vol. II, 86; and Fritz 2005: 73–6), though here it can also be construed as a preposition with ὤμοις (510n.).

510 From the horse's head we move down to its shoulders.   ὤμοις: the dative can be construed with ἀμφί but can also stand on its own, as a locative; cf. 509n., Chantraine 1948–53: vol. II, 84.   ἀΐσσονται: the mane lit. 'darts' on either side, i.e. flows in the wind; the middle forms of ἀΐσσω tend to refer to the swift movement of body parts, as here. At *Aen.* 11.496 Virgil uses *emicat*, a close equivalent of Greek ἀΐσσω, of the whole horse rather than its mane.   ὃ δ' ἀγλαΐηφι πεποιθώς 'confident in his splendour', cf. Paris at 505n.: ποσὶ κραιπνοῖσι πεποιθώς. Paris, like the horse, is beautiful and fast. The word ἀγλαΐη is rare in the *Iliad* (only here and at 15.267); though more common in the *Odyssey*, where it occurs only in character speech, conveying a subjective impression of beauty and well-being: e.g. *Od.* 15.78 (also in conjunction with κῦδος, as here), 17.244 (of a self-satisfied man), 18.180–1, 19.81–2 (of women), *Od.* 17.309–10 (of a dog). The rare verb ἀγλαΐζεσθαι is associated with horses at *Il.* 10.329–31. The old ending -φι can be used as a dative or a genitive, singular or plural. Here it serves as a metrically distinct alternative to the dative singular in -ῃ; cf. Chantraine 1948–53: vol. I, 237; Ruijgh 1995: 72.

511 The description of the horse climaxes with this entirely dactylic, 'galloping' line: Kirk 1990: 226.   ῥίμφά ἑ γοῦνα φέρει: the phrase poses two problems, one semantic, one grammatical. (1) the expression 'swiftly his knees carry him' is unusual: knees are not otherwise said to carry or convey anyone in Greek epic. (2) the nomina-tive participle πεποιθώς in 510 made us expect the horse to be the subject of the main verb, but in fact the horse is the object. Zenodotus tried to address both difficulties by reading ῥίμφ' ἑά, which makes matters worse. In fact, there is no problem: (1) is easily solved if we compare the new Cologne Papyrus of Sappho, line 13, γόνα δ' οὐ φέροισι (see Gronewald and Daniel 2004: 5 and 7). What we evidently have here is an expressive variation on the common πόδες φέρον; cf. 514n. below. Problem (2) exemplifies the malleability of Homeric syntax, where abrupt changes of subject reflect the structures of the spoken language; cf. Slings 1992: 96–101, with detailed discussion of 6.510–11. Here, however, the loose syntax seems stylistically motivated, rather than simply a matter of spoken language (see Chantraine 1948–53: vol. ΙΙ, 356; and Kirk 1990: 226). Ennius' *fert sese*, which is correct Latin, stems from a creative misunderstanding of φέρει ἑ; cf. Eustathius II, p. 377: 8–9 van der Valk. For the accentuation of ῥίμφά ἑ, cf. 251n. (ἔνθα).   ἤθεα καὶ νομόν 'the familiar pastures'. In epic, ἤθεα often means 'dwelling place'; it thus suggests that the horse is returning to where he belongs; cf. Virgil's *flumine noto* at *Aen.* 11.495.   ἵππων: mares, according to Virgil (*Aen.* 11.494), who perhaps takes inspiration from Homer's analogy between Paris, the womaniser, and the horse. Homeric ἵππος can be either masculine or feminine.

512–14 Paris' shining appearance evokes images of Achilles at the height of his powers, shortly before he kills Hector: see 505n. (ποσὶ κραιπνοῖσι πεποιθώς), and 513n. Paris' own approach to Hector in the next lines, however, reveals his vanity and insecurity: there is a sharp contrast between Paris' appearance and his words at 517–19n; cf. the depiction of Helen in this book: she looks like the perfect wife (323n., 324n., with 318–24n.) but does not talk like one (337–9n. and 349–53n.).

512 ὥς picks up ὥς at 506; cf. 149 with 146n.   υἱὸς Πριάμοιο: the only time in the *Iliad* that Paris is honoured with this epithet; contrast, e.g., 12.93–5. Now that Paris is ready to fight, the poet emphasises his connection to Priam, and to his brother Hector, cf. ἀδελφεόν at 515–16n., and see also 76n. (Πριαμίδης); earlier in the book Paris seemed hateful and isolated from the rest of his family (see esp. 280–5n.).   κατὰ Περγάμου ἄκρης: Pergamos is the name of the Trojan acropolis, where Paris had his house built: 317n. (ἐν πόλει ἄκρηι). It is rare in Homer and tends to be associated with Priam and his family, as here, or with Apollo. For further discussion, see Stoevesandt 2008: 159.

513 ~ 19.398, of Achilles: 512–14n. The main verb, in necessary enjambment, is further postponed by a participle phrase and by another short simile. The effect is ebullient: it suggests sparkling beauty and barely contained high spirits.   τεύχεσι παμφαίνων: shining Hector took off his gleaming helmet in order to reassure his son (472–3n.). Now Paris' appearance helps to restore the impression of brilliance that characterises the heroes, cf. 31n. (δῖος) and Introduction 2.6.   ὥς τ᾽: another simile, introduced by the generalising epic τε; cf. 127n.   ἠλέκτωρ: epithet of the sun at 19.398 and *Hom. Hymn* 3.369; its precise meaning was debated also in antiquity, cf. ΣD *ad* 6.513. It is clearly related to ἤλεκτρον, 'amber', possibly understood as 'sun drops': *LfgrE* s.v. ἤλεκτρον. The parallels at 19.398 and *Hom. Hymn* 3.369 suggest power as well as brilliance.   ἐβεβήκει: cf. 312–13n.

514 καγχαλόων 'exulting' takes up κυδιόων at 509n., in the same metrical position. This unusual verb normally expresses triumphant joy at a victory (e.g. 10.565, *Od.* 23.1, etc.); here it seems a little premature. For the diectasis (-όων) see 148n. (πηλεθόωσα).   ταχέες δὲ πόδες φέρον: a variant of common πόδες φέρον, in the same metrical position. The phrase, even without ταχέες, suggests swiftness: 13.515 (ῥίμφα), 15.405 with 402 (σπεύσομαι), 17.700 with 691 and 698 (αἶψ᾽ . . . θέων, βῆ δὲ θέειν), etc.   αἶψα δ' ἔπειτα: as in the formula αἶψα δ' ἔπειθ' ἵκανε (370n.), the three words introduce a swift arrival.

515–16 This is the only explicit reference to the encounter between Hector and Andromache in the *Iliad*, and it marks a change of tone in the main narrative. The perspective is now that of men who are about to face death on the battlefield: to them, the encounter between Hector and Andromache is 'love talk'; see Introduction 5.   ἐτέτμεν: 374n.   ἀδελφεόν after the main verb, and the main caesura, gives the traditional Ἕκτορα δῖον a more personal inflection. Hector goes on to tell Paris how hard it is to be his brother: 523–4n.   εὗτ' ἄρ ἔμελλε picks up ἔμελλε at 393n.: the verb frames, in ring composition, the drawn-out, painful encounter between Hector and Andromache. The particle ἄρ (2n.) draws attention to the sudden encounter between the two brothers.   στρέψεσθ' ἐκ χώρης ὅθι 'to turn from the place where'; cf. *LfgrE* s.v. στρέφω B I 2 b α; the closest parallel is *Od.* 16.352. Hector was looking at Andromache when she left (496n.) and now is still facing in the direction of the city. After moving quickly for most of book 6, in order to return to the battle, he now seems painfully still; Paris, by contrast, is galloping towards the plain.   ὀάριζε γυναικί describes an intimate conversation; see esp. 22.126–8 (Hector realises he cannot sweet-talk Achilles; for the relationship between that passage and the present line, see N. J. Richardson 1993: 120); cf. 13.291 and 17.228, where – in the context of battle exhortation – references to ὀαριστύς seem grimly sarcastic; for further discussion: Loraux 1995: 81; and Van Nortwick 2001, esp. 221–2 and 233–4. The focus is now exclusively on the couple (the baby and the nurse do not feature); and this highlights Hector's delicate position.

517–19 At 341n. Paris boasted that he would catch up with Hector. Now, as he runs towards the Gates and sees his brother – seemingly idle, and facing towards him (515–6n.), he states that, surely, he has made Hector wait. The tone of this remark is difficult to gauge and was debated also in antiquity: ancient readers thought that Paris was disingenuously asking a question: 518n. (ἦ μάλα δή). Although his speech is, formally, a statement, Paris may be indirectly asking for a compliment. He thus comes across simultaneously as self-defeating and boastful, insensitive towards Hector and afraid of him.

517 The fact that Paris now speaks first confirms that he has caught Hector at a difficult moment: 122n.   τόν: cf. 9n.   Ἀλέξανδρος θεοειδής: cf. 290n. The formula, like the simile at 503–14, draws attention to Paris' beauty – and hence to his devastating role in the downfall of Troy.

518 Paris now claims he is holding up Hector, in his impetus to return to the battlefield. In fact, the immediate context suggests the reverse: Paris is running towards the battlefield but now stops in order to talk to Hector.   ἠθεῖ' is generally used to address an older brother, or somebody senior, with the intention to help: cf., e.g., 10.37–41 (Menelaos to Agamemnon); 23.94–6 (Achilles to Patroclus); Hes. *Sc.* 103–14 (Iolaos to Heracles); 22.229–31 (Athena, disguised as Hector's favourite brother Deiphobos); for discussion see Bettini 1988.   ἦ μάλα δή: the exact force of this expression is unclear, but cf. 255n., where it also introduces a supposition that is in some way problematic for the speaker, and the addressee; translate: 'I assume', 'surely'. ΣAbT *ad* 6.518*c* claim that ἦ is interrogative: 'Did I make you wait?' The expression ἦ μάλα δή, however, does not introduce a question anywhere else in Homer.   **καὶ ἐσσύμενον** 'even though you are rushing forward'. This statement seems disingenuous: Hector did leave his own home in a rush (390n.: ἀπέσσυτο), but he is now standing still, in the place where he met Andromache (515–16n.).   **κατερύκω:** all the people Hector encountered in the city tried to hold him back (258n., 340n., 354n., 431n.), but this is not the case now.

519   δηθύνων: Paris flatly contradicts the poet's assertion that he wasted no time in getting ready: 503n. His own words thus seem insincere or insecure and designed to elicit a compliment: 520–9n.   **οὐδ'. . . ἐκέλευες:** Paris did actually follow Hector's commands.   **ἐναίσιμον:** adverbial, 'at the right time'. The adjective is not otherwise used as an adverb, nor does it normally refer to time; ἐναίσιμος generally implies a judgement about what is 'according to fate' (cf. 62n.), and hence just and proper (cf., e.g., 2.353, where it is used of signs from the gods; and 24.40, where it characterises basic human decency). Paris judges his own timely arrival as a matter of great significance. Hector responds by using the same word, ἐναίσιμος, in order to describe an objective judge of his brother's character: 521n.

520–9   Hector immediately responds to the main thrust of Paris' speech (517–19n.) and pays him a compliment: any fair and objective man would agree that Paris is brave (522n.). This is a surprising statement, and Hector immediately qualifies it (523n.) – and then remembers his own anguish when the Trojans criticise Paris (524–5n.). Hector is concerned with what others say and think, and he lets their opinions shape his own response; cf. the τις-speeches embedded in his own earlier statements at 460–1n., and 479n. Now he suggests a contrast between what an objective judge of Paris' abilities might say, and what the Trojans actually say about him: it is down to Paris to confirm one opinion or the other (523n.). Hector also lets his brother know that he too faces a dilemma, for he understands the soldiers who risk their lives for Paris but also feels loyal to his own brother: 524–5n. He then moves swiftly on: ἀλλ' ἴομεν (526n.); any difficulties can be solved later – if Zeus grants them victory, and a chance to celebrate together ἐν μεγάροισιν (528n.). Structurally, this speech echoes Hector's earlier address to Paris (325–31n.), in ring composition: both start with δαιμόνι' (326n., 521n.), emphasise the plight of the Trojans (327n., 524–5n.) and press for swift action (331n., 526n.). The final images, however, are different: at 331n. Hector describes Troy going up in flames; whereas now he holds on to an image of victory, and peace. He needs hope in order to face the enemy: 526–9n. Hector's speech ends the book; unusually, the speech-concluding line starts the next book; no parallels in the *Iliad*, but cf. *Od.* 8.586–9.1, 12.453–13.1. On book division, see further Introduction 3.

520   One of the most common speech introductions in epic; see M. Parry 1971: 15–16. Here it presents Hector's speech as a neutral response; for a similar effect, cf. 359n.   **ἀπαμειβόμενος** 'in reply'. The compound form ἀπό + ἀμείβομαι ('exchange') is only used of speech.

521 δαιμόνι᾽: Hector used the same word when he addressed Paris in his previous speech; for discussion, cf. 326n. The expression δαιμόνι᾽ οὐ . . . seems to have formulaic integrity in itself: 2.190, 6.326, *Od.* 18.15, 23.174.   ἄν: the particle with the optative does not describe a remote or general possibility, but rather someone's ability to express a positive view of Paris: Willmott 2007: 138–40.   τις: cf. 520–9n.   ὃς ἐναίσιμος εἴη: Hector responds to Paris' own use of the word (519n.) and corrects it.

522 ἔργον ἀτιμήσειε μάχης: the verb ἀτιμάω/ἀτιμάζω usually takes the person that is slighted in the accusative; but there are parallels for Hector's impersonal, more tactful, phrasing: cf. μῦθον ἀτιμήσει᾽/ἀτιμήσαιτε at 9.62 and 14.127. For the manly expression 'war work', cf., e.g., μέγα ἔργον Ἄρηος at 11.734, and φυλόπιδος μέγα ἔργον at 16.208. The phrase πολεμήϊα ἔργα and related expressions are often used to describe characters who are not suitable for war: e.g. 2.338 (boys), 5.428 (Aphrodite), 7.236 (a woman), 11.719 (a young man), 13.730–4 (men with other talents).   ἄλκιμός ἐσσι 'you are brave' (< ἀλκή; cf. 112n.). Hector's claim is at best controversial. Several characters, in the course of the poem, claim the opposite, including Hector himself at 3.45; cf. also Helen's assessment at 3.428–36. The spear is the only weapon that takes the adjective ἄλκιμος (3.338, 10.135 = 14.12 etc.), and Paris has damaged his when fighting against Menelaos: 322n.

523 Hector now explains his previous claim: Paris does not have the will to fight. This is an attempt to hold Paris accountable for his past behaviour (cf. 328–9n.) but Hector does not linger on that point now, also because Paris seems, for once, ready to fight. At 3.38–75 Hector criticises his brother harshly and at length, and Paris resists and corrects his remarks; for the difficulties of holding Paris responsible for his actions, see also 7.347–79 and 13.769–88.   ἑκὼν μεθίεις echoes μεθιέντα at 330n., but with an emphasis on choice (e.g. 23.585, *Od.* 2.132–7; Hes. *Theog.* 232 and *Op.* 282–5). The expression is almost paradoxical: it describes wilful neglect; cf. 13.232–4, *Od.* 4.371–4.   οὐκ ἐθέλεις: at 281–2n. Hector ardently hoped that Paris would 'want' to listen to him (αἴ κ᾽ ἐθέλῃσ᾽ εἰπόντος ἀκουέμεν), at 336n. Paris revealed that he stayed away from battle because he 'wanted' to abandon himself to grief (ἔθελον δ᾽ ἄχεϊ προτραπέσθαι). Now Hector again emphasises that everything depends on what Paris wants.   τὸ δ᾽ ἐμὸν κῆρ marks a shift of focus to the speaker's own emotions; cf. the related phrase αὐτὰρ ἐμὸν κῆρ at 19.319, *Od.* 4.259; cf. also *Od.* 9.459. The basic meaning of κῆρ is 'heart' (cf. Cheyns 1985: 29–42 and 67–73; Sullivan 1996; and Clarke 1999: 53–4, 74, 79).

524–5 The scholia bT *ad* 6.523–4 rightly point out that Hector has recently been criticised for the behaviour of his brothers (see 5.473–6) and more generally assume that he feels obliged to defend Paris. For Hector's feelings of frustrated loyalty, and powerlessness in relation to Paris, see esp. 280–5n.   ἄχνυται ἐν θυμῶι: the verb ἄχνυμαι/ἄχομαι/ἀκαχίζω/ἀχέω/ἀχεύω (< ἄχος; cf. 336n., 486n.; Mawet 1979: 330–49) is typically used together with the noun θυμός (51n.), or with a word denoting the 'heart' (κῆρ, κραδίη, ἦτορ). Here Hector refers to both his spirit and his heart, emphasising his great distress; for the heart being located in the θυμός, see Jahn 1987: 17–18.   ὑπὲρ σέθεν 'for your sake', 'on your behalf'. Hector does not simply hear 'about' Paris (περί); he suffers because of him; cf. Chantraine 1948–53: vol. II, 137. The old separative ending -θεν is treated as a genitive: 62n. (ἔθεν).   αἴσχε᾽: 351n.   πρὸς Τρώων: the addition, in progressive enjambment, draws attention to Hector's complicated relationship with the Trojans; cf. 361n., 362n., as well as 441–6n. and 442n. For πρός + genitive, see 57n.   οἵ . . . σεῖο: this remark echoes 328–9n., but – as the scholia T *ad* 6.525 point out – Hector now pleads for understanding.   πόνον: cf. 77n. The present passage shows that, Aristarchus' theory notwithstanding, πόνος does have connotations of suffering in Homer.

526–9 Hector now briskly turns to action and dismisses his previous concerns: his final image of future peace is in stark contrast with the present reality. (The city and the halls are now the domain of women: Introduction 3.3.) It also contradicts Hector's earlier visions of the future, esp. 447–9n., but Hector now insists that he does not know what will happen (αἴ κέ ποθι Ζεύς: 526n.; cf. οὐ γάρ τ᾽ οἶδ᾽: 367n.), and his predictions are in part designed to make the present bearable; cf. his prayer at 475–81n. and 22.226–53, esp. 253, where Hector needs to believe in the possibility of victory in order to stop running away from Achilles.

526 ~ 4.362; cf. *Od.* 22.55. The parallels suggest that Hector comes close to apologising.   ἀλλ᾽ ἴομεν: formulaic in this position; cf. 10.126, 251, 11.469, *Od.* 2.404, 10.549 and 24.437 – all of which call for action at the end of a speech. For the subjunctive with short vowel, see 230–1n.   τὰ δ᾽ 'those things'; Hector remains suitably vague: cf. 70n. (καὶ τά) and 441n. (τάδε πάντα).   ἀρεσσόμεθ᾽: future of ἀρέσαι (aorist), 'make amends' (cf. ἀραρίσκω, 'join'); for discussion see Pernée 1988, and Scodel 2008a: 102–3. Hector takes responsibility, though the 1st pers. plur. suggests a certain vagueness (cf. 4.362 but contrast 9.120 ~ 19.138; *Od.* 8.396 and 415).   αἴ κέ ποθι Ζεύς 'if somehow Zeus . . .' The phrase is used of wishes whose fulfilment seems unlikely but not impossible. Homeric πόθι and ποθι correspond to ποῦ = 'where?', and που = 'somewhere, somehow'; and they are clearly used in that sense at *Od.* 1.170 (πόθι) and *Il.* 19.273 (ποθι). LSJ offer the translation 'at some time' for this passage, following early readers who glossed ποθι = ποτε, 'at some point, ever' (ΣD *ad* 1.128); but the temporal emphasis is almost certainly misleading: cf. *LfgrE* s.v. πόθι, ποθι B 2 b. For αἴ κε with the subjunctive see Chantraine 1948–53: vol. II, 211; cf. 94n.

527–9 A very compressed description of a thanksgiving ritual; cf. *Od.* 2.431–2. Hector offers only a fleeting image of victory.

527 δώῃι: cf. 1.129, *Od.* 12.216, 22.253. For forms of διδόναι in prayers and related contexts see 307n., 476.   ἐπουρανίοισι . . . αἰειγενέτῃσι: this unusual phrase, with two weighty epithets, extends Hector's wish into the next line. θεοῖς αἰειγενέτῃσι is formulaic in the context of prayer (3.295–6, 20.104–5), sacrifice (3.295–6 *Od.* 14.446) and libation (*Od.* 2.432), i.e. when the gods are imagined as accessible and beneficial; for the exact meaning of the epithet, which was debated also in antiquity, see *LfgrE* s.v. αἰειγενέτης Σχ and B; translate 'everlasting'. The adjective ἐπουράνιος, which is here displaced from its normal position at the end of the line, describes the gods as awesome, unapproachable beings: it is not used in the context of prayer or sacrifice, but rather when human beings come into conflict with the divine; cf. 128–9n., 131–2n.

and *Od.* 17.484–7. The unique combination of these two epithets may reflect Hector's precarious state of mind, between hope and despair.

528 κρητῆρα: mixing bowls unite the people who draw their drink from them. They are used for many different purposes: 3.295–6 (confirming a truce), 10.578–9 (thanksgiving after a successful expedition), *Od.* 3.393–4 (a drinks party in the house of Nestor), *Od.* 7.179–81 (welcoming a stranger) and 13.49–56 (after-dinner drinks in the house of Alcinous), etc. Hector refused to drink wine or make a libation at 264–8; now he looks forward to a time when he will be able to drink together with the other Trojan men. In the *Iliad* descriptions of mixing bowls are common on the Achaean side, but the only time a κρητήρ features on the Trojan side is when the ill-fated truce between the two sides is sealed: 3.245–8 and 295–6.   στήσασθαι: for 'setting up' a mixing bowl (ἵστημι), cf. 9.202.   ἐλεύθερον: cf. ἐλεύθερον ἦμαρ ἀπούρας (455n.). Here the mixing bowl marks the day on which the Trojans finally celebrate their freedom; see Raaflaub 1981: 191–2.   ἐν μεγάροισιν: the normal place for drinking parties; though in this time of war, the city and its halls are the domain of women: 286–7n., 371n.

529 Hector offers a fleeting image of victory also at 15.497–9, in order to motivate the Trojans to risk their lives.   Τροίης: cf. 207n.   ἐϋκνήμιδας Ἀχαιούς 'well-greaved Achaeans' (< κνημίς, greave; cf., e.g., 3.330); a common noun–epithet phrase in this position; in the *Iliad* the adjective is used exclusively of the Achaeans.

BIBLIOGRAPHY

Adkins, A. W. H. 1960. *Merit and responsibility: a study in Greek values*, Oxford

Albrecht, M. von. 1969. 'Ein Pferdegleichnis bei Ennius', *Hermes* 97: 333–45

Alden, M. J. 1990. 'The Homeric house as poetic creation', in M. Païzi-Apostolopoulou, ed. *Ὁ Ὁμηρικός οἶκος. Ἀπό τά πρακτικά τοῦ Ε' συνεδρίου γιά τήν Ὀδύσσεια (11–14/09/1987)* (Ithaka) 57–67

    1996. 'Genealogy as paradigm: the example of Bellerophon', *Hermes* 124: 257–63

    2000. *Homer beside himself: para-narratives in the Iliad*, Oxford

Alexiou, M. 2002. *The ritual lament in Greek tradition*, 2nd edn rev. by D. Yatromanolakis and P. Roilos, Lanham, MD

Allen, T. W. 1931. *Homeri Ilias*, Oxford

Allen, W. S. 1973. *Accent and rhythm. Prosodic features of Latin and Greek: a study in theory and reconstruction*, Cambridge

Aloni, A. 1986. *Tradizioni arcaiche della Troade e composizione dell'Iliade*, Milan

Alpers, K. 1969. 'Eine Beobachtung zum Nestorbecher von Pithekoussai', *Glotta* 47: 170–4

Andersen, Ø. 1978. *Die Diomedesgestalt in der Ilias*, Oslo

Andronikos, M. 1968. 'Der Totenkult in den Epen', in F. Matz and H.-G. Buchholz, eds. *Archaeologia Homerica*, vol. III, ch. w: *Totenkult* (Göttingen) 1–37

Antonaccio, C. M. 1995. *An archaeology of ancestors: tomb cult and hero cult in ancient Greece*, Lanham, MD

Arend, W. 1933. *Die typischen Scenen bei Homer*, Berlin

Arnould, D. 1990. *Le rire et les larmes dans la littérature grecque d'Homère à Platon*, Paris

    2002. 'Du bon usage du vin chez Homère et dans la poésie archaïque', in J. Jouanna and L. Villard, eds. *Vin et santé en Grèce ancienne: actes du colloque organisé à l'Université de Rouen et à Paris (Université de Paris IV Sorbonne et ENS) par l'UPRESA 8062 du CNRS et l'URLLCA de l'Université de Rouen, 28–30 septembre 1998* (Athens) 7–10

Arthur Katz, M. 1981. 'The divided world of *Iliad* VI', in H. Foley, ed. *Reflections of women in antiquity* (New York) 19–44

Assunção, T. R. 1997. 'Le mythe iliadique de Bellérophon', *GAIA: Revue interdisciplinaire sur la Grèce archaïque* 1: 41–66

Astour, M. C. 1967. *Hellenosemitica: an ethnic and cultural study in West Semitic impact on Mycenaean Greece*, 2nd edn, Leiden

Aura Jorro, F. 1985. *Diccionario Micénico*, vol. I, Madrid

Austin, N. 1994. *Helen of Troy and her shameless phantom*, Ithaca, NY and London

Avery, H. C. 1994. 'Glaucus, a god? *Iliad* Z 128–143', *Hermes* 122: 498–502

Bakker, E. J. 1988. *Linguistics and formulas in Homer: scalarity and the description of the article 'per'*, Amsterdam

    1993. 'Discourse and performance: involvement, visualization and "presence" in Homeric poetry', *Classical Antiquity* 12: 1–29

1997a. *Poetry in speech: orality and Homeric discourse*, Ithaca, NY and London

1997b. 'The study of Homeric discourse', in Morris and Powell 1997: 284–304

2005. *Pointing at the past: from formula to performance in Homeric poetics*, Washington, DC

Bakker, E. and Kahane, A., eds. 1997. *Written voices, spoken signs: tradition, performance, and the epic text*, Cambridge, MA

Baldacci, P. and Roos, G., eds. 2007. *De Chirico*, Padova

Ballof, R. 1914. 'Zu Schillers Gedicht "Hektor's Abschied"', *Euphorion* 21: 298–9

Barchiesi, A. 1998. 'The statue of Athena at Troy and Carthage', in P. Knox and C. Foss, eds. *Style and tradition: studies in honor of Wendell Clausen* (Stuttgart and Leipzig) 130–40

Bartoloni, P. 1995. 'Techniques et sciences', in Krings 1995: 354–61

Basset L. 1989. *La syntaxe de l'imaginaire. Étude des modes et des negations dans l'Iliade et l'Odyssée*, Lyon and Paris

Bassett, S. E. 1934. 'The omission of the vocative in Homeric speeches', *American Journal of Philology* 55: 140–52

Bassi, K. 1997. 'Orality, masculinity, and the Greek epic', *Arethusa* 30: 315–40

Beazley, J. D. 1958. 'Ἑλένης ἀπαίτησις', *Proceedings of the British Academy* 43: 233–44

Beck, D. 2005. *Homeric conversation*, Washington, DC

2008. 'Character-quoted direct speech in the *Iliad*', *Phoenix* 62: 162–83

Bergren, A. L. T. 1975. *The etymology and usage of πεῖραρ in early Greek poetry: a study in the interrelationship of metrics, linguistics and poetics*, New York

1979–80. 'Helen's web: time and tableau in the *Iliad*', *Helios* 7: 19–34 (Reprinted with revisions in Bergren 2008: 43–57)

1983. 'Language and the female in early Greek thought', *Arethusa* 16: 69–95 (Reprinted with revisions in Bergren 2008: 13–40)

2008. *Weaving truth: essays on language and the female in Greek thought*, Washington, DC

Bermingham, A. and Brewer, J., eds. 1995. *The consumption of culture, 1600–1800: image, object, text*, London

Bernsdorff, H. 1992. *Zur Rolle des Aussehens im homerischen Menschenbild*, Göttingen

Bethe, E. 1929. *Homer. Dichtung und Sage*, vol. II, 2nd edn, Leipzig and Berlin

Bettini, M. 1988. 'ΗΘΕΙΟΣ', *Rivista di filologia e di istruzione classica* 116: 154–66

Beye, C. R. 1984. 'Repeated similes in the Homeric poems', in Rigsby 1984: 7–13

Bichler, R. 2007. 'Über die Bedeutung der Zimelien in der Welt der Odyssee', in E. Alram-Stern and G. Nightingale, eds. *Keimelion. Elitenbildung und elitärer Konsum von der mykenischen Palastzeit bis zur homerischen Epoche (Akten des internationalen Kongresses vom 3.–5.2.2005 in Salzburg)* (Vienna) 31–9

Blanc, A. 2007. 'Rhythme et syntaxe dans l'hexamètre. Les datifs pluriels des thèmes sigmatiques', in A. Blanc and E. Dupraz, eds. *Procédés synchroniques de la langue poétique en grec et en latin* (Brussels) 13–26

Block, E. 1982. 'The narrator speaks: apostrophe in Homer and Virgil', *Transactions of the American Philological Association* 112: 7–22

Bloedow, E. F. 2007. 'Homer and the *depas amphikypellon*', in S. P. Morris and R. Laffineur, eds. *Epos. Reconsidering Greek epic and Aegean bronze age archaeology.*

Proceedings of the 11th International Aegean Conference, Los Angeles 20–23/04/2006 (Liège)
87–95 and plates XXII–XXIII

Blok, J. H. 1995. *The early Amazons: modern and ancient perspectives on a persistent myth*,
Leiden

Blum, H. 1998. *Purpur als Statussymbol in der griechischen Welt*, Bonn

Boedeker, D., ed. 1997. *The world of Troy: Homer, Schliemann, and the treasures of Priam*,
Washington, DC

Bohn, W. 1975. 'Apollinaire and de Chirico: the making of the mannequins', *Comparative Literature* 27: 153–65

Boime, A. 1987. *Art in an age of revolution. 1750–1800*, Chicago, IL and London

Bolling, G. M. 1923. 'A peculiarity of Homeric orthography', *Classical Philology* 18:
170–7

1944. *The athetized lines of the Iliad*, Baltimore

Borchhardt, J. 1972. *Homerische Helme. Helmformen der Ägäis in ihren Beziehungen zu orientalischen und europäischen Helmen in der Bronze- und frühen Eisenzeit*, Mainz

1977. 'Helme', in H.-G. Buchholz and J. Wiesner, eds. *Archaeologia Homerica*, vol. I,
ch. E: *Kriegswesen, Teil I: Schutzwaffen und Wehrbauten* (Göttingen) 57–74

Borchmeyer, D. 1972. 'Hektors Abschied. Schillers Aneignung einer homerischen
Szene', *Jahrbuch der Deutschen Schillergesellschaft* 16: 277–98

Bouvier, D. 2002a. *Le sceptre et la lyre. L'Iliade ou les héros de la mémoire*, Grenoble

2002b. 'Présence ou absence d'armes dans les tombes héroïques', in Montanari
2002: 535–45

Bowden, H. 1993. 'Hoplites and Homer: warfare, hero cult and the ideology of the
polis', in J. Rich and G. Shipley, eds. *War and society in the Greek world* (London)
45–63

Brandenburg, H. 1977. 'Μίτρα, ζωστήρ und ζῶμα', in H.-G. Buchholz and
J. Wiesner, eds. *Archaeologia Homerica*, vol. I, ch. E: *Kriegswesen, Teil I: Schutzwaffen
und Wehrbauten* (Göttingen) 119–43

Braswell, B. K. 1988. *A commentary on the fourth Pythian ode of Pindar*, Berlin and New
York

Bremer, D. 1976. *Licht und Dunkel in der frühgriechischen Dichtung. Interpretationen zur
Vorgeschichte der Lichtmetaphysik*, Bonn

Brillante, C. 1996. 'La scrittura in Omero', *Quaderni Urbinati di cultura classica* 52:
31–45

Broccia, G. 1956/7. ' Il posto della Ἕκτορος καὶ Ἀνδρομάχης ὁμιλία nell'*Iliade* e nel
corso della vita eroica di Ettore. Nota sul pensiero della morte nell'*Iliade*', *Atti
della Accademia delle Scienze di Torino, Classe di Scienze morali, storiche e filologiche* 91:
165–203

1963. *Struttura e spirito del libro VI dell'Iliade. Contributo allo studio del problema omerico.
Parte prima: dalle androctasie del preludio alla homilia*, Sapri

1967. *La forma poetica dell'Iliade e la genesi dell'epos omerico*, Messina

Brunius-Nilsson, E. 1955. Δαιμόνιε: *an inquiry into a mode of apostrophe in old Greek literature*,
Uppsala

Bryce, T. R. 1986. *The Lycians: a study of Lycian history and civilisation to the conquest of Alexander the Great*, vol. 1: *The Lycians in literary and epigraphic sources*, Copenhagen
   1992. 'Lukka revisited', *Journal of Near Eastern Studies* 51: 121–30
Burgess, J. S. 2001. *The tradition of the Trojan War in Homer and the epic cycle*, Baltimore, MD
Burkert, W. 1955. *Zum altgriechischen Mitleidsbegriff*, Diss. Erlangen
   1976. 'Das hunderttorige Theben und die Datierung der Ilias', *Wiener Studien* n.s. 10: 5–21
   1985. *Greek religion*, trans. J. Raffan, Cambridge, MA
   1998. 'La cité d'Argos entre la tradition mycénienne, dorienne et homérique', in V. Pirenne-Delforge, ed. *Les Panthéons des cités des origines à la Périégèse de Pausanias. Actes du Colloque organisé à l'Université de Liège du 15 au 17 mai 1997 (2e partie)*, Kernos Supplément 8 (Liège) 47–59 (Reprinted in C. Riedweg, ed. *Walter Burkert. Kleine Schriften I* (Göttingen 2001) 166–77)
Buxton, R. 2004. 'Similes and other likenesses', in R. Fowler, ed. *The Cambridge companion to Homer* (Cambridge) 139–55
Cairns, D. L. 1993. *Aidōs: the psychology and ethics of honour and shame in ancient Greek literature*, Oxford
   ed. 2001. *Oxford readings in Homer's Iliad*, Oxford
Calder III, W. M. 1984. 'Gold for bronze: *Iliad* 6.232–36', in Rigsby 1984: 31–5
Calder III, W. M. and Cobet, J., eds. 1990. *Heinrich Schliemann nach hundert Jahren*, Frankfurt
Calder III, W. M. and Traill, D. A., eds. 1986. *Myth, scandal and history: the Heinrich Schliemann controversy and a first edition of the Mycenaean diary*, Detroit, MI
Cantarella, E. 2009. 'Friendship, love, and marriage', in G. Boys-Stones, B. Graziosi and P. Vasunia, eds. *The Oxford handbook of Hellenic studies* (Oxford) 294–304
Capettini, E. 2007. 'La "vera" Andromaca (Eur. Tro. 731–732)', *Materiali e discussioni per l'analisi dei testi classici* 58: 217–23
Carlier, P. 1984. *La royauté en Grèce avant Alexandre*, Strasbourg and Paris
   2006. 'Ἄναξ and βασιλεύς in the Homeric poems', in S. Deger-Jalkotzy and I. S. Lemos, eds. *Ancient Greece: from the Mycenaean palaces to the age of Homer* (Edinburgh) 101–9
Carrara, P. 1997. 'L'addio ad Andromaca e ad Astianatte nell'*Ettore* di Astidamante', *Prometheus* 23: 215–21
Casabona, J. 1966. *Recherches sur le vocabulaire des sacrifices en grec. Des origines à la fin de l'époque classique*, Aix-en-Provence
Cassio, A. C. 1999. 'Epica greca e scrittura tra VIII e VII seculo a.C.: madrepatria e colonie d'Occidente', in G. Bagnasco Gianni and F. Cordano, eds. *Scritture mediterranee tra il IX e il VII sec. a.C. Atti del seminario. Università degli Studi di Milano, Istituto di Storia Antica, 23–24 febbraio 1998* (Milan) 67–84
   2002. 'Early editions of the Greek epics and Homeric textual criticism', in Montanari 2002: 105–36

2006. 'La Tessaglia, l'isola di Lesbo e i dativi plurali del tipo "epeessi" ', in M. Vetta and C. Catenacci, eds. *I luoghi e la poesia nella Grecia antica. Atti del convegno Università 'G. D'Annunzio' di Chieti-Pescara (20–22 aprile 2004)* (Alessandria) 73–84

Càssola, F. 1975. *Inni omerici*, Milan

Caswell, C. P. 1990. *A study of* thumos *in early Greek epic*, Leiden

Cavafy, C. P. 1992. *Collected poems*, ed. G. Savidis, trans. E. Keeley and P. Sherrard, rev. edn, Princeton, NJ

Caylus, A. C. P. de Tubières, comte de 1757. *Tableaux tirés de l'Iliade, de l'Odyssée, et de l'Enéide*, Paris

Ceccarelli, P. 2002. 'Message épistolaire et message oral au Proche Orient ancien et en Grèce archaïque et classique', in E. Gavoille and L. Nadjo, eds. *Epistulae antiquae II, Actes du IIe colloque international 'Le genre épistolaire antique et ses prolongements européens', Tours, 28–30 septembre 2000* (Louvain and Paris) 11–26

Chadwick, J. 1990. 'The descent of the Greek epic', *Journal of Hellenic Studies* 110: 174–7

1996. *Lexicographica Graeca: contributions to the lexicography of ancient Greek*, Oxford

Chantraine, P. 1937. 'Grec μειλίχιος', *Annuaire de l'Institut de Philologie et d'Histoire Orientales et Slaves de l'Université Libre de Bruxelles* 5: 169–74

1946–7. 'Les noms du mari et de la femme, du père et de la mère en grec', *Revue des études grecques* 59–60: 219–50

1948–53. *Grammaire Homérique*, 2 vols., Paris

1999. *Dictionnaire étymologique de la langue grecque: histoire des mots*, 2nd edn with supplement by A. Blanc, C. de Lamberterie and J.-L. Perpillou, Paris

Cheyns, A. 1985. 'Recherche sur l'emploi des synonymes ἦτορ, κῆρ et κραδίη dans l'*Iliade* et l'*Odyssée*', *Revue belge de philologie et d'histoire* 63: 15–75

Ciani, M. G. 1974. φάος *e termini affini nella poesia greca. Introduzione a una fenomenologia della luce*, Florence

Cingano, E. 2002. 'I nomi dei Sette a Tebe e degli Epigoni nella tradizione epica, tragica, e iconografica', in A. Aloni, E. Berardi, G. Besso and S. Cecchin, eds. *I Sette a Tebe. Dal mito alla letteratura. Atti del seminario internazionale (Torino 21–22.2.2001)* (Bologna) 27–62

2002–3. 'Riflessi dell'epos tebano in Omero e in Esiodo', *Incontri triestini di filologia classica* 2: 55–76

2004. 'Tradizioni epiche intorno ad Argo da Omero al VI sec. a.C.', in P. Angeli Bernardini, ed. *La città di Argo. Mito, storia, tradizioni poetiche. Atti del convegno internazionale, Urbino, 13–15 giugno 2002* (Rome) 59–78

Clader, L. L. 1976. *Helen: the evolution from divine to heroic in Greek epic tradition*, Leiden

Clampitt, A. 1997. *Collected poems*, New York

Clark, M. 2004. 'Formulas, metre and type-scenes', in R. Fowler, ed. *The Cambridge companion to Homer* (Cambridge) 117–38

Clarke, M. 1995. 'Between lions and men: images of the hero in the *Iliad* ', *Greek, Roman and Byzantine Studies* 36: 137–59

1999. *Flesh and spirit in the songs of Homer: a study of words and myths*, Oxford

2004. 'Manhood and heroism', in R. Fowler, ed. *The Cambridge companion to Homer* (Cambridge) 74–90

Clay, J. S. 1983. *The wrath of Athena: gods and men in the Odyssey*, Princeton, NJ

1989. *The politics of Olympus: form and meaning in the major Homeric hymns*, Princeton, NJ

2003. *Hesiod's cosmos*, Cambridge

2007. 'Homer's Trojan theater', *Transactions of the American Philological Association* 137: 233–52

Clingham, G. 2000. 'Translating difference: the example of Dryden's "Last parting of Hector and Andromache" ', *Studies in the Literary Imagination* 33.2: 45–70

Cobet, J. 1997. *Schliemann: Archäologe und Abenteurer*, Munich

Cobet, J. and Gehrke, H.-J. 2002. 'Warum um Troia immer wieder streiten?', *Geschichte in Wissenschaft und Unterricht* 53: 290–325

Cobet, J. and Patzek, B., eds. 1992. *Archäologie und historische Erinnerung: Nach 100 Jahren Heinrich Schliemann*, Essen

Cohen, D. 1991. *Law, sexuality, and society: the enforcement of morals in classical Athens*, Cambridge

Coin-Longeray, S. 1999. ' Ἄφενος et ἀφνειός chez Homère: la richesse prestigieuse', in *Lalies: actes des sessions de linguistique et de littérature 19 (Aussois, 24–29 août 1998)* (Paris) 279–88

Collins, D. B. 1998. *Immortal armor: the concept of alke in archaic Greek poetry*, Lanham, MD

2004. *Master of the game: competition and performance in Greek poetry*, Washington, DC

Collins, L. 1987. 'The wrath of Paris: ethical vocabulary and ethical type in the *Iliad* ', *American Journal of Philology* 108: 220–32

1988. *Studies in characterization in the Iliad*, Frankfurt

Crielaard, J. P. 2003. 'The cultural biography of material goods in Homer's epics', *GAIA: Revue interdisciplinaire sur la Grèce archaïque* 7: 49–62

Crotty, K. 1994. *The poetics of supplication: Homer's Iliad and Odyssey*, Ithaca, NY and London

Currie, B. 2005. *Pindar and the cult of heroes*, Oxford

Dalby, A. 1995. 'The *Iliad*, the *Odyssey* and their audiences', *Classical Quarterly* 45: 269–79

Danek, G., trans. 2003. *Bosnische Heldenepen*, Klagenfurt

2005. 'Antenor und die Bittgesandtschaft. Ilias, Bakchylides 15 und der Astarita-Krater', *Wiener Studien* 118: 5–20

2006a. 'Antenor und seine Familie in der Ilias', *Wiener Studien* 119: 5–22

2006b. 'Die Gleichnisse der Ilias und der Dichter Homer', in F. Montanari and A. Rengakos, eds. *La poésie épique grecque: métamorphoses d'un genre littéraire* (Entretiens sur L'Antiquité Classique 52) (Vandoevres-Geneva) 41–71 and 72–7 (Discussion)

Davidson J. 2001. 'Homer and Euripides' *Troades*', *Bulletin of the Institute of Classical Studies* 45: 65–79

Davies, M. 2000. 'Homer and Dionysus', *Eikasmos* 11: 15–27

Davies, M. I. 1977. 'The reclamation of Helen', *Antike Kunst* 20: 73–85

Denniston, J. D. 1954. *The Greek particles*, 2nd edn, Oxford

Deoudi, M. 1999. *Heroenkulte in homerischer Zeit*, Oxford

Detienne, M. 1996. *The masters of truth in archaic Greece*, trans. J. Lloyd, New York

Detienne, M. and Vernant, J.-P. 1978. *Cunning intelligence in Greek culture and society*, trans. J. Lloyd, Hassocks and Atlantic Highlands, NJ

Di Benedetto, V. 1998. *Nel laboratorio di Omero*, 2nd edn, Turin

Dickey, E. 2007. *Ancient Greek scholarship: a guide to finding, reading, and understanding scholia, commentaries, lexica, and grammatical treatises, from their beginnings to the Byzantine period*, Oxford

Dindorf, W., ed. 1855. *Scholia graeca in Homeri Odysseam*, 2 vols., Oxford

Dodds, E. R. 1951. *The Greeks and the irrational*, Berkeley and Los Angeles

Dönike, M. 2005. *Pathos, Ausdruck und Bewegung. Zur Ästhetik des Weimarer Klassizismus 1796–1806*, Berlin

Donlan, W. 1989a. 'Homeric τέμενος and the land economy of the Dark Age', *Museum Helveticum* 46: 129–45

   1989b. 'The unequal exchange between Glaucus and Diomedes in light of the Homeric gift-economy', *Phoenix* 43: 1–15

Donner, H. and Röllig, W., eds. 2002. *Kanaanäische und aramäische Inschriften*, vol. 1, 5th revised and expanded edn, Wiesbaden

Dörr, V. C. and Oellers, N., eds. 1999. *Johann Wolfgang von Goethe. Sämtliche Werke. Briefe, Tagebücher und Gespräche*, part 2, vol. v (32): *Johann Wolfgang Goethe mit Schiller. Briefe, Tagebücher and Gespräche vom 24. Juni 1794 bis zum 9. Mai 1805. Teil II: Vom 1. Januar 1800 bis zum 9. Mai 1805*, Frankfurt

Douglas, M. 2007. *Thinking in circles: an essay on ring composition*, New Haven, CT and London

Drerup, H. 1969. *Griechische Baukunst in geometrischer Zeit*, Göttingen (= F. Matz and H.-G. Buchholz, eds. *Archaeologia Homerica*, vol. ii, ch. O)

duBois, P. 1982. *Centaurs and Amazons: women and the pre-history of the great chain of being*, Ann Arbor, MI

Dué, C. 2001a. 'Achilles' golden amphora in Aeschines' *Against Timarchus* and the afterlife of oral tradition', *Classical Philology* 96: 33–47

   2001b. '*Sunt aliquid manes*: Homer, Plato, and Alexandrian allusion in Propertius iv 7', *The Classical Journal* 96: 401–13

   2002. *Homeric variations on a lament by Briseis*, Lanham, MD

Duentzer, H. 1848. *De Zenodoti studiis Homericis*, Göttingen

Duffy, C. A. and Graziosi, B. 2005. 'Homeric encounters', *Omnibus* 51: 6–8

Easterling, P. E. 1984. 'The tragic Homer', *Bulletin of the Institute of Classical Studies* 31: 1–8

   1991. 'Men's κλέος and women's γόος: female voices in the *Iliad*', *Journal of Modern Greek Studies* 9: 145–51

   1995. 'Holy Thebe', in A. Fol, B. Bogdanov, P. Dimitrov and D. Boyadzhiev, eds. *Studia in honorem Georgii Mihailov* (Sofia) 161–7

Easton, D. F. 2002. *Schliemann's excavations at Troia 1870–1873*, Mainz

Ebbott, M. 2003. *Imagining illegitimacy in classical Greek literature*, Lanham, MD

Ebeling, H., ed. 1880–5. *Lexicon Homericum*, 2 vols., Leipzig

Edmunds, S. T. 1990. *Homeric nēpios*, New York

Edwards, M. W. 1970. 'Homeric speech introductions', *Harvard Studies in Classical Philology* 74: 1–36

   1986. 'Homer and oral tradition: the formula, part I', *Oral Tradition* 1: 171–230

   1987. *Homer: poet of the Iliad*, Baltimore, MD

   1988. 'Homer and oral tradition: the formula, part II', *Oral Tradition* 3: 11–60

   1991. *The Iliad: a commentary*, vol. v, Cambridge

   1992. 'Homer and oral tradition: the type-scene', *Oral Tradition* 7: 284–330

   2002. *Sound, sense, and rhythm. Listening to Greek and Latin poetry*, Princeton, NJ

Eiselen, F. C. 1907. *Sidon: a study in oriental history*, New York

Ekroth, G. 2002. *The sacrificial rituals of Greek hero-cults in the archaic to the early Hellenistic periods*, Liège

Elliger, W. 1975. *Die Darstellung der Landschaft in der griechischen Dichtung*, Berlin and New York

Elmer, D. F. 2005. 'Helen *epigrammatopoios*', *Classical Antiquity* 24: 1–39

Erbse, H., ed. 1969–88. *Scholia Graeca in Homeri Iliadem (scholia vetera)*, 7 vols., Berlin

Erbse, H. 1979. 'Hektor in der Ilias', in H. Erbse, ed. *Ausgewählte Schriften zur klassischen Philologie* (Berlin) 1–18 (First published in H.-G. Beck, A. Kambylis and P. Moraux, eds. *Kyklos. Griechisches und Byzantinisches. Rudolf Keydell zum 90. Geburtstag* (Berlin and New York 1978) 1–19)

   1986. *Untersuchungen zur Funktion der Götter im homerischen Epos*, Berlin and New York

   2000. 'Beobachtungen über die Gleichnisse der Ilias Homers', *Hermes* 128: 257–74

Erren, M. 1970. 'Αὐτίκα "sogleich" als Signal der einsetzenden Handlung in Ilias und Odyssee', *Poetica* 3: 24–58

Espermann, I. 1980. *Antenor, Theano, Antenoriden. Ihre Person und Bedeutung in der Ilias*, Meisenheim

Fagan, P. L. 2001. 'Horses in the similes of the *Iliad*: a case study', Diss., Toronto

Fagerström, K. 1988. *Iron age architecture: developments through changing times*, Göteborg

Fantuzzi, M. 2001. ' "Homeric" formularity in the *Argonautica* of Apollonius of Rhodes', in T. D. Papanghelis and A. Rengakos, eds. *A companion to Apollonius Rhodius* (Leiden) 171–92

Farmer, M. S. 1998. 'Sophocles' Ajax and Homer's Hector: two soliloquies', *Illinois Classical Studies* 23: 19–45

Farron, S. 2003. 'Attitudes to military archery in the *Iliad*', in A. F. Basson and W. J. Dominik, eds. *Literature, art, history: studies on classical antiquity and tradition in honour of W. J. Henderson* (Frankfurt) 169–84

Felson, N. and Slatkin, L. M. 2004. 'Gender and Homeric epic', in R. Fowler, ed. *The Cambridge companion to Homer* (Cambridge) 91–114

Fenik, B. 1968. *Typical battle scenes in the Iliad: studies in the narrative techniques of Homeric battle description*, Wiesbaden

1986. *Homer and the Nibelungenlied: comparative studies in epic style*, Cambridge, MA and London

Fensham, F. C. 1962. 'Widow, orphan, and the poor in ancient Near Eastern legal and wisdom literature', *Journal of Near Eastern Studies* 21: 129–39

Ferrari, F. 1986. *Oralità ed espressione: ricognizioni omeriche*, Pisa

Fineberg, S. 1999. 'Blind rage and eccentric vision in *Iliad* 6', *Transactions of the American Philological Association* 129: 13–41

Finkelberg, M. 1988. 'From Ahhiyawa to Ἀχαιοί', *Glotta* 66: 127–34

2005. *Greeks and pre-Greeks: Aegean prehistory and Greek heroic tradition*, Cambridge

Foley, H. P. 2001. *Female acts in Greek tragedy*, Princeton, NJ

Foley, J. M. 1991. *Immanent art: from structure to meaning in traditional oral epic*, Bloomington, IN and Indianapolis, IN

1999. *Homer's traditional art*, University Park, PA

Ford, A. 1992. *Homer: the poetry of the past*, Ithaca, NY and London

Fornaro, S. 1992. *Glauco e Diomede. Lettura di Iliade VI 119–236*, Venosa

Forssmann, B. 2005. 'Das Verbum οἴγ- "öffnen" bei Homer', in G. Meiser and O. Hackstein, eds. *Sprachkontakt und Sprachwandel. Akten der XI. Fachtagung der Indogermanischen Gesellschaft (Halle a.d. Saale, 17.–23.9.2000)* (Wiesbaden) 105–15

Foster, B. R. 2005. *Before the Muses: an anthology of Akkadian literature*, 3rd edn, Bethesda, MD

Fowler, R. L. 1987. *The nature of early Greek lyric: three preliminary studies*, Toronto

Fränkel, H. 1921. *Die homerischen Gleichnisse*, Göttingen

1955. 'Die Zeitauffassung in der archaischen griechischen Literatur', in F. Tietze, ed. *Wege und Formen frühgriechischen Denkens. Literarische und philosophiegeschichtliche Studien* (Munich) 1–22 (First published in *Beilagenheft zur Zeitschrift für Ästhetik und allgemeine Kunstwissenschaft* 25 (1931) 97–118)

Fraenkel, E., ed. 1950. *Aeschylus: Agamemnon*, vol. II, Oxford

Friedrich, R. 2007. *Formular economy in Homer: the poetics of the breaches*, Stuttgart

Frisk, H. 1960. *Griechisches etymologisches Wörterbuch*, vol. I, Heidelberg

Fritz, M. A. 2005. *Die trikasuellen Lokalpartikeln bei Homer: Syntax und Semantik*, Göttingen

Gaertner, J. F. 2001. 'The Homeric catalogues and their function in epic narrative', *Hermes* 129: 298–305

Gagliardi, P. 2006. 'I lamenti di Andromaca nell'*Iliade*', *GAIA: Revue interdisciplinaire sur la Grèce archaïque* 10: 11–46

Gaisser, J. H. 1969. 'Adaptation of traditional material in the Glaukos–Diomedes episode', *Transactions of the American Philological Association* 100: 165–76

Gartziou-Tatti, A. 1992. 'Pâris-Alexandre dans l'*Iliade*', in A. Moreau, ed. *L'initiation: actes du colloque international de Montpellier (11.–14.4.1991)*, vol. I: *Les rites d'adolescence et les mystères* (Montpellier) 73–93

Garvie, A. F. 1994. *Homer: Odyssey books VI–VIII*, Cambridge

Gates, H. P. 1971. *The kinship terminology of Homeric Greek*, Baltimore, MD

George, C. 2005. *Expressions of agency in ancient Greek*, Cambridge

Golden, M. 1988. 'Did the ancients care when their children died?', *Greece and Rome* 35: 152–63

Goldhill, S. 1990. 'Supplication and authorial comment in the *Iliad*: *Iliad* Z 61–2', *Hermes* 118: 373–6.

1991. *The poet's voice: essays on poetics and Greek literature*, Cambridge

Görgemanns, H. 2001. 'Hektor's Entscheidung', in S. Böhm and K.-V. von Eickstedt, eds. *IΘAKH: Festschrift für Jörg Schäfer zum 75. Geburtstag am 25. April 2001* (Würzburg) 115–20

Granata, G. 1991. 'Dioniso tra Pilo e Omero: una nota', *Athenaeum* 69: 623–33

Graver, M. 1995. 'Dog-Helen and Homeric insult', *Classical Antiquity* 14: 41–61

Graziosi, B. 2001. 'Competition in wisdom', in F. Budelmann and P. Michelakis, eds. *Homer, tragedy and beyond: essays in honour of P. E. Easterling* (London) 57–74

2002. *Inventing Homer: the early reception of epic*, Cambridge

2004. 'La definizione dell'opera omerica nel periodo arcaico e classico', in G. Zanetto, D. Canavero, A. Capra and A. Sgobbi, eds. *Momenti della ricezione omerica: poesia arcaica e teatro* (Milan) 2–17

2007. 'The ancient reception of Homer', in L. Hardwick and C. Stray, eds. *A companion to classical receptions* (Oxford) 26–37

Graziosi, B. and Haubold, J. 2003. 'Homeric masculinity: ἠνορέη and ἀγηνορίη', *Journal of Hellenic Studies* 123: 60–76

2005. *Homer: the resonance of epic*, London

2009. 'Greek lyric and early Greek literary history', in F. Budelmann, ed. *The Cambridge companion to Greek lyric*, (Cambridge) 95–113

Grethlein, J. 2006a. *Das Geschichtsbild der Ilias. Eine Untersuchung aus phänomenologischer und narratologischer Perspektive*, Göttingen

2006b. 'Individuelle Identität und Conditio Humana. Die Bedeutung und Funktion von ΓΕΝΕΗ im Blättergleichnis in Il. 6,146–149', *Philologus* 150: 3–13

2008. 'Memory and material objects in the *Iliad* and the *Odyssey*', *Journal of Hellenic Studies* 128: 27–51

Griffin, J. 1980. *Homer on life and death*, Oxford

1986. 'Homeric words and speakers', *Journal of Hellenic Studies* 106: 36–571

1992. 'Theocritus, the *Iliad* and the east', *American Journal of Philology* 113: 189–211

ed. 1995. *Homer: Iliad, book nine*, Oxford

Griffith, M. 1983. 'Personality in Hesiod', *Classical Antiquity* 2: 37–65

2009. 'Greek lyric and the place of humans in the world', in F. Budelmann, ed. *The Cambridge companion to Greek lyric*, (Cambridge) 72–94

Gronewald, M. and Daniel, R. W. 2004. 'Ein neuer Sappho-Papyrus', *Zeitschrift für Papyrologie und Epigraphik* 147: 1–8

Hackstein, O. 2002. *Die Sprachform der homerischen Epen. Faktoren morphologischer Variabilität in literarischen Frühformen: Tradition, Sprachwandel, sprachliche Anachronismen*, Wiesbaden

2007. 'La paréchèse et le jeux sur les mots chez Homère', in A. Blanc and E. Dupraz, eds. *Procédés synchroniques de la langue poétique en grec et en latin* (Brussels) 103–13

Hagen, H. 2000. 'Die Diskussion um Ἄρτεμις ἰοχέαιρα im homerischen Epos', *Glotta* 76: 53–8

Hainsworth, J. B. 1988. 'The epic dialect', in Heubeck, West and Hainsworth 1988: 24–32

1993. *The Iliad: a commentary*, vol. III, Cambridge

Hajnal, I. 2003. *Troja aus sprachwissenschaftlicher Sicht. Die Struktur einer Argumentation*, Innsbruck

Hall, E. 1989. *Inventing the barbarian: Greek self-definition through tragedy*, Oxford

Hall, J. 2002. *Hellenicity: between ethnicity and culture*, Chicago, IL and London

Halliwell, S. 2008. *Greek laughter: a study of cultural psychology from Homer to early Christianity*, Cambridge

Hansen, W. 2002. *Ariadne's thread: a guide to international tales found in classical literature*, Ithaca, NY and London

Hanson, V. D. 1999. *The wars of the ancient Greeks*, London

Hardwick, L. 2007. 'Singing across the faultlines: cultural shifts in twentieth-century receptions of Homer', in B. Graziosi and E. Greenwood, eds. *Homer in the twentieth century: between world literature and the western canon* (Oxford) 47–71

Harries, B. 1993. 'Strange meeting: Diomedes and Glaucus in *Iliad* 6', *Greece & Rome* 40: 133–46

Haslam, M. 1997. 'Homeric papyri and transmission of the text', in Morris and Powell 1997: 55–100

Haubold, J. 2000. *Homer's people: epic poetry and social formation*, Cambridge

2002. 'Wars of *Wissenschaft*: the new quest for Troy', *International Journal of the Classical Tradition* 8: 564–79

2005. 'Heracles in the Hesiodic *Catalogue of Women*', in R. Hunter, ed. *The Hesiodic Catalogue of Women: constructions and reconstructions* (Cambridge) 85–98

2007. 'Xerxes' Homer', in E. Bridges, E. M. Hall and P. J. Rhodes, eds. *Cultural responses to the Persian Wars: antiquity to the third millennium* (Oxford) 47–64

Heiden, B. 1998. 'The placement of "book divisions" in the *Iliad*', *Journal of Hellenic Studies* 118: 68–81

Heinhold-Krahmer, S. 2003. 'Zur Gleichsetzung der Namen Ilios-Wiluša und Troia-Taruiša', in Ulf 2003: 146–68

Heitsch, E. 1968. 'Ilias B 557/8', *Hermes* 96: 641–60

2001. 'Der Zorn des Paris. Zur Deutungsgeschichte eines homerischen Zetemas', in E. Heitsch, *Gesammelte Schriften*, vol. I: *Zum frühgriechischen Epos* (Munich and Leipzig) 178–209 (First published in E. Fries, ed. *Festschrift für Joseph Klein zum 70. Geburtstag* (Göttingen 1967) 216–47)

Henrichs, A. 1974. 'Die Proitiden im hesiodischen Katalog', *Zeitschrift für Papyrologie und Epigraphik* 15: 297–301

1994. 'Der rasende Gott. Zur Psychologie des Dionysos und des Dionysischen in Mythos und Literatur', *Antike und Abendland: Beiträge zum Verständnis der Griechen und Römer und ihres Nachlebens* 40: 31–58

Herman, G. 1987. *Ritualised friendship and the Greek city*, Cambridge

Hershkowitz, D. 1998. *The madness of epic: reading insanity from Homer to Statius*, Oxford

Hertel, D. 2003. *Die Mauern von Troia. Mythos und Geschichte im antiken Ilion*, Munich
    2008. *Troia. Archäologie, Geschichte, Mythos*, 3rd edn, Munich
Herter, H. 1973. 'Der weinende Astyanax', *Grazer Beiträge* 1: 157–64
Herzhoff, B. 2008. 'Der Flußkatalog der Ilias (M 20–23) – ältestes literarisches Beispiel
    geometrischer Raumerfassung?', in J. Althoff, S. Föllinger and G. Wöhrle, eds.
    Antike Naturwissenschaft und ihre Rezeption 18 (Trier) 101–38
Heubeck, A. 1979. *Schrift*, Göttingen (= F. Matz and H.-G. Buchholz, eds. *Archaeologia
    Homerica*, vol. III, ch. x)
Heubeck, A., West, S. and Hainsworth, J. B., eds. 1988. *A commentary on Homer's Odyssey*,
    vol. I, Oxford
Higbie, C. 1990. *Measure and music: enjambement and sentence structure in the Iliad*, Oxford
    1995. *Heroes' names, Homeric identities*, New York
Hijmans, B. L. 1975. 'Alexandros and his grief', *Grazer Beiträge* 3: 177–89
    1976. 'Archers in the *Iliad*', in J. S. Boersma, W. A. Van Es, W. C. Mank *et al.*,
    eds. *Festoen. Opgedragen aan A. N. Zadoks-Josephus Jitta bij haar zeventigste verjaardag*
    (Groningen) 343–52
Hiller, S. 1993. 'Lykien und Lykier bei Homer und in mykenischer Zeit', in J. Borch-
    hardt and G. Dobesch, eds. *Akten des II. internationalen Lykien-Symposions (Wien,
    6.-12.5.1990)* (Vienna), vol. I, 107–15
Hillgruber, M. 1994–9. *Die pseudoplutarchische Schrift De Homero*, 2 vols., Stuttgart and
    Leipzig
Hinderer, W. and Dahlstrom, D. O., eds. 1993. *Friedrich Schiller. Essays*, New York
Hirsh, J. 2004. 'Representing repetition: appropriation in de Chirico and after', in
    L. Somigli and M. Moroni, eds. *Italian modernism: Italian culture between decadentism
    and avant-garde* (Toronto) 403–49
Hoekstra, A. 1965. *Homeric modifications of formulaic prototypes. Studies in the development of
    Greek epic diction*, Amsterdam and London
    1969. *The sub-epic stage of the formulaic tradition. Studies in the Homeric Hymns to Apollo, to
    Aphrodite and to Demeter*, Amsterdam and London
Hogan, J. C. 1981. '*Eris* in Homer', *Grazer Beiträge* 10: 21–58
Holeschofsky, K. 1969. 'Orientteppiche in der klassischen Antike', *Wiener Studien* n.s.
    3: 166–80
Holmes, B. 2007. 'The *Iliad's* economy of pain', *Transactions of the American Philological
    Association* 137: 45–84
Horrocks, G. 1997. 'Homer's dialect', in Morris and Powell 1997: 193–217
Horsfall, N. 1979. 'Some problems in the Aeneas legend', *Classical Quarterly* 29: 372–90
Huehnergard, J. 2005. *A Grammar of Akkadian*, 2nd edn, 2nd printing, Winona Lake,
    IN
Hughes, L. B. 1997. 'Vergil's Creusa and *Iliad* 6', *Mnemosyne* 50: 401–23
Hunter, R. 2004. 'Homer and Greek literature', in R. Fowler, ed. *The Cambridge
    Companion to Homer* (Cambridge) 235–53
Hurst, A. and Kolde, A., eds. 2008. *Lycophron: Alexandra*, Paris
Ieranò, G. 2002. 'La città delle donne: il sesto canto dell'Iliade e i Sette contro Tebe
    di Eschilo', in A. Aloni, E. Berardi, G. Besso and S. Cecchin, eds. *I Sette a Tebe.*

Dal mito alla letteratura. Atti del seminario internazionale (Torino 21–22.2.2001) (Bologna) 73–92

Ingalls, W. B. 1998. 'Attitudes towards children in the *Iliad*', *Échos du monde classique (Classical Views)* n.s. 17: 13–34

Irwin, E. 2005. *Solon and early Greek poetry: the politics of exhortation*, Cambridge

Jacquinod, B. 1992. 'La liberté dans les poèmes homériques', in R. Sauter, ed. *Visages de liberté. Recherches lexicales et littéraires* (Saint-Étienne) 17–27

   1994. 'Homère Z 396 et l'attraction inverse', in D. Conso, N. Fick and B. Poulle, eds. *Mélanges François Kerlouégan* (Paris) 289–95

Jahn, T. 1987. *Zum Wortfeld 'Seele-Geist' in der Sprache Homers*, Munich

Jäkel, S. 1994. 'The phenomenon of laughter in the *Iliad*', in S. Jäkel and A. Timonen, eds. *Laughter down the centuries*, vol. 1 (Turku) 23–7

Janko, R. 1982. *Homer, Hesiod and the Hymns: diachronic development in epic diction*, Cambridge

   1994. *The Iliad: a commentary*, vol. IV, Cambridge

   2002. Contribution to 'Seduta di chiusura', in Montanari 2002: 653–66

Janz, R.-P., ed. 1992. *Friedrich Schiller. Theoretische Schriften*, in O. Dann, H. G. Ingenkamp, R. P. Janz et al., eds. *Friedrich Schiller. Werke und Briefe in zwölf Bänden*, vol. VIII, Frankfurt

Jensen, M. S. 1980. *The Homeric question and the oral-formulaic theory*, Copenhagen

   1999. 'Dividing Homer: when and how were the *Iliad* and *Odyssey* divided into songs?', with contributions by Ø. Andersen, A. Ballabriga, C. Calame et al., *Symbolae Osloenses* 74: 5–91

Jidejian, N. 1971. *Sidon through the ages*, Beirut

Jones, P. 1995. 'Poetic invention: the fighting around Troy in the first nine years of the Trojan War', in Ø. Andersen and M. Dickie, eds. *Homer's world: fiction, tradition, reality* (Bergen and Athens) 101–11

de Jong, I. J. F. 1987a. 'Silent characters in the *Iliad*', in J. M. Bremer, I. J. F. de Jong and J. Kalff, eds. *Homer, beyond oral poetry. Recent trends in Homeric interpretation* (Amsterdam) 105–21

   1987b. 'The voice of anonymity: *tis*-speeches in the *Iliad*', *Eranos* 85: 69–84

   1997. 'ΓΑΡ introducing embedded narratives', in A. Rijksbaron, ed. *New approaches to Greek particles* (Amsterdam) 175–85

   ed. 1999. *Homer: critical assessments*, 4 vols., London and New York

   2001. *A narratological commentary on the Odyssey*, Cambridge

   2004. *Narrators and focalizers: the presentation of the story in the Iliad*, 2nd edn, Bristol (First published Amsterdam 1987)

   2007. 'Homer', in I. J. F. de Jong and R. Nünlist, eds. *Time in ancient Greek literature* (Leiden and Boston) 17–37

de Jong, I. J. F. and Nünlist, R. 2004. 'From bird's eye view to close-up: the standpoint of the narrator in the Homeric epics', in A. Bierl, A. Schmitt and A. Willi, eds. *Antike Literatur in neuer Deutung. Festschrift für Joachim Latacz anlässlich seines 70. Geburtstages* (Munich and Leipzig) 63–83

Jörgensen, O. 1904. 'Das Auftreten der Goetter in den Buechern 1-μ der Odyssee', *Hermes* 39: 357–82

Kakridis, J. Th. 1949. *Homeric researches*, trans. A. Placotari, Lund (Originally published in Greek as Ομηρικές Έρευνες, Athens 1944)

Kamptz, H. von 1982. *Homerische Personennamen: Sprachwissenschaftliche und historische Klassifikation*, Göttingen

Karadžić, V. S. 1953. *Srpske narodne pjesme*, vol. II, ed. S. Matić, Belgrade

Karp, A. 1994. 'The harmony of *eleos* and *aidôs* in the moral universe of the *Iliad*', *New England Classical Journal and Newsletter* 21.3: 106–10.

Katz, J. T. 1998. 'How to be a dragon in Indo-European: Hittite *illuyankas* and its linguistic and cultural congeners in Latin, Greek, and Germanic', in J. Jasanoff, H. C. Melchert and L. Oliver, eds. *Mír curad: studies in honour of Calvert Watkins* (Innsbruck) 317–34

Kauffmann-Samaras, A. and Szabados, A.-V. 2004. 'Rites et activités relatifs aux images de culte: vêtements, parures', *Thesaurus Cultus et Rituum Antiquorum* 2: 427–37

Kelly, A. 2007. *A referential commentary and lexicon to Iliad VIII*, Oxford

Kennedy, G. A. 1986. 'Helen's web unraveled', *Arethusa* 19: 5–14

Keulen, A. J., ed. 2001. *L. Annaeus Seneca. Troades. Introduction, text and commentary*, Leiden

Kirk, G. S. 1962. *The songs of Homer*, Cambridge

   1985. *The Iliad: a commentary*, vol. I, Cambridge

   1990. *The Iliad: a commentary*, vol. II, Cambridge

Kitts, M. 1994. 'Two expressions for human mortality in the epics of Homer', *History of Religions* 34: 132–51

   2005. *Sanctified violence in Homeric society: oath-making rituals and narratives in the Iliad*, Cambridge

Klein, J. S. 1988. 'Homeric Greek αὖ: a synchronic, diachronic, and comparative study', *Historische Sprachforschung* 101: 249–88

Konstan, D. 1997. *Friendship in the classical world*, Cambridge

   2001. *Pity transformed*, London

Kossman, N., ed. 2001. *Gods and mortals: modern poems on classical myths*, Oxford

Kotsidu, H. 1991. *Die musischen Agone der Panathenäen in archaischer und klassischer Zeit: eine historisch-archäologische Untersuchung*, Munich

Krauskopf, I. 2001. 'Thysthla, Thyrsoi und Narthekophoroi: Anmerkungen zur Geschichte des dionysischen Kultstabes', *Thetis (Mannheimer Beiträge zur klassischen Archäologie und Geschichte Griechenlands und Zyperns)* 8: 47–52

Kretschmer, P. 1912. Review of P. Cauer, *Grundfragen der Homerkritik*, 2nd edn, Leipzig 1909, *Glotta* 3: 307–9

Krings, V., ed. 1995. *La civilisation phénicienne et punique: manuel de recherche*, Leiden

Krischer, T. 1971. *Formale Konventionen der homerischen Epik*, Munich

Kühner, R. 1904. *Ausführliche Grammatik der griechischen Sprache. Zweiter Teil: Satzlehre. Zweiter Band*, 3rd edn by B. Gehrt, Hannover and Leipzig

Kullmann, W. 1960. *Die Quellen der Ilias (Troischer Sagenkreis)*, Wiesbaden

Lanfranchi, G. B. 2007. 'The Luwian-Phoenician bilinguals of ÇINEKÖY and KARATEPE: an ideological dialogue', in R. Rollinger, A. Luther, and J. Wiesehöfer, eds. *Getrennte Wege? Kommunikation, Raum und Wahrnehmung in der alten Welt* (Frankfurt) 179–217

Lang, M. L. 1975. 'Reason and purpose in Homeric prayers', *The Classical World* 68: 309–14

1989. 'Unreal conditions in Homeric narrative', *Greek, Roman and Byzantine Studies* 30: 5–26

1994. 'Lineage-boasting and the road not taken', *Classical Quarterly* 44: 1–6

Lange, V., Becker, H. J., Müller, G. H., Neubauer, J., Schmidt, P. and Zehm, E., eds. 1988. *Johann Wolfgang Goethe. Sämtliche Werke nach Epochen seines Schaffens. Münchner Ausgabe*, vol. VI.2: *Weimarer Klassik 1798–1806*, Munich

Lardinois, A. 1997. 'Modern paroemiology and *gnomai* in Homer's *Iliad*', *Classical Philology* 92: 213–34

2000. 'Characterization through *gnomai* in Homer's *Iliad*', *Mnemosyne* 53: 641–61

Larson, J. 2001. *Greek nymphs: myth, cult, lore*, Oxford

Laser, S. 1968. 'Sitzmöbel bei Homer und im älteren Epos', in F. Matz and H.-G. Buchholz, eds. *Archaeologia Homerica*, vol. II, ch. P, *Hausrat* (Göttingen) 34–45

Latacz, J. 1977. *Kampfparänese, Kampfdarstellung und Kampfwirklichkeit in der Ilias, bei Kallinos und Tyrtaios*, Munich

ed. 2000a. *Homers Ilias. Gesamtkommentar. Prolegomena*, Munich and Leipzig

ed. 2000b. *Homers Ilias. Gesamtkommentar*, vol. I.2, Munich and Leipzig

ed. 2003. *Homers Ilias. Gesamtkommentar*, vol. II.2, Munich and Leipzig

2004. *Troy and Homer: towards a solution of an old mystery*, trans. K. Windle and R. Ireland, Oxford

Latacz, J., Blome, P., Luckhardt, J., Brunner, H., Korfmann, M. and Biegel, G., eds. 2001. *Troia: Traum und Wirklichkeit*, Stuttgart

Lateiner, D. 1997. 'Homeric prayer', *Arethusa* 30: 241–72

2005. 'Proxemic and chronemic in Homeric epic: time and space in heroic social interaction', *The Classical World* 98: 413–21

Lavelle, B. M. 1997. '*Epikouros* and *epikouroi* in early Greek literature and history', *Greek, Roman and Byzantine Studies* 38: 229–62

Leaf, W., ed. 1900–2. *The Iliad*, 2nd edn, London

Lebessi, A. 1992. 'Zum Phalos des homerischen Helms', *Mitteilungen des Deutschen Archäologischen Instituts, Athenische Abteilung* 107: 1–10

Lefkowitz, M. R. 1996. 'Women in the Panathenaic and other festivals', in J. Neils, ed. *Worshipping Athena: Panathenaia and Parthenon* (Madison, WI) 78–91

Lehrs, K. 1882. *De Aristarchi studiis Homericis*, 3rd edn, Leipzig

Lesky, A. 1961. *Göttliche und menschliche Motivation im homerischen Epos*, Heidelberg

2001. 'Divine and human causation in Homeric epic', trans. L. Holford-Strevens, in Cairns 2001: 170–202 (Originally published in German in Lesky 1961)

Lessing G. E. 1962. *Laocoön. An essay on the limits of painting and poetry*, ed. and trans. E. A. McCormick, Indianapolis, IN

Létoublon, F. 1985. *Il allait, pareil à la nuit. Les verbes de mouvement en grec: supplétisme et aspect verbal*, Paris

ed. 1997. *Hommage à Milman Parry: le style formulaire de l'épopée homérique et la théorie de l'oralité poétique*, Amsterdam

2003. 'Ilion battue des vents, Troie aux larges rues: la représentation de Troie dans l'*Iliade*', in M. Reddé, L. Dubois, D. Briquel, H. Lavagne and F. Queyrel, eds. *La naissance de la ville dans l'antiquité* (Paris) 27–44

Leumann, M. 1950. *Homerische Wörter*, Basel

Levine, D. B. 1982–3. 'Homeric laughter and the unsmiling suitors', *The Classical Journal* 78: 97–104

Lévy, E. 1983. '*Astu* et *polis* dans l'*Iliade*', *Ktèma* 8: 55–73

Lilja, S. 1972. *The treatment of odours in the poetry of antiquity*, Helsinki

Link, S. 1994. '*Temenos* und *ager publicus* bei Homer?', *Historia* 43: 241–5

Logue, C. 2001. *War music: an account of books 1–4 and 16–19 of Homer's Iliad*, London

Lohmann, D. 1970. *Die Komposition der Reden in der Ilias*, Berlin and New York

1988. *Die Andromache-Szenen der Ilias: Ansätze und Methoden der Homer-Interpretation*, Hildesheim

Löhneysen, W. Frhr. von, ed. 1965. *Propyläen: Eine periodische Schrift, herausgegeben von Johann Wolfgang von Goethe. Erster, zweiter und dritter Band*, Stuttgart

Lomax, J. 2000. *Temple Newsam paintings*, Leeds

Long, A. A. 1970. 'Morals and values in Homer', *Journal of Hellenic Studies* 90: 121–39

Longley, M. 2006. *Collected poems*, London

Lonsdale, S. H. 1990. *Creatures of speech: lion, herding, and hunting similes in the Iliad*, Stuttgart

Loraux, N. 1995. *The experiences of Tiresias: the feminine and the Greek man*, trans. P. Wissing, Princeton, NJ

Lord, A. B., ed. 1974. *Serbocroatian heroic songs*, vol. iii: *Weddings of Smailagic Meho*, Cambridge, MA

1991. *Epic singers and oral tradition*, Ithaca, NY

2000. *The singer of tales*, reprinted with introduction and cd-rom by S. Mitchell and G. Nagy, Cambridge, MA (First published Cambridge, MA 1960)

Lorimer, H. L. 1950. *Homer and the monuments*, London

Lossau, M. 1994. 'Retter-Licht (φόως, φάος) bei Homer und den Tragikern', *Eranos* 92: 85–92

Louden, B. 1993. 'Pivotal contrafactuals in Homeric epic', *Classical Antiquity* 12: 181–98

1995. 'Categories of Homeric wordplay', *Transactions of the American Philological Association* 125: 27–46

Lowry, E. R. 1995. 'Glaucus, the leaves, and the heroic boast of *Iliad* 6.146–211', in J. B. Carter and S. P. Morris, eds. *The ages of Homer: a tribute to Emily Townsend Vermeule* (Austin, TX) 193–203

Luce, J. 1984. 'The Homeric topography of the Trojan plain reconsidered', *Oxford Journal of Archaeology* 3: 31–43

Ludwich, A. 1885. *Aristarchs homerische Textkritik*, vol. ii, Leipzig ed. 1887. *Homeri Iliadis et Odysseae periochae metricae: editae ad celebrandam diebus XI m. Martii, XXI et XXIII m. Maii, XXIII m. Junii memoriam virorum illustrium Caelestini de Kowalewski, Jacobi Friderici de Rhod, Friderici de Groeben, Joannis Diterici de Tettau,* Königsberg

Lynn-George, M. 1988. *Epos: word, narrative and the Iliad,* Basingstoke

Lyons, D. 2003. 'Dangerous gifts: ideologies of marriage and exchange in ancient Greece', *Classical Antiquity* 22: 93–134

Mack, M., ed. 1967. *The poems of Alexander Pope,* vol. VII: *Translations of Homer,* London and New Haven, CT

Mackie, H. 1996. *Talking Trojan: speech and community in the Iliad,* Lanham, MD

Macleod, C. W., ed. 1982. *Homer: Iliad XXIV,* Cambridge

Macrakis, A. L. 1984. 'Comparative economic value in the *Iliad*: the oxen-worth', in Rigsby 1984: 211–15

Maehler, H. 1982. *Die Lieder des Bacchylides. Erster Teil: Die Siegeslieder,* vol. II: *Kommentar,* Leiden

Maftei, M. 1976. *Antike Diskussionen über die Episode von Glaukos und Diomedes im VI. Buch der Ilias,* Meisenheim

Marinatos, S. 1967. 'Kleidung', in F. Matz and H.-G. Buchholz, eds. *Archaeologia Homerica,* vol. I, ch. A and B: *Kleidung, Haar- und Barttracht* (Göttingen) 1–66

Marmorale, E. V. 1950. ed. *Naevius poeta. Introduzione bibliografica, testo dei frammenti e commento,* Florence

Maronitis, D. N. 2004. *Homeric megathemes: war – homilia – homecoming,* trans. D. Conolly, Lanham, MD

Martin, R. 1989. *The language of heroes: speech and performance in the Iliad,* Ithaca, NY and London

Matthaios, S. 1999. *Untersuchungen zur Grammatik Aristarchs: Texte und Interpretation zur Wortartenlehre,* Göttingen

Mawet, F. 1979. *Recherches sur les oppositions fonctionnelles dans le vocabulaire homérique de la douleur (autour de πῆμα-ἄλγος),* Brussels

Mazon, P. 1948. *Introduction à l'Iliade,* Paris

Meier-Brügger, M. 1989. 'Episch μητίετα (Ζεύς) und das Suffix -(ϝ)εντ-', *Historische Sprachforschung* 102: 207–10

Meister, K. 1921. *Die homerische Kunstsprache,* Leipzig

Mellink, M. J. 1995. 'Homer, Lycia, and Lukka', in J. B. Carter and S. P. Morris, eds. *The ages of Homer: a tribute to Emily Townsend Vermeule* (Austin, TX) 33–43

Mellor, A. K. 1995. 'British romanticism and gender', in Bermingham and Brewer 1995: 121–42

Merkelbach, R. 1952. 'Die pisistratische Redaktion der homerischen Gedichte', *Rheinisches Museum* 95: 23–47

Meyer, J. H. 1800. 'Preisaufgabe fürs Jahr 1800', *Propyläen* 3: 167–8 (Reprinted in von Löhneysen 1965: 879–80)

Minchin, E. 1995. 'Ring-patterns and ring-composition: some observations on the framing of stories in Homer', *Helios* 22: 23–35

2001. 'On declining an invitation in Homer and in everyday talk: context, form, and function', *Antichthon* 35: 1–19

2007. *Homeric voices: discourse, memory, gender*, Oxford

Mirto, M. S. 1997. *Omero. Iliade. Traduzione e saggio introduttivo di Guido Paduano. Commento di Maria Serena Mirto*, Turin

Mondio, A. 1996. 'Lessico economico greco: il βοῦς "res" economica e misura di valore nei poemi omerici e nella rilettura dei commentatori', *Atti della Accademia Peloritana dei Pericolanti, Classe di Lettere, Filosofia e Belle Arti* 72: 219–23

Montanari, F. 1979–95. *Studi di filologia omerica antica*, 2 vols., Pisa

ed. 2002. *Omero tremila anni dopo. Atti del congresso di Genova, 6–8 Luglio 2000*, Rome

Morris, I. 1986. 'The use and abuse of Homer', *Classical Antiquity* 5: 81–138 (Revised and shortened version published in Cairns 2001: 57–91)

Morris, I. and Powell, B., eds. 1997. *A new companion to Homer*, Leiden

Morris, S. P. 1992. *Daidalos and the origins of Greek art*, Princeton, NJ

Morrison, J. V. 1991. 'The function and context of Homeric prayers: a narrative perspective', *Hermes* 119: 145–57 (Reprinted in de Jong 1999, vol. III, 284–97)

1992. 'Alternatives to the epic tradition: Homer's challenges in the *Iliad*', *Transactions of the American Philological Association* 122: 61–71

1999. 'Homeric darkness: patterns and manipulation of death scenes in the *Iliad*', *Hermes* 127: 129–44

Most, G. W. 1997. 'Hesiod's myth of the five (or three or four) races', *Proceedings of the Cambridge Philological Society* 43: 104–27

Moulton, C. 1977. *Similes in the Homeric poems*, Göttingen

Muellner, L. C. 1976. *The meaning of Homeric εὔχομαι through its formulas*, Innsbruck

Mülke, C. ed. 2002. *Solons politische Elegien und Iamben (Fr. 1–13, 32–37 West)*, Munich

Müller, H. W. 1979. 'Bas-relief et peinture', in J. Leclant, ed. *Le monde égyptien. Les pharaons*, vol. II: *L'empire des conquérants* (Paris) 67–138

Murnaghan, S. 1999. 'The poetics of loss in Greek epic', in M. Beissinger, J. Tylus and S. Wofford, eds. *Epic traditions in the contemporary world: the poetics of community* (Berkeley and Los Angeles) 203–20

Murray, G. 1934. *The rise of the Greek epic*, 4th edn, Oxford

Nagy, B. 1979. 'The naming of Athenian girls: a case in point', *The Classical Journal* 74: 360–4

Nagy, G. 1983. '*Sema* and *noesis*: some illustrations', *Arethusa* 16: 35–55

1996a. *Homeric questions*, Austin, TX

1996b. *Poetry as performance: Homer and beyond*, Cambridge

1999. *The best of the Achaeans: concepts of the hero in archaic Greek poetry*, 2nd edn, Baltimore, MD

2003. Review of West 2001 in *Gnomon* 75: 481–501

2004. *Homer's text and language*, Champaign, IL

Nahler, E. and Nahler, H., eds. 1992. *Schillers Werke. Nationalausgabe*, vol. XXVI: *Briefwechsel. Schillers Briefe 1.3.1790–17.5.1794*, Weimar

Naiden, F. S. 2006. *Ancient supplication*, Oxford

Nannini, S. 2003. *Analogia e polarità in similitudine: paragoni iliadici e odissiaci a confronto*, Amsterdam

Nappi, M. P. 2002. 'Note sull'uso di Αἴαντε nell'*Iliade*', *Rivista di cultura classica e medioevale* 44: 211–35

Neils, J. 1992. *Goddess and polis: the Panathenaic festival in ancient Athens*, Princeton, NJ

Nesselrath, H.-G. 1992. *Ungeschehenes Geschehen*. *'Beinahe-Episoden' im griechischen und römischen Epos von Homer bis zur Spätantike*, Stuttgart

Neumann, G. 1991. 'Die homerischen Personennamen. Ihre Position in Rahmen der Entwicklung des griechischen Namenschatzes', in J. Latacz, ed. *Zweihundert Jahre Homer-Forschung. Rückblick und Ausblick* (Stuttgart and Leipzig) 311–28

Nickau, K. 1977. *Untersuchungen zur textkritischen Methode des Zenodotos von Ephesos*, Berlin and New York

Nimis, S. A. 1999. 'Ring-composition and linearity in Homer', in E. A. Mackay, ed. *Signs of orality: the oral tradition and its influence in the Greek and Roman world* (Leiden) 65–78

Notopoulos, J. A. 1949. 'Parataxis in Homer: a new approach to Homeric literary criticism', *Transactions of the American Philological Association* 80: 1–23 (Reprinted in de Jong 1999: vol. IV, 94–112)

Nünlist, R. 2000. 'Homerische Metrik', in Latacz 2000a: 109–14

    2006. 'A neglected *testimonium* on the Homeric book-division', *Zeitschrift für Papyrologie und Epigraphik* 157: 47–9

Ong, W. J. 1988. *Orality and literacy: the technologizing of the word*, New York

Ormand, K. 1999. *Exchange and the maiden: marriage in Sophoclean tragedy*, Austin, TX

Osborne, R. 2005. 'Ordering women in Hesiod's *Catalogue*', in R. Hunter, ed. *The Hesiodic Catalogue of Women: constructions and reconstructions* (Cambridge) 5–24

Otto, W. F. 1965. *Dionysus: myth and cult*, trans. R. B. Palmer, Bloomington, IN and London (German edn, Frankfurt 1933)

Page, D. 1959. *History and the Homeric Iliad*, Berkeley and Los Angeles

Paladino, I. 1978. 'Glaukos, o l'ineluttabilità della morte', *Studi storico-religiosi* 2: 289–303

Pantelia, M. C. 1993. 'Spinning and weaving: ideas of domestic order in Homer', *American Journal of Philology* 114: 493–501

    2002. 'Helen and the last song for Hector', *Transactions of the American Philological Association* 132: 21–7

Parker, R. 1998. 'Pleasing thighs: reciprocity in Greek religion', in C. Gill, N. Postlethwaite and R. Seaford, eds. *Reciprocity in ancient Greece* (Oxford) 105–25

Parkinson, R. B. 1997. *The tale of Sinuhe and other ancient Egyptian poems 1940–1640 BC*, Oxford

Parks, W. 1990. *Verbal dueling in heroic narrative: the Homeric and old English traditions*, Princeton, NJ

Parry, A. 1972. 'Language and characterization in Homer', *Harvard Studies in Classical Philology* 76: 1–22

Parry, M. 1971. *The making of Homeric verse: the collected papers of Milman Parry*, ed. A. Parry, Oxford

Passa, E. 2001. 'L'antichità della grafia ευ per εο, εου nell'epica: a proposito di una recente edizione dell'*Iliade*', *Rivista di filologia classica* 129: 385–417

Patterson, R. D. 1973. 'The widow, orphan, and the poor in the Old Testament and the extra-Biblical literature', *Bibliotheca Sacra* 130: 223–34

Payton, R. 1991. 'The Ulu Burun writing-board set', *Anatolian Studies* 41: 99–106

Pelliccia, H. N. 2002. 'The interpretation of *Iliad* 6.145–9 and the sympotic contribution to rhetoric', *Colby Quarterly* 38: 197–230.

Perceau, S. 2002. *La parole vive. Communiquer en catalogue dans l'épopée homérique*, Louvain and Paris

Perna, M. 2007. 'Homer and the "folded wooden tablets"', in S. P. Morris and R. Laffineur, eds. *Epos. Reconsidering Greek epic and Aegean bronze age archaeology. Proceedings of the 11th international Aegean conference, Los Angeles, 20–23/04/2006* (Aegaeum 28) (Liège) 225–30 and table LVIII

Pernée, L. 1988. 'Ἀρέσαι dans l'*Iliade* et l'*Odyssée*', *Les études classiques* 56: 67–72

Peters, M. 1998. 'Homerisches und Unhomerisches bei Homer und auf dem Nestorbecher', in J. Jasanoff, H. C. Melchert and L. Oliver, eds. *Mír curad: studies in honour of Calvert Watkins* (Innsbruck) 584–602

Pfeiffer, R. 1968. *History of classical scholarship: from the beginnings to the Hellenistic Age*, Oxford

Piccaluga, G. 1980. 'Il dialogo tra Diomedes e Glaukos (Hom. *Il.* VI 119–236)', *Studi storico-religiosi* 4: 237–58

Pisanello, P. 1999. 'Il comico e il serio-comico nei poemi omerici', *Rudiae* 11: 91–102

Plath, R. 1994. *Der Streitwagen und seine Teile im frühen Griechischen. Sprachliche Untersuchungen zu den mykenischen Texten und zum homerischen Epos*, Nürnberg

Pontani, F., ed. 2007. *Scholia Graeca in Odysseam*, vol. I: *scholia ad libros α–β*, Rome

Powell, B. B. 1991. *Homer and the origin of the Greek alphabet*, Cambridge

Pratt, L. 2007. 'The parental ethos of the *Iliad*', in A. Cohen and J. B. Rutter, eds. *Constructions of childhood in ancient Greece and Italy* (Princeton, NJ and Athens) 25–40

2009. 'Diomedes, the fatherless hero of the *Iliad*', in S. R. Hübner and D. M. Ratzan, eds. *Growing up fatherless in antiquity* (Cambridge) 141–61

Prauscello, L. 2007. ' "Dionysiac" ambiguity: *HomHymn* 7.27', *Materiali e discussioni per l'analisi dei testi classici* 58: 209–16

Prieto, M. L. 1996. *Ares en Homero: función del dios de la guerra en la Ilíada y la Odisea*, Amsterdam

Privitera, G. A. 1970. *Dioniso in Omero e nella poesia greca arcaica*, Rome

Probert, P. 2003. *A new short guide to the accentuation of ancient Greek*, London

2006. *Ancient Greek accentuation: synchronic patterns, frequency effects, and prehistory*, Oxford

Pulleyn, S. 1997. *Prayer in Greek religion*, Oxford

Quasimodo, S. 1982. *Iliade. Episodi scelti e tradotti da Salvatore Quasimodo con 26 tavole di Giorgio de Chirico*, Florence

Raaflaub, K. A. 1981. 'Zum Freiheitsbegriff der Griechen. Materialien und Untersuchungen zur Bedeutungsentwicklung von ἐλεύθερος/ἐλευθερία in der archaischen und klassischen Zeit', in E. C. Welskopf, ed. *Soziale Typenbegriffe im alten Griechenland und ihr Fortleben in den Sprachen der Welt*, vol. IV (Berlin) 180–405

Rabel, R. J. 1990. 'Apollo as a model for Achilles in the *Iliad*', *American Journal of Philology* 111: 429–40

Race, W. H. 1982. *The classical priamel from Homer to Boethius*, Leiden

Radif, L. 1997. 'Gli avverbi in -θεν da nomi propri in Omero', *Orpheus* 18: 435–41

1998. 'Significato e funzione di alcuni avverbi omerici in -ξ (-ψ)', in U. Rapallo and G. Garbugino, eds. *Grammatica e lessico delle lingue 'morte'* (Alessandria) 33–46

Radt, S., ed. 1985. *Tragicorum graecorum fragmenta*, vol. III: *Aeschylus*, Göttingen

Rank, L. P. 1951. *Etymologiseering en verwante verschijnselen bij Homerus*, Assen

Redfield, J. 1994. *Nature and culture in the Iliad: the tragedy of Hector*, 2nd edn, Durham, NC and London

Reece, S. 1993. *The stranger's welcome: oral theory and the aesthetics of the Homeric hospitality scene*, Ann Arbor

1999–2000. 'Some Homeric etymologies in the light of oral-formulaic theory', *The Classical World* 93: 185–99

Reichel, M. 1994. *Fernbeziehungen in der Ilias*, Tübingen

Reichel, M. and Rengakos A., eds. 2002. *Epea pteroenta. Beiträge zur Homerforschung. Festschrift für Wolfgang Kullmann zum 75. Geburtstag*, Stuttgart

Reinhardt, K. 1997. 'The judgment of Paris', trans. G. M. Wright and P. V. Jones, in *Homer: German scholarship in translation* (Oxford) 170–91 (translated from K. Reinhardt, *Tradition und Geist*, Göttingen 1960, pp. 16–36; first published in *Wissenschaft und Gegenwart* 11, Frankfurt 1938; reprinted in de Jong 1999: vol. III, 47–65)

Rengakos, A. 1993. *Der Homertext und die hellenistischen Dichter*, Stuttgart

2002. Review of West 2001 in *Bryn Mawr Classical Review* 2002.11.15

Reynolds, L. D. and Wilson, N. G. 1991. *Scribes and scholars: a guide to the transmission of Greek and Latin literature*, 3rd edn, Oxford

Richardson, N. J., ed. 1974. *The Homeric Hymn to Demeter*, Oxford

1993. *The Iliad: a commentary*, vol. VI, Cambridge

Richardson, S. D. 1990. *The Homeric narrator*, Nashville, TN

Riggsby, A. M. 1992. 'Homeric speech introductions and the theory of Homeric composition', *Transactions of the American Philological Association* 122: 99–114

Rigsby, K. J., ed. 1984. *Studies presented to Sterling Dow on his eightieth birthday*, Durham, NC

Rijksbaron, A. 1992. 'D'où viennent les ἄλγεα? Quelques observations à propos d'ἄλγε' ἔχειν chez Homère', in F. Létoublon, ed. *La langue et les textes en grec ancien: Actes du colloque Pierre Chantraine (Grenoble: 5–8 septembre 1989)* (Amsterdam) 181–91

1997. 'Further observations on expressions of sorrow and related expressions in Homer', in E. Banfi ed. *Atti del secondo incontro internazionale di linguistica greca* (Labirinti 27) (Trento) 215–42

Risch, E. 1974. *Wortbildung der homerischen Sprache*, 2nd edn, Berlin and New York

Robertson, C. 2002. 'Wounds and wounding in the *Iliad*', *The Ancient History Bulletin* 16: 103–10

Rohde, E. 1925. *Psyche: the cult of souls and belief in immortality among the Greeks*, trans. W. B. Hillis, London (German edn. 1898. *Psyche. Seelencult und Unsterblichkeitsglaube der Griechen*, 2nd edn., Freiburg)

Roisman, H. M. 2005. 'Nestor the good councillor', *Classical Quarterly* 55: 17–38

2006. 'Helen in the *Iliad*; *causa belli* and victim of war: from silent weaver to public speaker', *American Journal of Philology* 127: 1–36

Rollinger, R. 1996. 'Altorientalische Motivik in der frühgriechischen Literatur am Beispiel der homerischen Epen', in C. Ulf, ed. *Wege zur Genese griechischer Identität. Die Bedeutung der früharchaischen Zeit* (Berlin) 156–210

Romilly, J. de 1997. *Hector*, Paris

Roth, C. P. 1990. *'Mixed aorists' in Homeric Greek*, New York and London

Rougier-Blanc, S. 1996. 'ΠΡΟΔΡΟΜΟΣ et ΑΙΘΟΥΣΑ: remarques sur les distinctions sémantiques et fonctionnelles entre deux termes d'architecture domestique employés chez Homère', *Revue des études grecques* 109: 44–65

2002. 'Maisons modestes et maisons de héros chez Homère. Matériaux et techniques', *Pallas* 58: 101–16

2005. *Les maisons homériques: vocabulaire architectural et sémantique du bâti*, Nancy

Roussel, L., ed. 1960. *Eschyle: Les Perses*, Montpellier

Rowe, C. J. 1983. 'The nature of Homeric morality', in C. A. Rubino and C. W. Shelmerdine, eds. *Approaches to Homer* (Austin, TX) 248–75

Ruijgh, C. J. 1971. *Autour de TE épique: études sur la syntaxe grecque*, Amsterdam

1995. 'D'Homère aux origines proto-mycéniennes de la tradition épique. Analyse dialectologique du langage homérique, avec un *excursus* sur la création de l'alphabet grec', in J. P. Crielaard, ed. *Homeric questions* (Amsterdam) 1–96

1996. 'L'emploi de HTOI chez Homère et Hésiode', in A. Rijksbaron and F. M. J. Waanders, eds. *Scripta minora ad linguam Graecam pertinentia*, vol. II (Amsterdam) 519–34 (First published in *Mnemosyne* 34 (1981) 272–87)

Rutherford, R. B., ed. 1992. *Homer: Odyssey. Books XIX and XX*, Cambridge

Salazar, C. F. 2000. *The treatment of war wounds in Graeco-Roman antiquity*, Leiden

Sammons, B. 2010. *The art and rhetoric of the Homeric catalogue*, Oxford

Saunders, K. B. 2003. Appendix to W. H. Friedrich, *Wounding and death in the Iliad: Homeric techniques of description*, trans. G. Wright and P. Jones (London) 131–67

Schadewaldt, W. 1943. *Iliasstudien*, 2nd edn, Leipzig

1959. 'Hektor und Andromache', in *Von Homers Welt und Werk*, 3rd edn. (Stuttgart) 207–33 and 457–8 (Reprinted in de Jong 1999: vol. III, 27–46)

1970. 'Hektor in der Ilias', in R. Thurow and E. Zinn, eds. *Hellas und Hesperien. Gesammelte Schriften zur Antike und zur neueren Literatur in zwei Bänden*, vol. I: *Zur Antike*, 2nd edn. (Zurich and Stuttgart) 21–38 (First published in *Wiener Studien* 69 (1956) 5–25)

1997. 'Hector and Andromache', trans. G. M. Wright and P. V. Jones, in *Homer: German scholarship in translation* (Oxford) 124–42. (Originally published in German in Schadewaldt 1959: 207–29)

Scheid-Tissinier, E. 1994. *Les usages du don chez Homère. Vocabulaire et pratiques*, Nancy

Scheidig, W. 1958. *Goethes Preisaufgaben für bildende Künstler 1799 bis 1805*, Weimar

Schein, S. L. 1976. 'The death of Simoeisios: *Iliad* 4.473–489', *Eranos* 74: 1–5

1984. *The mortal hero: an introduction to Homer's Iliad*, Berkeley and Los Angeles

2002. 'The horses of Achilles in Book 17 of the *Iliad*', in Reichel and Rengakos 2002: 193–205

Schliemann, H. 1880 *Ilios: the city and country of the Trojans*, London

Schlunk, R. R. 1974. *The Homeric scholia and the Aeneid: a study of the influence of ancient Homeric literary criticism on Vergil*, Ann Arbor, MI

Schmidt, M. 1976. *Die Erklärungen zum Weltbild Homers und zur Kultur der Heroenzeit in den bT-Scholien zur Ilias*, Munich

2002. 'The Homer of the scholia: what is explained to the reader?', in Montanari 2002: 159–85

2006. 'Some remarks on the semantics of ἄναξ in Homer', in S. Deger-Jalkotzy and I. S. Lemos, eds. *Ancient Greece: from the Mycenaean palaces to the age of Homer* (Edinburgh) 439–47

Schmit-Neuerburg, T. 1999. *Vergils Aeneis und die antike Homerexegese. Untersuchungen zum Einfluss ethischer und kritischer Homerrezeption auf imitatio und aemulatio Vergils*, Berlin and New York

Schnapper, A. 1982. *David*, trans. H. Harrison, New York

Schofield, M. 1999. '*Euboulia* in the *Iliad*', in *Saving the city: philosopher-kings and other classical paradigms* (London and New York) 3–30. (First published in *Classical Quarterly* 36 (1986) 6–31)

Schulze, W. 1892. *Quaestiones epicae*, Gütersloh

Schwyzer, E. 1939. *Griechische Grammatik auf der Grundlage von Karl Brugmanns Griechischer Grammatik*, vol. I, Munich

1950. *Griechische Grammatik auf der Grundlage von Karl Brugmanns Griechischer Grammatik*, vol. II, completed and edited by A. Debrunner, Munich

Scodel, R. 1980. *Euripides' Trojan trilogy*, Göttingen

1992a. 'Inscription, absence and memory: epic and early epitaph', *Studi italiani di filologia classica* 10: 57–76

1992b. 'The wits of Glaukos', *Transactions of the American Philological Association* 122: 73–84

2002a. *Listening to Homer: tradition, narrative, and audience*, Ann Arbor, MI

2002b. 'Homeric signs and flashbulb memory', in I. Worthington and J. M. Foley, eds. *Epea and grammata: oral and written communication in ancient Greece* (Leiden) 99–116

2008a. *Epic facework: self-presentation and social interaction in Homer*, Swansea

2008b. 'Zielinski's law reconsidered', *Transactions of the American Philological Association* 138: 107–25

Scott, W. C. 1974. *The oral nature of the Homeric simile*, Leiden

Scully, S. 1990. *Homer and the sacred city*, Ithaca, NY and London

Seaford, R. 1994. *Reciprocity and ritual: Homer and tragedy in the developing city-state*, Oxford.

ed. 1996. *Euripides: Bacchae*, Warminster

Segal, C. 1971a. *The theme of mutilation of the corpse in the Iliad*, Leiden
 1971b. 'Andromache's *anagnorisis*: formulaic artistry in *Iliad* 22.437–476', *Harvard Studies in Classical Philology* 75: 33–57
Shear, I. M. 1998. 'Bellerophon tablets from the Mycenaean world?: a tale of seven bronze hinges', *Journal of Hellenic Studies* 118: 187–9
Shelmerdine, C. W. 1995. 'Shining and fragrant cloth in Homeric epic', in J. B. Carter and S. P. Morris, eds. *The ages of Homer: a tribute to Emily Townsend Vermeule* (Austin, TX) 99–107
Sicking, C. M. J. 1993. *Griechische Verslehre*, Munich
Sider, D. 1996. ' "As is the generation of leaves" in Homer, Simonides, Horace, and Stobaios', *Arethusa* 29: 263–82
Sifakis, G. M. 1979. 'Children in Greek tragedy', *Bulletin of the Institute of Classical Studies* 26: 67–80
Skutsch, O., ed. 1985. *The Annals of Q. Ennius*, Oxford
Slatkin, L. M. 1992. *The power of Thetis: allusion and interpretation in the Iliad*, Berkeley and Los Angeles
 2007. 'Notes on tragic visualizing in the *Iliad*', in C. Kraus, S. Goldhill, H. P. Foley and J. Elsner, eds. *Visualizing the tragic: drama, myth, and ritual in Greek art and literature* (Oxford) 19–34
Slings, S. R. 1992. 'Written and spoken language: an exercise in the pragmatics of the Greek language', *Classical Philology* 87: 95–109
Snodgrass, A. M. 1974. 'An historical Homeric society?', *Journal of Hellenic Studies* 94: 114–25
 1980. 'Iron and early metallurgy in the Mediterranean', in T. A. Wertime and J. D. Muhly, eds. *The coming of the age of iron* (New Haven, CT and London) 335–74
Sourvinou-Inwood, C. 1995. *'Reading' Greek death*, Oxford
Stadtmueller, H., ed. 1906. *Anthologia Graeca epigrammatum Palatina cum Planudea*, vol. III.1, Leipzig
Steiner, D. T. 1994. *The tyrant's writ: myths and images of writing in ancient Greece*, Princeton, NJ
Stoevesandt, M. 2004. *Feinde – Gegner – Opfer. Zur Darstellung der Trojaner in den Kampfszenen der Ilias*, Basel
 ed. 2008. *Homers Ilias. Gesamtkommentar. Herausgegeben von Anton Bierl und Joachim Latacz*, vol. VI.2, Berlin and New York
Strömberg, R. 1961. 'Die Bellerophontes-Erzählung in der Ilias', *Classica et Mediaevalia* 22: 1–15
Sullivan, S. D. 1988, *Psychological activity in Homer. A study of phrēn*, Ottawa
 1996. 'The role of *kēr* in Homer and the Homeric hymns', *Euphrosyne* n.s. 24: 9–31
 1997. 'The effects of wine on psychic entities in early Greek poetry', *Eirene* 33: 9–18
Susanetti, D. 1999. 'Foglie caduche e fragili genealogie', *Prometheus* 25: 97–116
Sutherland, C. 2001. 'Archery in the Homeric epics', *Classics Ireland* 8: 111–20
Taplin, O. 1990. 'Agamemnon's role in the *Iliad*', in C. Pelling, ed. *Characterization and individuality in Greek literature* (Oxford) 60–82

1992. *Homeric soundings: the shaping of the Iliad*, Oxford

2009. 'Hector's helmet glinting in a fourth-century tragedy', in S. Goldhill and E. Hall, eds. *Sophocles and the Greek tragic tradition* (Cambridge) 251–63

Tatum, J. 2003. *The mourner's song: war and remembrance from the Iliad to Vietnam*, Chicago, IL and London

Thalheim, H.-G., ed. 1980. *Schiller. Sämtliche Werke. Gedichte*, Berlin and Weimar

Thiel, H. van, ed. 1991. *Homeri Odyssea*, Hildesheim

ed. 1996. *Homeri Ilias*, Hildesheim

2000a. 'Die D-Scholien der Ilias in den Handschriften', *Zeitschrift für Papyrologie und Epigraphik* 132: 1–62

ed. 2000b. 'Scholia D in Iliadem secundum codices manu scriptos (Proecdosis 2000, adiuverunt N. Conrad et S. Matthaios)', http://kups.ub.uni-koeln.de/volltexte/2006/1810/ (accessed 10 May 2010)

Thomas, B. M. 2002. 'Constraints and contradictions: whiteness and femininity in ancient Greece', in L. Llewellyn-Jones, ed. *Women's dress in the ancient Greek world* (London and Swansea) 1–16

Thompson, S. 1946. *The folktale*, New York

1955–8. *Motif index of folk-literature*, 6 vols., rev. edn, Copenhagen

Thornton, A. 1984. *Homer's Iliad: its composition and the motif of supplication*, Göttingen

Traill, D. A. 1993. *Excavating Schliemann: collected papers on Schliemann*, Atlanta, GA

1995. *Schliemann of Troy: treasure and deceit*, New York

Trümpy, H. 1950. *Kriegerische Fachausdrücke im griechischen Epos. Untersuchungen zum Wortschatze Homers*, Basel

Tsagalis, C. C. 2004. *Epic grief: personal laments in Homer's Iliad*, Berlin and New York

2008. *The oral palimpsest: exploring intertextuality in the Homeric epics*, Washington, DC

Tzamali, E. 1997. 'Positive Aussage plus negierte Gegenaussage im Griechischen. Teil I: Die ältere griechische Dichtung', *Münchener Studien zur Sprachwissenschaft* 57: 129–67

Tyrell, W. B. 1984. *Amazons: a study in Athenian mythmaking*, Baltimore, MD

Ulf, C., ed. 2003. *Der neue Streit um Troia. Eine Bilanz*, Munich

Ulf, C. and Rollinger, R., eds. 2010. *Lag Troja in Kilikien? Der aktuelle Streit um Homers Ilias*, Darmstadt

Uther, H.-J., ed. 1996. *Grimms Kinder- und Hausmärchen*, vol. I, Göttingen

van der Valk, M. 1963–4. *Researches on the text and scholia of the Iliad*, 2 vols., Leiden

ed. 1971–87. *Eustathii archiepiscopi Thessalonicensis commentarii ad Homeri Iliadem pertinentes*, 4 vols., Leiden

van Leeuwen, J. 1890. 'Homerica', *Mnemosyne* 18: 265–99

Van Nortwick, T. 2001. 'Like a woman: Hector and the boundaries of masculinity', *Arethusa* 34: 221–35

van Otterlo, W. A. A. 1948. *De ringkompositie als opbouwprincipe in de epische gedichten van Homerus*, Amsterdam

van Wees, H. 1992. *Status warriors: war, violence and society in Homer and history*, Amsterdam

1996. 'Growing up in early Greece: heroic and aristocratic educations', in A. H. Sommerstein and C. Atherton, eds. *Education in Greek fiction* (Bari) 1–20

2004. *Greek warfare: myths and realities*, London

2005. 'Clothes, class and gender in Homer', in D. Cairns, ed. *Body language in the Greek and Roman worlds* (Swansea) 1–36

Venturi Bernardini, I. 1999. 'Le epiclesi di Atena in Omero', *Studi e materiali di storia delle religioni* 23: 41–97

Vermeule, E. 1974. 'Der Götterkult bei Homer', in F. Matz and H.-G. Buchholz, eds. *Archaeologia Homerica*, vol. III, ch. V, *Götterkult* (Göttingen) 76–132

1979. *Aspects of death in early Greek art and poetry*, Berkeley and Los Angeles

Vernant, J.-P. 1991. 'Feminine figures of death in Greece', in F. I. Zeitlin, ed. *Mortals and immortals: collected essays* (Princeton, NJ) 95–110

Visser, E. 1987. *Homerische Versifikationstechnik. Versuch einer Rekonstruktion*, Frankfurt, Berne and New York

1997. *Homers Katalog der Schiffe*, Stuttgart and Leipzig

Vox, O. 1975. 'Epigrammi in Omero', *Belfagor* 30: 67–70

Wachter, R. 1991. 'The inscriptions on the François Vase', *Museum Helveticum* 48: 86–113

2000. 'Grammatik der Homerischen Sprache', in Latacz 2000a: 61–108

2001. *Non-Attic Greek vase inscriptions*, Oxford

Wackernagel, J. 1916. *Sprachliche Untersuchungen zu Homer*, Göttingen

1926. *Vorlesungen über Syntax*, vol. I, 2nd edn, Basel

1953. 'Zum homerischen Dual', in *Kleine Schriften*, 2 vols. (Göttingen) 538–46 (First published in *Zeitschrift für Vergleichende Sprachforschung* 23 (1877) 302–10)

Wagner-Hasel, B. 2002. 'The Graces and colour weaving', in L. Llewellyn-Jones, ed. *Women's dress in the ancient Greek world* (London and Swansea) 17–32

Wathelet, P. 1988. *Dictionnaire des Troyens de l'Iliade*, 2 vols., Liège

1991. 'Dionysos chez Homère ou la folie divine', *Kernos* 4: 61–82

1992. 'Argos et l'Argolide dans l'épopée, spécialement dans le Catalogue des vaisseaux', in P. Marcel, ed. *Polydipsion Argos: Argos de la fin des palais mycéniens à la constitution de l'État classique: actes de la table ronde Fribourg (Suisse), 7–9 mai 1987* (Fribourg and Paris) 99–116

Watkins, C. 1995. *How to kill a dragon: aspects of Indo-European poetics*, Oxford

Wehr, O. 2006. 'The judgement of Paris in Homer: re-examining *Iliad* 8, 548–552 and 24, 27–30', *Journal of Ancient Civilization* 21: 41–60

Weil, S. 2003. *Simone Weil's The Iliad or The Poem of Force: a critical edition*, ed. and trans. J. P. Holoka, New York

Weiler, G. 2001. *Domos theiou basileos: Herrschaftsformen und Herrschaftsarchitektur in den Siedlungen der Dark Ages*, Munich and Leipzig

Weise, E. A. 1965. 'Terms of address in the *Iliad*: an interpretative study of their relevance to their contexts', Diss., Columbia

Wendel, T. 1929. *Die Gesprächsanrede im griechischen Epos und Drama der Blütezeit*, Stuttgart

West, M. L., ed. 1966. *Hesiod: Theogony*, Oxford

ed. 1978. *Hesiod: Works and Days*, Oxford

1982. *Greek metre*, Oxford

1985. *The Hesiodic Catalogue of Women: its nature, structure, and origins*, Oxford
1995. 'The date of the *Iliad*', *Museum Helveticum* 52: 203–19
1997a. *The east face of Helicon: west Asiatic elements in Greek poetry and myth*, Oxford
1997b. 'Homer's metre', in Morris and Powell 1997: 218–37
ed. 1998–2000. *Homeri Ilias*, 2 vols., Stuttgart and Leipzig
2001a. *Studies in the text and transmission of the Iliad*, Munich and Leipzig
2001b. 'The fragmentary Homeric *Hymn to Dionysus*', *Zeitschrift für Papyrologie und Epigraphik* 134: 1–11
ed. 2003. *Homeric Hymns with Homeric apocrypha and Lives of Homer*, Cambridge, MA
2004. 'West on Rengakos (*BMCR* 2002.11.15) and Nagy (*Gnomon* 75, 2003, 481–501) on West', *Bryn Mawr Classical Review* 2004.04.17
West, S. 1967. *The Ptolemaic papyri of Homer*, Cologne and Opladen
White, J. A. 1982. 'Bellerophon in the "land of Nod". Some notes on *Iliad* 6.153–211', *American Journal of Philology* 103: 119–27
Wickert-Micknat, G. 1982. *Die Frau*, Göttingen (= H.-G. Buchholz, ed. *Archaeologia Homerica*, vol. III, ch. R)
Willcock, M. M. 1976. *A companion to the Iliad, based on the translation by Richmond Lattimore*, Chicago
1992. 'Nervous hesitation in the *Iliad*', in J. Pinsent and H. V. Hurt, eds. *Homer 1987. Papers of the third Greenbank colloquium (April 1987)* (Liverpool Classical Papers 2) (Liverpool) 65–73
2002, 'Menelaos in the *Iliad*', in Reichel and Rengakos 2002: 221–9
Williams, G. 1968. *Tradition and originality in Roman poetry*, Oxford
Willmott, J. 2007. *The moods of Homeric Greek*, Cambridge
Wilson, D. F. 2002. *Ransom, revenge, and heroic identity in the Iliad*, Cambridge
Winkler, M. M. 2007. 'The *Iliad* and the cinema', in M. M. Winkler, ed. *Troy: from Homer's Iliad to Hollywood epic* (Oxford) 43–67
Wöhrle, G. 1999. *Telemachs Reise. Väter und Söhne in Ilias und Odyssee oder ein Beitrag zur Erforschung der Männlichkeitsideologie in der homerischen Welt*, Göttingen
Wolf, F. A. 1985. *Prolegomena to Homer, 1795*, ed. and trans. A. Grafton, G. W. Most and J. E. G. Zetzel, Princeton, NJ (Latin edn. 1795. *Prolegomena ad Homerum*, Halle)
Worman, N. 1997. 'The body as argument: Helen in four Greek texts', *Classical Antiquity* 16: 151–203
2001. 'The voice which is not one: Helen's verbal guises in Homeric epic', in A. Lardinois and L. McClure, eds. *Making silence speak: women's voices in Greek literature and society* (Princeton, NJ) 19–37
Wülfing-von Martitz, P. 1972. 'Ennius als hellenistischer Dichter', in O. Skutsch, ed. *Ennius* (Entretiens sur L'Antiquité Classique 17) (Vandoeuvres and Geneva) 253–83 and 284–9 (Discussion)
Yamagata. N. 1989. 'The apostrophe in Homer as part of the oral technique', *Bulletin of the Institute of Classical Studies* 36: 91–103
1994. *Homeric morality*, Leiden
1997. 'Ἄναξ and βασιλεύς in Homer', *Classical Quarterly* 47: 1–14

Zajko, V. 2006. 'Hector and Andromache: identification and appropriation', in C. Martindale and R. F. Thomas, eds. *Classics and the uses of reception* (Oxford) 80–91

Zanker, G. 1992. 'Sophocles' *Ajax* and the heroic values of the *Iliad*', *Classical Quarterly* 42: 20–5.

Zarker, J. W. 1965. 'King Eëtion and Thebe as symbols in the *Iliad*', *The Classical Journal* 61: 110–14

Zielinski, T. 1899–1901. 'Die Behandlung gleichzeitiger Ereignisse im antiken Epos', *Philologus Supplement* 8: 105–49. Selections reprinted in English as 'The treatment of simultaneous events in ancient epic', trans. C. Krojzl and S. R. van der Mije, in de Jong 1999: vol. IV, 317–27

Zimmermann, B. 2002. 'Der tragische Homer. Zum Aias des Sophokles', in Reichel and Rengakos 2002: 239–46

   2006. *Die griechische Komödie*, 2nd edn, Frankfurt

Zink, N. 1962. *Griechische Ausdrucksweisen für warm und kalt im seelischen Bereich*, Diss. Mainz, Heidelberg

INDICES

References in italics are to pages of the Introduction; references in roman type are to lemmata in the Commentary.

GENERAL

enjambment, *12–13*, 37–8, 53–4, 134, 159, 240, 387, 392–3, 408, 445, 450, 478, 496, 507, 509; corrective, 125, 260; introduces further information about a character, 13, 154, 299, 395–8, 395; necessary, *12*, 11, 130–1, 135, 139–40, 150–1, 157, 180, 222–3, 230–1, 281–2, 324, 362, 408, 409, 412, 477, 482–3, 513; progressive, *12*, 13, 126, 137, 154, 195, 299, 328–9, 395–8, 396, 410, 413, 430, 461, 492–3, 524–5; repeated use of, *13*, 29–36, 31, 33, 36, 61–5, 138, 325–31, 327–30, 407–13, 506–11
Ennius, *52*; *see also* Index of passages
Ephyre, 152
epic cycle, *28*, 465; *see also Aethiopis, Cypria, Epigoni, Iliou Persis, Little Iliad, Thebaid*
Epictetus, 492–3
Epigoni, 222–3; *see also* Index of passages
epigram, 460–1, 460
epithets, *14–16*; ancient explanations of, 162, 186, 288, 311, 400, 428; and context, *15*, 160, 186, 199, 235, 251, 381, 390, 473, 498; and focalisation, 134, 374, 400–3; artificially formed, 292; characterising war, 1, 16–17, 124–5, 185, 254, 330; clusters of, 155, 190, 266, 440, 466; distinct use in singular and plural, 73, 282–3, 299, 461; distinctive and/or generic, 8, 12, 22, 29, 31, 44, 205, 220, 234, 267–8, 269, 282–3, 290, 315, 397, 416, 428, 454, 466, 529; effect in character speech, 377, 416, 423, 436–7, 437, 481, 527; elaboration of, *14–15*, 466, 469–70; gendered use of, 31, 92; lack of, 160, 163, 476, 512; meaning of, 23, 26–7, 34–5, 88, 89, 92, 96, 111, 168, 171, 184, 350, 367, 371, 377, 380, 442, 467, 468; obscure, 269, 513; *see also* Artemis, Athena, Bellerophontes, Hector, Helen, Hephaistos, Hera, Heracles, patronymics, Theano, wine, Zeus
Erichthonius, 461
Eteocles, 237–41
Ethiopians, 111
Euboean dialect, 22
Eumaeus, 334
Eumelos, 130–40; *see also* Index of passages
Euphorbos, 481
Euripides: *Alexandros*, 7, *41*, 280–5; *Andromache, 49*, 456, 471; *Bacchae*, 132; *Hippolytus*, 160–5; *see also* Index of passages
Europa, 198
Euryalos, *17*, 5–36, 20–8, 20, 28
Eurycleia, 381–9
Eurydice, *50*
Eurynome, 136

Eurypylos, 36
Eurysaces, *49*
exhortation, *16*, *17*, 58, 66–71, 66, 71, 83, 84, 99–100, 103, 105, 110–18, 110, 113, 114, 515–16

Fantuzzi, M., *57–8*
fate, *26*, *46*, 62, 146–9, 155–205, 200, 241, 280–5, 357, 407–13, 408, 412, 443, 454–63, 458, 485–93, 487, 488, 519; determined at birth, 345, 489
fathers, *15*, *19*, *37*, *38*, *46*, 46, 47, 119, 155–205, 155, 206–11, 207, 209, 222–3, 251, 292, 317, 400–3, 403, 429–30, 437, 441–6, 474, 475–81, 479; Homer as father, *56*; *see also* Diomedes, Glaukos, Hector, patronymics
fig tree, *33*, *45*, 237, 433
flyting, *16*, *36–7*, 123–43, 211
focalisation, *19*, *32*, 166, 374, 400–3, 404, 452–3, 470, 482–3, 484
Foley, H. P., *49*
folk tale, 155–205, 160–5, 170, 171, 178–86, 178, 187–90, 191–5, 191, 192, 193, 200–2, 414–28, 421
Ford, A., *24*
foreshadowing, *25–6*, *33*, 405, 481
formulae, flexibility of, *13–16*, 32, 49, 51, 175, 187, 222–3, 241, 245–6, 260, 311, 372, 381, 390, 473, 495, 502, 504, 514; in character speech, 413, 423
funeral lament, *18*, *30*, *32*, *46*, 47, *55*, 405–39, 407–13, 410–11, 464, 494–502, 499

gender roles, *29–32*, *45–46*, 160–5, 161, 336, 464–5, 482–93, 490–3
genealogy, *17*, *37*, *38*, 20–8, 145, 150–211, 154, 196–9, 206–11, 211
Gilgamesh, Poem of, 175; language of, 22
Glaukos, son of Hippolochos, *15*, *17*, *27*, *34*, *36–40*, 119, 125, 154; and his father, *15*, *37*, 119, 155–205, 206–11; and Sarpedon, *37–8*, 55, 198–9, 199; and the gods, 140–1, 153, 155–205, 183, 191, 200–2, 200, 203–5; armour of, *38–9*, 123–43, 236; as narrator, *37*, 185, 190; characterisation of, *37*, 127; use of language, *13*, *21*, 160–5, 162, 163, 170, 172, 203–5; views on the human condition, *37–8*, 146–9, 147, 147–8, 150–211
Glaukos, son of Sisyphos, 154
glory, *see* Index of Greek words s.v. κλέος
gods, *26–9*, *36–7*, 1–4, 1, 14, 76, 82, 115, 123, 128–9, 130–40, 171, 203–5, 269, 349, 356, 419–20, 438, 475, 487, 499, 527; associated with gold, 3, 236; carefree, 138; difficult to identify, 108; divine justice, 160–5; do not

PASSAGES DISCUSSED

GREEK WORDS